THE PRINCIPLE OF HOPE

THE PRINCIPLE
OF HOPE

Volume Two

Ernst Bloch

Translated by Neville Plaice,
Stephen Plaice and Paul Knight

The MIT Press
Cambridge, Massachusetts

Third printing, 1996
First MIT Press paperback edition, 1995

Written in the USA 1938–1947
revised 1953 and 1959;
first American edition published by The MIT Press, 1986
English translation © 1986 by Basil Blackwell, Ltd.
Originally published as *Das Prinzip Hoffnung,* © 1959 by
Suhrkamp Verlag, Frankfurt am Main, Federal Republic of Germany.

Library of Congress Cataloging-in-Publication Data

Bloch, Ernst, 1885–1977
   The principle of hope.

   (Studies in contemporary German social thought)
   Translation of Das Prinzip Hoffnung.
   Includes index.
   1. Hope.   2. Imagination.   3. Utopias.   4. Creation
(Literary, artistic, etc.)   I. Title.   II. Series.
B3209.B753P7513   1986   193   85-23081

ISBN 0-262-52199-7 (volume 1)
      0-262-52200-4 (volume 2)
      0-262-52201-2 (volume 3)
      0-262-52204-7 (3-volume set)

Printed and bound in the United States of America

CONTENTS

PART FOUR

(*Construction*)

OUTLINES OF A BETTER WORLD

(MEDICINE, SOCIAL SYSTEMS, TECHNOLOGY, ARCHITECTURE,
GEOGRAPHY, PERSPECTIVE IN ART AND WISDOM)

PART FOUR

(Construction)

OUTLINES OF A BETTER WORLD

(MEDICINE, SOCIAL SYSTEMS, TECHNOLOGY, ARCHITECTURE, GEOGRAPHY, PERSPECTIVE IN ART AND WISDOM)

The act-content of hope is, as a consciously illuminated, knowingly elucidated content, the positive utopian function; the historical content of hope, first represented in ideas, encyclopaedically explored in real judgements, is human culture referred to its concrete-utopian horizon.

The Principle of Hope, Vol. I, p. 146

Too many are queuing up outside. From him who has nothing and is content with this shall be taken away even that which he has.* But the pull towards what is lacking never ends. The lack of what we dream about hurts not less, but more. It thus prevents us from getting used to deprivation. What hurts, oppresses and weakens us all the time has to go.

Just a short breathing-space, this never sufficed for long. Above all, dreaming always outlived the brief and private day. So this is the beginning of something other than the desire to dress up, to see ourselves as our masters wish to see us. A larger image is sketched in the air here, a wishfully deliberate one. Even with this deliberate element mistakes have often been made, but it cannot so often be used to deceive. Nor will it be cheaply fobbed off, its will aims at something more, and everything that it attains tastes of this something more. So that it seeks to live not merely beyond its own means, but beyond the poorly available means of conditions as a whole. Longing holds strong and true, especially when it is deceived, even when it is racing aimlessly now in one direction, now in another. All the more so, when the path leads unerringly and caringly forwards.

PHYSICAL EXERCISE, TOUT VA BIEN 34

Fresh, frank, frolicking, free. *Motto*†

Only what is little moves downwards. The child has no say, the woman cooks and washes. The poor man stands hunched up, not many people eat their fill even once a day. How do we stay healthy, that is the question, how do we feed ourselves well and cheaply. Where is the leafy bough, others can be seen on it, they are sitting pretty. A fortnight off, that is already a great deal for most people, then back to a life that nobody wants. Fresher air here stands for much that could sparkle.

It is freely available to the body, and everyone has a body after all. Sport

* Cf. Matthew 25, 29: 'but from him that hath not shall be taken away even that which he hath'.
† 'Frisch, fromm, fröhlich, frei.' Motto of a nineteenth-century gymnastic movement in Germany.

has never been more desired, practised, planned than today, and never have more hopes been pinned on it. It is regarded as healthy, the athlete's heart has ousted the enlarged heart of the beer-drinker. A suntan automatically creates a healthy glow, brings back in the flesh the South or the mountains. The price paid for this is that in backward bourgeois conditions sport often stultifies the mind, and for this very reason is promoted from above. It is not just free competition, for which there is now no room, that is replaced in the search for records, but also the real struggle for improvement. A powerful need drives the masses out into the open air, but water only cleanses their bodies, and the home to which the outdoor type returns in the evening has not got any fresher. Though in the Vormärz,* when gymnastics appeared on the scene, the jolt it gave to leaden limbs still seemed to be bound up with another kind of jolt. Let steel spring from rust, from wineskins the must, through the mist blows a wind from the east, down with the frost, so went a song in the days when gymnastics replaced drill. Storm and Stress† of the body came to the fore among bourgeois youth; Jahn, the so-called father of gymnastics, wrote in 1815: 'The soul of gymnastics is the life of the people, and this only flourishes in public, out in the air and light.' Thus dangerous ideas were spawned by the straightened back or associated with it, and the young gymnast thought of freedom. Though what he meant by freedom was walking upright, the strength not to cower before the enemy but to hold his own, manly pride before royal thrones, and the courage to stand up for his beliefs, none of which followed, as we know. This freedom also remained poor later on, especially amongst the Germans, because there was a double layer of lords and masters here, the bourgeois and the feudal. Thus the tradesman himself emerged as a hero, the bourgeois himself doing the goose-step, and the Nazis, even citing Jahn as their authority, completed all this. Exercise of the body without the mind ultimately meant being cannon-fodder, and thugs beforehand. There is no unpolitical sport; if it is free, then it is on the left, if it is blinded, then it hires itself out to the right. And only in a nation that is not cowed, where the able body is neither abused nor stands as a substitute for manly pride, does Jahn's wish become meaningful. It is only when the swimmer also parts the given in other ways that he has swum free and loves the deep water.

Even athletic exercise remains wishful, hopeful. It does not merely seek

---

* The period of political ferment in Germany leading up to the revolution of March 1848.
† A reference to the 'Sturm und Drang', the revolutionary movement in literature and drama in Germany in the latter half of the eighteenth century.

to gain control over the body so that there is no fat on it and every movement is pleasantly uninhibited. It also seeks to be able to do more, to be more with the body than this body seemed to promise at birth. Genuine athletic postures are very different from cosmetic postures in front of the mirror, from make-up that is wiped off a woman's face again at night, or from other rebuilding which is dismantled when we take off our clothes again. The body should not be concealed at all but rather shed the distortions and disfigurements which an alienating society based on the division of labour has inflicted on it too. The wish is to give it a 'return to health' with so many exercises formerly confined to chivalry and so many newly discovered ones too in the new society. Namely a return to health which does not presuppose any illness at all, but is rather the verb, the action of health itself, a healing precisely without an illness. Whereby sport is also relieved of its emergency function in bourgeois society to create a so-called balance with the predominantly sedentary way of life, in both the narrow and broad sense, typical of the indoor worker. There will always be a sedentary way of life, but not always the unpleasant consequences which arise from the lack of open air of any kind. The sportsman wishes to have such control of his body that, even on the ski-jump when he is flying through the air, every situation is familiar, even the new, exaggerated one. Thus the mind certainly does not build the body, but it keeps it in shape, often beyond its innate capacity.

Nothing ventured, nothing gained; it is easy enough to say this of course. It is presented as if it was also easy to do, indeed as if this saying illustrated the best thing to do here. For apparently there is another way to make the body powerful, namely that which cheerfully and blindly disregards it. Coué* adopted this approach, with his motto: Tout va bien (not to mention utterly silly faith-healers). Fortune favours the brave in this kind of world, even though no-one needs to be particularly brave. Colds and more serious illnesses are supposed to be driven away by means of Tout va bien, in a light-headed way so to speak. The famous rider on Lake Constance is the prime example here: since he rode over the danger so staunchly and unsuspectingly, it simply did not arise, and the ice did not break beneath him. This is the dangerous example of disregarding the trouble; it is as if, by being ignored, it does not exist. Though the whole thing does also acquire a dash of truth the moment the courage is not blind or cheap but – again in a truly sporting way – goes under the name

* Emile Coué, 1857–1926, French psychologist, whose popular books advocating psychotherapy through autosuggestion enjoyed a vogue in the 1920s.

454 OUTLINES OF A BETTER WORLD

of 'Chin up'. The brighter the mood here, and the more hopes are pinned on 'Chin up', the more this insistence combats listlessness. And this listlessness can even be the beginning of an illness, not just its effect. Tout va bien certainly does not mean that everything is as right as rain, but even here the dream of a better life entails that a will is following its path. Also, not even our body is so constituted that it can get by unchanged, unextended as it were. This man can definitely be helped,* and so can the woman, along the road that can be planned.

STRUGGLE FOR HEALTH,   35
MEDICAL UTOPIAS

Once cured, the patient must feel a new man, he ought to be healthier than before.   *Inscription*

A warm bed

The physically weak must exercise instead of relaxing. They cannot wish to rest without completely rusting. But the sick man insists on resting and relaxing, his bed both hides and shelters him. And when asleep the sick man also feels healthy, that is, he does not feel at all. He is then like the sound body itself, which does not even have a sensation of itself when it is awake. It is seemingly very simple to prolong this, to shake off discomfort as a dog shakes off water. Illness does not belong to us, there is even something shameful about it, it resembles a kind of nightmare, it has got to disappear overnight. At first we wish for nothing more than its mere disappearance, just as sleep gets rid of tiredness. The aching tooth has to go, even a diseased limb has to go, this desire to shake them off can itself be diseased. As in the case of a randy woman who would take her skin off too if she could. Or even as in the case of fat people who would like to see themselves as skeletons if they could. So the sick man has the feeling not that he lacks something but that he has too much of something. His discomfort, as something which is hanging around him and superfluous, has to go; pain is proud flesh. He dreams of the body which knows how to keep comfortably quiet again.

---

* An allusion to the final line of Schiller's play 'Die Räuber'.

Lunatics and fairytales

Thus every sick man wishes to get well again in a flash. An honest doctor
cannot give him this, but this sudden recovery has always been pictured.
Swimming around in blood in the morning, healthy and up and about at
midday. Even doctors indulged in dreams of this kind, mostly deceitfully,
often themselves deceived. The two most general favourite wishes of
mankind are to stay young and live long. And a third is precisely to achieve
both, not in a painful roundabout way but with a fairytale quality of
surprise. As the sick man does not skip and leap around, his wishes do so all
the more. The quack lives off this will for abrupt recovery, and now comes
the really lunatic stuff. A doctor rushed out into the street in his nightshirt
and shouted that the fiery owl had arrived, death and disease were abolished.
Healing potions, healing lotions, what a short cut, how literally condensed
they seem, how intensively the fairytale has been preoccupied with them.
There is the ointment that heals injuries at a stroke, there is the fountain
from which old people emerge rejuvenated, which is particularly good for
preserving the fleeting quality of female beauty. A Cockaigne of healthiness
is spread before us, without pain, with bounding limbs and a stomach that
is always merry. It is no accident that quacks are closely linked with the
medical fairytale, with magic ointments, wands, and lotions; they are all
living dispensers of old wives' tales. Count St Germain, who in the prime of
life claimed to be many hundred years old, used to sell a 'tea for long life';
it was a mundane mixture of sandalwood, senna leaves and fennel. On a
higher plane, Mesmer belonged to the guild of the half-deceitful, half-
utopian short cut; he believed he could cure diseases by stroking and soft
tones, hypnotically in other words. A perfect example of the business of
physical renewal in Mesmer's day was Dr Graham's 'Celestial Bed', which
was supposed to have the capacity to rejuvenate the person lying in it by a
pleasant shock; electric currents, perfume and glass domes were built into the
frame. The belief in magic herbs seems older and sounder as it were; it is
shared by the fairytale and folklore alike: this same impatience for a sudden
cure also characterizes the hope in medicinal herbs, the breakthrough which
changes everything: the leaves of the box-thorn, for example, are effective
as plasters against ulcers, one quick wash with its decoction is said to be good
against infected ears and rotten gums, bad eyes and shrivelled lips; even such
a common plant as this seems as if it had been brought over from distant
islands. It is as if herbs from Frau Holle's meadow were standing around all

over the place, and it was just a matter of knowing which ones to pick. Extraordinary things were hoped for and demanded, not just in lunatic medicine but also in this kind that resembled colportage, as it were. But we must not forget that extraordinary things, on a highly changed path, have also accompanied all major medical plans. There is always an element of adventure and strangeness in them, in the poison that does not kill but frees from pain, in the knife that does not murder but heals, in borderline creations like the artificial stomach. The fact that what is patched up or replaced in this way does not last particularly well and is definitely not better than the healthy organ does not lessen the adventure, certainly does not make it a failure. Disease is not abolished, but its end, death, is amazingly pushed back. If the exploited lives to which so many are returned were worth something, and if a war did not make up in days for years of lost death, then doctors could be half content with the course of the last hundred years. This is the place to die – this inscription at any rate no longer belongs over hospitals but over the states in which they stand. Healing is a waking dream which is only brought to an end by restoring the old state of health; and is there an old state of health? The real medical dreams surface here, they surge around a rock which is itself not as permanent as it seems. The couch from which the sick man arises would only be perfect if he was refreshed instead of merely patched up.

Medicines and planning

This means nothing less than rebuilding the body. Conducting life into channels where it has not flowed before or not so *easily*. New from the start, and added to the body, are pain-killing drugs. They have been sought from the beginning; in addition, there is the sick man's dream of not being present during the operation on his body. The body too can sometimes deaden its pain, as in the shock after an accident. But no doctor will operate while this shock lasts, the number of fatalities is too great. It is different in the case of anaesthetics, this unnatural relief added from outside. And most medicines, vegetable and metallic, come from outside, including many re-addressed poisons. The poison of the foxglove, for example, protects it from being eaten by animals, in drug form it helps to fight heart disease: what a roundabout method, what far-fetched aid. This is even more true of cutting into life, removing diseased tissue, stitching up the opened body after changing its contents, antiseptic treatment, the fight against germs. All this is artificial and does not proceed along the lines of the self-protective mechanisms which exist anyway, of the regeneration which is possible anyway. It took bold planning, a far cry from accepting things as they are. Wishful images of combatting disease must be the oldest along with those of combatting hunger, and from the start healing was regarded as winning a battle. On the other hand, the frail body also pursues the brightest dreams of a better life; thus even fairytales of an ideal state, in which there are no longer any other deprivations, cannot avoid considering disease and the role of the doctor. Plato's 'Republic' (Book 3) even demands that the ideal doctor 'must also experience all diseases himself in his own body and not have a totally healthy constitution himself'. For only in this way can he assess diseases from within, from his own experience, with a soul which has remained spotless and 'which certainly must not be in a bad state, otherwise it cannot possibly produce a good cure'. However extravagant this demand that the doctor must know at first hand in his own body the diseases that he cures, indeed all diseases, Plato nevertheless also includes as part of the disease the treatment which is imposed all too indifferently by the all too healthy doctor. And the treatment can in fact be not only more painful but also more dangerous and longer lasting than the disease itself. The more recent fairytales of an ideal state, More's 'Utopia' and especially Bacon's 'New Atlantis', also make medicine easier, less painful, more of a short cut, an art of newly constructed life or, if life cannot be preserved, of effortless death. Instead of gloomy medieval infirmaries, More portrays friendly, roomy hospitals for all on a happy island. Bacon adds food and drink which do not encumber the body at all any more, together with wholesome mountain air, artificially produced, serum and vaguely described baths which are nevertheless supposed to make everybody into a Hercules. This is all the more necessary as the existing body itself in these utopias does not live up to the level of the rest of existence, which is imagined as running so smoothly. That is why in the background even here, precisely here, there is the wish to develop a body less susceptible to illness. This finally emerges, quite openly, in a very late social utopia, Swesen's 'Limanora, The Island of Progress', 1903. The people on this island laugh at the idea that medicine is merely therapeutic. They are well 'over the crude stage of mere cure of disease', they intervene in the mere laissez faire, laissez aller of the body, restraining, promoting, stimulating, arranging and re-arranging. Thus the doctor is never conceived here as a cobbler who patches up the old again after a fashion. But they wish him to be an innovator, liberating the flesh not only from its acquired, but even from its innate weakness.

For even the healthy body could be helped much further. Along these lines are all plans which are not preoccupied with each single case of healing but with striving to abolish generic ills. These are: influencing gender, artificial selective breeding, and the abolition of the ageing process. These plans, utopian as they are, still partly cast a reactionary shadow of course. It is no accident that the phrase 'toughening up' temporarily smacks more of cannon fodder than of the superman. The greatest silence now surrounds the plan for influencing *gender*, though it was the loudest plan of all for a long time. This dream is mostly a bourgeois conformist one, it seeks male sons and heirs for Smith and Jones, as if there were a coat of arms and sword to be passed on. It is pointless in any case; for even if more boys than girls were born in accordance with the wishes of their parents, the girls would become particularly coveted, and therefore particularly precious, and in the course of time the fruits of love would never escape this constant alternation of genitals. Secondly, the plan for *efficient breeding* existed even prior to the Nazis, it is reminiscent of an agricultural research station. After all, none of our nutrient and ornamental plants is the same as it was in its natural state, all of them are artificially cultivated and changed. As are most domestic animals, they too were grafted on to one another so to speak and interbred, until the fattest pig or the fastest racehorse or even simply the most patient mule emerged. In accordance with Mendel's rules of heredity, this is now to be applied to human beings, it is a question of consciously planned interbreeding, a question of a better sorted blend of genetic inheritance. But this sorting occurs by means of intrusions on human love, which does not consist as such in a particular selection of mutual germ cells. And it would then be only logical to abolish love and, as in the breeding of thoroughbred horses, to use the Pravaz syringe, filled with the sperm of the best breeding stallions, by-passing the remaining men who are not so pure-blooded. In his authoritarian novel of an ideal state 'Civitas solis', 1623, Campanella had the time of sexual intercourse determined by astrologers; these astrologers have now become the strict breeding masters and gamekeepers. And they do not merely choose the hour of mating, but the couples themselves, according to the auspices of the genetic inheritance. This with regard above all to a product which is useful to the ruling class, in the age of the little man on the conveyor belt. Such selective breeding is to occur before birth, though after it Mendel's rules, which are complicated anyway, no longer hold, but the simple ones of murder instead. This is practised on all those who stand outside the norm, and the norm for the Nazis was simply the ass at the bottom, the beast at the top. The Babbitt is the measure of this in the still inhibited bourgeoisie; all the rest, after assessment by the same type, are to be exterminated when it becomes uninhibited. Thus so-called eugenics has degenerated to this level; Beethoven, the son of an incurable drinker, would never have been born according to this scheme of things, and even if this had occurred, 'war the breeder' would have obliterated him. Only a society which was no longer a capitalist one would be able to put everything to rights in the problem area of eugenics, with other means and standards of selection. While the best eugenics presumably consists in good board and lodging, in an unspoilt childhood. This promotes successful development, and also makes super- fluous that selection according to the strange tincture that has been called pure blood and that presumably only stems from inbreeding, with its rare advantages, and vast dangers. The nobility has propagated itself eugenically along these lines for a very long time, and it has not, in purely physiological terms as it were, proved to be gold, which has retained its value throughout the long series of individual recastings or even become more and more purified. What distinguished and singled out the nobility as such, namely not as individuals but as a group, was solely the class code which gave it obligations and standing, was primarily good upbringing, and therefore not heredity. And that quality in King Lear's face to which one would like to say Sire does not stem from his family tree; on the contrary, his family tree produced despicable material enough in the shape of his two daughters. Thus even the chances of nobility do not stem from breeding; it is rather that social hygiene, a society in which an upright posture is not suppressed any more, in which no mean trick pays off any more, reveals noble behaviour anyway, indeed it is truly revealed by that society alone. Only here does the 'breeding' of geniuses really succeed, of these true and solely desirable 'blood minorities'. At least so long as the peculiar kind of 'hormone', or whatever we like to call that which gives rise to creative talent, is physiologically unknown with regard to both its nature and the conditions in which it arises. Certainly, from father comes our stature, from little mother our cheerful nature,* or also, in many other cases: little mother showed signs of hysteria, and this now seems like a prerequisite for the brilliant birth. Yet on the other hand, how many meticulous fathers and fantasizing mothers have merely produced incon- spicuous creatures, or possibly even meagre and frail ones? The mixture of blood which produces great talent therefore still lies too much in the dark for this talent to be promoted and encouraged physiologically with

---

* Allusion to lines from Goethe's 'Zahme Xenien VI'.

any prospect of success. Whereas after the brilliant birth has occurred, history is crammed with those unfavourable circumstances which prevented the great talent from even being aware of itself, and then from developing. Most of the goldfish have always swum at the bottom, there have been thousands of Solons who were cowherds, of Newtons who were day-labourers, and nobody knows their names. Efficient breeding would have a social field here to keep it busy for a long time, before entering or being able to enter the still largely opaque field of controlled insemination. The control of the individual biological disposition and the abolition of the element of 'fate' about it are certainly a goal, but first this planning will pull down the real slums before it approaches the slum of the puny body. There is everything to be said for reducing the aggressive drives and promoting the social ones even by means of organic breeding; just as the nutritional value of cereals and the sweetness of cherries has been improved. But the breeding society must first be bred itself, in order that the new human nutritional value is not determined by the demands of the cannibals.

The third kind of planning finally looks purer, i.e. without cannibals: the *fight against old age*. It probably strikes out most boldly of all, it begins early in women. It does not want to leave the peculiar wound unattended which the body inflicts on itself. As far as the renewal of lost or damaged organs is concerned, human nature is the most obdurate of all. Only in his brain is man the most highly developed living organism, not in other organic capa-bilities however. After all, progress frequently also represents a certain retrogression in organic development as a whole, by concentrating on one-sided training. By allowing organs to become over-specialized, so that development in a direction other than the one that has become established stops, and even capabilities of an earlier level are lost. The capability of regeneration in particular constantly decreases at higher organic levels: in the case of the earthworm a few rings are sufficient to produce the rest, in the case of newts legs and eyes grow again, the same is true when lizards lose their tails. In the case of mammals however, in the case of human beings, mother nature is by no means generous in this respect. When they lose a limb, human beings are dependent on artificial ones, and the strongest wear and tear of all: ageing, which begins so much later in many animals anyway, is for them the most severe. The wishful dream of the fountain of youth was placed in this field, and the route towards it was constantly cultivated, by quacks or others. Count St Germain's 'tea for long life' has been mentioned above, as has Dr Graham's 'Celestial Bed' from the so enlightened eighteenth century. From Persia came the advice to use

breathing techniques, from Tibet the control of one's breathing, from the
faith-healers the belief that one will soon be immortal in the flesh. Compared
with advice like this, that of Hufeland in his 'Macrobiotics' of 1796 sounds
modestly correct: 'Sleep and hope are the two best elixirs.' But the more
rational wishful path was not lacking even amongst more material elixirs: the
Chinese used to take the sex glands of stags and monkeys, the Indians those
of tigers; and in 1879 Brown-Sequard actually did discover the supposed
material of rejuvenation in the sex gland, the hormone. The further assumption that every organ produces the substances which will heal it when
diseased ('dentine' in the tooth, 'cerebrin' in the brain) quickly fell by
the wayside; although it was defended by Bier, in a somewhat modified
form, even as late as the Twenties. But the hope which the sex gland
had kindled was not completely illusory in the case of substances which
are extracted from the glandular organs themselves, they permit diseases
to be treated successfully from the hypofunction of these glands at least.
Since then a totally new medical dreamland has opened up here: in 1922
a hormone against diabetes was obtained from the pancreas, in 1929 an
ovary hormone from the urine of pregnant mares, which is six times as
strong as the natural one. All diseases which are based on the hypofunction
of the endocrine glands (pituitary gland, parathyroid gland, thyroid gland,
suprarenal glands, ovaries and others) can in fact be treated by preparations
from these glands. It is precisely with the dream of most general interest,
with the active substance against old age, that expectations have not yet
been realized, despite mobilization on all fronts. Steinach tied the spermatic
cord, and thereby achieved a growth of the puberty gland, the hormones
produced to excess passed into the blood, while Voronov transplanted sex
glands from monkeys. Both efforts were in vain, rejuvenation did admittedly
occur, but such a momentary one that it seemed as if the cause of ageing
did not lie in the sex glands at all and as if the wear and tear on them
was itself simply an effect of unknown causes. Though dreams are still
left surrounding the thymus gland, the growth gland till puberty, at sixteen
it is used up and then only has some functions during pregnancy which
have not been adequately clarified. It is here, and not in the sex glands,
that rejuvenation is said to lie waiting, and means are being sought to
keep this organ functional up to a ripe old age, so that if this ripe old
age is not a fertile one, it is still an upright, sprightly, open-minded one.
The utopian apple of rejuvenation nevertheless still hangs quite a long way
off, and – as far as the examination of heart and kidneys* is concerned

---

* Bloch is playing on the metaphorical meaning of this expression here, i.e. a thorough examination.

– old age remains almost the same as it was in grandfather's day. What has changed is the way of handling it, which is no longer hypochondriac, no longer exaggerated. But this is a psychological intervention, not one from the standpoint of the substructure, of the glands and internal secretion, from which vitality is probably fed. The most conscious and also the most felicitous fight against the degrading effects of old age is to be found in the Soviet Union; and this for reasons which capitalist society cannot allow itself at all. In the latter, as a competitive society, old people have to make room, stand down, simply so that so-called younger blood can take their place. From a socialist point of view, however, the fight for a healthy vigorous old age becomes the same as the fight for the preservation of valuable cadres in all areas of the great programme of construction. 'Old age', as Metshnikov said, 'which under all previous circumstances has been a superfluous burden for the community, now becomes a particularly useful period of work from a social point of view. It can devote its indispensable experience to the most difficult tasks of the life of society.' A future is indicated here in which a significantly possible ageing has replaced the pathological kind, and even physiological decline is no longer acknowledged to be inevitable. The successful Soviet attempts at resuscitation shortly after death has occurred even challenge the most definitive fact to be found in the lives of human beings, and show it to be premature. To drive life beyond its previous limits, beyond those which are much too narrow for our capabilities, unachieved works, and ranks of purpose, this is the wish that includes that of healing and clearly surpasses it.

Hesitation and goal in actual bodily rebuilding

The wishes of the sick man himself do not extend so far. His main concern is that his complaint is cleared up, that is enough. He wants to be restored to health, is content if he is rid of his affliction, if he can get up and be his old self again, and does not immediately demand any more than this. Equally the plans of the doctor, at the patient's bedside, are far more subdued than the general ones for rebuilding mentioned above. In each particular case, with each actual illness (ageing is not an illness) it is enough for him to restore the former state of health. The surgeon by no means regards his work as a process of rebuilding and improving, but as a stopgap measure. The artificial stomach in no way surpasses the one we are born with, good enough if a person can hold out for a few years with such artificial aids and limbs without complaint. And good enough for the general practitioner if a patient returns from the interesting skittle-alley of surgical possibilities to his last. Perhaps even Götz von Berlichingen of the Iron Hand, although knocking off table-ends with it and acting as a pulverizer, did not feel this artificial limb to be solely a source of strength. So here is a countermovement against the utopian rebuilding of the body, against that rebuilding that has ventured so far forward in the case of generic ills (artificial selective breeding, the fight against the ageing process). The general practitioner essentially contents himself with forcing back the end of the disease, i.e. death, he fights against the acquired weakness of the flesh, not against the innate one. His medicine does not yet undertake to assume the high office of being an improver of the body on the same scale as the rebuilding and improving of society and the vast bold changes of inorganic technology. This is a powerful distinction between medical wishes, in so far as they are individual and practical, and those of the more far-reaching attempt to change the world. Thus, however bold the operations and changes may be, in the consciousness of most doctors the goal itself is a stationary one: namely the restoration of the status quo ante. This is also why doctors often succumbed much more easily to the fascist slogan of Blood and Soil than other less restoratory professions. And it is why the doctor is given a significant, thoroughly incisive role in most *social* utopias, but few or no purely *medical* utopias have appeared; unless Hufeland's or Feuchtersleben's tranquil works are seen as such. One will not find explosive dreams in them, both Hufeland's 'Macrobiotics' and Feuchtersleben's 'Dietetics of the Soul' contain little more than the wishes and images which a clever man had recourse to anyway during the age of spas in the colonnades of the Biedermeier period. One reason for this utopian hesitation may possibly lie in the caution and responsibility of the medical profession. Another reason possibly lies in the empirical sense which is closely related to caution and which acts like a lead weight on the inspired flights of the mind. But the final reason for this astonishing utopian reserve which is often even salutary itself, alongside all 'creative' medicine, must be philosophical, whether it is conscious or not: the origin of European medicine among the Stoics. This school trusted in the natural course of things, did not want to explode it at any point but to act in accordance with it in every particular. Hippocrates, the older medical teacher, was active before the Stoics of course, but he too came down to us through Galen, the head of the Stoic school of healing. In its view, health is the right mixture of the four main humours of the body (blood, yellow bile, black bile and phlegm), whereas disease is the disturbance of this balance. This already contains the belief in balance as a condition which can merely be disturbed but not ventured beyond. Galen, however, also added the whole Stoic trust in nature, the striven-for harmony with nature, without the slightest deviation or overhauling. 'The world has everything it needs within it', Plutarch says in totally Stoic fashion, and our little world, the body, is also just as undemanding. This conviction did not of course prevent the Stoics from thinking up a very much better model as far as the state is concerned, a kind of universal fraternity, but the bodies within it, if they lived 'sensibly', i.e. naturally, were regarded as all right the way they are. Even diseases were for the Stoic doctor not just ills but a piece of healing themselves, namely of the disorder that has invaded the body; for a long time even chemical cures were rejected by the Galenists as artificial. Two kinds of antidotes to utopian and all too utopian boldness ultimately continued to be influenced by the Stoics: bon sens and trust in the natural powers of healing. A good doctor follows nature, supports it, never contradicts it: this is the Stoic legacy. 'Peu de médecin, peu de médecine':* with this maxim from the eighteenth century, the heyday of enemas, the doctor finally made himself superfluous, even the empirically spirited one, not just the utopistically high-spirited one. And so-called nature-healing began with bon sens enough to do justice to the instinctive desire for air, light and water, but also with mad dilettantism enough to end up treating patients with curd cheese. Thus once again a utopian streak emerges here after all, the worst kind though, one of ignorant wishful thinking, with hopes which soon become superstitious. This sort of thing is as different as can be from the nevertheless innate medical utopia: *the ultimate rebuilding of the body*, in fact it is the opposite. But the blow against this utopia still comes from an attitude of devotion to nature, in practical empirical terms and also suggested above all by the Stoic legacy. And the good thing about this attitude is undoubtedly that it has almost always hampered abstract notions of improvement in the medical profession. If there are few purely medical utopias, there are also no abstract ones, like the fairytales of an ideal state. So the lower utopian awareness of the general practitioner is itself partly salutary; for everything which is separated too far, too artificially from the usual life of the body becomes gangrenous like a limb with a tourniquet on it. Responsibility and the Stoic legacy maintained the contact with the objectively possible; unlike what often happened in eugenics and the fight against old age. Only this attitude must not be allowed to interrupt the utopian

---

* 'Few doctors, few medicines.'

courage which is thorough in a different way and without which nothing great happens, even in the art of medicine. This courage refers in a specifically non-utopistic way to the *causal* liberation from physical ills. Since the final cause here does not lie in bacilli or in the strange 'imperialist' growth of individual cells and groups of cells, as with cancer, but precisely in the corruptible susceptibility and frailty of the flesh itself, the wishful dream of rebuilding it still remains inevitable and therefore – even when we look away from it – in the background. Indeed a suspicion arises that the medical caution which is aimed to such a great extent merely at the status quo ante is itself rather fishy. We may finally risk the proposition that precisely because the doctor, even at the individual sick-bed, has an *almost crazy utopian plan* latently in view, he ostensibly avoids it. This definitive plan, the final medical wishful dream, is nothing less than the *abolition of death*.

The sick man who has recuperated wants to feel as if he were newborn. This means more than restored to health again, although the sick man is pleased if this is the case all the same. Well pleased, as they say, he can now go about his business again. Restored to health again certainly, but to which Again in the course of his life? Is there such a thing as an old state of health at all, which only has to be restored? Is it a permanent rock, firm at all times, as firmly fixed as it is firmly agreed upon? It is not, health is a wavering notion, if not directly in medical terms, then in social terms. Health is by no means solely a medical notion, but predominantly a societal one. Restoring to health again means in reality bringing the sick man to that kind of health which is respectively acknowledged in each respective society, and which was in fact first formed in that society itself. Thus even for the mere purpose of restoring to health again, the goals of this Again are variable, but more than that: they are themselves first posited as the 'norm' by each respective society. In capitalist society health is the capability to earn, among the Greeks it was the capability to enjoy, and in the Middle Ages the capability to believe. Illness was then regarded as a sin (hence above all the terrible treatment of lunatics, in chains and dungeons), thus the person with least sins was the best-developed. Thus Katharine of Siena, who is a hysteric for every bourgeois enlightened doctor of today, was regarded as absolutely normal. It would never have occurred to any medieval doctor to want to cure this sort of thing, nor would it have been the restoration of a so-called original condition, but the transformation into a much later one normal for the modern age, which hardly existed at that time. Even faith-healing, however much Jesus assumes the role of a doctor here and his church that of a chemist's, would have been totally incomprehensible in religious times, as far as its notions of health are concerned. For the Middle Ages may also have counted among its prayers those which were sudorific, laxative and sedative, but none with the goal of making a businessman efficient again. Even the so-called earthiness of that time was, from a modern point of view, by no means a 'prototype' of health; for it produced the Children's Crusade, the flagellants and more besides. This sort of health contradicts the bracing air of the forest and yet in its day it was considered as precisely that of the real Christ-child, of the real forest hermit. And what of the so-called primitives themselves? – they rebuild their body so magically that it is hardly recognizable any more, they chisel and colour their teeth so that they do not, as they say of the Europeans, 'look like dogs', they aspire to and revere a kind of health which more closely resembles that of a somnambulist than that of an athlete. A health that is presupposed and remains constant is thus non-existent; unless in the universally materialistic, and only in this respect eternally youthful, formula: A merry head sits on a full belly. But every text that expands on mens sana in corpore sano is not actual experience but an ideal, and furthermore a different one in each respective society. Thus the doctor in each respective society, instead of restoring a primary general health, rather gives the sick man an additional one. He simply builds up that state of normality again which is socially in vogue at the time, and he is able to build it up again simply because the human body is also capable of functionally changing, and possibly improving itself. Up to now the body has been orientated solely towards limited, even dubious kinds of health, and society has also made possible a lot of diseases (venereal, tubercular, neurotic) of which the animal world knows little or nothing at all. But then the organic wishful dream at least imagined a body on which *only pleasure, not pain* is served and whose old age *does not have frailty as its fate*. So it is this fight against fate which links medical and social utopias in spite of everything. The power of replacing lost parts is not so great in the human body as it is in the lower animals, but in return it is only in man that the utopian power directed towards what he has never previously possessed takes effect. It is unlikely that this strength so fundamental to man, the strength to venture beyond and form anew, stops at his body. The exploration of this tendency is of course impossible without knowledge of what is already predisposed towards it in the body itself; everything else would be folly. As the body of all multicellular beings is predisposed to death, even the most secret medical plan, the abolition of death, is so far up in the air it becomes dizzy.

For this very reason such a plan appears crazy and, although it hovers at least before the fight against the ageing process, it is never seriously admitted. Which is understandable, even ante rem, because continuation in the flesh even as a wishful dream does not occur without mixed feelings, nor without horror; the legends of the Wandering Jew and the Flying Dutchman demonstrate this. We do not even first need to imagine the social non-sense of an earth which is incessantly becoming overcrowded: no entrance without any exit, no possible society without a spacious graveyard. All in all, even without grotesque visions, every organic desire for improvement remains up in the air if the social one is not acknowledged and taken into account. Health is a social concept, exactly like the organic existence in general of human beings, as human beings. Thus it can only be meaningfully increased at all if the life in which it stands is not itself overcrowded with anxiety, deprivation and death.

Malthus, birth-rate, nourishment

So hardly any of the ills of the body are removed when it is seen in isolation. That is why all improvers of our situation who merely concentrate on health are so petit-bourgeois and odd, the raw fruit and vegetable brigade, the passionate herbivores, or even those who practise special breathing techniques. All this is a mockery compared with solid misery, compared with diseases which are produced not by weak flesh but by powerful hunger, not by faulty breathing but by dust, smoke, and lead. Of course there are people who breathe correctly, who combine a pleasant self-assurance with well-ventilated lungs and an upright torso which is flexible to a ripe old age. But it remains a prerequisite that these people have money; which is more beneficial for a stooped posture than the art of breathing. The splendid Franziska Reventlov wrote a book along these lines about the money complex, the root cause of which nobody can ask their doctor to remove; it is the true glutton, the main problem, ninety per cent cancer. All the more interested, of course, was and remained the capitalist desire to cut into the social tumour by purely medical means. Breeding, or rather that which was perpetrated with it, only constitutes the most immediately repulsive, not the sole example. But no less repulsive is the great-grandmother of imperialist decimation, Malthus's theory of population. While no elaborated, purely medical utopia exists, a social utopia here appeared as it were with a medical base; by an economist, incidentally, who was no longer one at all, but already the first hired champion of the capitalist economy. Malthus decided in his 'Essay on the Principle of Population', 1798, that the reason for misery lies in the 'natural' contradiction between man's boundless striving for propagation and the limited increase in means of nourishment. Malthus promises: mass misery will only exist until a nation sensibly recognizes this connection and restricts reproduction to a degree which corresponds to the degree of loaves of bread available. Thus it is proletarian lechery, not capital, which produces social misery; and the so-called law of diminishing crop yield plainly passes sentence on the proletarian scapegoat. The crisis also simply appears as a shortage crisis, on the assumption of very slowly increasing forces of production, not as one of surplus. This theory was nevertheless modified many times, indeed a so-called academic socialist, Adolf Wagner, was preaching as late as the Nineties that Malthus was right in all essentials. But the most essential part of his theory only came into its own when the capitalist age was fulfilled, and only baseness can drag it out further by means of lies and murder. From the outset Malthus's theory was inherently misanthropic and bigoted, Marx had already certified its distinguishing feature to be 'a profoundly low level of thought', in both the moral and the scientific sense. Consequently its brutality broke out completely in the imperialist stage of capitalism; it is not only fêted among American murderers however, but it is also at least excused by right-wing socialists, like Eduard Heimann, and even ennobled in Georgian* fashion by particularly slimy fascists, like Edgar Salin. This renewed Malthusianism justifies war, the scrapping of the 'superfluous' unemployed, the fascist extermination of entire nations, and at the same time it is designed to distract from the true causes of capitalist misery those proletarians whose existence is tolerated after they have been subjected to the numerus clausus† of profit interest. All this recommends Malthus to the final spurt of capitalism; the latter is no longer capable of producing original ideas anyway, not even about its baseness and in the service of it. As soon as the wish is no longer a progressive one, it does not even become the father of an idea, but of a plot, or at least of a cover-up. The Malthusian approach, as a diagnosis diverted towards insufficient, socially isolated causes, is thus not just confined to a theory of overpopulation. For even in circles which know nothing about and want to have nothing to do with the hiring

---

* A reference to the German poet Stefan George.
† Restricted entry to German universities.

of champions, the purely medical recourse replaces or suppresses the recourse to the social causes of misery. The lever to improvement is here always placed as far down, as far beneath the real man and his milieu as possible. Hence, even without a literal Malthus, the interested or at least ignorant narrow view which, from a drop of blood as it were, sent in to the laboratory, thinks it can discern the entire sickness of mankind. The whole living sufferer is overlooked, but also particularly the circumstances in which he finds himself. Hence the overestimation of bacilli as the sole causes of epidemics; the microbe above all concealed other attendant symptoms of the disease, bad milieu and the like; it thus relieved people of the duty to look for the causes there as well. Consumption, for example, rages chiefly amongst the poor, but if that were taken into account, then poverty would have to be combatted, as a particularly damp patch; for which bourgeois medicine shows less inclination. A one-sidedly medical abortion of these ills is thus often only an intentionally or unintentionally chosen means of not having to remedy the real ills (ut aliquid fieri videatur, as it says on false prescriptions). Thus the entire Malthusian system, even apart from the man himself and his theory, epitomizes a whole area of repression. A mere mechanistic first-aid chest, without primacy of the social milieu and without plans to change it, without Pavlov and knowledge of the whole human being as a creature who is cerebrally and socially controlled, – this prevents the co-operation of doctor and red flag, with the latter leading the way. The social question is solved least of all by the poor exercising sexual self-control, we must intervene in production in a different way, and in a different production. An element of Malthus also had an effect on Darwin, who projected overpopulation back into the animal kingdom; Soviet Darwinists have recently rid Darwinism of its Malthusian mistakes. What remains is merely the plan for a birth control which for many people would certainly be beneficial and hence progressive. Namely as long as there is a capitalist society, and life within it is so precarious that such a society needs this kind of limitation or abortion. As long as it remains in the state it is in today: namely that of no longer being able to feed its slaves. The earth has room for everyone, or it would have, if it were run by the power of satisfying people's needs instead of by satisfying the needs of power.

The doctor's care

Only then would the doctor's work really make a clean start. The doctor

washes his hands before he begins, all the instruments are shiny, but that
is no good on its own. Society itself is dirty and diseased, it is the first
thing that needs clinical attention and planning. From this point of view
disease is really to blame, not that of the individual but of the group itself.
That ought to be obvious to the doctor too, whenever he enters the slums.
And even during treatment everything makes a mockery of his medical
conscience: the poor devil with diseased kidneys rides on the rattling lorry
so as not to lose his wages, clenching his teeth in pain, while the rich
man rests beneath his quilt. And after treatment: what is the life of most
people, for which the doctor makes them 'fit for work' again? What is
a health which merely makes people ripe to be damaged, abused, and shot
at again? A German paediatrician wrote even in 1931, with a common
sense which was to lead to certain non-bourgeois conclusions: 'To cure,
curare, to take care of somebody, means to see that their health is not
disturbed in any way. If this has happened though, the cura of the doctor
should be directed towards bringing the patient into circumstances which
are as favourable as possible for him.' A splendid goal, an economical one
in human terms, but one which is only attainable in socialist society. The
message is clear as things stand now (America leads the world in the number
of its citizens who are mentally ill): capitalism is unhealthy – even for
the capitalists. And the dreams of surgical intervention and organic
rebuilding are only really detoxicated in a different economy to that based
on profit. This holds true from the cradle to the grave, indeed even before
the cradle, all this as support for the political animal, but the right one.
The Marxist approach is consciously to make history and no longer to
suffer it passively. And the Marxist approach is also consciously to intervene
even in the *preconditioning* from which human beings emerge and in which
they physically live before they surface historically at all. This is their
existence in the womb, furthermore the physical state given to them at
that time. The idea of no longer putting up with it, in the form it has
assumed, suggests itself to the man who never accepts the idea of fate.
The bold plan suggests itself to him of seeking to set the course of the
body before birth in its very predispositions, just as we do with time when
we set a clock. To continue to mould it consciously after birth, in a possibly
changing and vital way, by means of controlled internal secretion or through
as yet unknown shaping energies. All this not in order to make people
the same, of which there is no prospect and for which there is no cause,
but rather so that their organic start is not much more unhampered than
their social one. So that they do not remain slaves to their own bodies

after they are no longer the slaves of society. They would all like to turn out well, in the measure of freedom which is socially in store for them and becoming clear to them. But for all that, the most visible hope remains the centrally steering influence of life in a society which has become healthy on the very diseases associated with being born and being grown up, especially on their prevention, and on our lifespan. There is a long way to go and one which, as far as sensitive flesh is concerned, it may not be possible to cover very satisfactorily for a long time to come. It is certainly not covered within the mere fitness for work in capitalist enterprise; for health is something which should be enjoyed, not abused. A long painless life to a ripe old age, culminating in a death replete with life, is still outstanding, has constantly been planned. *As if newborn: this is what the outlines of a better world suggest as far as the body is concerned.* But people cannot walk upright if social life itself still lies crooked.

FREEDOM AND ORDER, 36
SURVEY OF SOCIAL UTOPIAS

The earth belongs to nobody, its fruits belong to all.

John Ball

I simply cannot imagine the present situation of mankind as being the one in which it will now remain, simply cannot imagine it as being its whole and final destiny. Everything would then be a dream and an illusion; and it would not be worth the trouble of having lived and having joined in this constantly recurring, fruitless and meaningless game. Only in so far as I can regard this state as the means to a better one, as the crossing-point to a higher and more perfect one, does it acquire any value for me; I am able to bear it not for its own sake, but for the sake of the better life for which it prepares the way.

Fichte, The Destiny of Man

In place of the old bourgeois society with its classes and class differences there arises an association in which the free development of every individual is the condition for the free development of all.

Communist Manifesto

I. Introduction

A frugal meal

Many things would be easier if we could eat grass. In this respect the poor man, kept as a brute animal in other ways, does not have it as good as that animal. Only the air is readily available, but the soil first has to be tilled, over and over again. In a stooping, painful posture, not as one grows choice fruit upright against the wall. The days of collecting berries and fruit, and of free hunting have long been a thing of the past, a few rich people live off a lot of poor people. Constant hunger runs through life, it alone compels us to drudgery, only then does the whip compel us. If our daily bite to eat was as certain as the air, then there would be no misery. As it is, bread grows like leaves on the trees only in dreams. Nothing of this sort exists, life is hard, and yet there has always been a sense of escape, and that it is possible. Since this escape route was not found for so long, dreamy courage swarmed out on all sides.

The roast pigeons

A body which is full should have nothing to complain about. Provided it does not lack clothing and shelter, almost everything in other words. Provided there is no lack of friends and provided life proceeds easily and peacefully instead of being the stormy ride accorded to most people. But only the fairytale, which is always instructive, and the fairytale of an ideal state can tell us about the Magic Table, and the Land of Cockaigne. Just as the fountain of youth reaches into medical wishful images, so the Land of Cockaigne reaches into social ones, is a cheerful prelude to them. All human beings are equal there, i.e. well off, there is neither effort nor work. Roast pigeons fly into people's mouths, every pigeon in the bush is already like one in the hand, all things and all dreams are ready to hand as commodities. Thus those in Cockaigne lead a pleasant life, they are no longer prepared to let the rich tell them how unenviable riches are. How unhealthy a lot of sleep is, how deadly leisure is, how much we need deprivation so that all life does not come to a standstill. The people have merrily embroidered on their most nourishing fairytale, their most obvious utopian model, and even caricatured it: the vines are tied together with sausages, the mountains have turned into cheese, the streams are flowing with the best muscatel. The Magic Table and Indian magic meadows here exist as a public institution, as a state of happiness per se.

Lunacy and colportage even here

The fiery owl undeniably flies into these images too. It flies further than it did in the medical dreams, and an end to deprivation does not sound mad. But several world-improvers were paranoid or in danger of being so, in a way that is not wholly incomprehensible. Lunacy, as a loosening up for an invasion of the unconscious, for possession by the unconscious, also occurs in what is Not-Yet-Conscious. The paranoiac is often a project-maker, and there is occasionally also a mutual connection between the two. So that a utopian talent slips off the rails in a paranoid way, indeed almost voluntarily succumbs to a delusion (cf. Vol. I, p. 92ff.). An example is furnished by one of the greatest utopians, Fourier; in his work th strangest images of the future grow alongside a sharp tendency-analysis. Concerning not society but nature, in so far as it is included in our own harmoniously polite order and sings along with it as it were. Thus, as a bonus to social liberation, Fourier plans a North Pole Crown, that is to say a second sun which will provide the North with Andalusian warmth. The Crown emits a fragrance, warms and glows, an aura emanates from it which desalinates the ocean, in fact improves it into lemonade. Herrings, cod and oysters will immeasurably increase, by a shifting of the faulty position of the earth's axis, whereas the sea-monsters will perish. These monsters are replaced by an anti-shark, an anti-whale, friendly paradisial creatures 'who pull the ships when they are becalmed'. But on the land Fourier prophesies 'an elastic conveyance, the anti-lion, with which a rider who sets out from Calais in the morning has his breakfast in Paris, spends his afternoon in Lyon and his evening in Marseilles'. Though – in the case of great utopians – we see that there is also method in their madness, not merely its own method but also the technological one of a later age: the anti-whale is the steamship, the anti-lion is the express train, indeed the motor-car. Just as foolish, just as anticipatory is Fourier's theory that man will develop a new organ, even though it will be on the end of a tail which he will grow (Daumier supplied a drawing of this fantasy). By means of this organ, people absorb the 'ethereal auras', are able to

contact the inhabitants of other stars, while the planets copulate. The
'ethereal auras' have since been received through the radio, although the
rapport with the stars is still a shambles, the technological body and the
copulation of the planets even more so. These fairytales are not so very
different in appearance from those of Jules Verne, or at least from the
starrily utopian colportages in Lasswitz, and especially Scheerbart. But all
playfulness is lacking in Fourier; the paint-pot of this seriousness stands
in the realm of paranoia, not just in that of colportage, though of course
this colportage is also coloured by paranoia. Is there not a sense of the
fine element of madness that even tinged the liberal utopianizing Freemasons
of the eighteenth century, the bourgeois with their set squares and
pyramids? Is there not a kind of jester's cap perched on the whole
ceremonial, on the preparations and symbols which are supposed to lead
the young Mason towards 'the realm of Astraea'? Even Saint-Simon, the
great utopian, in his last works concerning the pope of industry, quietly
touched on the delusion which occasionally threatens world-improvers;
his disciple Auguste Comte was completely lost in it, in his final phase.
Comte extended Saint-Simon's Church of Intelligence so far that not only
humanity but also space and the earth were supposed to be worshipped.
Humanity as the 'Great Being', space as the 'Great Medium', the earth
as the 'Great Fetish'; Clotilde, Comte's dead mistress, became the new
Virgin Mary. These are the bizarre ideas which adorn some of the most
energetic castles in the air. Yet, as noted above, they are also not wholly
unrelated to colportage, that colportage touched on and occasionally
incorporated in a fruitful way by the novel of an ideal state. Almost all
older utopias use space-machines, almost all newer ones the time-machines
of an exotic imagination, when they travel into the social dreamland. Many
seek, in their titles at least, to give the happy island the sparkle of lurid
colportage. Thus there is a 'Kingdom of Macaria',* an 'Isle of Felsenburg't
which was so famous, a 'Crystal Age':‡ names like those of booths at
a fairground in which mermaids from distant shores are displayed; even
the secret tones of an invisible lodge,§ a long way out, were not lacking.
The fairytales of wonderlands, of wishful times and wishful spaces give
a sparkle here; since Alexander the most beautiful utopias are set in South

---

* Samuel Hartlib, 'A Description of the Famous Kingdome of Macaria', 1641.
† Johann Gottfried Schnabel, 'Insel Felsenburg', 1731–43.
‡ W. H. Hudson, 'A Crystal Age', 1887.
§ A reference to the title of Jean Paul's early novel 'The Invisible Lodge', 1793.

Sea islands, in a Ceylon of the Golden Age, in the wonderland of India. Sailor's yarns lend the trappings even to important social utopias, as in that of Thomas More; happiness appears in this setting long before the times were ripe for it; for more than two thousand years the exploitation of man by man has been abolished in utopias. Social utopias contrasted the world of light with night, broadly pictured their land of light, with the sparkle of justice in which the man who is oppressed feels uplifted, and the man who goes without feels content. The fact that this fantastically pictured state of affairs was so often conceivable only in colportage, as the sole remaining form of adventure and of evidently good victory, is not surprising. It is the state of affairs which even today the soldier in Brecht's 'Threepenny Novel' dreams has finally come about: 'Baseness lost its high fame, the useful became famous, stupidity lost its privileges, people had no dealings with brutality any more.' Once the islands of the sun are reached, through lunacy, sailor's yarns or even simply, in the latest social utopias, in the work of Bellamy or Wells, through magnetic sleep, then things are by no means so lively on them any more, apart from the splendours of nature, things are more normal. For one would think it is surely normal, or ought to be so, for millions of people not to allow themselves to be ruled, exploited and disinherited for thousands of years by a handful of upper class. It is normal for such a vast majority not to put up with being the damned of this earth. Instead, the very awakening of this majority is the utterly unusual occurrence, the rare event in history. For a thousand wars there are not even ten revolutions; so difficult is walking upright. And even where they succeeded, as a rule the oppressors turned out to be exchanged rather than abolished. An end to deprivation: this did not sound at all normal for an incredibly long time, but was a fairytale; only as a waking dream did it enter the field of vision.

New Moral Worlds on the horizon

Only far away from here does everything seem better, things are held in common. This is how the citizens live in the work of Thomas *More*: moderate work, not above six hours a day, the proceeds are distributed equally. There is no crime any more and no compulsion, life is a garden, cosy and noble happiness hang around openly. Things are strict, however, in the great counterpart to More's Utopia, in *Campanella's* City of the Sun. The happiness of all is here set straight not by means of freedom but by means of an order which is planned down to the slightest detail. Despite even shorter working hours than in More, only four hours a day, and a communist distribution of the proceeds once again, the beneficial burden of rules lies on every hour, and also on every pleasure. The rules are ascertained and upheld by savants, particularly astrological savants; the City of the Sun is precisely fitted into the universe. It is a long way from here, via 1789, via the formal freedom and equality of all which followed and turned into the cruellest misery, a long way to the utopians of the industrial age, to Owen, Fourier, Saint-Simon. Natural Right lies on this path, and also *Fichte's* dream of a closed commercial state in which everyone possesses de jure, and thus in utopian terms in facto, the provisions and goods to which he has a fundamental right. But in the meantime cash payment had become the sole link of society, a different link was sought, the forgotten one of fraternity for example. *Owen* at first turned directly to the workers and remained active in their midst, not just as a factory owner. Private property, the Church and the prevailing form of marriage destroy human happiness; in New Harmony they do not exist any more. The capitalists of distribution and production: merchant and factory owner, are regarded as dispensable phenomena; bazaars are to arise in their place, in which the worker receives in exchange the commodity which other workers have produced and which he needs, in accordance with the number of hours of work he has put in. *Fourier,* the other, harsher utopian, pre-Marxist in the sharpness of his analysis, Fourier constructed the Nouveau Monde industriel et sociétaire not so much on philanthropy as on criticism. On criticism of bourgeois civilization, as the last order that has appeared. It is the curse against which Fourier sets the vision of gentleness, of the disappearance of the fear of life. Fourier was the first to see how in present society poverty springs from affluence itself; the remedy is a departure to communist islands, to the social islands which Fourier calls phalanxes; and they are all attuned to one another as if under world-leadership. A kind of harmonic theory of passions completed the smoothly designed economy; the new world was to be as clearly tuned as a harp. Owen and Fourier designed their state (more a happy group than a happy state) along federalist lines; in *Saint-Simon,* however, it appears in centralized form, again closer to order than to individual freedom. Almost more fervid than in Owen and Fourier is the hatred here of unearned income and the misery it presupposes, of the feudal and bourgeois men of private means, as painted by Goya and Daumier. All love is reserved for work, and the magic word for Saint-Simon is l'industrie. For him workers are of course also the factory

owners, merchants, bankers; thus the 'Industrial System' fell back behind
Owen, who managed without these types. But Saint-Simon's industrialist
does not remain private, he becomes a public official, and society as a whole
a Church of Intelligence. Exploitation is eradicated, because individual
economy is eradicated, in its place blossoms the red dawn of planland,
the blessed gift of industry – with a social high priest at its head.

All this consequently leaves the old land, more or less peacefully and
rapidly. Comfort seemed to be most rapidly attained when new inventions
also came to its aid. The newer fairytales of an ideal state are often inter-
spersed with them, More paints flat roofs and large windows of light into
his dreamland, Campanella even motor-cars. There are also fairytales of
an ideal state which do not so much picture social dreams as technological
ones instead. As does *Bacon's* 'New Atlantis', the land beyond the Pillars
of Hercules, beyond the known world. A happy people lives there, happy
above all because it does not content itself with that which nature casts
off as flotsam and jetsam as it were. But the Atlantians delve into the
natural forces themselves, with senses sharpened to the extreme by instruments, and after they have taken a deep look they utilize what they have
seen. New plants and working animals surround man, life is chemically
prolonged, even the old dream of being a bird is realized there, by carriages
which rise into the air. A social section of this novel, with its many open
doors to tomorrow, remained unwritten; so it is not known by which
means the Magic Table that has grown enormous only yielded good things,
and not also, for hostile wishes, poison as well. Purely technological images
of progress have thus always made progress appear too cheap, too linear;
just as today, presented in isolation and with social change left out, they
are delusions or means of deception. In the honest, yet abstract utopias
the technologically supported belief in progress has very often facilitated
the illusion of undisturbed success and advance. Among all the utopians
only one, Fourier, has maintained that even in the better future every
phase has its ascending line, but also the danger of a descending one. An
abstract utopia, even the so-called socialist state of the future, namely that
which is only for our grandchildren, very rarely knows any real danger;
even its victory, not just its path, then seems undialectical. This even
though a more sorrowful than trusting mood undoubtedly hangs over
the first and most famous, though coolest utopia: that of *Plato*. Of course,
unfriendliness is here transferred from the existing state to the ideal one
anyway: the aversion of the upper classes to the masses. The wishful image
does not serve the latter, the farmer class, they are to be kept in their

place instead. A military state is dreamed up which is also an inward one, with Brahmans of this world at its head. It is the idealized Doric state, even though crowned with philosophy, from which Sparta was far removed. And the 'Let everything be in common', which is not lacking in Plato, and indeed through him became the most distinguished utopian catch-phrase, this dangerous phenomenon was confined to the two upper classes; it was a monastic privilege, not a democratic demand. Thus the restraint in this utopia, though admittedly at the cost of its being the most re-actionary, is not one in the fairytale sense at all, in the sense of the Golden Age. And there is restraint even in the second most famous utopia of the ancient world, in *Augustine's* City of God. It was of course originally designed in its salvation for Adam and Eve, but their Fall prevented it, and since then the City of God has been making a pilgrimage on earth. It cannot appear as an earthly state, for it embraces only the chosen few, it is a Noah's Ark. Its peace is threatened and lonely, sunk into the ocean of sorrow and injustice of which the world consists. But neither Plato's restraint, which was certainly dearly paid for with its reactionary foundation, nor the pessimistic restraint of Augustine have deeply affected the carefree nature of the social-utopian image of happiness. The novels of an ideal state very often saw all contradictions resolved by their prescriptions, health has become paralysed in them as it were. No fresh questions, no different countries appear in the margin any more, the island, although a future one itself, is largely insulated against the future. This is connected in many ways with technological optimism, as noted above, but it is ultimately connected above all with the contraction which the utopian has undergone in this its most obvious expression: utopia was confined to the best constitution, to an abstraction of constitution, instead of being perceived and cultivated in the concrete totality of being. Thus apart from levity or fanatical abstraction the utopian has also received from the novel of an ideal state a departmental character totally inappropriate to its raw material which permeates all spheres. Instead utopian organization, that is, the intended complete satisfaction of needs, without the empty wishes which are to be forgotten, with the profound wishes which are still to be wished and the gratification of which leads to the so unbluntable happiness of an ever-increasing intensification of human profusion, must be comprehended as a Totum on which the social utopias themselves depend. And into which they also finally wanted and had to overshoot within their department, with socially radical, necessarily good conditions in mind. This Totum ensures that the old fairytales of an ideal state are still new and meaningful, that even their mistakes are instructive and their claims are binding. They make the claim to which Oscar Wilde's proposition refers: *no map of the world which does not contain the country of Utopia is worth looking at.* The old social dreams painted the isle of abstraction and love; because of these two qualities nothing was to be difficult on it either.

Utopias have their timetable

The dreams of living together in a better way were for a long time only thought out internally. Yet they are not arbitrary, not so completely free-rising as it may occasionally appear to the originators themselves. And they are not disconnected with one another, as if they only had to be empirically enumerated like odd events. On the contrary: in their apparent picture-book or revue character they show themselves to be rather precisely socially conditioned and coherent. They obey a social mandate, a suppressed or only just evolving tendency of the imminent social level. They give expression to this tendency, even if mixed with private opinion, then with the dream of the best constitution per se. Of course, the social utopias do not reflect the existing tendency with nearly the same tenacity or even sharpness typical of a different form of anticipation: bourgeois Natural Right. Yet they are by no means independent of the surge towards the next level, despite all skimming, all romance of an unconditional social happiness. They speak with consternation, even if seldom in concretely mediated terms, of what is imminent, they couch their communist final happiness in forms of the next tendency in each case. This is so in Augustine, and clearly so in Thomas More and Campanella, in Saint-Simon. Augustine's work is influenced by the incipient feudal economy, that of More by free trading capital, that of Campanella by the absolutist period of manufacture, and that of Saint-Simon by the new industry. Although in a transparent way each time, with heaven on earth and nothing less in mind. Thus even utopias have their timetable, even the boldest are tied to it in their direct anticipations. Differences in respective location also play a part, it influences the Englishman More and the Italian Campanella most decidedly. More's utopia of freedom thus corresponds in its non-communist sections to the coming parliamentary form of English domestic politics, as does Campanella's utopia of order to the absolutist one on the Continent. Such things show that however privately the dream rises it contains the tendency of its age and the next age expressed in images, though in overshooting ones even here, images almost always overshooting into the 'original and final state'. So much for the social mandate and coherence in the series of social utopias; it is always stronger than the individual characteristics of the utopians. And utopias are taken even less from the drawers of *a priori* possibilities for instance, independently of history, than they are from the depths of sheer *private* feeling. All possibilities only attain possibility within history; even the New is historical. Even the Novum of an abolition of private property (which is anticipated by most social utopias, in that no longer topical section which transcends to the final level), even this Novum is not a priori unalterable. It looks very different in the work of the not very liberal Plato than in that of Thomas More, and very different again in his work than in that of Robert Owen. Not even the New itself, in its respective dimension, not even the utopian element, as pertaining to the superstructure, is invariant. The 'future ages' which Jacob shows to his sons on his deathbed are not the same, either in their content or in their concept of the future, as those which the chiliast Joachim of Calabrese had in mind in the thirteenth century, let alone those meant by Saint-Simon. What is invariant is solely the intention towards the utopian, for it is continuously discernible throughout history: yet even this invariance immediately becomes variable when it gets beyond expressing the first word, when it speaks the contents which are always historically varied. These contents are not at rest like Leibniz's possibilités éternelles, from which the anticipator selects now this one and now that, they move solely in the history which produces them. Which is true of all utopian contents, not merely of the social-utopian ones of the best of all societies. The social waking dreams themselves, of course, are not yet the most significant or profound amongst the structured ones, yet in return a utopian element develops in them at its social base. Thus they do not merely exhibit the largest scope, but together with technological utopias they are also the most practical manifestation of human wishful landscape. A proud one too; for social utopias, even in their tentative beginnings, were always capable of saying no to the despicable, even if it was the powerful, even if it was the habitual. The latter is in fact subjectively even more of a hindrance for the most part than the powerful, since it presents itself more continually and therefore less dramatically; since it numbs the awareness of contradiction, and reduces the cause for courage. But social utopias have almost always arisen in contrast to this numbness, in contrast to that kind of habit which among despicable acts, especially among intolerable ones, constitutes half of moral unimaginativeness and the whole of political stupidity. Social utopias functioned as a part of the power to be amazed and to find the given so little self-evident that only changing it can clarify it. Changing it into a state of society which, as Marx says, does not merely end the isolation from the political community, but the isolation from essential humanity. The social dreams have developed with a wealth of fantasy, but at the same time, as Engels adds, with a wealth 'of brilliant germs of ideas and ideas bursting out of their fantastic cloak'. Until the designing of the future is concretely corrected in the work of Marx and brought into the truly comprehended timetable of a due tendency, so that it does not stop but only now vigorously begins. Without the growing wealth of anticipations, of still abstract plans and programmes, which are now to be recalled, the final social dream would not have come either. It is now to be found at the height of consciousness and thus becomes, really full of planning at last, social awakening.

II. Social Wishful Images of the Past

Solon and the contented medium

As long as we are children, we will not put up with a lot. A poor man who has been made to get used to pressure takes things differently. Only late in life comes a feeling of how badly people behave and a glimpse of how things could be different. At first this glimpse is fugitive, evasive, the individual falls back on himself as quickly as possible, without needs. Thus Bias said that he carried all his possessions with him; he did not need much and did not ask much of others. Life without luggage appeared to be the best from both an economic and a social point of view, this sort of thing was never wholly forgotten. Friction becomes slight, envy and cheating come to an end, there is no cause for either among those who are idle. Epigrams from the time of the Seven Sages were all of the same opinion in this respect, in a figurative sense they all wish that man should be contented. He can be happy with a little and only with a little; too much property, says Solon, should be shared. It is not riches that are desirable for us, but virtue, and that alone makes communal living easy. Nobody is to be considered happy before his death, this maxim also means that there is no relying on riches, that they are advisable neither for an

individual nor as the condition of lots of people. As general and condescend-
ing as all this is, it still seeks a quiet medium. This medium was to feature
that happiness which grants the same thing to everybody and thus persists.

Diogenes and the exemplary beggars

If life that was too fat was made lean, then where was the place to stop?
Certainly not at anything to which man had previously been accustomed,
nor at sweet contentment. Diogenes lived out everybody's wish of going
to the dogs,* for man and the group he forms are the false, devious animal
that has become artificial. Antisthenes, as head of the Cynics, taught from
the start that the real community was like that among dogs who know
how to beg and are not shy of doing so; a free herd, satisfying its simple
needs. All people should live together as this loose herd, and no nation
should be separated by borders from another. Gold is abolished, marriage
and households too, and extreme absence of needs (something which dogs
do not possess of course) frees people from one another and from their
surroundings. Since the man dreamed as a dog is no longer involved in
unnecessary pleasure, his other involvements come to an end. He becomes
independent of the circumstances which stand around life, he and his kind
are at home in every situation, as long as it is an undisturbed one, one
which has as little to do with the state as possible. Freedom therefore begins
here by no means boldly and lavishly, it begins fugitively and offensively.
Thus among other things Diogenes publicly masturbated from his barrel,
and also regretted that he could not drive away his hunger just as simply.
Krates and Hipparchia, a girl from a wealthy family who adopted the life
of a beggar with the Cynic, publicly consummated their sexual relations
in a pillared hall. Apart from dogs the simple manners of their forefathers
served as a model, satisfied with life and unafraid of it. The olden days
with rye bread, milk and turnips were the only healthy, natural ones, and
people who declare their faith in them get along with one another as easily
as all those who have eaten their fill. Also almost all work becomes
superfluous amongst those without needs, only a little splashing on the
water is needed to keep the naked swimmer afloat. And a city of barrels
for the free man to live in makes it easy enough to keep envy at bay.
Above all, the man who is frugal in this way sleeps soundly at night, and

* In this section, Bloch plays on the original meaning of the word Cynic; dog-like.

walks upright during the day; for he does not settle in the vicinity of
conditions over which he has no power.

Aristippus and the exemplary scroungers

But parallel to this ran the lure of the merry life which goes short of nothing.
The original golden age was then conceived not as that of frugal equality
but as that of lavish equality. Instead of a rugged bohemia, one of pleasure
and scrounging here fills a proper existence. It taught that pleasure is the
human share, enjoyment for its own sake, independently of stilling our
needs, that is what distinguishes man from the animals. The power of
enjoyment, it was affirmed here, elevates man above dogs, above animals,
above the satisfied ascetic (Marx would by no means have denied this).
Human wishes unlike animal ones ultimately aim at orgy, and they are
completely natural in this respect. Thus Aristippus, the head of the
Hedonists, taught that not absence of needs but the unlimited, shrewd
capacity for enjoyment was the natural human condition; and that it should
be cultivated. A Hedonist breed thus arose, in contrast to the Cynic one,
and its state is dreamed as one of mutual or patronizing egoists. The best
of all communities is that which is least of a hindrance to the highest possible
pleasure of its citizens. The Hedonist group demands no individual sacrifice,
recognizes neither family nor fatherland, least of all prohibitions which
hamper an individual's desire for happiness or even simply determine it
from the start. This links Cynics and Hedonists, the freethinkers of absence
of needs and of pleasure; they are both anarchic. Their own lives are to
be the state that is organized, social life is to be unobtrusive like strolling
in the marketplace. Aristippus delighted in his social independence which
allowed him to wear the beggar's cloak and fine clothes with equal pro-
priety. He delighted, as Xenophon relates, in the political independence
of his roving life, in his ubi bene, ibi patria, and he set it up as an example.
Dependence was allowed at most within friendship, a later Hedonist by
the name of Annikeris even taught that a city of friends should be established, not because of its usefulness but because of the self-generating
goodwill and the pleasure that results from it. The democratization of
this essentially aristocratic image of enjoyment was furthered by the fact
that even the poorer citizen benefited from slavery; on this basis a commune
of enjoyment could be generally conceived. But above all, the Hedonistic image corresponded much more exactly than the Cynic one to the

conceptions of the Golden Age, to those that still remained vivid. In his malicious comedy 'The Birds', Aristophanes indicated the scale and the power which the popularity of this image of pleasure had assumed. The image of pleasure became a rebellious one in the play in so far as it was never accommodated, never remained undisturbed. After all, the heroes of the comedy, Euelpides (Hopegood) and Peisthetairos (Trusty Friend), who were little satisfied with the earthly Fortunate Islands, decided to remain in the clouds with the birds and to propose that they found a new state in the air. Yet the different, considerably more earthly and actually existing utopia of that time is also already cited in the comedy. It is really against this that Aristophanes directs his armoury of wit:

> A man will never die of want any more,
> Because everything is the property of everybody,
> Bread, cake, garments, salted meat,
> Wine, peas, lentils and garlands.

This verse – one like it has already appeared in connection with derided wishful images (Vol. I, p. 436) – undoubtedly refers to recollections of the Golden Age which were beginning to grow dangerous and serious at that time. The verse satirizes the plebeian 'natural state' with its reference to lentils, and with the profusion of other goods it satirizes the Hedonist ideal, or rather: the democratic sell-out of this ideal. The violent belching which fills such travesties is Epicurus among the people as it were; freedom is meant to appear as gluttony. It appeared among the Hedonists themselves as wine for all, in so far as they are human beings and not slaves. The freedom of pleasure was democratic, despite boundless egoism; for happiness was conceived in generous terms once again, in terms of live and let live, with polite good manners.

Plato's dream of the Doric state

It is one thing to mock such wishes, another to render them harmless. Plato undertook to do the latter, in such a way that he both took up the utopian drive and reversed its trend towards freedom. Plato wrote the first detailed work on the best state, the 'Republic', and this work is as well thought-out as it is reactionary. Here there are no vague dreams any more, no vague notions dreamed through to the end, but neither is some original golden age longed for and extolled. Lost freedom (of a rustic or lavish kind) is replaced by unattained order: the dreaming is consolidated by its content and becomes imperious. And it is even based on an empirical model here, a model which is found very close at hand (with a realism which is surprising in this great idealist), namely in Sparta. The love for Sparta and its aristocrats began to answer the interests of the Athenian upper classes after the Peloponnesian War, their interest in dismantling democracy. The ruling class always tends towards the dismantling of democracy as soon as conditions arise like those described by Plato: 'The present state is falling into two states, that of the poor and that of the rich, who pursue one another with implacable hatred.' At such times there is a tendency towards total state authority, towards a police state, one based on order. Thus Plato's utopia (the paradox of a utopia of the ruling class) became an idealization of Sparta; the growing tension between classes recommended Sparta as the strictest Greek state, as the remedy based on authority. Farmers, guardian-auxiliaries, guardian-rulers, these three castes of Plato's ideal state have their prototypes on the Peloponnese; they are the Helots, the Spartiates and the Council of Elders (Gerusia). Thus Plato takes up the popular dreams of an ideal state and reverses them; thus he builds a splendid social-utopian ship and gives it a headwind; thus he transposes the land for which the ship is destined and replaces the Golden Age with that of black soup. Only in passing does Plato also recall the Golden Age as that of plenty, indeed he adds that only through the 'worsening of the world' had authorities and laws become necessary. And the famous verdict on the natural state as being one of pigs refers not to its obscene but to its undemanding character. Socrates gives an account of these undemanding creatures in the second Book of the 'Republic', and how their healthy state is to be described: 'We will give them peas and beans, and they are to roast myrtle-berries and acorns at the fire and wash them down with a sip of wine.' And Glaucon then calls this 'a state of pigs, for these are just the things we would throw down for them to eat as well' – whereby the Cynic state is therefore also rejected from the angle of its undemanding nature, not merely from that of its lack of discipline and its bohemia. But immediately afterwards, in the same Book of the 'Republic', Socrates also tackles the Hedonist state, the state of gluttons. He treats its effeminate happiness ironically: 'We must introduce painting and gold and ivory and everything like that. . . This also includes all heroic hunters, the imitative artists, the poets and their servants, the rhapsodists, actors, dancers, showmen, artists in all sorts of fields, among others those who make jewellery for women.' And a higher happiness was only granted to the Golden Age in so far as people in those days exploited the advantages of their situation in order to gain higher knowledge. So there is no room for any Saturnalia in Plato's temple state, no carnival of nature, none of art and superfluous beauty: a thoroughly ruled world arises, the rational structure of a permanent realm. Its people have a Doric toughness, its order remains precisely that of Spartan aristocratism. Even the holding in common of women and other things (among the upper castes), even this so apparently dangerous similarity of Plato's ideal state to the anarchy of Cynics and Hedonists stems from the Spartan camp. In Sparta too an elderly man could supply his wife with another man, and an unmarried man could borrow the wife of his friend; in Sparta too the possession of gold and silver was forbidden the warrior caste, the provisions and tools of others could be shared. The Gerusia though, Lycurgus' Council of Elders, only provided the framework for the upper caste in Plato's state, the philosophical caste; for even the eldest members of the Gerusia were not Plato's academicians, quite the opposite. So when Plato called for the Philosopher Ruler, when he taught that the state would not become a good one until the regents became philosophers or the philosophers became regents, the anti-intellectual model of Sparta is certainly abandoned in this one point, as far as the content of the framework provided by members of the Gerusia is concerned. But it is noteworthy that even the caste of philosophers in Plato's utopia does not last: the deeply disappointed work of his old age, the 'Laws', wholly does without an aristocracy of education. Instead, in this work the ideal society is posited entirely as a police state, now incidentally retaining private property and marriage. The 'Laws' are instructive as a restrained, and as it were burnt-fingered social utopia; they content themselves with the design of a second- or even third-best state. Of course in this diminished ideal, precisely because it is diminished, the growth of reaction is particularly strong, extending as far as a criminal law against political and particularly cultural innovators; so that it almost seems as if even Plato – who had become highly conservative as a result of his pessimism – no longer regarded such an ideal of order as – an ideal. However, definition of the state and criticism of the state in the 'Republic', and even more so in the 'Laws', are exclusively orientated around the idea of tiered architecture, tiered human architecture.

And what is more, this structure is already supposed to be exactly predetermined in the human predisposition. Man accordingly has three forces or parts in his soul, desire, courage, and reason. These three active voices are arranged in order of value from bottom to top, thus there is a various order of rank even here. Desire, courage, and reason are allocated to the loins, chest, and head; as each predominates they form the fiery character of southern peoples, the bold one of northern peoples, and the level-headed character of the Greeks. They constitute the three kinds or directions of level-headedness among the Greeks: the level-headedness of desire is obedience, that of courage bravery, that of reason wisdom. Greek virtue derives from level-headedness: the virtue of obedience thus further constitutes the farmers, the virtue of courage the military class, and the virtue of wisdom the class of philosophical legislators. So in this way a state willed by nature so to speak is supposed to arise, a state whose laws so little contradict nature that they complete and crown nature in the social stratum. Very much unlike the Cynics and Hedonists, Plato consequently deduces no libertine Natural Right from nature, but a directly hierarchical one: the principle of suum cuique is contained in physis itself. The third Book of the 'Republic' even maintains, in a literal sociological application of chemistry, that those who are suited to be regents have had gold added to their souls, the warriors silver, and the traders copper and iron. So the suum cuique certainly seems easy; Plato also adds that as a rule children will resemble their parents, so that 'by nature' a son from a lower class would only rarely fit into a higher one or even a soldier's child into the trading class. Statecraft in general is the fusing of basic characterological-social circumstances into a harmonious whole, into the harmony of 'justice'. We will often encounter the structure of Plato's ideal state later on; for it is that of a longed-for 'state morality'. The fact that (along with the slaves) there was the broad exploited mass of peasants and traders in this ideal state, this pervasive immorality was cloaked by the ideology of a tiered justice; and the exploitation here, as is obvious, was ideologized by the doctrine of an innate servant soul (of base metal). The upper classes are completely supported economically by the work of the third class, and their communism is not one of work but one of non-work: of the police and the learned Gerusia. It is not as if Plato did not want to 'tax' the lower class with the military and monastic communism of the upper classes, for instance; as if it were too tough. He sees it instead as too noble, the philistines are not worthy of it, they must definitely continue to have cares, unlike the aristocratic commune which has no cares any more, but takes care, of its state. Even the task which Plato assigns to the upper classes of watching 'that poverty and wealth do not creep into the state unnoticed',

– even this variety of financial asceticism, applied to the third class, simply means letting no rich and hence dangerous plebeians appear on the scene. Despite these not exactly revolutionary contents, Plato's 'Republic' subsequently continued to act like a socialist, indeed communist work. It was regarded, particularly in the Renaissance, as a kind of set of instructions for socialism, supported by the powerful authority of the great philosopher. Thomas Münzer, the theologian of the German peasants' revolution, also cites Plato's utopia, moreover in the spirit of Omnia sint communia, not in the spirit of suum cuique. This is a productive misunderstanding: the image of the Golden Age, which Plato had given a Spartan turn, was now again recalled in terms of primitive communism, and as if Plato, by distinguishing the commune as what was best for his nobility, had also been the guide to this best form of society for all. Thus the 'Idea' as it were of social utopia, one without classes and stations, was restored in this version of the great idealist. There and then, Plato's best state looked different of course; he had the wishful dream, in the framework of Sparta, of a medieval, indeed military-clerical ecclesiastical realm rather than a socialist construction. And long before freedom found its novel of an ideal state, Plato's 'Republic' utopianized order. A perfect Spartan order, with people as pedestals, walls, and windows, where all of them are only free to be supporting, protective, and illuminating in the ranked limb structure.

Hellenistic fairytales of an ideal state, Iamboulos' island of the sun

The more lively and more popular wishes persisted, as if nothing had happened. If they were not accommodated at home, then they sought their ideals in the distance and not just in the Golden Age of long ago and tomorrow. But this temporal distance cloaked itself in a spatial one, it became that of a remote wonderland. The decisive factor here was the broadening of the geographical horizon by the campaigns of Alexander. The accounts of Arabia and India, which Nearch, Alexander's admiral, sent back home, gave a solid footing, as it were, to the hopes of the Golden Age. The Hellenistic utopia was reinforced and illustrated by the discovery of India in much the same way as the modern one was by the discovery of America: the space of the ideal state found a geometrical locus. Also there is only one single utopian account, that of Theopompos concerning the fabulous Meropis, in which the land of happiness is assigned to the dim and distant past (as in Plato's 'Critias' concerning Atlantis). But the strange novel by Euemeros 'Holy Inscription' (around 300 B.C.), which has survived in fragmentary form, is the first to have the fiction of a present-day utopia. An almost paradoxical gain results from the connection with sailors' yarns: utopian graphicness. From Arabia, Euemeros sails to a previously hidden land, the island of Panchaea; there things are produced in common, the proceeds evenly distributed, the soil (this motif also appears for the first time) yields fruit without cultivation and sowing. A people lives here whose happiness and prosperity stem from their connection with the days when Zeus was still on the earth. Kingship and authority, apart from the mild one of priests, are unknown and superfluous: for Zeus had taught the principles of bliss so perfectly that no further interventions from above were needed. But Euemeros was not merely giving an account of the social utopia of a far-off land, this social utopia itself was again the veiled expression of an educational fairytale about Zeus and the gods. For it is in a temple that Euemeros claims to have discovered the 'Holy Inscription' from which his utopia gets its name: the history of the gods from primeval times, from which the secluded happiness of Panchaea has survived. Uranus, Cronos, Zeus, and Rhea were princes and princesses, only later were they elevated to the status of gods – exactly like Alexander and the Diadochi* in the days of Euemeros. This is sheer atheism, the gods became beneficent human local dignitaries, have nothing to do with running the world, heaven and the like, are products of Fame. On this point Euemeros was close to the Hedonistic school, particularly to the precursor of Epicurus, the first Greek atheist Theodoros. Accordingly the happy land of Panchaea was also mentioned in the great Epicurean didactic poem by Lucretius (De rerum natura, 2, 417); an incense land of this world. Happy utopia and religious enlightenment become one and the same in this land: the earthly tyrants and the gods, above all the stern, aloof ones, fall at the same stroke. It was, after all, precisely the temple of Zeus in Panchaea that contained the document which caused Zeus and all the gods to be worshipped as former human beings, as people from a milder, almost matrilinear age, from an age when even Zeus still presided over agriculture. Now Euemeros fundamentally continued to have an influence only with this derivation of the gods from good kings, not with his dream of an ideal state; but Hellenism also produced another dream of an ideal state,

---

* Diadochi: the Macedonian generals amongst whom the empire of Alexander was divided after his death.

in which there was only pleasure and plenty. Unencumbered with holy inscriptions, but provided in an intensified way with *good* nature, with that outside man, which Euemeros had also trusted. It is Iamboulos' 'Island of the Sun', a communist and collective feast; hence thoroughly popular and yet new in its political festive character.

Wishes that were more than popular, namely rebellious ones, may also have played a part here. Iamboulos displays no frivolity, the surviving fragment of his work is at once vigorous, ceremonial and cheerful. It sweeps away slaves and masters, posits mutual work and joy, is consistent in both. That is why this novel of an ideal state also continued to be recalled for centuries, it was almost placed beside that of Plato. The fragments were well-known to the Renaissance, and also circulated in Italian and French translations. Some influence on Thomas More and his 'Utopia' is probable; Campanella's 'Civitas solis' has points of contact with Iamboulos not just in its title but also in its collective ethos. The collectivism in Iamboulos is more detailed and better thought-out in economic terms than that in Euemeros. Though a fabulous nature myth, in the shape of a thousand-fold fertility, is not lacking here either. This tropical element is conditioned in terms of the novel by the situation of the 'Island of the Sun', in practical terms it is a stopgap for still undeveloped forces of production. The Dionysian cult and the cult of Helios, from another age than the patriar-chal age or age of masters, may of course also have influenced the Hellenistic utopia. Such cults were still alive around the eastern Mediterranean, as cults of Dionysian liberation in fact, as the cancellation of all class differences in intoxication and feasting. Iamboulos transfers his novel of an ideal state to seven equatorial islands: the happiness of all is established there by the total lack of property. By alternating work in regular rotation, by doing away with the division of labour, and by deliberate education towards agreement and harmony. Slavery is likewise abolished, as is every kind of caste and Platonic utopia based on caste; everyone is subject to the same requirement to work, a totally unprecedented demand, isolated in a backward and forward direction, both in antiquity and in the feudal society which followed it. The fact that in this connection no separate economic systems remain even for house, home, and family rounds off the collective image of this utopia, the last and most radical to have been devised by antiquity. The uniting element still contained in the feast was also meant to enliven and cheer the requirement to work; tropical nature helped things along, added plenty and ease to the rotation of work. The seven equatorial islands thus thoroughly give the impression of lying in the land of the shortest shadow, in the land of wine without mine and thine, where a Dionysian sun still shines, one which melts together. Helios here beams equally on the just and unjust, does away with the justice of suum cuique, as if he really was a benefactor from the Golden Age, in fact the Golden Age itself.

The Stoics and the international world-state

In a way, the dreams considered so far were still modest in one respect. They settled on an island or in a city, did not go beyond this. The island was admittedly the model one per se, it provocatively demonstrated how a community ought to be, indeed almost how it could be. Yet the model kept its humble proportions, it never outgrew the Greek city-state. That all changed with the Stoic designs for an ideal state, they have larger spaces in their favour, ultimately even Roman ones. Though this was at the expense of detailed, certainly of radical content, and also of the fire which usually radiates from a person, not from a school. Stoic literature is long and multi-layered, it was in fact more effective than Plato and Aristotle put together, but unlike their schools it has no first-rate star in the middle (like the multi-layered neo-Platonism in Plotinus). In addition there is the threefold, though coherent phenomenon of the school: the Greek one with Zeno and Chrysippos, the Hellenistic one with Panaitios and Poseidonios, and the Roman one with Epictetus and Seneca. But despite this multi-layered aspect the Stoics exhibit as a historical phenomenon something of the concentrated and imperturbable qualities which they assigned to the wise man in their teachings. Thus they outlast pedantic Alexandrianism, that strange winter garden of Greece, and by no means become intricate and weak in the antiquarian hothouse. In the enormous processing of material, in which the Stoics competed with Alexandria and also agreed with it in many ways, they by no means become lifeless, scholarly and disengaged themselves. They retain their masculinity, a connection with practice, for all their abstraction, attain a relevance both to the present and the future, are ripe for Rome, and even for the Christian break with Rome. The Stoics, particularly in their social dreams, draw the logical conclusions from historical changes, they ideologize and utopianize the tendency of these at one and the same time. This is precisely the case in the image sketched by Zeno around 300 B.C., in the image of the *ideal world-state*, of the *humanitarian* state (this concept was first developed by

OUTLINES OF A BETTER WORLD

Panaitios in the society of the younger Scipio). The ideal state was to be so great and so good that nothing else at all could rank alongside it; it was the first utopia to raise the banner of a universal republic, and later of a universal monarchy. Plato's utopian polis sought to have a timeless existence like the Idea of the good; the empire of Alexander and the Roman empire added utopian breadth. The departure from humble dimensions already began in Zeno's social utopia; as the decline and transition of the Greek polis, even the utopianized one, into the supranational empire of Alexander. Plutarch's speech 'De fortuna Alexandri' still brings together the history of Alexander with recollections from Zeno's 'Politeia' in a late retrospective glance, with the usual causal inversion of reality and reflection. Alexander appears here as the accomplisher of the Stoic ideal state, he is portrayed as bringing together the life, ethos, marriage, and way of life of nations 'in one festive krater'.* As teaching them always to regard those who are good as relations, those who are bad as strangers, and the oecumene as their fatherland. The empire of Alexander very quickly disintegrated into individual states again, but after the Punic Wars Rome rose to power, and its imperialism brought with it a much more colossal krater. For Rome too: just as the Greek nation was submerged in the empire of Alexander, so was the Latin nation in Caesar's Mediterranean monarchy. Destiny itself, the Tyche so important to the Stoics and which still appeared to them to constitute order, seemed to contain the Roman expansion. The historian Polybius,† who had close connections with the Stoics, thus dates a very different world situation from the Second Punic War onwards: previously events were dissipated, now they cohere physically as it were, in a grand successful sweep. In Polybius the Tyche causes the ways of the world to converge, and creates a spatial-temporal overall destiny for all: Rome. Pax romana and the Stoic universal state complemented one another to such an extent in the end that it is hardly possible to distinguish where the submissive or conversely patriotic compromise of the Stoic literati begins when their cosmopolitan utopia ultimately looks like the Roman Empire itself ('disregarding its human weaknesses', as Cicero says). It is certainly not the crushing military might, but rather the universal element, the oecumene, which made Rome so seductive in the eyes of the Stoics. And an admittedly rigorous, but hair-splitting and by no means rebellious school found it perfectly tolerable when this

* A large bowl in ancient Greece in which the wine was mixed with water.
† Polybius: ?205-?123 B.C., Greek historian under the patronage of Scipio the Younger. He wrote in forty books a history of Rome from 246 to 146 B.C.

seduction was of service to it; when the utopia of fraternity, in countless rhetorical presentations, later turned into eulogies of the Roman Empire. Zeno had already prophesied the world-state; this in marked contrast to the restricted nature of Plato's polis, and also to its restricted castes. And if Zeno had even linked individuals with the universe by skipping over nations, then he had already done so all the more by skipping over borders.

He started out from individual, inward, morally liberated human beings. They were to be formed into an enormous association in which those who were less wise were educated by example. Zeno tolerates no coinage in his 'Politeia', no power over other people, no law courts, not even schools of wrestling. Chrysippos said that all existing laws and constitutions were wrong, chiefly because of the power which they contain, and with which they are maintained. An existence is imagined without fixed law, without war, the Golden Age all over again, and friendship, both in small circles and in large associations, guarantees an undisturbed coherence. The surviving fragments provide only a dim picture of the particulars of this utopia, and of the fantastic parts as well. But because of the inwardness from which it starts out, because of the indifference of the Stoics towards external circumstances and because of their feigned and genuine contempt for them, it is probable that this utopia remained unrealized at least in economic terms. And as far as the political aspect is concerned, the 'best constitution', the Stoics soon became eclectic, despite Chrysippos. They preached mixtures of democracy and aristocracy, following a non-utopian like Aristotle in this respect. They were even well-disposed towards monarchs, in fact they finally praised the uniform head of the ideal centralized state. So that a king among the Diadochi devoted to the Stoics, Antigonos Gonatas, was the first to describe kingship as a 'glorious act of servitude' (to the people); the emperor Marcus Aurelius even more emphatically derived a morality of the ruler from the Stoic ideal of the state. Thus far does a social utopia here plunge into given fact; the oecumene alleged to be moral does not yet break - as the religious one does later, under Augustine - with Caesar. But the significance of the Stoic utopia does not lie in its institutions anyway, nor in the consistent communism which it declaims. Its significance lies in the programme of world-citizenship, which here means the unity of the human race. At the bottom the individual remains its representative; the 'superior state' begins as the selection of individuals for moral education and non-violent communal life. But it by no means ends there; it is one-sided and exaggerated when Wilamowitz remarks on one occasion that Plato's ideal construct is a community, but Zeno's is an individual. Even

in the ideal of the wise man the non-personal, typical characteristics of
a general rational rule of life predominate. And even in the Stoic state
there is much more pathos of communal life, appropriate to the general
law of reason which has to permeate it, than cultivation of inwardness
from which the Stoics started out. This communal life is not even confined
to the human sphere, instead the human sphere is backed up by the cosmic
sphere, of which it forms a part. The most important part; for according
to the image of the Stoic Kleanthes, the earth is 'the common hearth of
the world', and above this hearth, linking men and gods, reigns systematic
reason. It gives its uniform law of life to all human beings, demands the
International of all rational beings, fits things into the cosmos as the
'supreme community', as the 'city of Zeus', from which the individual
states are to form their individual houses. This cosmic reason 'at the
common hearth of the world' even exhibits matrilinear characteristics in
the Stoics; they had already become apparent in the agricultural Zeus of
Euemeros, the Stoic utopia intensified them in general. Bona Dea and Zeus,
the cosmos as city of Zeus and as mother house, world reason and the
most trustworthy Mother Nature who settles everything, here often become
interchangeable. And this strengthens the footing of the Golden Age in
the universe itself, in the syncretistic notion of Zeus, kind as a Demeter
of heaven. The existence without money, law courts, war, power, which
Zeno had imagined, obtains in this 'worldly megalopolis' the footing,
believed to be cosmic, which it had not been given in economic and political
terms. The cosmos in the state now levels all social distinctions, even that
of the sexes: man and woman, Greek and barbarian, freeman and slave,
all distinctions due to limitation vanish in the intellectually and quantitatively
unlimited realm. Even blood and family, the ties from the age of agriculture
and the polis, do not hold the new human beings together, instead equality
of moral inclinations determines the bonds in megalopolis. The difficulties
are solved by the Law of Large Numbers* as it were, or rather: by the
expansion which has a cosmomorphic effect, by world harmony. This is
'the grand systema, uniting the gods and the divine in man', in the words
of Poseidonios; a pantheon on earth, at the common hearth of the world.
This is the new natural state, that in which physis stands against the statute
(thesis), but coincides with the right law (nomos). A far-reaching equation;
it had less of an influence on the later social utopias, but a decisive one
on Natural Right. Though in individual practice the Stoics hardly championed this Masonic state any more than could be expected, given its formal

---

* Cf. Vol. I, p. 311n.

inwardness together with the colossal cosmos. Thus the sense of brotherhood remained unrealized in economic terms, the preached superiority to external circumstances allowed these to persist unchallenged alongside utopia. Even Stoics outside the upper classes, such as the slave Epictetus, were as far away from social revolutionary activities as their inwardness or even their world reason was from the suffering earth. So from this point of view as well a compromise with Rome must have been easy, apart from the gratitude with which prophets are stirred when their prophecy (here that of the world-state) seems partly fulfilled. In addition there is the markedly antiquarian sense which the Golden Age and the identification of the wishful state with it had gradually assumed. For the Golden Age was regarded by the Stoics as irretrievably lost, only a new course of the world could set it in motion again, and this new course presupposes nothing less than Zeus taking the entire world back into himself again through world conflagration. And even then, after this somewhat too violent upheaval which is also independent of human beings, the Golden Age – restored again in the new world – will not last: nor is it known why this should be so, in the doctrine of universal optimism like that held by the Stoics. Again it is precisely this emphatic peace with statically celebrated world perfection, this pantheistic acclimatization to approved fate, which is averse to change, unless it is a mitigation or reformation (influences on slave economy, married life, and even the running of the state are discernible here). If diseases look like a kind of purgative in Stoic medicine, with which rational nature heals itself as it were, law and justice are of course shown no such mercy, but neither are they attacked anything like as much as in other utopias. The whole is held up to them as an example, a prevailing model, so that the parts keep and are kept to it. Nor is the utopia of the Stoics directed towards what is explosive but rather towards what is complete, towards an increasingly improved harmony with the existing God-nature that is the world. Pretended world perfection thus prevents the intended world change, just as it seeks to govern it; this makes the Stoics, even their utopia, strangely reformist and conformist at the same time. There are a few exceptions: the tutor of the Spartan king Kleomenes, who ordered a kind of socialist economy, was the Stoic Sphairos, a pupil of Zeno; and he is said to have influenced the king with Zeno's 'Politeia'. The tutor of the tribune Tiberius Gracchus was the Stoic Blossius, and the result: the call for a sharing out of the land, the fight against the patrician upper classes, was different at any rate from the result in the case of Marcus Aurelius, who did not shake up the Roman Empire as everybody knows. The Stoic utopian concept of oecumene above all had an inspiring effect, it outshone the mere ideologization of the Roman Empire undertaken by later Stoics, and it also had an effect outside the Stoic school. As in Judaism, touching on old prophetic universalisms again, which the Jewish national church state had buried, after the return from Babylon. It is more than probable that the world-citizenship supported by St Paul in contrast to St Peter was produced, or at least strengthened, by Stoic influences. His quotation from Kleanthes or Aratus, in the speech to the Athenians (Acts of the Apostles 17, 28), proves that St Paul had read Stoic writings; and the quotation refers to the unity of the human race in the world reason of Zeus. But in early Christianity, partly even in St Paul, the explosive element was considerably clearer than the element of reformatory completeness which is part of Stoicism, even where it converts to Christianity. This is the end of the resemblance, to which St Paul had alluded, of the Stoics, the Freemasons of antiquity, to early Christianity; the Stoic utopia seeks transfiguration through correspondence to nature, the Christian utopia does so through the critique and crisis of nature.

The Bible and the kingdom of neighbourly love

What do the Scriptures tell us, immediately after they become historical? They tell of the sufferings of an enslaved nation; they have to haul bricks, labour in the fields, the Egyptians 'made their lives bitter'. Moses appears, kills an overseer; it is the first act of the future founder; he has to leave the country. The God he imagines when he is abroad is in his very origin no masters' God, but one of free Bedouins, in the Sinai region of the Kenitic nomadic tribe into which Moses had married. Yahweh begins as a threat to the Pharaoh; the volcanic God of Sinai becomes Moses' god of liberation, of flight from slavery. An exodus of this kind gives the Bible, from here on, a basic resonance which it has never lost. And there is no book in which the memory of nomadic, and thus still half primitive communist institutions remains so strongly preserved as it does in the Bible. A community without division of labour and private property still appears to be God's will for a long time to come, even when private property had emerged in Canaan and the prophets accepted it, on a modest scale. Jeremiah called the period in the desert the bridal period of Israel (following in the footsteps of the elder Hosea), and this was not only because of Yahweh's greater proximity, but also because of economic innocence. In the Promised Land of course, after they had settled down, the communal life quickly came to an end. From the conquered Canaanites, who had long reached the agricultural and urban stage, farming and wine-growing were adopted; crafts and trades, rich and poor developed, in glaring class distinctions, and debtors were sold abroad as slaves by their creditors. The two Books of Kings are as full of famine as of the glitter of wealth which produced it. On the one hand: 'And there was a sore famine in Samaria' (1 Kings 18, 2), on the other hand, King Solomon 'made silver to be in Jerusalem as stones' (1 Kings 10, 27). In the midst of this exploitation, and thundering against it, the *prophets* appeared, drew up the notion of judgment, and in the same breath the *oldest outlines of social utopia*. And they did this – giving proof of continuity with the semi-communist Bedouin period – in connection with semi-nomadic opponents still close to the Bedouins, with cumbersome and isolated figures, the so-called Nazarites. There was also a connection with the Rechabites, a tribe in the south, which had held aloof from the opulence and money economy of Canaan, and remained faithful to the old desert god. The Nazarites themselves were also externally recognizable by their desert clothing, their hair cloaks and unshorn hair, and they abstained from wine; their Yahweh, still a stranger to private property, became for them the god of the poor. Samson, Samuel, and Elijah were Nazarites (1 Samuel 1, 11; 2 Kings 1, 8), but so was John the Baptist (Luke 1, 15): all of them enemies of the Golden Calf, and also of the opulent masters' Church which stemmed from the Canaanite Baal. Thus a single line, full of twists and turns, but recognizably the same, runs from the half-primitive communism remembered by the Nazarites to the preaching of the prophets against wealth and tyranny, and to the early Christian communism founded on love. It runs almost unbroken in the background, and the famous prophetic depictions of a future kingdom of social peace take their colour from a Golden Age which was not just a legend. Similarly their criticism of the 'apostasy' from Yahweh takes its bearings from Nazaritism: for this apostasy is a turning from the pre-capitalist Yahweh so to speak towards Baal, and also towards that masters' Yahweh who conquered Baal at the price of becoming a god of luxury himself. Accordingly, prophets arose in times of great internal and external tension, admonishing people to change their ways. Amos, who says of himself that he is a poor cowherd who picks mulberries, is the oldest of the prophets (around 750 B.C.), and perhaps the greatest: and his Yahweh sets things alight. 'But I will send a fire upon Judah, and it shall devour the palaces of Jerusalem...because they sold the righteous for silver, and

the poor for a pair of shoes; That pant after the dust of the earth on the
head of the poor, and turn aside the way of the meek' (Amos 2, 5-7).
And further, annihilating the masters' Church: 'I hate, I despise your feast
days, and I will not smell in your solemn assemblies...But let judgment
run down as waters, and righteousness as a mighty stream' (Amos 5, 21
and 24). This is the same spirit in which Joachim of Fiore, the great chiliast
of the High Middle Ages, later says: 'They deck the altars, and the poor
man suffers bitter hunger.' This god is extremely ill-disposed towards a
discussion of religion with expropriators, his colleagues are neither Baal
nor Mercury. 'And he looked for judgment', cries Isaiah, 'but behold
oppression; for righteousness, but behold a cry. Woe unto them that join
house to house, that lay field to field, till there be no place, that they
may be placed alone in the midst of the earth!' (Isaiah 5, 7f.). Yahweh
is thus invoked as an enemy of the expropriators of peasants' land and
of the accumulation of capital, as an avenger and tribune of the people:
'And I will punish the world for their evil, and the wicked for their iniquity;
and I will cause the arrogancy of the proud to cease, and will lay low
the haughtiness of the terrible. I will make a man more precious than
fine gold; even a man than the golden wedge of Ophir' (Isaiah 13, 11f.).
But Deutero-Isaiah, the mystery man, adds: 'But this is a people robbed
and spoiled; they are all of them snared in holes, and they are hid in prison
houses: they are for a prey, and none delivereth; for a spoil, and none
saith, Restore.' (Isaiah 42, 22). Until the time of happiness and wealth
for all, it is characterized as socialist wealth: 'Ho, every one that thirsteth,
come ye to the waters, and he that hath no money; come ye, buy, and
eat; yea, come, buy wine and milk without money and without price.'
(Isaiah 55, 1). The day is certain when the spirit of liberation will be revived,
with Yahweh as the god of exodus. He is the centre of the famous utopia
to be found almost word for word in Isaiah and the slightly younger Micah,
and which may even have been taken from a still older prophet: 'For out
of Zion shall go forth the law, and the word of the Lord from Jerusalem.
And he shall judge among the nations, and shall rebuke many people: and
they shall beat their swords into plowshares, and their spears into pruning-
hooks: nation shall not lift up sword against nation, neither shall they
learn war any more. But they shall sit every man under his vine and under
his fig tree; and none shall make them afraid' (Isaiah 2, 4; Micah 4, 3f.).
This is the original model of the pacified International which forms the
core of the Stoic utopia: with real influence, the passage from Isaiah formed
the basis of all Christian utopias. It is of course open to question whether

the concept of the future, and therefore of time, of the ancient Israelite prophets (and in a broader context of the ancient Orient) coincides with that which has developed since Augustine. The experience of time has certainly undergone many changes, the Futurum above all has only recently been augmented by the Novum and become charged with it. But the content of the biblically intended future has remained intelligible to all social utopias: Israel became poverty as such, Zion became utopia. Necessity is the mother of messiahs: 'O thou afflicted, tossed with tempest, and not comforted, behold, I will lay thy stones with fair colours, and lay thy foundations with sapphires...In righteousness shalt thou be established: thou shalt be far from oppression; for thou shalt not fear; and from terror; for it shall not come near thee' (Isaiah 54, 11 and 14). An aura of this light in the night lies above social utopias again and again, right down to Weitling.

The Romans came into the Promised Land, which had become less and less of one. The rich did not get on badly with the foreign occupiers, who protected them from desperate peasants and patriotic resistance fighters. They protected them from prophets, who could quite unreservedly be called agitators now. The Nazarite John the Baptist preached at this time among the common people and promised an end to their misery. 'And now also the axe is laid unto the root of the trees: therefore every tree which bringeth not forth good fruit is hewn down, and cast into the fire.' (Matthew 3, 10). In those days there was more than enough room for glad tidings, of a social revolutionary, national revolutionary kind; change seemed imminent. 'He that cometh after me', said John, 'Whose fan is in his hand, and he will throughly purge his floor, and gather his wheat into the garner; but he will burn up the chaff with unquenchable fire.' (Matthew 3, 12). And the coming of Jesus himself was by no means as inward and other-worldly as a reinterpretation since St Paul, which always suited the ruling class, would have us believe. His message to those that labour and are heavy laden was not the cross; they had that in any case, and in the terrible cry: 'My God, why hast Thou forsaken me?'* Jesus experienced the crucifixion as a catastrophe and not in a Pauline way. The great logion in Matthew 11, 25–30 is of this world, not the other world, it is the edict of the royal Messiah who puts an end to suffering in every form and does so on earth, as a man to whom a change in all things is entrusted: 'My yoke is easy, and my burden is light.' Jesus never said: 'The kingdom of God is within you'; instead, the momentous phrase (Luke 17, 21) literally reads: 'The kingdom of God is among

* Matthew 27, 46.

you'; and it was said to the Pharisees, not to the disciples. It means: the
kingdom is already alive among you Pharisees, as the chosen community, in
these disciples; the sense is therefore a social one, not an inwardly invisible
one. Jesus never said: 'My kingdom is not of this world'; this passage is
interpolated by St John (John 18, 36), and it was designed to be of use to
Christians in a Roman court. Jesus himself did not attempt to give himself
an alibi in front of Pilate with such cowardly pathos of the other world. This
would have contradicted the manifest courage and the dignity of the founder
of Christianity, and above all it contradicts the sense which the words 'this
world' and 'the other world' possessed in Jesus' day. This sense is a temporal
one and stems from the astral-religious speculations of the ancient Orient,
that is, the theory of world cycles. 'This world' is synonymous with that
which now exists, with the 'present aeon', whereas 'the other world'
is synonymous with the 'future aeon' (thus Matthew 12, 32; 24, 3). What
is therefore intended by these contrasting terms is not a geographical division
between this world and the other world, but a *chronologically successive one
in the same arena, situated down here.* 'The other world' is the utopian earth,
with a utopian heaven above it; in accordance with Isaiah 65, 17: 'For,
behold, I create new heavens and a new earth: and the former shall not
be remembered, nor come into mind.' The aspiration is not another world
after death, where the angels are singing, but the equally terrestrial and
supra-terrestrial kingdom of love, of which the early Christian community
was already supposed to represent an enclave. The kingdom of the other
world was interpreted as other-worldly only after the catastrophe of the
Cross, and above all after the Pilates and especially the Neros had become
Christians themselves; since for the ruling class everything depended on
defusing the communism of love and rendering it as spiritual as possible.
The kingdom of this world was for Jesus the kingdom of the Devil (John
8, 44), which is precisely why he nowhere stated that it should be allowed
to persist; he never concluded a non-intervention pact with it. Armed force
is rejected, – though not always: 'I came not to send peace, but a sword'
(Matthew 10, 34) – but the rejection of armed force, in the Sermon on
the Mount, significantly places the Kingdom of Heaven at its immediate
end in every Beatitude (Matthew 5, 3–10). So armed force is rejected because
it is superfluous for Jesus the *apocalyptic thinker*, because it is already obsolete.
He expects an upheaval which will leave no stone standing on another
anyway, and he expects it at any moment, from nature, from the super-
weapon of a cosmic catastrophe. The eschatological sermon has precedence
for Jesus over the moral one and determines it. The money-changers will

not only be driven out of the temple with a whip, as Jesus did to them,
but the whole state and temple will fall, totally, through a catastrophe,
before long. The great eschatological chapter (Mark 13) is one of the best-
attested in the New Testament; without this utopia, the Sermon on the
Mount cannot be understood at all. If the old fortress is to be so soon
and so totally razed to the ground, then economic questions also seem
pointless to Jesus, who regarded the 'present aeon' as finished in any case
and believed in the immediately imminent cosmic catastrophe; thus the
phrase about the lilies of the field is much less naive, or at least surprising
and disparate on quite a different level, than it appears. And the instruction:
'Render therefore unto Caesar the things which are Caesar's; and unto
God the things that are God's' was uttered by Jesus out of contempt for
the state and with a view to its speedy destruction, not as a compromise,
as St Paul would have it. A natural catastrophe is of course a substitute
for revolution, but an extremely extensive one, and in this appeal to the
Last Judgment it does of course defuse every real revolt, as it does even
in the account of the old servant in 'Cabal and Love' (Act 2, Scene 2),*
but it still did not make any truce with the existing world, there was
no forgetting the 'future aeon'. The catastrophe of the kingdom of this
world is even cruelly fulfilled according to Jesus, there is little more talk
of loving one's enemies when it comes to the Last Judgment. The new
team owed its allegiance solely to Jesus; the new social community,
redeemed from the previous aeon, exists through him, in him, for him.
'I am the vine, ye are the branches' (John 15, 5), the founder had ordained;
thus Jesus merged into the community just as much as he encompassed
it. 'Inasmuch as ye have done it unto one of the least of these my brethren,
ye have done it unto me' (Matthew 25, 40): this saying grounds the social
utopia intended by the early Christians in its communism of love and in
the International of whatever bears a human face, however poor. The saying
also adds, in a momentous way, an element that was completely lacking
in the Stoics: a social mission from below and a mythically powerful person
to watch over it. Even where the social mission had almost disappeared,
as in the case of Augustine, the opposition to the power of this existing
world and to its misanthropic content remained predominant; throughout
all church-building and all compromises. As it certainly did in the Christian
revolutions, bearing in mind the killing of the Egyptian overseer, the
exodus, the thundering prophets, the expulsion of the money-changers

* A play by Schiller.

and the promise to those that labour and are heavy laden. The Bible did not elaborate any social utopia, and it is certainly not exhausted by the latter, nor does it constitute its decisive value; to believe that would be both a false overestimation of the Bible and a shallow approach. Christianity is not just an outcry against deprivation, it is an outcry against death and the void, and inserts the Son of Man into both. But even if the Bible contains no elaborated social utopia, it does point most vehemently, in both negative and positive terms, to this exodus and this kingdom. And when the scouts told of the land flowing with milk and honey, there was no shortage either of warriors who wanted to conquer it, nor afterwards, when the land proved to be no Canaan, of tough and ardent dreamers who sought for it further and further afield, lavished more and more stirring superlatives on it, and wanted to bring it ever closer to mankind. No mercy was shown to the great Babel: 'Babylon the great is fallen, is fallen...And the kings of the earth...shall bewail her, and lament for her...And the merchants of the earth shall weep and mourn over her; for no man buyeth their merchandise any more' (Revelation 18, 2ff.). But the kingdom is nowhere regarded in the Bible as a baptized Babel, not even – as Augustine later regarded the millennium – as a Church.

Augustine's City of God from rebirth

Nearly all the forward dreams of the Greeks were well and truly directed towards this world. Life itself, without any outside contribution, was to be improved in them, in a sensible though colourful way. Even the distant islands in the pagan wishful image lay in a still coherent world, together with their happiness. This happiness, with its institutions, was immanently inserted into existing life, and held up as an example to it. But to the Rome which was going to pieces nothing could be set up as an example of an immanent kind any more. A completely different example, something completely new, was longed for; in the end, in the competition between various salvations, Pauline Christianity – making political use of this new element – was triumphant. Jesus had by no means demanded the leap, as we have seen, out of this world into inwardness and the other world, but the fresh leap on to a new earth. The Christian-utopian wish for community formed around the core of Jesus, though in such a way that it shifted more and more into the other world, into an inwardly transcendental gathering, and empty promises. Instead of a radical renewal of this world, an institute of the other world appeared: the Church; and it applied the Christian social utopia to itself. This was joined by references to the Stoic utopia, in the form of the 'superior state', as already taught by Chrysippos; his oecumene – apart from the Roman Empire – provided the framework. But it was precisely in the Stoic utopia that the leap into the new was lacking: the ordinary world was presented as complete in itself. Unable, and in the whole disposition of antiquity also unwilling, to develop new dispositions, tasks, let alone breakthroughs from within itself. For this an impulse towards exodus was necessary which was not to be found on pagan soil. Only the impulse of Jesus cancelled what was complete, posited the explosive: the city of reason, in the world, with Zeus, became the city of God, against the world, with Christ. Augustine's utopia 'De civitate Dei' (around 425) gave the most powerful utopian expression, though of course also a Church-building one, to the new earth as an *other world* on earth.

Earthly wishes can only be considered incidentally here, can never be fulfilled. They are bad, as such they have had their fling up till now, driven off course from the right life. Their location is the secular state, and the will that makes the latter is wicked. Thus it cannot be improved, it must be converted, both the previous will and the previous state. The target of this conversion is Jesus, though to begin with Augustine still admits the necessity which compels the good to live together with the wicked. Their two states are still intertwined, and the holy-desired one must accept the evil of the unholy one for the time being. Though at this point (Augustine is still a disciple of the Pauline social compromise throughout, here) this Father of the Church even goes so far as to condone slavery, which almost all the Stoics had rejected. Our duty is to be contented, it is still better to serve a foreign master than our own lusts. Augustine further ascribes the right of punishment to the existing authorities, as a good pater familias – no one knows why; and this even in connection with so-called salvation history. For the secular state is the bad one, but not the worst; below the civitas terrena there is still the completely diabolical primordial condition, the anarchic one. Accordingly there is, if not salvation history, then certainly healing history * even in the existing states on earth; home and family offer the first refuge; tribal association and city-state (civitas as urbs) the second, and the international state of peoples (civitas as orbis)

---

* Bloch is here punning on the words 'Heilsgeschichte' (an interpretation of history stressing God's plan of salvation within it) and 'Heilungsgeschichte' (the process of history healing itself).

the third. The Roman Empire is instantly recognizable in this international
state, the very same Empire which Augustine contemptuously opposes
from the standpoint of the utopia of the civitas Dei. Unlike other Fathers
of the Church, particularly Tertullian, Augustine has no longing for an
initial Golden Age, which for him lies before every kind of civitas whatsoever, and is hence never otherwise described than as a diabolical animal
kingdom. But instead, the practical prince of the Church – against that
antithesis of civitas terrena and civitas Dei to be discussed in a moment
– took the Roman Empire as the *basis* of the ecclesiastical oecumene. Almost
as the later Stoics connected Rome with their 'superior state'; with the
difference though that this 'superior state' was politically powerless in
Rome. Whereas Augustine placed the Church above the Empire, and could
almost actually do so, placed the superior *home of salvation* supposedly set
up by Christ above the dubious *home of healing*. This marks the end of
the relative recognition of the earthly state in Augustine; circumstances
were not yet conducive to a more extensive levelling. The relations between
church and state were as yet so little consolidated that Augustine as
accomplisher of the Christian utopia is in direct opposition to the practical
prince of the Church. The shrewd though disgusted admiration for Rome
gives way in the further progress of the civitas Dei to totally dualistic
hatred, adopting the tension between night and light, Ormuzd and Ahriman
from Augustine's Manichaean youth. If Jesus and Jesus alone is the target
of this conversion, if there is only salvation history and no healing history:
then the historical states, including Rome, are exclusively enemies of Christ;
they themselves, not just the anarchy from which they arise, are the
kingdom of the Devil. This is the decisive idea in Augustine's work, beyond
its compromise, and it is presented as a process: political utopia appears
for the first time as history, indeed generates it, history emerges as *salvation
history towards the kingdom*, as an unbroken uniform process, harnessed
between Adam and Jesus, on the basis of the Stoic unity of the human
race and the Christian salvation it is to attain. So two states have always
been struggling irreconcilably with one another in humanity, the civitas
terrena and the civitas Dei, the community of sinners hostile to God and
that of the chosen ones (chosen by divine grace). Augustine's philosophy
of history claims to be a record of this struggle: the *self-decay of the earthly
states, the budding victory of the kingdom of Christ* are antithetically elucidated
by means of forceful examples. The first part of the work 'De civitate
Dei' (Augustine himself calls it a 'magnum opus et strenuum'), in Books
1-10, contains a critique of polytheistic paganism as such: the pagan gods

are here evil spirits, and in this capacity they already rule the community of the damned on earth. The second part however, from Books 11–19, develops the antithetical process of salvation in history, by dividing it up into periods which take their decisive turning-points and the visual horizon of their historical contents mainly from the Old Testament. Humanity appears – from the Fall to the Last Judgment – as a single condensed individual, thus the historical division into periods is carried out on the analogy of the various stages of life; it is a credulous philosophy of history of the Bible. According to this, the stage of childhood lasts from Adam to Noah, boyhood from Noah to Abraham, youth from Abraham to David, manhood from David to the Babylonian captivity; the two last periods extend to the birth of Christ and from there to the Last Judgment. With regard to the kingdom of God and the history of its breakthrough, this means that the civitas terrena (the sinful state) was destroyed in the Flood, the civitas Dei was preserved in Noah and his sons, but even in their children the curse of the false state was revived. The Hebrew Jews assembled once more beneath the baldachin, 'ye shall be unto me a kingdom of priests, and an holy nation'; while all other nations, the Assyrians most bitterly of all, succumbed to the rule of evil, the power-state which is the Devil's. Thus through the entire civitas Dei, and summing up its philosophy of history, there runs a critique of violence, a critique of the political state as a crime. The anger of the prophets thunders once more over Babylon and Assyria, Egypt, Athens and Rome (in which Christianity had nevertheless become the 'official state religion'): 'The first city and the first state were founded by a fratricide; an act of fratricide also sullied the beginnings of Rome, sullied them to such an extent that one can say: it is a law that wherever a state is to arise, blood must have been shed beforehand' (De civ. Dei XV). This is supported by the famous passage which is an example of a realistic critique of the state on the basis of such an unrealistic utopia: 'What are the earthly states since justice has vanished from them but great dens of robbers? Remota igitur justitia quid sunt regna nisi magna latrocinia?' (De civ. Dei IV). Justice must of course be understood in the Pauline sense here; it is justification through submission to God's will for salvation and harmony with it; justitia is justificatio. But the political state is filled with nothing but squabbles over worldly goods, political discord at home and abroad, power struggles remote from God; it is filled with the essence of pride and the Fall. So little does Augustine, as a thinker desiring salvation, remain well-disposed towards the existing state ('Deum et animam scire cupio; nihilne plus? nihil omnino', 'I desire to know God and the soul; nothing else? nothing else at all'). So acute is the tension at work within him, stemming from the Manichaean convictions of his youth, between the god of light and the god of night, between Ormuzd and Ahriman, a political tension. The City of God is an ark, often also a mere catacomb hidden over and over again; its revelation occurs only at the end of present history. Which is why even the Church does not completely coincide with the civitas Dei, at least since the Church extended the right of forgiveness of sins to mortal sin as well, and also to apostates (since the Decian persecution of the Christians), and consequently comprises a very mixed society. Only as the number of the Chosen, as the corpus verum, is the Church wholly the City of God, whereas the existing Church, as the corpus permixtum of sinners and Chosen, does not coincide with the City of God, but only borders on it in a preparatory way. The existing Church does of course coincide in Augustine with the millennium, as the first awakening, the first resurrection before the second definitive one (Revelation 30, 5f.); this first awakening is initiated and maintained by the Church's means of grace. Chiliasm is thereby defused, yet civitas Dei is not handed over to the existing Church; instead, civitas Dei builds itself up for heaven from Abel onwards, in fragments, and only reveals itself as complete with the appearance of the Kingdom. Civitas Dei is a foundation like Plato's ideal polis, but more consistently than the latter in its complete orderliness it is not conceived as being founded by men but as being founded in a God of order. Every utopia of order of a pure kind, so that it does not fall into the opposite of its order, namely into the merely arranged and not ordered character of chance or fate, Tyche or Moira, presupposes an economy of salvation which founds the order and in which the utopia itself is founded. This fundament of transcendentally communicated or inspired order, without any admixture of chance and Moira, was not to be found in Plato's idea of the polis and god of the polis, nor in that of the Stoics; it was only to be found in the Christian concept of God. It is not in and not behind the existing world, but after it that the civitas Dei, as the timeless-elapsed polis in its highest form, becomes completely manifest. And the basic utopian goal of society, towards which only the Church can lead us, remains *the acquisition of the divine image for man* (De civ. Dei XXII). This is the radically supra-temporal directing and ordering principle of the one and only best state as against the others, the systems of sin. Civitas Dei was quite literally conceived as a piece of heaven on earth, from the angle of happiness and above all from that of cleanliness, which does not make people into angels of course, but into saints, and thus into something greater according to Catholic doctrine. Augustine's dark pessimism with regard to the worldly life of the state is countered by a kind of priestishly ardent yet space-making, and even in the following period richly secularizable optimism of the civitas Dei, founded on the existence of saints and their growth in the Church. Casting off the works of the old Adam, putting on Christ, in short the hopes for a spiritual rebirth of more and more people, thus became a utopian political issue in Augustine's City of God.

And yet it is strange how these dreams are not automatically directed towards the future. They rush ahead as anywhere else, but the future apparently cloaks itself in present existence. The question thus becomes possible: is civitas Dei strictly speaking a utopia? Or is it the manifestation of an already existing transcendence circulating in this world? Is the waking dream of a socially Not-Yet-Become really developed here, or is a finished transcendental whole ('ecclesia perennis') sunk into the world? Often of course the City of God seems to be only germinating in Augustine's history, and therefore future-utopian. But it often also seems to be an existing great power, great anti-power, which has come into existence in the same way as the other dramatis persona, the City of the Devil. Civitas Dei is celebrated in the work of Augustine as almost present, in the Jewish Levite state and in the Church of Christ. Precisely such a powerful dream of the future as that of the millennium is sacrificed to the Church, in which it is supposed to be already fulfilled. And a major point here is that the existence of the civitas Dei ultimately poses as a fixed pattern of grace, embracing the predestined chosen few. Whether they wish to be citizens or not, whether they aspire to, dream of, or work for the kingdom of God or not. One can no more work for the kingdom of God than for any other good in Augustine's theology, it comes from grace and exists by virtue of grace, not of good works. Thanks to divine predestination the outcome of historical discrepancy (between civitas terrena and civitas Dei) is also fixed from the start; just like grace, its content of light and heaven is irresistibly victorious. All this actually distances Augustine's ideal state from the truly utopian will and conceptual plan: *and yet the civitas Dei is a utopia.* It is of course not one which wills change, according to Augustine there is just one freedom, that of psychological willing to will, but since Adam's fall there is no freedom of moral ability to will (non possumus non peccare). But as grace stirs man not merely to do good but to be prepared to do good, so the city of God marches ahead of man and is an active utopian force within him; as an expectation predestined in the chosen few. And its basic substance is that the community of perfect individuals and saints on earth appears, as we recall, only at the end of present history. Civitas Dei only wholly emerges when the secular state goes to the devil, to whom it belongs. Thus civitas Dei does not merely circulate in history as a distinct dramatis persona, it is also produced, or more cautiously: turned out, by history as the 'acquisition of the divine image'. And it hovers above the historical process as a whole, it is 'the eternal corporation, where nobody is born because nobody dies, where true and strong happiness prevails, where the sun does not rise on the good and the wicked alike, but the sun of justice shines on the good alone' (De civ. Dei V). This is certainly transcendence, but not one which has a fixed existence and thus contradicts utopia. Socialis vita sanctorum is historical-utopian transcendence, since it is, in contrast to St Paul's, located on the earth again. St Paul also uses the expression city of God, but – as is characteristic of the road from Jesus to St Paul – in the purely transcendental sense as a 'state in the heavens', cut off up above; Augustine on the other hand posits something like a new earth again. This is precisely why his transcendence can be utopian, for it is entwined with the productive hope of *human history*, experiences contact, danger and triumph within it, and not, like pure transcendence, already a determination, i.e Fixum. Consequently, civitas Dei in Augustine is only present as a bone of contention and a highly threatened pre-appearance: it will only be a utopia at the end of present history. Indeed Augustine sets a further goal even for the perfect city of God; it too is only a preliminary stage towards this goal. For civitas Dei is not the kingdom which is asked for in the Lord's Prayer; this kingdom is called regnum Christi in the work of Augustine. Civitas Dei is admittedly also called this occasionally, with apologetic embellishment, but the regnum is never called civitas in Augustine; for it no longer stands within time. So just as the earthly Sabbath for Augustine is a utopian festival in expectation of the heavenly one, civitas Dei, which only seemingly exists as complete, itself still contains its utopia within it: namely regnum Christi as the final, heavenly Sabbath. The seventh day of Creation still remains open, above it Augustine placed precisely the most central utopian statement: 'We ourselves will be the seventh day, Dies septimus nos ipsi erimus' (De civ. Dei XXII). This is a kind of transcendence which, when it has broken through in man, simultaneously arouses his desire, contrary to Augustine's understanding, to have made the breakthrough himself. The alleged fact that 'We cannot not sin' (non possumus non peccare) was little hindrance here, especially as the radical

moral unfreedom of the will did not even gain acceptance in the Church.
The defusing of the millennium into the Church was little hindrance,
especially as civitas Dei, being such a high vision, constantly gave the lie to
the corrupting Church's claim to be the millennium. Chiliasm broke out in
all periods of unrest again, the kingdom of God on earth became the revolutionary magic formula throughout the Middle Ages and the early modern era,
right up to the pious radicalism in the English revolution. Civitas Dei in the
work of Augustine himself is more lasting in its definition of the power-states
than in its apologia for the Church, more lasting in its utopia of brotherliness
than in its theology of the Father. Human beings were henceforth utopianized
as brothers even where a Father was not believed in any more – civitas Dei
remained a political wishful image even without God.

Joachim of Fiore, the third gospel and its kingdom

It all depended on whether people were serious about what they were
expecting. The revolutionary movements were in this position, and they
created a new image of the kingdom. They also taught another kind of
history, one which animated the image and held out the promise of its
incarnation. The most momentous social utopia of the Middle Ages was
drawn up by the Calabrian abbot Joachim of Fiore (around 1200). He was
not trying to purge the Church, or even the state, of their atrocities; they
were abolished instead. And the extinguished gospel was rekindled, or
rather the lux nova within it: what was called by the Joachites the Third
Kingdom. Joachim teaches that there are three stages of history, and each
one is closer to the viable breakthrough of the kingdom. The first stage
is that of the Father, the Old Testament, of fear and of known Law. The
second stage is that of the Son or the New Testament, of love and the
Church, which is divided into clerics and the laity. The third stage, which
is yet to come, is that of the Holy Spirit or the illumination of all, in
mystical democracy, without masters and Church. The first Testament
gave the grass, the second the ears, and the third will bring the wheat.
Joachim elaborates on this sequence in many ways, mostly with direct
reference to his age, believed to be a final apocalyptic age, and with the
political prognosis that the masters and the priests will no longer be able,
and the 'laity' will not want, to go on living as before. Joachim's sermons
thus dealt, in an early-bourgeois visionary way, with the curse and radical
end of the corrupt feudal and ecclesiastical kingdom; with an anger born
of hope, a satis est, which had hardly been heard since the days of John

the Baptist. This also accounts for the strength of the watchwords in his
three categories: the age of rule and fear = the Old Testament, the age of
grace = the New Testament, the age of spiritual perfection and love = the
rising final kingdom ('Tres denique mundi status: primum in quo fuimus
sub lege, secundum in quo sumus sub gratia, tertium quod e vicino expecta-
mus sub ampliori gratia...Primus ergo status in scientia fuit, secundus
in proprietate sapientiae, tertius in plenitudine intellectus').* Two persons
of the Trinity have already appeared, the third: the Holy Spirit, can be
expected at an absolute Pentecost. The idea of the third Testament, which
Joachim thus elaborates in his work 'De concordia utriusque testamenti',
goes back in its foundations – but not in its social-utopian power – to
the third century, to Origen, the Father of the Church by no means canonized by his Church. For the latter had taught that there were three possible
ways of interpreting the Christian records: a physical one, a mental one,
and a spiritual one. The physical interpretation is the literal one, the mental
interpretation the moral-allegorical one, but the spiritual interpretation
(pneumato intus docente)† reveals what is meant in the Scriptures by the
'eternal gospel'. At the same time though, this third gospel was for Origen
only a mode of interpretation, even though the highest, it was not itself in
the process of developing, within time. Nor did the third gospel in Origen
emerge from the New Testament, as one which was given as complete to
the end of time. Joachim's greatness consists in having transformed the
traditional trinity of mere *viewpoints* into a threefold gradation *within history
itself.* Connected with this, and with even more momentous consequences,
was the complete transfer of the kingdom of light *from the other world and
the empty promises of the other world into history*, even though into a final
state of history. The ideal community lay for Iamboulos (as later for More,
Campanella and often later for others) on a distant island, and for Augustine
in transcendence: but utopia for Joachim, as for the prophets, appears
exclusively in the mode and as the status of historical future. Joachim's
chosen few are the poor, and they are to go to paradise in the living body,
not just as spirits. In the society of the third Testament there are no classes
any more; there will be an 'age of monks', that is universalized monastic
and consumer communism, an 'age of the free spirit', that is spiritual

---

* 'There are three states of the world: the first in which we were under the law, the second
in which we are in grace, the third we next expect in which we will be in expanded grace...Thus
the first state was in knowledge, the second in possession of wisdom, the third in the fullness
of intellect.'
† 'with the spirit teaching us from within'.

illumination, without sundering, sin and the world that goes with it. The body too thereby becomes guiltlessly happy, as in the original state of paradise, and the frozen earth is filled with the appearance of a sacred May. There is a hymn by the Joachite Telesphorus (end of the fourteenth century) which begins: 'O vita vitalis, dulcis et amabilis, semper memorabilis – O lively life, sweet and lovable, always memorable' – the 'libertas amicorum' is not puritanical. Its theme is precisely the exodus from fear and servitude or the Law and its state, the exodus from the rule of clerics and the immaturity of the laity or loving grace and its Church; so Joachim's doctrine, with its band of brothers, is not a flight from reality into heaven and the other world. On the contrary: the kingdom of Christ is for Joachim more decidedly of this world than anything since the days of early Christianity. Jesus is once again the Messiah of a new earth, and Christianity operates in reality, not just in ritual and empty promises; it operates without masters and property, in mystical democracy. This is what the third gospel and its kingdom aim to achieve, even Jesus ceases to be a leader, he dissolves himself in the 'societas amicorum'.

It is hardly possible to determine all the paths taken by this extremely historically oriented dream. It spread through long periods and into far-off countries, genuine and forged works by Joachim were circulated for centuries. They spread to Bohemia and Germany, and also to Russia, the early-Christian oriented sects show clear influences of Calabrian preaching there. The kingdom of God in Bohemia – as it did a hundred years later for the Anabaptists in Germany – signified Joachim's civitas Christi. Behind it lay the misery which had long prevailed, within it lay the millennium whose arrival was in the air: thus people struck out to greet it. Very particular attention was paid to the abolition of rich and poor, the preaching of the apparent fanatics took the notion of fraternity by the pocket and at its word. Augustine had written: 'The City of God attracts citizens during its travels on earth and gathers friendly pilgrims in all nations without regard to the differences in customs, laws and institutions which promote acquisition and safeguarding of earthly peace' (De civ. Dei XIX). The City of God of the Joachites, on the other hand, turned a very sharp regard on institutions which promoted acquisition and exploitation, and it practised that tolerance which was necessarily alien to an International of the Church, namely towards Jews and heathens. The citizenship of the forthcoming City of God was not determined by baptism but by perceiving the fraternal spirit in the inner word. According to Thomas Münzer's great supra-Christian definition, the future kingdom will be formed 'of all the chosen ones among all scatterings or races of every kind of faith'. Joachim's Third

Kingdom clearly continues to exert an influence here: 'You should know',
says Münzer in his work 'On fictional faith', praising the testimony
of the genuine Christian against the lackeys of princes and against scribbling
priests, 'You should know that they ascribe this doctrine to the Abbot
Joachim and call it an eternal gospel with great scorn.' The German
Peasant War very much dispelled this scorn; even the radicals of the
English revolution, the agrarian-communist Diggers, the millenarians and
Fifth-monarchy men all bear the legacy of both Joachim and the Baptists.
Only when the Joachite-Taborite spirit was eliminated from the Baptist
movement, by Menno Simons, did the western sects, and not just the
Mennonites, become quiet, particularly quiet, evangelical communities.
But even the other irredenta, that which was detached from the Baptist
movement, the incipiently rational, no longer irrational utopia of the
modern age, abandoned the millennium; Plato and the Stoics triumphed
over Joachim of Fiore, even over Augustine. In this way a greater precision
of institutional details developed in utopias, a connection with bourgeois
emancipation arose, which was already fully utopianized into socialist
tendencies, but the elements of a final purpose and final goal, as contained
in Joachim's utopia, were toned down. They were turned – in the work
of rational utopians like Thomas More, and also Campanella – into social
harmony; a liberal or even an authoritative future state thus became heir
to the millennium. The mythologizing Christian way of thinking in the
medieval Christian utopias certainly did not specify the element of a final
purpose, but nor did it ever lose sight of it. It persisted in the fermenting,
dream-laden red dawn which filled the Joachite and the Baptist utopia to
the brim and turned the whole sky into an eastern glow. This way of
thinking had less elaborated social utopia than Plato or the Stoics, let alone
the rational constructions of the modern age, but it had more utopian
conscience in its utopia than they did. Conscience and the problem of the
final What For thus remain indebted to the chiliastic utopias; quite independently of the intolerably mythological designations of their content.
And Joachim was cogently the spirit of *Christian revolutionary social utopia*:
it was in this spirit that he taught and continued to have an influence.
He first set a deadline for the Kingdom of God, namely for the communist
one, and called on people to observe it. He deposed the theology of the
Father, relegated it to the age of fear and servitude, but dissolved Christ
into a commune. Here as nowhere else the social expectation was in earnest
which Jesus had placed in the new aeon and which had been turned into
hypocrisy and cliché by the Church. Or as Marx says quite rightly on

this point, concerning the Christianity of the ecclesiastical centuries (Nachlaß II, p. 433f.): 'The social principles of Christianity have now had eighteen hundred years to develop... The social principles of Christianity justified slavery in the ancient world, glorified medieval serfdom and are likewise prepared to defend the oppression of the proletariat if necessary, even if they adopt a rather piteous expression. The social principles of Christianity preach the necessity of a ruling and an oppressed class, and for the latter they merely express the pious wish that the former may be charitable. The social principles of Christianity consign the consistorial councillor's compensation for all infamies to heaven and thereby justify the continuance of these infamies on earth. The social principles of Christianity declare all despicable acts of the oppressors to be either a just punishment of original sin and other sins, or to be trials which the Lord in his wisdom imposes on the redeemed. The social principles of Christianity preach cowardice, self-contempt, degradation, obsequiousness, humility, in short all the qualities of the rabble, and the proletariat, which does not want to be treated as a rabble, is far more in need of its courage, its self-esteem, its pride and its sense of independence than of bread. The social principles of Christianity are cringing, and the proletariat is revolutionary; so much for the social principles of Christianity.' All this applies to the Church, or what for eighteen hundred years has been called Christianity, ex cathedra or ex encyclica; and if he returned, Joachim of Fiore, along with Albigensians, Hussites, and militant Baptists, would understand this critique of Christianity very well. Even if for his part applying this critique to the ecclesiastical centuries and above all deriving the critique from the very Christianity which interrupted the ecclesiastical centuries with Joachim, Albigensians, Hussites and Baptists. All Joachitism actively fought against the social principles of a Christianity which since St Paul has allied itself with the class society through thousands of compromises. A Christianity which itself constitutes one long catalogue of sins in its practice of salvation on earth, down – or up – to the final entry: the sympathy of the Vatican for fascism. And to the mortal enmity of the second or priest kingdom in Joachim's sense towards the third that is starting to begin in the Soviet Union and is not understood by the forces of darkness or is very well understood and slandered. The so-called Natural Right of property, even the 'sanctity' of private property are a central social principle of this Christianity. And the monstrance which priests of this Christianity show to those that labour and are heavy laden testifies to no new aeon but gilds the old one. Together with the cowardice and obsequiousness which the old aeon needs in its victims, but without the day of judgment and the triumph over Babel, without intending towards a new heaven and a new earth. Resignation to fear, servitude and empty promises of the other world are the social principles of a Christianity which are despised by Marx and cast into Orcus by Joachim; but they are not the principles of a long-abandoned early Christianity and a social-revolutionary history of heresies that sprang from it. In his expectation of the kingdom, Joachim of Fiore merely expresses the continuing influence through the centuries of the eschatological preachings of Christ, what he said about a future 'Spirit of truth' (John 16, 13), and what did not seem to be concluded with the first pouring out of the Holy Spirit at Pentecost (Acts 2, 1–4). The western Church declared such things to be concluded, the only thing that was unconcluded was its compromise with the class society; the eastern Church at least left open a continuation of this pouring out. After the Lateran Council of 1215, the western Church put all monasteries under the spiritual control of their diocesan bishop; even after it had adopted the western order of the sacraments, the eastern Church had to allow a charismatic and often heretical independence to monasticism, and the sects. The western Church confined enthusiasm to apostles and the ancient martyrs, in order to deprive Adventist beliefs of any kind of sanction; the eastern Church, on the other hand, which is so much less thoroughly organized, teaches a continuing presence of the Spirit outside the priestly Church, among both monks and laymen. It thus lacks the monopoly of administering the host, the whole legally established or screwed-in business of redemption; Russian Orthodoxy under the Tsars was too ignorant for this anyway, it had no scholasticism, let alone the legal sharpness and dogmatic formulations of scholasticism. Instead, out of reach of the Holy Synod, a constant unwritten essence of Joachim of Fiore lived on in Russian Christianity: it lived on in the easily kindled feeling of brotherhood, in the Adventist beliefs of the sects (the sect of the Chlysts has a doctrine of Russian Christs, of which it lists seven), in the basic motif underlying everything: in the unconcluded revelation. Several great peculiarities were thus able to spring up in Christo-romantic fashion on Bolshevist soil; the indisputable Bolshevik and equally indisputable chiliast Alexander Blok gave an indication of this, thoroughly in the Joachite spirit. When in Blok's hymn, the 'March of the Twelve', that is, of the twelve Red Army soldiers, a pale Christ precedes the revolution and leads it, this kind of presence of the Spirit is just as remote from the western Church-combines as it finds the eastern Church at least theologically open to it. Only the heretical sects, with Joachim among them, allowed revelation to spring up anew even in the west, and the Holy Spirit accordingly recommended astonishing Pentecosts to them. It recommended social principles of Christianity which, as the example of Thomas Münzer indicates, were not cringing and did not treat the proletariat as a rabble. This was heretical Christianity and ultimately revolutionary Adventist utopia; with the social principles of Baal they would not have arisen. They blossomed in the preaching of Joachim, to such an extent that a single antithesis exposed the masters' Church here: 'They deck the altars, and the poor man suffers bitter hunger.' This very antithesis sounds, as we have seen, as if it was from the Bible, from Amos, from Isaiah, from the Jesus quoted by Münzer. In fact even the ideal states constructed out of pure reason, which prepared the way for socialism from the sixteenth century on, are themselves, for all their rationality, still built into the third aeon. They no longer keep this space occupied, but they still keep it, despite an unspoken finality, at bottom: there are no such utopias without an unconditional element. The will to happiness speaks for itself, but the plans, or contemporary images of a New Moral World speak differently, i.e. chiliastically. However secularized and finally, eventually, set on its feet, the social utopia since Joachim has the societas amicorum within it, this Christlikeness turned into a society. Happiness, freedom, order, the whole regnum hominis, resound with it, in its utopian application. A remark by the young Engels in 1842 (MEGA I, 2, p. 225f.) contains an echo from Joachim, only a few years before the Communist Manifesto: 'The self-confidence of humanity, the new Grail around whose throne the nations jubilantly gather...This is our vocation: to become the Templars of this Grail, to gird our swords about our loins for its sake and cheerfully risk our lives in the last holy war, which will be followed by the millennium of freedom.' Utopian unconditionality comes from the Bible and the idea of the kingdom, and the latter remained the apse of every New Moral World.

Thomas More or the utopia of social freedom

The bourgeois citizen got moving, went in search of his Own, in which he could flourish. He was in favour of work, making way for efficiency, and the end of class differences. The work of the English Chancellor Thomas More, 'De optimo rei publicae statu sive de nova insula Utopia' (Concerning the best condition of the state or concerning the new island of Utopia), appeared in 1516. For the first time in ages the dream of the best state is here once again presented as a kind of sailor's yarn. More's island is called U-topia, No-where, with a fine, slightly melancholic, but acute title. The Nowhere is conceived as a postulate for the Where in which people actually find themselves. Once assured of not being disturbed, a globe-trotter here tells his friends about the distant happy island. The sailor's yarn that More uses once again following on from the utopian fables of Euemeros and Iamboulos is even based on a careful report; as has been proved, in his book More used the memoir by Amerigo Vespucci of his second voyage to America. Vespucci had said of the inhabitants of the New World that only there do people 'live naturally', that they 'are rather to be called Epicureans than Stoics', and they also manage without separate property. And the humanist Petrus Martyr, a contemporary historian of the new discoveries, praised the condition of the American islanders as one 'without the curse of money, without laws and unjust judges'. It may come as a surprise that Thomas More, the courtier and the subsequent martyr of the Church (against the 'Reformer' Henry VIII), was so well-disposed towards the primitive communism of these reports and furnished the 'New Island of Utopia' with it. The egalitarian tendencies, directed against class prejudices, of the incipient bourgeoisie must be taken into account here; up until the Thermidor, equality was a serious watchword, however formal it may have remained, of capitalist liberation. In the century of the 'Utopia' itself, around 1550, a democratic work had been written by a friend of Montaigne: Etienne de La Boëtie's 'The contrary man or the will to bondage'; More drew on the same content. One sentence from this rhetorical but interesting work is enough to show how little the cultured Renaissance had to be aristocratic: 'Nature cast us all in the same mould, so that each can recognize a likeness, or rather: his brother, in the other.' One may further point to the absence of property among the upper classes in Plato's 'Republic', that book so highly esteemed by humanists; More, who does not follow Plato's ideal state in other respects, takes the idea of refined communism from it, but turns it from the privilege of a few into the right of all. One may point not least to the Christian More's love for the early Christian community; it is easier for a camel to pass through the eye of a needle than for a rich man to enter the kingdom of heaven* – no Pope will give dispensation from this saying even to the most faithful son of the Church. What remains striking though is the Epicureanism revelling in this world, which likewise animates the

---

* Matthew 19, 24.

communist island; it stands as an extremely secular heaven above Utopia. Even more striking is the abolition of religious controversy: Thomas More, since 1935 a saint of the Catholic Church, seems with his tolerance almost like an early Roger Williams, not to say Voltaire. Certainly on this point he is a close forerunner of Jean Bodin, the ideologist (though for different reasons) of a non-denominational state. This surprising contradiction enabled a late bourgeoisie no longer interested in utopias to turn More solely into a churchman and to disinfect him of any revolutionary odour. Among other things a philologist with capitalist interests, Heinrich Brockhaus, furnished a hypothesis which considers precisely this communist-Epicurean-tolerant 'foreign body' in the 'Utopia' and carefully eradicates it. For according to Brockhaus (Thomas More's Utopia-work, 1929) More's work, as it exists and has had a continuing influence down the centuries, as a democratic-communist document, is supposed to be a forgery. According to him, More was not the author but only the official editor, or rather: More also wrote a 'Utopia', but what was later circulated under this name is no longer the original but a distortion of the original Utopia perpetrated by another hand. The other hand is that of Erasmus of Rotterdam; the Epicureanism of the work originates from him, not from More, as well as the communism, the six-hour day, the religious tolerance. Eradicated by Erasmus, however, was 'the main sharp reforming content', that is to say the non-political, exclusively religious interest which is allegedly supposed to have motivated More in the drafting of his original Utopia. This interest is interpreted by Brockhaus on the assumption that More wanted to restore to the Church at the last moment the ascetic conscience and its salutary dignity, a year before the catastrophe of the violent, schismatic Reformation occurred in 1517. Accordingly, it is not England that is supposed to have been criticized in the original Utopia but the Pontifical State, and above all: the model for this ideal was by no means the primitive commune of American islanders but – the monastery on Mount Athos. Instead of England and the primitive commune, More is solely supposed to have contrasted the two centres of Christianity: Rome and Athos; Utopia is nothing other than 'the land of Athos reconstructed with the help of additions'. Hence it was not an outline of the best state that More intended, in particular and in general, but a reform of the Church; but Erasmus spoilt this plan by spoiling the plan of the original Utopia, which already lay ready for dispatch to the decisive council in the Vatican. Thus Brockhaus's theory would like to rid More of the foul odour of communism, as well as the zest for life, as well as religious tolerance;

all these main ideas of the 'Utopia' (which have become historically effective)
are 'distortions' by Erasmus. And it is not as if this was a case of an
unimportant exchange of names in the province of the same work (as in
the Shakespeare-Bacon controversy, for example), on the contrary: the
works themselves are as different as a freethinker and an angel. There is
actually an original Utopia, one indisputably written by More, and this
work is simply a religious document, unlike the political tract by Erasmus,
– the kingdom of 'Utopia' is not of this world either. So much for
Brockhaus; the social brief of this kind of philology is quite obvious: one
of the noblest precursors of communism is to have his words cut short.
But this suspect hypothesis is useful in that it focuses attention more sharply
than before on the collaboration of Erasmus and thereby removes undeniable
difficulties. The fact that Erasmus edited the 'Utopia' before it was printed
was well-known; certain elements of lightness, indeed of ironic playfulness
(which are inappropriate to Thomas More) must have been incorporated
by the great man of letters. Erasmus could be tolerant, for he had said
that the Holy Spirit wrote very bad Greek in the New Testament. Erasmus
could be epicurean, for he is the author of the most unprejudiced pedagogical
'Colloquia' (they contain a didactic discussion on the manners of young
people in a brothel). The tone in the two parts of the 'Utopia' is also
strangely different: the first part contains fierce condemnations of social
conditions in England (certainly not in the Pontifical State), whereas the
second part, which was after all supposed to proclaim the ideal, indulges
in a genially refined mixture of playfulness and seriousness, and it avoids
the expected organ-tones of hope. At any rate, the Thomas More who
demonstrated by his martyr's death what it meant to believe in a cause
does not merely make the best state into a fairytale, as noted above, in
harmony with late classical forms, but he inserts, beyond this harmony,
elements of a courtly dramatic fable. But above all, the Thomas More who
advertises in the 'Utopia' the results of a social revolution is a different
man to the one who a few years later, when this revolution had broken
out in Germany, defended the existing state, kingship, the clergy, in short
the very fortress of property which was missing in 'Utopia'. And the
content for which the martyr ultimately died was not that of social, let
alone religious tolerance; he died a faithful supporter of the papal Church,
whose memory has remained preserved solely in this form for Catholicism.
On top of this there are incompatibilities in the work itself, especially
in its second part; dissonances by no means just between the tone of a
courtly fable and communism, but between humaneness and indifference,

between social paradise and the old class world. The first part had explained crime in terms of economic causes, and accordingly demanded the humane treatment of prisoners; the second part recognizes criminal slaves in the midst of 'Utopia', who have to perform heavy labour in chains. The warfare of the Utopians and their desire for annexation seem a related inconsistency: 'They regard it', More remarks, 'they regard it as a highly just reason for war if a nation seeks to prohibit the use and possession of land, which it does not need itself but leaves barren and unproductive, by another nation which according to the dictates of nature should draw its subsistence from it'. Hermann Oncken rightly stresses in his edition of the 'Utopia' that this martial passage no longer has anything whatever in common with the isolated and exemplary peaceful existence of the Utopians, but rather with the later practice of England: 'The communist and primitive-agrarian ideal state, which already revealed itself as a class state in the question of slaves, now shows itself to be a state based on domination and power politics with the first signs of a capitalist imperialism which seems almost modern.' Thus 'Utopia' by no means appears of a piece, by no means as if it has sprung from one single person and his socially conscious love of Christ. But the eminently English nature of many of these inconsistencies once again does not argue in favour of Erasmus but shows that More too could accommodate breaks in his work, and further that the abolition of private property (with all its consequences) is an anomaly within bourgeois anticipations which even the noblest faith in Christ cannot dispose of. Dreams of the early bourgeoisie, in which the bourgeois himself disappears as a class, cannot avoid irony and dissonances. Thus the explanatory value of Brockhaus's hypothesis is very much reduced even over and above the suspicious nature of its social brief: a series of difficulties certainly arises not just from the editing by Erasmus. No ideology is more English than that of a morally justified colonial war, as taught in 'Utopia', none could be further from the monastic republic on Mount Athos. The 'Utopia' is most probably a hybrid creation with two authors, but England is already criticized by More, not just by Erasmus, and it is once again exclusively England, not Rome, that is to become the best state. The 'Utopia' is and remains, with all its dross, the first modern portrait of democratic-communist wishful dreams. In the womb of capitalist forces that were only just beginning, a future and supra-future world anticipated itself: both that of formal democracy, which delivers capitalism, and that of material-humane democracy, which cancels it out. For the first time democracy was here linked in a humane sense, in the sense of *public freedom and tolerance*, with a collective economy (always easily threatened by bureaucracy, and indeed clericalism). In contrast to the previously imagined collectivisms of the best state, in the work of Thomas More freedom is written into the collective, and genuine material-humane democracy becomes its content. This content makes the 'Utopia', in substantial sections, into a kind of liberal memorial and memorable book of socialism and communism.

People are only made wicked by deprivation, 'why punish them so severely'? More commences with this question, he immediately makes the surroundings responsible for the individual. 'The gallows are appointed for thieves, whereas we should much rather see to it that they can make a living, so that none of them faces the dire compulsion of first having to steal, and afterwards to die.' Right next to this, More portrays the world which allows the poor man to become guilty and sets itself up as a judge: 'How great is the number of noblemen who, themselves as idle as drones, live off the work of other people, and make them sweat blood; but on top of this they gather a swarm of wastrels and satellites around them.' And the end of the first part of the 'Utopia' states openly: 'Where private ownership still exists, where all people measure all values by the yardstick of money, it will hardly ever be possible to pursue a just and happy policy... Thus possessions certainly cannot be distributed in any just and fair way, and mortal happiness cannot be established at all, unless property is done away with beforehand. As long as it continues to exist, poverty, toil and care will hang instead an inescapable burden on by far the biggest and by far the best part of humanity. The burden may be lightened a little, but to remove it entirely (without abolishing property) is impossible.' More puts all these words into the mouth of the globe-trotter, whom he introduces as a reporter from 'Utopia' and who now, from the standpoint of the best state, regards the English one in horror. The cautious Chancellor calls the man Raphael Hythlodaeus (which means 'windbag'), but Raphael undoubtedly represents More's most radical opinions. The island of 'Utopia' then, of which the reporter gives an account in the second part of the book, is above all a humane one because its inhabitants are so largely free of drudgery. Six hours of moderate effort are sufficient to satisfy all urgent needs and also to produce enough provisions for the comforts of life. Then life beyond work begins; it is a life of the happy, liberal family unit, in a beautifully kept house which unites several families like guests. So as to suppress even the semblance of private property, the houses are exchanged every ten years by drawing lots; in the forum there are free eating-houses, educational establishments for all and temples. 'The economic system of Utopia focuses on the primary goal of giving all citizens as much free time as possible for the cultivation of spiritual needs.' Not the least aspect of this cultivation of spiritual needs is the art of eating and drinking, together with the worship of physical strength and beauty; there is a sharp rejection of asceticism at this point: 'To wear oneself out without being of any use to anybody, merely for the sake of an empty shadow of virtue – this seems quite absurd to the Utopians: an act of cruelty towards one's own person and the deepest ingratitude towards nature.' There is no sharing of women in Utopia of course, on the contrary: adulterers are punished with the harshest slavery, and with death if they repeat the offence. Yet marriages can be dissolved and are only entered into after the bride and bridegroom have seen each other naked; 'since the Utopians think that nature herself has marked out pleasure for us as the goal of our actions, and living in accordance with her dictates they call virtue'. Admittedly other passages in the work continue to extol monastic renunciation, the delight in painful, even disgusting and unnatural work; but despite these inconsistencies, Epicureanism remains dominant. 'These are the views of the Utopians on virtue and pleasure, and unless a religion sent down from heaven should inspire man with more pious thoughts, they think no views are to be found which could come closer to the truth in accordance with human reason.' Even Christianity does not seem to the Utopians to contain 'more pious thoughts'; they have adopted the Christian religion chiefly only 'because they heard Christ had sanctioned the communist life-style of his disciples'. Otherwise there is room for all religions in a splendidly uniting tolerance, even sun, moon and planet worship. The Utopians have agreed on a common cult which every faction fills out in its own sense and with particular forms of ritual; Utopia is the Eldorado of religious freedom, not to say the pantheon of all good gods. 'Since it is one of the oldest constitutional provisions of the Utopians that nobody's religion must cause them any harm... The founder of Utopia made this provision not merely with a view to peace, but because he was of the opinion that such a stipulation also lay in the interests of religion. He did not have the presumption to make any final provision about religion, since he was not sure whether perhaps God himself may desire a varied kind of worship and thus gave this inspiration to one person, and that to another.' These sentences are certainly most astonishing from the mouth of a subsequent martyr of the Roman Church; they call into question the absolute supremacy of Christianity itself. They not only give a first whiff of the Enlightenment, but immediately give its full aroma; they break the authoritarian state in two at its toughest point, that of constraint of religion and conscience. But the strength for this freedom in More's case springs over and over again from the abolition of property, and furthermore from a general abolition, not from mere cloister communism. Property alone creates masters and servants, creates factions among the masters themselves, the need for power and authority, wars about power and authority, religious wars and unchristian extortion by state and Church alike. Thus a premonition of surplus value appears at the end of the 'Utopia': 'What are we to say about the fact that the rich squeeze a bit more every day out of the daily wages of the poor, not just by means of private fraud but even on the strength of public laws?' Likewise – isolated both backwards and forwards – a kind of pre-Marxist concept of the class-state gleams through: 'When I consider all our states which are flourishing anywhere today, I come across nothing other than a conspiracy of the rich, who abuse the name and legal title of the state in order to ensure their own advantage. They think up all conceivable methods and tricks, firstly to hold on to their possessions, which they have amassed by reprehensible means, without any danger of losing them, and then to buy and abuse the effort and labour of the poor as cheaply as possible...But even when these abominable people have divided the goods of life amongst themselves which would have sufficed for all, – how far away they still are from the happy condition of the utopian state!' This salutary and festive book concludes with a hymn to that state: 'What a weight of vexations is shaken off in this state, what a tremendous crop of crimes is rooted out, since avarice has been eliminated there along with the use of money. For who can fail to see that fraud, theft, robbery, feuds, rebellion, squabbling, murder, treason and poisonous intrigue, now simply more avenged than checked by daily punishments, would all have to die out at once with the elimination of money, and furthermore that fear, sorrow, worries, torments and night-watches would also have to disappear at the same moment as money?' In acknowledging Raphael's account, Thomas More finds there is a great deal in the constitution of the Utopians that he would like to see introduced in our own states, though he adds that this is more of a wish than a hope. A wishful construction arose, a rational one in which there is no longer any kind of chiliastic certainty of hope, but in return this construction postulates itself as one that is capable of being produced by its own efforts, without transcendental support or intervention. 'Utopia' is projected a long way into the Unbecome on earth, into the human tendency towards freedom – as a minimum of work and state, as a maximum of joy.

Counterpart to More:
Campanella's City of the Sun or the utopia of social order

The bourgeois blossomed later on, precisely by affirming new constraint. Imposed by the king on the small feudal lords and their splintered economy. This was the case in the seventeenth century, when production changed from manual crafts to large workshops, to manufacture. When it consequently moved, in advanced countries, towards a large, uniformly run economic body. The Baroque is the age of centralized royal power, and it was progressive at that time. A totally authoritarian and also bureaucratic utopia: Campanella's 'Civitas solis', published in 1623, now corresponded to the harmony of bourgeois interests with the monarchy. Instead of freedom, as in More, the tune that now rings out is that of order, with rulers and supervisors. Instead of a president of the Utopians, in a simple Franciscan cloak, with a harvest crown, a ruler appears, a world pope. And what Campanella found most seductive about America was no longer, as in More, the paradisial innocence of the islanders, but the highly constructed Inca empire of the past. Lewis Mumford, in 'The Story of Utopias', 1922, calls Campanella's utopia nothing short of a 'marriage between Plato's Republic and the court of Montezuma'. After all, as noted above, Plato's 'Republic' was the first utopianizing order, long before there was a novel of an ideal state based on freedom. In its title as in its geographical situation, Campanella's 'City of the Sun' touches on that of Iamboulos; though the Sun in Campanella's City does not shine with effortless Hellenistic-oriental abundance, but simply with centralized rigour, of the sort which was also practised in truly Campanellan fashion by the artificial Jesuit state in Paraguay. Campanella's dreams as a whole were connected with contemporary power units; he projected these on to a utopian screen. Not in order to ideologize them, but he believed in the coming of his dream kingdom and emphasized the existing great powers solely as instruments for hastening its arrival. Although he spent twenty-seven years in the dungeons of Spanish reaction, which did not trust him, Campanella, who is first supposed to have had relations with the Turks, wildly acclaimed Spanish world-domination, and ultimately that of France, but in both cases exclusively as places of preparation for the messianic

kingdom of the sun. He still characteristically ended the dedication to
Richelieu of his work 'De sensu rerum et magia', newly published in 1637,
with a messianic claim, not with courtly flattery: 'The city of the sun,
devised by me, to be established by you'; in this arrogant hope Campanella
also welcomed the birth of the future Louis XIV, who was later actually
called the Sun King. Looking at it in more detail, the work about the 'City
of the Sun' is a meticulous account given by a widely travelled Genoan to
his host. The Gubernator Genuensis relates how on a voyage round the
world he landed on the island of Taprobane (Ceylon) and fell into the
hands of a band of armed men who had conducted him to the City of the
Sun and explained its institutions to him. For all its boldness and the usual
novelistic trappings, the account has a feel of technical engineering about
it: the civitas is constructed like a contemporary plan of fortifications by
Vauban. On the whole, Campanella's utopia must be understood in conformity with the world system of its creator; apart from Bacon and the
Fichte of the 'Closed Commercial State', Campanella is the only philosopher
among the more modern utopians. It was no accident that the 'Civitas
solis' was published as the appendix to a 'Philosophia realis', that is, as
a paralipomenon, but also as a means of putting to the test a natural and
moral philosophy. Just as man is a likeness of God, so is his extension,
the state; accordingly, this social utopia descends from the supreme being
to the state and seeks to show that the latter, conceived as perfect, resembles
the radiations of a divine solar system. The communist features of such
a utopia of domination may cause surprise; only in fact it is not a utopia
of freedom at work here, but one of impersonal order, conceived in terms
of an international state. Its thorough administrative organization was
reflected in a model island, and the contradiction between a universal
kingdom and an island city is suppressed. Life runs like clockwork in a
military monarchic fashion, the strictest punctuality and pre-orderedness
demonstrate their technical efficiency in terms of time, administration and
economy. The incipient manufacturing system, which brought together
workers and technological means of production in large workshops, is utopianized along the lines of state socialism. On the other hand, Campanella
transfigures the Hispanicization of the continent at the time, the deliberate
intolerance (though with contents of his own, not with those of the
Inquisition). A state socialism appears, or rather: a popish one, with a lot of
Byzantine and astrological pathos behind it. With the pathos of *the right
time, the right situation, the right order of all people and things*; a commanding
centre establishes order in a classless but extremely hierarchical way.

If things are run in this way, then there are neither rich nor poor, private property is abolished. All citizens have to work, a four-hour day is enough, exploitation and profit are unknown. Each trade is a communal enterprise, under supervision and without individual gain, the highest task is the common good. Current states are riddled with selfishness: 'But if there is no private property any more, then it becomes pointless and disappears.' The vices of poverty and the greater ones of wealth have vanished, the only quarrels are those on points of honour: 'The Solarians claim that poverty makes people low-minded, cunning, thieving, homeless and mendacious. But wealth makes them impudent, arrogant, ignorant, treacherous, boastful and heartless. In a true community, however, everybody is rich and poor at the same time – rich because they do not wish for anything that they do not have in common, – poor because nobody possesses anything, and consequently the Solarians are not enslaved to things, but things serve them.' But while private property has thus died out, the state is not diminished as well, as it is in More, but it becomes instead the highest purpose of society; ascending from the provincia to the regnum, to the imperium, to the monarchia universalis and finally to the papal kingdom. The state guarantees precisely the pleasant part of order, the distribution of goods: 'The Solarians receive everything they need from the community, and the authorities strictly see to it that nobody gets an excessive amount, and nobody is denied anything they need.' Above all, Campanella's state also seeks its power in the present metaphysics it portrays, in the image of God, in accordance with Campanella's philosophy. The authorities reflect the primary forces of cosmic order, those three 'primalities' of being which govern human experiences and spheres of activity. These are Sapientia, Potentia, and Amor, their unity is God, they reach and emanate from God, through four worlds growing ever more corporeal, into their respective historical existence, the 'mundus situalis'. Within it the 'primalities' themselves need an embodiment to create the order which can always only be one of the right coordination: God becomes the papal world-ruler, also called Sol or Metaphysicus in Campanella's utopia. Subordinate to him are three princes whose sphere of activity exactly corresponds to the regions of Sapientia, Potentia, and Amor, as in a cabbalistic space. History becomes the production of this state space, which is the only veritable, i.e. vertical one; just as space in general is celebrated throughout Campanella, 'as an immortal and almost divine, all-pervading receptacle of things', which itself strives for fulfilment and fills the horror vacui, the horror of chaos and nothingness. Necessity as the expression of divine Potentia conquers the case of chance (contingentia), certainty (fatum) as the expression of divine Sapientia conquers the individual case (casus), but order (harmonia), above all, as the expression of divine Amor conquers the case of luck, of vicissitude (fortuna). Thus in Campanella (as earlier in Cusanus) the rising bourgeoisie stands firmly in the struggle against nothingness; unlike the declining, panchaotic bourgeoisie, wallowing in nothingness. But Campanella's order of wisdom, power and love, i.e. that of the three 'primalities', is opposed to the chaotic: to the case of chance, the individual case, and the case of vicissitude. And this order is precisely *active* in its opposition, since contingentia, casus, and fortuna are supposed to be merely 'a nihilo contracta', simply the remnants of the dead nothingness (De monarchia, p. 1) from which God called the world into existence. Though in a truly *emanatistic* fashion, Campanella ultimately sought to conquer the nothingness or non-ens in the world by an irradiation of the ens, the Sol, the solar essence. It therefore comes as no surprise that the further directive of such a thoroughly ruled world could become the myth of *astrology*; for it above all guarantees dependence on above. Astrology corresponded to the fanaticism of this order, it casts man along with all things among planets and the ruling houses of the zodiac. Both the domestic and the public life of the Solarians, the traffic and the lay-out of the city, even baths, meals and the right moment for sexual intercourse are governed by the stars: 'Men and women sleep in two separate chambers, and await the moment of their fruitful union: at a specified time a matron opens both doors from outside. This time is specified by the doctor and the astrologer, who try to hit the moment in which Venus and Mercury stand east of the sun in a favourable house, in the auspicious aspect of Jupiter.' Freedom of choice and freedom in general are thus taken away from man, not in a mechanizing way but rather in the manner of a dictatorship of the stars, from above, on all sides. Nowadays astrology is just a ruin of superstitious architecture, but in those days it was still alive and accepted, a kind of class meeting-house, extending with its patri-archalisms through the whole world. And only incidentally do a few exemptions – not freedoms – lodge in the total hierarchy, they are solely missing prohibitions. There are several such missing prohibitions: 'The Solarian can spend his free time with pleasant studies, walks, mental and physical exercises and with pleasures.' Likewise the mount of Venus does not attain the height of the other pedantry, the astrological rules for sexual intercourse are only obligatory for prospective parents: 'The rest, who associate with those who are infertile or prostitutes either for pleasure or on doctor's orders or as a stimulant, disregard these customs.' In fact there is even an illusion of liberalism at the point where the state is most seriously in evidence, on the occasion of a death sentence: 'The man found guilty must in this case make his peace with his accuser and witness by kissing and embracing them, as the doctors of his illness so to speak. Moreover, the death sentence in Solaria is not carried out on any condemned man until he himself has become convinced by superior reasoning that it is necessary for him to die, and until he has been brought to the point of wishing for the death sentence to be carried out himself.' Rousseau's 'Contrat social' admittedly makes a similar demand, but the difference between the attitude of the latter and that of Campanella could not be greater. Rousseau wants to preserve self-determination even in the act which destroys it, whereas Campanella uses liberality as an aid to the strongest triumph of authority. For the rightly condemned individual here wants to see himself destroyed as a deviation, or in the language of the Church: laudabiliter se subjecit. Subjectivity precisely exists only in so far as it agrees to its own extermination. That is, it is even deprived of the refuge of being able to be a rebel or a persistent heretic. Thus total conformism triumphs exactly where it seems to suffer an exception; even in its humaneness, Campanella's 'City of the Sun' represents the most extreme antithesis to the utopia of freedom. Order is virtue itself and its assembly: 'The Solarians have as many authorities as we have names of virtues: magnanimity, bravery, chastity, generosity, cheerfulness, sobriety and so on. And they are chosen for posts according to whether they betrayed the greatest tendency to this or that virtue even as children at school.' Even in this harsh utopia, happiness remains the summum bonum, but it is precisely the happiness of servitude, harnessed to a divine service which – with the total unity of spiritual and temporal power – is the same as service to the state. So much for Campanella's future state, it contains an intoxication of constraint which is unparalleled, it surpasses Plato's ideal of Sparta by using the whole Byzantine and Catholic hierarchy which had arisen since then. Apart from the distribution of property, life is only so bad because people are not in their place, because mundus situalis, the mere situational state of life, totters into the situational accidents of its semi-nothingness. Because no concord prevails and no agreement with the ruling celestial forces, no harmony with them; because the state is not on an even keel. This is time and again the basic contrast to the utopias of freedom, in such various forms, from the Cynics to Thomas More, and ultimately to anarchism; in Campanella the contrast breaks out consciously.

The abolition of private property does not dissolve the contrast: for while in More this abolition overcomes subordination and superiority in general and posits total equality, in Campanella this equality becomes the very foundation soil on which a new hierarchy arises, that of talents, virtues and 'primalities'. If we clarify this contrast between More and Campanella in terms of the two more competing than connected natural myths of their time, then we can say that More or the utopia of *freedom* corresponds almost as much to *alchemy* as Campanella or the utopia of *order* corresponds in fact to *astrology*. More never mentions alchemy, if only because gold is despised on his island and because the refining of metals in the symbolic sense, as a refining of the world, no longer seems to be necessary there. But when More relates right at the beginning that the founder of his island first blasted it away from the mainland, and when, as More says, it is isolated precisely from the world of the 'plumbei' or leaden ones, then these passages were soon interpreted alchemically and could be interpreted like this, in the sense of the later Rosicrucians or initiated 'general reformers' (Andreae, Comenius). 'Utopia' is distilled from the evil world like gold from lead, – alchemy was regarded as the mythology of this liberation. Campanella on the other hand certainly does mention alchemy, even the golden lustre in Sol and Civitas solis suggested this reminiscence, but the continuous pathos of astrology in his work prevented the liberation of social gold from breaking out of its pre-ordered space and exploding it. In Campanella, the harmony of the world below was also still to be founded, but the 'Civitas solis' remains strictly chained to the regency of the stars. Utopia does not have to be processed out here, but it is cosmic harmony, and there has been not too much but too little government in society up to now, and consequently too little astrology. Thus the contrast between More's model and that of Campanella is also a mythological one; and it extends – without a mythological cloak – into all following utopias. Liberal-federative socialism (from Robert Owen onwards) has More as its ancestor, while centralist socialism (from Saint-Simon onwards) has points of contact with Campanella, with a broad-based, high-built system of rule, with social utopia as strictness and arranged happiness.

Socratic inquiry into freedom and order, with regard to 'Utopia' and 'Civitas solis'

The bigger the words, the more easily alien elements are able to hide in them. This is particularly the case with freedom, and with order, of which everybody often has his own idea. The island on which the one or the other has settled, despite its smallness, does not diminish the extensive ambiguity of these principles. A man like Socrates pretended to be ignorant about concepts which everyone thought they understood, and he ironically sought advice from so-called experts. But they quickly became entangled in contradictions, became confused, and reflection finally got under way. Freedom too, and then constraint and order must be questioned in this way so as not to be slogans for mere, and often deceived opinions. While Thomas More assumes democratic freedom, and Campanella authoritarian order, to be synonymous with social happiness, these political issues also underwent and signified very different things both beforehand and afterwards. The problem of freedom is its ambiguity and the particularly great change in its function during the course of history. Thus we do not only have to differentiate psychological freedom or freedom of choice, political freedom or freedom of self-determination from one another. Even within freedom of self-determination everything depends on the group that is striving for it, on the respective state of the society in which the call for liberté is still a virgin one. Thus it ranges from free competition, economic Manchesterism to the struggle against precisely these liberal masters. It ranges from the bourgeois-revolutionary act which established free competition in the face of barriers set up by the guilds and feudal patronage, to the free revolutionary action of the proletariat, which emancipates precisely from the emancipated bourgeois again. The call for freedom ranges from the 'Liberty' of the German territorial princes, stabilized against the Emperor in Vienna, to the opposite – the abolition of the princes, and of the dominant class-state as a whole. Freedom: it is demanded by the neo-feudal liberty of the princes of industry and monopolies, and it fulfils, with a radical contrast, the programme: expropriation of the expropriators. The Phrygian cap covers both the national war of liberation and the revolutionary civil war against the Gessler class within the nation itself. All this shows freedom to be a concept of relation variable in its contents; even the formal aspect of this relation is still different according to whether liberation from something or to something is aspired to. Private ownership of the means of production necessitates ipso facto the oppression of those whose labour is the only capital they possess. A call for liberté, however radically intended, if it occurs within a society based on property, only changes the dependence of economically weaker classes, below the victorious liberating class, or posits new slaves, like the industrial proletariat. The freedom of acquisition, by not becoming a freedom from acquisition, manifestly ended in tyranny, one which was particularly oppressive; capitalist democracy is plutocracy, so Socrates would have discovered little concurrence and true emancipation in the many kinds of economic and political freedom, save in the emancipation from the property-masters, as the source of every political non-freedom. Everywhere else there exists only the special interest in a freedom which is the freedom of a special interest. On the other hand, where property is removed, freedom – in its political and social application – yields the common element which Socrates had intended in his questions, or at least something of this enterprise. This is what makes More an example of the utopias of freedom in spite of everything and attacks the master-servant relationship. Intrinsically alive in freedom is the opposition to anything pre-ordered without assent, to the social fate which overcomes and has come down to those who are dependent. Intrinsically at work in freedom is the countermove of a subjective factor to that necessity to which people are chained without their will, against their will and without any conception anyway. The subjective factor does not need to be that of the individual, it is more certainly that of the community which is oppressed in corpore and rises up in corpore against oppression, liberating its individuals as it does so. The necessity, on the other hand, does not only have to be absolutely hostile, as in its superannuated periods, when it is artificially upheld solely by means of tyranny. It can also be that blind necessity in society and in nature which is blind in so far as it is not comprehended. Socio-political freedom takes up the fight against this necessity, and it only becomes freedom in its complete or characteristic sense by concretely mediating itself with the forces of necessity. Engels thus defines social freedom in concreto in his 'Anti-Dühring': 'The objective alien powers which have dominated history up to now will come under the control of mankind itself. Only from that point on will mankind make its own history itself in full awareness, only from that point on will the social causes it has set in motion also, predominantly and to a constantly increasing extent, have the effects it desires. It is the leap of humanity out of the realm of necessity into the realm of freedom.' There are still thousands of problems with this freedom, i.e. of its What For and content, of the self that is determined in the self-determination, but there is no ambiguity any more. One of its prerequisites, in More and most utopias, is the abolition of private property and the classes this has produced. Another prerequisite is the consistent will towards the negation of the state in so far as it rules individuals and is an instrument of oppression in the hands of the privileged. In Engels the state is not primarily negated, but ultimately brought back to the running of affairs and the management of the processes of production; even here it does not have any pathos any more, the state becomes intangible, its pressure dies away.

The harsh word constraint seems not so much ambiguous as downright reactionary, it scares us. And yet there is something shaky even here, however much everything looks like a screw, nothing like freedom. For we must take into account who is imposing the constraint, and therefore the maintenance of order, and for what purpose order is being imposed. If we take this into account, then it is clear that order too has several faces, and the state that is formed by it does not remain the same. There is an order of pure constraint, with which a bad community asserts itself against some of its wolves, but chiefly against all of its victims, and another order which emerges from the community itself, from its support and structure. In the *first case* there is no real order at all, but only regulated or rather forcibly maintained disorder. Even the capitalist community then only becomes possible by individual freedom, here that of the owners of goods, being restricted in the so-called state under the rule of law to a level which leaves the equally individual freedom of every other citizen untouched. This restriction is not taken from this freedom, although this is asserted in liberal Natural Right, but hovers over it, is imposed on it as a state of emergency. This state of emergency is called bourgeois order: as constraint it is opposed to those who are oppressed economically anyway and to their rebellion, as cunning it is in league with the strong and their competition. The order in the *second case*, in the case of a socialist economy and society, proves to be quite different. It does not then appear as pure constraint or an enforced state of emergency, nor as the condition of social life, or even of the community itself. But community is then primary in any case, and man, as Marx observes on this point in his work 'On the Jewish Question', has recognized and organized his forces propres as social forces. He thus no longer separates off social force as political force, as an abstract political state based on order, in contrast to its egoistically economizing elements. Order then loses the constraint of individual restriction; for the situation of homo homini lupus is brought to an end, restriction of the earning citizen by an abstract citizen of the state is no longer necessary. Everybody has the opportunity to be a human being, because nobody any longer has the opportunity to be a monster; thus the social order loses both its character of constraint and its abstract ideality. The social individual has taken back into himself, and taken himself up into, the abstract citizen of the state; thus community becomes self-evident, order concrete. As soon

as the capitalist threat on its borders has ceased, this order no longer has
to maintain itself with arms, against an oppressed class, but shows itself,
once the cause for oppression has disappeared, to be a mutually agreed
organization and encirclement. Such concrete order is ultimately the same
as the classless society, is the structure of this non-antagonistic community
per se. Concrete order appears in the unessentially Become as the control
of processes of production and, in the essentially Permanent, as the construction of a more and more central unity of goal in the human race or
as the construction of the *realm* of freedom. This clearly constitutes a
different concept of order from that of pure constraint and of restriction;
order operates in the community itself, as its immanent support. Order
does not thus become a game of course, on the contrary it retains its *character
as organization and realm*. Precisely as organization it does not therefore
necessarily contradict the most important motif in Campanella's utopia
of order: the abolition of uncontrolled cases of chance, individual cases,
cases of luck (contingentia, casus, fortuna); the will to set things to rights
from a central vantage-point. And it is no accident that apart from the
tolerant element as it were that expresses itself in the realm of *freedom*,
Marxism is also animated by the cathedral element as it were, which
expresses itself precisely in the *realm* of freedom, in freedom as a *realm*.
The paths to it are likewise not liberal; they are the capture of power
in the state, discipline, authority, central planning, a general line, and
orthodoxy. And the goal which gives support to every future freedom
likewise shows no affinity whatsoever with the liberalism of dissociation;
on the contrary, total freedom in particular does not get lost in a swarm
of frisking caprices and in the insubstantial despair in which they end,
but triumphs solely in the will to orthodoxy. Thus order is likewise not
a simple concept, and Socrates would have needed a lot of the midwife's
art before its essence finally appeared. An essence which in any case – even
more clearly than freedom – can only unfold in a propertyless, classless
society. The essence of freedom has the will behind it, the emotional intensity that seeks to break through and boundlessly to realize itself; whereas
the essence of order has perfect logic on its side, the *tangibility of what
has come good or been achieved*. Even the experiment of order in all possible
fields and spheres lives off this in the end, from cleanliness and punctuality
to the survey of the manly and the masterly, from the ceremonial to
architectural style, from the numerical series to the philosophical system.
In some of these arrangements the order is only external or imposed, like
the laws of state in oppressive and class societies. But in other arrangements,

above all in those with artistic precision and in those of philosophical systems of quality, the order already comes partly out of the material itself. In tendency it is inscribed within it, so that chaos, which is not or does not remain such, itself holds latent within it the star and the star-figure. Common to the manifestations of freedom is the desire not to be determined by something alien to or alienated from the will: but common to order is the value of builtness, the elapsion in need of no emotion any more. It is this element of release and of having found its place, indeed this realm-like element, which in other worlds lying less in wickedness* than the political one indicates best repose and indicates it as the best; as in Giotto, as in Bach. The essence of order – and all essence is something different from appearance – thus remains the *utopia of chancelessness, of situationlessness*. Even in the abstract orders or those of constraint in class society, this realm-spirit is a tribute of vice to virtue. It constitutes the seduction or half-truth in Campanella's pathos of strictness, pathos of social construction, in harmony, which rises out of the mundus situalis against contingentia, casus, fortuna and posits Being of situationlessness. In this respect order is opposed to freedom, namely to freedom in the bourgeois antagonistic sense, with nothing but capitalist individual cases as its vehicles and the happiness of acquisition as its goal. Bourgeois order was of necessity already partly opposed to this kind of freedom; *but concrete order is not opposed to concrete freedom*. For concrete freedom is the socially succeeding will which has become communally clear, just as concrete order is the successful figure of the community itself; both, including freedom, are now constructive. Concrete freedom and concrete order are connected in this postulate of independence, in the utopia of a situationless Being, which governs the postulate of freedom and order. This connection is no unspoken identity (as in Kantian ethics for example, when it presupposes the identity of its freedom with the moral law). But rather the connection is dialectical: freedom and order turn into one another over and over again, to produce situationlessness. Freedom is brought to an end by order, which makes it land in a *built* space or realm, instead of freedom endlessly continuing in volitional time. Order in turn finds its end in freedom, namely its *sole content*, or the one thing that needs to be in order: the human will, the intrinsic self and What of this will. This ultimately points order towards freedom, towards that which is *certainly the sole substantial element of order*, whether it is freedom of the oppressed class or finally of individuals who

---

* 'And we know that we are of God, and the whole world lieth in wickedness.' 1 John, 5, 19.

have become classless, with a collective which springs from them. Only freedom the will has a content, order the logos has no content of its own; in other words: the realm of freedom does not contain another realm, but it contains the freedom or that Being-for-itself towards which things are solely organized and ordered. Marx equally connected and overcame the free-confederative element in More and his successors, and the ordered-centralist element in Campanella and his successors. Order is here the Novum: *democratic centralism*, it is common organization of the processes of production, a common unified plan of human information and cultivation. Just as the detached political state dies away, so culture now loses its detached reification and hovering abstractness; it acquires a concrete framework, a concretely cohesive relief. Culture loses the arbitrary and aimless element, it gains the sharply orientating background of a What For; a new order of salvation, namely for human material, approaches. Solely through this order does freedom attain its content, a defined, or at least more and more precisely articulated one. But what possibly emerges in the figure of order is and remains precisely nothing other than defined freedom; order is in contrast solely the space, which is nevertheless indispensable, for the defined freedom-content. Only the path via 'Campanella' (conceived as a pathos of order) thus leads to a democracy of 'More' (conceived as a pathos of freedom), in which no liberalist juste milieu is possible, in whatever form, but a realm of individuals could begin who have left behind them the freedom of isolated robbery and mild unorderedness and know well the best legacy of federation and centralization: profusion in unity. This is the same as *solidarity*, the richly animated harmony of individual and social forces. Freedom and order, harsh contrasts in the abstract utopias, thus merge into one another in materialist dialectics, and assist each other. Concrete being free is order, that of its own field, concrete being ordered is freedom, that of its sole content.

Continuation: social utopias and classic Natural Right

Dreams did not always have to be of things far off in order to see light. Particularly not when a *demand* was made for something better, instead of it merely being pictured. Something closer, seemingly remembered, certainly evident always then appeared, namely the so-called right, born with us. Which is or ought to be unchangeable and as *natural right* superior to all arbitrary statutes. It justifies, and even encourages where necessary, resistance to statutes, from a higher position than that of written law. This age-old Antigone motif, typically defined in matrilinear terms, gained a new lustre in the sixteenth century, mediated by Stoic Natural Right. Its matrilinear features, though still clearly recognizable in the Stoics, almost disappeared of course. Almost, but not entirely; for they are still clearly at work in Rousseau, in his praise of nature as both benevolent and egalitarian. But Natural Right immediately takes a tough line, by becoming revolutionary and hostile to tyranny in the strengthening bourgeoisie. It is made of sterner stuff than the social utopias, although their wishful goals are related, and temporarily replaced them. Such strange bedfellows as Huguenots (after the St Bartholomew's Massacre) and Jesuits (in the fight against heretical states) prepared the way for the theory of bourgeois revolution by legally justifying tyrannicide; Natural Right as against the written kind acquired from then on its politically and methodically distinct form. Althus (Politica, 1610) taught that resistance to unjust masters was not rebellion but the protection of one's own violated rights. In doing so, he used the Epicurean doctrine of the contract which people *voluntarily* entered into on founding a state. There was no talk yet in Epicurus of a termination of this contract; but Althus uses it to justify resistance. If the contract is broken on the side of the authorities, if they no longer govern in accordance with the will and welfare of the people, then it is no longer binding on the other side either. The people then rightly resist the authorities who have become unjust, they revoke their authority. The logicized dream of what is right in Grotius (De jure belli et pacis, 1625) appears with the theory of resistance tempered down, but with an increased distinction between positive and unwritten law; this dream saw the beginning of modern Natural Right as a system. That is to say, the drive and its intention, with which a *communal contract* was concluded here, appear together as the 'principle' from which the tenets of Natural Right are deduced a priori. The origin of the state which justifies it in this way is the appetitus socialis, the drive towards an ordered and peaceful community; consequently injustice becomes everything which disturbs this community or makes it impossible (like breaking promises, and the appro- priation of other people's property), and justice, a justice which must be eternally demanded, remains everything which keeps this community going in accordance with the initial principle. This ideal justice is clearly bourgeois- democratic, not only in the protection of private property, but above all in the call for universality, for the general validity of these tenets of justice for all. In this respect Grotius' theory is more advanced than his political

opinion, which in many aspects was still class-bound, still represented the
private interests of the republican aristocracy in Holland. But theoretically
Grotius definitely seeks generally-correct reason in commands and prohibitions, the 'recta ratio', as he says with Cicero. In his interpretation of the
'oecumene' of his Natural Right, which was equally valid for all men, he
clearly followed the Stoics. They had, after all, first portrayed Natural Right
as being the same at all times and in all nations, beyond human arbitrariness,
beyond changing opinions and beyond interests (which shaped positive law).
Grotius takes up the Stoic doctrine of the consensus gentium, as an empirical
proof of Natural Right, and the doctrine of the communes notiones, which
only have to be brought to scientific consciousness, as a priori notions. The
agreement in the certainty of what is right is thus founded in the nature of
reason, in the reason of nature as the causa universalis (l.c., Proleg. 40). There
is no dispensation from this rational law which universally prevails, although
repeatedly obstructed by particular interests; it is like two times two equals
four, and therefore could not even be changed by God, but would indeed be
lex divina even if God did not exist (l.c., Proleg. 71). The strange thing is
that the a priori construction did not even result in quite the opposite when
the content of its 'principle' was changed. As in the case of Hobbes (De cive,
1642, Leviathan, 1651), the original advocate of the Royalist party in
England, the fiercest champion of absolute central power and yet a – democrat. The basic drive and intention natural to man are now no longer the
appetitus socialis, which is friendly and optimistic, but boundless selfishness,
hence homo homini lupus, hence bellum omnium contra omnes as the state
of nature. The same selfishness consequently concludes the state-contract not
as one of *unification*, but of *subjugation*, of the deliberate suppression of
wolfish nature. This nature is entrusted to one person who keeps it and now
only uses it de jure: for oppressing all subjects, for establishing peace and
the security which seeks self-preservation, in accordance with its 'principle'.
There is no law at all outside the state, and within it everything is law that
the ruler commands, though in accordance with the 'principle' of peace
and the security of all – 'auctoritas, non veritas facit legem'* (Leviathan,
cap. 26). Of course democracy emerged here too in the end, even a more
unlimited kind than in the aristocratically class-bound politician Grotius;
an awkward democracy certainly, but one which nevertheless caused Charles
II to exclaim of Leviathan: 'I never read a book which contained so much
sedition, treason and impiety.' If people come together with the intention

---

* 'Authority, not truth, makes the law.'

of setting up a state, then this basic act is itself a democratic one; 'But we understand that to be the will of the council, which is the will of the major part of those men of whom the council consists' (De cive, 5, 7). The nullity to which all are reduced in the face of absolute state authority further breaks down feudal class differences: all people are equal, because all people are nothing in the face of the ruler; the generality of the law proves complete in this paradoxical way. But above all, Hobbes did not portray absolute kingship as demonstrable, but solely the absolute sovereignty and unity of state authority. The latter was feasible even in republican form; even in his work 'De cive', Hobbes had compared the democratic state with the aristocratic one as having fundamentally equal rights; also the definition of monarchy as received wolfish nature was incompatible with anointed dignity by the grace of God. So strangely did the bourgeoisie smooth the way for itself here, interpreting those who ruled over it totally cynically; and Leviathan, the state, is a monster. The enmity of the nobility and the Church towards Hobbes certainly did not prevent all future Natural Right from appearing as anti-Hobbes in its wording. This is clearly the case even in Locke (Civil Government, 1689); he returns to Grotius: the origin of society, and therefore the measure of its correctness, is once again mutual goodwill, not mutual fear. Here, in Locke, not in Rousseau, the natural goodness of man is monstrously exaggerated, one does not know how an emergency and despotic state could ever arise at all. Where Hobbes introduces a wolfish capitalism, which did not even exist in his day, into his portrayal of the state of nature, Locke introduces a utopia which is reminiscent of that of More; the state of nature is 'peace, good will, mutual aid, protection'. This felicitous element continues to have a normative influence in the established legal position and above it: 'The state of nature has a law of nature to govern it, which obliges every one: and reason, which is that law [again a literal agreement with the logos-nature of the Stoics] teaches all mankind, who will but consult it, that being all equal and independent, no one ought to harm another in his life, health, liberty, or possessions.' Clearly nature is a guiding idea throughout here, but still not a contrasting idea to bourgeois society. Also the whole nation, undiminished so to speak, is still by no means the vehicle of the ideal of rational law but only a representative part of it, in classes or in a parliament built on the class system.

Only in the final, fieriest figure of classic Natural Right, in Rousseau (Contrat social, 1762), does the nation appear with total power, undivided into classes, unrepresented. The citizen wanted to see that things were right himself, did not wish for anybody to take his place any more. As

the upper classes have disregarded his will, he does not want to engage
any new suspicious advocate to distort it. Hence Rousseau's Swiss preference
for small states, small towns, where the public will can declare itself and
intervene directly. Hence his mockery of the English parliament and the
democratic farce which the upper classes act out with it. The Genevan's
insight is amazing on this point: the English nation, jeers Rousseau, thinks
it is free, but is so only at the moment of elections; when these are over,
'it is a slave, it is nothing'. The completely new feature of Rousseau's
Natural Right is the doctrine of the inalienable nature of freedom; to
preserve it and it alone is the purpose and measure of the true state. And
just like freedom in the individual, sovereignty is untransferable, indivisible,
irreplaceable, illimitable in the nation. A person can therefore no more enter
into slavery on a contractual basis than a nation can place itself in the hands
of a prince: any addition of a contract based on rule consequently drops
out of the contrat social, it remains even more than in Grotius a *contract
of unification*. And Rousseau's great question reads: 'How can a state be
created in which there is not a single unfree person any more, in which
the individual in the community does not sacrifice anything at all of his
fundamental right to freedom' (Trouver une forme d'association qui défende
et protège de toute la force commune la personne et les biens [!] de chaque
associé et par laquelle chacun s'unissant à tous, n'obéit pourtant qu'à lui
même et reste aussi libre qu'auparavant? Tel est le problème fondamental
dont le contrat social donne la solution [Contrat social I, 6]). The answer
to this tremendous question is understandably less exhaustive, in keeping
with the bourgeois class-content; it reads: as relinquishment occurs in
everyone, in the whole community, the individual himself remains an
equal part of this totality and gets back from the complete wealth of freedom
it has received exactly as much as he has given up. Through this reciprocity
freedom is supposed not to be given up, and the constraint which is adopted
by the state-contract is supposed to be none other than the general will
constraining its member to be free (on le forcera d'être libre). This response
is as formally arithmetical as it is over-subtle; in concrete terms it means
little more than the guarantee of individual free enterprise by a syndicate
of free entrepreneurs acting in solidarity. The general will, the volonté
générale, now becomes as it were only the moral Natural Right still missing
in the mere, morally neutral state of nature. For it can only be inferred
from 'Emile' and other works by Rousseau, but by no means from the
'Contrat social', that man, and consequently the nation, is good at all
events. According to the 'Contrat social', man in the state of nature

is 'ni bon ni méchant'; he is also only made the latter by an evil society, by the social arousal of selfishness, by the inequality of property, the separation of the classes. If then, according to the 'Contrat social', man is neither good nor bad in himself, his articulation and organization in the volonté générale is nevertheless simply good. Volonté générale cannot err (II, 3), it is the language of real justice (II, 6), it is reason itself, by which it is determined with the same necessity as the law of nature in the physical world (II, 4). And the general will, otherwise directed towards a rough equality of private property, may possibly also know all about socialism, at least according to 'Emile'. Here the man who was otherwise the ideologist of private property almost touches on the basic communist motif of most utopias: 'The sovereign power (volonté générale) has no right to touch the property of one or several individuals. But it has every right to appropriate the property of all (in a simultaneous act of general dispossession)' (Emile V). This is admittedly, if not the only place, then one of the few places in which systems of Natural Right contain the idea of expropriation. It was suggested to Rousseau by Morelly's 'Code de la Nature', 1755, besides Mably, the most important forerunner of utopian socialism, with complete égalité in economic life. But the strength of classic Natural Right lay not in the fact that it rebelled economically but that it did so politically, in other words: that it eroded the respect for authority. It built subjective public rights into the so-called basic rights of the individual, codified in the Droits de l'homme of the French National Assembly. These Droits de l'homme (Liberté, propriété, sûreté, résistance à l'oppression)* are the postulate, in places also even the legal superstructure, of an overdue bourgeoisie, of a breakthrough of the individual-capitalist mode of economy against guild barriers, a class society, and a controlled market. But this ideology in fact shows a surplus which aroused enthusiasm; the ideal of freedom aroused this enthusiasm, in so far as it was not completely covered or discharged by mere freedom of movement or by free competition. It committed itself in revolutionary Natural Right to the individual (and to the nation as an aggregate of individuals), only the personal pathos employed was far older, derived from Christianity, from its metaphysical estimation of the individual soul. The Droits de l'homme themselves are also just as influenced in historical and literary terms by the religious idealism of the young American states and their constitution as they are by Rousseau's Natural Right. All this exploded the doctrine of the divine right of authority, in its own field; but it also

---

* 'Freedom, property, security, resistance to oppression.'

exploded the legal system of a police state, according to which only the state exists sui juris, in its own right, whereas the subject merely exists alterius juris, by derived right. The whole cleansing power of Natural Right only becomes clear against the contemporary background of arbitrary despotism; Beaumarchais and the young Schiller put Rousseau in context. The spirit of idolizing princes, which at that time was not found only in police states, was combatted by Natural Right; it stands diametrically opposed to Versailles. In the face of the double barrage of a state-contract and natural human rights, the particularly precious material of kings and masters was rendered defenceless. The old framework of injustice collapsed, reason and nature became the banners beneath which a world of human dignity proposed to come marching in. This dignity was interpreted purely individualistically at that time and could not be otherwise, corresponding to the private mode of economy that was breaking its way through and to which it was still related. But for this very reason this dignity, as one of individual freedom, was aimed precisely at feudal oppression, and also at the patriarchal system of enlightened despotism. This kind of hostility to the state broke through even in Prussia at that time, even if only in literary terms, in W. v. Humboldt's 'Ideas for an attempt to define the limits of the effectiveness of the state', 1792. Chapter 15 decrees (ineffectively of course, both in the aristocratic book itself and in Prussian reality): 'Even if the state constitution, whether through superior strength or violence or habit and law, insists on a certain attitude in its citizens, there is a different attitude as well, voluntarily chosen by them, infinitely varied and often changing. And it is actually the latter, the free working of the nation amongst itself, which protects all possessions, the longing for which leads people to enter into a society. The actual state constitution is subordinate to this purpose within it and is always chosen only as a necessary means, and since it is invariably connected with the restriction of freedom, as a necessary evil.' Junkerdom, which still lies before the progressive tendencies of bureaucracy, and the hopes of Rousseau, which already combat the incipient military state and denounce it, are strangely combined in this book of liberty. But it simultaneously reveals a consequence inherent in the dream of dignity itself: Natural Right as democracy means an aristocracy bestowed on everybody. Free working of the nation amongst itself is not trading here, was not conceived as a market, but invoked as an agora in the Greek-urbane, utopian-urbane sense: so that everyone may walk upright. The idea of everyone walking upright is of course an illusion in the very class society in which Natural Right blossomed, but the heroic illusion of a world without corruption and pressure, with human dignity. Natural

Right fully constructed this world as a world of still bourgeois-humane, socially guaranteed (not just permitted) licence to want.

Enlightened Natural Right in place of social utopias

It is very constructive to consider from this point of view the attitude which classic Natural Right adopts to the social-utopian project, with which it has an affinity anyway. It does not claim to be merely wished like the latter, its dream is not lavish. What was right emerged among its champions with sparing dignity, not pictured but *sharply thought out*. What has been thought out by deduction claims to be binding, absolutely valid, instead of the nowhere of reason there appears its *deducible everywhere*. That is why Natural Right also intervened much more closely, and also partly of course more approvingly in the current circumstances of the time than novels of an ideal state. Though, as we have seen, these also have their age within them and the immediately following age above them, yet they skim over both at the same time. Whereas Natural Right sharpened, took aim, demanded there and then, intervened in bourgeois constitutions, wrote new ones. International rights were drafted by Grotius along the lines of his Natural Right, indeed the French Revolution drew its most vital impulse from Rousseau and particularly also the wording of its principles. Paragraph 6 of the 'Déclaration des droits de l'homme' decrees word for word from Rousseau: 'La loi est l'expression de la volonté générale.'* Even in Germany, which never brought off a revolution, Natural Right still influenced reform legislation like that of Stein-Hardenberg and, mediated by Anselm Feuerbach, the liberal Bavarian Criminal Code of 1813. Even the General Prussian Common Law of 1794 borrowed at least the form of its organization from Natural Right – a tribute of the benevolently patronizing police state to formally inevitable reason. This influence is admittedly bought at the price of Natural Right also being less of a social utopia, in so far as it is more alert to half-realized tendencies than to future ones, especially to radical future ones. Because this is the other way round in social utopias, because they do contain the tendency to the immediately following stage, corresponding to the timetable of utopias indicated above, and express their excessive wishful dream largely in this merely relative one, but in doing so seldom forget the excessive wishful dream, which in almost all social utopias is a communist one: because social utopias thus transcended into the unconditional and treated existing overdue material

---

* 'The law is the expression of the general will.'

only very immediately or incidentally or instead as clothing the unconditional, they inevitably did not have nearly as much influence on the liberation of the bourgeois forces of production as the much more localized Natural Right and they hardly occur even nominally during the French Revolution. As a whole, justice is a topic much closer to the class society than utopia is, and there is certainly no Christian, let alone chiliastic utopia in justice. Jesus expressly denies that it is his job to administer justice (Luke 12, 14), and the vernacular retains the old saying 'Men of law – Christians poor'. And only the Natural Right of the sects, i.e. that which was not legally implemented, by going back to the primal state of paradise as a standard, kept aloof from amalgamation with the law of property, the law of bonds, debt, punishment and the like. Inherent in implemented classic Natural Right is the budding entrepreneurial interest; hence its almost continuous protection of privacy, hence its liberalist eggshells. But, as noted above, this is joined by the excess in the ideal of freedom, that male pride before royal thrones which does not wholly coincide with ideology in favour of free competition and individual economy. And from this excess the great bourgeois-revolutionary expansion is ultimately derived which Natural Right afforded to subjective public right in its influence on empirical circumstances. Social utopias therefore have nothing to set alongside this, because they hardly deal with revolution itself, because they already assume that its imaginary result has happened. However much more future social utopias contain, this future is certainly more one of happy human flora than of demands that have been forced through. Things are different in the trenchant concept of justice* which has been developed in terms of Natural Right; since it has a provocative ambiguity of postulation about it right from the start. Justice as *individual justification* and justice as the alleged representation of a general interest, as an *objective legal prescription* from above: these two elements have a strange equivocation in the identical expression: justice. This was not as yet the case when subjective right merely represented a claim by creditors to debtors and merely a justification to force other private individuals to meet an obligation; at this unpolitical stage justification and legal prescription, facultas agendi and norma agendi, were still opposite sides of the same coin. Justinian's legal code saw in private law and constitutional law (the law of the state) merely two positions within the same area (Inst. V I, 4): 'Publicum jus est, quod ad statum rei Romanae, privatum, quod ad singulorum utilitatem pertinet' (Public law is that which refers to the Roman state, private law that which

* Bloch uses the same word 'Recht' here, which has to be rendered variously in this section according to the English context as 'right', 'justice' or 'law'.

refers to the benefit of individuals). If, however, tension arises between an economically progressive class and the state as the representative of an economically outdated class, then justice as justification and justice as an objective system of laws no longer look like opposite sides of the same coin. Then neither of them are equivocal any more in terms of content, the two legal branches become separately manifest, and on the one sits the nation, on the other the authorities. Then Natural Right can develop a postulative-revolutionary force of which social utopias, with their mere invitation or even incitement to their pictured happy goal, were incapable. It was precisely classic Natural Right which equipped subjective right with the whole excess of the ideal of freedom: *right becomes essentially the right to something, and furthermore from the point of view of what has formerly been governed*. Subjective right ceases to be a mere permitted exception, a mere exception from the sphere of being governed. Natural Right made this exception the rule and main point: facultas agendi demolishes the previous authoritarian norma agendi and sets up its own democratic legal norms. The theory of the French Revolution ultimately developed out of this: as the liberation of the bourgeoisie, but also, as Kant says of the Enlightenment, as the emergence of human beings from an immaturity which is their own fault. And a further point appears here as to why the social utopias in the eighteenth century were unable to provide the same kindling force as Natural Right: the latter showed, in the framework of the overdue resistance movement, the stronger *moral pathos*. The utopias are less approving of the circumstances and the immediately due tendency within them; they are more alert to radical future tendencies, as is demonstrable from Diogenes down to the last pre-Marxist blueprints of an ideal state, but they also stake more on human flora as opposed to the iron aspect and to character. The accents are different in which the best constitution is expressed, in social utopian terms on the one hand, in terms of Natural Right on the other. The social utopia predominantly aims at *human happiness* and considers, in more or less *novelistic form*, its economic-social form. Natural Right (with only the partial exception of Hobbes) aims predominantly at *human dignity* and, in as *reasoned a deduction* as possible, derives from the concept of an a priori free subject of a contract the legal conditions in which dignity is socially secured and maintained. Only Thomasius (Fundamentum juris naturae et gentium, 1705) teaches happiness as a target of Natural Right, but even here happiness is never without backbone. Hence a social utopia like the Stoic one, in which Natural Right prevails, shows far more pathos of male pride than comfortable institutions or occupied seats. Because of this republican character (compare in bourgeois-revolutionary drama the heroes of Alfieri, Odoardo from Lessing's 'Emilia Galotti', Verinna from Schiller's 'Fiesco', and also Tell) – and also because of this iron aspect, Natural Right largely replaced social utopias, during the bourgeois struggle against the upper classes. And the highly individual, non-communist content gave its blessing to this replacement, gave its ideological recommendation to this pathos of character. It is true of course that almost three times as many utopias appeared in the eighteenth century as in the seventeenth, but utopias in particular must be weighed rather than counted. Even such a noble creation as Fénelon's 'Aventures de Télémaque', 1698, merely adapts Thomas More in its two chapters on the land of happiness, in a classically proportioned way. Even an undoubtedly interesting dictatorship utopia like 'L'Histoire des Sévérambes', 1672, by Vayrasse is a combination of More and Campanella; the rest of what appeared is essentially satire or else mere fantasizing. Only a single social utopia towers in its institutions out of the seventeenth over into the eighteenth century as well, which is otherwise so purely one of Natural Right: Harrington's 'The Commonwealth of Oceana', 1656; in fact, this novel of an ideal state was even the force behind the American Constitution. But this very fact indicates that it was a novel of an ideal state only in its most superficial guise: 'Oceana' is in reality a single constitutional project, with a Lower House, Senate, and short-term presidential election, and only as such a blueprint ('society of laws') did the book gain its bourgeois-revolutionary influence. Harrington's 'Oceana' thus represents nothing short of a usurpation of lavish social utopia by precise Natural Right on that utopia's own territory. Here it is particularly clear that only bourgeois-delimited Natural Right, not the almost always communist-excessive utopia, was able to provide an outline for capitalist democracy; just as on the other hand this outline would not have arisen without Natural Right. And the classic text-book of bourgeois economics, Adam Smith's 'Inquiry into the Nature and Causes of the Wealth of Nations', would not have been possible at all without Natural Right in its progressive significance, in the 'natural system' as which the individual unleashing of the forces of production at that time was able to swagger. But this necessitated the whole pathos of entitlement, pathos of certainty in the phrase Law of Nature; this alone was able to develop the acutely topical formulae and hopes of the bourgeois revolution. Social utopia, however, dreamed of an economy which satisfied people's needs and was free of entrepreneurs, that is, a happy communism, long before this was empirically possible; so this utopia had little say in the eighteenth century. Only at the beginning of the nineteenth century, with Owen, Fourier, and Saint-Simon, did the picture change again, when More and Campanella found worthy successors. For the 'natural system' of capitalism was disturbed by quite astonishing problems, Ricardo and Sismondi developed the first theories of crises within this system. It was therefore precisely the economic tendencies of the age which slowly started to find that a good many things in the old communist cloud-cuckoo-land were not quite so remote or fictional. But between Campanella and Owen there is characteristically a space almost devoid of original social utopias, in keeping with the requirements of bourgeois emancipation. As has become clear, Natural Right came much closer to them; it is much nearer to ideology, even if by no means coinciding with it. *The inheritance of Natural Right: the thought-out facultas agendi* – was not amassed by social utopia, it is merely entered into by that utopia, under banners which are not capitalist any more.

On the whole, as noted above, the dream in search of justice was by no means lavish. Instead it remains conceptual, never departs from hard work and cold theoretical effort. A novel of an ideal state may perhaps still have been able to develop the theory of an original social contract, but not the *strict conclusions* on which Natural Right intrinsically depends. In any case, the original contract is not essential to Natural Right; after all, the former is first found in Epicurus, who needs no Natural Right at all, whereas the copious Natural Right of the Stoics knows nothing of a contrat social. In any case, the theory of a contract is the weakest in terms of logic in Natural Right: since the contract, as a highly developed instrument of law, already presupposes the whole legal sphere which is first supposed to be formed and legitimated by the contrat social. So what is and remains essential to Natural Right is not the original contract, this component that seems as if it is from a prehistoric novel of an ideal state, but the rational construction of the best constitution – with an axiom of nature, with a nature based on principles and capable of being deduced, not with a tropically fruitful and transfigured nature, as on the sunny islands in the novel of an ideal state. The rational unity of Natural Right thus demanded the development of all conclusions from a single principle if possible (the will for usefulness or the will for community or the will for security); it did this in the strictest deductive fashion, in accordance with the law of non-contradiction and of sufficient reason. The model for classic Natural Right was mathematics, and Natural Right came closest to this example among all the geometrically treated sciences of this period. Certainly, the social utopias were constructive too, but loosely, they were constructive, so to speak, only through the imagination of pure reason, not through its logic. Classic Natural Right, however, represents at least since Pufendorf one of the most conscious attempts at applied logic, and from this angle its relation to the social utopias is like that of a strict canon to a song or like that of a drama by Racine to a vaudeville. And it was the mathematician Leibniz who asserted the following to the lawyer of this period: 'One can draw firm conclusions from every definition, by using indisputable logical rules. And one does precisely this in the construction of necessary sciences based on rigorous proof, which are not dependent on facts but on reason alone, as is true of logic, metaphysics, arithmetic, geometry, the science of motion and also the science of law. For all these do not have their foundations in experience and facts but serve to account for the facts and to regulate them in advance: and this would be true of justice even if there were no laws in the whole wide world' (Leibniz, Hauptschriften, Meiner, II, p. 510f.). The calculus within the rising bourgeoisie therefore serves not only the mathematical analysis of the turnover of goods but also – in a less outwardly formal way – the antithesis to facts which hinder the rise of the bourgeoisie. Here, in Natural Right, pure reason is revolutionary; and instead of bowing to facts it posits security in nature. In a nature which is composed in a highly varied way: in one with rationally coherent laws, and then of course also, in Rousseau, in one of opposition to all artificiality, in nature as simplicity, wildness, unspoiltness. Rousseau's concept of nature has almost completely lost the character of rational laws, instead it is closely connected with all the enthusiasm at that time for simplicity and democratic generality, with natural language, natural poetry, natural religion, and natural education; all these ideals were monstrances in the axiom of nature. Thus, from this point of view as well, Natural Right acquired a lustre which social utopias, after their chiliasm was toned down, could not match for a long time. But as far as the *revolutionary effect* of Natural Right at that time is concerned, it certainly remained historically limited and extended less than social utopias into the future. Consider the close links of Natural Right with immediate currents of society at that time, with thoroughly individualistic ones as well: could social revolution borrow something from these? The case is undoubtedly complicated, Marx very often treats Natural Right as if it had been put on file for good, on bourgeois file. On the other hand, bourgeois reaction throughout the whole of the nineteenth century speaks of Natural Right only with contempt and hatred. Does not this hatred do credit to Natural Right, does it not indicate a possible inherited substratum in it, one worth thinking about? And if its older opponents, from Hugo (Textbook of Natural Right, 1799) to Bergbohm (Jurisprudence and the Philosophy of Right, 1892), condemned Natural Right from the standpoint of 'law become historical', modern 'sociologists' like Pareto or even Gentile do the same from the standpoint of their vitalism or of the fascist theory of elitism. This is something that speaks very much in favour of Natural Right; its rationalism is still dangerous to the hereditary whip and a strangely lively enemy to industrial feudalism. Natural Right therefore seems to have not only confined itself to the almost achieved tendencies of its time, or to those which already have one foot in the door anyway. Despite its bourgeois substructure, despite the static unity of its abstract-ideals, it has that very excess which makes all revolutions appear related to one another. Thus the *declaration of subjective public rights in totality* that has occurred in terms of Natural Right occasionally displays economic individualism less as a substructure than as a temporary measure. The declaration of subjectively public rights posited these as a cadre into which rights against the employer could also be inserted, not just those against the authorities. Hence the right to strike, the right of combination, the principle of equal rights for all human beings and nations, in short the former code of bourgeois human rights, on the state of which Stalin still had this to say: 'The banner of bourgeois-democratic freedoms has been thrown overboard. I think that you, the representatives of communist and democratic parties, must raise this banner again and carry it before you, if you want to gather the majority of the nation around you. There is nobody else who could raise it.' Natural Right was a declaration of these rights, it made it possible to express them, that is and remains its legacy. Even its pathos of the free individual seems like a warning against any confusion or mixing up of collectivity with the herd and herd character. The very reference of concrete order to the will-content of concrete freedom maintains the legacy of Natural Right against every collective conceived in merely abstract and isolated terms, against a collective which is contrasted with individuals instead of springing from them, from classless individuals. The goal defined in communist terms: 'From each according to his abilities, to each according to his needs' itself clearly preserves a mature Natural Right – even if without recourse to nature and perhaps without the permanent necessity of a right. So the problem of Natural Right – the problem which formerly had a revolutionary character, not of course the 'eternal law' of the capitalist so-called constitutional state – is not yet settled, although it does not precede Marxism as precisely as the social utopias do, either in chronological or factual terms. These utopias instantly emerged again when questions arose which could not be reconciled with legal exposure. The dream of protected human dignity did not in the long run replace the more urgent, if not more central dream of human happiness.

Fichte's closed commercial state
or production and exchange in accordance with rational law

It is surely deprivation which most makes people cower in an undignified way. The poor man is totally incapable of holding his head up as high as his pride demands. So what if it were above all right for every person to live as pleasantly as possible? If proper justice were brought to bear precisely on happiness too and on its starving opposite? If dignity itself regarded deprivation and misery as a situation which follows from it least of all, indeed is incompatible with it? These were questions which were bound to lead from considerations of original rights to economic considerations. Far beyond older concerns and moderate pangs of conscience or respectabilities, along the lines of a fair price and the like. There thus arose the new phenomenon of an economic, not just political legal claim, a critique of the market in terms of Natural Right. In its wake arose the strange hybrid: a legal social utopia; Fichte elaborated it. His work 'The Closed Commercial State', 1800, appeared as an 'Appendix to Jurisprudence', but also, in a distinctly utopian manner, as the 'sample of a politics to be supplied in the future'. The differences in method and portrayal between Natural Right and social utopia are not removed but toned down in Fichte's hybrid. A better constitution is here both sharply thought-out and visibly pictured, both portrayed as absolutely and universally valid and yet once more transferred to a kind of island, namely into an enclosed state. A legal claim a priori announces its arrival throughout, a claim not just to dignity but expressly to happiness. Indeed to socialist happiness, without that species of male pride which in Natural Right, among other things, had cloaked free enterprise. 'Live and let live', that is the rule according to which Natural Right here lines up socially, not individualistically. According to which it lines up above all eudemonistically, as in social utopias: 'Everybody wants to live as pleasantly as possible: and since everybody demands this as a human being, and nobody is more or less of a human being than anyone else, all are equally right in this demand' (Werke, Meiner, III, p. 432). And the state is not presented as a protector of the property which it finds and leaves unequally distributed, but on the contrary, it becomes 'the destiny of the state first to give everybody what is theirs, first to set them up in their property, and only then to protect them' (l.c., p. 429). Thus deduction from pure legal maxims and social utopia here merged into one another, with the early intention of uniting both. As early as 1793 Fichte had written to Kant that he was fired by the great idea 'of tackling the problem of Plato's Republic, of the rational state'. And the fruits were a total paradox: state socialism in the spirit of Rousseau, portrayed in both a deductive and colouring way. This was of course joined by a third element which sought to detach Fichte's procedure, that was otherwise so little empirical or amicable to the given, from previous utopianizing and from previous Natural Right. A glance at existing conditions was added, with the intention of acting practically within them, without belonging to them, and of drawing them closer to the ideal state. The speculative politicians, says Fichte, have remained fictitious, and 'as surely as there is order, consistency and certainty in their ideas, as surely do their regulations, in the way they have been drawn up, only fit the state of things presupposed and invented by them, in which the general rule is portrayed, as in a sum in arithmetic. The practising politician does not find this presupposed state of things waiting for him, but a very different one. It is no wonder that a regulation does not fit the latter when that regulation is not designed for it in the way it has been drawn up' (l.c., p. 420). Though what Fichte uses to replace the pure world of ideas is – as is natural in a Germany so little developed in economic and political terms – once again ideas with general-abstract definitions, except 'that these are further defined for a given actual state of affairs'. If, however, idealism does not become practice in this way, it does develop as criticism in the work of Fichte, the angry man of virtue. Fichte takes up the indirect criticism which the image of a utopian land of happiness implicitly portrayed concerning conditions at home. And he takes up the direct criticism which the rationality of Natural Right explicitly applied to the irrationality of the existing constitution of the state. This made Fichte's criticism all the sharper as he completely transformed Natural Right into rational law, i.e. severed it from all primordial and prehistoric fictions. There is in the work of this great nature-hater no freedom at all in and through nature; existence in animal or primitive society is not Arcadian, but coercive and despotic; only social life makes it possible to think of freedom. An Elysian goal remains, not one given as workless or existing somewhere, but rather, in connection with Fichte's radical-idealist philosophy of 'active deeds', a generated goal.

This in a constructive, but partly also in a technical working sense: 'Unless either the forces of our own nature increase enormously, or unless the nature outside us transforms itself without our assistance by a sudden miracle and destroys its own previously familiar laws, we cannot expect that prosperity from it, we can only expect it from ourselves; we must earn it ourselves through work' (l.c., p. 453). This is a kind of introduction of the theory of labour value into utopia, into a utopia which no longer lives off raw materials or even manna. But the pathos of active reason nevertheless remains so idealistic in Fichte that it does not develop its social utopia economically but – syllogistically, in the form of logical conclusions. In this too the exercise of Natural Right is stronger than a genetic development from the point of view of the work process. Fichte's work thus begins with a major statement as the first main part: 'What is right as regards commerce in the rational state.' This is followed by a specific minor statement as the second, critical main part: 'On the condition of commerce in current actual states.' This is followed by the concluding statement as the third, ideally resulting main part: 'How the commerce of an existing state is to be put in the constitution required by reason.' The whole thing aims at freedom, but at freedom which only finds room through economic restraint. It is an open question whether the ethical individualist Fichte became an economic socialist because he saw his ethical individualism threatened by economic individualism. But even in the case of Fichte himself it is evident that *socialism is what has been sought in vain for so long under the name of morality*.

The individual person is still taken throughout as the basis in all this, everything follows from him. From him alone as a thinking being the shape which justice has to take is developed. Original rights are those of the rational individual, and it is his 'I think' which not only has but develops these rights. Fichte distinguishes three original rights: the individual's power to dispose of his body, his property, and his sphere as a person. These are supposed to be boundless freedoms, and they are only limited by the freedom of all other individuals, and hence by nothing alien to the original rights. In order that people are able to live together, the freedom of the individual must be rendered finite, but in such a way that it may be restricted firstly only by freedom and secondly only for the sake of freedom. Striking conclusions are drawn here from the original right to property, not at all private capitalist conclusions. In Fichte there is no right of ownership of things but only of actions, so that nobody else is to be authorized to cultivate this piece of land, or only one group is to be allowed to manufacture shoes.

Old guild rights are thus functionally renewed, as the guaranteed ability of the individual 'exclusively to pursue a greater art'. In the case of land there is absolutely no ownership, it belongs to nobody and to the farmer only in so far as he cultivates it (and is consequently not an idle feudal lord). After Fichte has thus brought possession and ownership out of the law of property into a kind of law of production, he progresses to logical socialist conclusions. Precisely because of the original right to property, it must be given to everyone by the state: 'If someone does not have enough to be able to live, then he does not have what he is entitled to have; he does not have what is his. In the rational state he will receive it; in the division which was made by chance and force before the awakening and the rule of reason everyone certainly did not receive it, because others took more for themselves than was due to them' (l.c., p. 433). And further on in this state-socialist text: 'The task of the state has been only one-sidedly and half understood up to now, as an institution for keeping the citizen at the same proprietary level at which we find him, by means of the law. The more deep-seated duty of the state first to establish everyone in the possession of what is due to him has been overlooked. But the latter is only possible if the anarchy of commerce is abolished in just the same way as political anarchy is gradually being abolished, and the state closes into a commercial state just as it is closed in its legislation and its judicial offices' (l.c., p. 483). Fichte thereby extends, in his postulated ideal state, the generality of the law which had abolished the rights of class and privilege to a generality of job creation. In addition, as a means towards this, there is the elimination of free enterprise, the shut-down of free competition. In addition there is the abolition of the open market, in short: the destiny of the ideal state to be a controlled economy. This in a Germany which still hardly exhibited one exponent of free enterprise and which therefore invited more easily than the advanced western states a kind of pre-capitalist anti-capitalism; as has already become apparent in Fichte's work-guilds. The Romantic transfigurations of medieval society which Novalis had expressed shortly before this ('Christendom or Europe', 1799) also probably had an influence here. A single common interest, said Novalis, connected the remotest provinces of this broad spiritual realm. Fichte, so little of a Romantic in other respects, was in any case one of the first to touch on the backward-looking anti-capitalist utopia which is not entirely lacking in Saint-Simon and which still emerged in Ruskin or William Morris as a kind of Gothic socialism. It would be erroneous, as Mehring says, in the case of the closed commercial state to think of a mere idealization

of the 'state of Frederick the Great'; it would have been belated even in
Germany. And then above all, this is contradicted by Fichte's intention
'first to establish everyone in the possession of what is due to him'; which
was the least of the concerns of the manufacturing period. Fichte's concern,
social in character, made him particularly bitter in this connection against
the Manchesterism of the advanced capitalist countries. In the second and
third parts of his utopia there is a critique of the evils of free competition
(stagnation, unemployment), which anticipates Fourier's critique in many
respects. The 'harmony of interests' presupposed by the great economist
Adam Smith was seen through by Fichte before it had even made its whole
deception apparent in practical terms. An economic layman, but a speculative
politician turns against the speculators and their so-called play-drive: 'As
a result of this inclination they seek to achieve nothing in accordance with
a rule but everything by cunning and luck, by intrigue, favouring others,
and chance. It is these people who are incessantly calling for freedom,
freedom of trade and earnings, freedom from all order and morality. For
these people the idea of an arrangement of public trade in which no giddy
speculation, no chance profit, and no sudden enrichment takes place any
longer can be nothing other than repugnant' (l.c., p. 541). In keeping
with this antipathy towards 'Gründerjahre' which were still so far away,
Fichte preaches a relative utopia of order, the first since Campanella, instead
of the bustle of supply and demand (after Adam Smith), instead of the
free struggle of interests. With three main working classes, all under the
supervision of the government (the real working class, the proletariat, is
not yet in evidence). The organization of working conditions appears as
the organization of the conditions of trade and industry, with the abolition
of the military and of the feudal aristocracy. One class is responsible for
obtaining raw materials, another for processing them, and a third for the
equal distribution of available products to all at a stable basic price. But
barter and distribution by private individuals takes place only within the
state, not beyond the national boundary. The (much to be restricted)
purchase of foreign raw materials and products is handled solely by the
government, which has a monopoly of foreign trade. Of course it might
be asked at this point in Fichte's utopia why the government does not
handle domestic trade as well, and hence make the class of businessmen
superfluous. But Fichte very much suppresses business houses as such, they
become mere channels of a closed, regulated market low in profit. They
are merely haulage firms so to speak, not speculative firms, they are
mediators within an economy which exclusively satisfies people's needs,

'because the permitted production and manufacture is already calculated in the basis of the state' (l.c., p. 443). So Fichte's state believes that it does not have to take on domestic bartering, it contents itself with the social supervision of the implementation of contracts entered into. It contents itself with this if only because the really supreme or state class in this utopia, as in Plato, consists of teachers and scholars; but these have Fichte's 'Theory of Science' in mind, not book-keeping, financial exchange, discount credit. The state's monopoly of foreign trade is also simply conceived as a defensive measure, as the protection of the production budget against 'the uncontrollable influence of the foreigner'. And precisely from this will towards overall control there now follows the most radical conclusion of the plan, that most reminiscent of the happy isle again: *autarky*. The world currency of gold and silver is abolished, a domestic currency of worthless material takes its place, which cannot be hoarded and which is unsuitable for the purchase of foreign products. Perhaps, says Fichte, there will then be no furs and silk clothes any more in a utopian Germany, and certainly no Chinese tea, but nor will there be any economic wars and wars of conquest. Foreign credits are to be handed over to the government (an amazing anticipation of foreign exchange legislation), in fact Fichte even indicates the home production of substitutes for cotton and other imported materials (an amazing anticipation of synthetic chemistry). The Chinese wall, the patriotic wall thus becomes utopian: 'There is a specific goal which the government must resolve to attain before completely closing off the state: namely, that everything which is being produced anywhere at the time the state is closed off is produced from now on within the country itself, as far as at all possible in such a climate' (l.c., p. 532). This idea of autarky is known to have kindled reactionary fervour in the semi-fascist Brüning period of the Weimar Republic. It recommended itself as a means of running the economy without gold backing, without international clearing, of preparing a war economy. But it recommended itself to Fichte on account of the closed unity which every system of organized work needs as long as it is not introduced in other states as well, and then of course on account of patriotism. Under the influence of the Napoleonic Wars, Fichte increasingly abandoned his initial principle: ubi lux, ibi patria. But the so-called transition from cosmopolitanism to nation-state in Fichte's utopia must not be over-estimated; even the Germanness only proves and justifies itself here so as to be most universally human or the strongest Humanum. The basis of Fichte's distinction of Germanness from foreignness, even in his Speeches

to the German Nation, lies in 'whether we believe in an original element
in man, in freedom, infinite capacity for improvement and the eternal
progress of our race, or whether we do not believe in all this'. And the
right to turn towards the particular state where light prevails, outside our
native state, is only limited by the hope that Germany itself is most devoted
to the light. It is assessed by the permanent nature-hater not as native
soil but as a source of moral light: 'Of all the nations, you are the ones
in whom the seeds of human perfection most decisively lie.' Only on the
basis of this hope did Fichte place the nation, particularly the German one,
between individual and mankind; Germany was not to stand in isolation
but in an exemplary and most human fashion within the human race.
National honour, national character, all closed elements like these derive
their sole value in the work of Fichte from the humane idea which moulds
them; and science remains international in any case. 'No closed state will
abolish this connection; on the contrary, it will favour it, since the enrichment of science by the combined strength of the human race even promotes
its separate earthly aims' (l.c., p. 542). And ultimately Fichte's utopia does
not, in its state socialism, want the state to be made absolute any more
than it wants patriotism of the soil. This would conflict with the original
right of freedom or with the principle already mentioned that this freedom
may only be restricted for the sake of freedom, within human coexistence.
Thus even the closed commercial state is not eternal, behind its utopia
another one is at work. This state is only regarded as a transition from
the tyrannical or emergency state to a rational state in which, with growing
freedom and morality, no constraint is necessary any more. Lenin once
said we must get to the stage where every cook could govern the state;
Fichte, who lacked all the economic prerequisites and knowledge for such
a hope, would nevertheless have approved of the cook as a sign of realized
political wisdom. And he prophesies: 'The easiness of administering the
state, as of all work, depends on setting to work with order, an overall
view of the whole, and in accordance with a firm plan' (l.c., p. 537). What
thus emerges as a rational state renders itself superfluous as a state by means
of reason (which generates the content of authority). 'The art of reason'
emerges or the harmony of educated, morally responsible individuals as
a realm of beautiful souls. In fact in the late Fichte an almost Joachite
music invaded these noble rooms, the drawing-rooms of the art of reason.
His 'Political Science' of 1813 transforms the social conductors of the future
into bridge-builders of eternity: 'The community of scholars is the teaching
corps of Christianity, of the kingdom of God, the beginning of society,

from the unbroken continuation of which those sovereigns and creators in the kingdom described will emerge' (Werke, Meiner, IV, p. 615). Though Fichte explains little or nothing about practice: how and by what means it may come even to the beginnings of a closed commercial state, let alone such an enthusiastic art of reason. In the Germany of that time no proletariat had yet appeared, and it was already a great deal for Fichte to admit and condemn the fact 'that the combined mass of owners could forcibly prevent the weaker individual from proclaiming his legal rights' (l.c., p. 475). Even this slight hint of social revolution, as the expression of legal rights, was abstract at that time, was almost as speculative as Fichte's entire design itself. Thus his designer is content with the fact that the whole thing 'may remain a mere school exercise without success in the real world'. He is astonished at existing conditions and finds in this astonishment that philosophical spur which could only become a practical one much later on. Although Fichte considers his socialist conclusion, like all that have been correctly deduced, to be conceptually necessary, state socialism in this world is still only considered to be abstractly possible, only to be 'demanded by the rule of law'. Anything other than proposals and demands was not submitted by Fichte's later disciples either, by Rodbertus for example, the ancestor of academic socialists. And even Lassalle, who was influenced by Fichte in many ways, did not get beyond reformist agitation, despite proletarian contact. In fact, Lassalle endorsed the current state more than Fichte, especially the authoritarian Prussian state. Workers' productive co-operatives with state credit were to form a transition to the future socialist society: Fichte's utopia certainly could be misused on behalf of this substitute for revolution. But a socialism in the Germany of 1800 has a historical freshness and distinction which cannot be misused at all. It exhibits precisely the brilliant naivety, the intuitive youthfulness, which were lacking in a Lassalle around 1860, and which were lacking in the later reformism even as an excuse. The closed commercial state remains the first system, deduced from original rights and pictured in a utopian way, of organized work. More than this: Fichte's work considers socialism to be possible in a single, sufficiently large and autarkical country.

Federative utopias in the nineteenth century:
Owen, Fourier

Misery did not remain idle in the meantime, it grew disturbingly. While its bearers had so far been peasants, they were now joined by the worker.

Precisely the more economically advanced a country was, the more gruesome
the situation of its poor became. The serf had things hard enough, suffering
seemed to have reached its height. But even the worst period of deprivation
for the medieval peasants is surpassed by the misery of the first factory
workers. The early factories were the same as galleys; a starving, sleepless,
desperate proletariat was chained to machines. Entrepreneurial profit knew
no mercy nor let-up, daily work lasted eighteen hours and over, a filthy
work beyond compare. Never were such a large number of people so
unhappy as in England around the turn of the eighteenth century. The
first man to come out against it was a doctor called Hall, he saw the country
rotting to the core. In 1805 his work 'The Effects of Civilization' appeared;
in it, besides medical and moral indignation, there are several utopian
proposals for improvement. The poor, says Hall, barely receive an eighth
of the proceeds of their efforts; it is the trend of the times to make the
rich ever richer, and the poor ever poorer. The only salvation is to reduce
industrial development, but not in order to bring back the so-called good
old days. Hall already saw that all is not yet won if the factories disappear
but the lords of the manor remain. The soil should be shared out again
in equal portions among all the families in the country: beyond machine-
wrecking there thus arises a future full of free peasants. If this protest
against the misery in factories had met with little response, emanating
from a mere philanthropist, the appeal of a factory-owner himself met
with a much greater one, above all since it was linked with an extremely
useful example. The example that a well-fed and not discontented worker
accomplishes the same and better work than a galley slave in half the time.
Robert Owen had made this discovery, but not only this one: Owen, an
anima candidissima, 'a man with a simplicity of character that was childlike
to the point of sublimity, and at the same time a born leader of men',
as Engels says, also became one of the first utopians of the nineteenth century
with a federative-socialist objective. Pre-eminent among his many works
are 'The Social System', 1820, and 'The Book of the New Moral World',
1836; in the former he turns away from patriarchal social welfare towards
communism, and in the second work he seeks to recommend it to his
professional colleagues, from the standpoint of kindness. But if the utopian
thus saws off the bough on which he is sitting as a capitalist, it was absurd
to demand the same of capitalists who were not even utopians as a sideline.
Owen still considered social well-being to be attainable through reforms;
he rejected strikes, even the struggle for political freedoms, he sought reconciliation, he expected dukes, ministers and manufacturers to renounce

capitalism out of sheer insight and love of mankind. Owen the industrialist also had a curiously low opinion of the future role of industry; admittedly he demanded the introduction of steam power and machinery into the household, he never advocated machine-wrecking, but big industry still played no major role in the factory-owner of New Lanark's dreams of the future. Despite these weaknesses Owen organized his philanthropic communism, in contact with Quakers, from whom however he moved on to the works of Winstanley, the agrarian communist of the English Revolution. Above all, Owen adopted Ricardo's theory of labour value which had just been published, with all that it entailed, without a trace of any special privilege for 'leading businessmen'. Ricardo had discovered that the only yardstick of a product is the amount of work contained in it; on this theory Owen built the plan of a future community in which everyone attains the full enjoyment of the amount of value he has produced, with the removal of capitalist profit which stems from unpaid work. The path to this community is still completely reformist though: by setting up a large storehouse, every producer is to be enabled to deposit the commodities he has manufactured. In recompense for this he receives a work-note which corresponds to the value of the work embodied in the delivered product and entitles him to withdraw products of equal value. Such an exchange bazaar was actually set up by Owen in London in 1832, as a labour exchange in which producers came together without the mediation of capitalists and endeavoured to avoid the surcharge of profit. It is not surprising that this naive organization collapsed after a few years, specifically because of that still pre-capitalist utopia which sought to regulate the economy on the basis of distribution instead of production. So the surplus of capitalist anarchy continued in the exchange bazaar; despite the 'district councils' which Owen introduced, 'with overall control of existing needs'. The actual future community was more radically conceived than the consumer co-operative; here we find, as Engels says with just as much mockery as admiration, 'the complete elaboration of the edifice of the communist community of the future, with ground plan, elevation and bird's eye view'. With the total abolition of private property a new system of production is to be founded on co-operative settlements, though even this system does not permit large-scale production, on an agrarian skilled basis. And without the family; Owen came out more vehemently than any other utopian against the existing form of marriage. For him it was a life-long sexual and social slavery, it was the lie which makes a borderline case of lasting love into a norm and fakes it into a convention. Owen called private property, marriage, and positive religion the 'Trinity of evil', all three are idols, and only create human unhappiness. Thus the agrarian skilled basis reproduces nothing of its old social forms, despite the old village structure that was planned. Federated groups of three hundred, at most two thousand people will cover the earth, with a collective readiness to help in and among themselves. Though the only settlement which covered the earth in this way, New Harmony in Indiana, associated with the 'neighbourhood ethic' of the American pioneering age, perished even more decidedly than the London exchange bazaar; for the age of sectarian colonies was over. In an age of mature capitalism such small structures were not able to transcend their capitalist environment, in fact they remained – at least in terms of technological production – a long way behind it. But Owen did not primarily want to improve production, in order to pave the way for an improved human situation, from the outset he wanted to improve the noblest means of production: man, and to lift him, cleansed, out of the dirt of the factory. Hence the restriction to small, humanly achievable spheres of life; hence not least Owen's *pedagogical* dream on a large social scale, the dream of forming a new humanity. According to Owen's theory, human beings do have a character which is innate in outline, but this outline is finally determined only by the circumstances in which the individual ends up. If the circumstances come out all right, then the person also comes out all right, he becomes cheerful and good. This healing is therefore to be best accomplished in small federated communities, without division of labour, without separating urban economy and agriculture, without bureaucracy. Precisely because of the pedagogically humane goal, which seemed to need close human contact, there is no coherent large-scale manufacture in Owen's wishful dream, but the International disintegrates into federated islands.

All these good things were to come, to be founded all at once. Life so far was for Owen a single motionless night, the new life is abruptly set off against it. Owen thinks almost completely unhistorically; this distinguishes him from the other great federative utopian, from *Charles Fourier*. Even his first work: 'Theory of the four movements', 1808, criticizes the present on a historical basis. Fourier later rejected this work, yet it remains the basis of his other major works. Both 'Treatise on the domestic agricultural association', 1822, and 'The New Industrial World', 1829, contain, like his first work, criticism of contemporary life, history, and choruses of the future all in one. More specifically, there are four epochs according to Fourier, the earlier striving towards the later one in each case,

and the later one can no longer be rescinded. The first epoch is that of
the happy early communist age of instinct, the second that of piracy and
direct barter economy, the third that of patriarchy and the development
of trade, the fourth that of barbarism and economic privileges. The latter
continue in the fifth epoch (which still largely coincides with the fourth):
in the age of capitalist civilization, which is the present. It epitomizes
Fourier's historical force that he does not criticize this present like all earlier
utopians from the standpoint of an ideal state, but as a product of degeneration at that very time and place, as an intolerable intensification of barbarism.
Fourier proves 'that civilized order raises every vice practised by barbarism
in a simple way to a complex, ambiguous, equivocal, hypocritical mode
of existence'; in this historically sound fashion, he becomes not just a satirist,
but a *dialectician*. Although Fourier does not represent, any more than
Owen, the class interests of the proletariat in the sense of the class struggle,
he does not believe that bourgeois society can be improved as such or
through its own resources. Without any knowledge of Hegel, and more
than a generation before Marx, Fourier discovers the extraordinary proposition that 'in civilization poverty springs from affluence itself'. Misery is
no longer regarded (as it is in the work of bourgeois economists even decades
later and even in America today) as a temporary condition which would
be removed as a matter of course by the cornucopia of growing riches.
On the contrary, misery is the dialectically necessary reverse side of capitalist
splendour, posited along with it, inseparable from it, growing with it;
that is why capitalist civilization never can nor will eliminate poverty.
The same dialectical genius made Fourier keenly alive to the tendencies
which are forcing their way to maturity and to sudden change within
the present 'incohérence industrielle' itself. As far as the more immediate
future of capitalism is concerned, Fourier predicted as early as 1808 the
ultimate end of free competition, the formation of monopolies. With a
quite incredible perspicacity he prophesied, in an age which had only just
broken the guild barriers and saw the beginnings of free competition, the
bankruptcy of economic liberalism. Fourier hoped here that even before
the formation of monopolies a social upheaval would abolish 'commercial
anarchy' and grant mankind a guaranteed existence beyond capitalism. This
guarantee was also inherent in the tendencies of capitalist civilization, so
that Fourier stipulates: 'Civilization in itself, in accordance with the will
of nature, strives towards guaranteeism.' Clearly though, Fourier's
historical-dialectical mediation broke off here, at the end of his critique,
and prophecy; purely subjective wishful fantasy dictated its images to the

future. The goal was a co-operative organization of the manufacture and distribution of goods; strangely enough, Fourier saw the beginnings of this in the existing savings-banks, in co-operative insurance companies and similar bourgeois caricatures of a socialist guaranteeism. Although Fourier foresaw later stages of production: specifically the formation of industrial monopolies, he simply feared them and did not, like Saint-Simon and especially Marx, welcome them and include them in his utopia as riper stages. Fourier's outlook and evaluation here remained fixedly petit-bourgeois, and moreover anarchist sympathies made their presence felt in his federalist guaranteeism. Like Owen he plans small communes, so-called phalanstères, in fact even without the total abolition of private property – an anomaly in utopias. Instead, the man of the future is also to be allowed to gain his independence by acquiring a small fortune; certainly not for the exploitation of others (there is no private ownership of the means of production), but rather with the aim of preventing individual nullification in the collective. Even the phalanstères are nothing but individually autonomous communities, manageably intimate communes of one and a half thousand people or a little more; every phalanx preserves within it a careful balance between individual and collective. Even amongst themselves, the phalanstères are only associated, although under a fantastically embellished world-leadership; no *other socialism* than the *personal-federative* one is permitted here. The business of agriculture and skilled trades in the phalanstères, and the absence of large-scale industry, was to preserve for the community the sweetness of a pastoral in the midst of a socialist front. Two hours work are enough, so that work should remain a pleasure, and an abundant change of occupation is likewise envisaged – in keeping with the 'butterfly passion' of human beings and the makings of at least thirty jobs which everyone has in him according to Fourier. At this point the utopian becomes almost American: the resourcefulness and versatility of the pioneer is introduced not into the prairie, of course, but rather into the safe garden cities of the future phalanstères. Also, just as in Owen, all this freedom without the division of labour and this pronounced *federative* utopia serves not so much a lavish production as the victory of our 'basic passion'; according to Fourier – with a sudden astonishing optimism – this is the Christian love of mankind. Capitalist civilization does of course already bear within it the tendency towards the new phase of society (just as every epoch has inherent within it the one which follows), despite the feared monopolies, those which are already to be nipped in the bud by socialism: but with more than historical, with 'geometrical necessity' Fourier's future state flows from the 'supreme principle of Christianity'. Fourier conceives his commune as a music of sheer Christian harmony, and the voices which clamour for this higher federation are not only individual human beings, but also the individual drives within those human beings. Thus Fourier even designed a kind of anthropological counterpoint, with twelve passions and no less than eighteen hundred characters; all of these flourish into a universal love of mankind, once society is attuned and dissonant deceit removed. A rich unison altogether is the destiny of man, for himself and in relation to the world. 'His industrial destiny is to harmonize the material world; his social destiny is to harmonize the emotional-moral world; his intellectual destiny is to discover the laws of universal order and harmony.' Accordingly, Fourier's utopia constructs out sheer connections in which consonance necessarily reigns; utopia is medicine and instruction for agreement. Without poverty, without that division into jobs which carves up man himself; here the federative commune, the happy structure could almost come from a kind of early Walt Whitman America, though without capitalism.

Centralist utopias in the nineteenth century: Cabet, Saint-Simon

That which brings happiness instead of misery does not always need to be friendly itself. Likewise the plan which means to abolish the harshness of life is not always soft. In Owen and Fourier the better life appears as individual and federative, its framework is loose. The centralists, however, who now emerge, closer to industry, make freedom organized, and stress the power of solidarity. They do not think in terms of settlements but of large economic complexes, and instead of Owen's 'district councils' a strict system of administration arises. One could even say that a stricter order arises in freedom again, freedom is no longer affirmed as economically individual but solely as social, i.e. orientated towards common goals. It is thus more than indicative, it is decisive that the centralist utopians no longer furnish their dreams with field, house and workshop, with a cast of peasants and craftsmen. But they affirm the collective means of production of industry, they deny only the 'subjectivism' with which these are used and administered. *Cabet* was one of the first to turn to workers in this way and was felt to be a spokesman of their powerful future.

Though he too believed, still believed, that the tension between rich and poor was based on a kind of misunderstanding which could be cleared up without a class struggle. He no longer put his trust in the zephyr of a humane torrent of words, of course, but instead he hoped that the crises would suffice to appeal if not to the capitalist's conscience, then to his common sense. But apart from this, Cabet's utopia lies thoroughly on the strict, unsentimental, organizational side. His 'Voyage to Icaria', 1839, only appears to provide a new dream of an island settlement; his Icaria was modern and complex instead. In this spirit Cabet first used the word communiste, in his programme of 1840; Heine introduced the neologisms communiste, communisme into German. No communités partielles are to cover the earth, Icaria is a uniform, highly industrial creation, supported by a mighty nation of workers. Cabet praises industry and its revolutionary power: 'By plain fire and simple water the aristocracy will be blasted into the air and smashed into the earth. There are the four ancient elements, but steam is a fifth and no less important than they are, for it is creating the world of the future, it is separating our present from the past.' The future state, which was to spring from organized industry, was devised with all the elegance and precision of the decimal system. A dictator was to create the political standard metre, the decimal system itself signifies the most clearly arranged logic of order. The projected country is divided into a hundred provinces, of roughly the same area and population; each of these provinces is again split into ten communes; provinces and communes are ruled by the working brain of their city, at the very top by Icara, the centre, a crystal completely rationalized throughout. The day is meticulously regulated, a seven-hour day of early risers, a Campanella day, filled from top to bottom with work-uniforms and committees. There are only official newspapers and no other aid to organized criticism either; engineers and civil servants govern a technical world – the contrast to Fourier's phalanstères could not be sharper. The clock of duty ever set the same* was totalized in no other utopia with so little aversion, with so much idolization of exactness. But throughout – an element of reality alongside this idolization – a socialist planned economy prevails: an industry committee fixes in advance the number and kind of goods which have to be produced in the year. Thus production manages without the crises which destroy welfare and make their system a hell for the capitalists

---

* Schiller, Max in 'Piccolomini' I, 4.

themselves. The capitalists were not, however, inclined to allow themselves to be rid of their disease by having their lives taken: there is no voluntary Icaria. Thus Cabet experimented for bad and all, wholly against his doctrine, with settlement plans of the most minimal kind, exactly like Owen. Icaria was designed as a glorious workers' state with a metropolis in the middle; it became in reality a laborious colony, established on the banks of the Missouri by communist pioneers. Despite steam power, extensive mechanization, and attempted model factories it perished, swallowed up by swamp and prairie. In any case, Little Icaria was always conceived as a substitute; the real Icaria lies on the Seine, was conceived as the perfect France of the decimal system and the departments, from which, after all the medieval mess or confusion, even the accidents of private property have been removed.

Steam overturned things at that time more quickly and more thoroughly than anyone had dreamed. Not yet for the better, as far as the workers were concerned, for the time being that was only a hope. It was championed particularly by *Saint-Simon*, he glows with praise of industrial life even more than Cabet. But then Saint-Simon again interpreted this life, in so far as it was an active one, too broadly, too indiscriminately: he also utopianized the employer along with the worker. This contemporary of Fourier did not have his dialectical perspicacity; thus he failed to notice the creation of misery by wealth, the contrast between proletariat and bourgeoisie. Thus he backed a 'working class' per se, as the 'working parts of the nation'; these also included, because their interest in profit did not seem to be idle at any rate, the capitalists, peasants, workers, traders, employers, engineers, artists, scientists – all types without inherited feudal privilege belonged for Saint-Simon to the creative part of humanity, and consequently to its future. Saint-Simon did not yet comprehend the bourgeoisie as a separate class, and hence, although all his life he wished to stand on the side of 'those who are most numerous and most poor', a peaceful balance between capital and work likewise seemed to him to be possible. What today is demagogy or the harmonizing stupidity of the backmost table reserved for regulars, was at that time still bedazzlement by young, up-to-date industry, by the modernity of all those who were occupied with steam power, with industry and progress. Workers and employers were simultaneously at the head of the development; thus they stood out equally from rotten feudality. Property earned by one's own efforts, without the right of inheritance, was different from that handed down by titled landowners, by parasites with twenty ancestors; the power of wealth by virtue of one's own labour was more progressive than the wealth of power by virtue of feudal tradition. There remains the proletariat; but the latter, in its weakness and immaturity at that time, still appeared to Saint-Simon, in his 'Reorganization of European Society', 1814, to be completely passive and sheep-like. 'Heroes of industry' were called for, who were to transform the proletariat from an object of exploitation into an equally passive object of happiness – in the 'progress of the industrial revolution'. In this belief, Saint-Simon and his disciples touched on much that is practised or hoped for by technocrats today (who have also half vanished again); it was disciples of Saint-Simon who first devised plans for the Suez and Panama canals, and all in the framework of social world-improvement. Saint-Simon himself praised the 'capacité administrative' in the active representatives of the rising bourgeois class; the bankers in particular, as representatives of the central institutions of modern economic life, are seen as being chosen to lend their aid to the nation, to become public servants of national industrial community. Bazard, the theorist of the school, declared that the bankers could deprive kings and feudal parasites of their money; banking institutions in general were the 'germes organiques' of the social system of the future. All this despite the fact that Bazard was the first Saint-Simonist to abandon his master's belief in a uniform 'industrialism' and to portray the class struggle within industrial society. Louis Blanc on the other hand, the late and dubious practician from Saint-Simon's school, thought he could make capitalist institutions into socialist ones by throwing out of them all private concerns, even the banking institutions, and replacing them with the state. The state is to cancel private competition with competition of its own, 'national workshops' for producing goods will be opened with state loans, the government itself is the supreme organizer of production. In this way there arises, in Lorenz von Stein's sympathetic phrase, the Novum of a 'governmental socialism'. But, even in the heart of Louis Blanc, this is more easily attainable by a coup d'état than by a revolution. Saint-Simon's admiration for the 'capacité administrative' of the bankers appeared in Louis Blanc for good and all not even as state socialism any longer, but as state capitalism, with the paradoxical task of functioning in a socialist way. Every connection of socialism with state capitalism, as capitalist exploitation along official paths, every masking of state capitalism with socialism occurs along the path indicated by the compass of Louis Blanc. Here too, of course, 'society takes over the means of production', but precisely a society which has no social revolution behind it, which is the old one in an intensified form and would like to make the system of profit consistent, strike-free, and formidable by means of a cross-mixture of socialist manners and political police. Saint-Simon's splendid insight – a true Frontal idea – that big business itself contained socialist elements degenerated into such questionable notions and concealed itself among such strange notions as these. Saint-Simon lags far behind the social criticism of his contemporary Fourier, but he far surpasses even the federative socialist in his premonition that it is not association but organization which brings us closer to socialism.

Yet the Count's hatred of our former masters in so far as they are brazen tyrants is as genuine as it is mottled. It is no accident that Saint-Simon presented himself under *two titles*, namely both as a 'soldier under Washington' and as a 'descendant of Charlemagne'. As the former, as a fighter of Lords, he portrayed the drawbacks of industrial concerns, which he cannot deny, exclusively as preserved or revived forms of the old serfdom. Accordingly Saint-Simon considers every exploitative employer to be a neo-feudalist, i.e. it is not industry which is the primary source of exploitation and oppression but simply the feudal disposition within industry. According to Saint-Simon, even economic liberalism appears as such a disposition, skilfully borrowed and transformed, that attitude in other words which we are used to regarding as the extreme opposite of the guild and class world of the past. Liberalism is stated to have been this opposite even in its beginnings, it overthrew feudalism, but in many ways only with the aim of putting itself in its place by equally merciless means of oppression. 'The true motto of the leaders of this party is: Ôte-toi de là que je m'y mette',* – with this statement Saint-Simon in fact superbly described in advance the new robber barons, and also the neo-feudal power ideologies and luxury forms of capitalism in the nineteenth and especially the twentieth century. Only Saint-Simon believes that the total extortion of the weak is not essential to the 'industrial system': so if the right of inheritance and other lordly forms of unearned income are abolished, then the blessings of industrialism can begin at once. So much for the pure hatred of feudality; but it is followed by the *second form* of this hatred, namely the *love-hate of feudality*, and the condemnation of liberalism provides an astonishing bridge to this. Count Saint-Simon, the alleged descendant of Charlemagne, lived in the middle of the Restoration period;† if only for reasons of the 'capacité administrative', but especially of centralism, he was not impervious

---

* 'Get down so I can set myself up there.'
† Bloch again refers to the ultra-conservatism associated with the restoration of the Bourbon monarchy in France after the fall of Napoleon and until the Revolution of 1830.

to authoritarian ideas. Thus on the other hand he thought he discovered precisely in the pre-capitalist system (and the Catholicism connected with it) considerably more tenable elements than mere hostility to the people and oppression. The *prophet of industry* never shows any mercy to feudalism, but the *prophet of the centralized collective* sees in the Middle Ages, restricted as it is, the better Europe. Saint-Simon coincides at many points here with the Restoration thinkers of his age, with the haters of revolution and 'traditionalists' like de Bonald and de Maistre, with the reactionary anti-capitalists and preachers. Compare this with de Maistre's hope: 'Tout annonce que nous marchons vers une grande unité'* or the other one, from his 'A Study of Sovereignty', full of the Holy Alliance: 'Le gouvernement est une vraie religion, il a ses dogmes, ses mystères, ses prêtres.'† This is a mystified pathos of order, firmly in the style of Campanella, and now Saint-Simon also describes an arc towards it, in the midst of industry, an industry to be organized. Namely by overthrowing the feudal lords, liberalism only did half the work even where it did not take over their positions, for its product is negative or the mere destruction of what has been. Economic and other 'subjectivism' (contained in the Manchesterist principle, in laissez faire, laissez aller) dissolved and atomized society; in the midst of the unleashed upturn in industry reign chaos and anarchy. Saint-Simon's intention was to eliminate them and to put in charge of the unleashed forces of production that 'capacité administrative' which has nothing in common precisely with Jacobin ideas. Which creates order instead, an overall view from the heights of a central institution, a new hierarchy in fact. This is in Saint-Simonism a highly momentous, highly paradoxical encounter between reaction and socialism, united in their hatred of individual economic freedom. Not only is the caricature 'feudal socialism' encountered here, which the 'Communist Manifesto' derides in the French and English 'legitimists', but the nasty reverse of the paradox continued its influence right up to Lassalle's flirtation with Bismarck, right up to the various alloys of 'Prussianness and socialism', of state capital and socialism. But the centralist Saint-Simon took up illiberal Romanticism while completely ignoring its reactionary application and naturally without a reactionary brief. He wanted to change the function of illiberalism in order to *reach right through it to the light and the humane value of bondedness* Like Fourier, Saint-Simon was also convinced that no earlier epoch could

---

* 'Everything suggests we are marching towards a great unity'.
† 'The government is a true religion, it has its dogmas, its mysteries, its priests.'

be restored as such; and like him he took his conviction from a system of phases of history itself. So in spite of everything the soldier of Washington *finally triumphs* over all kinds of inherited descent from Charlemagne; and through the *historical consciousness* which here seeks to signify progress, and by no means Restoration: 'The waters of the past have extinguished the fires of chivalry, and Nôtre Dame, a born ruin, became a real one.' For history passes through three stages here: a theological one which presents the world as having been created by gods, a metaphysical one which deduces it from abstract natural forces or from ideas, and a positive one which grasps it through the analysis of facts and on the basis of immanent causes. Now modern industrial society is the positive one, therefore it has totally emerged from the religious and semi-religious mythology of the first two stages, and therefore it can no longer return to the essentially religious-metaphysical idea of life at the heart of feudalism. But it can still regain on the basis of knowledge the social and spiritual bond (substance) which formerly existed on the basis of faith. Industry and science have taken the place of feudality and the Church, materiality that of religious metaphysics; but materiality itself demands a central structure in which – and here again we have a secularized Middle Ages thought to have been detoxicated – it can distribute a variety of intelligent sacraments through the 'capacité administrative'. Saint-Simon's 'Industrial System', 1821, and above all his last work 'New Christianity', 1825, thus aspire to a strictly hierarchical division of industrial functions and a centralized end to amateurish disruptive freedom, to freedom as anarchy. Intellectual authority, which was vested in the clergy in the Middle Ages, passes to the researchers and scholars; the organized industrial state becomes – and moreover immortally, eternally – the 'Church of Intelligence'. A social high priest, a kind of industrial pope, will be at the head of it, the spirit of a rejuvenated Christianity will guide it. These are all ideas which recurred a generation later in the final period of Auguste Comte's philosophy, and they fill over and over again the fantastic dream-weddings between sacred socialism and profane Vatican. Protestantism is here a laxly individual half-measure, deism a laxly agnostic generality; without hierarchy there is no religion, and hence none of the new intelligence either. The English natural scientist Huxley called this sort of thing Catholicism minus Christianity, and from the school of Comte there then came a correction which was a confirmation: the positive future religion was Catholicism plus exact science. If this is true of Comte, it certainly is not true of Saint-Simon of course; his social papism was by

no means intended to do without Christianity. It was not based on
hierarchical architecture alone, but on a sharpened, thoroughly organized
Christian humaneness. The precursor of all these churches of the future
or of intelligence was – despite Comte's anti-deist frame of mind – naturally
a deist, and moreover in the spirit of so-called natural religion: John Toland.
In his 'Pantheistikon', 1721, he had not only already demanded, like all
deists, a religion which by completely disposing of other-worldly revelation
'agrees with scientific reason'. Toland also erected to his natural god ('the
universe from which everything is born and to which everything returns')
a cult of his own, that 'of truth, freedom and health, the most valuable
possessions of the sages'. And above all he installed, just like Comte, new
saints and Church Fathers, namely 'the exalted spirits and the finest writers
of all ages'. This is already the 'Church of Intelligence', Saint-Simon added
the industrial pope in the age of factories and Romanticism and of course
certain continuing correspondences of bondedness which did not exist
before: the correspondences between socialism and church organization.
Apart from this, the pathos of social organization, here also that of a social
state industry, is conceived in a gloriously illiberal way all the same. Saint-
Simon's utopia is considerably closer to Campanella than to More and
contains within it all the advantages and also dangers of a collective idea
which is not provided in its centralizing organization with democratic-
federative elements, and does not in fact build up with them in a spirit
of solidarity the strictness of the organization itself.

Individual utopians and anarchy:
Stirner, Proudhon, Bakunin

Does not the life which is free of violence seem the best of all? Being
one's own master, independent, unrestricted, growing wild, or at least
growing to standards of one's own. Even Saint-Simon said on his deathbed: 'My whole endeavour is summed up in the one idea of securing for
everybody the freest development of their talents.' The guardian, even
the social one, who turns out to be the best is the one who, at a stroke,
no longer exists. The anarchists, of course, who deliver this stroke in utopian
fashion, always display, despite all their defiance, petit-bourgeois behaviour.
Not because of their background which is predominantly of this kind,
but because of their immediate goals; for these often seem to come from
an 'independent' private world like that of a man of leisure. *Stirner*, more

a wild old primary school teacher than a lion, began with the call for the ego as such, for the owner of one's self. This owner is one of the heroes in Marx's 'Holy Family'; that strange work 'The Lone Individual and his Property', 1844, wants to free the individual, and nobody else, from the last 'quirks' or 'ghosts' which have been left over from the other world. Thus, from the standpoint of the completely private person, it is the social and moral quirks which have been left over. The lone individual scorns to have himself trained any further for such ideal service, for a service to his neighbour, to the nation, to humanity. The lone individual is already a human being, he does not need to become one first by fulfilling so-called general, and therefore spectral duties. Every super-ego disappears and every demand it makes: 'I do not live for a job any more than the flower grows and is fragrant for a job.' The ego is its own super-ego and also its own utopian state, it maintains with others of its kind at most a 'contact or association', just as long as the latter aids self-benefit. As soon as the association becomes fixed, as soon as it threatens to become a society or even a state, it must be terminated by the lone individual. In short, the lone individual who only enters into the contrat social for himself is a free outsider not merely in existing society but in every conceivable one. He also demonstrates of course how much society and the fact of being an outsider are correlatively connected: the lone individual is himself only a social phenomenon. Stirner's individual and his association has much in common with that of the Cynics, apart from absence of needs; the Cynic also became a complete cynic. Naturalist drama particularly liked to portray such lone individuals, only they did not turn into a future state of their own. But into scornfully unhappy bohemians, or moving bankrupt ones, or simply cynics of the living lie (Braun in Hauptmann's 'Lonely People', Ulrik Brendel in Ibsen's 'Rosmersholm', Relling in the 'Wild Duck'). And the counterpart of the lone individual, in the same sphere, is the philistine: his total freedom, if it is no other than that of the private sphere, contains just as much total limitation. The released individual even as a social dream gets no further than the society of private entrepreneurs, or even small investors, which delivered him. The lone individual and his property, – this inscription logically adorns not only the coat of arms of libertinism but also the house sign of philistinism; and the latter is wholly the case with the anarchist *Proudhon*. Originally of course, in its infancy as it were, Proudhon's song still sounded rough, in fact his lyrics, which soon became so petit-bourgeois, appeared to be full of power, an attack on property such as had not yet been made before. Proudhon's first work posed the basic question even in its title: 'Qu'est-ce que la propriété?' and answered it with the statement that has since become famous: property is theft. This slogan, however general it was kept for the most part, seemed not only shocking but sacrilege against the bourgeoisie and desecration of the assumptions of the bourgeois individual as such. Meanwhile Proudhon, the later target in Marx's 'Poverty of Philosophy', already gave a more sympathetic origin to la propriété in his second memorandum; he says: 'Property has its roots in the nature of man and in the necessity of things.' The basis of the bourgeois individual is thus preserved, though on a broad utopian scale: all human beings are elevated to modest proprietors, the property of the proprietor must only be kept so small that it constitutes no means for subjugating others. Even Fourier, even Saint-Simon did not completely do away with private property, but this anomaly is also one within their own theory, stands in contradiction to it, and does so wholly en passant. In Proudhon, however, the preservation of property follows from a rule, from a system of principles a priori, which is characteristic of anarchism. It stems from the abstract liberalism of the eighteenth century, to which anarchism is so close, and is strangely reminiscent of antiquated deductions of Natural Right, applied to utopia. Thus Proudhon's utopia is based on nothing but 'axioms' and 'principles', on bourgeois-revolutionary ones of course, but on those which are just as statically idealistic. The first axiom posits the self-satisfaction of individuals, with which every inequality caused by social circumstances is incompatible. The second axiom posits the idea of justice as the power, inherent in the individual, of respecting and promoting human dignity in every other individual. So much for the axioms, these are joined by principles, above all for a historical application, namely for recognizing the driving forces of history. Proudhon even equates the abstract concept which appears to him to be the principle or the main economic category of an age with the driving force in that age; he thus confuses the cognitive basis, indeed the mere slogan of summary condensation with the real basis. Dialectics is admittedly to be found in the realm of these principles, but it is one which is misunderstood: Proudhon does not regard the economic contradictions as enzymes of change, but he keeps them in a simple static contrast, in mere duality: dialectics means nothing but the light and shady side of every economic category. That is to say: property, value, division of labour, credit, monopoly and so on each have their positive and negative aspect; the negative aspect is judged and eliminated by the two 'axioms'. In the 'System of Economic Contradictions or Philosophy of Poverty',

1846, but above all in his major work 'On Justice in Revolution and in the Church', 1858, Proudhon develops this notion of 'consistent future harmony'. It will bring a social existence which has found its centre, its middle class, and runs as smoothly here as a wheel around a hub; it will bring a society without friction, therefore without power, and therefore without a state. All this is constructed on the basis of the two 'axioms': on the individual independence of the producers conceived as smallholders and petit bourgeois; on the reciprocal appreciation of the individual and of the mutualité or mutual aid which springs from it. Private property, which is derived from the axiom of the self-satisfied individual just as much as it guarantees this individual freedom again, must of course be purified. It is polluted firstly by the phenomenon of minted money, and secondly by the interest on capital loans. Both desecrations of private property are to be remedied by means of an extensive social credit, precisely in the spirit of mutual aid. To be more exact: in the shape of an exchange bank which issues circulation vouchers instead of money, to the value of the goods deposited. Proudhon's utopia thus seeks to abolish capitalism and the proletariat at one and the same time, and hence not first capitalism for example (by proletarian action), and then the proletariat (by the self-cancellation of this final class into the classless society). But a levelling or harmony of the centre occurs: the bourgeoisie and proletariat dissolve into the petit propriétaire rural ou industriel. Marx once speaks of the petit bourgeoisie as the stratum in which the contradictions of two classes simultaneously blunt one another: this very situation is immortalized in Proudhon's ideal, the de-proletarianized, de-capitalized centre. Or as Marx said more specifically of Proudhon and his proclaimed 'equality of possessions': he removes national-economic alienation within – national-economic alienation. Though anarchy in particular certainly does not remove all contradictions, namely that of the bourgeois bough on which it is sitting and which it is sawing off at the same time. The anarchists do of course reject the external features of bourgeois justice: state constraint and laws, but they allow its internal essence to persist: the free contract between independent producers or those feigned to be independent. This becomes very clear in the case of Proudhon in particular, as the theorist of the 'lone individual and his association'; in the case of Bakunin or Kropotkin this sort of thing is blurred in the larger world of fire or love. Proudhon, in his 'General Idea of the Revolution', declares at one point: 'I want a contract and not laws; in order for me to be free, the whole social edifice must be rebuilt on the basis of the mutual contract' (p. 138). Later however, when it is a question of something so essential to the contract from the start as fulfilment, the anarchist has to add in the same book: 'The norm according to which the contract is to be fulfilled shall not rest exclusively on justice (the second axiom), but also on the joint will of the people who are living together. This will shall even enforce the fulfilment of the contract with violence if necessary' (p. 293). No axiom had mentioned violence, not even a joint will. But no social utopia can in fact be founded on the contract, as the centre of bourgeois civil law, without the consequences of the violent society coming to the fore again. Anarchism cancels itself out in this contradiction; the individual of the free contract – however much of an ideal petit bourgeois he may be – cannot manage without constraint. That which emanates from the basic legal instrument of a society based on property cannot land up in non-violent associations. An American disciple of Proudhon, the anarchist Josia Warren, did admittedly confess, still wholly in the spirit of Stirner: 'Every man should be his own government, his own law, a system within himself!' But the radical slogans of freedom ultimately dissolve in the ideal of the family hermit and in the cultural backwater of bourgeois conformism in which he feels at home. The outcome of Proudhon's utopia would be the all-pervading power of the provinces and hence, since precisely the middle classes are immortalized as the majority, a dictatorship of mediocrity. The threat of this dictatorship of mediocrity is incidentally to be found everywhere where a democracy is based on broad middle strata of society and inevitably absorbs their parlour infection, a mixture of resentment and lack of culture. There is then – in the spirit, though not in the letter of Proudhon's work – a kind of draped communism transplanted into the petit bourgeoisie. Proudhon's anarchy, with its philistine content and the cheapness of the common sense that corresponds to this content, bears within it in any case a system of bohemian Babbittry and also revolutionary kitsch.

For the fact that this is nevertheless not all that anarchy amounts to and that it appeared as a bogey of the bourgeoisie, for a short time, it has to thank its most vehement exponent: *Michael Bakunin*. He did not call upon the centre but upon unruly elements which wish and know how to live precisely in an unsecured way. He kept the fire in the so-called federations or trade associations, and taught a dangerously empty enthusiasm. The wild woods and the free steppes, together with the life of South Russian robbers were occasionally incorporated but mostly only rehearsed in it. From Bakunin comes the abstract proposition that the pleasure of destruction is a creative pleasure, and he applied this 'dialectics' to reactionary thinking in Germany. This gave rise to the violent propaganda of direct action by means of which individuals wanted to destroy the state by exterminating individuals. But also from Bakunin comes the nervous statement (in 1868, in a letter to Chassin, a member of Bakunin's 'Fraternité international'): 'Proudhon, the great teacher of us all, said that the most disastrous combination that could arise was that of socialism with absolutism: the endeavours of the nation towards economic liberation and material prosperity with dictatorship and the concentration of all political and social powers in the state. May the future protect us from the favours of despotism; but let it preserve us from the fatal consequences and stultifications of doctrinaire or state socialism...Living things and human beings cannot prosper outside freedom, and a socialism which expelled it from its midst or did not adopt it as its sole creative principle and as its basis would lead us straight into slavery and bestiality.' There is a complete monomania of hatred of authority in these lines, and at the same time they contain the declamatory stridency and the unconsidered sense of freedom, exhausting itself in immediacies, of anarchist utopia. For this, the main evil is not capital but the state; Bakunin's hatred is primarily fixed on the latter, everything else appears an evil of secondary rank, a derivative one in fact. If the state is abolished, then capital perishes too, for it lives solely by the grace of this conglomerate of prisons, soldiers and laws, and is allegedly derived from it, the oldest oppressor. According to anarchist theory, the state was solely created by conquerors and imposed on subjects who had first been reduced to drudgery and helotism by this very means. Accordingly, the state as political oppressor chronologically and causally precedes exploitation and remains ranked above it. Consistent with this, Bakunin diagnoses the state, a mere economic function in Marx, as the seat and origin of the entire system of exploitation and, in contrast to the Marxists, focuses on the abolition of this function. In the Marxists the state does not even have the honour of being specially abolished, instead it dies out of its own accord, in Engels' famous phrase, with the disappearance of classes. This interpretation is an economically realistic one; according to the anarchists, however, profit, the stock market, and accumulation are set in motion by the state, and even by the other world to some extent. For the instrument of the state is also made more and more of a fetish here: Bakunin's 'Dieu est l'état',* 1871, traces the source of oppression back to God himself; belief in God (i.e. a mere false consciousness) is the

---

* 'God is the state.'

feudal lord of all authority, all right of inheritance, hence of all capital. In the anarchist image of the future, Church and state are replaced by the free, godless Workers' International, furthermore it replaces them immediately, not through seizure but through the demolition of state power; economic freedom then directly follows. Bakunin, in his abstract hatred of power, despite the propaganda of direct action rejects power even when it has become revolutionary, governmental control in the hands of the victorious proletariat. From the very first day the 'égalisation des classes', cohabitation, and spontaneous fraternity will begin in the new community, merely by abolishing authority. In fact, as soon as the ship of state sinks, in a way the whole inhospitable ocean will sink and disappear, the ocean of heteronomy, with its sharks and its night; voluntary solidarity will blossom beneath the sun of autonomy. This is anarchist faith, founded, as is obvious, on the conviction that human nature is originally good and only corrupted by the master-servant relationship. So on the whole the anarchist image of freedom remains partly superannuated individualistic ideology from the eighteenth century, partly a bit of future in the future, for which no present prerequisites exist anywhere at all. Except in the putsch, the rash heroic deed, and in political lyricism which knows nothing about epic poetry and even less about the dialectics of history. Thus anarchy homelessly describes a vitalist-idealistic curve, without matter, without detective knowledge of economic matter. Though if their upheaval succeeded for once, then certain anarchic themes, being applied in the right place, would also become Marxist ones. In fact, they are already to be found in Marxism, sensibly enough not as present postulates but as prophecies and conclusions. The above-mentioned prediction by Engels is relevant here, his hope that the state will die out one day, that it will pass from ruling over people to running affairs. All the more relevant here is the formula which Lenin cites in 'State and Revolution' as summing up the communist goal: 'Everyone producing according to his abilities, and consuming according to his needs.' Though of course this formula which sounds so anarchic – the quintessence of non-constraint – does not stem from anarchists at all, but strangely enough from a Saint-Simonist, from Louis Blanc, the otherwise very questionable inventor of national workshops. To sum up, we can say that the dream of a society without rule is, when interpreted tactically, the surest means of not realizing this dream; when fundamentally understood, after the economic foundations of the state have been removed, this dream becomes a matter of course.

Proletarian castle in the air from the Vormärz:
Weitling

Shortly before people wake up, they usually have the most colourful dreams. Weitling, one of the last purely utopian thinkers, gave not the richest but probably the most ardent and warmest picture of a new age. He was a proletarian by birth, and this fact alone already distinguishes him from the other world-improvers treated here. Proudhon was also of plebeian origin of course, but he soon worked his way up into the petit bourgeoisie and spoke from its standpoint. Proudhon, the owner of a printing works, spoke from the standpoint of his credit problems, the *travelling journeyman Weitling* spoke from the standpoint of proletarian misery and of the dawning awareness of his class. Accordingly the tone of pity is also absent here which more aristocratic utopians so often show towards those who are very poor; in Weitling bitterness and hope come from his own suffering. Weitling, as Franz Mehring says, 'threw down the barrier which separated the utopians of the west from the working class'; that is his historical contribution. Weitling did not of course become the head and leader of the German working class, this was only just beginning to develop in the Germany of the Vormärz. But there was a contact here, even an identity, of a man from the disinherited class with its then existing clarity about itself. Accordingly, Weitling presents both a penetratingly genuine and a backward aspect; his pathos is related to that of another early proletarian spokesman, that of Babeuf. Weitling is the earliest proletarian voice in Germany, Babeuf one of the earliest in France, and he was certainly the first person after the stifling of the French Revolution to represent those demands for real equality out of which the bourgeois had cheated the citoyen. So there are connections, both of purity and primitiveness, between the head of the 'Égalitaires' and Weitling. The early proletarian manifesto of 1795 issued by the 'Égalitaires' is unjustly half forgotten; Weitling also shares their emotions (one might say: their confused far-sightedness and radicalism). Take a few sentences from Babeuf's manifesto on this subject: 'The French Revolution is only the forerunner of a much greater, much more serious revolution, which will be the last. No individual ownership of the soil any more, the soil belongs to nobody, we demand, we want the common enjoyment of the fruits of the earth, the fruits belong to all. Away with the outrageous distinctions between rich and poor, between rulers and the ruled. The moment has come to form a republic of equals,

the great hospitable house (hospice) that is open to all.' Though this
'republic of equals', given the state of the forces of production at that
time, could only present itself in the same light as that in which the petit
bourgeois imagined the 'future state' during the whole of the nineteenth
century: as one of sharing, sharing out, levelling. Thus Marx mocks the
'raw, ascetic egalitarianism' of Babeuf; a mockery which he did not bestow
on the equally pure, equally primitive performance of Weitling. Marx was
even initially inclined to overestimate Weitling, and he wrote of his
'Guarantees of Harmony and Freedom' of 1842: 'If we compare the sober,
sheepish mediocrity of German literature with this boundless and brilliant
debut of the German workers: if we compare these gigantic children's
shoes of the proletariat with the dwarfishness of the worn-out political
shoes of the bourgeoisie, then we must prophesy an athletic figure for
the German Cinderella.' Later, though, Marx was more inclined to
underestimate him: 'Weitling's utopian arrogance could no longer be cured,
and so there was no other choice but to clear this impediment out of the
way of the development of the proletariat.' Indeed, Weitling had become
a member of a really crazy and vague 'League of the Just', Proudhon's
influence was not lacking, and their slogan ran: 'All men are brothers'.
The difference of this slogan from that stressed by Marx : 'Proletarians
of the world, unite' is the difference of militant socialism from that which
is still lyrical. Weitling also finally became addicted to social experiments,
in Columbia he founded a trade exchange bank, this even for the purpose
of a harmonious co-operation between bourgeoisie and proletariat. All the
same, this professed purpose must have been a tactical, if not demagogic
one; Weitling (he died in 1871) also set in motion the beginnings of the
German labour movement in the United States. Also Weitling, although
influenced by Proudhon, is not at all anarchistic; the influence of Saint-
Simon is greater and brought order into social freedom. Even his first work:
'Mankind, as it is, and as it ought to be', 1838, portrays a 'constitution
of the great family league of mankind', in which working hours are precisely
regulated and production is precisely adapted to consumption. Regulation
and adaptation occur on a technical basis and in such a way that the 'two
essential conditions of human life: work and pleasure' are treated in a
general, equal order. 'The one is the family order or the order of pleasure,
the other the business order'; the former consists of families under the
supervision of elders, the latter of farmers, manufacturers and teachers and
the industrial army. 'The future community of property is the common
right of society to be able to live without care in permanent prosperity;

and the majority will never make an attempt to destroy this right, because it is its own right, the right of the majority.' This is naive and stirring popular language, full of the old original state of things and Christian dreams; but as for bringing this state of affairs about, Weitling the proletarian talks considerably less naively than most bourgeois utopians. He has the realism of the afflicted man, even more than that: of the capitalist victim, he no longer believes in socialist measures 'with the aid' of the ruling class. In this respect, Weitling the proletarian is far superior to previous illusionists, he sees through the sly believers, criticizes the dilettante believers of every kind of socialism from above. This is shown by the following sentence: 'Let us mistrust the reforms intended by means of capital, as well as the financiers, we cannot expect perfection from either but rather the same traps, of which the good can never be wary enough.' Here is a warning not to allow ourselves to be diverted from the hard path on the march to the land of happiness by something worse than false prophets: by false friends. This warning is accompanied by less realistic pieces of advice, but all unbowed and demonstrating a Christianity which has not been heard for a long time. As in the 'Gospel of the poor sinner' and especially in the 'Guarantees of Harmony and Freedom', 1842, an association of dreams which is frequently reminiscent of the hopes of the German Peasant War. Act and content of social revolution are concisely expressed in two sentences: 'Fear is the root of cowardice, and the worker must eradicate it, this poisonous plant, and allow courage and brotherly love to take root in its place. Brotherly love is Christ's first commandment, the wish and will and therefore the happiness and the welfare of all that is good is contained within it.' There is also a hint of adventist hope, shortly before the 'peoples' spring' of 1848: 'A new Messiah will come, to implement the teachings of the first. He will demolish the rotten structure of the old social order, channel the springs of tears into the ocean of oblivion and transform the earth into a paradise.' Weitling was no great architect, but his castle in the air has particularly humane dimensions. There is something of the fair hand of women in it, a piece of female-maternal utopia, which loathes war and brutality, exploitation and tyranny from the bottom of its heart. And Weitling's structure certainly also contains a piece of the work of the carpenter's son, an element of early Christian love. Saint-Simon had also tried to restore the connection between Jesus and the tribune of the people, but the result was not so much a new Christianity as a new kind of Church. Weitling's more gentle dream never builds into the world of masters, not even into the socialist one of

Saint-Simon; he is a bosom companion, friendly by nature, but for the first time in ages again, and for the last time for ages, he knows how to read the Bible as it was read by a Baptist. From the aspect of an undeveloped proletariat, of course, what emerged was more the image of a society of ordinary people than a classless one; in fact, not even the society of ordinary people could be realized in this way. But 'the great family league of mankind', made possible by a 'co-operative business order', is nevertheless more than the Biedermeier style in utopia. It has the grace and purity of this style, but it does not lack crude greatness, thorough aspiration and within it a problem which radical movements were to disregard for a century. It is the problem of the carpenter's son and socialism, or Christ's homecoming to those that labour and are heavy laden. Weitling sought a red trade union of Jesus the proletarian, he intended a socialism which does not even guard against being devotional. Weitling's dream, with much bitterness and purity, glanced into a Promised Land at a time when Marx and Engels had just begun to discover and to open up the real entrances to it.

A conclusion:
weakness and status of the rational utopias

It comes as a constant surprise that great hatred can still remain trusting. Many of the visionary thinkers who have appeared so far found themselves in this situation, they were ultimately conciliatory. The same deadly enemies of exploitation who have just portrayed its merciless horror turn to the exploiters and suggest that they put an end to themselves. With their hearts the utopians condemned injustice, and wished for justice, with their minds they sought – as abstract utopians – to construct the better world, and in their hearts again they hoped to kindle the will for this world. A few friendly, and also snobbish exceptions, a few deserters from 'fawning commerce' were made the rule; the appeal, for all that, was to justice and reason. Only around 1848 did the experience open up more generally which Herwegh expressed as follows: 'Only the lightning which strikes them can illuminate our masters.' But just as the employers were to be persuaded into their opposite, so the rest of reality, society as a whole, was to be turned into its opposite, immediately, as if by abruptly breaking a spell. Although a few utopians, such as Fourier and Saint-Simon, explored historical mediations and premonitions of existing tendencies, even here the essentially private and abstract fathoming of an imaginary state independent of history and the present (of the 'dross of the present') wins the day. Fourier, the only dialectician in this group, took most notice of real tendencies; yet even in his case we find more decrees than insights, more abstract than concrete utopia. The dream lantern shines into an empty space in the case of the abstract utopians, the given has to bow to the idea. Thus the constructive wishful images were applied unhistorically and undialectically, abstractly and statically to a reality which knew little or nothing about them. Though this weakness is only rarely a personal one of the utopians; rather, it was precisely here that the conception did not attain reality because the reality at that time did not attain conception. Industry was undeveloped, the proletariat immature, the new society barely visible in the old. Marx comments on this in his 'Poverty of Philosophy' (admittedly only contra Proudhon, but also describing all the older utopians): 'As long as the proletariat is not yet sufficiently developed to be constituted as a class, and hence the struggle of the proletariat still bears no political character, as long as the forces of production are not sufficiently developed even in the bosom of the bourgeoisie itself to allow the material conditions to shine through which are necessary for the liberation of the proletariat and for the creation of a new society, these theorists will simply remain utopians who, in order to remedy the needs of the oppressed class, devise systems and search for a regenerating science. But to the same extent that history progresses and with it the struggle of the proletariat becomes more clearly apparent, they no longer need to search for this science in their minds; they merely have to account for that which is taking place before their eyes, and to make themselves a mouthpiece of it. As long as they search for this science and only construct systems, they will only see the misery in misery, without perceiving the revolutionary aspect within it which will throw out the old society. From this moment on science becomes a conscious product of historical movement, and it has ceased to be doctrinaire, it has become revolutionary.' And the old utopias were doctrinaire because they combined their otherwise so highly imaginative, indeed fantastic nature with the rationalist style of thought of the bourgeoisie. Up to the end of the eighteenth century, the fundamental discipline of the bourgeoisie was mathematics, not history; but the method of this mathematics was formal, was the 'creation' of the object from pure thought. It was not least the methodical model for the deductions of Natural Right, this strict cousin of the utopias. However little utopistic construction has in common with exact mathematical construction, and even that of

Natural Right, however little utopianism in general represents a science, it does occasionally proceed in logical constructions (even with a basis of 'axioms' in Proudhon), as if it too were a formal science. This constructive nature had such a powerful effect that both the existing state and especially the utopian 'rational state' could be presented as a mechanism, and the modern utopian was a social engineer (out of pure reason). He no longer waited for Jerusalem to descend by an act of grace, he exchanged a poorly functioning social machine for a perfect one. And none of the utopians completely understood why 'the world' took no interest in his plans and why it gave so few orders to carry out the new design.

Yet these dreamers have a status which nobody can take away from them. Their very will for *change* in itself is unquestionable, and despite their abstract appearance they are never simply contemplative. This distinguishes the utopians from the political economists of their time, even from those who are most critical (to whom they are so often greatly inferior in knowledge and research). Fourier rightly says that the political economists (his contemporaries Sismondi and Ricardo for example) had only exposed the chaos, but he wanted to lead the way out of it. This will for practice almost never erupted of course; because of the weak connection with the proletariat, because of the scanty analysis of the objective tendencies in existing society. But there is also the fact of course that increased attention to these tendencies can, if it is mechanically increased, if it turns into economism, weaken the will for practice all the more. It can weaken it far more thoroughly than abstract utopia, it can cause the socialist (or to be more precise: the social democrat), as a completely non-utopian type, to become a slave to the objective tendencies. Objectivist idolatry of the objectively possible then waits winking until the economic conditions for socialism have become completely ripe, so to speak. But they are never completely ripe or so perfect that they are in no need of a will to action and an anticipatory dream in the subjective factor of this will. Lenin, as is well known, did not wait until the conditions everywhere in Russia gave leave for socialism, in a comfortably distant age of his children's children: Lenin surpassed the conditions, or rather: he helped them to ripen by means of surpassing targets of a concrete-anticipatory kind, which are likewise a part of ripeness. And when the realization that with the rule of monopolies capitalism had reached its final stage, that of death and decay, that the chain had to break at its weakest link, when this realization was also certain of the objective conditions of revolutionary victory, how could the hour of the Great October Revolution have been seized and how could power have been maintained without the surpassing goal-image of socialism, without the subjective factor in the highly organized, disciplined, conscious form of the Party? Marxism is instruction for action; but if it becomes both subjectless and alienated from its goal, then a fatalistic anti-Marxism arises, that degenerates into the justification for not having acted because the process was already under way of its own accord. Such automatism therefore becomes a cookbook of missed opportunities, a commentary on wasted chances, vacated positions. But Marxism is only an instruction for action when its grasp is simultaneously a grasp ahead: the concretely anticipated goal governs the concrete path. Hence, even more decisive than the will for change is the *pathos of the basic goal*, which is usually so instructive for the status of the old utopians and for the significance which is still due to them today, and indeed makes them into allies against so-called social democracy, for which since Bernstein the movement means everything but the goal means nothing. Regardless of the fact that the goal-pathos of the utopians, being all too direct, is questionable in a different way because it replaced the path, it skipped over it abstractly. It operated above all as a static pathos, as one of the mere exposure of existing cathedrals; it posited good order as readily available, a ready alternative. In this respect there is very often no genuine, historically new future at all in the goal of utopians, but a false, non-new future; bad utopians like Proudhon even imagined a mere transfigured petit bourgeois into the Idée générale de la révolution. And even great utopians decorated, indeed overfilled their constructions with false ideals, i.e. with those which in terms of content (essentially) were exactly known and complete, only not yet realized so to speak. But if instead of such ideals (they all stem from a static theory of two worlds) Marx teaches the work of the next step and determines little in advance about the 'realm of freedom', this does not mean, as we know, that these goal-substances were missing in his work. On the contrary, they move within the entire dialectical tendency as its ultimately inspiring purpose, they establish the spirit of the entire revolutionary work. Marx likewise uses ideals as a measure of criticism and direction, only not transcendentally introduced and fixed ideals, but those to be found in history and thus unfinished ideals, i.e. those of concrete anticipation. This was clearly distinguished above as the warm stream of Marxism (cf. Vol. I, p. 210f.), as the 'theory-practice of reaching home or of departure from inappropriate objectification'. If Marxism did not have its dialectical materialist humanism, in historically dawning, and also inheriting anticipation: then we could never speak of capitalist 'alienation', 'dehumanization';

Marx even teaches a 'restoration of man'. Except that this human element or the complexities of a realm of freedom as a whole are not rigid genera, but ensembles of social conditions, and above all that they do not stand behind history as an unchangeable essence, existing like a Golden Fleece which only has to be fetched from existing Colchis after it has been described and depicted. This was the plan of the abstract utopias, but not in fact their only one: the intention towards the better world itself is by no means discharged, it and it alone is a major invariable in history. Without such anticipation in general there is no undisappointability, no belief in the goal, no distributable abundance of belief. 'And even if Marx rightly assigned the stimulus to the new life decisively to the homo oeconomicus, to the control of points of economic interest, in order to conquer the paradisial order, beyond the world and assumed to be all too Arcadian, of rational and at heart chiliastic socialism in a harsh manner and with a worldly-wise struggle against the world: one surely does not die merely for a thoroughly organized production budget, and even in the very Bolshevist fulfilment of Marxism the old Taborite-Joachite type, aggressive towards God, of radical Baptism recognizably recurs, with a still hidden, secret myth of the What For, for which chiliasm nevertheless constantly figures as a prelude and a corrective' (Ernst Bloch, Thomas Münzer als Theologe der Revolution, 1921, p. 128). *The abstract element is the defect, the remorseless and unconditional element is the power of great old utopian books.* And as a condition of this unconditional element they almost always named the same thing: Omnia sint communia, let everything be in common. It is a credit to pre-Marxist political literature to possess these isolated and rebellious enthusiasms among its many ideological insights. Even if they did not seem to contain a shred of possibility, and naked appearances, and all the more so those cloaked in ideology, contradicted their reveries. After all, the society projected within them managed without self-interest at the expense of others and was to keep going without the spur of the bourgeois drive for acquisition. For thousands of years this hope of the social utopias in particular was passed off as particularly unworldly and much laughed at. Until this sort of thing actually started to begin in a vast country, instead of on a dream island; whereupon the laughter stopped. So there was ultimately also insight in these enthusiasms after all and despite everything a great deal of reality: at first one which was still immature, which confined the better world to an abstractly pictured, immediately anticipatory system in the mind of its creator, but then a forcibly prevented reality which, however difficult its birth, finally breaks through. Since Marx the abstract character of utopias has been overcome; world improvement occurs as work in and with the dialectical coherence of the laws of the objective world, with the material dialectics of a comprehended, consciously manufactured history. Since Marx, mere utopianizing, apart from still having a partial active role in a few struggles for emancipation, has turned into reactionary or superfluous playful forms. These do not lack a seductive quality of course, and are at least useful for diversion, but this is precisely why they have become mere ideologies of the existent, beneath a critical-utopian mask. The work of the genuine social dreamers was different, honest and great; this is how it must be understood and taken to heart, with all the weaknesses of its abstractness and its all too nimble optimism, but also with its cons-tant insistence on: peace, freedom, bread. And the history of utopias demonstrates that socialism is as old as the western world, much older in fact in the archetype which continually accompanies it: the Golden Age.

III. Projects and Progress Towards Science

Topical remnants: bourgeois group utopias

Previous sociable dreams were not separately inviting. They did not concern themselves with a particular, or smaller group. Instead they wanted to cure the whole of society, the lives of everyone, even if a single discontented stratum was to see to this. But now groups appear on their own and peel themselves, with supposed or genuine individuality, out of the whole in order to seek and picture ahead what is *specifically* best for them. They separate themselves in a longitudinal section which is supposedly to go through all classes; they were linked by organic and national characteristics. And of course by those of oppression or persecution, like young people, the female sex, and especially the Jews. Quite late social utopias thus arose here, alongside Marx so to speak, those of a group emancipation. It operates as the *youth movement*, as the *women's movement*, and as *Zionism*; gulfs lie between them, but also the common element of feeling oppressed in existing society by virtue of a single characteristic. The programme of these groups does not contain revolution but *secession*, exodus from a manifold ghetto. What they strive for and dream of is of course an influence on society, in a way a new virtue pouring out of youth, womanhood, and national

Judaism. Thus it wants or wanted to escape from mustiness, pressure, and also the atmosphere of lazy scepticism. But the will towards *rebuilding the whole of society*, that was usual in the great social utopias, is lacking. It is nevertheless remarkable that the programmes confined to groups have a certain specialist status: they know their way around in their groups and undertake utopian gleaning there. Many elements from these specialized utopias were even included in Marxism, which did not happen with any bourgeois full-scale utopia after Marx. These emancipatory plans are certainly not lacking in the short-sightedness which characterizes every mere reformism, but they do lack or did lack deceit. They are thus as different from the bourgeois full-scale utopias of the present as the patch on a dress from the festive garb of finished rags. Utopian remnants, as dished up by capitalist democracy and later by fascism, were sheer deceit, either of an objective kind, with private self-delusion, or of a thoroughly conscious, deliberate kind. One only has to compare with the specialized short-sighted character of the group utopias cited above the totally bogus character of the bourgeois full-scale utopias which have recently sprung up. A future as envisaged by Moeller van den Bruck in his 'Third Reich', and Rosenberg in his 'Myth of the Twentieth Century' is capitalism plus murder. Ernst Jünger's imagined unity of workers and soldiers is the same demagogy in its tone of command which Rosenberg demonstrated in blood and flickering flames. What Spengler called 'Prussianness and socialism' even around 1920 is a dream of the future which rightly followed the decline of the western world. Even earlier, Kjellén, another utopian reactionary, had declared the 'ideas of 1914' to be superior to those of 1789, indeed to be Prussian salvation, a 'third Rome' in Brandenburg; thus full-scale utopia had a fascist appearance. There remains the bourgeois-democratic future, with H. G. Wells as its first champion. It certainly does not wear such a war-like death-mask as fascism. Instead it wears moral make-up, and feigns human rights as if the capitalist whore could become a virgin again; Wilson's fate showed what comes out of this.* Freedom from fear cannot be brought by those who themselves represent and produce the cause for fear; freedom as the utopia of western capitalism is chloroform. Thus the smaller or *group utopias* still stand out as honest exceptions to this, they really wanted to reach the light. Once again a dream of the better life surfaced here, even if by unsuitable means, on soil that had

---

* Thomas Woodrow Wilson (1856–1924), whose 'Fourteen Points' were the basis on which the League of Nations was established. They were presented at the Paris peace conference in 1919.

become wholly unsuitable. All the same, a cause for the dream existed
and a goal of freedom; there also is or was real movement there and behind
it, which is lacking in all bourgeois full-scale utopias after Marx. Escape
from minority, from the doll's house, from being a nation of pariahs was
what was longed for in these movements; this is the aim of the special
utopia of their programme. The women's movement even contains its
own utopian question: that concerning the border of sex, and it entertains
the doubt whether such a border exists at all. A piece of Thomas More,
a late romantic stirring of liberalism circulates in these movements for the
last time. In places, that 'draught of fresh air' blows through them which
a man like Ibsen wanted to send in all its lively purity through the bourgeois
home and community. But the movement ends at the bourgeois barriers
erected for it and which tolerate only corruption or abstractness. Life was
to resemble nothing but the nobility, nothing but Sunday weather, but
they did not see the connection whereby bourgeois life is not like that.
For the liberal abstract element to come to an end, the necessary information
still lies solely in socialism even for these social dreams. Both things lie
in socialism: the end of their movement and the end of the deprivation
which caused this movement to begin. The partial utopias of today
repeatedly exhibit dreams of emancipation which are a sequel to or an afterripening of the eighteenth century; although or because the latter, apart
from a few points in the programme of the Sturm und Drang, still did
not in the least dream of such far-reaching emancipation.

Beginning, programme of the youth movement

The child is only to speak when it is spoken to. Even when growing up,
it belongs to its parents, has always been more or less kindly enslaved.
But around 1900 a will surfaced among young people, on a fairly broad
scale, to belong to nobody but themselves. Youth experienced itself as
a beginning, wore its own costume, loved travel, cooking in the open
air, and was consciously green. It wished for a new life of its own, different
from that of adults and better in everything, namely informal and sincere.
Family pressure was felt here to the same extent that it decreased. For
only those parents no longer sure of themselves, only the home no longer
stable itself had children who renounced them and joined their contemporaries to make a fresh beginning. The former bourgeois home as well
as the school corresponding to it still at least gave a support which did

not merely coincide with constraint or with empty habit. The fathers still set an example, the teachers by virtue of their strictness towards themselves and their knowledge of their subjects were such that young people trusted them and allowed themselves to be guided by them. It was only possible to become widely disrespectful and to set one's own goals when the old simply knew how to oppress and to lie, and not to guide any more. Above all when new paths seemed to open up, on which the old in their insecurity were unable to find their way. An open field lay ahead, it only seemed to be accessible and indeed visible to the young. First boys and then also girls banded together and emigrated as it were.

Green, that was the approved colour, in order to begin afresh. In order to remain fresh and not to grow wooden, not even later on as a man. Everyone was a scout, the leaders developed out of the circle. The youth movement, in this contrast to the old, is historically new. Only the student fraternity of the Vormärz may come close to it, but it was politically more distinct, i.e. not separated from its older men of freedom, with full beards. The federated form of the 'free youth movement' is also old, even very old, it has been placed alongside the elemental community, alongside the so-called organic community, full of customs, sustained and held together by tradition. But the earlier federations, precisely when they contained young people, were intermediate forms, they prepared them for adult life. As is self-evident in a restricted society, and all the more so in the horde, in the primitive tribe. However carefully the original male federations were cut off from older age-groups, unmarried young people by themselves, no path led from here out of the customs of the old, nor was one sought. Also, the bachelors of the male federation were by no means always young men; the primitive only marries at around the age of forty, so the young people of that time were strongly mixed with men of mature years. The tension is quite different which the modern youth federations with their utopian goals felt between themselves and the older world. From this tension came the enthusiasms in the war directed against the functionally rational society, often intoxicated, streams of love or hatred pouring from the 'heart' or 'soul'. Though this took forms which frequently copied and even helped the society against which they were protesting. After all, this society itself was no longer solidly respectable, dignity loved to make itself up to look young, and even rebellious youth, if confused and rebellious, slowly began to seem quite useful to it. The federated emotional haze in which young people fought before, without seeing their real opponent, could be easily combined with the intoxicated fascist haze. The SA had long been tolerated and allowed out into the forest before it was called together and put to use, before they were no longer made to ramble but to march. The Wandervogel* is not just a German phenomenon but above all a petit-bourgeois one, hence the blurred nature of his dream both in terms of class and content. This kind of fuzziness is different from youthful vagueness, and it is only roughly connected with the striving for candour, with student fraternities, hatred of everyday life, and the longing for elemental, unbroken life. One particular reason for it lay above all in the fact that youth was not merely experienced as a condition but wrongly as a class of its own. Or also: a purely organic longitudinal section was drawn through all classes: that which fell on the side of youth thereby already seemed to have contents of its own, not just its own tempo. Schultz-Hencke, one of the leaders at the time, thus spoke of an 'overcoming of parties by youth'. A petit-bourgeois sense of harmony, a petit-bourgeois deadening thus pretended to be Young German,† Free German,‡ an 'advance guard', even a 'fountain of youth' or various other things. That is why the youth movement could be so easily captured, there were denominational federations, again in accord with the family, especially when the mother had an earphone hairstyle herself, and the father plucked the lute himself. The longing for a community such as did not exist among adults finally listened to Hitler; for if there were no new contents to counter old people, there were still new burning-blowing-overblown words, and to counter those old people who were not yet fired with blood lust there was power. The tension between father and son and the revolt of the son against the oppressive father was replaced by the parents' fear of the member of the Hitler Youth. With him the seemingly changing society enters the home; relationships which had been faltering for a long time through bourgeois insecurity were now completely and most alarmingly overturned. The fact that the Father-Ego, against which the dream of the young was fighting, had merely been replaced by the much harsher one of a murderous state did not occur to them. The young petit bourgeois obviously was not himself brought on to the path that could help him by his youth alone, by the reform of life which was to pass through all classes with a green light. Silt, mud, mustiness, and business were little affected by cooking in the open air in the forest and by the open country that shone beyond it;

---

* Literally 'bird of passage', a member of the Wandervogel youth movement.
† A reference to Das Junge Deutschland, a revolutionary group of writers after 1830.
‡ A reference to Freie Deutsche Jugend, a youth movement in East Germany.

the pot of dreams was filled with even more mud, and finally with his own blood. Although the open country was certainly meant to be liberal originally, with people who did not belong to everyday life as guides to it and no everyday life within it. The Wandervogel had moreover found a certain nest in new schools, likewise longitudinally through the classes, founded for the sons and daughters of liberal families. These were forest schools, Wyneken's free school community, and also a federation of determined school reformers belonged here, represented by Danziger and Kawerau. Education was no longer handed down from above; the cultivation of individual life, and a community spirit were attempted in these emphatic schools of youth. Noble general goals hovered about the picnic and the lamp of evening gatherings, comradeship and even courage were cultivated. As was the love of verse; only the life itself which was afterwards in store remained unrhymed and absurd. It lay behind a glimmer which lasted no longer than the youth that created it.

Which did not prevent this youth from feeling very rebellious. Especially as the city, seen from the campfire, seemed particularly corrupt and stunted. The word bourgeois acquired a special resonance in the youth movement, Blüher spoke of the atrocities of the bourgeois type. He was regarded primarily as the aged and senile type, his thrifty, economical, calculating, zestless nature was derived from this alone, and likewise the herd of bourgeois conformists: bourgeois society. There was far less talk of exploitation, in fact the other side of the bourgeois, so lovingly elaborated even by Sombart: that of the entrepreneur, the man who takes risks, the conqueror – met with sympathy. The hostility towards the bourgeois was therefore certainly not proletarian or akin to the proletariat; the bourgeois was regarded instead as the counterpart to their own bohemian world, that of knights of chivalry. The society dreamed up by this kind of youth was to be ultimately ardent and strict, anarchistic and class-bound at one and the same time. Nevertheless there was and is also a proletarian youth movement, only not an independent one, with a childish land of its own. The young worker feels no more discriminated against by adults as such than the female worker does by men as such. The enemy of both is the employer, their idea of the bourgeois primarily refers to the capitalist, not the nasty bourgeois conformist. Also the tension between father and son is absent or is powerfully diminished in the working-class family; for whereas the bourgeois sees in his son only the heir, the class-conscious proletarian brings up his son to be a comrade. Bourgeois youth thought it was being unbourgeois by carving people into age-groups, and by contrasting its rosy cheeks with the pallor of adults; whereupon they turned out to have little more in common than a fresh skin and a general air of the March revolution. Proletarian youth, however, does not create any fictitious contrast to its class, but identifies itself with it. It sees the latter as just as young and futurist as itself, and just as preoccupied with the morning of life, with the life of tomorrow. What it brings to that class is therefore not a goal of its own but an unbroken impetus towards the common proletarian goal. Sorrow however, greatness, noble-mindedness, all naive and high-vaulted, do not constitute a future on their own. The good of not being cheated of our youth will only be achieved when nobody can be cheated and deprived of their rights any more.

Struggle for the new woman, programme of the women's movement

Woman lies at the bottom, she has long been trained to do so. She is always available, always serviceable, she is the weaker sex and tied to the home. Serving and the obligation to please are related in female life, since pleasing also makes for servitude. The young girl had to be provided for through marriage, so she sat on the perch, and had to wait for a husband. Or she captured men with cunning and herself as the bait, remained a minor even then, without a hunting licence. If her catch was not successful, or if the virgin was too choosy, then she suffered a barren mockery: the woman ranked as an old maid. Sexual life, if it was present, as it mostly was, was not allowed to be shown. A job was regarded as indecent right down to the lower petit-bourgeois levels of society. But courageous girls and women drew a different conclusion, dreams of the new woman began. Around 1900, a little before and afterwards, a light flared up here which retains its attraction. The free girl announced her arrival, but so too did the masculine woman, both no longer inclined to be oppressed or even misunderstood. The incipient disintegration of the bourgeois home and the growing need for employees facilitated or justified this path into the open. New love, new life were demanded, a thoroughly self-chosen love, without the official stamp of approval. But what seemed more important, and certainly more strongly affirmative was the access to public life, to a job. The longing was to enjoy life to the full, happy brooding on the nest was no longer the goal. This lay instead outside the limits of the family, outside all the limits which had previously determined woman by hemming her in. The bourgeois girl who did not yet need to earn her living was different in this connection from poorer and bolder women. The latter had mostly broken with the family completely and bore the consequences; they adopted the masculine course, that of the professional person, entirely. The young ladies who no longer wanted to be so merely got over-excited, but the masculine woman acted differently, the leading woman of the time, the incipient suffragette. The intention of this female protester was, unconsciously and very often consciously, to go her own way, to attain masculine superiority. An undeniable hatred of men was a strange mixture here of hatred by those who were oppressed and of reluctant recognition at the same time; hence their envy, their emulation, indeed their grotesque will to outdo men. Suffering from their own sex made them prone to this, and in turn their own sex was to be led to victory, against itself. This broken wish did not prevent the female protester of the time from providing and sustaining the boldness of the call for the new woman. The free girl also blazed up now, as only young boys would do as a rule, and the masculine woman, in her new haircut, thoroughly sharpened the dream of being a woman in a different way.

But it turned out that the rebellious life did not remain fresh for long. The more workers were needed, the less room there was for the so-called free girl, the less reason the female protester had to be one. The bourgeois young woman who was capable of working for a living came to stand on her own two feet, but this only made her seemingly more independent. Instead of the right to self-chosen love and a free life there arose the tedium of the office, mostly with a subordinate position as well. Hardly had she gained the right to vote, than parliament had less say than ever before; hardly were the lecture halls opened up to women, than the crisis of bourgeois science began. At the same time capital, when it 'opened up jobs' for women, was interested in removing everything that smacked of the desire for freedom, and especially everything neighbouring on thorough emancipation, on socialist emancipation. The tamer female leaders now arose: Helene Lange, Marie Stritt, and finally Gertrud Bäumer, all for a movement without 'aberrations'. Around 1900 the aberrations had been secessionist, the hatred of the juste milieu. At that time the new woman had her utopia of water-lilies and sunflowers together with the Art Nouveau man; it was a bohemian literary one, but for this very reason not a tame one. The background of the future dreamed up for women was filled with festive-Dionysian images of revolution, of which little more remained a generation later than the liberation from the corset and the right to smoke, to vote and to study. When Bebel wrote 'Woman and

Socialism' in 1899, he recognized woman as the first creature to be oppressed, oppressed earlier than the male slave, and the question of women's rights was still inflammatory and shocking. But soon afterwards, when the spoons had been won, there was no millet gruel; and the bourgeois women's movement now defended the right to keep itself clear of socialism. Helene Lange fought for the goal that the headship of the secondary school for girls should be entrusted to a woman. Marie Stritt was satisfied with 'women's education – women's studies' in general, and Gertrud Bäumer saw the fulfilment of the new woman in the citizenship of the Weimar Republic. All this had not been foreseen of the movement, neither by the suffragettes nor even by the earliest champions of the second sex. After all, the movement which seeks to advance the organic and political limits of woman in a utopian fashion is actually as old as the struggle for freedom itself. Instead of being confined to Art Nouveau, this movement extends from the Athenian Ecclesiazusae mocked by Aristophanes into the Ottonian age, into the Renaissance and its virago, into the programmes of the Sturm und Drang, into the Young Germany of the Vormärz. The passionate Mary Wollstonecraft had published a fundamental book about women's rights in 1792, which radically applied the human rights of the time to women. George Sand had made the connection between the July Revolution of 1830 and women, in fact a sentence from her novel 'The Miller of Angibault', unlike the 'Daughters of the American Revolution' (who belong to the most reactionary group in America and are not confined to America), posits subversion on the horizon of the women's movement too: 'The violent, terrible blow to all egoistical interests must give birth to the necessity of a universal change.' One German female pioneer from the Vormärz is quite astonishing: Luise Otto, a red democrat. She was the one who, when the revolutionary struggles broke out in 1848, founded the first German women's magazine, with the motto: 'I recruit female citizens for the realm of freedom.' The first number declares to these female citizens: 'When the times grow forcibly loud, it is inevitable that women too should hear their voice and obey it.' In 1865 Luise Otto summoned the first women's conference to Leipzig, founded the General Association of German Women and ensured that the representation of female workers and their rights also became a point in its programme. But bourgeois liberalism, still so heated before 1871, very soon became a pillar of the state in the empire; an association of women who knew what was seemly especially moderated its demands. The realm of freedom in its political aspect found few female citizens among the female citizens, their freedom

was shattered not on the barrier of sex but on that of class. The class
barrier was clearly apparent in 1896, and therefore in the early light of
the new woman and her struggle for freedom, it was apparent in the strike
of the female clothing workers in Berlin. Women were forbidden by law
to participate in political associations; a deprivation of rights against which
radical bourgeois women were the first to act. But the same bourgeois
women used this law at the time as a pretext to leave the striking female
workers in the lurch; – the class barrier cut through the claims of the
heart or the seemingly general female solidarity. Thus the question of
women's rights is a function of the social question; as had already occurred
to George Sand. And also to almost all earlier utopians: Thomas More
demanded total equality, and Fourier taught that the degree of female emancipation was the natural measure of general emancipation in a society. A
state which appears in the guise of Papua down below will not be able
to release women from their minority either, not even from their gilded
minority in the ruling class.

   In spite of all this, the question remains as to the moving force in this new
departure by women. Sex is in fact the moving force within it, but one
which steps forward and seeks to be determined in social terms. It is false
of course that only the old maid or even the masculine woman had rebelled.
It was predominantly young women who were stirred by the strange movement in the Nineties. There have always been old maids and masculine
women, but for many centuries women were silent in the community.
And women's revolt, although it occurred again and again in between
times, had no breadth up to the end of the last century. It only gained
support, and also the aspect of a thorough social utopia, when the capitalist
need for forces of production gave it a permit; when the interest in freedom
of movement released even this kind of serf. Though in this connection
no more was asked about the moving force in this new departure by women,
about the *submerged* or *remotely possible* contents of the sex, than capital
asks on the whole about the unusable qualities of its employees. People
were measured by results, ultimately only the flexibility of women was
taken into consideration, which was present and treasured in male law
even before this so-called emancipation. It was good for badly paid jobs,
for voluntary subordination; this is also a reason why the women's movement went flat. In fact, an undeniable insipidity of women, which the
cult of the Virgin Mary so vehemently refused to admit and which is not
predetermined in utopian terms either, was rewarded by capitalist objectification. And politically nothing actually changed when women were

given the right to vote, except that the votes for all previous parties doubled. Reactionary thinking was even rather more than doubled; no explosive or even just particularly humane impact of the political woman is discernible on bourgeois life. The senior female office clerk thus triumphed over what the lover not unreasonably saw in the first fictional, varied women created by this emancipation, in Ibsen's Nora, Hauptmann's Anna Mahr ('Lonely People'), Wedekind's Franziska. Thus in the bourgeois women's movement the contents of the sex certainly did not become manifest: and yet from the beginning they were intended as never before, and yet they were rejected by the opponents of emancipation, as if the movement was not heading for the office hours in which it died, but as if it was a recollection of *Carmen* on the one hand, and of *Antigone* on the other, in fact a utopian conjuring up of the *hetairan age* on the one hand, and of *matriarchy* on the other; and above all as if the women's movement were that of a specific human totality and fullness, which for this very reason, in its remotely possible contents, is inconsistent with soulless capitalist enterprise, as the mortal enemy of art and woman. The bourgeois male hatred of the women's movement announces all these themes again and again e contrario, devaluing them; and the devaluation of woman here into a hetaira seemed the cheapest and most ambivalent of all, with simultaneous reduction to no more than this, and stabilization within it. Weininger proceeded in this direction with total obsession (Sex and Character, 1903): W, the essence of woman, is accordingly downright lechery, without ego, memory, or loyalty, the totally opposite spirit to Jesus in man or to purity. Carmen thus appears as a genuine woman who has had no voice in civilization and is not at home in accepted morality: 'The need to be engaged in coition herself is woman's intensest need, but it is only a special case of her deepest, her only vital interest, which is in coition in general: of the wish that there should be as much coition as possible, by whomsoever, wherever, whenever it may be... And this characteristic of woman to be the envoy and agent of the idea of coition is also the only one which is present at all ages and even survives the menopause: the old woman goes on prostituting, no longer herself, but others' (l.c., p. 351ff.). And even more wildly: 'The education of woman must be taken away from woman, and the education of the whole of mankind must be taken away from the mother' (l.c., p. 471); for only woman as hetaira is the truth, woman as madonna is a creation of man, there is nothing that corresponds to her in reality. So much for the most vehement misogyny known to history, a single anti-utopia of woman, in the middle of the period of secession,* also during the incipient playing down of woman into a grey sister of reform. But precisely in this abyss of negation it is evident at the same time what unknown, unobjectified elements are on the move in the women's movement. After all, it was itself conceived as an emancipation of humanity from woman, that is, from the woman whose voice has been heard up till now. Its basic question was always that concerning the limits of sex, and whether these limits existed at all; whether, if she could not jump over the sexual barrier, woman could make it into a stepping-stone that would lead to hidden-untrodden contents of humanity itself. Extravagant dreams undoubtedly, aimed at an awakening of half the earth, yet with a historical and social depth, the very depth unwillingly sensed by Weininger's hatred of hetairai. Fundamentally, in accordance with its demonstrable utopia the women's movement did in fact keep the idea of *Carmen* alive, i.e. recollected *hetairanism*, but also the essence of *Antigone* as well, the second primitive woman before the age of men: recollected *matriarchy*. Both forms of life in fact preceded the patriarchal one: the irregular mixture of the sexes, which corresponded to the gathering and hunting stage, and matriliny with the primacy of woman and the earth, which corresponded to the agricultural stage. Both recollections revived again in the women's movement, explicitly and implicitly, and occupied archaic-utopian unfilled imagination. The hetairan age was interpreted by Bachofen in terms of mythical-ornamental swamp symbols (reeds, jungle), the matriarchal age in terms of night and earth symbols (moon, cave, ear of corn). The hetairan age, with an interchangeable female and male community, preceded marriage, the matriarchal age posited marriage, assigning the family and indeed the entire community to the mother. While Bachofen discovered these relationships and undoubtedly transfigured them beyond what was historically provable, he only expressed what dawned ahead on the subsequent women's movement as archaic utopia: Dionysian life on the one hand, regaining the night of Demeter on the other. Both forms of life are assigned to a 'language of the womb', which was later no longer heard in the world of male law, unless in maenad-like outbursts or in tributes of the strict masters' law to the equally older and milder law of the Bona Dea. The myth of the *female lover* thus sounds as follows in Bachofen: 'For this, Helen, who is not so richly endowed in order that, given up to the exclusive possession of one man alone, her beauty should fade, is

---

* Bloch is again referring to the breakaway movement among groups of artists in the 1890s.

the great model of every mortal woman, the symbol of every Dionysian woman.' And the myth, or rather the archaic utopia of woman as a *ruler* announces itself in Bachofen as follows: 'The relationship by means of which humanity first grows up to civilized behaviour, which serves as the starting point of the development of every virtue and the cultivation of every nobler side of existence, is the magic of motherhood which acts in the midst of a life full of violence as the divine principle of love, of agreement, of peace' (Preface to 'Matriliny'). Sex of a quite unfinished kind, one which sought to be recollected in non-capitalist terms and further determined in social utopian terms, was thus on the move in the women's movement throughout, it was not confined to old maids and masculine women. It was full of unobjectified expectation, no longer and not yet announced in previous objectivities. Woman, after such a long period of minority, had the fine presumption to want to introduce a past and never realized island of the great mother into the patriarchy.

The movement is at once outmoded, replaced and postponed, all with good reason. It is *outmoded* because it has pushed open bourgeois doors that were already open, and behind which there then proved to be nothing. The sexless worker bee is not the goal for which we started out, we cannot get any further now in bourgeois terms. It is irrelevant whether woman has the same value as man if both are employees of a firm which does not value them at all, but squeezes them dry. The movement is *replaced* because a struggle against the sexual barrier becomes pathetic without a struggle against the class barrier. The female worker does not feel discriminated against by the men of her class, any more than the young worker feels discriminated against by adults as such; thus an important element of the proletarian youth movement recurs in the proletarian women's movement. The semi-colonial status of women in general cannot be specially lamented by those who, like the working man, are themselves, if not even more so, kept as coolies. The female worker measures herself jointly with poor male workers against rich men and women, and the old social democracy already supported the programmatic statement: 'The question of women's rights coincides with the question of workers' rights.' The Soviet Union faces no question of women's rights any more, because it has solved the question of workers' rights; where master and servant cease, the lower stratum: woman also disappears. A third problem, though, a separate *problem of content*, continues to be sex, which determines woman far more extensively, but also far more indecisively than man (Gottfried Keller spoke of the 'unfathomable half-measure of woman'). This means that the women's movement, even where it is replaced by the proletarian one, is still only *postponed*. That is to say: woman the sexual being, so little clarified in previous male societies and so little defined beyond the mere family, emerges as a problem again even beyond economic and social liberation. The very decline of female oppression does not create, per se ipsum, the decline of female content. Lover, mother, even objectified worker have never yet shaped this content let alone exhausted its utopian possibilities. It is not even shaped in the categories of lover and mother, however poetically condensed; not to speak of new, previously unknown and yet possible categories. The levelling of sexual differences which appeared in the Soviet Union during the first urgent general programme of construction did not go very deep. Precisely where it depended on less regimented intervention, specifically female attitudes and energies appeared and are proving themselves over and over again. The mother, as Gorky presents her in his realistic novel, knew how to do her revolutionary work differently from her male comrades; the nature of her kindness, of her hatred and of her understanding could not be replaced by a man. On the whole, the difference between the sexes lies in a different field to the artificial differences which the class society has produced; thus it does not disappear with the latter. Sexual difference disappears so little that female nature can only become clear in socialism. Enough of it remains in any case to refurbish it in its content, to have it as Eve in search of her form. The largely ambiguous element remains, the fermenting half-decisive, wrongly decisive, indecisive muddle and tangle in woman, as the previous society delivers it to a coming one. It is something gentle and wild, destructive and compassionate, it is the flower, the witch, the haughty bronze and the efficient life and soul of business. It is the maenad and the ruling Demeter, it is the mature Juno, the cool Artemis and the artistic Minerva and all sorts of other things. It is the musical capriccioso (the violin solo in Strauss' 'Heldenleben') and the prototype of the lento, of calm. It is finally, with an arc which no man knows, the tension between Venus and Mary. All this is incompatible, but it cannot be corrected let alone abolished with a stroke of the pen through the problem of the content of woman. This is even less the case with that which has not yet been announced in woman up to now, that utopian-indefinite element which caused the great variety of previous definitions in the first place. As if they were mere attempts and experiments with names, in which the main thing has still not been named and revealed at all. Has not been nearly as revealed as in the case of man and his predicates; although the latter also has a great deal of distinctions and a great deal of unfinished material behind him, with historical guiding types like warrior, monk, citoyen and so on. The women's movement is therefore still sufficient to form a partial utopia, just as it formed one in the previous full-scale utopias. This specifically announced and hoped for element will still call for advice and action even in the classless society, as a special problem which is the legacy of history and prehistory. Consider the hetairan features in the Cynic, and in parts also in the libertine-anarchistic utopia; they have not been dealt with. Consider the matriarchal features in the Stoic social utopia and its after-effects, down to Natural Right and Rousseau's notion of a benevolent Nature; they have not been completed. Thus elements from the female partial utopia have certainly already made a contribution to previous full-scale utopias, one of unrest and of collection, and also of the distant attractive ideal (for Goethe, in his own words, 'always conceived in female form'). And the fragrance, fullness, melody of this genre continue to have an effect, mutatis mutandis, in the utopia which has progressed towards science; there thus remains a special contribution of the female-utopian content to the realm of freedom.

The desire to escape from confinement has come to an end in bourgeois society, and will only return in a classless society. Only here will there be a new tide, an open voyage, and correctly placed orders for a women's movement too. Which utopian forces and values will then begin can only be stated, like classless man as a whole, in terms of direction and not unemptied content. It is a direction which leads out of the previous bad breadth, the incompatible muddle of female types. It leads out on to an existence where the unfathomable half-measure, and also the unaimed art of experimentation disappears which in fact first made possible the false abundance of female predicates and types. An abundance whose falsity and indefiniteness is already discernible in the swift transition of one type and its attitude into another, wholly incompatible one. Since the flower-like quality in existing woman can become the 'Set it alight, set it alight!' of the witch, since the efficient life and soul of business almost effortlessly turns into a maenad, and even Venus into Mary, these individual definite characteristics often appear so provisionally, as if they were not even irregular experiments of female Being, but mere masks. 'Chaste Luna has capricious moods',* this statement, whispered by Mephisto, shows what this hysterical abundance and false breadth of variation is all about. Female emancipation

---

* 'Faust', Part II, 4955. Mephisto is prompting the Astrologer as he speaks.

of a concrete kind aims instead at genuine tests of utopian essentials; it brings out of the muddle of types the real abundance of female nature within human nature. All the more reliably as the various and alienating categories of goods and categories of rule which have helped to model the female types which have so far appeared, chiefly in capitalism, vanish in a society that is becoming classless. Then a real legacy arises beside the previous, so frequently disguised and diverted predicates of femininity, and is able to arise from them. The real Possible is more unformed in woman than in man, but also intended from time immemorial, in all visions of female perfection, as more promising; it reaches more powerfully into well-founded imagination. Just as the musical is more promising than the poetic, which is already coined by its precise statement. And just as music, where it is already formed, can go deeper than even a lot of verbal poetry, so the utopian element in woman, where it valuably appears in advance, signifies a countenance of central human depth and a comforting depth. The gentle and the compassionate element operate more intensively in the female version of mankind; the qualities once ascribed to Artemis have no equal in pure coolness among young boys; the female saint displays a Christian condition in its full glory. The bourgeois women's movement, being bourgeois, indicated little or nothing of course of such possibilities or that which may correspond to them in a new guise; it hardly got beyond contrasting trivialities like free love and suffragettes. If a human spring begins with the classless society, then so does the prospect of venturing beyond an undetermined sexual barrier, of dispelling frozen vagueness. A society without an assignable dark side of life will undoubtedly be the first to give femininity probation and licence. And woman as comrade will be that part of society which keeps her full of subject and unobjectified in every respect.

Old New Land, programme of Zionism

There is no suffering that can be compared with that of the Jews. Other small nations were also dispersed, led away from their soil, but then they quickly perished. Not even the names of the other tribes which had been dragged off to work by the Nile have come down to us. The Jews did not allow themselves to be gobbled up, as we know, although they were constantly between the teeth of their host nations. Devoted to trade and the Scriptures, they rescued their fearful existence in the face of endless killing, until after long centuries the air outside the ghetto seemed a little less dangerous. The Jew was now simply beaten, despised, but no longer burnt to death. This patronage further increased, in the course of bourgeois liberation, the yellow patch was removed from the caftan, the latter also disappeared, and around 1800 the Jewish fellow citizen emerged in the West. He took up his new position trustingly, and since doings and dealings prevailed in the world outside anyway, and also the more chivalrous or official professions continued to remain closed to him, the start was for the most part commercial. He entered existing capitalist society, no longer, as in the Spanish heyday, a feudal and ecclesiastically learned society. This causes distinctions; they are not simply a burden to those Jews who so smartly went into general business life, the station of the cross is also important at which the long life of suffering finally stops. This station was the capitalist one, for the same reason that it was the provisionally liberating one: free competition requires the legal equality of its partners. Amongst these partners the best Jewish element did not always come to light, any more than the best German or French element. The stock market does not look good from all angles, and it was the columns of the liberal press from which the breath of the age blew most fiercely. The Jewish spirit came to be one which gabbled everything to pieces, which produced solely for the market, and distinguished itself in this respect. Only in the beginning, when liberation arrived, this sort of thing did not yet become apparent. The fall of the walls which had surrounded so much oppression and of course also so much seriousness and devout strictness seemed even biblical. It was a first red dawn, that of conformity; behind it nothing but democratic happiness was suspected, new life after long paralysis. It was not just the Jews however, but also the Gentiles who did not, as we know, wholly achieve what was hoped for in this liberation. The equality of Jews with others, if it ever existed, was a temporary exception, it never became a rule. In the end that which seemed unthinkable only to the fools who believed in an empty rolling progress returned, returned in an intensified form: extermination. The liberal citizen stood by, arms at the ready, in so far as he was not himself aiming his rifle at Jews. There seemed or seems nothing left for it but to separate for good from fellow citizens who endangered their lives, a homeland* gleams before them.

---

*Bloch is not using his own concept 'Heimat' here for 'homeland'. We translate it thus in this section in view of the language of the Balfour declaration discussed below.

This had been longed for for ages, even when conformity flourished. Many would not have chosen to be Jewish of course, but now nothing could be done about it they pretended to be proud of the fact. This was a false pride, and they only paid lip-service to the Promised Land. Just as many Jews have now become extremely Zionist who do not want to emigrate at all from the country where they are getting on tolerably well. They are Zionist partly out of sympathy for exiled racial comrades, partly out of the passion with which one usually takes out accident insurance. And for the last two thousand years orthodox Jews have been expressing the wish in their prayers: next year in Jerusalem; although a strong aversion to actual return emanated from these very circles. Nevertheless, the dream of a restored kingdom of David had never wholly died in political terms; there were military adventurers like David Reübeni (around 1530), who called upon the nation so long unaccustomed to arms to undertake a kind of Jewish crusade against the Turks. There was the false Messiah Sabbatai Zewi (around 1640), who first wanted to call Israel home to Jerusalem in the campaign of redemption. Provided that a nation still felt itself to be such and still had coherence, it seemed hard to take away from it the memory of the soil where it took root and, in frequently deceptive memory, was happy. Even the exiled Spanish Jews were consumed by longing, if not for Palestine, then for Spain, and have often remembered down to the present day the names of long-vanished streets, and long-collapsed houses in which their ancestors had lived as señores. Thus even real naturalization, when the bourgeois sky still had a friendly aspect, did not prevent wishes to return in everyone, in this case without lip-service, wishes which were even passionately genuine. Astonishingly it did not even prevent a varied, leading, teaching connection with the international labour movement. On the contrary, the socialist Moses Hess, the former friend and precursor of Marx and Engels, the later friend of Lassalle, admittedly a permanently idealistic dialectician, wrote in 'Rome and Jerusalem', 1862, the most moving Zionist dream-book. He was aided in this by the simultaneously warm and obscure manner in which he believed in race as a source of inspiration. Hess was an upright revolutionary to the end, but nevertheless belonged to the 'brainspinning' of the left-wing Hegelian school. He belonged to the 'true socialism' whose economic ignorance, speculative cobwebs, and practical naivety were afterwards so sharply criticized by the 'Communist Manifesto'. Hess remained within idealistic dialectics although, indeed because he wanted to intersperse Hegel's self-movement of reason with that 'of energy and the will'. With this 'philosophy of action' he went back far more to Fichte's active deeds than forward to a comprehension of the economic-material factors of history. He adopted Marx's economic-materialist interpretation of history, but almost at the same time accused Marx and Engels of having 'exchanged the nebulous standpoint of German philosophy for the narrow and petty standpoint of English economics'. Economics was thus defined by Hess himself in the narrow sense, not in the total social sense of Marx; he regarded it as the typical class science of the bourgeoisie. Consequently even 'energy and will', the driving forces in dialectics activistically introduced by Hess, were not primarily understood in terms of radical economic change but ethically, approximating to Fichte's active deeds, and finally in terms of racial theory. Alongside the proletariat, which is still celebrated as the real subject of radical practice, race was the shaping force of history for the later Moses Hess. Of course, Marx and Engels also discussed race, as a kind of inner aspect of nature, and this must not be forgotten. In a letter of 1894, Engels acknowledged race 'as an economic factor', and Marx also declared economic development to be 'dependent on the favourable nature of the circumstances, on the racial character'. There were nations with more or less 'temperament and disposition for capitalist production', and Marx names the Turks among the less disposed. But Marx and Engels made race neither into an intrinsically determining factor nor into a constant factor within history; racial fetishist ideas are totally smashed. The racial disposition is also historically redisposed again and again in Marx by man's work: 'Because he acts through this movement on the nature outside him and changes it, he also changes his own nature at the same time.' It is different in the case of Moses Hess, different because apart from appearing as an economic factor race also appears in his work as a factor independently shaping ideology, even with the same economic substructure: and for him the strongest spiritual race is and remains Jewish. There have been several small Near Eastern nations with a fairly similar agrarian economy and political constitution but, Moses Hess adds, 'only the Jews have carried the banner which the nations are following today'. It is the moral-prophetic banner, and only for its sake, for the sake of the inscription: Zion, are Jews to be planted in their old soil again. Thus Zionism wanted this to be done on the basis of Zion and not on that of a chance sojourn of the Jews in Palestine two thousand years ago: 'Carry your banner high, my people', Hess demands in 'Rome and Jerusalem' – 'The living corn is stored in you which, like the seed corns in Egyptian mummies, has lain dormant for thousands of years but has not lost its powers of germination...Only from national rebirth will the religious genius of the Jews, like the giant who touches native soil, draw new strength and be filled by the holy spirit of the prophets again.' But the content of these emotive expressions or missions, of this rather long-winded edification, remains socialism alone for Hess the revolutionary: he was one of the first to apply Judaism, as he knew it from the works of the prophets, to the cause of the revolutionary proletariat. Socialism becomes for Hess 'the victory of the Jewish mission in the spirit of the prophets'; only to this end did this international socialist plan 'an action centre in Palestine, in which the spirit of the Jewish race can rise again'. Admittedly with the aid of France, though not of imperialistic France but that of the great Revolution, which Hess thought was still at work within it. 'Once on its own soil again, once lifted back on to the rails of world history again', the Jewish nation was to astonish the House of Rothschild: 'The social animal kingdom, which lives off the mutual exploitation of human beings, is coming to an end.' So much for the Zionist utopia of Moses Hess, dreamed and designed as a socialist one ab ovo, based on the prophets.

But the western Jews were mostly bourgeois, there were not many workers among them. The Zionist dreams therefore only gained influence on these middle classes in so far as they no longer had a socialist ring, but were moderate and liberal. Long after Hess, a generation later, Theodor Herzl appeared, the originator of the only Zionist programme to become effective, maybe with Jeremiah, but without Isaiah. This for two reasons, one political and one ideological, both in keeping with the situation of a Jewish bourgeoisie to which Zionism passed, very much without socialism. Politically, in the wake of the crises of the middle classes, the thin liberal pro-semitism of the surrounding world had swiftly been completely undermined again. Ideologically, liberal Judaism itself wanted to know very little about committed love, about the revolutionary love which its prophets had preached and which would have cost more money than suited mere charity. Politically it promoted Herzl's success that a so-called Anti-Semitic League had arisen, that trials for ritual murder advanced from Russia and Rumania to Hungary and Germany. Herzl saw in the Dreyfus trial that even the classic bourgeois land of human rights no longer remained what it was, and he drew from this no conclusions about the citizens themselves, on whose side he remained, but about their character as Gentiles. What was ideologically decisive for Herzl's influence on the Jewish bourgeoisie was in fact the bourgeois détente, the liberal level of enlightenment which was given here to the dream of Zion. Above all, Herzl removed every connection with the social radicalism of the prophets, with socialist mission and other so-called extravagances of Moses Hess; Zionism thus became acceptable to the liberal Jewish bourgeoisie. Now Herzl found the model for a separate Jewish state in the manifold irredentist movement as which the Austro-Hungarian monarchy masqueraded; like Czechs, Poles, Ruthenians, Rumanians, Serbs, and Italians, the Jews were also to return home to their own nation-state. Not even the ancient golden sound of Jerusalem was heard at first; Herzl's utopia wavered initially, in search of the land of the future, between Argentina and Palestine. And the paths to Canaan were political realist and diplomatic ones, cleverly taking into account existing shady deals and imperialist interests of several great powers: 'The Jewish question is a national question; in order to solve it, we must above all make it into a world question which will have to be solved in the council of civilized nations.' Moses Hess, as we have seen, also had international political aid in mind, that of France; but what was naivety or a kind of Romanticism in Hess, stemming from 1789, became capitalist approval in Herzl. The only alternative for Judaism seemed extinction through intermarriage or national rebirth: Herzl preached the latter, but in the form of a capitalist-democratic miniature state by the grace of England or even Germany; under sovereignty of the sultan. There thus appeared 'The Jewish State', 1896, worked out as a scheme in considerable detail, co-operative private capitalism with land reform, the land is public property, and is only leased for fifty years at any one time. The entire civilization of the turn of the century is transferred: 'When we troop out of Egypt again, we will not forget the fleshpots.' Thus 'the fairytale will come true', if the Jews want it to, and a utopian novel 'Old New Land', 1900, further pictured the bourgeois land of progress, sitting in one's own tent, beneath one's own vine, at home as before, so to speak, in Europe, but now by oneself. In keeping with the slight economic change in the model Jewish state, this utopia is set not far in the future: it claims to be a report from the year 1920. Even in the 'Jewish State', critics like Achad Haam had found few Jewish elements, almost none, which would have differed from the business of western civilization other than through the admittedly invaluable security with which this business was now to be continued on their own soil, in their own cities. In modern Hebrew, certainly also with the hoped-for 'de-complication' through agriculture, dairy co-operatives and other kinds of return to the land, which every bank manager finds a sound proposition. Herzl's Zion was thus a utopia of the immediately

attainable, with a capitalist-democratic background; firmly rooted in the
soil, the only thing it did not yet have, it did not tilt at any windmills.
If it thus recommended itself to the specific idealism of the Jewish
businessman, and lawyer too, then as far as the national element is concerned this utopia cut very sharply through assimilation, much more sharply
than Moses Hess; pride, not a sense of mission was the substance of Jewish
national consciousness according to Herzl. The diaspora with its thousands
of distortions and forms of pariahdom was to be reversed, but so was Moses
Mendelssohn or assimilation, as a false red dawn, in which the diaspora
had not been cleared but affirmed. Instead the second and true red dawn
now seemed to be breaking with Zionism or anti-Mendelssohn: 'a homeland
for the Jewish nation in Palestine protected under public law'. In spite
of the fact that at least the immigrants keen on investment and most
certainly the fleshpots of Egypt presuppose and profit by a strong assimilation. The Hasidim would not have founded a Tel Aviv, the study of the
Talmud would not have deposited an Einstein manuscript in the University
of Jerusalem, and there would not be any professors of the cabbala there,
but cabbalists. Jewish fascism in particular, as a consequence of the adopted
contemporary capitalist-democratic state, would be totally unknown
without such an adoption. Herzl's utopia is in nuce itself more of an
assimilation than the apparently much more assimilated utopia of the
romantic Zionist Moses Hess. The latter was much more closely connected
with the old Messianism, a believer in the social Zion, who fought in
the labour movement up to the moment he died, and who believed he
was activating the spirit of the prophets precisely in his connection with
the international labour movement. As Hess, unlike Herzl, tried to show,
there is clearly a Zionism for which the family grave is less important than
resurrection. If not that of the Jewish national consciousness of the
bourgeoisie, then that of a very old, frequently submerged faith. If this
faith, because it is still a utopia, also sought an 'action centre in Palestine',
then this centre was clearly conceived as radiating outwards, as an appeal
to the world and not as a miniature state. The element of social mission
and prophetic legacy which is still at work in Judaism and which makes
it uniquely important was proclaimed by Moses Hess far from Palestine,
and made current by Marx even in total alienation from Palestine. For
them, Zion was everywhere where the 'social animal kingdom' is destroyed
and the diaspora comes to an end: that of all the exploited.

When the dream had been turned into a bourgeois one by Herzl, it immediately began to work. It was undoubtedly skilfully nurtured, from 1897 Zionist congresses regularly took place in Basle. The movement grew, a voluntary transplantation of minorities such as had not yet occurred before. It also came close to success again and again, and this was owing to a totally unsentimental trend which promoted it even among Gentiles. If there had in fact even been sentimental trends towards Zionism among Gentiles, then this was also true of millenarians in the English revolution and of other Adventist sects, again and again. But this sort of thing was powerless, temporary and mystical, the ruling class is not expecting Elijah. On the other hand, the English ruling class had long been interested in safeguarding the overland route to India, and Palestine fitted the bill. Hollingworth, a political writer, suggested a Jewish state in this spot even earlier than Hess, let alone Herzl (Jews in Palestine, 1852). Lords Palmerston, Beaconsfield (the latter admittedly flirting with a highly illustrious Israelite tribal feeling), and Salisbury were already negotiating with the Porte* over the concession. It is true that England was not only interested in the overland route, in 1903 it also offered Herzl land in East Africa, for which colonists were lacking and which it did not want to populate with convicts as was once the case with Australia. Besides, it was not just England that was interested in Palestine, Wilhelm II and German imperialism also had Zionist sympathies; in 1898 the Kaiser discussed with Herzl a Jewish Palestine under German protection and Turkish sovereignty. The reason for this was the interest, which has become proverbial, of the Deutsche Bank in the Baghdad railway and all that was connected with it; it was the whole German legacy-hunting around Turkey, the Sick Man of Europe. Thus Zionism was certainly entrusted on several sides to 'the council of civilized nations', as Herzl had said, a piece on the board of imperialist politics. But when German imperialism lost the game and Turkey stood there without this 'patron of Islam', the thing which had been waiting for so long in the files of the Foreign Office for its moment to come was proclaimed in 1917: the Balfour Declaration. A British mandate of Palestine was declared as a homeland for the Jewish nation under public law. Parts of Herzl's programme thereby admirably suited imperialist England, magnanimous as always, and the realization, if we can call it that, of the Zionist dream arrived in time to establish a refuge for the later victims of fascism. Or rather, it would have arrived in time if the

---

* The Sublime Porte, the central office of the Ottoman government. An old diplomatic term derived via the French from the Turkish title.

England which opened the homeland had not closed it at the very moment when it was most urgently needed. But in 1939, the appropriate year, a White Paper appeared to the following effect: in the next five years at most 75,000 Jews will be admitted, and after that no more without Arab consent, hence no more in fact. A peaceful business situation in Arab Egypt and Moslem India was automatically dearer to the hearts of the English philanthropists than saving the lives of the European Jews – 'and', said Churchill, 'the logic in doing so is simple'. It simply left several million Jews to be slaughtered by the Nazis, and in fact, it drove them back into their hands again by preventing them from landing in Palestine; England aided and abetted the murder which, moral as always, it so hotly condemned. The homeland from the period of the Balfour Declaration was immediately interpreted as an 'Arab state', and its Jewish population was not allowed to amount to more than a third of the Arab one. Herzl's Jewish state had thus resulted in a numerus clausus of the Jewish right of abode, which was unknown in any other country before the Jewish state, apart from Tsarist Russia. The reality which came about accordingly corresponds to Herzl's means of realizing it: the land of the Jews became one from which politically awkward Jews could even be deported as troublesome foreigners. Certainly, the means do not always ruin the end, the relationship between cause and effect does not hold good here, where causa aequat effectum, but different means can also possibly lead to a good end; but then the end itself must be a powerful one and not a begging one. If it is not powerful, then it does not use the means but the means uses it, and if it is constructed on exactly the same capitalist-democratic lines as the England whose imperialism it uses as a means, then the interest of the stronger capital must triumph over the programmes of the weaker one. Zion thus became a fraction of the business to be attended to in the English empire, and Jewish secession, since it occurred as an invasion, became an object of hate for the Arab national revolutionary movement, which for its part represents in turn a card in the game of British imperialism. Now the Jews who escaped from fascism or even simply social discrimination have a new conflict with the Arabs, and the planned Jewish state is more precarious than any assimilation ever was, up to Hitler. The difficulties here by no means appear to be temporary ones, unless geographical Zionism itself becomes a mere – programme once again, that is, after the end of Hitler's fascism only a handful of Jews from capitalist countries demands admission to Palestine again. Or far more thoroughly: the difficulties decrease because a general social upheaval also solves these

miniature problems dripping with blood. And it is not then Herzl the
Jew from the New Free Press who will be responsible for this upheaval,
but Marx the Jew, who was not merely no Zionist but only became what
he is and was able to do what he did because he was not a Zionist. Precisely
the originally better, subjectively pure, though false will at the outset of
Zionist enthusiasm: that of a real new beginning in Palestine, with a very
different nervus rerum than before, does not come with Herzl's blessing,
let alone as a result of it. Tremendous enthusiasm poured with Jewish
youth into the cultivation of the old earth, agrarian communes were formed,
related in their intention to those of Owen or Cabet in North America,
and in places even attempted collective farms; very far at any rate from
Tel Aviv, the real contemporary expression of the bourgeoisie and speculation. But all this only promoted the fact that the state of Israel, populated
by the flight from fascism, has itself become a fascist state. And at this
bitter end, which was not yet foreseen even by Herzl, Israel even became
the – not even well-kept – cur of American imperialism in the Near East.
Both the archetype of Moses, and the other of Egypt – the desert – Canaan
have developed a different power and hope in revolutions. But the Jewish
state looks as if these archetypes of its own have become alien to Judaism
itself; which is not always the case, however, as the example of Marx
shows. Here, too, the conclusion remains that there is no isolated solution
to any problem of minorities or nationalities as such. This means that there
is no solution to the so-called Jewish question, in so far as it exists, without
an overall solution to the economic and social one. Zionism is not even
possible in Palestine without such a settlement; there is no pax Britannica
any more, let alone a pax Americana. And however many psychological,
anthropological or even mythological secondary causes anti-semitism, a
stubborn and conspicuous phenomenon, may have, its basis is the precarious
economy. It was after all precisely a Russian Zionist in the days of Lenin
who felt compelled to observe that Bolshevism was beginning to realize
what the old prophets had preached; the Soviet goal was biblical, whether
people knew it or not. If that is so, then Judaism in the spirit of Moses
Hess is intact and has new things to do, even without its own miniature
state. Zionist utopia was not alone in cultivating the special distinction
of being transfigured past and hoped-for future at one and the same time;
this is cultivated by other national and minority utopias too. Such as the
Wends in Prussia, the Czechs, the Poles before 1918, they all had a
traditional-utopian dream of resurrection; even the Germans had it, in the
imperial dream between 1806 and 1871, in its various patriotic fantasies.

So a mere irredentist movement does not distinguish the Zionist group utopia from others or do it credit; even if the Jews were only regarded as Ahasueruses* where the Poles, divided up among three empires, were still at home. On the other hand, the unique feature of the Jewish utopia is the obligation, posited along with it and stressed not for the first time by Moses Hess, to act in accordance with the intention of the prophets; and this obligation, as a result of the revolutionary situation which has ripened in Europe since the days of Moses Hess, certainly needs no 'action centre in Palestine' any more. It needs no geographical Zionism; in an extensive liberation movement the Jews have room at any time to make the last ghetto superfluous. To line up with the movement towards the light, in every country to which we belong, this seems the genuine homeland of the Jews. Provided that Judaism not only represents a more or less anthropological quality, but a certain messianic emotion, *one for the genuine Canaan*, which is no longer restricted in national terms; *Thomas Münzer, 'with the sword of Gideon', displayed it, the House of Rothschild did not.*

It is mostly right to explain hatred in economic terms from the start. What can be directly seized, often what is someone else's, and even better what is weak, simply gives grounds for giving vent to it. For ages it was easiest to vent hatred and rage on the Jews, on poor ones as well as and even better than on rich ones; it remains the simplest thing to blame them for disaster. They are not as conspicuous as the gypsies, let alone the negroes, but they are more popular scapegoats, precisely because of their familiar strangeness as it were. Until the Nazis arrived, they were not charged with such monstrous things as witches had once been, but instead they are more credible as mischief-makers to an enlightened rabble as it were. There are wishes and non-wishes, images on which what was wished for was unloaded, and images on which what was not wished for was unloaded, and the Jews, as Musil splendidly remarks on one occasion, provided the non-wish image, which was formerly the fetish that the sorcerer pulled out of the sick man's throat. The human delight in a whipping boy was therefore undoubtedly added to economic distress, a very old and stubborn delight. All this is true, and yet without famine, without fine gentlemen and deflectors there would not have been this fattening of scapegoats. The motivation of anti-Semitism changed three times in the course of time, even its intensity was different in each case, but in spite of all this its essential feature remains recognizable. In antiquity the alleged arrogance was regarded as provocative

* Ahasuerus: the Wandering Jew.

with which the Jews cut themselves off from the Gentiles, had their own
rules about food and their own feast days and other things as well. Philo the
Jew even maintained that Plato owed his best work to Moses, which was
undoubtedly going too far, especially in a Rome still little influenced by the
Middle East. In the Middle Ages, Judas furnished the motive for anti-
Semitism, despite the fact that all the other disciples were also Jews, like Jesus
himself. In the age of fascism, though, racial theory and the wise men of
Zion make up the business of anti-Semitism; for the crucifixion of Jesus the
Jew no longer enrages fascists at all, they sympathize with it instead, indeed
the blood of the whole of Jewry is to be drained with his blood, so that
the Aryan is finally redeemed. Incompatible motives obviously and yet,
as the anti-Semites say, united in their instinct against the Jew. So that
the Jew still offered a unique starting-point for false consciousness and
the ideology surrounding economic grounds for a pogrom. As if there
really was something in this group of people which has condemned them for
two thousand years to allow themselves to be treated as the guilty cause of
every problem. This broad availability of the Jews for the purpose of the
bogeyman almost represents a counterpart to the broad availability which
the Bible has found in the entire white race for the purpose of edification.
And it is unprecedented that the authorship of that same Bible is granted to
the Jews, but they are still cheated of the honour this brings with it. This can
also be expressed in poetic terms, as Beer-Hofmann has done in 'Jacob's
Dream', where the devil prophesies: 'People may well incline to your word/
But they will smash the mouth to pulp that spoke it:/You shall be a nation
from which everyone takes the spoils.' This double view of Judaism, this unprecedented split consciousness in the apperception of Judaism undoubtedly
indicates an uncanny hatred of the object, a hatred which has become almost
autarkical, within which the economic diversionary tactics could only succeed.
All this is true too of course, just as true as the delight in a whipping boy,
and yet even the not very rational source of offence which the Jewish object
may represent would never have been effective without a profit economy.
The fact remains that the economic-social revolution sweeps the Jewish
question in an instant under the table. Anti-Semitism is not an eternal
institution, as the Zionists would have us believe, and if it were one, then
it would not be mitigated by the invasion of an Arab country, with new
frictions, and a new protective Judaism, but solely by the self-banishment
of the Jews to a desert island, without windows and doors. Which would
be neither capitalist-democratic, in the sense of Theodor Herzl, nor by
any means socialist, in the grand sense of Moses Hess; the latter would

now no longer locate his imagined Jerusalem in Jerusalem, in the age of
the Soviet Union and the movement towards Soviet Unions. The end of
the tunnel is in sight, certainly not from the standpoint of Palestine, but
from Moscow; – ubi Lenin, ibi Jerusalem. It is not in question whether
the Jews are still a nation or not; if they had ceased to be a nation, as
is totally the case in Western Europe, then what they had lost could certainly
be regained through renewed separation, and in Palestine something of
the kind has clearly succeeded in the Hebrew-speaking generation that was
born there. This may be gratifying and even necessary from a national
Jewish standpoint, but it is no more moving than the preservation of other
small nations. Judaism still claims in its Bible at least a *more specific pathos*
of its existence, without which pathos its existence would be immaterial.
So what is in question is solely this: do the Jews, whether a nation or
not, still as such have a consciousness of what the God of exodus said
to his servant Israel, not as a promise, but as a task: 'I have put my spirit
upon him: he shall bring forth judgment to the Gentiles' (Isaiah 42, 1).
With the apostrophe to the very nation for which misery has been prophesied and which has learnt better than any other nation what it is all
about: 'To open the blind eyes, to bring out the prisoners from the prison,
and them that sit in darkness out of the prison house' (Isaiah 42, 7). The
Jews also did this kind of missionary work, though on nothing like the
Christian or Moslem scale. Nubian tribes accepted the Mosaic Law, in
the second century A.D. the Jewish religion spread to China, and in the
eighth century the Chazar empire, with its capital Astrakhan, went over
to Judaism. All this occurred late of course, and probably not because of
an actual agitation; the diaspora also became less and less inviting. And
almost all scriptural texts only tackle the idea of a mission as that *messianic
tendency* and the future of its expansion which is to be kept open by Jews:
'They shall not hurt nor destroy in all my holy mountain: for the earth
shall be full of the knowledge of the Lord, as the waters cover the sea'
(Isaiah 11, 9). The memory of such tendencies can be just as burning in
Jews who do not have any trace of Zionist national consciousness as it
is in Joachim of Fiore. Conversely it can be totally lacking in Jews who
merely apply the age of a highly intensified nationalism to themselves and
confuse every future International with the cosmopolitanism of commercial
travellers. Or with the opinion that the International would be nothing
but all the national flags sewn together; then it would be important of
course to have a blue and white Zionist flag in the combine too. But if
Judaism is a prophetic movement, that is, a movement towards that which

has been conceived as Zion for three thousand years, then it definitely belongs among the nations and not to an English protectorate at the eastern corner of the Mediterranean. In which it is not foxes and wolves who say good night to one another, but the Suez Canal and Mosul oil, Arab tension and the British sphere of influence, the sinking empire and the American monster who say good day to one another. This sort of thing is rather too little to suit the idea of Moses Hess, or too much. If a Jewish nation still exists, then its liberation coincides with social liberation, or its state is an invention in which the British speculative buyer has no longer shown such an interest as in 1917, as in the solvent age of the Empire, and which is now leading America into atomic war. If a Jewish nation no longer exists, then experience shows that there remains an old affinity in the best Jews with everything which suggests the destruction of the great Babel, and a New World. This dream has its action centre where the country of their birth and education is, where it helps to build the language, history, and culture of the latter, where it participates both patriotically and expertly in the struggle for a new earth. Hic Rhodus, hic salta, Zion is everywhere according to the intention of the prophets, and the local mount in Palestine has long since become a symbol. Nazi Germany was its strongest counter-blow, the Soviet Union defeated this counter-blow, for all the oppressed in the world, including the Jews, in harmony with the universalist hope of the prophets. In short, this partial movement could come to an end without a Jewish component itself coming to an end, whether as a nation, whether – in a considerably more genuine fashion – as witness to and evidence of a messianic cast of mind; Zionism flows out into socialism, or it does not flow out at all.

Novels set in the future and full-scale utopias after Marx:
Bellamy, William Morris, Carlyle, Henry George

It was some weeks later. It was now the middle of November, and Mr Britling, very warmly wrapped in his thick dressing-gown and his thick llama wool pyjamas, was sitting at his night desk, and working ever and again at an essay, an essay of preposterous ambitions, for the title of it was 'The Better Government of the World'.   *H.G. Wells, Mr Britling Sees It Through*

Since everything grows worse in bourgeois terms, the dream does not come to an end even here. But it is only reasonably fresh when it announces itself in a group and subsequently for it. If a tomorrow is pictured as a whole however, then this mostly becomes deceit in late bourgeois terms, and at best it becomes a game, or romantic. We shall possibly have to speak about these last two varieties later, at least they kept utopian inclination afloat. The prophetic light novel provided this kind of thing among non-proletarian strata, in the inquisitive petit bourgeoisie. Hertzka's 'A Journey to Freeland', 1889, belongs here, with a girl from Freeland in it, mildly advocating agrarian reform. Even a private-capitalist fairytale of an ideal state ventured forward, rare even in ancient times, and bold so to speak today: Thirion's 'Neustria', 1901, devoted to a new Gironde. The capitalist future was seen in a better light in Tarde's 'Underground Man', 1905: images of attempted restoration arise where the past is concerned, but solely those of underground escape where the future is concerned. Air, light and sunshine, however, are to cure the defects at home in Ebenezer Howard's 'Tomorrow', 1898, and also in his 'Garden Cities of Tomorrow', 1902. The first garden city is pictured in the latter, organized according to nothing but 'social functions'; what keeps the chimneys burning* is rather less clear. Weak in insight, rich in ideas, such an organization is to be established and to succeed.

And as usual it is not at all clear by what means life is radically changed into something better. The American *Bellamy* still appears the most sympathetic of all here with his once famous book 'Looking Backward', 1888, published in German by Dietz as 'Ein Rückblick aus dem Jahr 2000'. The story in which it is cloaked is well-tested colportage: a rich Bostonian, Mr Julius West, is buried shortly before his wedding, after he had sunk into a magnetic sleep; he is dug up in the year 2000, the magnetic sleep has conserved his body, and Mr West becomes a citizen of the American ideal state which has arisen in the meantime. The reader can now inspect this construct of the future as if through opera glasses; more than in any previous utopia that which is dreamed appears as a fabulous present. Thus Bellamy satisfies the demand rejected by Marxists to give a picture of future society; his sensational novel, for all its shallowness and the superficiality of its civilization, is not without agile socialist imagination. It hallucinates, knowing Marx at best by hearsay, an egalitarian organization of economic life, without slums, banks, stock markets, and courts; America (!) is regarded here as a 'pioneer of general radical change'. There is no money

---

* The general meaning of the German phrase alluded to here, 'damit der Schornstein raucht', is 'to keep body and soul together'.

any more, only goods and credit notes for the work accomplished. Not higher wages but social competitiveness in the service of the nation and degrees of distinction provide the impetus in the general army of workers. Like working hours, the horde of civil servants is amazingly reduced, a simplified, clearly arranged, generous administration prevails on all sides, a kind of card-index of the distribution of goods is started, statistics of supplies. Even at the beginning of the twentieth century, Bellamy relates, capital had passed out of the hands of a few, in which it was concentrated, to the state, and what is more 'without any violence'. State socialism has arisen since then, that is, the state has transformed itself into a large business association, to whose profit and savings all citizens have an equal right. Thus Bellamy propagates a kind of centralist socialism, though rather within the framework of Babbitt-wishes. Bellamy's utopia lies flawlessly in the line of extension of the modern world, it is fundamentally satisfied with the disposition of capitalist civilization. The nationalization of private property only removes the social defects and hindrances from the current state of affairs, but it does not change the general style. The earth becomes a gigantic Boston or better still Chicago with a bit of agriculture in between; the latter region was formerly called Nature. Many 'good Europeans', incidentally, viewed America as mechanized like this anyway, but in a bad sense, even the America that already existed; so that Bellamy's utopia produced a flood of other contrasting utopias and the old Europe so to speak rose up against the American's socialism of the business association, with a romantic counter-move.

Not only is the stock market then supposed to disappear, but the very steel and iron in which it deals. The most significant rejoinder to Bellamy's steam-association was called 'News from Nowhere', 1891, and was written by *William Morris*, the great innovator in English industrial art, the friend of Ruskin and the romantic anti-capitalist. Morris, architect and draughtsman, maker of glass and ceramics, producer of furniture, fabrics, carpets, and wallpaper, was in agreement with Ruskin: only work done by hand puts things right, machines are hell. So the driving force here is not sympathy with the poor, or rage against the rich, but a previously unfamiliar note is struck in a social-utopian fashion: Morris is a socialist craftsman, a homespun socialist. 'News from Nowhere' is thus not merely a contrasting utopia to Bellamy, it is a campaign against the whole mechanization of existence. The world of profit leaves a lot to be desired not only in moral, but also in aesthetic terms, and this was the source of the anger with capital here. Or as the architect van der Velde expresses it in his essay on Ruskin: 'Towards the end of the last century the situation was such that we were suffocating beneath the burden of the ugliness of things. Never, at any moment in world history, had the decline in taste, the weakness of ideas and the indifference towards work and materials reached such a low level.' Thus capitalism is fought by Morris not so much because of its inhumanity as because of its ugliness, and this is measured against the old craftsmanship. This is why 'News from Nowhere' no longer contains any profiteering of course, any degrading and uninspired work, indeed any money and wages; but of equal importance here is the fact that there should be a terracotta frieze of figures beneath the tiles of every house. Morris prophesies the revolution as the fruit and self-destruction of 'unnatural' industrialism, and he welcomes the revolution, though only as an act of annihilation. For once it has died down, not only the capitalists but also the factories will be destroyed, in fact the whole plague of civilization in the modern age will have been removed. Revolution therefore appears to this machine-wrecker to be a sheer turning back of history or a dismantling; once it has done its work, the world of craftsmanship will return, people will stand – after the modern age has disappeared – on the colourful ground of native Gothic, which was only disguised in the English renaissance. In other words, of half-timbered houses seen from a socialist perspective, of old market-places and inns, with massive fireplaces and their chimney-hoods, of country mansions and Oxford colleges. And on related ground Morris' utopia dreams up a new construction in the twenty-first century, it follows in the direction of medieval tendencies, but de-feudalized and secularized. The towns are dispersed in a clear re-agrarianization, a rural life in the midst of nature dispenses with the noisy and unnatural, truly diabolical machines which stifle the happiness of mankind and kill beauty. The modern age was the age of diminished human beings, regulated and boxed up in tenement houses like anthills: this age of insects passed away in the twenty-first century as if it had never been. Thus the earth is freed of factories and urban monsters, capitalism and industrialism are abolished, complete human beings and old craftsmanship flourish again in place of mechanical horrors. This backward-looking utopia is reminiscent of the longings at the time of the Restoration, of the Romantic infatuation with the Middle Ages and the wish to see it approaching again from the future. But the conservative political brief which the Romantics had over a hundred years before is missing; Ruskin's and Morris' backward utopia was not intended in a politically reactionary way. It wanted progress from the standpoint of an abandoned position, agrarian-artisan reaction for the sake of a revolutionary new beginning. The old Romanticism had still lacked this agrarian-artisan longing; there was no cause for it as yet amongst the profusion of well-preserved country towns and the peaceful beauty of life. Seldom has a utopian homespun city appeared more tasteful than in William Morris, but seldom too has it been directed at such a small circle, with its simultaneously naive and sentimental intellectual mixture of Gothic revival and revolution. The circle has admittedly increased since the Gothic revival was obliterated and the aversion to the haste, enervation and artificiality of mechanical life grew along with this. Especially since the lost goods of a more peaceful distant past have been sought by all kinds of mottled reactionary thinking in rectified capitalism, instead of in capitalism which has been surmounted and driven to abrupt change. The bourgeois utopias now end; with his neo-Gothic Arcadia Morris supplied the last original, though redundant motif.

Unless we also include *Carlyle* and the obsession with heroes which he conjured up. This was likewise opposed to the industrial world, but only ostensibly, since this exhorter did not so much look at grey misery from behind as look down on it from above. His puritanical sermons on working and not despairing were precisely associated with the imperialist kind, which by no means want to shut down the factories but rather the class struggle. This plan is also relevant here; it was after all Carlyle, in conjunction with Nietzsche, who contributed a lot directly after Marx to a utopian, and then terrible cult of the leader. Of course, Carlyle is still pure, is very much a moral person, as they say, an individualist and later definitely a patriarchalist. He definitely sought 'the happiness from which all life streams' only in individuals, but in those who make a fine combination. He suffered like Ruskin from the new factory civilization, and he coined the undoubtedly anti-capitalist phrase that cash payment was the sole connecting link in modern society. He hated Manchesterist liberalism, described the misery of the English working classes and not just the ugliness of the factory buildings, and utopianized a world which 'is no longer surrounded by cold general laissez faire'. He understood the French Revolution as the breakthrough of the industrial age and of its anarchy, but unlike Ruskin and Morris he did not evaluate it solely in negative terms but also positively, without any longing for the stale Middle Ages: 'French Revolution means here the open violent Rebellion, and Victory, of disimprisoned Anarchy against corrupt worn-out Authority.' Above all, the power of industry cannot be removed by anything any more; Carlyle, with his puritan work ethic, is not sparing in his contempt for 'the lazy and phantom aristocracy

since the end of the Middle Ages'. Nevertheless, the same friend of
the victims of industry, the same enemy of both liberalism and feudalism,
produced out of blazing ignorance one of the most reactionary late utopias;
in so far as this sort of thing can still be called utopia, let alone 'eutopia',
the land of happiness. Carlyle was the first to posit the leader-workforce-
relationship, and hence the industrial neo-feudalism which was slyly rampant
even before the days of fascism and merged with it in a systematic and
violent manner. He was the first to posit the 'captain of industry'; despite
Saint-Simon, who had underestimated the proletariat and had likewise
advocated that the big employers should become the leaders of the nation.
But in the days of Saint-Simon it was still possible to believe in the weakness
of the working classes, whereas Carlyle lived in the middle of the period
of social struggle and heightened proletarian class consciousness. And
then Saint-Simon considered the exploitation by employers to be a remnant
of the actual and only age of oppression, the feudal one, which would
vanish from industry with progressive political liberation, whereas Carlyle
thought that liberalism itself was the root of all evil and therefore –
applied feudalism to it. The way was thus prepared for the fascist theory
of elitism (the demigod who earns a lot): Carlyle sees his ideas of leadership
and proletarian vassalage in thoroughly individual terms; there thus arose
the paradox of an individualistic neo-feudalism. His later works in particular
('Past and Present', 1843, 'The History of Frederick II of Prussia', 1858)
give way in a utopian manner to enlightened industrial despotism. In
'Past and Present' he conjures up the noble employer, who is summoned
away from 'Midas-eared' Mammonism towards the exemplary heroism
kindled by prophets, poets, and statesmen.* Welfare institutions are
prophesied, cheerful communal evenings of the patriarchal entrepreneur
with his worker-children; we all know the outcome. Even Carlyle himself
did not cherish very great expectations with regard to such an ethicizing
relationship between employer and employee; he writes in his 'French
Revolution', and he writes this not just as a puritan: 'In such prophesied
Lubberland,† of Happiness, Benevolence, and Vice cured of its deformity,
trust not, my friends.' The beginning of winter thus descends on the

---

* The passage from Carlyle Bloch seems to have in mind here is: 'in whirlwinds of fire, you
and your Mammonisms, Dilettantisms, your Midas-eared philosophies, double-barrelled
Aristocracies shall disappear!'
† Bloch uses the word 'Schlaraffenland' to translate Carlyle's 'Lubberland'. Elsewhere in Bloch
we have translated 'Schlaraffenland' as 'The Land of Cockaigne'.

bourgeois utopia, for the first time in its existence, and in fact a Lubberland did not arrive with this utopia. The appeal to the philanthropy of the exploiters, common to all pre-Marxist plans for world-improvement, also wrecked this world-improvement; not only did nothing come of this Lubberland, it became a hell. So much for Carlyle, as a side utopia to Ruskin's neo-Gothicism and to the Old New formations of Morris. All other latecomers, after Morris, tread a familiar beaten track in their utopias, and are – at least in so far as they still remain liberalism – a diluted modernization of Thomas More. In the *twentieth century H. G. Wells* leads the way in the fabrication of these peepshow images of a better future. Half a dozen dream-trains, time-machines, and Mr Britlings who write until daybreak were dispatched into the future by Wells and brought back snapshots. And it is characteristic here that hardly one of these snapshots shows related landscapes, apart from the liberal lilac; and even that is perforated with sarcasm in the 'Time Machine', which is interesting from a technological-utopian point of view. Among other things, Wells wrote the idyll of the future with Greek embellishments 'Men like Gods', 1923, a frolicking life like that of naked piano-teachers in Arcadia. Bourgeois utopias thus end in skylarking, imagination has disappeared too, and the so-called noble future, which dodges Marxism because of its own vagueness and especially its bourgeois substitutes for socialism, becomes odd or epigonic. Thus what remained in the end was dilettantism and chaff; the grain of the social utopias has been removed along with Marxism. Even socialism then becomes, in the mocking words of Engels, nothing other 'than the existing social order minus its defects'; in this way of course bourgeois-liberal utopianizing still finds adherents.

Otherwise it would be totally inconceivable to want to improve the economy in such a particularly silly way, i.e. piecemeal. And all this sort of thing, even when it is dressed up in a particularly naive Anglo-American fashion, follows the lead of one of the most dubious utopians, Proudhon. In this way, strange dwarfish creations like the free money and shrinking money* utopia appeared, building socialism on mere currency. Capital is 'abolished' in Silvio Gesell's dream of free gold by a kind of legal inflation; thus it does not breed interest any more. Similar measures are taken against ground rent, relations of 'free money – free land' to the older utopia of

---

* References to Silvio Gesell's economic theory.

agrarian reform emerge. *Henry George* was the advocate of this, and in his influential book 'Progress and Poverty', 1879, he taught that the increase in mass poverty and the industrial crises were primarily caused solely by the private ownership of landed property. Ground rent gives landowners the power to make life intolerably more expensive; in order to establish a paradise for the poor, George demands the confiscation of this rent, and indeed 'nationalization' of the land, in the case of uncontested profit from industrial and commercial capital. And since only land capital was fought in this way, and not productive capital, manufacturers were able to join forces with the working classes on the basis of Henry George, particularly in England. The English proletariat, the majority of which had so little class consciousness and Marxist training anyway, was thus further diverted from its direct exploiters. In 1887 the English Trades Union Congress adopted a resolution in favour of the nationalization of the land; its effect was nothing more than a heavier taxation of ground rent. The following instructive sentence from John Stuart Mill stands at the head of a chapter of George's book (it mocks itself without knowing it): 'When the object is to raise the permanent condition of a people, small means do not merely produce small effects; they produce no effect at all –'. This is in fact a motto against the whole of reformism and its utopia. But Anglo-Saxon socialism as a whole, in the English and especially American economy, for so long the most progressive, managed only partially if at all even just to understand, let alone to implement, the conclusions which Marx drew from this very economy. The taste for delay, compromise, and appeasement in English business life and its politics, the cunning evolutionism with which the ruling class forestalled every revolutionary will, in so far as it existed at all, and defused it, this hesitation and Fabianism, together with the Labour Party of the time, but above all the illusory existence of a workers' aristocracy, owing to colonial exploitation: all this preserved, in one and the same act, capitalism and a pre-Marxist utopianizing, as if scientific socialism did not exist at all. These are the consequences when social utopia lags behind Marx, it then even lags behind Owen, and behind Thomas More, it falls totally outside the socialist tradition. All the more so when the eternal waverers, posing as men of private means, or when artificial stick-in-the-muds, posing as renegades, when these disappointed or kept lovers of a so-called 'third force', 'against fascism and Bolshevism', 'against every dictatorship, whether it comes from the right or the left', fool themselves with a belated Lincoln utopia, or allowed themselves to be fooled in Atlantic terms for a terribly long time, in order to stoke up murderous hatred of the Soviet Union with the notion of 'freedom' as well, and at least to indulge in both the easing of their conscience and a 'socialism of the heart' (which even Bellamy had scornfully derided). Reformism of the Henry George type is, in comparison with all this, still totally innocent, unless the petit-bourgeois patchwork as a whole contains the elements of deception which not only promote the anti-Soviet philistine or snobbish renegade but which led to SA-fascism, which was and is pictured and introduced in the name of socialism, and to USA-fascism, which was and is pictured and introduced in the name of freedom. But reformism in the narrow sense always remains the art of not admitting contradictions between capital and work, between the compulsion to export and peace, and the site of its seduction is precisely the middle class in which, according to Marx, the contradictions and the interests of two classes still both take the edge off one another. Thus a utopian 'synthesis' emerges of the era of the man in the street and large profits, of overproduction and guaranteed employment, of the atom bomb and a united world. The Archimedean point from which fear and privation, tyranny and the catacomb life of truth could be removed has long since been discovered in the meantime, there would be no need for any extravagances at all. But if the position of this point was avoided by the frivolous utopians after Marx, as if they could not see it, it is avoided by the surrogate utopians because they can see it. With the danger, which has here likewise already occurred, that the edifice of hope, occupied by thoughts of improvement, will totally collapse. What remains left over is then nihilism, so that it shall swallow up the salvation of those who are lost and deceived as well. Social utopia without frivolity and error can only operate in so far as it is concrete, as the progress from it towards science, with the undeceivable mandate of the revolutionary proletariat behind it. This is the result of the history of utopias before Marx, and especially of their history of decay and ultimately of opium after him. Progress only counters Poverty when reforming Progress no longer produces Poverty, but active Poverty produces Progress.

Marxism and concrete anticipation

To think our way into what is right, this will has to remain more than ever. Since it was so powerfully alive in the earlier, really flourishing forward dreams, these deserve to be remembered with special emphasis. Remembered all the more fondly as the progress of socialism from utopia towards science has long been a decided one. Sentimental and abstract world-improvement is played out; disciplined work in and with actual tendencies has taken its place. Existing misery is not lamented and left at that, but it appears, when it becomes aware of itself and of its causes, as the revolutionary power to cancel itself out causally. Marx likewise never allowed his subjective indignation to pose as an objective factor and thus to deceive itself about the actually existing revolutionary factors. He never taught, like Owen and Proudhon, and also like Rodbertus and especially Lassalle, that because workers receive unfair wages in capitalist society a new society must therefore be created, with fair wages for instance. But the Must discovered by Marx is quite different from that of the introduced moral demand. It lies within the economically immanent manifestations of capitalist society itself and causes the latter to collapse only in immanent-dialectical terms. The subjective factor of its destruction lies in the proletariat, which is simultaneously produced by capitalist society as its contradiction and becomes aware of itself as a contradiction. The objective factor of its destruction lies in the accumulation and concentration of capital, in monopolization, in the crisis of affluence which stems from the contradiction between the attained collective mode of production and the retained private form of acquisition. Such are the new rudiments of an immanent economic critique; they are almost entirely lacking in the older utopias, they are characteristic of Marx. Marx's critique displays no recesses of the heart, as Hegel would say, but it displays all the more sharply the recesses, fissures, cracks, and contrasts incorporated in the objectively existing economy. For this very reason, as far as the so-called State of the future is concerned, there is also no detailed specification privately introduced from outside, ante rem, of an abstract-anticipatory kind, as in the old utopias. The abstract utopias had devoted nine tenths of their space to a portrayal of the State of the future and only one tenth to the critical, often merely negative consideration of the present. This kept the goal colourful and vivid of course, but the path towards it, in so far as it could lie in given circumstances, remained hidden. Marx devoted more than nine tenths of his writings to the critical analysis of the present, and he granted relatively little space to *descriptions* of the future. Hence, as has justly been remarked, Marx called his work 'Capital' and not 'Appeal for Socialism' for instance. It contains an overall view of economic life, for the first time since Quesnay's 'Economic Tableau', and on a much higher level. It

FREEDOM AND ORDER, SOCIAL UTOPIAS

does not picture a paradise on earth, it reveals the secret of profiteering and the almost more complicated secret of profit distribution. Marx applies Ricardo's law of value to labour as a product, he discovers the dialectics of the product by means of exchange value and within it, he discovers profit as extorted surplus value and the strange average rate of profit as the basis of the class solidarity of capitalists. In this way he first lays the material foundations of the dialectics of history which leads to tensions, utopias, and revolutions. He substantiates and amends the anticipations of utopia by means of economics, by means of the immanent radical changes in the mode of production and exchange, and he thereby cancels out the reified dualism between what is and what ought to be, between empirical experience and utopia. He thus fights against both clinging empiricism and skimming utopianism. What counts instead is actively conscious participation in the historically immanent process of the revolutionary re-organization of society. All this as realism full of future, in the most thorough investigations, with breath-taking sharpness and breadth, for the purpose of real revolution, as both its general staff office and arsenal. And just as, from the standpoint of attained realism, there was no longer any justification for the novelistic goal-images of the old utopias, so there was still no cause at that time to specify the construction of socialism already in a concrete-processive way. The humane conditions behind the nationalization of the means of production are still barely indicated, for all the comprehensiveness of the mode of investigation. Engels speaks in general terms of the realm of freedom, Marx posits little more than the sparse concept of the classless society, even though it is powerfully differentiated from what has gone before. Actual *descriptions* of the future are deliberately missing, as noted above, and they are deliberately missing precisely because Marx's whole work serves the future, and can only be comprehended and implemented at all in the horizon of the future, yet one which is not pictured in a utopian-abstract way. But a future which is illuminated in historical-materialist terms in and by the past and present, and hence by the tendencies which operate and continue to operate, in order to be at last a knowing future capable of being shaped. Nothing was more necessary than this emphatic contrast to the imagined phalanstères or New Harmonies; than the rejection of all fantasies of the so-called State of the future; than the omission of the field to come, together with the restrained style which is in keeping with it. But in fact this omission occurred solely for the sake of the future, a comprehended future into which it was finally possible to travel with a map and compass; the omission certainly did not occur for the sake of the revisionists who confused concreteness with empiricism because they did not want to travel at all. In their case though, the faintness of the descriptions of their goal was turned into one of the goal itself, and the desired omission – in Marx essentially a *keeping open* – lost its critical shades of value as well in an age which was not threatened by dreams anyway but abandoned itself to a flat empiricism. The movement became everything for the reformists, as noted above, and the goal became nothing; and the path itself thereby came to an end. In fact, the meeting of extremes even resulted in ostensibly radical sectarianism likewise sinking into empiricism, and thus robbing Marxism of its very richness and the life of profundity which this sectarianism does not understand. But Marx, when he set dialectics on its feet and combatted the cloud formations in the sky of his still thoroughly idealistic age, definitely had not preached empiricism and the mechanistic philosophy analogous to it (a halved world). Occasionally such an undernourishment of revolutionary imagination occurred and a comfortable, i.e. schematically pragmatic reduction of totality; despite Lenin's call to bear this totality in mind both in the subjective and in the objective factor. Thus a far too great progress of socialism from utopia towards science occasionally appeared, such that the pillar of fire in utopias, the thing which was powerfully leading the way, could also be liquidated along with the cloud. Instead it must be repeated that Marxism is *not no anticipation (utopian function), but the Novum of a processive-concrete anticipation.* Likewise, this is precisely why it is part of Marxism that enthusiasm and sobriety, awareness of the goal and analysis of the given facts go hand in hand. When the young Marx called on people to think at last, to act 'like a disillusioned man who has come to his senses', it was not to dampen the enthusiasm of the goal, but to sharpen it. With all this what Marx had established as the 'categorical imperative' first became and becomes accomplishable: namely 'to overturn all circumstances in which man is a degraded, a subjugated, a forsaken, a contemptible creature'; what is best in utopia is given a firm practical footing. Thus from Marx onwards the inserting of the boldest intending into the occurring world elucidates itself, the *unity of hope and knowledge of process*, in short, realism. Everything inflamed in the forward dream is thereby removed as is everything mouldy in sobriety. The concrete dream makes itself sound and valid all the more unmistakably, and its performed content developed, its unperformed content works, all the more powerfully in reality.

To think our way into what is right, this will has to operate more than ever. The sound dream actively follows what is historically due and under way in a more or less hindered fashion. Concrete utopia is therefore concerned to understand the dream of its object exactly, a dream which lies in the historical trend itself. As a utopia mediated with process, it is concerned to deliver the forms and contents which have already developed in the womb of present society. Utopia in this no longer abstract sense is thus the same as realistic anticipation of what is good; which must have become clear. There is processive-concrete utopia in both basic elements of the reality discerned by Marxism: in its *tendency*, the tension of what is due though hindered, and in its *latency*, the correlate of the not yet realized objective-real possibilities in the world. Wherever so much is constructed into the mediated-blue, a utopian ground is required; if it did not exist, nothing of value could be created. Every dream of a better, of a higher, of a fulfilled life would be confined to a separate, inner, slender, and quite mysteriously isolated enclave. But a great suggesting and an intending of the still unarrived runs through the whole world: concrete utopia is the most important theory-practice of this tendency. Accordingly, utopian intention is confined neither to the mere inner dream-enclave nor to the problems of the best social constitution either. On the contrary, its field is broad in social terms, it has all the object worlds of human work in its favour, it extends – as must be remembered and as is to be demonstrated in what follows – no less into technology and architecture, into painting, literature and music, into ethics and religion. There are technological wishful images as well as social ones, they are not inferior to these in boldness, and have always been intertwined with them, in so far as they push back the barriers of nature and fashion a world for us. And every work of art, every central philosophy had and has a utopian window in which there lies a landscape which is still developing. Even natural forms, apart from what they are as forms that have become, constitute a cipher in which a Not-Yet-Become, an object-based utopian element circulates, which is first only present as a latent form; natural beauty, and also natural mythology gave and give access to these real-utopian ciphers. Just as a Not-Yet-Conscious, which has never been conscious before, dawns in the human soul, so a Not-Yet-Become dawns in the world: at the head of the world-process and world-whole is this Front and the vast, still so little understood category of the Novum. Its contents are not merely those that have not appeared, but those that are not decided, they dawn in mere real possibility, and contain the danger of possible disaster, but also the hope of possible, still not thwarted happiness, capable of being decided by human beings. So far does utopia extend, so vigorously does this raw material spread to all human activities, so essentially must every anthropology and science of the world contain it. *There is no realism worthy of the name if it abstracts from this strongest element in reality, as an unfinished reality.* And certainly only the socially successful utopia, allied with the technologically successful one, can precisely enable us to define that pre-appearance in art, let alone religion, which is not illusion, let alone superstition. But Marxism is the first door to the position which removes the root cause of exploitation and dependence, and consequently to an incipient Being like utopia. It posits liberation from blind fate, from unfathomed necessity, allied with a concrete act of pushing back the barriers of nature. Since human beings here consciously make history for the first time, the appearance vanishes of that fate which has been produced by human beings themselves, in class society, and ignorantly made into a fetish. Fate is unfathomed, uncontrolled necessity, freedom is controlled necessity, from which alienation has vanished and real order emerges, precisely as the *realm* of freedom. Utopia that has become concrete provides the key to this, to unalienated order in the best of all possible societies. Homo homini homo: *this is therefore what the outlines of a better world suggest, as far as society is concerned.* And only when the interhuman relation has duly been put in order, the relation to man, the most powerful thing alive, can a truly concrete mediation also begin with the most powerful thing that is not alive: with the forces of inorganic nature.

WILL AND NATURE,   37
THE TECHNOLOGICAL UTOPIAS

Beneficent is the fire's might
If man controls and guards it right.   *Schiller*

Better like this though:

Sublime spirit, you gave me, gave me all
For which I asked. You did not turn in vain
Your countenance to me within the fire.
You gave me glorious nature for my kingdom,
The strength to feel and to enjoy it. Not
Just cold astonished visits do you allow,
You let me look into her breast so deep
As if into the bosom of a friend.   *Goethe*

In the language of the old legends the task of man with regard to nature involved nothing less than propagating and spreading a paradise over his earth; in other words, man's vocation as a heavenly body of the earth was no less than to help this earth to bring forth heavenly fruits and forms and thus to perform a similar service for it, only in a higher sense, as the external heavenly body, the sun, performs for it: which likewise not only liberates and releases the sealed earthly powers from their chains – like the vanished and fettered spirits in fables – but also gives them the necessary restoration for growth, for blossoming and bearing fruit. Just as in the rising of the external solar image the entire external organism unfolds, so in the rising of the divine image in man this external nature was to be equipped and fortified for the unfolding and consequent effects of an internal, higher organism.

Franz von Baader, On the Foundation of Ethics through Physics

It is characteristic of the ideology of a decaying class that it is incapable of imagining the harmony between human beings and the universe. The contradictions in the system oppose the conscious mastery of the forces of nature. The world seems to be hostile to a society which is paralysed by internal disorder.

Roger Garaudy

The *human* essence of nature only exists for *social* man; for only here does she exist for him as a *bond* with man, as existence for the others and of the others for him; only here does she exist as the *basis* of a *human* existence. Only here has his *natural* existence, his *human* existence and nature for him become man for him. Thus *society* is the perfect essential unity of men with nature, the true resurrection of nature, the implemented naturalism of man and the implemented humanism of nature.

Marx, Economic and Philosophic Manuscripts

I. Magic Past

Plunged into misery

Our bare skin absolutely forces us to invent. Man as such is strangely helpless, even against the weather. He only progresses in regularly warm regions, and could not survive a single winter. The south permits us to walk about naked of course, but not to walk about unarmed. The teeth of the apes receded in primitive man, even the manliest fist is hardly any use against a single wolf. For protection and attack it must grow further, into something which did not grow with it, into the club, into the stone axe. As long as these had not yet been invented, it is strange that men remained alive at all. Since then at any rate they preserve themselves only by working a thing, by planning something better.

Fire and new armament

Our nakedness is now covered, not of our own accord, but only from outside. The alien skin is put round our shoulders, and the cave from which the bear and lion sometimes first had to be driven away was replaced by the house, made of wood or large stones. Birds also build a nest, but it is only used for rearing their brood, not for extending the fortification of the body like human implements and houses. The ant, the bee, the badger, and especially the beaver all build structures and partly even actually like an extension of their body, like an artificial shell as a fortress, but everything essential to technological invention is lacking: implements and their conscious use. Man is the only animal who makes implements, who intensified the nail into a file, the fist into a hammer, the teeth into a knife. Only self-made man utilized fire, which cooks the food, smelts the ore, and scares off every predator. And even more quickly than the plundered raw materials grew the art of making something out of them that never existed before. Since then, invention means procuring additional strength or comfort from organic or dead resources outside the body by processing them. Whereby, after the host of commodities has arisen, it becomes essential for invention to add something new to these as well, which has not been found among them up till now. The German patent journal of 1880 gives an adequate supplementary definition along these lines: 'Invention is the production of a new kind or a new kind of production of artifacts.' The first can be the zip-fastener for instance, the second a different method from previous ones of fastening the heel of a shoe to the sole. The whole of life is thus surrounded by a belt of artificial creations which have never existed before. The human house is vastly extended by them, it becomes more and more comfortable and adventurous.

Lunacy and Aladdin's fairytale

Almost everything was dreamed in this field which has since come to exist. And more as well, if only because the fiery owl of delusion is particularly inventive. It prompted one of the lunatics to invent a bed which is both a kitchen and a lake to bathe in. A schizophrenic tailor kept in a thimble 'water mixed with childlike innocence', which washed up the plates and cleaned the suits in a flash. Stain-removers are popular, which in addition to cleaning change cotton into silk. A hunter who suffered from paranoia even invented a lamp by means of which he hatched eagles from hen's eggs. But all these foolish tricks are taken from an area which, as was seen in the case of medical wishful dreams and those of an ideal state, has long been occupied by the fairytale, and occupied in particular detail on the technological level. The needle which sews by itself, and the saucepan which puts on and cooks the meal on its own, is incomparable fairytale invention. As is the mill which even grows out of the corn itself, and threshes and grinds it, as is the fruit loaf which always grows again provided just a little crust of it is left over, and which replaces all other foods. Thus Grimm also explains the social aspect of the fairytale of the Land of Cockaigne in technological terms: 'The human imagination here satisfies the desire to wield the big knife which cuts through all barriers with total freedom for once.' From the family of the knife from Cockaigne come the wishing hat, the magic hood and so much else from the witch's store, the magic table, the seven-league boots, the cudgel from the sack and the alchemical ass Bricklebrit who pours forth gold when all ends well. Said in Hauff's fairytale blows the silver whistle which the fairy gave him as a present, and the waves immediately subside; the piece of wood to which the shipwrecked sailor clings becomes a dolphin that carries him to the shore. The magic table also turns up here again, this time from the waves, but as dry as if it had stood in the sun for a week, and laden with the most delicious foods. Said's whistle has distinguished relations, they are all gifted not just musically but with magic technology: Roland's horn in the valley of Roncesvalles already half belongs here, but above all the magic flute and Oberon's horn. The full glory of technological wishful images erupts, in keeping with its more luxurious needs, in the oriental fairytale. There the magic objects are even comparatively rationalized and amassed into a technological treasure chamber. The fairytale of Prince Ahmad and the fairy Peri-Banu contains an ivory tube through which one can see whatever one wishes to see, even if the object of one's wishes is hundreds of miles away. This fairytale contains the flying carpet which carries its owner in a moment, even if he only utters his wish in his thoughts, to the goal revealed to him by the ivory tube. The fairytale contains winged giants who not only carry people over immense distances like lightning, but also bring up treasures so rich that people would hardly dare to wish for them from underground, in fact, as in the case of Aladdin and the magic lamp, from the void. That which appears impossible, that which is almost deliberately arranged to be impossible is thus created with effortless ease, above all also by means of imaginary instruments. Difficulties fall away on all sides, nothing sounds fantastic in such fairytales, everything sounds plausible. Gigantic forces of nature, pictured as spirits, are immediately and slavishly at the command of Aladdin, the master of the ring and the lamp. Or of Hassan the Basorite, the master of the magic rod, he strikes the ground with it: 'Then the earth gaped open, and out came ten Ifrits, whose legs still stuck in the bowels of the earth while their heads towered far above the clouds' ('The Arabian Nights'). The fairytale of the ebony horse hallucinates technological wishful images even soberly as it were, in detail: the magic horse has a lock of hair for ascending and descending, it can be steered according to the direction in which its head is turned, and it is so well equipped for every purpose that the rider carries off the king's daughter from the inaccessible castle or ascends and escapes from the ranks of his enemies. A Chinese fairytale on the other hand, called 'The Suit of Leaves', enchants with the magic of a raw material which can be transformed at will, almost as infinitely usable as the above-mentioned all-purpose artificial bed of the lunatic. The fairy here makes a suit of green silk for her human lover out of banana leaves, cakes are baked out of the same foliage, a hen and a fish are cut and cooked, and finally donkeys are carved, on which the lover rides home with the children who have been born in the meantime. It is again a fairy (the wish for superhuman, more superhuman powers) in a fairytale by Lagerlöf who bestows the gift of new creation. So that a blacksmith successfully sets about producing another sun, in the middle of the northern winter; one which does not forsake people for half the year like the celestial one. Magic tables, Aladdin's lamps, divining rods at every turn, along with Medean cauldrons, caps of Fortunatus, Oberon's horns in the legends and so much more; obstacles are removed from the course of things in a wishful magic way. Sluggish time is overtaken, heavy matter is to settle lightly and transparently around all wishes. The most popular expression of this, which no longer had an improbable fairytale quality, was in the novels of Jules Verne, and partly in those of Kurt Lasswitz. The journey 'Around the World in Eighty Days' is already long out-of-date, that to the centre of the earth and to the moon is still to come. But all this sort of thing, whether it is a crazy device, whether it is an even crazier success with it, is, as Baroque title-pages used to say, not only pleasant but useful to read. It is sometimes the future of human ability, asserted and described as if it already existed now.

'Professor Mystos' and invention

In addition, there are now also those eccentrics who seduced others and even themselves. Often deceitful, occasionally obsessed and then not wholly capable of recognizing their suspect trade. Crooks and dreamers are among them, boasters as a whole, distributing unlaid eggs with open hands. Alchemists formerly used to be at their head, better people by and large than the quacks of today. For all around them even learned men believed in spirits, in a summonable something which flutters up above, and digs down below, and above all they believed in the philosopher's stone. Though porcelain was invented in this connection quite by chance, and also ruby glass, the discoverers, the court adepts Böttger and Kunckel, who had the philosopher's stone in mind, were honestly disappointed, so to speak. The alchemist Brand first produced phosphorus from human urine in 1674, instead of the philosopher's stone; but it seemed to Brand as if he had found a she-ass instead of the expected kingdom. Even the swindler Cagliostro, in his by no means scientific awareness, believed some of the tales of alchemists and ghost-seers which a greedy, corrupt, and bored aristocracy so willingly swallowed from him. The contemporary and as it were liberal occult freemasons were also up to so many cranky tricks, with coffins, lights, hermetic arts, that Cagliostro, their so-called 'Grand Cophta', could almost appear as a serious case among mere scene-painters. It is altogether strange how at that time two or three trends could run alongside and even into one another in this variously inventive sorcery: First the rising bourgeois tendency towards promoting the technological forces of production, but then the obscurantist addiction to miracles of the declining feudal class, which produced the appearance of Cagliostro himself – in a way reminiscent of Rasputin at the court of the Tsar. But these are joined by a third component, the cabbalism which still had a continuing influence precisely from the Renaissance again, from its witches' kitchens and incantations. Though witch-burnings themselves had also become rarer of late, the belief in helpful spirits had not; a book against ghosts like Balthasar Bekker's 'Enchanted World', which denied the pact with the devil, still seemed bold and almost paradoxical around 1690 and later, outside the highest academic sphere. The magical Renaissance and the theosophical seventeenth century lived on for such a long time; the dividing line between freemasonry and the Rosicrucians was still often blurred. Swedenborg, deep in the Age of Enlightenment, best demonstrates what a strange background open to wonders had still remained to Reason. In fact, *mechanics itself* occasionally still had a ghostly element of its own at that time, one which was not even that far-fetched. It joined the old one surrounding the clock, this strange life-simulating phenomenon, above all the church clock and its lonely dark activity. Surrounding the clicking and shifting of the wheels up in the casing, surrounding the whole mechanical life-in-death and its aura. Thus cogwheels, gears, pulley blocks stare out at us from woodcuts of this period, all natural, all as if from the belfry, all spooky. Even L'Homme machine, the materialist catchphrase of La Mettrie, which seemed to break the spell so thoroughly around 1750, produced a new shudder of horror, one which until then was even unknown, for the diversely uncontemporary bizarreness which persisted even during the bourgeois Enlightenment. It was a mixture of a bit of the Golem legend with the metaphor of the clock with which the Baroque is filled, particularly in its dramas: Hallmann's 'Marianne' talks of the body as 'practicable clockwork', and Lohenstein gathers up the wheels of his fallen 'Agrippina', the female tyrant, 'who had the strange idea the clockwork of her brain/Was powerfully to revolve the orbit of the stars'. But the new element was in fact added as the shudder of exposure, precisely in mechanics: the fact that living man is a piece of clockwork which is self-winding. This sort of thing seemed to become apparent in the automata which emerged at that time: in the singing nightingale, the mechanical violin-player, the mathematical wizard, all made of wax and inside only clockwork, but all alive as it were. It was characteristic that the clockwork was not concealed, it was merely draped with Rococo clothes or rich Turkish costume and thus doubly apparent. The mechanism was emphasized in a downright coquettish fashion in all these figures, the skirt or curtain drawn back from the wheels displayed the mechanics precisely as a new magic abyss. There is an echo of this in the keeper of the stool-shop from the 'Tales of Hoffmann': with a barometer, hygrometer, and glasses, whoever looks through them sees everything that is dead as alive; all the more so in Doctor Spallanzani, the physicist who hatches automata. There is still an echo in the advertising preparations of modern chemical laboratories: the sparkling glass itself, and the bright mechanistic light reaches into old, strangely increased imagination. At any rate, mechanics also seemed to reveal something secret, a land of adventure and hubris beyond the frontiers, in the midst of sobriety. The golem was to be found in there too, not just in the pre-mechanical region in which rabbi Löb as a cabbalist wanted to attempt the business of creation, with a lump of clay and a magic slip of paper. Thus the various Cagliostros were not made totally impossible even by the Enlightenment, especially when they used a mechanical-technological language apart from the magic one.

Moreover, even today we still say that a liar 'invents' something. The strange, bad and good ambiguity of this word particularly found adherents at that time, among bankrupt and bored princes. And it was the age of the rising bourgeoisie, very interested in profitable inventions. But inventing was still bizarre, so to some extent it was uncritically merged in human consciousness as something à la Münchhausen and as something technological. Consequently, adventurers of the kind that were called 'projectors' in the Baroque also moved into technology; as much on a wishful basis as on one of swindling and shudders of horror. These project-makers or 'donneurs d'avis' effortlessly switched at that time from the domain of state finances, where they were never at a loss for any 'invention', to the domain of technology, again with an often complicated mixture of conning and ardent enthusiasm. The same type who concocted patent economic remedies, and often sold them at great profit (to himself), also had technological arcana for sale. One of these project-makers, his name was Bessler and he later called himself, probably crossing Orpheus and zephyr, Orphyré, also Dr Orfyréus, first eked out a living as a wood turner, clockmaker, and grinder, switched over into a quack, astrologer, and alchemist, and then united this versatility in the business of a charlatan engineer. As such he created the 'curious and duly appointed running pearl, called Orfyréi Perpetuum mobile'. Around this he wrote a trashy piece of technological colportage in 1720, with the fairground title: 'The eight hidden chambers of the edifice of nature'. This was then described like one of those fairytale castles in which entry into one chamber, of special luxuriousness, was not permitted. The edifice of nature of Dr Orfyréus had eight such chambers all at once, they contained curiosities and utopian gadgets, in one chamber there was the squaring of the circle, in another the hyperbolic mirror, in the third the solution to the problem of making a jet of water rise out of a pond without using pipes. In the fourth there was inextinguishable fire, and so on through to the last one where the model of the said Perpetuum mobile stood. It is precisely this which Orfyréus claims to have stolen from its chamber of nature, he set it up, 'after a thorough inspection of the works', first in Gera, and then in a summer residence of the Landgrave of Hessen-Kassel. There the machine is said to have been on show for a long time 'in perfect running order' and even 'to have performed some work'. An unknown trick aided the illusion, and the public was blinded by the illusion. Perhaps there was a hunchbacked dwarf hidden in the impossible object, who could be packed into it particularly easily, as in another famous contemporary automaton, the invincible chess-player. Every Perpetuum mobile was interesting anyway; since it fulfilled in the most radical fashion the mission of newly-begun capitalism: cheaper production. The same Orfyréus, he was also called Professor Mystos, planned to place orchestrions with windmill sails on high towers, and in stormy weather an organ concert would peal in fortissimo above the town. A plan which shows that the fiery owl, when it adopts windmill sails, seems quite splendid, almost American. If even seven-league boots were technologically promised and exhibited to good effect, then the style of Orfyréus was always present, with and without the title of doctor. The 'Cosmic Universal Powers' in particular, discovered over and over again although always given a different name, remained immortal. The 'fluid' of old Mesmer was newly revived anyway when it was able to adopt the scientific language and the electricity of the nineteenth century. And the transition to the really and truly revived 'radiation magnetism' of today was represented by an otherwise very proficient natural scientist with an equally proficient eccentricity, the chemist Reichenbach, the discoverer of paraffin and creosote; he provided the transition through the 'discovery' he also made of the 'world-od'. This was actually the sought-after original radiating force, which spiritualists were soon able to use too ('Physical-physiological investigations into the dynamics of magnetism, electricity, light etc. in relation to the life-force', 1845); it ranges from protoplasm and the fuel of machines animated like the golem and operating instinctively, to the 'cause' of the halo. And part of the most recent bombast of the 'fluid', one which now even makes its Perpetuum mobile again in a roundabout psychoanalytical way, is the so-called 'orgone' of W. Reich. That is: a juicy 'world-od', from the wedding night of Being, or the biological-cosmic potent and orgasmic force par excellence. Moreover, this orgasmic force is visible, it appears both in the 'blue colouring of frogs during coition' and in the St Elmo's fire on ship's yards, as well as in the likewise bluish twinkling of the stars. 'Orgones' and several other things of this kind (sheer cosmic super-vitamins for that kind of hope which does not run out) were also collected by America in 'accumulators', which draw the priceless but saleable substance from the air, after which it remedies every kind of debilitation, sexual, spiritual, social, and cosmic all at the same time. All this is the style of Cagliostro and Orfyréus, introduced into the epigonic light of hazy blue nonsense in the world. Nevertheless, the Cagliostro approach belongs, even in the form of the petit-bourgeois humbug of today, to the region of technological dreams; it constitutes its old traces of magic, even though they are grotesquely decayed. But just as Gothic capitals often display little grotesque figures, with their heads looking out between their open legs or making other faces, the ever-recurring Professors Mystos also have exactly this traditional place in the technological-utopian structure. And a permanent attribute of this kind of inventor, apart from the 'world fluid' mentioned above, is not least the old alchemical gold-making, in the most comprehensible meaning of the word. So as not to tire ourselves out with too many tripods in the modernized junk shop, let us indicate only one new motif of ancient alchemy. Typical of the continuing appeal of the cheap witches' kitchen was the activity of the alchemist Franz Tausend, one of the last of the breed. With a host of people behind him, right up to the 'highest circles', right up to the German general staff, who invested capital in the business, so that although never coming to an end it started up all over again. Tausend certainly introduced a particularly acoustic attraction into the old magic, namely a kind of musical reform. Gold-cooking was namely transferred from its traditional furnace to tuning forks, and in fact achieved by merely changing keys. For according to Tausend every element is formed by a characteristic frequency of oscillation; hence by means of chemical-musical modulation it can be readily transformed from its original element-key into another one. Corriger la fortune: this unites the cheats with the old grave court adepts and their shoddy Pythagorean descendants down to the very end. The correction would be perfectly good, if only the means were as good, the unsuitable means for inventing things which are not possible as such.

Andreae's 'Chemical Wedding of Christian Rosenkreutz anno 1459'

The most tempting idea remained that of baking money out of the muck that is lying around. If everyone forges his own happiness, then it is best forged at its metal origin. Thousands upon thousands have worked before the furnace, with abstruse means to a very generally comprehensible end. And further, what is rarer, more interesting, and mostly overlooked today: if most necromancers merely wanted gold, then several others wanted something more than this: the transformation of the world. The 'Chemical Wedding of Christian Rosenkreutz anno 1459' appeared in 1616, it aims at a broader 'refinement' than that of base metal into gold. The author of this anonymously published work is almost certainly Johann Valentin Andreae, Swabian poet, churchman, theosophist, utopian. The work sharply criticizes the bad gold-cookers, in places it can even be interpreted as mocking the whole hermetic craft. But more striking than the undeniable presence of an element of satire is the solemn *significance* which the 'Chemical Wedding' gives to the path of gold and to the allegorical knight who takes it. In two earlier works, the 'Fama Fraternitatis' and the 'Confessio Fraternitatis', Andreae had already invented and introduced Rosenkreutz, a founder of an order. Born in 1388, the latter travels to the East as a young man, is there initiated into the occult sciences and into a 'reformation', of which the transformation of metals is only the beginning. The 'Chemical Wedding' shows the same Rosenkreutz as an old man, engaged in a new journey, on the eve of Easter Day, to the royal castle where a wedding is to be celebrated. He is admitted to the mysterious castle, undergoes a kind of ordeal of fire and water, then afterwards, adorned with the Golden Fleece, attends the seven-day wedding celebration as chief guest, has a vision of death and afterwards the resurrection of the royal couple. The guests are dubbed Knights of the Golden Stone, but Christian Rosenkreutz, having forced his way into a chamber where he found Lady Venus asleep, is induced, as the wedding is in full swing, to remain in the castle as a doorkeeper or as Peter. 'Alchymia' gives away the bride at the wedding, she is the 'parergon to the ergon of the seven days'. On the whole the alchemical meaning in Andreae's allegory is clear, but not as one which refers exclusively to metallurgy. If it is confined to the latter, then the 'Chemical Wedding' bears no or only very little relation to gold-cooking. If, however, alchemy is conceived as giving away the bride of a trans-formation of the world or 'general reformation', then it is understandable that contemporary believers saw in the novel, even if it is typically a fragment, the most sublime allegory of the 'work of perfection', of the extraction of philosophical gold. A Rosicrucian by the name of Brotoffer published an interpretation in 1617: 'Elucidarius major or Synopsis of the Chemical Wedding F.R.C., in which praeparatio lapidis aurei is very neatly described.' This interpretation openly explains the seven days of the wedding as the seven stages of the alchemical process, spiritually brought to light: as destillatio, solutio, purefactio, nigredo, albedo, fermentatio, and projectio medicinae (tincture of gold). It is even correct that the 'Chemical Wedding' was not only intended as allegory but as symbolism in the comprehensively final sense, i.e. as metaphorical reference to an ultimate Unitas, to the fermenting golden Pan. So, in alchemy of *this* kind, this was supposed to be the solemn *significance* announced above: that of an *Easter Day* to be fantastically created against ice and barriers. The bourgeois impulse towards the 'Freedom of the Christian Man'* that did not arrive now adopted such strange paths and naturally-adorned disguises in the so-called hermetic societies of the German Baroque and their stated symbolism. A reveille was intended which was to resound through the *whole earthly layer*, an 'Awake, frozen Christian', through lead, creation, society and the remaining Alteritas. *The preparation of gold and the promotion of humanity* are jumbled together in Rosicrucianism from then on, constitute the peculiar quality of its mixed fantasy. In 1622 the since famous Society of Rosicrucians was founded in The Hague, though the name of the order itself is older than the Fama and Confessio which Andreae produced about it. Paracelsus

---

* Luther's 'Freiheit des Christenmenschen'.

cites a Rosicrucian lodge in Basle in 1530, not wholly unequivocal manuscripts from the beginning of the twelfth century tell of lodges of this name in Germany. Not content with this, Rosicrucians from the time of Andreae, and even from that of the Magic Flute, claimed to have preserved that 'veram sapientiam' for thousands of years 'quae olim ab Aegyptiis et Persiis magia, hodie vero a venerabili fraternitate Roseae Crucis Pansophia recte vocatur'. *
But however old the name Rosicrucian is and however far the emblem may go back into utopianizing or utopianized myths: only Andreae with his 'Chemical Wedding' gave it the sense, claimed to be rising or humane, of 'higher alchemy'. We must continue even further, into the peculiar connection which exists, through Andreae's link of a 'general reformation', between something as superstitious as alchemy and something as sunlike and crystal-clear as the – Enlightenment, this battle of light against superstition. For the pathos of light itself, as the 'birth', as the advancing 'process' of light (gold), comes from alchemy: 'Enlightenment' itself is originally an alchemical concept, just like 'process' and its 'result'. Conversely the strange connection of freemasonry, and even the Enlightenment with occultism arises from this, of course; even Andreae mixed his fraternities with magic rites. The golden dream of a societas humana thus found its philanthropic alchemical conventicles in Germany, but also in the strangely theosophical England throughout the whole of the seventeenth and eighteenth century. There was a secret society called Antilia, another called Makaria, a 'brotherhood of the celestial wheel for the restoration of hermetic medicine and philosophy'. There was, with a mixed social-cosmological dream, the collegium lucis which was founded by no less a person than Comenius, the disciple of Andreae; and all these sections set up the Rosy Cross or the 'higher alchemy'. They all wanted to turn the course *of society and of nature* towards the original state of paradise, where social equality and unfallen or golden nature were one and the same. The dream of these alchemical sects thus remained general reformation throughout, in the sense of the restoration of the original state of paradise, and above all of leading the fallen world over to Christ; which is why the Rosicrucians were also continually compared with the Anabaptists by their enemies at the time. Gold-cooking became chiliastic or, as a hostile tract denounced it at the time: 'Turning the whole world upside down before the Day of Judgement into an earthly paradise such as Adam occupied before the Fall, and the restitution of all the arts and wisdom possessed

---

* 'which was rightly called 'magia' in former times by the Egyptians and Persians, today 'pansophia' by the true and venerable fraternity of the Rosy Cross'.

by Adam, after the Fall, Enoch and Solomon.' *Alchemy and chiliasm together* thus entered the hermetic sects, with the transformation of metals as a prelude to the 'true' homunculus or to the birth of the new man. A late after-image of this is still to be found in Goethe's fragment 'The Mysteries', concerning the dream of a chemical kingdom. The wanderer, 'exhausted by the day's long journeying/He undertook upon impulse sublime', here sees a mysterious image on the monastery gate, sees the cross entwined with roses, 'and light celestial clouds of silver float,/To soar into the sky with cross and roses'. Thirteen chairs are standing in the monastery hall, at their heads hang thirteen shields with unmistakably alchemical allegories: 'And here he sees a fiery dragon pause/To quench his raging thirst in wild flames;/And here an arm caught in a bear's fierce jaws,/From which the blood is pouring in hot streams.' The images on the shields signify in this order thirteen stages of turning to gold, and thus they are the ancestral hall which the old man in the monastery tells the wanderer about. But then the wise man, who has such diverse ancestors behind him, is called Humanus in Goethe's strange poem; and this very name has also been claimed in the Rosicrucianism of Andreae to be the final name and content which rises from the transformation of metals and the world. Cross and rose, the first the symbol of pain and of dissolution, the second the symbol of love and life, thus united allegorically in the 'work of perfection'. 'And a French philosopher', as Gottfried Arnold's history of heretics of 1741 relates, in the chapter on the Rosicrucians, 'has sought the secret of making gold in the name itself and suggested that rose comes from ros or dew, and crux means lux for them, which things the alchemists used most.' Thus again and again Rosicrucianism opened out into a kind of second storey of alchemy; the philosopher's stone in the Chemical Wedding was at the same time Christ the cornerstone. For lead and man and for the whole world: 'Vita Christi, mors Adami, Mors Christi, vita Adami',* ran the epitaph of the Rosicrucian and friend of Jakob Böhme, Abraham von Franckenberg. Or as the same Franckenberg, in connection with the Chemical Wedding, had taught: alchemy was 'renewal of the celestial lights, ages, men, animals, trees, plants, metals and all things in the world'. Moreover this kind of thing was levelled at any constraint or spellbinding by the *existing celestial lights*, and therefore, despite some cross-connections, at the mythology of fate at that time: astrology. Some cross-connections did exist of course, all metals bore planetary symbols and vice versa, the position of the planets was always taken

---

* 'Life of Christ, death of Adam, Death of Christ, life of Adam.'

into account when cooking gold. Nevertheless, the superstition of alchemy has always reserved to itself something distinctive from, even contrary to that of astrology, simply the act of intervention, combination, the changing process; all this was to be levelled precisely at the 'frozen heavens'. At the horoscope of the beginning, which also claims right at the beginning to be an epitaph as well, an unchangeable, inescapable one. The planetary symbols themselves, in metals and in the heavens, were to be 'chemically surmounted', namely by the sun or by gold. That is why Franckenberg's 'Oculus siderius' of 1643 boils down to this: 'Since we have been stuck long enough in the circumscribed cage or whitewashed imaginary vault of the frozen heavens and have fooled one another with all kinds of fantastic visions and constellations, we now need to rub the sleep of seven ages out of our eyes at once.' The hidden alchemy at work in Thomas More and his liberal utopia has already been referred to, as the 'mythology of liberation (cf. Vol. II, p. 528). This was in contrast to astrology, the characteristic guiding system in Campanella's authoritarian utopia; astrology is solely magic that descends from above, it does not, like alchemy, ascend from below into something better. Turning to gold as a whole was and remained for Andreae and his successors the transformation of the world, and metallurgy a mere vicarious test of this 'technology'. In the end, out of the really divined Pan, the world was to be rebuilt, by means of 'pansophy' and humanity.

The paths to this were clearly confused, and in a more familiar region they became conspicuously short. In 1619, three years after the anonymous 'Chemical Wedding', Andreae also published a social utopia: 'Rei publicae Christianopolis descriptio'. Outside the background we have just seen, it is not particularly important and is not independent in any case; that is also why we can talk about it only now, in connection with the Rosicrucians. The golden order has here become a kind of thoroughly Christianized city of artisans and schools, an island-city with a circular temple in the middle, with a market-, gymnastics- and pleasure-zone around it, with fields and workshops on the outskirts of the city. Admittedly there is no mention of alchemy even in the curriculum of the utopian school, even the undoubted dispersion of the city is surrounded by a kind of planetary circle, almost in the manner of the somewhat later 'Civitas solis' of Campanella. Nevertheless, an alchemical consciousness, opposed to the astrological one, is at work on this social utopia, as was already the case in that of More; for Christianopolis rises in an emphatically antithetical manner, as if processed out, from 'the dross of the topsy-turvy, completely corrupt world'. And the science of its wise men, divided into three stages, is not static and self-enclosed, as in Campanella, but the final lesson in the top class is called: 'Prophecy of the final status', 'prophetic theology'. With this the arc towards the 'general reformation' is described once again, towards Rosicrucianism, which combined superstition with light, 'pansophy' with the Day of Judgement in such a strange way. And in the end the most important disciple of Andreae: *Comenius*, the founder of visual instruction, but also of an 'Ecclesia philadelphica', also summarized the intention of Rosicrucian alchemy. Exactly like Andreae, Comenius also speaks ironically and not just enthusiastically about it, but even the irony shares the superstition-faith which it mocks. In 'The Labyrinth of the World and the Paradise of the Heart', 1631, the following is related of the Rosicrucians 'to the sound of trumpets': 'Making gold is the least among a hundred other things they can do; for since the whole of nature is an open book to them, they are capable of giving a particular form to every single thing at will and of knowing everything that happens within the whole circumference of the old world and in the new world, especially as they can speak to one another at a distance of a thousand miles. Then they possess the philosopher's stone, with the aid of which they cure all diseases and confer long life...and after they have kept themselves hidden for so many centuries and have worked quietly at the perfection of philosophy, they are willing, especially now everything is in order and in their opinion a powerful upheaval is in store for the world, not to remain hidden away any longer but to come out into the open, and are ready to communicate their most precious secrets to anyone who is worthy of them'. The 'precious secrets' are here always the same as the secret ways to turn the topsy-turvy world the right way up, so that the gold emerges from it. That very gold which for the very symbolic economic-technological enthusiasts of that time, apart from what it actually is, was also the solar symbol for what had blossomed out, was rounded, and luminous.

Alchemy again: mutatio specierum
(transmutation of inorganic species) and its incubator

The pupil first had to purify himself before he began this sort of thing outside. However sober and businesslike the impulse to make gold, the fields of gold had to be tilled with reverence. Otherwise, it was said (and all works, however confused, are agreed on this), no initiate may be accepted, and even less may a piece of the art be 'betrayed' to him. Often fasts, sexual abstinence and other solemn remittances were required; at least the pupil thereby attained an out of the ordinary, devoutly patient state of mind. And, in a business which could never come to an end anyway, there always remained the possibility of putting failure down to one's own impurity, to inadequate inner preparation. In addition, the fear of evil spirits played a part, in an age when the impenetrable night inhabited by demons already began three steps from the tallow candle and the hearth; when a hellish something croaked, groaned, threatened, hovered or groped in all dark corners. Thus it seemed advisable for the initiate just starting out to be clean himself, and unassailable so to speak; a pious heart was regarded as an amulet. But superstitious as all this was: some of these inward pieces of advice nevertheless seem strangely close to nature, subterraneanly close to nature as it were. The alchemist also changed his pupil's state of awareness so that he should attain an unconscious connection with his materials. The initiate just starting out therefore not only had to become just and pure of desires but also had to do justice to his material, connected in such a way with fire, lead, antimony, ductility and lustre as if they were 'fundamentally' a part of him. Then an 'imagination' of gold was pre-supposed, in reality probably one which was mostly very clear-cut, one of the very comprehensible exchange value, but according to the ideal regulation one which referred to gold, frankincense and myrrh, and thus almost to the birth of the Lord. This kind of thing is less blasphemous or even ideological than it sounds in view of the usual alchemical gold-making and hence money-making; for it belonged, according to the faith of the art, to the technological method itself. Here totally disregarding for the moment deeper allusions and intentions which became apparent in the case of the Rosicrucians. Gold was at any rate to be aroused and summoned with the volitional image of itself, with the preparation of an internal philosopher's stone, before the 'great metallic sound' could be evoked. Some regulations concerning this 'imagination' seem as if the whole passionate volitional subject itself had to enter into nature, 'sympathetically' linked with its own core or source, as if by a subterranean passage. Psychological, religious and natural categories frequently became inter-twined in alchemy just as in the contemporary cosmologies of Paracelsus and Böhme. This state of affairs can hardly be re-experienced scientifically any more, when the very independence from the experiencing and inter-preting subject is regarded as the criterion of knowledge. Above all, even the pictures of the lives of alchemists that have been preserved convey a dogged and single-minded character of course, but more rarely one which seems to have just taken Holy Communion or has even just come from the cave of the earth-spirit. Men like Ramon Lull, and also several of the later Rosicrucians, constitute a clear exception of course, and this counts. In the midst of the mess of his kitchen, of his boundless recipes and endless wrong paths, 'henosis' was required of the initiate, a neo-Platonic term which means simplifying oneself, concentrating on efficacity and seed.

Significantly, even the principal things which the pupil had to know were not all that complicated. This although the many swindlers deliberately obscured the business in order not to have to say what they did not know. And although even in the subjectively honest books the recipes and the pictures are often incompatible with one another, as well as being in a language which has become wholly strange. All the same, certain unified and almost well-formed basic concepts stir in the drapery, but they are by no means numerous. The whole thing is a pure searching, testing, and also uncertain re-testing of other people's experiments, with tremendous industry throughout ten centuries and more. Perhaps the alchemical dream goes back to the Bronze Age, when the first alloying into a golden gleaming metal was successful, and it was certainly widespread in all cultures from about 700 A.D. There is not only Arabian and European, but also Indian, Chinese, and Siamese alchemy; and even here the essential features are not so very different. This art always deals with releasing something that has Become in things again, with displacing something mixed up in them. What was sought in them, above all in those which were themselves already 'elementally' decayed, was at first a still totally featureless substance in itself, the virginal beginning. Everything in existence was tested in turn to this end, the duller or even the more decomposed and exhausted it appeared, the better: rainwater, urine, and excrement were promising when it came to finding the 'materia prima' and the 'enzyme' in them. The metals themselves, apart from this passive original substance, were supposed to be a mixture of three basic components, in varying proportions: of mercury (quicksilver), sulphur (brimstone), and sal (salt). The three do not coincide with naturally occurring deposits of mercury, sulphur, and salt, they are related to them roughly as carbon is related to coal, or rather: they are, in a magicized scholastic sense, their 'essence'. Mercury, the essence of quicksilver, was regarded as the most important component of metals; it consists of water and earth, facilitates ductility and fusibility. Because of these passive properties mercury was regarded as a feminine power, and thus it is closest to the 'materia prima'. Sulphur or the essence of brimstone consists of air and fire, an active masculine entity, it gives metals their colour, and above all their combustibility and transformability. Finally sal, the essence of salt, causes the calcinability and also the hardness and brittleness of metals; very old, magical high evaluations, even touched on in the New Testament ('salt of the earth'), occasionally even linked 'Sal philosophicum' with the philosopher's stone (cf. the healing powder 'with a decidedly alkaline taste' in Goethe's 'Poetry and Truth', book eight). But more crucial than all this was the belief that with the 'materia prima' and with the mixture of the three other basic components metals were not yet exhausted, not yet at the end of their being. Chemistry itself, until towards the end of the eighteenth century, believed in the three basic components of metals cited above (even 'phlogiston' or 'thermal matter', first disposed of by Lavoisier, still has sulphur as one of its ancestors); only, they were not struck by the flash or the will-o'-the-wisp of gold. Thus alchemy further added to the three basic components the highest 'essence' or the germ of gold which presses in all common metals, hindered in growth, an 'entelechy' which is not yet actualized. Like the featureless 'materia prima', the idea of the 'entelechy of gold' also went back to Aristotle, in an admittedly monstrous overwhelming of all other natural entelechies of species and genus. Aristotle had only called motion an 'unfinished entelechy', but for him there lay in matter itself the possibility of every higher form which is next in order; but then 'all matter is potentially gold, just as the egg is an unhatched bird'. This gold-entelechy was to be promoted and liberated by the 'red lion', the 'red tincture', the 'grand elixir', the 'magisterium magnum', which all means the same as the philosopher's stone. Welling's 'Opus mago-cabalisticum' of 1735 (the same which the young Goethe read with Fräulein von Klettenberg, the 'beautiful soul')* says the following on this point: 'The philosophers' stone is a substance which is skilfully composed of a highly refined animated mercurio and its living gold and combined together by means of a prolonged heating in such a way that it can never be separated again, in which form it can immediately produce, refine and tinct the other metals in such a way that they are raised into the nature of the purest gold.' At least descriptions of this fabulous stone exist, and in fact by very famous men; the descriptions

---

* Cf. Goethe's 'Wilhelm Meisters Lehrjahre'. On her death the character of Aurelie leaves behind a document entitled 'Bekenntnisse einer schönen Seele' – 'Confessions of a Beautiful Soul'. This was intended by Goethe as a posthumous tribute to his friend Susanne von Klettenberg.

tally to some extent, just as if each later one stood on the shoulders of the ones before. Ramon Lull compares the stone with a carbuncle; Paracelsus, in his 'Signatura rerum naturalium', states that the stone is heavy, in mass bright red as a ruby, transparent as a crystal, but also malleable as resin and yet fragile as glass; Helmont, the chemist and Paracelsian, relates that the stone, when he had it in his hands, was a heavy saffron-coloured powder, shimmering like not very finely ground glass (cf. Kopp, Die Alchymie, 1886, I, p. 82). Both silver and quicksilver as well as the 'unripe' metals, namely lead, tin, copper and iron, as well as brittle ones like antimony, bismuth, zinc and so on, permeated by the tincture and the stone, are supposed to turn to gold. This refining is caused by 'projection', i.e. by throwing the tincture on to the metal when it is in a state of flux, such that the tincture, according to the purity attained, can transform base metal up to thirty thousand times its own weight (cf. Schmieder, Geschichte der Alchymie, 1832, p. 2). But the alchemists always speak of this utopian, all too utopian jewel with a reverence which goes far beyond such lucrative metal miracles and also more particularly does not omit Gospel allusions to another cornerstone and saviour. Just as the 'materia prima' and more specifically Mercury are compared with the Virgin Mary, so is the stone to her son. Then there is a 'conception of the blessed stone', and *Robert Fludd* calls it 'the foundation stone of the inner temple, so that the whole work of the sun is done'. Then *Jakob Böhme* praises it as the 'root of a kingdom in which there is no longer any other element than the Son of Man'. Just as Böhme on the whole elaborated the outlines of his theosophy and theogony in accordance with alchemical operations; as if in the alchemical process man was only doing what God does in a similar or the same way in the created life of inorganic nature (cf. Harleß, Jakob Böhme und die Alchymisten, 1870, p. 46ff.). Angelus Silesius, in the wealth of his allegories, spurns the alchemical-Messianic ones least of all: 'I am myself the metal, the spirit is hearth and fire,/The tincture which transfigures body and soul is the Messiah' ('Cherubinical Wanderer' I, rhyme 103). But the cue for all this idolization of the stone and of what it brings was given by *Marsilio Ficino*, the neo-Platonist of the Renaissance; all the later allusions and transparencies are first found in his work. Whether still hesitantly veiled in a half gnostic 'Theologia Platonica', or openly in the treatise 'De arte chimica', as follows: 'The Virgin is Mercury, from here the Son is born to us, that is the stone, through whose blood the tainted lower bodies are led back into the golden heavens intact.' At the same time through this text, as it recurs word

for word or with Baroque embellishments in numerous alchemical Rosicrucian writings, the stone, the philosophical gold, and the golden heavens
are made one and the same. So when Andreae says: 'The red tincture is
the purple cloak around the appearing king', then the king is both the
stone and the heavenly-earthly gold itself which it releases from the world.
Chemical chiliasm certainly became one in which analytical chemistry, red
tincture, gold, and paradise at the end of time seem to coincide, in fact
the work of transmutation is regarded, in complete hubris, as the 'laboratorium Dei'. It is not astonishing that now also *all other myths*, whenever
metamorphosis occurred in them, seemed interpretable in terms of alchemy.
Circe and the voyage of the Argonauts, the march through the Red Sea
and the deeds of Hercules, King Midas and the Garden of the Hesperides,
the staff of Moses transforming bitter water into sweet, and the wedding-
feast at Cana: all this and much more besides had to serve the worship
of the stone for the best. Mythical archetypes of change have been most
powerfully preserved in the lavish allegory of alchemy, and if indeed the
Olympian gods breathed their last only in the eighteenth century as metallic
symbols, metallic souls, then the Persian-Jewish Messianic faith lived on
in such strange metallurgy not just in secularized form. Not just allegorically
either, but symbolically; for the transformation into essence lacks the
ambiguity which sends from one Alteritas to the other, it is characterized
in its *target* by unambiguity and undeniable fanaticism of the Absolute.
*Gold, happiness, eternal life are imprisoned in lead; the captive Christ, the gold-
entelechy of all things and beings, must be released from the dungeon of the status
quo by means of the general reformation of which alchemy is a metaphor.* Historical
improvement and the transfiguration of the world were thereby cross-
connected just as they introduced into one another an organic-inorganic
motif of the saviour. Thus it was no accident that Andreae adopted a motto
which was probably already instructive for the Renaissance visionary of
alchemy, the neo-Platonist Ficino; an ancient motto from the Messianic
'Odes of Solomon', stemming from Philo or from his school. It runs:
'Only the pure man, transformed by his own conversion, possesses the
resurrecting power to dissolve, to renew and to wake the substances sunk
like lead into the chaos. By means of the holy water, the logos spermatikos,
he returns them to existence and leads them in purified form upwards,
until all things below are transformed on high.' With this statement
alchemical utopia – the boldest and most mythological that was possible
at all in technology – is really characterized in toto; even beyond the 'Christ
of the unripe metals'. Finally it is characteristic that the pure man or Cathar,

who was found in the 'Odes of Solomon' and who is absent from Arabian and Christian alchemy of the Middle Ages, reappears in the age of the Reformation as does the 'kingdom element' within the essence. The pure man becomes in Paracelsus a chemical Elijah, 'Elijah Artista', and the work of alchemy as a whole becomes that of the 'great May' or simply of the 'kingdom'. Hence Paracelsus (Book Paragranum, Chapter 3) says of nature, in terms as Messianic as they are chemically chiliastic: 'She brings nothing to light that is perfect as it stands, but man must perfect it, and this perfection is called alchemy'; – this is the dies septimus or Sunday of the world, created by man. Not least, the influence of Joachim of Fiore and his 'Third Kingdom' is apparent in all mysticism of the stone during the Reformation and the Baroque; he and Ficino together are the first to produce this very complex alchemical Rosicrucianism.

The mists and the difficulties surrounding the usual greed for gold could thus hardly be more colourful and more convoluted. But in order that the ultimately uncomplicated, ultimately unambiguous nature of the alchemical wishful dream should emerge even at this final stage, we will further refer to two clearly Joachite books on mutation from the Baroque (the heyday of alchemy); to Sperber's 'Treatise on the three seculis', published in 1660, and to the work by Nollius 'Theoria philosophiae hermeticae', 1617. Sperber, one of the most genuine chiliasts, not only seeks to demonstrate 'that a golden age, as the third and final age, is still outstanding, and what it will be like', he also promises: 'The third gospel and the art of alchemy will emerge together.' Nollius, a systematic disciple of Paracelsus and persecuted Rosicrucian, gave the 'work of perfection' a total climax, referring to the general reformation; the philosopher's stone here becomes a series of stages itself, like its manufacture, it becomes the celestial stair of nature. The chemical climax to the final kingdom runs: 'Verus Hermes, Portae hermeticae sapientiae, Silentium hermeticum, Axiomata hermetica, De generatione verum naturalium'* and finally: 'De renovatione'.† Likewise, the golden dream, apart from the metallurgy in which it was technologically immersed, was everywhere really a kind of mythology of liberation as well. It was never more than, at best, a mythology, but also seldom less than one of liberation. Something like the catharsis of objects, together with that of souls, did not lose its main alchemical sense from the late Middle Ages up to the metaphors of classicism, and especially Romanticism. Even Goethe, in

---

* 'True Hermes, Gates of Hermetic wisdom, Hermetic silence, Hermetic axioms, On the generation of true natural things.'
† 'On renovation.'

his history of the theory of colours, when dealing with the alchemists, still alludes to these connections; he even interprets them by means of a kind of Kantianism: 'If those three sublime ideas most intimately related to one another, God, virtue and immortality, have been called the highest demands of reason, then there are clearly three corresponding demands of a more sensory kind: gold, health and long life.' Alchemy certainly did not find any gold, nor was it capable of finding this goal with its fantastic process-methods. Nevertheless it can be justified not merely as a forerunner of modern chemistry, and even its more specific plan: the transmutation of metals (elements) as a plan itself sounds by no means grotesque any more in the age of the splitting of the atom, and of the transfer of electrons in the elements. On the contrary, it was grotesque that in the last century, in Darwin's century of the 'transmutation of species', the inorganic elements themselves were regarded as unshakable and the wholly identical term 'mutatio specierum' (it first occurs in alchemy) was not understood at all. But above all, as has become obvious, the purpose of alchemy is by no means exhausted by partial transmutations, at least not in the century shortly before the Enlightenment. Instead, the inscription on the gate of this disreputable technological wishful dream ran, in a quite total fashion: Jehi Or, Let there be light; – this therefore lay in the horizon of the fantastic mutations. The vast majority of the gold-cookers were undoubtedly searching for nothing other than a purse that is always full, and here fooled neither themselves nor others with anything much grander. The enthusiasts in this area however, sitting in front of the same furnace, and also thoroughly inclined towards the prospect of as many ducats as they liked, also had in mind another transfiguration of nature as a goal of metamorphosis.

Unregulated inventions and 'Propositiones' in the Baroque period

It was always possible to plan into the mere blue, arbitrarily and also shakily. But sounder technological dreams and those directed towards an extension of implements appear only sparsely before 1500. However remarkable Roman plumbing, Chinese paper and gunpowder (only used for fireworks), and Egyptian cranes are: only with the mandate under capitalism did larger technological projects also get under way. Admittedly, around 550 in Byzantium there are already plans for a ship with paddle-wheels which are moved by oxen at a capstan; but it never got further than the planning stage. Miniatures based on the medieval legend of Alexander already portray a kind of submarine, in which Alexander sinks into the depths and observes their monsters; but the age was only interested in these ocean depths, not in the glass submarine. Roger Bacon, the empirical and scientific Franciscan, represents a solitary exception in the thirteenth century. In his 'Epistola de secretis operibus artis' he prophesied carriages which are moved without the aid of animals, 'with incredible speed', and also flying machines, 'in which a man who sits comfortably and thinks about everything beats the air in the manner of the birds'. But Roger Bacon, with these inventive dreams, met with no interest in a society which was just as class-bound and static as it was full of mistrust towards nature. Thus only in the Renaissance, only with the business interest and pursuit of profit of the capitalism which was getting under way at that time, was the technological imagination publicly acknowledged and promoted. The Renaissance and Baroque are both the age of technological wind-makers à la Dr Orfyréus, whom we have encountered above, and above all of practical and capable designers. They were dilettantes tinkering around in many areas, experimenting around in all areas, without sufficient mechanical knowledge, but overflowing with patentable ideas. At their head stood Joachim Becher (1635–1682), a splendid figure whom Sombart rescued from obscurity (cf. 'Die Technik im Zeitalter des Frühkapitalismus', Archiv für Sozialwissenschaft, Vol. 34, p. 721ff.), a lucky Sunday's child of inventiveness: Becher brought blueprints into the world by the dozen, new looms, water-wheels, clockwork mechanisms, a thermoscope, a method of extracting tar from hard coal, and so on. His book 'Foolish Wisdom and wise Folly or a Hundred at once Political and physical/mechanical and mercantilic Concepta and Propositiones', 1686, really raves in the realm of unlimited possibilities, unimpeded by mathematical and mechanical knowledge of the facts. This strange connection between dilettantism and technology, incidentally, lasted from the Renaissance until far into the eighteenth century. A doctor, a student of theology, an Egyptologist, and a young worker invented asphalt, the knitting machine, the magic lantern, and the steering mechanism of the steam-engine at that time, while the great natural scientists, like Kepler, Newton, and even Galileo, were interested in technology more as a side-line and only two scientists: Guericke, as the inventor of the air pump,* and Huygens, as the inventor of the pendulum clock, figure equally strongly in the history of physics and technology. The capitalist mandate was the same for technology and science, but for a long

* Otto von Guericke (1602–86). His air-pump, invented in 1654, preceded Robert Boyle and Robert Hooke's version, the 'Machina Boyliana' (c. 1658).

time technology was still connected with handicrafts, and almost only in
Agricola (De re metallica, 1530) was practical activity accorded the same status
as theory. There is also something else which, for their part, kept the majority
of inventors in those days aloof from mathematical and mechanical knowledge. For the magic natural background had still by no means collapsed for
them; the world of Paracelsus took root and survived for a long time precisely
in technological books. Above all in those dealing with mining; the earth-
spirit or a ghostly life in the depths had a naive effect on the technologists
at that time, just as it stirred the poets and the philosophers of nature sentimen-
tally again so much later, in Romanticism. The gases in the air were demons
who were after the miner's blood, the rising waters from the depths contained
a living water-spirit, whereas the falling waters which have to be raised were
therefore regarded as dead waters, in short, even in this direction technology,
and not just alchemy, lived in a qualitatively magical and not in a quantitatively
mechanical world. Almost solely in Italy, as the most advanced capitalist
country at that time, was invention linked with early calculation. Around
1470 the engineer Valturio sketched a car, called a 'storm carriage', with
windmill sails at the side, the drive was transmitted to the wheels of the
carriage by means of cogwheels, and the sketch was worked out mathematically. And when Brunelleschi put together the machines for building his
dome of Florence cathedral himself, they were combined levers and inclined
planes in a mathematically considered design. And as far as the bold technologist Leonardo da Vinci is concerned, he is the first purely immanent inventor
and scientist whatsoever, working on the basis of causality ('necessity'). Keen
observation and careful calculation assisted his varied plans; occasionally with
the errors of the pioneer, but without any dilettantism. Thus he designed
the first parachute, the first turbine (preserved as a sketch: 'Propeller in a
canal'), and the first flyover system (likewise preserved as a sketch: 'Design
for streets lying above one another'). He studied the flight of birds in order
to realize the human dream of flight, the oldest of all the technological wishful
images: 'I intend to make the big artificial bird take his first flight; it will
fill the universe with amazement, and all works with its fame; eternal glory
will be accorded to the nest where it was born.' The bird was to rise in
Florence, but it never got beyond a plan, and Icarus did not even fall, so little
did he rise from the ground. And of course the mathematical mechanics on
which Leonardo wanted to base his inventions was only developed after his
death. And furthermore even Leonardo, despite the mathematically constructive instinct which so characteristically distinguishes him, did not wholly
emerge from the organic view of nature of the Renaissance. On the contrary:

'The sea of blood which lies around the heart is the oceanic waters, its breathing and the waxing and waning of blood through the pulses is in the earth the ebb and flow of the ocean, and the warmth of the soul of the world is the fire inherent in the earth, and the fires which breathe into spas from various parts of the earth are the abode of the vegetative soul' (Richter, 'Literary works of Leonardo da Vinci', 1883, p. 1000). Thus even Leonardo himself had a more 'sympathetic' than quantitative attitude towards nature, although and indeed because he believed that it was already written in numbers. But the inventive will in the Renaissance and the Baroque as a whole remains essentially in the impromptu, with the belief that inventing is a mysterious process, as is ultimately the nature into which it delves. Joachim Becher, who was regarded as the greatest inventive genius of his day, himself speaks in deeply moved tones of the gift granted to him which cannot be acquired, the 'donum inventionis'. For Becher it is not tied to professional knowledge: 'There is no respect of person or profession here; kings and peasants, the learned and the unlearned, heathens and Christians, the devout and the wicked have been endowed with it.' Inventiveness built into the unknown for a long time to come and thereby made it known for the first time, it produced the unprecedented, additional working capacity of the machine, but often without seeking to have more contact with existence than that of the gift, the lucky touch and the chance which turns out lucky for the gift.

Bacon's Ars inveniendi; survival of the Lullian art

Conscious invention also appeared at first only as dream and planning. As in Francis Bacon, in his 'Novum Organum scientiarum', 1620, and the inductive information still imparted in very general terms there. There is a call for experiments, operational knowledge of the laws of nature, the renunciation of myth, and caution with respect to teleological explanations. Tricks of the trade are omitted, as are trade secrets, based on merely manual skill or chance recipes, especially magical-theosophical backdrops. Admittedly Bacon does not speak in an unfriendly fashion of alchemy in his posthumous work 'Sylva sylvarum or a Natural History', he thinks that gold-making is possible, as a ripening of the 'lighter metals', but he mocks the methods used, particularly the desired 'projection' with the philosopher's stone, these 'few drops of elixir'. He mocks this as he does everything abrupt and miraculous; that is why the connections often claimed to exist between Bacon and the Rosicrucians are also dubious. Only Bacon's aim of a 'regnum hominis' touches on the 'higher alchemy', but the regnum was conceived as the mastery of nature, not as the transfiguration of nature or as Joachim's 'Third Kingdom'. Especially the 'Ars inveniendi' in the 'Novum organum scientiarum' seeks to found theoretical finding and practical inventing wholly on experience (instead of on something beyond the sensory world) and on regular induction (instead of on deductions which trust written authority). Only through observation and analysis are the 'constant properties', the 'primitive forms' of all things discernible; only thus is the goal of knowledge achieved: 'the production of artefacts'. Knowledge of earlier inventive dreams is also supposed to be useful for this, but essentially so that they can be used to emphasize that which seemed daring or impossible to men and which was nevertheless to be found in their technological dreams. The record of realized, and particularly of unrealized plans also gave useful hints for inventive ideas which hitherto lay 'beyond the Pillars of Hercules': but only the ship of the real art of experimentation will reach the golden Gardens of the Hesperides. Only *in this way* according to Bacon do the old fairytales come true, they are not realized by continually being told walking the same old treadmill in an increasingly garrulous, increasingly epigonic fashion. And just like irregular anticipation, the quarrelsome lumber of words and deductions has an unfruitful effect: 'So that the state of learning as it now is appears to be represented to the life in the old fable of Scylla, who had the head and face of a virgin, but her womb was hung round with barking monsters, from which she could not be delivered. For in like manner the sciences to which we are accustomed have certain general positions which are specious and flattering; but as soon as they come to particulars, which are as the parts of generation, when they should produce fruit and works, then arise contentions and barking disputations, which are the end of the matter and all the issue they can yield' (Magna Instauratio, Preface). Knowledge is power, also the power to fulfil the old dreams of inventors, and indeed those of magic, if not to surpass them in boldness: 'For as for the *natural magic* whereof now there is mention in books, containing certain credulous and superstitious conceits and observations of Sympathies and Antipathies and hidden properties, and some frivolous experiments, strange rather by disguisement than in themselves; it is as far differing in truth of nature from such knowledge as we require, as the story of king Arthur of Britain, or Hugh of Bordeaux, differs from Caesar's commentaries in truth of story. For it is manifest that Caesar did greater things *de vero* than those imaginary heroes were feigned to do.'* The term 'magia naturalis' stems from a work by the neo-Aristotelian della Porta from the Renaissance and it was already directed in his work against the cabbalists and believers in magic at that time. In terms of detail, of course, Bacon exhibits rather than fills the gaps in previous knowledge, and gives desiderata himself rather than building up 'natural magic'. Also his technique of induction, directed towards the discovery of 'primitive forms', is still itself far more scholastic than scientific. Also he regarded mathematics as a mere appendage to physics and by no means as its methodical basis, which to his contemporaries appeared to be a downright backward element in this 'Novum Organum', this 'Nova instauratio scientiarum'. Though he did this on the still wholly organic, natural-philosophical grounds that 'the mathematicians spoil physics', because the latter 'deals with the qualitative' (with the 'form of heat' for example). But Bacon showed, with enormous foresight, if not the ways then the various and at that time still wholly untrodden cadres and areas in which modern science itself was to develop, with a purely causal-mechanical technology.

Regulated invention therefore here presupposes passing from the particular to the general. But however sound the inductive conclusion is, it neither seeks nor is able to go beyond a more or less high degree of probability. In the strict sense it is valid only for the sum of individual cases observed, but not for all the other unobserved ones to which the general law obtained is now extended. Whereas the very deduction rejected by Bacon brings necessity with it, at least in terms of formal logic: if according to the major premise all men are mortal, then Caius as a man not only probably but necessarily has to die. And as far as this kind of propagation of science is concerned, even in the Middle Ages, as Bacon himself reminds us, and hence in reasonable proximity to Arthur's Round Table, there was an Ars inveniendi, which even appeared in the shape of a machine. It was the so-called Lullian art or the technologically manufactured seven-league boot of the *deductive concept, of the syllogism*. Even the Middle Ages, though hardly technologically active at all, was interested in such instruments: as those of knowledge, not of change. The strangely

---

* 'The Advancement of Learning', Bacon's works, ed. Spedding, Vol. III, p. 361. Bloch is using an inferior German translation of Bacon. His quotation suggests natural magic can perform great deeds, combined with science, whereas Bacon's original states that it is inferior to real truth and knowledge. In Bloch's version natural magic is thus compared with the true deeds of Caesar, whereas in Bacon it is compared to the legends of Arthur, i.e. exactly the reverse.

rationalist scholastic Ramon Lull had made a device around 1300 by means of which every kind of deductive derivation was to be discovered and checked. The device ('Instrumentum ad omnis scibilis demonstrationem') consisted of a system of concentric circles, on each of which a group of concepts was spread in the shape of a fan. By moving these circles all possible combinations whatsoever between subject and predicate were supposed to be achieved; whereby the number of possible subjects and that of possible basic predicates (predicables), and consequently the quantity of discs was fixed. There was thus a Figura Dei which 'contained' the whole of theology, a Figura animae which 'contained' the whole of psychology, and a Figura virtutum with the seven virtues and deadly sins in alternately blue and red chambers (v. the details in J. E. Erdmann, Grundriss der Geschichte der Philosophie I, §206, 4–12; table in Stöckl, Geschichte der Philosophie des Mittelalters II, 1865, p. 936). The Lullian art thus sought to give instructions for discovering what is categorially definable, scientifically distinguishable, combinable, and provable in every object. And Lull's hope was simply that the deduction machine of knowledge should encompass and exhaust every variation of cognition that was at all meaningfully possible. It demonstrates literally ad oculos, so that anyone eager for knowledge can also see and not merely understand the arch-rationalist derivation of individual definitions from ideas. All this in the most abbreviated mode of deduction, based on Aristotelian topics, though also not unconnected with the Plotinian, indeed cabbalistic doctrine of emanation of the world from ideas. At any rate the most astonishing machine was in fact produced, that of an 'Ars magna' as both Ars inveniendi and Ars demonstrandi, portrayed in symbols, circles, tables, in the reductions of a kind of logical logarithmic clock. Giordano Bruno sought to improve the Lullian art by decreasing the circles, and Pico della Mirandola connected it for the first time with Pythagorean arithmetic. The need in bourgeois calculation for an arithmetical universal derivation of all that is given from a few logical elements or principles ('first truths') ensured that the Lullian art was not forgotten anyway, at least with regard to its intention. Leibniz began his career with the work 'De arte combinatoria', 1666, in which, following Lull and Bruno, he treated the modes of combination of concepts as calculable; so that one would be able to demonstrate an error in reasoning with the same clarity and certainty as an arithmetical error. Throughout his life Leibniz searched for the valid combination theory composed of an 'alphabet of ideas', according to which new truths can be found mechanically as it were. This 'Ars combinatoria' survives in an extremely elementary form even in the diverse calculating machines; though not in order to discover new truths but, as the so-called Maniac (Mechanical and Numerical Integrator and Calculator) has succeeded in doing, in order to multiply two ten-figure numbers in less than a thousandth of a second. Pascal had constructed the first mechanical calculator, with rotating wheels, and today Lull's arithmeticized dream has been turned into a whole intellectual industry, with speed as witchcraft. Even the newest American mechanical engineering, which has culminated for the moment in Norbert Wiener's 'Cybernetics', still incorporates a portion of Lull's mechanical idea. His plan never aimed at such automatisms though, even a mathematical 'alphabet of ideas' still lay beyond the horizon of the Lullian art, in view of the time at which it arose. Instead, Lull originally had a – missionary purpose with his machine; the invention was planned as a kind of deductive apostle of the faith. Thus Lull had intended to convince all unbelievers of the truth of the Christian religion by means of the irrefutable demonstrations of his machine, free of every error in reasoning. This aim is of course also as remote as possible from Francis Bacon and his 'natural magic', even more remote than it is from Leibniz. Bacon thus speaks almost contemptuously of Lull, and not only because of the scholastic mythology itself, but also because of the curious *deduction* and *subsumption* in which its machinery moves. Nevertheless, because of its technical nature Lull's invention would also have cut quite a good figure in Bacon's 'Ars inveniendi', and especially in his utopian hall of instruments (Theatrum mechanicum). Not even the passionate praise of induction stands in the way of this; for even Bacon's *induction* still seeks to explore 'the basic form of things' and finally, although the word deduction is deliberately absent, permits 'descending', namely from the law of forms to the experiment of their self-application in appearance. Only in this, in contrast to purely flat empirical progress, is the regulated art of the inventor completed for Bacon: 'But after this store of particulars has been set out duly and in order before our eyes, we are not to pass at once to the investigation and discovery of new particulars or works...For our road does not lie on a level (neque in plano via sita est), but ascends and descends; first ascending to axioms, then descending to works' ('Novum Organum' I, Aph. 103). In this 'descendendo ad opera' the 'Ars inveniendi' was for Bacon a portion of Lull's 'Ars magna' as well; directed against the method of testing, failure, and renewed testing (trial and error method) of the philistines, – not just the superstitious ones. But the goal of knowledge for the English project-maker was not knowledge for its own sake, but – very much in the manner of Marlowe's Doctor Faustus – power through knowledge, a new Atlantis, where everything serves man, serves him for the best.

New Atlantis, the utopian laboratory

And if perhaps a hundred years
From now an airship with Greek wine
High-laden through the red dawn steers –
Who would not be the ferryman?

Gottfried Keller

But the hearth still lies far off on which the new useful things develop. In Bacon's dream of distant shores, shipwrecked people reach an island in the South Seas, and are there introduced to inventing as it ought to be. What was hesitantly and haphazardly begun elsewhere is completed on the 'clever island'; a separate class of natural scientists achieves incredible things there. Bacon's 'New Atlantis', 1623,* which appeared at the same time as Campanella's 'Civitas solis', was supposed to answer two questions according to the plan of its author: that concerning the best research institute, and that concerning the best state. The unfinished work only answers the first question, it portrays a 'Solomon's House', vast, bright and wide. What the wise king knew and could do by means of magic, according to the legend, is here actually carried out, in so far as it lies within human ability and advantage. The voice of the birds is not understood, no spirits are invoked, but the hyssop which grows on the wall is recognized all the better. The legendary accomplishments of the Atlantians are also recalled, of which Plato gives an account in his Critias, with their skills in making canals and working in bronze. But in Bacon it is a question not of vanished but of utopian splendour, not of a pre-Mycenean but of a post-Gothic age. In his new Atlantis Bacon describes successful inventions which are partly still to come, and he outlines them with amazing anticipation. Even though merely anticipating the result, and not the means to achieve it for instance, as intended by the author

* The first edition of Bacon's 'New Atlantis', edited by William Rawley, actually appeared in 1627 appended to the 'Sylva Sylvarum'. There is some doubt as to its actual date of composition. Spedding suggests it was written in 1624.

of a 'Novum Organum'. Disdain for mathematics prevented Bacon from having a vision of production, but his vision of the fruits is all the richer. Bacon's technological prophecy is unique; his 'book of desiderata' more or less contains modern technology in wishful outline and goes beyond it. The head of Solomon's House declares they have means of producing artificial rain or even snow and artificial mountain air. They cultivate new varieties of plants and fruit in hothouses, they shorten the ripening process, mix the species of animals according to their needs, mineralize their baths, and produce artificial minerals and building materials.* Vivisection is not lacking: 'We try also all poisons and other medicines upon them [beasts and birds], as well of chirurgery as physic.' The Atlantians are acquainted with the telephone and no less so with the submarine: 'We have also means to convey sounds in trunks and pipes, in strange lines and distances (ad magnam distantiam et in lineis tortuosis)....we have ships and boats for going under water, and brooking of seas.' The microphone is not lacking either: 'We represent small sounds as great and deep; likewise great sounds extenuate and sharp'; Atlantis is even acquainted, incredibile dictu, with the most modern quarter-tone technique: 'We have harmonies which you have not, of quarter-sounds (quadrantes sonorum), and lesser slides of sounds.' There is a telescope and a microscope: 'We have also glasses and means to see small and minute bodies perfectly and distinctly; as the shapes and colours of small flies and worms, grains and flaws in gems, which cannot otherwise be seen; observations in urine and blood, not otherwise to be seen.' Solomon's House further harbours aeroplanes, steam-engines, water-turbines and still other 'Magnalia naturae', 'feats of nature', with it and beyond it. Thus 'New Atlantis' is not merely the first technologically reflective utopia, in fact d'Alembert called this work (thus surpassing the wishful models of fairytales themselves) 'un catalogue immense de ce qui reste à découvrir'.† Bacon's work is, even subsequently, the only utopia of classical status which gives decisive status to the technological productive forces of the better life. Unlike in real life at any rate, the mechanical world and the economic-social one were not always linked in utopias. Bacon's 'New Atlantis' would have deserved emulation here, one seriously corresponding to technological development and its immanent possibilities.

---

* Bloch gives a direct quotation here, but the unreliable translation he is using has again condensed the original. The full text in which these ideas are found is not included here because of its length. It may be found in Spedding's edition, Vol. III, pp. 157-62. We have set the 'quotation' in indirect speech here.

† 'an immense catalogue of what remains to be discovered'.

Apart from the fact that the technological component never appeared in
any novel of an ideal state other than as ornamentation, social utopias,
as is clear in the case of Owen, often even lagged behind the technological
level attained by their age. Aside from Bacon, only Campanella at best
forms an exception here, in so far as he too dreams of unborn technology,
indeed of unborn architecture, though without Bacon's powerful wit.
Delighting in invention almost as much as Bacon, he predicts in the 'Civitas
solis' that 'the development of the printing press and of magnetism will
fill the coming centuries with more history than the world foresaw in
four thousand years'. But Campanella's utopia could exist even without
these breakthroughs in existing nature, it even contradicts them in its
astrologically static form. Whereas 'New Atlantis' seeks to lie in every
respect beyond the Pillars of Hercules, i.e. beyond the binding of given
nature. Bacon's fragment, in its technological optimism, does not even
recognize catastrophes any more, there is no longer any firedamp in the
controlled earth. There is of course no mention of the firedamps which
fill not nature but uncontrolled human *history*, of the various burning Troys.
Fate appears to be so restrained in purely technological terms that *Solomon's
House* already seems to have coped with it before *Solomon's State* has even
developed. The question as to what men should do with their knowledge
and power, within the social nature which Bacon, the fallen Lord
Chancellor, had not found to be wholly without catastrophes, is not yet
posed by Bacon the philosopher in this fragment of his; shortly before
the question concerning the best state the 'New Atlantis' breaks off. But
the outlines of the unwritten sequel, concerning Solomon's kingdom, can
be guessed perfectly well from the philosopher's other works. Guessed
in contrast to a mechanization made absolute; for Bacon, contrary to popular
opinion, is neither a pure utilitarian nor a pure empiricist. However much
he praises the life of active invention, he still gives precedence to the life
of reason: 'So must we likewise from experience of every kind first
endeavour to discover true causes and axioms; and seek for experiments
of Light, not for experiments of Fruit.'* Only a balance between the
contemplative and the active life appears correct and salutary to the dreamer
of the 'New Atlantis': 'But this is that which will indeed dignify and
exalt knowledge, if contemplation and action may be more nearly and
straitly conjoined and united together than they have been; a conjunction
like unto that of the two highest planets, Saturn the planet of rest and

* 'Novum Organum', Aphorism 70.

contemplation, and Jupiter the planet of civil society and action'.* But Solomon's House is incorporated into an ultimately calm kingdom: *the control of nature* (in which privation and catastrophes come to an end) *serves in Bacon the establishment of a 'regnum hominis'*. This kingdom and goal of knowledge is in Bacon filled with the hopes which early capitalism was still able to cherish for mankind through the unleashing of the forces of production: 'Now the true and lawful goal of the sciences is none other than this: that human life be endowed with new discoveries and powers.' ('Novum Organum', Aph. 81).† Mankind was to emerge from a world full of epidemics, shortage crisis, and underproduction, from a world to which Bacon's admired Montaigne had called out: Grâce à l'homme, into the affluence which only seemed attainable to earlier utopias by transferring them to a 'paradisial nature', into the affluence which precedes the regnum hominis as dinner precedes the dance. The plan of 'Solomon's House' has been fulfilled in the meantime by technical colleges and laboratories, beyond Bacon's dreams; there is still a long way to go as regards the regnum hominis. And even the 'production of artefacts' in Bacon's sense, a not only Promethean but also artificial production, has not subsequently abolished catastrophes in technology. Admittedly the contact with nature remained in the bourgeois economy and society which arrived, but it remained sufficiently abstract and unmediated. Bacon's great maxim: 'Natura parendo vincitur', nature is conquered by obedience, remained active, but it was crossed by the interest of an 'exploitation' of nature, and thus by an interest which has nothing more to do with the natura naturans which Bacon still knows and singles out as the 'causa causarum', let alone being allied to it. In this way there arose, alongside all the blessings, such a peculiarly artificial-abstract character in bourgeois technology that it can doubtless also seem, in many of its cunning inventions, still 'unnaturally' founded and not just still inhumanly managed. 'Solomon's House', so it seems, cannot do without Solomon after all, that is, without natural wisdom. It contains, like all wisdom, reference to its opposite number, nature; the regnum hominis attained within it too, and not merely above it, would then have it easier.

---

* 'The Advancement of Learning', Spedding, Vol. III, p. 294.

† Bloch quotes a much longer passage here, again from an unreliable translation. After the first sentence, it bears no relation to Bacon's Aphorism 81. We have omitted the extraneous material and give only the opening of the original aphorism here.

II. Non-Euclidean Present and Future, the Problem of Technological Contact

Plans must also be spurred on

There is no inner urge as such to invent something. A mandate is always necessary for this which pours water on the planned wheels. Every implement presupposes exact needs and has the precise aim of satisfying them; otherwise it would not be there. Hunger started everything off at this very point, the earliest implements are those for hunting and fishing, the former also served as weapons. The plough, the invention of spinning and weaving, pottery: even if some of this was covered with ornament, the latter was never primary, or it served a useful purpose itself, as a supposed magic symbol. And to this day the inventor, even as a dreamer, is a practical man. At the same time he is more conscious than any other intellectual maker of not being a wheel that rolls of its own accord. If the English mines had not been in danger of flooding, then Watt, like so many others before him, would have watched the hissing kettle in vain, a legendary kettle anyway. And without a social mandate the image of the knitting machine or chain towing would not have flashed into the mind of any inventor, out of inner vocation for instance. It would not have flashed through his mind without a mandate any more than the invention of artificial raw materials or even of atom bombs today. Unrecognized inventors are therefore, in a particularly clear way, those who come too early or also, as in the stagnant business of the West today, too late. Here there are only two kinds of ideas, those which can be bought and those which cannot be bought; the latter do not really exist even as blueprints. An inventor cannot do anything superfluous, nor has one ever had it in mind to plan such a thing.

Late bourgeois curbing of technology,
apart from the military kind

The bourgeois mandate to invent has been characteristically waning for a long time. Before the last crisis too much was produced for capital to be able to cope with it. Famine began, not because of crop failure as in earlier times, but because the granaries were too full. As is evident and well-known, the private capitalist economy has itself become a chain for the production which it once unchained. Only new means of death are interesting, shortly before and during the war, war technology is booming, the peaceful kind follows in its wake. And there is also a second motive for this curbing, one from a wholly opposite, namely socialist area. Socialism at the present time is more urgently interested in changing backward society than in changing a technology which is advanced enough anyway and can be readily adopted. Technology is already collective: the individual workshop in which the master craftsman still collaborates with his few journeymen has long since become the factory of hundreds and thousands. But the private owner of the factory who does not collaborate in the production is still thoroughly individual – for social, not for technological reasons. It is in fact precisely the contradiction between the maturity, and also the long since collective form of production and the antiquated private capitalist form of appropriation which particularly demonstrates the nonsense of the capitalist economy. Technology, in so far as it represents a technology of the means of existence and not the means of death, is itself cum grano salis already socialist; it therefore needs less future planning than society. All this combines to make technological utopias nowhere near as exciting as they were even in the time of Jules Verne. Not merely because the sky is teeming with fake birds, by means of which it is possible to go around the world in a considerably shorter time than eighty days, but above all precisely because even in utopian terms a temporary moratorium on technology has occurred. The term moratorium on technology stems from the long period of crisis before the Second World War and is in this respect far more pertinent than the jubilation over production fleetingly aroused by a so-called economic miracle as a result of the Second World War, with which it is wholly in character. A crisis of surplus, the more than cyclical fate of monopoly capitalism, stands in the way of the green light over and over again, of the mandate which capital, in its progressive period, had given to technological daring. The contrast to the pace of invention from 1750 to 1914 is and remains a piercing one; no investment of today feels anything like as electrified any more. Wholly contrary to hasty appearances and propaganda, the vaunted pace of technology, as far as changes in *civilian life* are concerned, rather advances like that of a mail-coach, compared with that of the Industrial Revolution and with the nineteenth century. Look what became of Papin's old steam digester once capital was interested in making steam do some work. And what a long

way in a short time from Newcombe's steam-engine, which hardly managed
to drain a mine, to Watt's steam-engine, with slide valves, eccentrics,
flywheels and the industrial consequences. Look what became of the rubbed
amber of the past and of the magnet once the interest in the working
power of electricity joined the interest in steam. What a powerful corpus
the magnet became in the dynamo, what changes this induced electric system
rapidly introduced into the world, into a world which still sought to unleash
the forces of production. Thirty years after the opening of the first stretch
of railway line, Europe was covered with rails in all directions, and not
even as much time as that elapsed after the invention of the first induced
electric devices before there was barely a village without a telephone and
not a town without an electric power station. Whereas the new, the colossal
discovery of our age: atomic energy, certainly more revolutionary than
steam power and electricity together, was described apart from the atom
bomb by American technical journals merely as 'the next century's power'.
Since at the time of this prophecy there was more than half of the present
century to go, the revolution by the new force of production is not even
shifted on to children but on to great-grandchildren; the Soviet Union,
however, erected the first atomic power station. Practical difficulty is by
no means involved in America's hesitation, for it was the first to produce
the atom bomb, by virtue of the imperialist mandate. What is involved
remains instead a state of society which no longer easily endures the glorious
chapters of technology, as they used to say in the nineteenth century. Despite
the diversion which technological progress, or rather the praise of
technological progress, achieves in ideological terms. Despite the possibility
of oil and coal capital also cashing in on atomic energy, so that it can
be channelled capitalistically after a fashion, as long as it possibly can. For
fear of further overproduction, even the development of long since
introduced inventions is astonishingly slowed down, even if it cannot be
prevented. Chemistry continues the invention of substitutes of course, which
the nineteenth century had started with artificial indigo. It synthetically
manufactures rubber, oil, and textiles, it even makes inroads into steel
and cement, presumably entire cars can be pressed out of the new material
'plastic', and lifting cranes, trains, tenement houses, skyscrapers baked
out of it. Beyond the aeroplane there is the threat or fascination of adventurous rocket propulsion, with 'supply rockets', 'multistage rockets', and
a 'space station' (artificial earth-moon); this is all the more inexorable as
precisely this sort of thing invites imperialist war-interests. Nevertheless
the pace of installation and industrialization in the previous century is

lacking; the leap from the mail-coach to the train was an incomparably greater change in living conditions than the leap from the train to the aeroplane. And we do not even need to consider here the hail of bombs beneath which the aeroplane has been encountered by most people and has also possibly transported them, to kingdom come. The latent Luddism of late capitalism everywhere counteracts the progression of what is Edison-like, although once it has got under way it is not that easy to stop. On the whole, however, invention will only have real utopia at heart again when an economy directed towards the satisfaction of needs is pursued instead of a profit economy. When the law of socialism: maximum satisfaction of needs at the level of the highest technology, has finally superseded the law of capitalism: maximum profit. When consumption is capable of assimilating all products, and technology, regardless of risk and private profitability, is once again given a mandate for boldness, without any imperialistically promoted demonism.

De-organization of the machine; atomic energy, non-Euclidean technology

This is all the more likely as another trend is stirring beneath the present crust. Far beyond substitute materials, however much it may lie in their field, namely in that which is *no longer natural*, but artificial or all too artificial. The unnatural element already began when men invented the wheel, which is not found on their body. Usually, as we know, implements and machines arose from imitating parts of the body, the hammer is the fist, the chisel the nail, the saw the row of teeth and so on. But great progress occurred only when this sort of thing was abandoned, when the machine solved its task with means of its own. The sewing machine does not operate like sewing by hand, nor the type-setting machine like hand-setting; the aeroplane is not an imitation of a bird, on the contrary its wing is inflexible, and its propeller is not a wing. Only in the steam-engine and locomotive does a semblance from the old organic series still continue to operate. Hissing, boiling, breathing, with connecting rods like arms at the side; children playing are thus still induced to imitate locomotives. And how organically familiar the description can still be which Joseph Conrad bestows on the ship's engine-room in 'Typhoon', the pale long flames on the brightly polished metal, the enormous crank-heads emerging from the flooring, and sinking down again, the big-jointed

connecting-rods, reminiscent of skeleton limbs, which thrust down the
crank-heads, and pull them up again: 'And deep in the half-light other
rods dodged deliberately to and fro, crossheads nodded, discs of metal rubbed
smoothly against each other, slow and gentle, in a commingling of shadows
and gleams.' This sort of thing, in its expressive and unerring movements,
still looks like an artificial organism or also like a natural mechanism. But
the technology which has developed in the present century shows less and
less resemblance to *human limbs and proportions*, and the steam-engine only
gives a final greeting, itself only the semblance of a greeting to the old
organoid series. The retort is no longer a mixing bowl or kneading-trough
in which given existing substances are combined and remodelled into forms
which are not very remote from them; and the big machine disposes of
the final organic resemblance. If the rod, shaft, bearing, ball-bearing, wheel,
cogwheel, transmission and all other machine components were already
the beginning of de-organization, this is all the more true of their combination, the machine as work-transformer. Not merely is the *organic guideline*
broken down in it, but another break or constraint redisposes things here,
one in the *physical guideline* itself. A machine as a whole, as defined by
Reuleaux, 'is a combination of resistant elements which are so arranged
that by means of them mechanical forces are compelled to operate under
set conditions'. Although this definition, in accordance with the nineteenth-
century way of thinking, omits any human final designation, and hence
the social, unnaturalistic purpose which mechanical forces are compelled
to achieve, it is still evident that machinery itself is already an *unnaturalistic
occurrence*, a kind of *unnatural physics*. And within it the repulsion to the
given naturalistic element increases even further; organic projection is
increasingly abandoned or transcended. The electric locomotive is a colossus
from no man's land, and the rocket-propelled aircraft that shoots through
the stratosphere is not even like a propeller and wing in relation to the
bird, but like a meteor. This is all the more true of the possible technology
derived from the hitherto remotest power drives: the sub-atomic ones,
and from the transformers into which these are conducted. With this
technology, not just organic projection is abandoned but also partly the
realm of the *at least three-dimensional mechanical world*, in which the electric
locomotive, the diesel engine, and the rocket-propelled aircraft are still
located. Graphic classical mechanics itself is thereby abandoned: in the
electron 'nothing looks like anything at all any more', electrons and protons
are no longer the matter of the old physical world. Even if they are
by no means, as their idealistic interpreters say, 'mathematical-logical

structures', the former ether, which conjured up notions of gas for so long, has nevertheless become a synonym for an n-dimensional field, for an electro-magnetic structural field. If a real radiation industry was to arise, still within capitalism, or, as now already emerging for peaceful purposes, in the Soviet Union, then a substantial departure from classical mechanics and its projection would be added to the abandoned organic projection. Classical mechanics was and is that of our mesocosmic visual space, between the inhuman 'four-dimensional world continuum' and the inhumanly realized abyss of 'atomic space'. But since future technology must essentially feed on sub-atomic impulses, and therefore on precisely this grotesquely dimensioned atomic centre, compared with the present one it uses a totally different world, into which it is translated and transposed. The technology that can be expected is not just like the difference between wireless telegraphy and the acoustic hand-bell, but by means of annihilation radiation any parts of terrestrial matter can be transformed into the condition of the matter of fixed stars: it is as if factories stood directly above the orgies of energy of the sun or of Sirius. Synthetic chemistry, which produces raw materials not yielded by the earth, cheaper and occasionally better ones, is joined in atomic physics by a kind of analytical gain of energy *which is not at all of this earth, the hitherto familiar earth.* Though this presupposes a society which can endure this upheaval in the forces of production, and this includes that kind of nature which even the old society called up from the depths of nature.

The still uncanny path began when substances were successfully annihilated by radiation. It had long been conjectured that the gaseous state of a body was not its last. Faraday gave this state, suspected but not experimentally proven by him, the name 'radiant matter'. The series of astonishing discoveries is well-known which led from cathode rays to X-rays, to Becquerel rays and from there to the so-called radioactive rays emitted by the self-decay of a very heavy element, uranium. In 1919 Rutherford first succeeded in splitting the atom, and thus the energy from annihilation radiation was released by artificial means, though still in a minutely small quantity. Rutherford did not yet think that a practical energy source could be obtained from atomic decay, but the energy obtainable theoretically was already well-known: one gram of radium emanation contains a work capacity of 160 million hp, and therefore enough power to drive a ship with a cargo of a thousand tons for six hundred nautical miles. According to the theory of relativity, the energy of a stationary body with a mass of m grams is: $E = m.c^2$, where c signifies the speed of light, expressed in kilometres per hour; c^2 is therefore an enormously large number, and its multiplication even with the smallest mass in grams reveals latent quantities of energy of cosmic proportions in every large stone. Thus the successful practice of the atom bomb, the so disgracefully perverted fore-runner of sub-atomic forces of production, displayed the same basic energy which builds, sustains and can destroy the universe. The neutrons in the exploding uranium bomb had the speed of 6210 English miles a second; a completely unearthly hurricane at the root foundation of the world, and one started by human beings. For the elements 95 and 96, which are provisionally used in the manufacture of the atom bomb, the names 'pandemonium' and 'delirium' were suggested, which have since been replaced by the names 'americium' and 'curium'; the delirium in the chain reaction is in fact solely imperialistic. Just as the chain reactions on the sun bring us heat, light and life, so atomic energy, in a different machinery from that of the bomb, in the blue atmosphere of peace, creates fertile land out of the desert, and spring out of ice. A few hundred pounds of uranium and thorium would be enough to make the Sahara and the Gobi desert disappear, and to transform Siberia and Northern Canada, Greenland and the Antarctic into a riviera. They would be enough to present mankind with the energy, which would otherwise have to be obtained in millions of hours of labour, ready for use in slim containers and in highly concen-trated form. Together with all this the de-organization of technology, of one which is no longer Euclidean, would be complete to its remotest extent; it would project from our mesocosmic world into an immeasurably different one, not just into a sub-atomic, but also into a macrocosmic one. A near future which can also best illustrate to itself, namely through practice, the quantum theory and what is tenable in the theory of relativity, the new theory of gravitation, will raise the possibilities of a *non-Euclidean technology*, as it is pursued in the radiation industry, out of the realm of fantasy into almost sound, almost already delineable prospects. If it were at all conceivable to apply the spatial and temporal relations of Einstein's world to our own, paradoxes would appear which not only surpass all the visions of technological fiction but almost the classic books of ancient magic. Outside our three-dimensional world, more generally: in all spaces with an even number of dimensions, spaces would remain bright even when the light-source disappeared; which is supposed to be deducible from the wave equation of light as soon as it is applied to n-dimensional space (cf. Herm. Weyl, Philos. der Mathematik und Naturwissenschaft, 1927, p. 99). The indifference of mathematical-physical laws towards the number of dimensions ceases at a deeper level; something impossible in three-dimensional classical mechanics can thus be valid, become technologically possible. It can do this in a way which is at least no longer absolutely out of the question; the utopia which has begun of a non-Euclidean technology already has limits which have been pushed extraordinarily far forward. In return, of course, there is also the danger cited above of ever greater artificiality, of projecting ever further into a mathematicized no man's land. And this *artificiality* is in fact at the same time the Negativum emerging at the end ever more clearly in the *break in the graphically physical guideline* itself. A Negativum which indicates *likewise at this end a future shift* in the expansion of technological space which is so highly important and so highly progressive in itself. Only this shift will no longer be able to occur on the basis of the bourgeois relation to human beings and to nature, i.e. within that component of the relation to nature which belongs to bourgeois ideology and thus shares the rest of the *abstractness (alienness) of the bourgeois material relation.* But just as it manages atomic energies humanely, a no longer imperialistic society will *mediate* to itself this material, however non-Euclidean it may be, as one *without ultimate alienness.* Also connected with this abstractness is the peculiar pathos of non-graphicness which has filled all non-Euclidean physics up to now. What is meant by this is not non-graphicness in the simple sense, namely the obvious kind inherent in all occurrences outside three-dimensional visual space. But that other non-graphicness is meant here which is the same as unmediatedness of the independent object with the thinking subject, of the thinking subject with the independent object. In so far as a non-Euclidean physics, despite constant recourse to observation, still constructs its world as a mere reification of mathematical symbols, the abstractness has grown so great that subject and object no longer meet at all, indeed that the non-Euclidean object precisely as real kinetic matter totally drops out of sight. Complete unmediatedness with content thus appears here – an ideological analogue to the totally alienated, de-realized functional operation of late capitalist society, projected into nature. An idealism of method thus still increases that whereby even a non-Euclidean technology still towers so strangely into the unmediated and into what is downright disparate to concrete mediation. Certainly the ideological component is only the one in de-humanized physics, and the other one, irrefutable by ideological analysis, is the dictate of observed nature to do theoretical justice to it. But neither are both components already sharply separable nor can the real threat of a lack of mediation be overlooked in the whole trenchant business of abstraction. However, *the very triumph of non-Euclidean practice*, represented by the technology of annihilation radiation, now brings *salutary anticipations from the image of a no longer apparatus-ridden society into the arena*. These concrete-utopian outlines spring in technology particularly clearly from the task of a *concrete subject-object-relation*. So that the subject is mediated with the natural object, the natural object with the subject, and both no longer relate to one another as to something alien. De-organization which completely abandons the organic and ultimately the mesocosmic must not lose the connection with the *human subject* which precisely in technology, in the fine phrase of Engels, seeks to transform things in themselves into things for us. And for the same reason de-organization must prove the *depictive contact with the object*, with its real obedience to dialectical laws, which combines nature and history in the same connection, but also – of which more in a moment – with *that nuclear and agent immanence* of the really naturalistic connection of the object, which was once half-mythically described as 'natura naturans' or also hypothetically as 'subject of nature' and which is certainly not yet settled by the questionable character (but also that worthy of question) of these descriptions. It became apparent at any rate, for all its progressiveness, how much abstractness and what an abyss of uncontrolled disparateness still lies in de-organization. De-organization only becomes a blessing when apart from social order it also has the final anticipation of 'natural magic', to use Bacon's term, in its favour: *the mediation of nature with the human will - regnum hominis in and with nature*.

Subject, raw materials, laws and contact in de-organization

Bourgeois thinking as a whole has distanced itself from the materials with which it deals. It is based on an economy which, as Brecht says, is not interested in rice at all but only in its price. The transition from use to barter is an old one, but only capitalism introduced the transformation of all bartered goods into abstract commodities and of the commodity into capital. Corresponding to this is a calculation alienated not only from human beings but also from things, one indifferent to their content. Thus a non-organic, de-qualifying spirit has been spreading ever since the end of the original accumulation of capital, and hence since the concentrated production of commodities and the corresponding commodity-thinking. From the seventeenth century on, the qualitative concepts of nature disappear which had still been cultivated by Giordano Bruno and even by Bacon himself in places. Galileo, Descartes, and Kant are united in the idea that only what is produced mathematically is recognizable, and only what is comprehended mechanically is scientifically understood. But sugar as an abstract commodity is different from real sugar, and the abstract laws of mechanistic natural science are different from the substratum of content with which these laws maintain no relation. What is true of theory is all the more true of technological practice, it contents itself with laws about sheer contingency. Poincaré, who only believed in conventions anyway and not in material laws, once remarked that one could not help being surprised to see how little a man needed to know of nature in order to tame it and make it serve his will. Steam and electricity appear solely as quantities of working power, which are defined in terms of physical-technological units of measurement and of production costs. Thus bourgeois technology itself stands in a pure commodity-relation, one alienated from the start, to the natural forces with which it operates from outside. And the very relation of content becomes all the smaller, the further technology has advanced beyond harnessing the organic horse towards the internal combustion engine or gains a foothold on the ultraviolet volcano of atomic energy. In any case, bourgeois society relates in an abstract way to the substratum of things which affect its thinking and behaviour. Thus even a working substratum of nature, that aspect of it which has elsewhere been called efficacity and seed, remains without relation. But this problem of relation is the most urgent one for every technology that is becoming concrete; for it is that of technological hope itself. It remains instructive here and will become ever more instructive that even the technological system of production, however abstract, will never attain or seek to attain Münchhausen's total lack of contact, pulling himself out of the swamp by his own pigtail. But even perfect artificiality, despite all technological nihilism, still definitely uses nature, and cannot avoid this support from outside. If we *first* take *raw materials*, then even the greatest cunning with substitutes cannot succeed in a vacuum. If synthetic chemistry manufactures other raw materials or existing ones in a different way, then it does of course secure independence from the natural occurrence or growth of these materials, but not from natural elements of relation in general. It obtains dyes from tar, petrol from coal, fertilizers from Thomas slag, rubber from grain, potatoes or other basic materials rich in carbohydrates; it produces textiles from milk, why not butter from the nitrogen in the air. But only the basic or initial materials have changed in this way, and only the process is a different one from the slow development of nature. Only the starting point is moved back, only fewer and fewer 'finished products' of nature are used as raw materials. But however bold the new formation, water, air and earth at least remain indispensable. However synthetic the chemistry, no cornfield will grow on the flat of the hand, which is to say: the link with what has prevailed, which can only be better managed when allied with itself, still does not come to an end here. This is even more true of the experiment which advances far more precariously than synthetic chemistry: of possible radiation technology; of the problem as to how classical mechanics is to be abandoned technologically as well, and how machines are to be established on the non-Euclidean margin. Even then the forces used remain derived from nature, although from a particularly sinister fund: and the process whereby new work-transformers are built into previously undreamt-of effective powers and miracles can by no means remain disparate to the impulse-matter in the non-Euclidean segment of nature. *Secondly* though: even more false than an abstract omission of raw materials is an omission of what has differently prevailed: of the natural *laws*. It is a purely subjectivist state of affairs if the laws are merely regarded as 'imaginary things', and especially as fictitious 'models', in accordance with which a succession or a simultaneity of perceptions is arranged 'with economy of thought'. This fideism then of course reveals, in all its variations, a particularly loudmouthed and ostensible freedom in the object space which has been idealized away. A freedom à la Simmel with regard to history, since 'the mind itself maps out its shores and the rhythm of its waves'. But then also a freedom à la Bertrand Russell with regard to nature and its laws, as supposedly 'purely logical structures which consist of events, i.e. perceptions'; according to which these laws certainly reflected nothing real that exists independently of methodical consciousness. The consequence for technology here would be that the de-organization, still projecting in a dangerously ungraphic fashion as it is, would now completely end up in no man's land. It is true, however, that all recognized laws reflect objective-real conditional connections between processes, and human beings are thoroughly embedded in this element independent of their consciousness and will, yet capable of being mediated with their consciousness and will. All theorists have pointed out this both insuppressible and helpful objective character of these laws: of the economic laws of concrete construction, but also of the naturalistic laws of the technology which serves it. Not so that men should become slaves of these laws and make a fetish of them, but rather so that even in Marxist terms, precisely in

Marxist terms, no attempt to take these necessities lightly and superficially should gain ground. Thus it has been said not unjustly on this point, though too one-sidedly throwing almost everything on to the side of the object: 'Marxism interprets the laws of science – no matter whether it is a question of laws of natural science or of political economy – as those of objective processes, occurring independently of the will of human beings. Human beings can discover these laws, recognize them, investigate them, take them into account in their behaviour, exploit them in the interests of society..., give the destructive effects of many laws a different direction, restrict their sphere of action, pave the way for other laws which are pushing their way to the fore, but they cannot overthrow these laws' (Stalin, 'Economic Problems of Socialism in the USSR'). Otherwise putschism or adventurism arise, those exaggerations of the subjective factor which confuse changing the conditions with leaping over the framework of laws, within which these changes can alone be concrete-beneficial, concrete-real ones. Above all, since the necessity is solely interpreted as *external*, unmediated with the subjective factor, indeed operating against it, a possible *hostility* also arises to this necessity, and hence to the objective-real timetable of laws in general. And therefore this necessity appears to consciousness, however remote the latter may otherwise be from bourgeois-abstract consciousness, not as one to be *intrinsically* recognized and thus to be controlled, but – because of its *alienness* – solely as one to be exploded. Despite Engels' instruction: 'Freedom does not lie in the dreamed independence of the laws of nature, but in the recognition of these laws and in the possibility thus given to make them operate according to plan for specific purposes' (Anti-Dühring, Dietz, 1948, p. 138). Hegel's insight already pointed in this direction, though in such a way that his undeniable hostility to nature, that is, his relative rejection even of an internal necessity in the motions of nature, now again precisely understood the *control* of the laws of nature just as much and more in the sense of cunning than in that of matter having been penetrated in a concrete way. So that an early statement by Hegel admittedly skirts technological necessity, but literally only – skirts it, and thus again does not seek contact with its *substratum of content*. Thus the passage from Hegel combines the correct approach, that makes nature into a collaborator, and the false approach, that associates with nature in technological terms only through the abstraction of alienness, of *colonial cunning* as it were; it combines them in the following way: 'This passivity' (of the man who makes nature work for him) 'is transformed into activity,...so that nature's own activity,

the elasticity of the watch spring, water, wind is used to do something very
different in their sensory existence than they wanted to do, so that their
blind actions are made into purposeful ones, into their own opposite
...Nothing happens to nature itself, individual purposes of natural being
become general. The drive here wholly withdraws from the operation, it
allows nature to wear itself down, calmly looks on and merely controls the
whole thing with very little effort: cunning. The broad flank of force is
attacked by the edge of cunning. It is the distinction of cunning with regard
to power to tackle blind power on a flank so that it turns against itself,
to attack it, to grasp it as a certainty, to work against this or to make it
retreat into itself as a movement, to cancel itself out' (Hegel, Jenenser
Realphilosophie, Meiner, II, p. 198f.). And there is even more of the same
thing in the style of a pitfall which is prepared for nature, of a treadmill into
which duped nature is led: 'The cunning consists generally in the mediating
activity which, by causing the objects to influence one another and to wear
one another out in accordance with their own nature, without directly inter-
fering in this process, nevertheless only carries out *its* purpose' (Hegel,
Werke VI, p. 382). So the *edge of cunning* here is the equally shrewd and
abstractly incomplete term for the technological relationship to nature, to
this foundation of human activity. Cunning has the same relation to nature
in this passage from Hegel as Schiller's man to fire: 'Beneficent is the fire's
might, *if man controls and guards it right.'* The passage from Hegel does not
have Faust's attitude to fire: 'Sublime spirit, you gave me, gave me all for
which I asked. *You did not turn in vain your countenance to me within the fire.'*
Goethe's phrase is that of a rising trust in nature, finally expecting the bosom
of a friend; Schiller's phrase is not without that violence which draws
benefit from nature, like a tamed, guarded colony, only on condition of
dominion. The capitalist concept of technology as a whole (and Schiller and
Hegel react more like capitalists on this point than Goethe with the older,
Renaissance line in Faust) thus exhibits more domination than friendship,
more of the slave-driver and the East India Company than the bosom of a
friend. *Thirdly* and *lastly*, therefore, only the total penetration into the
essential necessity of processes could also preserve de-organization from non-
relation to the 'fire' of the nature-agent. In the sense that *the manufacturing
element in nature too* is increasingly felt, tracked down, and comprehended
in place of merely external necessity, and especially the agnostic model
extra rem. With the Renaissance dimension handed down by Leonardo, not

* 'Faust', Part I, 3217-20.

just in his paintings: 'The laws of nature compel the painter to transform himself into the spirit of nature and to make himself the mediator between nature and art.' With the Renaissance dimension recalled by Marx himself, a fact itself worth recalling over and over again, in his 'Holy Family': 'Among the properties innate in matter, motion is the first and most excellent, not just mechanical and mathematical motion, but even more the drive, living spirit, tension, and the torment – to use Jakob Böhme's expression – of matter.' This with all caution towards the numerous mythical traces in the concept of a gushing substratum, and indeed towards a pantheistic bogeyman which could likewise still haunt the concept of a natura naturans. Whether in its poorly cleansed entrances and forecourts, or by virtue of the 'theological inconsistencies' of which Marx also speaks in the passage cited above, even with reference to Bacon. Nevertheless, the difference between bourgeois-technological alienness to nature, especially unworldliness, and affinitive inhabitation of nature is crystal clear: natura naturans can be set on its feet, physical nihilism definitely cannot. Thus the problem of a centrally mediated relation to nature becomes the most urgent: the days of the mere exploiter, of the outwitter, of the mere taker of opportunities are numbered even in technological terms. Bourgeois technology as a whole was a type of outwitter, and the so-called exploitation of natural forces was not primarily related, any more than that of human beings, to the concrete material of what was exploited, or interested in being indigenous to it. But precisely activity beyond what has become, this so wonderfully strong impulse in technology, needs contact with the objective-concrete forces and tendencies; *it is the techologically intended 'super-naturation' of nature itself which demands inhabitation in nature.* Prometheus, when he fetched fire from heaven to animate his human creations with it, stole not only fire but – according to a phrase of Plato's in the 'Protagoras' which aims at all or nothing – also 'the ingenious wisdom of Hephaestos and of Athene', in order to give it to men together with fire. And the more technology loses the final traces of its old rootedness, or rather the more it gains new rootedness wherever it wants to, in the synthetic production of raw materials, in the radiation industry and whatever else in magnificent hubris: the more intimately and centrally the mediation with the interpolated system of nature must develop.

Only then can things also be changed at their root cause, instead of merely displaced from outside. Every technological intervention contains the will for change, without however the X of what is to be changed having to be familiar to the mere outwitter, or even having to exist. An agent of the phenomena is of course admitted, but only as one which is absolutely unrelated to us, alienated from us, and as one without a subject. Children and primitive people automatically insert a subject, corresponding to their own ego, into physical events. And less naively, less directly analogous to the individual ego, a subject is also to be found in later non-animistic conceptions of nature, provided that they are not quantitative. This is already the case with Thales when he ascribes a soul to the magnet, and it is the case in a big way in all panvitalist images of nature, in Leonardo, Bruno, and in the early Schelling. But a subject, in the empirical-organic sense, is fundamentally lacking – and this was a great advance at first compared with all animism – in the quantitative view of the world, and therefore also in classical mechanics. It is completely lacking where quantitative thinking totally passes into thinking which is theoretical in terms of relation and function: in non-Euclidean mechanics nature becomes an absolutely free-floating association of (relativized) laws. Kant admittedly based the physical association of laws on a 'transcendental' subject, as he did with every combination ('The I think must be able to accompany all my ideas'); and this would not of course be introducing a subject into the mechanics of nature, but rather a hopeless subject into the mechanical concepts of nature. However, the latter subject is, as a so-called transcendental one, least of all an empirical-organic one; nature is here rather something to which an empirical-organic subject can only be added *in the mind*, though it can be *added* in the mind; in other words, the extreme 'objectivity' attained by Newton's natural science does not so exhaust nature in Kant that there is no room for basic concepts of a less alienated kind as well in his view of nature, even though only conceivable, regulative, and not scientifically constitutive room. These basic concepts are above all 'those of an inner purpose of nature, with the final purpose of a realm of rational beings'; but this introduces, with an undoubtedly still cloudy teleology, a conceivable natural subject. The causal explanation is thus supposed to be supplemented by the inevitable, although only regulative definition according to a capacity immanent in nature which could pursue its causes as purposive causes. Which in analogy to the human type of will goes to prove that we 'conceive of nature as *technological through its own capacity*; whereas, if we do not attribute such a type of effect to it, its causality would have to be represented as a blind mechanism' (Kritik der Urteilskraft, Werke, Hartenstein, V, p. 372). Kant still had no or very few technological viewpoints, and therefore the cited as-if definitions were also aimed far more at organic than at inorganic nature. But as soon as the problem arises as to whether the eminent expediencies of human technology can have any contact with the production of physical processes or not: at this moment the problem of a natural subject which can be mediated with us emerges from the mere regulative addition to mechanics. The definition does not of course become as strict as mechanics even then, but more serious than the latter: for the problem of a concrete technology consists precisely in not allowing de-organization and its consequences to refer to a void. As questionable as it remains whether a subject of nature already exists as realized, this subject must just as certainly be left open as a driving predisposition, and furthermore as one which thoroughly works into all its realizations. But at this point there now arises – without any Kantian regulative element, if not theologizing 'additional thinking' – Leibniz's problem of energy: what he called 'inquiétude poussante'. Leibniz posits it as the nuclear intensity of all monads and at the same time as the explicating tendency of this nucleus of theirs itself. There is thus a combination here of the sharpness of Leibniz's equation of energy and that 'inwardness' of the monads which signifies subjectness in the objective sense as dynamic natural determination. The problem of the subject in nature is of course pluralized in Leibniz into a host of individual monads, but in this host the prototype of all this: the old natura naturans, is still clearly discernible. Animism may remain wholly absent here and no less the 'psychological' element as well in Leibniz's individual points on the problem of the subject. But the fact that Leibniz's equation of energy and subjectness retains its relative meaning, even if the utterly false combination of energy and the psychological element is omitted, is indicated by Lenin himself in an extraordinarily profound remark: 'There is indeed a subjective factor in the concept of energy which does not exist in the concept of motion, for example' ('Philosophical Notebooks'). Not even the so indubitable subject of human *history* exists as already realized of course, although it increasingly manifests itself in empirical-organic terms, and above all in empirical-social terms as working man. How much more therefore may that which is hypothetically described as the *nature-subject* still have to be a predisposition and latency; for the concept of a dynamic subject in nature is in the final instance a synonym for the not yet manifested That-impulse (the most immanent material agent) in the real as a whole (cf. Vol. I, p. 307).

In this stratum therefore, *in the materially most immanent one that exists at all*, lies the truth of that which is described as the subject of nature. Just as the old concept of natura naturans, which first of all signified a subject of nature, is of course still half-mythical, as noted above, but by no means posits (in an idealistic way) a psychological element as prior to natura naturata. On the contrary, the concept of natura naturans was from the very beginning, from its *originator, the 'naturalist' Averroës* onwards, applied to *creative matter*. Even if the remnants of mythology cited above are not lacking, which may return as a pantheistic bogeyman, and which have long accompanied the problem of the subject of nature at least as a secularized Isis. Which have nevertheless only accompanied, not exhausted and settled it; whereas a mere In-itself of nature, in which neither subject nor even object occur, rather leads to Sartre, i.e. to the world as a disparate stone wall surrounding human beings, than to Marxism. *Likewise: in place of the technologist as a mere outwitter or exploiter there stands in concrete terms the subject socially mediated with itself, which increasingly mediates itself with the problem of the natural subject.* Just as Marxism has discovered the really self-generating subject of history in working man, just as it only allows it to be discovered and to realize itself completely in socialist terms, so it is probable that Marxism will also advance in technology to the unknown, in itself not yet manifested subject of natural processes: mediating human beings with that subject, that subject with human beings, and itself with itself. The will which resides in all technological-physical structures and has built them must simultaneously have both a socially grasped subject behind it: for the constituent intervention, beyond the merely abstract-external one, and a subject before it which is mediated with it: for co-operation, for the constitutive contact with the intervention. And finally: the first subject, as that of human power, cannot be conceived in sufficiently influential terms; nor the second subject, as the root natura naturans, indeed supernaturans, in sufficiently deep and mediated terms. Technology of the will and concrete alliance with the hearth of natural phenomena and their laws, the electron of the human subject and the mediated co-productivity of a possible natural subject: both together prevent bourgeois reification from being continued in de-organization. Both together suggest the concrete utopia of technology, which follows the concrete utopia of society and is bound up with it.

Electron of the human subject, of technology of the will

There is an inner force which has not been purely applied up till now. It constitutes the so-called strength in man, and does not wholly coincide with his familiar will. It acts as a power which sweeps the body beyond weariness, sharpens it as an instrument and equips it with astonishing capabilities. It acts equally as a power directed outwards, as influence or weight of character, or however else this peculiarly tough substance has been described. Its *most usual* discipline is military, Spartan, a voluntary, extremely masculine renunciation of desires, which practises in obedience the beginnings of command. All soldiers bear Spartan features, they are unmistakable wherever they appear; they are marked with stringent force, authority of command. But this sharpening of energetic capacity to a kind of lance-posture and lance-head of itself is only a beginning of that which subjective force has believed it can do. In the Spartan-military posture the will remains only abstractly polished as it were, it is of course allied with believed images and ideas here too, but mostly in a superficial, at least not in a necessary way. Thus the will shaped in an abstract-Spartan fashion was often able to fight for or lend executive support to anything at all: officers, and also officials in the Baroque period, served in foreign service, an attitude that if you are not for us you are against us does of course exist, but its contents are still interchangeable here. Even the fealty of the knight was formal, it did not yet pull together directions of the will which remained separate (ma coeur à dame, au Dieu mon âme, ma vie au roi, l'honneur pour moi)* into an irresistible unity. Only the religious war was able to do this, hence the entry of a content-laden, object-based, indeed object-based demanding goal into the militarily sharpened will. The will with believed ideas now no longer becomes transportable to any foreign service, that is, whose content it finds unimportant. Instead it is *strictly fixed*, which means it becomes fanatical; and it is this fanaticism which, where it occurs, now first produces the most monstrous increase of force or kindling of force in man. The pure force of command is now joined by the strength, fixing in accordance with an idea, of an idée-force; it alone overcomes what was formerly insurmountable. Loyola gave the most impressive coinage of idée-force, moreover in the connection which remained with military discipline. The 'Exercitia spiritualia' of this former officer, and visionary fanatical founder of an order are technology of the will to the highest degree reached in Europe so far; punctuality, obedience, authority of command, cruel authority of faith become one and the same here. They are joined by imagination on command, inflamed by the service of Christ, by the image of heaven and hell, opened and capable of being switched off on the dot. What the heretical sects had carried into the field in the way of courage and obsession was now made up for against the heretics themselves. Above all Moslem influences were not lacking on

---

* 'To the lady my heart, the soul is God's part, my life for the king, but honour I'm keeping.'

Spanish soil: the fanaticism which had once produced the hallucinating and murderous sect of the Assassins was deployed against the different infidels, against the Giaours of Protestantism. The result of such training, of one which was often almost mechanically rationalized, was that human beings appeared as machines of the will, with no will of their own, but charged with the energy of a mission and goal they believed in. The attitude that if you are not for us you are against us became totally one of content, as an attitude to the kingdom of Christ on the one hand, to the kingdom of the Devil on the other, and the decision became fanatical through both. But all this is still Europe, of course, and hence – compared with the *far older, far more radical technology of the will in Asia* – still almost dilettantism. At least if the inner force which is practised by the trainers there can be compared with the European will, and above all if even just a couple of words are true in the reports which have been circulating for ages about inconceivable intensification of inner force in India, which has so little energy. Even in India only the former yogis come into question, not the charlatans and fakirs of nowadays, who are partly raw epigones, partly tourist industry; there is no way of checking past effects, of course. The purely ideological role of the yogi is clear: as his first duty he had to set an example of repose; he had to make 'higher knowledge' equally uncontrollably exclusive. But apart from this a subjectively genuine trance of the most disciplined kind exists here, in a form which is still inaccessible to Europeans despite the Jesuit spiritual exercises (cf. Ruben, Geschichte der indischen Philosophie, 1954, p. 210). The intention and the methodical seriousness of the former yogis are certainly true, however unverifiable and undiscussible for the enlightened European the traditional hair-raising effects may be. After all, the technique of yoga fashions a belief in willpower which thinks it can move real mountains, not just mountains of difficulties; thus for ages it has formed the centre of utopian idée-force. And the intention here becomes totally monomaniacal, it is obsessed with the most extreme utopia of the will: that of material intervention through pure resolve. Control of breathing became the main path of these spiritual exercises: for in man as in nature, prana, breath, is regarded as the prime mover or divine wind of life. Control of breathing in the body is now to cancel the external rhythm of time, dependence on the course of the stars; the yogi feels that he has become the breath of the world itself in the small world of his body. Abstraction from the body is aided by disciplined muscular contractions, the 'styles' or figures of posture; there are ten of them. The 'Light of Hatha-Yoga' teaches that they increasingly destroy old age and death, in the double sense that they grant perfect health, but above all that they place the initiates in the 'possession of the deathless element' which is hidden within themselves (cf. also Zimmer, Indische Sphären, 1932, p. III). What remains constantly strange here is the external technicity, i.e. the change from self-control to the control of things, with which such concentrated willpower proceeds in what it claims to do. To it, every physically erected and ordered barrier, indeed every natural power seems reduced to something powerless, helpless and insignificant. Admittedly by means of a mythical alliance with magic which is added to the will, in its superhuman intensification: the yogi attains rapturous power of the kind that Krishna ascribes to himself in the Bhagavad-Gita: as Vibhuti or the attribute of becoming a god. The initiate of secret world forces is thus not merely contemplative, with 'sense organs of the soul' or 'lotus flowers' which mediate communion with a 'spirit world', as an Indianizing theosophy trimmed it into a stereotype for Europe. But beyond so-called clairvoyance precisely the old magical technology was to be kept alive, with a concentration which commands the world forces and comprehends, and thereby breaks through, their order. The yogi is now no longer their underling, concentration of controlled breathing, right into the centre of the breath of the world, was to mark the point from which the world can be governed, and hence co-governed and turned round. This is Indian technology in Brahma; to Indian consciousness, to which all determination and all concepts of law are foreign, the Ananke or conformity to the law of nature did not seem uninterrupted anyway, least of all superior to the coherent will. Many hair-raising things were reported concerning the effects of this power attainable by yogis: concerning second sight, telepathy and even levitation. Concerning the removal of their body to any distant place they chose, outside the dimension of time, in a moment; concerning spring air surrounding the yogis of the Himalayas, in the middle of the snow region; concerning the lingering force of curses and blessings. To decide how much of this is exotic nursery tale and how much a remarkably developed force which European meditation never attained or sought to attain, neither the otherwise so reliable authorities of European experience are sufficient (especially if they harden into negative dogmatism a priori) nor in fact the existing evidence. Even our knowledge of the *actual complications* of trained willpower is not sufficient; possibly it still stands on the electrotechnical level of the Greeks, whose knowledge of the whole of electricity was confined to rubbed amber and who knew nothing about the dynamo. In fact, something similar to that signified by the electron

and amber in the early history of electricity could – in the utopian line
of extension – be signified by an *electron*, discovered in India, *of the volitional
subject in the history of the technology of the will which lies before us*. It is true,
of course, that no power of the Indian mind has so far mastered the bullet
of a single English infantry rifle; Indian magic works only as a private
or peaceful commodity. Nevertheless, this very thing could lie in its nature,
and also all magic presupposes the old environment in which and for which
it has been developed, in which it is effective. However monstrous the
demands which Indian tradition makes on common sense, and however
much use mere fantasy may make of the world of Maya or illusion into
which most Indian philosophy has volatilized everything that is empirically,
or mechanically given. But this can act as a temporary measure merely
in order to provide space for mental energy in general, the courage of
a space in which to operate; and the implemented doctrine of yoga, above
all that of Patañjali, paradoxically seeks to extract a material force from
its contempt for matter itself. Whereas the same subjective system to which
this force is ascribed is only regarded as spiritual in mechanically materialistic
Europe and thus remains unmechanized. In short, the goal in the 'temple
of awakening' may be of the most adventurous kind, but it is an adven-
turousness of technological power, not of spiritual self-cultivation, as in
the otherwise so materially active Europe. It is the goal of omnipotence
in the fantastic sense that every wished-for and imagined event can be
realized by virtue of the telepathy of the trained will and by virtue of
the conceit which believes it is able to blow away or remove the veil of
Maya whenever it wants to. Even Buddha, who has a very different
'blossoming of the lotus flower' at heart, speaks of the magical wish as
one which is allowed and of the technique of fulfilling it: 'If, you monks,
a monk should wish: "If only I could manage to experience the display
of power in a varied way: to become many when I am only one, for
example, and having become many to be one again or to become visible
and invisible; also to float through walls, ramparts, and rocks as if through
the air; or to surface and submerge on earth as if in water; also to walk
on water without sinking as if on earth; or also to fly through the air
sitting down like the bird with its wings; also for example to feel and
touch this moon and this sun, which are so huge, so powerful, with my
hand, and for example to have my body in my power even as far as the
worlds of Brahma'': if he should wish that, you monks, then he only
has to practise perfect virtue, to secure deep peace of mind, not to resist
contemplation, and to be a lover of empty hermitages' (Neumann, Die

Reden Gotamo Buddhos I, p. 71f.). So this is how far grotesquely magical wishful technology of the will, even if only one enumerated by Buddha, extends into a doctrine whose only wish is in fact to forget all wishes. But such faith in willpower rarely occurred even in self-hypnotic, subjectively magical *Western regions*, and then always only sporadically, as with individual miracle men like Apollonius of Tyana, never as a religious system. Judaism, Christianity, and Islam are, at least in their orthodox form, hostile to magic, they tolerate no shamans, not even yogis; thus magical technology of the will or technology of the subject was also prevented. Mystic contemplation intended only the constraint of heaven, not the constraint of matter, and also European subjectivity only reached during rare and disintegrated fits the beginnings of the state of awareness which is the normal condition for the yogi. Thus the only technology of the subject which could compare with the Indian in quality referred in Western regions to the production of brief ecstasy. And during the ecstasy it referred to intended skimming, not to intended overcoming of the world. Two more strange disciplines are relevant here though, *one Jewish, one Christian developed self-hypnosis*, both in contempt of orthodox anti-magic. From the Jerusalem of the first century A.D. an art of 'entering into paradise' is recorded, and in connection with the famous vision of Ezekiel (Ezek. 1, 15–21) it was called 'Maase Markaba', 'Work of the Wheels'. This was the secret doctrine of the habitation of God and the technique of finding, indeed of forming the entrances to it by means of a disciplined change of consciousness. Jochanaan ben Sakkai, the head of the Pharisees, is said to have concerned himself with such a 'Work of the Wagon', in the second century this so-called art was regarded as so dangerous that it was only mentioned reluctantly, and later it was totally disreputable. A *Christian equivalent* to this is to be found in the Byzantine mysticism of the fourteenth century, in the conscious technique of enlightenment practised by the Hesychasts on Mount Athos. They sought a kind of religious love charm, a 'philtre' which artificially evokes an ecstasy of light in man and causes Jesus to appear within it. Just as he appeared to his disciples on Mount Tabor, surrounded with light, transfigured. The technique of the Hesychasts touched on the technique of yoga through the method of contemplating the navel, hence of total self-concentration, but the force which was thereby to be exalted was not in fact that of any change of the world, but exclusively that of an intensified heaven-forcing. The Hesychasts were the strangest of all strange saints, namely synthetically self-manufactured ones; at any rate, the Byzantine mystic Kabasilas, as if reminded of Prometheus, called those in the grip of the philtre 'robbers of the kingdom of heaven'. Zoē and Phos, life and light are the basic characteristics of Christ; since there is no celestial life without the appearance of both in man, but every Christian is to partake of such a life, a teachable intensification of the energies of longing led to the artificial manufacture of vision. Thus technology of the subject here broke into the supposed supernatural world, and enforced the unenforceable per se: divine grace; but it also opened in an oddly mechanized fashion a strange, still thoroughly mythicized floodgate in man. Behind it latent physical energy is dammed up in many of the cases cited above. On bursting through, it changes the known state of consciousness and the previous world of consciousness constructed on it, where it does not – as the practice of yoga intends – seek to change parts of the external world itself. By virtue of a kind of energy which is a leap ahead of all the others, and therefore neither qualitatively measurable nor transformable into others, but fantasizes instead that it is even expert at telepathy.

Something in this alleged force is both decayed and always new, and thus it never becomes established. It is surrounded by endless cloudy gossip, but on the other hand it seems as if a fermenting element were super-annuated here so to speak. It is high time to put things right in this simultaneously superstitious and strange utopian field, to consider a seriousness which has been distorted in the matter. For at least a hundred years expectation has been rife that we are standing on the threshold of great psychodynamic discoveries. According to which only a little effort is needed to attain highly charged willpower even in Europe, that which is called in colloquial language, precisely with regard to people of this kind, rousing or even electrifying. Just as this sort of thing has in any case been the wish and in fact the will in America since pioneering days, manifesting itself in thousands of encouragements or dilettante sugges-tions. In America pioneering gave grounds for such things, then the former notion of make way for efficiency, as well as a course without historical inhibitions and ties. Success and failure thus seemed – in a healthy super-stition as it were – left up to self-persuasion, and therefore to the attainable power to persuade others, indeed the course of the world – 'there are no limitations in what you can do; think you can'. The American bestsellers already mentioned with regard to wishful images in the mirror (cf. Vol. I, p. 349ff.) are full of this kind of thing – a cheap yogism against despondency and doubt, but all the same, as now first emerges, a pledge of very old, never properly formulated hope. 'Once you learn a few simple secrets, you will be amazed to find how ideas begin fairly pouring into your brain': all America believes or believed in a psychic magnet and in the art of charging it. This includes sentences like these (they do not lose the 'hidden storehouse of energy' in translation): 'A wish, conceived and uttered, brings what is wished for closer, namely in proportion to the strength of the wish and the increasing numbers of those who wish.' Or: 'Every imagination is an invisible reality, and the longer, the more intensively it is retained the more it will be converted into that form which we can perceive with our external senses. According to the nature of our daydreams we pile up gold or explosives in our destiny.' Or: 'We must cling to the thought of happiness and of health with every fibre of our being, week by week, month by month, year by year dream up our own image, free of every evil, until this dream has become a fixed idea, second nature to us, and intervenes in destiny: – from castles in the air arise the palaces of this earth.' Prentice Mulford, a Californian journalist of concentration, wrote these sentences, as vested rights so to speak, indeed as native ideas of Americanism. They are taken from his work: 'Your forces and how to use them', 1887, a veritable investment of will in things, of things in will. A technical college of willpower is demanded, a theological laboratory as well, with departments as follows: 'The slavery of fear; The Religion of dress; Positive and negative thought; Immortality in the flesh; The doctor within; The church of silent demand'. It is a single capitalist Lord's Prayer and that of a pantheistic engineer as well: if his machine goes more slowly, man casts the will of his prayer like a transmission belt around the original dynamo of God. Or as it can only really be expressed in American Greek: 'The man feels synchronized with the rhythm of Life.' In this way the utopia of a psychodynamics surfaces in America, again and again with the hope of securing in practice a daily experienced force-factor. Thus ultimately a certain, namely totally wild kind of will-magic was not lacking even in the modern *West*, though without technology and system. As in America, it was not lacking in Europe either, although with less business sense and more interest in a newly redeemed spirit so to speak; it is nevertheless a related intention. And here it has contacts with the end of naturalism, with a soon used or misused, but not yet irrational-reactionary recourse to the soul. The neo-Romantic *Maeterlinck* thus wrote, at the turn of the century when mechanism was subsiding, of 'an enormous receptacle of power which lies on the summits of our consciousness', of 'psychic energy as an unexpected central property of matter at its highest level'. And the poet, when he called this power 'the transition of the world

to the motions of happiness', in an essay with the characteristic title 'The
olive-branch', – the poet found himself with this secessionist optimism
of his, as far as orbits of willpower are concerned, in far-reaching
philosophical company at that time, in such various and yet such
spontaneity-loving company as that of both James and Bergson. *James*,
on the strength of the practice of yoga among primitive peoples, arrived
at the assertion that the will, in so far as it was concentrated, had no limits.
Bergson proclaimed psychic energy to be the raising counter-force to
mechanical decline and sleep; it guaranteed, at the human extreme, the
struggle against stifling habit, as the constantly threatening subsidence
of life, and it used the brain and indeed all physical determinisms in the
same sovereign manner as a virtuoso uses his instrument. Finally, as far
as the often felt 'vital thrust' of a person is concerned, as a raw force as
it were, which is everywhere felt and nowhere explored, let us recall one
of the few inventories of this phenomenon itself. It comes from *Simmel*,
an impressionist of philosophy, for whom the 'abundance of life' admittedly
remained formal, but who turned to impressions from the above-mentioned
area in a thoroughly notational way. Simmel's impressionistic inventory,
concerning vital thrust as subjective energy, runs: 'I am convinced – naturally without the possibility of any proof – that the human individual does
not yet end so to speak where our senses of sight and touch reveal his
limits; but instead that beyond them there still lies that sphere, whether
it is conceived as substantial or as a kind of radiation, whose extent defies
every hypothesis and which is just as much a part of his character as the
visible and palpable nature of the body. It is related to these in the same
way as the infra-red and the ultra-violet rays, which we cannot see but
whose effectiveness is nevertheless undeniable, are related to the colours
of the spectrum. . . As extremely important for all real community life as
this component of individual existence appears to me to be – the mysterious
phenomenon of prestige, the antipathies and sympathies between people
which cannot be rationalized at all, the frequent feeling of being ensnared
as it were by the mere existence of a person, and much else which is often
decisive even in events which have become historical may be traced back to
this component –, this sphere still clearly defies tradition and reconstruction
more than the qualities of character accessible to the five senses and therefore
possessing a linguistic formulation. At any rate this sphere is probably
connected with the latter qualities, together with which it forms the totality
of man, linked in some way which still admittedly defies all conjecture
at the moment, so that sometimes a glimmer of this expanded region of

being touches us from that which survives of a human being, his speech, his actions, the description of his appearance' (Fragmente und Aufsätze, 1923, p. 174f.). Simmel sees the connection of this atmosphere with the visible character above all in the significant portrait; but precisely the less contemplative reference to a force field is not lacking, to what James and Bergson meant by technological spontaneity. And finally, though in a totally abstract, wildly indeterminist way which became objectless out of sheer subjective pathos, an anarcho-syndicalist like *Sorel*, in emulation of Bergson, completely exaggerated the will. It appears as a gigantic muscle of moulded power: 'force individualiste dans les masses soulevées' reverses the course of history which is inherently always sinking; 'accumulation d'exploits heroïques' always breaks through what is determined; a general strike is the electrotechnics of this spontaneity – the will knows no bounds. This is putschist, in this abstractly pure exaggeration, and could in fact become fascist, as actually opposing the course of history. But it still contains this element of reality that the subjective factor, though only allied with the objective tendency, has the strength to counteract fate and to accelerate the hesitantly Possible of a good kind. Thus an element of yoga-will, so to speak, also undoubtedly smoulders in our western world; it appears in the adventurous consequences of the former pioneering will in America, and it appears in European terms in the more or less vague notations of the will, or 'decisionisms' which so soon degenerated into fascism. A technique comparable to that of yoga is certainly never developed, despite Loyola's 'Exercitia spiritualia', and even these pay no attention to the source of their effects. Instead the partly reflected modes of spontaneity in Europe reveal a similarity to the Indian ones in the most dubious point: they all move in an objectively undetermined field or think they are able to move within it. Their supposed indeterminism is related to Indian acosmism, at least to the superstition that the external world, insubstantial and dispersable as the veil of Maya, is not insuperable to an energetic imagination. This is the price which has had to be paid up till now for every approximation to the 'hidden storehouse of energy'; and there is ultimately only *a single exception* to this. It lies typically enough in the springtime of the *Renaissance*, as daring as it was nature-seeking, and the exception is called *Paracelsus*. All the modern utopias of the will cited above seem like diminutions of the intentions, however forgotten, of Paracelsus anyway, *as the strategist of concentration in the human microcosm*. And he is the only one in whose work the contact with a presupposed natural subject is also not undeveloped; the contact which occurs at best mythologically in the

practice of yoga, as the transcendental process of becoming Krishna, as
the attainment of the divine Vibhuti, whereas the contact with a worldly
natural subject is lacking. Even in Paracelsus of course the pathos of velleity
in man himself is important at first and of the imagination which it releases.
In the books Paramirum and Paragranum he conjures up the conjuration
as follows: 'You should know that the effect of the will is a major factor
in medicine. It follows from this that one image conjures up the other,
not from strength of character or the like, through virgin wax, but the
imagination overcomes its (the image's) own constellation so that it becomes
a means to complete its heaven, that is, the will of its man. Just as a carver
takes a piece of wood and carves out of it what he has in mind, so the
imagination does the same with astral matter. All human imagining thus
comes from the heart: the heart is the sun in the microcosm. And from
the small sun of the microcosm imagining radiates into the sun of the
great world, in the heart of the macrocosm; thus imaginatio microcosmi
is a seed which becomes material. If we human beings saw its nature in
a true light, then nothing would be impossible for us on earth, the
ceremonies, circle-making, furs, seals and so on are sheer monkey-tricks
in comparison, and seduction. Imaginatio is confirmed and completed by
the faith that it will truly happen, for every doubt breaks the work; faith
must confirm the imagination, for faith resolves the will' (Werke, Huser, I,
p. 334, 375; II, p. 307, 513). But even in the subject such faith is not
so lacking in contact as in isolated technologies of the will and their will
armed only with itself. Instead the *contact ground of the interior* in which
the will is located is called the 'archeus' in Paracelsus, i.e. the subject of
nature in man as it were. Archeus is the working image according to which
organic matter combines during procreation, it dwells in the seed, then
later permeates, animates and preserves the body; but every will and every
imagination is located in the 'archeus', only has its power in *harmony with
it* and furthermore only in *harmony with the general cosmic natural force*, which
Paracelsus calls 'vulcanus'. In this double contact Paracelsus limits and founds
the imagination, with regard to its intention, and thereby rids it of its
later abstract crazed character, and also its lonely quixotry. However –
and this is decisive for the power with which the subject of 'natural magic'
is sharpened and emphasized here – Paracelsus did not allow any
technological work, whether medical or chemical, to succeed without the
participation of the 'lever to the archeus-vulcanus'. It was indicated above
that the European rejection of yoga-energy is the same, in terms of its
method, as if the Greeks, on the basis of their knowledge of the electrical

properties of amber, had rejected the possibility of a dynamo. This metaphor, elucidated with Paracelsus, has in fact another wholly literal meaning: there is indeed *an analogy of undeveloped subjective energy with the simple Greek electron, of the subjective energy developed in the future with the dynamo*. At any rate, the technique of yoga already seems to know what may be called, highly comparatively, the Leyden jar or the electrostatic generator of this level (though by no means any inductors or cathodes); but Europe, by looking exclusively at the merely external factors of nature, has blocked itself off from a solid and sustained pursuit of Paracelsus' intentions. Though what is termed vital thrust and energy of the will only developed with the *organic-psychological condition* of matter, and thus cannot be measured and treated at the level of mechanical energies at all, except in subordinate idle analogies; there is no equivalent of heat for willpower. Also, psychic energy is able to move mountains at best figuratively, and even here only with the most exaggerated metaphor: a magnetic current is able to rotate the plane of polarization of light, but the most concentrated will is unable to pick up a pencil from the floor. And precisely the physics of apparent telepathy, of induced electricity, delivered the maxim through Faraday, its discoverer: 'electrical action at a distance (i.e. ordinary inductive action) never occurred except through the influence of the intervening matter', and even more pertinently: 'If we succeeded in moving even just a blade of straw with the force of our will, our conception of the universe would have to be changed.' Intervention of the will in the world without the external machinery which the practice of yoga professes to exercise and which Paracelsus intends certainly presupposes no intervening matter, and all this kind of thing is incompatible more than ever with the world of mechanism or with the world conceived in purely mechanical terms. There is nevertheless a technologically utopian approach to the problem of a legitimate kind here, one which, within a no longer mechanistically cropped matter, is not afraid to announce will and imagination as factors of nature sui generis. This always stimulated the hope that the lever was in man by means of which the world can be technologically lifted on to its hinges. That there is a dormant potential in human matter which does not know its own strength, which occurs in a thousand irregular experiences but not in a single adequate theory. There is a future in all this, a legitimate problem of the future, and there is indeed an enormous receptacle of power which lies on the summit of our consciousness; people travel through it on their own account, on one different from that of the Become. With the objective sense which

Paracelsus himself teaches against exaggerations, as a magic realist, but still as a realist: spontaneity extends exactly as far as the reality allows it to *from whose strength it stems, and towards whose process it is correlatively directed.* And this reality is of course further advanced than that of mechanics which only represents the part of it which is turned away from man, indeed one which is often still artificially isolated and reified in this superficiality. Man's possible field of action in nature is definitely more extensive, more unenclosed; and it is able to be this – whereby the main theme returns – by virtue of that possible subject of nature which gives birth to and dynamizes itself in utopian terms not merely subjectively, but also objectively.

Co-productivity of a possible natural subject or concrete technology of alliance

Even the external forces do not always exist as unequivocally as it seems. Often they were just a name for that which cannot be explained, a flashy name as well, which concealed ignorance. Opium, for example, is soporific because it contains a 'vis dormitiva'; vital force also belongs in this series. What is to be explained is thus turned into the explanation itself, and analytical work stops at a mere word, quickly invented and turned into a 'capacity'. And there is something else behind this, something preserved in the linguistic form: the belief in spirits. The more specific a force appears (like the 'soporific force' of opium or, as in a joke by Mörike, that of scarlet fever, the wicked 'fairy Briscarlatina'), the closer it is to animistic ideas. That is why physics sought more and more to level the individually designated forces in general mechanical terms, along the lines of pressure and thrust. Chemical affinity is the real force by which the atoms stick together in the molecule, cohesion the force by which the molecules stick together, and its opposite, in gases, is then called expansive force. But as early as a hundred years ago Davy and Berzelius tried to explain chemical affinity further by means of electrical attraction or repulsion, an explanation which only foundered on the chemical combination of atoms of the same kind, namely of carbon atoms (into chains and rings); electron research working on the basis of quantum theory is on the point of tracing the so-called force of chemical affinity uninterruptedly back to sub-atomic processes. The general theory of relativity ultimately seeks to dismiss even the so-called force of gravity as a separate form of energy, indeed as energy itself, and explains it by the mathematical structure of a four-dimensional continuum. The fact that a body is attracted here means simply that it describes the shortest line in curved space, a geodesic line. Space is particularly curved in the vicinity of large masses, hence a body in this space simulates parabolas or ellipses. But they only appear as such to the Euclidean way of thinking, and make the assumption of a force of gravity necessary only in a plane space. The tendency in physics is to define all manifestations of force as local irregularities in a metric, non-Euclidean, curved continuum. Clearly at least the specific multiplicity of forces thereby disappears, just as their super- and subordination disappeared long ago. The prophecy of Newton himself in his 'Opticks' is thus fulfilled: 'To tell us that every Species of Things is endow'd with an occult Specifick Quality by which it acts and produces manifest Effects, is to tell us nothing: But to derive two or three general Principles of Motion from Phenomena, and afterwards to tell us how the Properties and Actions of all corporeal Things follow from those manifest Principles, would be a very great step in Philosophy, though the Causes of those Principles were not yet discover'd.' And yet: the specific forces, in so far as they characterize the unexchangeable effective form of a group of manifestations, are not yet bought up by this *generalizing quantification*; not even the notorious 'vis dormitiva' of opium is bought up by it. For quantification makes all cats grey, it ignores the various modes in which general natural force still appears and has its effects. It allows a mechanical monotony to triumph over the always qualitative stages of development, a theorem of the identity (not just the conservation) of energy over its always still fermenting core (inquiétude poussante, according to Leibniz) and its ever more highly qualified objectivizations (entelechies, according to Aristotle). The very reduction of the various force dominants to a single basic force of nature cannot merely be one which analyzes everything mechanistically to death. Nor can it merely be one in the sense of the electromagnetic theory of light, nor merely one in the sense of tracing all phenomena back to a simple universal field law. But 'charge', 'energy node', 'field', even the peculiar conception of 'energy levels' (in atomic structure, expressed by whole quantum numbers), all these new terms of efficacity and seed are predominantly abstract ideas instead of mediations. Despite their not merely quantitative but higher-mathematical abstraction, they are *quantifications*, kept isolated, *of a natura naturata, not penetrations into the producing element of a natura naturans*, at least conceived as an agent. But physics, precisely as a dialectical science, remains related to a nucleus of force like natura naturans, indeed to a qualitative one in itself and in its products. Even what occurs in the atom, this strange origin, obscure as every beginning which is kept isolated, will not be able to be conceived concretely without an attempted glance at qualitative features of the natural force which starts in this way. Especially something as objectively qualitative as a gale, or a thunder-storm and so on is an event which is not exhaustively covered and explained by ultra-violet radiation or ionization of the upper layers of air. To understand it in its grasped total manifestation was precisely the sort of thing which was sought in the Paracelsian approach, with regard to its intention, however little this emerged from the mythical: the essence of human force was sought in the specified 'energy node' of the 'archeus', and the essence of cosmic force in the general one of the 'vulcanus'. If archeus was supposed to be the individualized natural force, then vulcanus was supposed to describe the 'virtus of the elements', which circles, burns, rains, and flashes with lightning in the cosmos, and also the one, million-headed essence of nature whereby the coherence of the whole is established. These are certainly likewise mere words and names, mythological ones too, yet they do not conceal any ignorance but revolve around the region of the objectively possible contact or world concept for the subjective energy factor of the imagination. Archeus and vulcanus or what has since been named the 'productivity' of nature in a dynamically qualitative philosophy of nature: all these derivatives of Isis or Pan, however mythical they may be, are closer in what they describe non-mythically to the concretum of the experience of nature and the co-ordination with its productive factor than the abstract or partial truths of mechanism. The Paracelsian approach only stands as a symbol for this other side of nature, but as an admonitory one and one which cannot be mechanistically superseded. The dynamically qualitative philosophy of nature of Schelling, and also of Hegel, as one related to physical productivity, is thoroughly located in the Paracelsian approach and is itself only a symbol, but one for mediated nature, outside the mechanistic sector. Without such mediation the physical is indeed only the corpse of abstract reason, with this mediation the dialectical system of tension also opens out here for the first time, in actual realism, without any grey beneath the colourful, mechanistically disavowed surface, without sheer caput mortuum right at the first base of Being. If there is a hearth of production in nature, then the structure of this origin is not exhaustible with sub-atomic models or even with a universal field law. Particularly not that of an origin which, instead of being confined to beginnings, still moves with continually new commitment through world process and world coherence, in the tendency to manifest itself. All this is sealed to mechanism; the real problem of the agent which operates the turnover and dialectical switch of natural phenomena is an implication which also exists quantitatively but cannot be quantitatively pursued. It is part of mechanistics to confine itself to beginnings which are kept isolated, and it is all the more a part of it to forget the original relation of production itself in face of the product and its relations. But that which objectively corresponds to technological world change must be founded for concrete technology in an objective production tendency of the world, just as, mutatis mutandis, it is founded for concrete revolution in the objective production tendency of human history. Co-productivity of nature is required, that which Paracelsus himself had in mind when his nature already appeared to him as friendly or capable of being befriended in a utopian way, 'inwardly full of remedies, full of prescriptions and one big chemist's shop', a cosmos in which man opens up, just as the microcosm of man causes the world to come to its senses.

By being used co-operatively, the root of things seemed tangible. The experiment is mediator between human and non-human, and it would like if possible to go so deep that it tests the current in the non-human itself. So deep in fact that it tests the access to the hearth on which external things have been cooked and on which they should continue to be cooked, in alliance with the natural subject and the natural tendency. 'All corn', said Meister Eckhart (Sermon 29), 'all corn suggests wheat, all metal suggests gold, all birth suggests human beings'; developmental history itself, from Aristotle to Hegel, contains the objectivity of this suggestion, in contrast to static mechanics. And it was no accident that the activity of this suggestion at the hearth, naturalistic shaping and developing, was thought out at the moment when the methodical concept of generation was transformed by Fichte into the universal one of an 'active deed' (with priority of doing over being), and by Schelling even into that of an – itself still shapeless – 'original productivity' (with Renaissance of the natura naturans). Thus only an indifferent partial view regards nature as a product, speculative physics recognizes it as something productive and as tendency. Schelling makes the following contribution here – totally incomprehensible from the point of view of mechanics, and even from that of contemplative science: 'We know nature only as active, for we cannot philosophize about any object which cannot be activated. Philosophizing about nature means lifting it out of the dead mechanism in which it seems imprisoned, animating it with freedom as it were and initiating its own free development – in other words, it means breaking free from the common view which sees in nature only what happens – sees at most action as a fact, not the action itself within action' (Werke I, 3, p. 13). Whereas therefore in the usual view the original productivity of nature disappears in face of the product, in the philosophically concrete view the product must disappear in the face of productivity. Schelling and Hegel of course cause the history of the manifestation of nature to land in *existing man,* in fact at the conversion point of the *historical beginning,* and Hegel even more so than Schelling, who at least still sees in the 'varied and intricate monograms of objects' an undeciphered meaning, one which has not yet properly brightened in the human mind. In Hegel, nature, 'a bacchanalian god who does not restrain and compose himself', is already thoroughly restrained, composed and cancelled out in existing history, in such a way that no substantial traces remain within it whatever. This totally antiquarian explanation of natural productivity and its products in terms of the past and Becomeness is clearly different from the approach to the root of nature intended elsewhere in Schelling and Hegel; and approaching this root has no productive sense itself if it has withered. But in reality it has neither withered nor is human history in its corporeality, background and above all in its technology, obliged to nature only as one that is past. On the contrary: *finally manifested nature lies just the same as finally manifested history in the horizon of the future,* and the mediation categories of concrete technology which can well be expected in the future also run towards this horizon alone. The more a technology of alliance in particular were to become possible instead of the superficial one, a technology of alliance mediated with the co-productivity of nature, the more certainly the creative forces of a frozen nature will be released again. Nature is no bygone, but *the building site which has not yet been cleared at all, the building material which does not yet adequately exist at all for the human house which does not yet adequately exist at all.* The ability of the problematic natural subject to help to create this house is in fact the objective-utopian correlate of the humane-utopian imagination, a concrete imagination. Therefore it is certain that the human house not only stands in history and on the foundation of human activity, it also stands above all on the *foundation of a mediated natural subject and on the building site of nature.* A borderline concept for the latter is not the beginning of human history where nature (which has constantly been present during history, surrounding it) switches into the site of the regnum hominis, but into the proper one, and rises in an unalienated way, as mediated good.

Technology without violation; economic crisis and technological accident

Private property alienates not only the individuality of human beings, but also that of things.

Marx, Holy Family

It is still not possible anywhere for the force of fire not to have to be guarded. Steam, ignited gas, electric current, they are outwitted, chained, secured in the way they work, great slyness is incorporated. Contact with the nucleus of operating forces, as attempted in the Paracelsian approach, appears totally eccentric from the point of view of the present technologist. But it is just as easily apparent from the present state of technology that it is precisely this eccentricity which it lacks in order to be less – artificial. This artificiality is more than and something different from the human nest which is called a house, or even moving on wheels, although this too occurs in no living being. All this kind of thing still has a hold, just as our hands have a hold when they are playing the piano instead of gathering food or strangling enemies. Even de-organized technological existence does not yet need to be an artificial one, namely not when, and this is most decisive, it occurs in a socially mediated, in a not inhuman society and participates in this mediation. The artificiality meant here is based instead on the predominant abstractness of bourgeois, and above all of late bourgeois existence, an abstractness (unmediatedness with human beings and nature) to which the technology of cunning also belongs, alongside the so progressive unleashing of the forces of production it brought about. And thus bourgeois technology, for all its triumphs, appears both as poorly managed and poorly related; the 'industrial revolution' is concretely related neither to human nor to natural material. To it belongs the *misery* which it inflicted on people, right at the beginning and over and over again. Leisurely crafts became unremunerative, life in the English factories was hellish, work on the conveyor belt has become cleaner, but not more enjoyable. Hence, from the abstract profit drive, comes the *uglification* which machines and mechanical work have inflicted on the world. Capitalism plus machine goods brought about the destruction of the old towns, of the naturally beautiful houses and their furniture, of the imaginative silhouette of everything organically constructed. It was replaced around the middle of the last century by an advance architecture

of hell, in keeping with the situation of the working class, but also with
the place of work at which and as which the triumphant machine first
appeared. Dickens described this first industrial landscape so unforgettably
in 'The Old Curiosity Shop' that no electric power station of today,
however clean, is a match for this sediment of his, for 'the great manufacturing town, reeking with lean misery and hungry wretchedness', for 'that
endless repetition of the same dull, ugly form, which is the horror of
oppressive dreams', for 'the shrieking engines and the plague of smoke
which obscured the light and made foul the melancholy air'. This kind
of thing has certainly become more neat and orderly since then, aesthetic
Luddism has lost its modernity much more than the moral kind, Dickens'
mechanized landscape is only still to be found in abandoned waste zones
of the nineteenth century and even becomes, in its demonically grotesque
ugliness, a new aesthetic object, a surrealistic one: yet surrealism does not
justify its object but interrogates it, and the functional form, however
much it has been cleaned up, or so-called art of engineering of today cannot
conceal the desolation beneath, the alienatedness. It has, after all, advanced
to the same extent that machines have become refined and de-organized.
Technology, as an ever more advanced but also ever more lonely outpost,
lacks contact with the old natural world from which capitalism pushed
itself off, and also contact with an element in nature favourable to
technology itself, to which abstract capitalism can never find the possible
access. The bourgeois mechanical world stands half-way between what
is lost and what is not yet won; in view of its progressive character, of
its most far-reaching unleashing of the forces of production to date, it
will of course still have to remain in operation a long time in a no longer
capitalist society, but for all that it remains marked by the peculiar pallor
and lack of secretion in which the whole capitalist world lies. This
cadaverousness is also transmitted not least to present machine goods, in
most visible contrast to the old craft products; and it is not hidden by
the art of engineering, which extends from the manufacturing plants to
the products, by all this functional form and by the unimaginativeness
which is proud of it. Kant had described artistic genius as that capacity
which creates just like nature. Not just to the extent that it produces its
distinctive work involuntarily and necessarily like nature, but that even
its products, however much they surpass nature and have to surpass it,
'seem like nature and can be regarded as nature'. The technological
intelligence is of course not the same as the artistic one, it aims at additional
power, not at additional beauty, but it is nevertheless likewise one of

formation, of additional release and new formation in material. Thus Kant's aesthetic criterion, mutatis mutandis, more or less also holds good for the technological genius, wherever it endeavours to advance beyond the mere technology of cunning, as a future-concrete genius. This is not controverted by the fact that Kant regards a subject in nature (natura naturans) as something which can only be added to nature in the mind, like an immanent 'technology of nature' itself, as Kant says. Even the preponderance which the mere Newtonian mechanism of nature possesses in Kant cannot prevent in the 'Critique of Judgement' the – however reflexive or hypothetical – interpretation which is able to refer to a natura naturans, indeed natura supernaturans. Certainly, a subject of nature (the not merely secularized ancient Isis) remains problematic as long as no concrete mediation by man, as the youngest son of nature, has succeeded with it. Yet the possibility of this remains open and is mapped out in the object, not just in our ability to interpret it, in an interpreting ability which would not even be possible as a problematic one without the penetrating influence of natural material. To sum up, therefore, leaving aside all speculation: *there is the predisposition, the real possibility of a subject of nature*, by seizure it is brought into Faust's relation to fire, which only overcomes nature in order to mediate it with the best that is latent within it in our best interests.

If fire is only controlled and guarded, then it remains alien. The separate track on which it moves along is then a downright dangerous one, even if its additional force were to be better managed in social terms than it is now. In the society which is currently still continuing there is definitely nothing discernible of the related spirit who has turned his countenance to us precisely in the fire. There is a specific anxiety of the engineer that he has advanced too far, too unsecured, he does not know what forces he is dealing with. And from such non-mediation stems not least the most obvious effect of omitted content: the technological *accident*. This above all indicates how the content of natural forces, which is still so little mediated with us, cannot be abstracted away without great harm. In fact, in all accidents which happen to human beings, among one another and in their relation to nature, a strangely common factor which is most instructive emerges at the same time: the *technological accident is not wholly unrelated to the economic crisis, nor is the economic crisis wholly unrelated to the technological accident*. Certainly, the differences between the two are more apparent, and in places even greater than this relationship, and the comparison therefore sounds paradoxical. The technological accident appears as a co-incidental crossing of regular motions, as their outward, unforeseen point

of intersection; the economic crisis, however, develops totally uncoinciden-
tally within the mode of production and exchange of the capitalist economy
itself, as one of its steadily hardening contradictions. Nevertheless, both
catastrophes have a deep-seated correspondence to one another, for both
stem ultimately from a *poorly mediated, abstract relationship of human beings
to the material substratum of their behaviour*. There are some safeguards against
the technological accident, they are more prudent and also rather more
knowledgeable than the helplessness with which the bourgeoisie faces
economic crises, and the technological safeguards also increase to some
extent with improved testing of materials, sounding, and meteorology;
but nature has not therefore become good friends with its caning master,
and diminished risk does not save the bourgeois-technological relationship
to nature from abstractness. Even war technology, although it frankly
rationalizes the accident (of others), as a highly conscious technology of
catastrophes to the disadvantage of the enemy, is abstract, merely canalizing.
The atom bomb is of course the imperishable glory of American
Christianity, the radiance of its explosion has been compared with the
light surrounding Grünewald's Christ on the Isenheim Altar, but the
anxiety of the engineer, apart from the political one, remains here more
than ever. Even the synthetically manufactured catastrophe does not get
any closer to nature, whose stellar blast-furnaces it imitates, with extreme
cunning. Thus bourgeois technology has chance formation everywhere
in its horizon, chance formation from the blind, uncontrolled, unmediated
encounter of two merely external necessities. And this chance is not just
the reverse of external necessity, it shows in the latter at the same time
that man is not only centrally little mediated with natural forces, but that
the cause of nature itself is still unmediated with itself. Thus technological
catastrophe also implies every time the menacing Nothing, as definitive
unmediatedness; in all cases of destruction this chaos gives a sample of
what it can do. This was already evident above, in the 'foundation' (cf.
Vol. I, p. 310): 'Nor does the dialectical usefulness of the Nothing conceal
the completely anti-historical pre-appearance which the Nothing has as
downright destruction, as a den of murderers repeatedly opening up in
history.' The underlying technological unmediatedness is not diminished
even by the – however astonishing – case of a *superficial congruence*. Whereby
bourgeois-abstract calculation, which has been so powerfully developed
as a mathematical-physical one, finds a corresponding stretch in nature
itself, namely the mechanical one. As the theory-practice of modern industry
proves, there is a portion of concrete abstractness as it were in physical

nature; this is also why calculatory thinking will remain in force technologically long after the destruction of its bourgeois basis. But the purely mechanical has its law itself only as one above sheer contingencies, it is ahistorical, stereotyped and without content like chaos itself, whose become reification or crust it describes quite clearly by means of mechanistics. Thus even this partial congruence with an unreleased nature, with a nature without a counter-move to the Nothing, does not help abstract technology out of its abstractness. Unmediatedness with its material remains largely common to bourgeois economy and bourgeois technology; in the post-bourgeois world changes will therefore appear in technology along these lines. Certainly bourgeois technology, by virtue of its elective affinity with natural mechanisms, is considerably more sound than the capitalist-abstract economic system, even non-Euclidean acts of boldness are not denied to it, they stand out remarkably, as we have seen. However, crisis and accident are an insurmountable barrier to both abstractnesses; for both are contemplative, both are idealistic, both are characterized by the genuinely idealistic indifference of form to content. Not just in crises either, but also in the technological catastrophe; everywhere here the price is paid for the lack of mediation of the bourgeois homo faber with the substance of his works, and all the more so with the unfound productivity, with the tendency and latency in the natural matter itself. *And only when the subject of history: working man, has understood himself to be the producer of history and has consequently cancelled out fate in history, can he also examine the hearth of production in the natural world.* Marx defined historical matter as the relation of human beings to human beings and to nature; where this relation, as in bourgeois society, is thoroughly and per definitionem calculi abstract, the natural matter which collaborates in this relation still cannot be one of concrete blessing either. Marxism of technology, once it has been well thought-out, is no philanthropy for maltreated metals, but rather the end of the naive application of the standpoint of the exploiter and animal tamer to nature. The connection, detected despite all differences, of the bourgeois attitude of human beings towards human beings with that towards nature does not yet remove the technological alienation from nature, but rather its clear conscience. It is no accident that North America, which was born purely out of capitalism and has never experienced anything else, has no relationship to nature at all, not even an aesthetically mediated one. The current of nature as a friend, technology as the delivery and mediation of the creations slumbering in the womb of nature, this belongs to the most concrete aspect of concrete utopia. But even just the beginning of this concretion presupposes interhuman concretizing, i.e. social revolution; until this occurs there will not even be any steps, let alone a door, to the possible alliance with nature.

Chained giant, veiled sphinx, technological freedom

It is thus pointless to expect a certain good from inventing which stands on its own. It is not always better than the society which posits and uses it, even if it contains much more that can be adopted than this society. Jubilation at great technological progress is always futile if the class and the condition of the class for which the miracles are happening are not taken into account too. In the end there was gigantic war technology, and precisely when it functioned in capitalist terms without an accident it was a single enormous accident. Instead of one burning Troy there were thousands; the social crisis of capital turned of its own accord into the greatest of all accidents, into the social one of war. Thus very great retrogression of society can correspond to progress in the 'control of nature', and even the 'control of nature' then looks that way. As such it is a manifestation of a violent society anyway; the image: iron slave is taken from those of flesh and blood. And the technological relationship to nature repeats in a different way the bourgeois-social one to the misunderstood tendencies and contents in its own operation: in both cases the activity never gets beyond the mere exploitation of opportunities; in both cases there is no communication with the matter of occurrence. Though history and society nevertheless still represent what is made by human beings, but nature further represents what is unmade by man, what is largely unaffected by metabolism with him. The greater the gap is, the less a merely abstract relation is capable of bridging it. Violation and unmediatedness thus remain technologically affiliated in bourgeois society; every invention is determined and limited by this. Thus it becomes evident again and again that our technology up to now stands in nature like an army of occupation in enemy territory, and it knows nothing of the interior of the country, the fact of the matter is transcendent to it. A striking double aspect of this is provided by two figures on a thoroughly honest monument, on that of the chemist Bunsen in Heidelberg: a chained giant on his left, the overpowered force of nature; a veiled woman on his right, the sphinx of nature. *But if nature was not veiled, then the giant would not be chained*; the chains and veil are therefore allegories here of the same facts, and they are nowhere more certainly correlative to one another than in the society of thorough abstractness. As far as the latter is concerned with respect to the essence of nature, as everybody knows it has become incomparably greater since Bunsen, Helmholtz, Einstein, and Heisenberg; this is the other side of the otherwise so blossoming and bold new physics. The relativization of social connections and of the previous industrial calculation is reflected in the decay of all and every concrete relation to nature whatsoever. On the one hand, subjective idealism thus gains ground, Berkeley in physics, above all in England, where it has never died out. On the other hand, that of nature, even conceivable reality is ostensibly extinguished, not merely visual reality; the unmediatedness with natura naturans makes itself into a methodical point of honour and absolute at all events. These are the reflexes of a disintegrating society, of its crisis and of its own chaotic nature; they appear in the way it divides its physics in half. In the way it isolates it far from every microcosm-macrocosm relationship and especially far from the dialectics of nature, from the physical subject-object relationship. But neo-Berkeleyism has become the furthest thing of all to efficacity and seed, with interpretations which contain no statement of the philosophy of nature at all but simply a sociological one, so that the agnosticism and also the chaotic world of Jeans and Eddington, of Mach and Russell belong to late capitalist ideology, not to the philosophy of nature. Thus total alienation from the content of nature doubly makes technology into a trick, doubly stresses the relation between eternally veiled nature and eternally chained giant. De-organization, as the transition of technology into regions of nature ever more remote from human beings, has further reinforced the abstractness of technology. And with it, in an ever more precarious way, its homelessness; apart from the social basis, radiation machines now also lack a physically familiar basis. If, therefore, *de-organization* itself is to obtain the desired additional forces concretely from the world, then this surplus must *not only extend into the graphic but into the non-superficial, consequently again and again: in mediation with a no longer mythical natura naturans.* The social-political freedom which takes the societal causes in hand thus continues in a natural-political way. After all, this mediation is the technological and natural-philosophical counterpart of what Engels calls, in the relation of human beings to human beings, the leap out of the realm of necessity into that of freedom. Engels thoroughly stresses the parallel between merely external social and physical necessity: 'The socially effective forces operate just like the forces of nature: blindly, violently, destructively, as long as we do not recognize them and do not reckon with them. But once we have recognized them, comprehended their activity, their directions, and their effects, it merely rests with us to subject them more and more to our will and to achieve our aims by means of them' (Anti-Dühring, Dietz, 1948, p. 346). Equally the blind catastrophe-containing necessity in the social and physical area is broken in both cases by mediation with the forces of production. In the former case, by human beings becoming masters of their own socialization, i.e. mediated with themselves as the producing subject of history; in the latter case, by increasing mediation taking place with the previously obscure *productive and conditional basis* of the laws of nature. And Engels vigorously stresses that both areas, and therefore also both acts of mediation with them and in them, can be separated from one another at best in the imagination, but not in reality: existence in social freedom and that in harmony with the recognized laws of nature are connected. To avoid the issue in a putschist, i.e. abstract way is no solution in either case; even in the fiercest counter-move and move to overhaul the Become, changing the world lives off object-based tendency. Even chemistry, however synthetic, or radiation technology, however boldly extended, is, *in so far as it is concrete, allied with a synthetically extending element a posteriori in the world*, must and will be so. The synthetically extending element a posteriori is in the dialectical legality of nature itself, beyond its Become. With the merely superficially-legal grasp which has been developed by bourgeois natural science and its technology natural necessity is of course not yet centrally grasped and mediated; quod erat demonstrandum. This itself external necessity is still blind and in this respect still ever more classified with the concept of fate of primitive peoples and in myths, namely with the Moira of destiny, than with that truly recognized necessity, which is thus brought to freedom, whereby concrete technology can have its concept and its continuing creation in nature. Only when Tyche and Moira, chance and destiny no longer form the unsurmounted factors of a merely external natural necessity, only in this precise presence in the force of nature would technology have surmounted its catastrophic side and its abstractness. An unparalleled hook-up is intended here, a real installation of human beings (as soon as they have been socially mediated with themselves) into nature (as soon as technology has been mediated with nature). Transformation and self-transformation of things into goods, natura naturans and supernaturans instead of natura dominata: *this is therefore what the outlines of a better world suggest as far as concrete technology is concerned.* Even assuming the earth had a heart of gold, this heart was still by no means found to be such and will only acquire its kindness when it finally also beats in the works of technology.

BUILDINGS WHICH DEPICT A BETTER WORLD, 38
ARCHITECTURAL UTOPIAS

A building must be useful, durable and beautiful at the same time.

Vitruvius

Going through St Peter's church the knight began the beautiful passage through immortality. He entered the magic church with the awareness that, like the cosmic structure, it expands and withdraws more and more the longer one is in it. At last they stood by the high altar and its hundred lamps – how quiet it was! Above them the celestial vault of the dome, resting on four inner towers, around them a vaulted city in which churches stood. – They entered the Pantheon; there a holy, simple, free cosmic structure curved around them with its soaring celestial arches, an odeum of the music of the spheres, a world within the world.

Jean Paul, Titan

Since architecture is nothing other than a return of sculpture to the inorganic, the geometrical regularity which is only discarded at the higher levels must also still maintain its rights within it.

Schelling, Philosophy of Art

Urbs Jerusalem beata/Dicta pacis visio/Quae construitur in coelis/Vivis ex lapidibus.*

Early medieval hymn

I. Figures of Ancient Architecture

Glance through the window

We do not have to set our foot down immediately everywhere. How beautiful a sketched staircase looks, drawn in small. A special appeal of plans and elevations has always been noted. Most of it goes into the finished

---

* Blessed city of Jerusalem/Called the vision of peace/Which is constructed in the sky/From living stones.

house, and yet the creation on paper, so delicately traced, was different. Sketched interiors seem similarly fresh, occasionally also deceptive, as even real rooms do provided they are seen through shop-windows or are divided off by a barrier. Who would not want to rest in these nobly swelling armchairs, beneath the congenially placed lamp, in the evening room. If only its peace was ours, the whole room speaks of happiness. But this happiness lies in the mere glance from outside, occupants could only disturb it. So here too the appealing plan lives on, though one which has become corporeal; a striking freshness of design still lives on in the unentered room. This freshness becomes totally alluring in the dream house of the young couple, which they savour in the drawing, engrossed in possible happiness. The model provides something similar, the now totally embodied design on a reduced scale. For the model too, the house as a child, promises a beauty which is not always to be found afterwards, in the real building. There is everywhere a sense of an outset here, seeming more beautiful than much that has grown up afterwards and its purpose. The design retains the dream of the house; the glance through the window frames it, even the model stands there as if in a telephoto. A protective layer is at work, which is transparent of course but does not yet allow us to help ourselves or to step inside. That is why everything looks so much better behind glass, co-existing more easily.

Dreams on the Pompeian wall

Even with crayon and paint it was possible to build in a thrilling way at any time. That which is painted does not collapse, no house on the wall comes too expensive or is too bold. Pompeian painting is thus the most famous in this vein, it is nothing but a holiday city at home. A perspective view, vedutas run riot, fragilely beautiful, impossible building shapes are conjured on to the wall. Those that are not to be found on earth, and that could not even stand up; particularly on wall decorations of the second, and then again of the fourth Pompeian style. A villa in Boscoreale displays side by side a view of painted gardens, oddly foreshortened pillared halls, groups of houses full of nooks and crannies in the background. Perspectives overlap in a cheeky and enchanted way, parts of buildings that lie at the front are placed at the back and vice versa, charming balustrades, solitary elevated circular little temples mock the static rule. Despite the vulgar colours the life on the walls is extremely graceful, people could only float through these houses. The Pompeian playfulness has never been considered in its utopian aspect before, although the latter even appears in details, in a wholly tangible way: namely in the anticipation of later styles. Only the 'impracticable element' was noted, and Vitruvius already reproached this painted architecture on account of it. But precisely this unsound triviality allowed the painter to produce effects which were not yet due at all in a sound way. Thus the profusion of houses crookedly piled up in the decoration of Boscoreale displays a Gothic aspect. Even more undoubtedly, Baroque motifs appear: here in a sweeping row of pillars, there in broken or rearing gables, there again in bosquets and the like which the Rococo period was able to copy later, without breaking its style on this account. Ancient architecture was not familiar with this bizarre phenomenon at all, or it touched on it only very late, on the Syrian borders of the empire, in Baalbek or Petra. The circular temple in Baalbek displays the curved entablature in Pompeian drawings, the rock façade of Petra the truncated gable corners, with a turban-shaped rotunda in between. But this kind of thing only sporadically reached Rome and then long after the destruction of Pompeii, in Hadrianic buildings. And even in the latter there was only an occasional suggestion of what the central country town had so vividly executed on the wall. Only the late Italian and German Baroque produces the split gables and curved portals which Pompeian master whitewashers effortlessly put up. These master craftsmen very often used patterns from scene-painting of the time, and this origin explains both the shaky and the bold element. Delicate halls seem as if they have flown in out of coloured air, and thus bring dream-play with them.

Festive decorations and Baroque stage sets

With crayon and paint things were later built in a much more boisterous way. Namely where it was a question of forming a great mask, an open illusion. This is the case with the festival, and then on the stage; both use Pompeian games. To begin with the festival and with the manner of celebrating it, its intention in any case is to forget all everyday routine, it can never be original enough. The festive element is insatiably settled in the broad, playful or glittering realm of its pleasure. The orgy distinguishes man from animals, more clearly than reason; man does not stop when he has enough. The most brilliant age for celebrating festivals was at the close of the Middle Ages and in the Baroque period; at that

time the ruling class knew more about ostentatious display than ever before.
Enormous wealth, the capital of merchants and princes, flowed together
at a few points; often tasteless but never weary powers of enjoyment and
splendour were able to invest themselves in exuberance. The architect joined
forces with the maître de plaisir; crayon and paint, management and allegory
furnished the festival with every constructible dream magic it needed. What
was painted on the wall in Pompeii, in the way of buildings, and also
mythical scenes, here stood on the table or exalted the banqueting hall
and the guests, who had become set pieces of the decor, within it. At
a ball of the bishop of Sens around 1400 there was wine made of glass,
women disguised as their own rivals and finally as nudes which were
called clear evening. From a banquet given by the Duke of Lille in 1454
which was to announce a crusade against the Turks for the reconquest
of Constantinople, the following table decoration has come down to us:
a manned and rigged merchant ship, a meadow with trees, rocks, a spring
and the image of Saint Andrew, the castle of Lusignan with Melusine the
fairy, a windmill with a shooting-match, a wood with mobile wild animals,
a church with an organ and singers who, alternating with musicians who
sat in a pie, entertained the guests with religious music. As if this remote
world was not enough, united on the table, mobile pictures and statues
appeared all around the centre-piece, furnishing warlike wishful situations
and those of victory. At the climax of the feast Sainte-Eglise herself rode
in, sitting in a tower, on the back of an elephant led by a Turkish giant.
This is a Gargantua-world of the festival, and also a wealth of barbaric
longing for the wondrous and wonderful, for Castel Merveil, drawn from
late romances of chivalry and used for show, transformed into a spectacle.
For this reason the director of such princely revels had to be an expert
at creating more than the land of the Phaeacians, he cast the room together
with the guests into a supernaturally monstrous realm. Casanova still records
from the Rococo period, from a world which was in other respects no
longer expert at fortissimo, gigantic enchantments from the late Middle
Ages and the Baroque period. He records them of the spectacular fairy-
plays of Karl Eugen von Württemberg, a despot who mastered even better
than most other petty princes in Germany the alchemy of making gold
out of the sweat of his subjects, a fantast who knew how to make his
court, despite Versailles, the most brilliant in Europe. These festivals lasted
uninterruptedly for two weeks, the capacity for enjoyment of a hearty
country wedding was combined with the gifts and works of art of chivalrous

courtesy. The Duke led his guests through a thousand-foot long, brightly lit hothouse, he led them through orange and lemon groves, past thirty lakes and fountains. In the castle courtyard stood the table, clouds descended, clouds parted, the summit of Mount Olympus became visible, with its gods, framed by golden pillars, to one side the seats of the four elements, and Italian arias rang from Mount Olympus, siren music without any danger. A hidden machine set Venus with sixteen gods of love on to the decorated table; the lady yielded, the cavaliers smiled, and at the end of the festival the whole consumable universe was served on the woman's skin, on the man's pleasure. Never were more brilliant festivals celebrated than in the Baroque period, that theatrical age, and its distant echo in the Rococo period; never were they embodied with such refined extravagance – at a time of departing but all the more decorative feudal power. The French Second Empire obtained its already rotten highlights from this source, and even today all splendour – from New York ice revues in Madison Square to the coronation in London – loan spectacular fairy-plays of the Baroque period in a tortured fashion. But the non-tortured element is lacking, and the pleasure in decoration, however peculiar it was, of the age of Makart had nothing at all in common with genuine exuberance. The banquets of the former merely chewed over ancient lustre again and again and fraudulently copied it, whereas the Baroque festival had represented with the lavish vividness of its own age ancient themes and themes of its own with further superelevated reflection. Fancy-dress balls and sleigh parties, pleasure hunts and equestrian contests equally embodied that Baroque style which seeks marvels in architecture, unprecedented amazement in scene-painting. But the final festive dream of Baroque society was to be carried off to India, to the court of the Great Mogul. Even Greek mythology, which was used for disguise or allusion, lay in the latitude of Delhi. Festive architecture posited tropical colours and contours throughout in order to be at home in it ad libitum.

It is only a step from this remoteness to the colourful stage itself at that time. To the world on the boards which is appropriate to a lavish plot. And hence to the *posed* scene on which the portrayed festivity is framed, and whereby something else was so richly to prosper. Baroque stage sets far surpassed the preparations for a festival in dissipation beyond the familiar and its field of vision. Giuseppe Galli-Bibiena (1696–1757) was the genius of the operatic scene, of that enchanted all the more by means of optical tricks. Hence the idea of introducing the perspective of the character on the stage or an imaginary perspective, a perspective from a great lateral distance, instead of the simple perspective of the spectator. Galli-Bibiena removed the visual point lying in the axis of the theatre, turned the flats which had previously stood at right angles to the spectator, placed them diagonally with the wishful effect that the perspective, in contrast to the Renaissance stage, pointed completely towards what was oblique, displaced, and full of presentiment. This became the frame of the dramas about high matters of state, above all of the Jesuit opera, which was highly fantastic. A world beneath the magic wand arose in the stage and backstage area: angels and demons stretched their wings, magicians produced seas of flame and floods through which innocence strode all the more touchingly or all the more victoriously, Elijah ascended into heaven in a fiery chariot, and in the end the practice of hell and the radiance of heaven were constructed as strikingly as if people really were transported to another place. But the architect had to shape the space in which the incredible appeared credible and the spectacular fairy-play an attainable condition. The backdrops which have survived (cf. Josef Gregor's portfolio 'Monuments of the Theatre') show staircases, banqueting halls, subterranean vaults, magnificent churches in an almost unfathomable wealth of drawing, overlapping and of backgrounds. Classical or oriental buildings, beloved by the contemporary Baroque novel, were put up in a striking manner, and potentiated again in their legendary splendour: Nero's golden house, the palace of the Great Mogul, 'sugar-sweet pleasure' full of 'empurpled heaven' on earth, and it was reflected 'in crystalline waters'. This was, in the locus minoris resistentiae: theatre, the power of this elegant, not to say ethereal bombast. In its illusory architecture, though, the illusion did not serve to copy historical styles, as in the scene-painting of the nineteenth century, but a style of its own, the Baroque, continued to experiment in a utopian fashion within it. In fact the Baroque, as mannerism had already done before it, sought its reflection so eagerly itself that real architecture was able to go to school in the theatrical kind and learnt the sorcery of multiplying itself even more daringly. Hence also the *final intensification* of theatrical architecture: the *real* that merges into the *painted*, the *painted* that merges into the *real*. As in the case of Tiepolo when he doubles as it were in painting the banqueting hall of the Palazzo Labia in Venice: with fake windows and arcades, with illusory guests at the table, with the banquet of Cleopatra in the wide open wall. This illusion worked very convincingly high overhead, in the painted ceilings of the Baroque, combined with dome and lantern. Wall and ceiling are here supposed to appear as one, the real pilasters are continued as painted ones, painted buildings tower up into infinity, seen from below, with the most blatant foreshortening. All the methods of optical illusion, of double and treble perspective are summoned up to heighten the space, to free the ceiling from termination; the dome, formerly suspended so dispassionately on its stone ring, becomes a sucking funnel. Different degrees of reality appear in the transition from the architectural to the painted building and even within the painted building itself. The opposite tasks of filling the ceiling and opening the ceiling clash, the real light which enters through the windows of the lantern becomes the climax of the painted light. The first of these pleasant views above had already been managed by Mantegna in the bridal chamber of the citadel of Mantua, the last and strangest are to be found in Bavarian and Austrian Rococo churches, and also castles, as in the Weltenburg ceiling fresco of Cosmas Damian Asam. This kind of thing embodies, in a masterly unsound manner, nothing less than the wishful image again to live in a different space from the existing one, in fact in a deliberately impossible space. It is a daredevil architectural hurly-burly of perspective, it is simultaneously a work of art composed of exaggerating illusion, of architectural travelling. All this was accomplishable in an architecture which was the most sensationally breath-taking of all anyway, one of built-in perspective. The Baroque was after all related from birth to nothing but veduta, to standpoints from which the ensemble amalgamated into the stage, into the theatrical backdrop in the street. The whole creation was agitative, was propaganda for princely power and Catholicism; but the means of this creation, even outside the stage, was a theatre of intoxication which was to insert the capricious and the marvellous into art. There is nothing familiar and fixed which this style did not circumvent despite strict symmetry, which it did not interrupt with a billowing line, a built-in veduta; the Rococo period merely represents an intensification of this. So Baroque architecture also stands on the Baroque stage, conceals precisely its clear constructive points of support, places its masses in the air, as if in the process of ascending to heaven. This is not inconsistent with the feigned problems of support, the enormous pedestals, the double, treble pillars and pilasters pushed far forward. They do not support the miracle at all, they merely suggest and underline that so much mass would be necessary for support if all was well in this architecture, instead of in gloria et jubilo. Even the Baroque balcony springs from the wall, as Burckhardt says, to the sound of drums and trumpets. For this reason the transition at that time from the art of stage design to real building also proved so easy: the same Giuseppe Galli-Bibiena who painted his fantastic stage built the opera-house in Bayreuth, the most beautiful Italian theatre in the world. He built the opera-house in Dresden and connected it with the Zwinger,* another Galli-Bibiena built the Jesuit church in Mannheim, – sheer festive performances in stone. The buildings stand there in a sensory-supersensory way, and the beautiful which here celebrates consummation with the sacred does not rest itself, but sweeps and soars.

Wishful architecture in the fairytale

But people always managed to describe houses almost more colourfully than to provide them. *Fictitious* building then appears, of the kind conjured up in the fairytale. Thus there are also Pompeian games with words, they then set off entirely into the wide blue or even turquoise-green yonder. The German fairytale, which reveals so much that the heart desires, contains the forbidden room of the dream house at any rate and pictures it namelessly. But complete dream castles and also dream cities are found in the Arabian Nights, where the architectural models for the dream that extends them were more abundant anyway than in the north at that time. And it's better in the dream, the houses are here endowed with a beauty which cannot be found elsewhere: 'Within them are days and nights which do not seem as if they are to be ranked with this life.' The fairytale: 'The Tale of Janshah' ('The Arabian Nights'), from which this sentence comes, describes the jewelled castle of Takni, far, far away in the hidden world: 'When Janshah awoke he saw something glitter in the distance as if it was a flash of lightning, and it filled the firmament with its flashing. But he marvelled at what this light could mean, without suspecting that it was the castle for which he was searching. So he climbed down from the mountain and went towards the light that radiated from Takni, the castle of jewels. Now it was still a journey of two months away from Karmus, the hill on which he had landed, and the foundations of the castle of Takni were built of red rubies and its walls of yellow gold. And it also had a thousand towers which were built of precious metals and studded and sprinkled with precious stones from the sea of darkness, and that is why it was called the castle of jewels, Takni.' In addition to this there are inanimate but totally

---

* One of the finest Baroque palaces in Germany, built by M. D. Pöppelmann between 1711 and 1722.

preserved statues, as in the fairytale of the strange city of brass, situated in the desert between Egypt and Morocco, and filled with corpses and treasures: 'When the emir Musa saw this, he stood still and praised Allah, the Supreme Being, honoured him and contemplated the beauty of the palace, the weight of its construction and the magnificent perfection of its distribution.' Everything judged or announced or even bragged about in this way lies in the wishful line which finally leads to the palace of Aladdin, to the conviction of the beholders that nothing could be built to compare with it in the whole world. And however much half-preserved Greek and Roman cities in the desert which had formed around them contributed to the oriental fairytale of castles and cities, it is still clearly always the architecture of its own epoch which is completed by this kind of literary Fata Morgana. It is instructive here that the fictional edifices of all ages take a substantial part of their lustre from the miniature or ornamental world of existing architecture; for these small forms inherently gave more concentrated expression even to the artistic aspiration of their style. A piece of Persian chased work ornamentally surpasses the gateway of a mosque, and a monstrance, a tabernacle, a baldachin above the figure on a pillar are even more Gothic than a cathedral. Thus the miniature, which contained as it were the mosque or cathedral seen as remote, small and sharp on the horizon, provided special material precisely for the formation of literary essence. The influence of the ornamental world is recognizable in the Arabian Nights by the unrestrained use of gold and precious stones, of ivory lattices and stained-glass windows. This kind of thing becomes even clearer in the dream buildings of medieval epic poetry, in the secular ones and all the more so in the consecrated ones. Namely whenever fairytale images of a legendary kind are sprinkled into this epic poetry. The temple of the Grail in Wolfram's 'Titurel' appears as one big reliquary, chased like the latter and yet as huge as a cathedral, sumptuous, indeed esoteric even in its materials. Its walls and roofs are gold and enamel, the windows are crystal and beryl, molten blue glass is poured into the golden roof-tiles, emeralds form the keystones, and the boss on the tower is a carbuncle which illuminates the forest paths at night and guides those who have lost their way. The whole description is hyperbolic, and yet it presents proper architecture: that of the castle in the air of Gothic design, driven to its ultimate Gothic conclusion. And once again of course a historical contact is not lacking here, as with the castles of jewels and cities of brass in the oriental fairytale, a contact which for its part gives a magic form to the style of the period. If Arabian dream buildings continued to be influenced

by classical ruins, and perhaps also the dilapidated castles from the early
Arabian age of chivalry before Mohammed, all the palace-utopias of the
Middle Ages adopted the imperial castle in Byzantium. Its magnificence
became a legend, and sprouted into a miracle among the Franconian nations,
since the time of Charlemagne. But even with Byzantium fictitious
architecture, since the time of the Crusades, was governed by oriental
romanticism. And this was ultimately the case for an important reason,
for the same reason which caused the most highly imaginative stage sets
to blossom with a touch of Baghdad. For Byzantium seized the imagination of the architectural fairytale so strongly simply because it was so
close to the Arabian Nights beauty of the buildings of the Orient in its
power and dignity. And even to modern eyes, nothing seems to have risen
so directly from the oriental fairytale, indeed even from the German
one, as Moorish architecture. If architecture as a whole was called frozen
music, then Moorish architecture interrupts this image: it seems much
more like embodied fairytale; which is why this whole world, down to
the catchphrase, appears to be magical down to the Europeans. Thus it
is evident that *architecture in the fairytale* almost continually turns into
that *fairytale in architecture* as which Moorish architecture acts and exists.
Above all in the European view of it, in that Open-sesame wish which
conceived all fantastic beauty from Castle Grail to Armida's magic garden in
an orientally enchanted light. This sort of thing extends, though with a
fortissimo which does not really suit the fairytale and the Alhambra, to
the castles of the exotic Baroque novel, all the way back to Ibrahim Bassa,
to the Great Mogul. Then again, so much later, the Kronenburg in Arnim's
highly Romantic novel 'The Guardians of the Crown' masquerades on
European soil as a Moorish-inspired glass structure. The fictitious building
nevertheless remains in the line of the architectural style existing at the
time, but extends this line in a utopian way, on occasion incorporating
legendary architectural images, almost always in the direction of the world
of domes, of the pillared courtyard, and of blue-gold ornaments. So too
in Hoffmann's fairytale 'The Golden Pot' Lindhorst's azure room, with
the golden palm-trees, passes smoothly from the Empire style into the
Eastern style. A path which is the closest to the architectural fairytale
particularly in the northern mists. At any rate, almost all buildings are
magically coloured in the fairytale, whereupon they then look like the
Fata Morgana where it is at home.

Wishful architecture in painting

So much for fictional houses, but there is now the important new addition of painted ones. They did not serve merely to fill in the background, more frequently and authentically they also sought to be wishful building in their turn. There is a distinct series in which the architectural picture gains a nevertheless strange life of its own, with a special concentrated expression. This goes back a long way, much further than landscape painting; the Pompeian murals belong here again, and painted townscapes already seem late Gothic. Afterwards the architectural distant views in the pre-Baroque of the fifteenth century begin, the halls and streets in Raphael's 'School of Athens' open out, Dürer and Altdorfer set the tone for architecture depicted for its own sake. Altdorfer's detached Renaissance villa in the 'Bath of Susanna' gazes into the countryside as an individual subject, with highly exaggerated loggias. Architectural pictures became particularly numerous in the north from the middle of the fifteenth century; from Memling on, they all contain prophetic anticipations of the architectural style to come. Altdorfer, already living in the breakthrough of the Renaissance, a painter and architect as well, gives in his pictures, overdoing the architectural style that had arisen, a permanently strange portrayal of the Italian-German Renaissance as it had never been built so far north. Afterwards there follows the half naturalistic, half fantastic painting of buildings in Dutch mannerism of the seventeenth century, with Vredeman de Vries and others. Their portrayals, now simply called 'architectural pictures', with the building as sole subject and people at best as accessories, turn Altdorfer's Renaissance villa almost into a peepshow veduta, but also into a particularly closed Baroque gloria; it is as if there were nothing in the world but this painted palace courtyard, this castle-yard, this late Gothic imaginary church (cf. Jantzen, The Dutch Architectural Picture, 1910). Particularly interesting here, because of its space-making character also well-suited to a philosophical study, is a successful architectural picture by Hendrik Arts, repeated by Peter Neefs and then frequently after that. This hall church,* painted in treble perspective and correspondingly co-ordinated spatial style, admittedly anticipates no future architecture, but has a Romantic attitude to the late Gothic style, in the middle of the seventeenth century, in such a way however that the space seems to

* A church with nave and aisles of the same height.

disappear even more than it did then into angles and depths. Such church-paintings are reminiscent of Hegel's post festum description and yet festive description of Cologne cathedral: 'Its majestic and graceful quality – the slender proportions, their elongated quality, so that it does not so much rise as fly upwards. . . This is not a question of usefulness here, of enjoyment and pleasure, of satisfied need, but of a broad-cloaked strolling around in halls which do not care as it were whether people use them, for whatever purpose it may be; – this is a high forest, a spiritual, ornate one' (Werke XVII, p. 553f.). Painted architecture as such is of course only a coloured shadow cast by the real kind, but it can also produce, in the sense indicated above, variations on a theme which further develop this theme in easily co-existing forms. So easily co-existing, painted architecture may appear terribly unsound in several cases, statically unelaborated and untenable; but the statically habitable is not the purpose of these thoroughly individual structures. Furthermore, even seen purely in terms of painting, a subject which is itself already art cannot lead to such fundamentally increasing revelations as subjects like the nude, the portrait, and the historical scene or landscape; but instead the architectural picture provides in its signifi-cant examples precisely clarifications, if not elaborations sui generis in a different material, in painting technique, which can continue in a particularly related way the very morning charms of the architect's sketch. The archi-tectural picture cannot be confused here with illusionistically intended mural painting, like that of Tiepolo; its purpose is not the Baroque and late Baroque mixture of painted and real architecture. Its purpose is rather the imagination of an ideal architecture which is certainly not yet to be found on earth or not in such a pronounced fashion. Jakob Burckhardt was the first to draw attention to the value possessed by *architectural pictures for the recognition of the architectural wishful imagination of an age*. Likewise, the more distinctly the architectural style of an age changes, the more strongly it ferments in a utopian way in its painted architectures. And equally, the more maturely an architectural style has already developed, the more brilliantly this phenomenon can be doubled in the architectural picture, as if there was a painted entelechy of style. As evidence of this latter process Paolo Veronese's biblical banquet pictures are unsurpassable, like the most famous of all: 'Feast in the house of Levi'. The painted pillared hall together with the townscape behind it has here translated all the lustre of Renaissance society into itself; a Venice of Paolo's time has been doubled and rebuilt of fire and harmony of colour. And as far as the wishful line in architectural pictures as a whole is concerned, it does of course follow that of architecture in the fairytale, namely with regard to the fairy-like quality and even the peculiar exoticism which the architectural picture also lends to the buildings of its own age and of its own country. But the wishful building in the architectural picture – precisely as a shaped work of art sui generis – is related much more sharply than the wishful building in the fairytale to architecture that can be optically strolled through, referring to it concretely, indeed painting it on the wall.

Painting on the wall ultimately means condensing architectural forms. Moreover, into types of building which cut across all styles; as for example the house, the pleasure seat, the high tower, the temple. Let us select two of these always also archetypal forms of building here in the architectural picture: tower and temple. The painted images of these two are all the more vivid as they simultaneously touch on very old, legendary *pre-images* of architecture. The two examples of this are Brueghel's archetype: *the Tower of Babel*, and then, in a very different age, beneath a very different sky, the Assisi frescoes from the school of Giotto, which conversely picture a kind of civitas Dei with the archetype: *Solomon's temple*. Brueghel presented the oldest, bitterest of all architectural fantasies in the 'Tower of Babel'. He painted this Promethean structure in two versions, both times, corresponding to the Baroque, with a perceptible echo of a stage aspect. In the Rotterdam picture a kind of colosseum rises unfinished in fifteen storeys, between a hill-town and the sea; the heights of the building are surrounded by clouds. The Vienna picture, retaining the curve of an amphitheatre, with arches, windows, gates and balconies on the illuminated left-hand, almost already developed side, adds a vast rocky landscape as a foundation for the building, and portrays the hubris in other ways too with greater severity: – a safe stronghold is our Lucifer.* The rebellious structure itself (Genesis 11, 1–9), as everybody knows, only appeared as a fragment, though as a fragment which represents the work of Prometheus and Icarus in the Bible. The story, which is Yahwistic, has the same author as the tale of paradise; it was probably also originally connected with the tale of the lost paradise. But the entrepreneurial ideology of early capitalism and the varied ideology of the manufacturing period now supervened: the building that reaches up to heaven certainly lay close to the heart of the age of Faust, with its receding sense of sin. Following Paracelsus, Baroque theosophy also restored the connection of the tower-building motif with that of the Fall, and furthermore – a fact which is important for wishful

---

* A reference to the Luther hymn: 'Ein' feste Burg ist unser Gott'.

building – by no means with clear condemnation. So that, as in Brueghel's picture, there was the opportunity of portraying the safe stronghold of Lucifer not just as a fragment but as an unfortunately thwarted monument of an aspiration to create like God. An aspiration which, as Jakob Böhme teaches at the same time, admittedly has an 'arrogant outcome', but also a great goal and one which does not even need to remain a fragment. The arrogance itself is condemned by Böhme, but not the drive within it towards light and the heights: 'When they' (the luciferian spirits) 'rose in sharp inflammatory revolt, they acted against Natural Right as God their Father acted, and this was a source against the whole Godhead. For they inflamed the body and gave birth to a highly triumphant son, hard, rough, dark and cold, burning with bitterness, and fiery...So that the inflamed bride now stood like a proud beast and now thought she was above God, there was nothing to equal her...They' (the luciferian spirits) 'no longer wanted the old order, but they wanted to be higher than the whole Godhead and thought they wanted to have their dominion over the whole Godhead, over every kingdom' (Aurora: On the origin of sin). But in fire there is the light or: man reborn becomes Lucifer's heir by 'mastering the wrath of God, and a miraculous structure of free will emerges from him, who controls the world instead of the outcast Lucifer.' The building of the tower is also purified in this way, indeed through the soul-spirit of Christ in place of Lucifer it turns into the house of the world with heaven as the attained property: 'The whole of matter was to be a pleasure-house for spiritual bodies, and everything was to arise and develop in accordance with the pleasure of their spirit so that they should never ever have displeasure in any figure, but their soul-spirit was to be in the midst of all formation' (Aurora: On the soul-spirit). Thus subjective mysticism here attacked and adopted the old rebel motif, sky-blue motif, in the princely absolutism of the Christian man himself, in dialectical ambivalence between Lucifer and Christ, between the house that reaches to heaven and the Ascension of Christ. And the building of the tower half symbolized the infernal judge pointing upwards, and half a Jacob's ladder of defiance; this is precisely the case in Brueghel's picture, with the architect as a rival of God, and unmistakable wishful building. The tents of Jacob do not stand on this side though, and the leap from Brueghel's defiant tower to the other architectural archetype cited above: *Solomon's temple*, operative in the devout Assisi frescoes, seems a large one. Nevertheless, both are united by a spiritual wishful excess or the architecture of black magic on the one hand, and of white magic on the other. The

Assisi frescoes from the school of Giotto are likewise excessive, full of paradoxical architecture, they paint civitas Dei in a heavy or glistening statu nascendi. The one picture: 'Jesus' return to his parents' (in the lower church) shows buildings in which the upward drive is loaded full of wall. Behind elongated figures there rises the tower-, castle- and chapel-Gothic of a strange Jerusalem, one composed both of pressure and the other world. A kind of baptistry is formed in a particularly oppressive-sublime way, at the same height as the enormous city towers, it towers between them, colossal, against the sky. The other picture: 'Dream of the palace' (in the upper church) is already pointed by its subject towards a vision which did not want to rank among the architectural habits of this world. The Lord shows Saint Francis the treasure-house of the champions of religion, it is filled with weapons and shields, illuminated by a light in which the building does not merely lie but which, as the stormy light of the Day of Judgment, is inherent in it, radiates from it. The wall is menacingly dark, only within it gleam pillars and windows, of unearthly white; in fact, the archetype of Solomon's temple presses to the fore. It was regarded by the Christian world as the canonical archetype per se, as the absolute counterpart to the Tower of Babel. And since its dimensions stated in the Bible also seemed to give a hint to the imagination, the temple was figured out over and over again in Romanesque and Gothic terms, and even in classical terms as well – an architectural prototype from Jerusalem and with a very special vitality. Its new location, or rather: its highest equivalent would of course only be in a *Heavenly Jerusalem*. This 'urbs vivis ex lapidibus', as an early medieval hymn calls it, was itself never painted though, as if it stood before one's very eyes. These remotest pinnacles appear almost exclusively on glass windows, as in the late example of St Martin in Troyes, a medieval town, introduced into the magic square and the other world, with the light of the Lamb on high. Great pictures denied themselves the portrayal of this supreme Christian architectural archetype; even that on the Gent altar by van Eyck shows a Heavenly Jerusalem only on the horizon. The imagination of architectural painting here dropped anchor in advance, it left it to the architectural symbol, that is, as is now to be shown, to the forms of utopia *within architecture itself*, Gothic architecture in this case, at least to signify an 'urbs vivis ex lapidibus'.

The church masons' guilds or architectural utopia in actual construction

Painting and writing can prepare the house, and overplay it too. Only the effort of building, the actual constructive effort, causes us to be inventive in a durable way. Ce qu'il n'est pas formé n'existe pas,* and not just Being but also the utopian substance grows with formation, if it is a shaping one. This is all the more unencumbered as the dream in the case of major actual construction, instead of vanishing in the face of technology, uses it for its advancement. The intention of the old church masons' guilds also becomes important for this, which again means the *image of the building* which guided them as a perfect image in the work itself. The Gothic church masons' guilds worked, as the Egyptian ones did long before, according to certain secret 'rules'. Of course, as far as the canonical essence in the church masons' guilds is concerned, we must distinguish between their secretiveness and the secrets they actually believed in. Undoubtedly a lot of mere tricks or dodges were also kept concealed; thus they looked strange without being so. Likewise much of this kind of code, and of mere trademark, is to be found in the professional masonic symbols, and also in the so-called basic figure used by the masons' guilds. The masonic symbols were granted to individual journeymen and, alongside any other meaning they may have had, served to sign a work. The basic figure on the other hand, also called the 'just basis of stonemasonry', served among other things as a model to resolve in practice to some extent proportions which arose and were incommensurable at that time, such as those which led to the irrational numbers $\sqrt{2}$ or $\sqrt{3}$. These ratios already appeared in the diagonal bisection of a regular triangle or in boring a cube at an angle along its body-diagonal (the edge and body-diagonal of a cube have the ratio $1:\sqrt{3}$); but such irrationalities were a sealed book even to the theoretical mathematics of the Middle Ages, which was stagnant anyway. Thus the 'just basis of stonemasonry', alongside other things which it signified as well, overcame this with a certain professional practicality. Which consequently, in a description hedged by clauses, was to remain a trade secret and in this respect by no means contained 'rules' of a canonical architectural perfection. The late Middle Ages even imparted a good deal of practical masonic mathematics in print; as in the 'Büchlein von der Fialen Gerechtigkeit', a collection of mechanical formulae. But of course: apart from this kept or betrayed trade secret the Gothic masonic guilds explicitly

---

* 'What has not been formed does not exist.'

propagated other traditions as well, those of a thoroughly non-mechanical kind. In the case of such buildings Semper's theory, which was really salutary in its day, is not correct that raw materials, technology, and function are the sole basic determinants of actual construction. This restriction was justified with regard to the senselessly affixed ornamentations of Victorian and other kitsch, but it becomes senseless itself as soon as it is applied wholesale to ancient architecture. At that time a different artistic aspiration was at work from that of so-called functional art, and because it was an *artistic* aspiration it displayed the most important determinant apart from raw materials, technology, and function: that of the imagination. Here it was that of canonical architectural perfection, with regard to a supposed symbolic model. This model guided precisely the actual construction of the work, not just, like the archetype, its dream and plan ante rem, and it gave the rule to the rules of the master builders themselves. Hence the great architectural artistic aspiration in each case was the same as the symbolic intention in each case, which was traditionally operative in the ideology of the ancient building trade. But this intention sought with set-square and compasses *depictively to approach the dimensions of a structure of existence in general imagined as exemplary.* Unfortunately the material which has come to light so far is not yet sufficient for us to recognize the goal-images of the masons' guilds, apart from the general outline, in detail as well. In any case the subject has been ignored since the invasion of art history by positivism, whereas on the other hand art historians from the Romantic period, like Stieglitz and above all Schnaase, who were still in contact with the subject, did not get much beyond establishing and providing a framework for the subject. Romanticism, and particularly mysticizing freemasonry before it, also supplanted the genuine symbolic intentions of ancient architecture with false ones, from the spirit of their own age and its ideology; as with the Gothic towers 'pointing heavenwards', which in reality, there and then, were rather symbols of bourgeois pride and of 'arrogance' than of longing for heaven. Nevertheless, the existing genuine symbolic intention in the masons' guilds is settled neither by the understatement of positivism nor by sentimental additions from the Romantic age; the genuine architectural symbol is itself manifested too unmistakably in the actual constructions of its respective artistic form for that. Equally there is a never wholly broken recollection in the masons' guilds of that sacred tradition in which not even a path, let alone a temple, had been laid out without mythical rites and similar standard measures. The druidical stone pillars and the stepped Tower of Babel, the Egyptian pyramid and the humanly balanced Greek temple, the Roma quadrata and even the Slavonic circular market-place always obeyed, from the standpoint of their respective symbols in the superstructure, different classifications from those of raw materials, technology, and immediate function; and the Gothic cathedral was no exception to these classifications. Even more unmistakable in the Gothic symbolism of the masons' guilds is the after-effect of dualistic-gnostic mythology of numbers and figures, which had been kept alive in the Mediterranean countries, particularly in Provence, and spread north from there. Christ-like architecture differs here from the heathen-astral kind only in the totally different content of its mythical classification, not in the classification itself. A special image of classification is found in Greek architecture of course, namely a purely humane one, one with corporeal-human proportions, not with astral or Christian-otherworldly ones. This kind of classification arose from a society without a priesthood and makes Greek architecture into that urbane human style among architectures, which then – through related replacements or conquests of myth – largely became a world of proportions kept humane in the modern age. But around the Greek-built urbanum there runs the credited formula of all the masons' guilds and their architectural utopia: *the attempted imitatio of a cosmic or conversely Christ-like building, the one most perfectly conceived, for the purpose of a rapport.* The imitatio necessarily preceded the longed-for rapport, and thus it created in its most radical expressions the *crystal symmetry of the Egyptian pyramid* or conversely the *hieratically ordered vitality of the Gothic cathedral.*

Beautiful building thus also intended to do more than have an externally pleasing effect. Unfortunately, as was stressed above, nothing is sufficiently clear in detail as yet about the 'rules' which undoubtedly existed at one time. And unfortunately again, only the freemasons have made an incessant allusion to this something more, a dubious and largely falsified one. Nevertheless, their civilized-delusional mummery must be taken into account here, for there definitely must be something discarded from the masons' guilds in it. As everyone knows, masonry both uses the emblems of the building trade and above all fantasizes its history throughout the entire history of architecture. It is highly improbable that this bourgeois-aristocratic alliance itself, especially with its hocus-pocus, emerged from practical masonry. But it is even more improbable that the fundamental frivolous use it makes of architectural metaphors was purely its own invention. The Salvation Army did not emerge from the military either, yet without the military its lieutenants and majors would not exist; even the hallelujah girl who is a sergeant presupposes a sergeant somewhere else. And it is reasonable to assume that the deistic brothers of tolerance took some of their plagiarized architectural metaphors from the church masons' guilds; whereby at least a clouded access, not merely faute de mieux, may open up to the latter. The back-connection with the masons' guilds was perhaps supplied by Rosicrucianism, which may well go back to the late Middle Ages and from which the freemasons branched off at the beginning of the eighteenth century. In the Rosicrucian Comenius we find again for the first time a recollection of the 'cutting of the stone to just proportions'. Then in the freemasons, in the midst of all other mystagogy, so-called ancestors of masonry are listed; likewise with conspicuous reference to the church masons' guilds which in the eighteenth century had disappeared from view long ago. These ancestors were supposed to be: Moses and the Egyptian priest-architects; the Chaldaeans and magicians on the Euphrates and Tigris; Hiram, the builder of Solomon's temple; the Roman priest-king Numa Pompilius, first Pontifex, and his collegia fabrorum. These were joined by Erwin von Steinbach, the builder of Strassburg cathedral, and around him the whole 'Solomonic' tradition of the medieval 'basis of stone-masonry'. Pious legends were also added, like the Byzantine one that the ground-plan of the Hagia Sophia had been conveyed to its builder by the archangel Rasiel in a dream. From which therefore, by virtue of the harmony of this church with the divine ground-plan of heaven and of earth, the magical significance of its pillar positions and proportions originates and ensues in detail. Moreover, connections with the Order of the Knights Templar are not lacking in freemasonry either, and with its churches which were decorated with undoubtedly gnostic-cabbalistic emblems. But the peak of perfection for the freemasons was precisely the above-mentioned Solomon's temple: – this highest symbol of all for the church masons' guilds. The constitutional book of the first freemasons calls the temple 'the finest work of masonry on earth, from the beginning up till today', for the reason that Hiram's, the builder's, architecture 'stood under the special protection and guidance of heaven and the noble and wise counted it an honour to be the assistants of the astute master craftsmen and artisans'. Actually even the hyperbole 'of the finest work on earth' did not grow on the soil of freemasonry but is only used decoratively in it; it was at work in real terms throughout the entire history of Christian architecture. The ground-plan of Solomon's temple influenced the first Christian basilicas almost a thousand years after its destruction, and the medieval church masons' guilds saw it as the sacred model. Freemasonry did not fail to point out at least one piece of authenticated evidence of this succession, one which is merely mentioned as a bare fact in the history of art. On a doorway with a pointed arch in Würzburg cathedral there are namely two pillars decorated with strange plinths and capitals, on its coping stone one bears the inscription 'Jachin' (i.e. 'He shall establish'), the other 'Boaz' (i.e. 'In him is strength'), and these were the names of the two pillars before the entrance to Solomon's temple, perhaps even stemming from an early mountain-cult and hence sun-cult (2 Chron. 14, 2). The Würzburg plinths and capitals correspond to the chains and pomegranates of the original, and also to the biblical statement: 'And upon the top of the pillars was lily work: so was the work of the pillars finished' (1 Kings 7, 22).* The magical tradition of this work is so old that even Josephus (Antiqu. Jud. I, 2) claimed the pillars were 'founded' by Enoch; the masons' guild of Würzburg cathedral certainly applied the symbolic supports from this cabbalistic antiquity to its own building and thus denoted the whole church in fact as a Solomon's temple in Christ. The pathos with which freemasonry distinguishes Solomon's edifice points in any case precisely to the Hermetic pathos of the Christian masons' guilds, and incidentally also of the Islamic imitatio. In its utopian completion the temple was in fact regarded by all architectural styles whose religion or religious astuteness was based on the Bible as the revered image of the perfect plan of their own architecture. Indeed, a collection of solemn architectural dreams which is itself almost perfect would be that of the reconstructions which were bestowed on Solomon's temple right up to the nineteenth century; just as the supposed imitatio of the temple also extends from the mosque of Omar to the – Escorial (which rises as an edifice on the grill of St Lawrence as its groundplan, but in accordance with the 'reconstruction' of the temple by two Spanish Jesuits). Of course for all this the freemasons, in the kitsch of their theory of the consonance or concordance of every architecture 'from the time of Adam on', poured a totally absurd uniformity over the entire history of architecture. The Gothic masons' guilds did not feel inspired in the sense of the 'Egyptian priest-architects' or the 'Chaldaeans on the Euphrates and Tigris' at all; they were gnostic-Christian-dualistic, not cosmic-pansophic like Rosicrucianism since the Renaissance. 'Pow, pow, hold on, hold on to the discord of the cosmos', this prayer from the dualistic

---

* The German translation of the Bible Bloch is quoting from here gives 'wie Rosen', 'like roses', which the Authorized Version gives as 'lily-work'. This is significant in the context of the Rosicrucianism and Freemasonry Bloch is discussing here.

Gnosis precisely characterizes the exodus ideology in which Christian architecture, culminating in the Gothic, arose. But in fact, if freemasonry is mentioned here all the same, this occurs despite its silly occult historical misrepresentation for the sake of its recollection, not improbable in places, of ancient architectural metaphors. What matters is the revelation of actual architectural symbols there and then, the understanding of ancient architecture from the standpoint of goal-images of its actual construction which were undoubtedly effective. And however unimportant the invention of a pedigree by the freemasons may be as such, what still remains important is the fact that it could not have occurred either if tradition had not continued to maintain, both stubbornly and significantly, the contact of the masons' guilds with a certain spatial mythology, but also spatial utopia. There is an ancient consecration of the house, and one intended objectively, one in which the traditional precision, indeed pedantry in laying out a magical point of contact cannot be denied. The cheapened allegory of freemasonry and the way in which it was possible probably only isolated the element in sacred architecture which helped to form and overformed at all times: mathesis of a magic space, 'the pattern of the tabernacle' (Exodus 25, 9). As a very old superstructure, very slowly revolutionizing itself, standardly supplying various foundations, though with changing goal-relations of the standard. Structures like the Pantheon, the Babylonian stepped pyramid, the Hagia Sophia, the Cheops pyramid, and Strasbourg cathedral by no means arose outside the ideology of a strict world of faith and hope, one determining the work itself in an imitative fashion. In the case of the Babylonian stepped pyramid the astral-mythical character has long been established, in the case of the Gothic cathedral its architectural utopia must first be gauged from the logos-mythical character. But everywhere, in the entire *sacred masons' guild*, the artistic aspiration is an aspiration to correspond, *an actually constructed congruence with the utopianized space imagined as most perfect in each case*. And it can be said that as a stone dance-movement in keeping with the dimensions of this space, or as a sheer built dancing-mask of this kind, sacred architecture was ultimately born. Indeed, even the Greek edifice was ultimately born as such an imitatio, despite its never trancendent-sacred character. And hence despite its body-sculpture sustained in all temple proportions, whose divina proportio, as the Renaissance said later, stands out in such a nobly animated way from Egyptian crystal, in such a quietly harmonious way from Gothic vitality. There is imitatio even in this well-balanced level-headedness, this moderate coastal shipping, which does not exaggerate to death, around the natural bodily dimension, precisely that specific imitatio which instead of the crystal of the pyramid, instead of the later forest profusion of the cathedral resorts to the perfect bodily figure as its architectural symbol. As one in whose youthful and also abstract Humanum the Egyptian final clarity and the Gothic final profusion are still or already united in a certain corrective. But the architectural utopia of completion was no less involved in the building here, however much more subdued it may appear than that of the Egyptian and afterwards of the Gothic architectural symbol. And although, as will be shown, only Egypt realized the possibility of total geometrization, only Gothic the possibility of total vitalization as an architectural experiment. So that most other architectures of the world then contain within them the Egyptian geometrical element and the Gothic vitalistic element again and again as *wishful alternatives*, as *guiding images of the final architectural expression*; in different percentages, and also with a perpetual struggle, with one abstractly settled only in Greece itself, and then perhaps also in the early Renaissance. This is the sense in which we can speak of geometric or vitalistic ornamentation even in the art of the Stone Age, and thus, with powerful anachronism, of that which later reached its full composition in Egyptian or in Gothic terms. And why Romanesque architecture, via late Roman mediation, can also still Egyptianize, i.e. geometrize, just as the Baroque incorporates re-functioned Gothic. Likewise, Egypt and Gothic remain the only radical architectural symbols, and at the same time those of the radical difference in the content of their intended architectural perfection. Therefore the 'rules' of the Gothic and long before that of the Egyptian stonemasons' guilds there and then certainly already contain an element of that utopia of completion which prospectively fulfils the symbolic intentions on both sides. Equally, however, both symbols are by no means free-floating or objectless, but they denote, like all genuine symbols, *real possibilities in the world, answering counterparts from its aesthetic latency*. The Egyptian architectural symbol is, as will now be seen in more detail, that of the *crystal of death*, the Gothic that of the *tree of life* or, expressed in terms of medieval ideology: of Corpus Christi. This is the breadth of variation of sculptural-architectural utopias, especially of those whose particular sap also rises and falls in the religious superstructures of their society. In the architectural will of Memphis stood there and then the utopia of an *aspiration to become and a being like stone, of a transformation into crystal*. In the architectural will of Amiens and Reims, of Strasbourg, Cologne and Regensburg sprouted there and then the utopia of an *aspiration to become and a being like resurrection, of a transformation into the tree of the higher life.* Greek antiquity is the beautiful general-human stroke of luck and the happiness of a nowhere outsized balance between level-headed life and level-headed geometry. Thus it alone has a humane reference, though abstractly humane, and like beautiful but not exactly boisterous youthfulness is a standard ante rem. But only *Egypt and Gothic* are consistently composed right through, *over-rigidity on the one hand, over-profusion on the other.* Thus, as far as extreme architecture is concerned, the imitatio cited above of a cosmic or conversely Christ-like space culminates and alternates here, as the space conceived as most perfect in each case, for the purpose of an architectural rapport.

Egypt or the crystal of death utopia, Gothic or the tree of life utopia

It is impossible to build to last with living matter. The wall of leaves, the roof of blossoming branches, how soon they are yellow, the winter destroys them. Life is too frail for building: whereas what is dead lives here, because it lasts. The wall, although it cracks itself, must at least surpass the brief human life-span. The obligation to resort to dead matter or that which has become dead holds for every building, even for the wooden one, even for that which, despite the use of stone, is still organically blossoming. But it is one thing to have to resort to non-living matter, and another to avoid every semblance of life in the work itself as well. This happened in its most extreme form in Egypt, on this large scale of rigidity. In so far as organic motifs still occur, like lotus and papyrus in the capital, and the snake in the sun-sign, they are reduced to the severest outline, unblossoming, as if pressed. This severity corresponds to the absolutely despotic social system, with dignity and ceremonial through and through; which is why almost only portrayals of folk scenes remain 'alive' in Egyptian art. But the position of rest in high sculpture was achieved as situationlessly as possible, as stereometrically as possible. The statues of kings and aristocrats strive, despite all the resemblance which was employed on the features for magical reasons to promote the personal survival of the person portrayed, towards block unity, they are one with the stone. They are drawn into regular bodies, every movement is reduced to a standstill, to a stance, often even spellbound into a squatting cube; motionlessness is their glory. The Greek statue recalls and denotes a living body, the Egyptian one represents a dead body which is waiting to be

inspirited by magic power into its death, into a living death. The completion
of such sculpture must lie at the point where no organic body whatsoever
disturbs it any more but where it is totally hidden, that is, as Hegel says,
in the crystal in which a dead man dwells: i.e. in the pyramid. But Egyptian
art culminates in the latter, which was an expression of the unification
of the kingdom, of the central cult of the king, not just as ceremonial
art but – related to this – as the art of rigidity and death per se. No possible
recollection and reproduction of organic motifs whatsoever clings to its
smooth-jointed, empty walls, to its crystal form. But at the same time
something new is added with this form which far surpasses the mere will
towards rigidity and severity. The pyramids, presenting their triangle to
the beholder on all sides, are almost obtrusively significant structures. Their
immediate practical purpose: the burial chamber with unassuming entrances,
could also have been fulfilled, in keeping with the megalithic graves of
the Stone Age for example, in the form of banked-up mounds of earth
or even in cubic form. Instead of which the conspicuous triangle emerged,
existing in such purity only here, and since, in the Middle Kingdom, it
descends in size right down to miniature pyramids, it can scarcely have
been chosen in order to place a particularly high roof over the dead Pharaoh.
Along with the square, the small scale, and triangular spirit level, small
stone pyramids were put into the grave of the dead man in the New
Kingdom, and they are supposed, as a pyramid text says, to help the dead
man to see the sun when it rises and when it sets. It is absolutely certain
that the pyramids were supposed to be cosmically depictive as edifices too,
just like the sacred buildings of all astral religions, from the Celtic stone
circles, the cromlechs, to the Babylonian stepped towers. The Babylonian
stepped tower also sought to be a depiction of heaven, of the mountain
of heaven, as it rises in its seven planetary levels. Such stepped pyramids
also existed in Egypt, indeed pyramid-building in general first began with
the sixfold tower of Sakkara. But from the fourth dynasty on, the triangle
triumphs, in the Cheops pyramid almost reaching the height of Strasbourg
cathedral, the fourfold profiled triangle over the square, the mountain of
heaven in a regularized shape. A still not yet extinguished, though still not
yet clarified light dawned with the measurements which the English astro-
nomer Piazzi Smyth took at the Cheops pyramid. According to these it
was certainly 'the purpose of the Great Pyramid' to reveal in its proportions
those of the then known universe and to be in conformity with them. Door-
angles, axial directions, and vertical lines seemed uniformly aligned with
the positions of the stars, the height of the pyramid stands in a harmonious

ratio to the assumed circumference of the earth, and the inclination of the walls corresponds to the angle of Alpha Draconis, the Pole Star at that time, and so on (cf. Smyth, On the Reputed Metrological System of the Great Pyramid, 1864, and Our Inheritance in the Great Pyramid, 1880, p. 380 squ.). Many things have since been corrected in the measurements made by Smyth, his astronomical connections have been totally rejected by Egyptologists like Ludwig Borchardt, and by historians like Eduard Meyer, and consequently enormously exaggerated by dilettantes (cf. Nötling, 'The Cosmic Numbers of the Cheops Pyramid', 1921, and – with an anthroposophical point of view – Bindel, The Egyptian Pyramids, 1932). But despite the provisional official verdict, despite the dilettante-occult substitute, the pyramid retains its cosmomorphic direction and depictiveness, it stands silently and as a crystal remote from life in the astral myth which – even though in so many different forms – governed the hierarchies of the whole ancient Orient. For all his customary Hellenistic romanticism of Egypt, Plutarch was still drawing on existing and well-understood traditions when he says (De Isi et Osiri, cap. 56): 'Thus the Egyptians conceived the nature of the universe in the image of the most beautiful triangle.' The pyramid condensed heaven to a central point, an apex, from which inorganic repose radiates equilaterally down to the ground; the temple of Karnak displays the same ordered repose on its starry ceiling, its downward-leading walls and pillars, and its floor, whose plant decoration represents the flooded land of the Nile. The pillars, whose dimensions and quantities are accorded not just technological construction but supposed symbolic significance, the temple walls whose paintings and reliefs represent the impressions of heaven on earth, have become as it were the exoteric, empirically constructed sides of the pyramid; whereby even the outside of the walls stands at an angle. And this is not just because the embankments on the Nile furnished the model for this slope (there are many sloping embankments and escarpments on the earth, but only a few pyramids), but because here, as on the Euphrates, the wall preserved the angle of the pyramids. The fanatical geometrization of all Egyptian art expresses its architectural utopia: *the crystal of death as foreseen perfection, cosmomorphically reproduced.*

It is very different where stone is negated, and the hard edge is broken. The life which conceives and changes itself in Christian terms seeks no rigidity. But just the opposite, it seeks to be eternal; thus Gothic decoration became precisely the most excited and lavish of all, neither a straight nor a curved line is preserved in it. Blossoming in the thirteenth century, with

a great wealth of details, which stems from the incipient liberation from
the feudal order, and with a direct upward surge of all structural members
into the air, which stems from the liberation of the wealthy cities from
the clerical order, the Gothic style is an urbane-mystical structure and thus
different from the Romanesque style, this thoroughly feudal stronghold
of God, in a highly gleaming, highly dynamic way. Since the organic
movement continues transcendently, it foams and triumphs all the more,
with Christ-like unrest. Plants, the bodies of animals, even monsters, are
effortlessly accommodated in Gothic decoration, not pressed, not stylized
as reliefs. The outside and inside of the Gothic cathedral could therefore
be compared ad nauseam to a forest. Branches are indeed found to be incorporated with total elective affinity into the organic stone structure,
and the building ends at the top with a finial. The pillars shoot upwards,
their capitals are simply nodal formations in this movement, the ceiling
is one single collision of these unfinished verticalities, the wall is pierced
with the immensely high, legend-narrating blood-gold windows; devout-
orgiastic light shines in from another day than that of nature. Longing
for the inward and for the above, which is like the inward, becomes the
measure of all things architectural. This Gothic soaring tendency organizes
all architectural proportions: 'Now the craving picture-panels have space
within it, network and interlacement of the incredible art of stonemasonry
proliferates in crockets and capitals, intersperses the glowing windows with
tracery and rose; a vaulting arises, not a vault, and a vast dynamic pathos,
thrusting upwards in all parts, in the nave, and also into the depths of
the chancel; sin and repentance, gleaming devilish beauty and the realm
of the gentle, the curved, the calm soul meet in these vast figured cathedrals
on the very closest terms, make them into the petrified trend of the perfect,
the undergone Christian adventure' ('Geist der Utopie', 1923, p. 33f.).
It is a blend of excitement, as experienced by no previous art, and an
excessive ornamentation which does not calm the excitement but does justice
to it. This therefore is the contrast to the gently organic regularity of
the Greeks, to the measured growth of the Ionic column and the harmony
between it and the weight of the architrave, but above all it is the decisive
contrast to the strictly inorganic crystal utopia of Egypt. *In Egypt ornamentation, especially the blossoming, organic kind, is an anomaly, in Gothic it is the
architectural symbolism of buoyancy and jubilation itself.* The few inorganic
symmetries of the Gothic style are no match for this organically transcendent
profusion: the diminutive subdivisions of the same pointed arches and
pinnacles, the frequently divided, subsumed, even geometrized element

which is found on the outside. If the cap of the tower of Strasbourg cathedral forms a triangle, an acute-angled triangle, then it forms it by no means in a geometrically pure way, but carved out, perforated, with spirals on the sides, and the finial stands on top of it; this triangle is therefore, as such a blossoming one, at war with the pyramid and even as a triangle an anti-crystal. Thus Gothic displays a totally different imitatio to the cosmo-morphic, and ultimately always astral-mythical one; it displays, with a dynamism which under other symbols, with a mandate to intoxicate, was only attained again by the Baroque, the extreme antithesis to the Egyptian granite repose, it displays *radically organic order*. And this in turn determined almost all details of the church building symbolically in the direction of resurrection and of life, in such a way that the very plant ornamentation has a mystical reference, to a wondrous garden of the Mother of God, in the spirit of the transcendent botany which developed in the late Middle Ages. Of course, just as the building contains geometrical regularities of an inorganic kind, triangles, circles, it also displays some cosmological references: the wheel window corresponded to the zodiac, in other versions to the astrological wheel of Fortuna, and the chandelier to the planetary spheres stacked on top of one another. But the chandelier with its lights stacked on top of one another in the shape of a ring corresponded much more genuinely to an imitatio of the rose of heaven, and in the arrangement of the pillars, windows, of the whole space set in motion, every reproduction of world statics came to an end. Everywhere proportions and configurations triumph in the end which are paradoxical to those of the world: The ground plan corresponds to the body of Christ stretched out on the cross, with the altar as his head; the finial symbolizes the mystical larynx which gives birth to the Son as the Word by uttering him; the glass windows correspond to the precious stones in the walls of the heavenly Jerusalem (cf. Josef Sauer, 'The Symbolism of the Church-building', 1924). However large the amount of symbolically unrelated or symbolically exchanged parts of the building may have become during the long period of actual construction and the frequent change of plan: the supreme canon remained a magical Christ-likeness, 'in typo et in figura ecclesiae et corporis Domini',* according to Augustine's Gothically fulfilled demand. The proportions of the Gothic cathedral are the disproportions of the Christological order to the cosmic one; this is the truth there and then in the just basis of stonemasonry. An exodus from Egypt in architecture is really intended here, an imitation

---

* 'in the shape and figure of the church and the body of the Lord'.

of the resurrection from the grave, with the stone rolled away (Mark 16, 4).
So if Egypt was the crystal of death as foreseen perfection, Gothic is assigned
in utopian terms just as decisively to resurrection and to life. Its architectural
symbol is thus necessarily the expulsion of death, anti-death, is *the tree of life
as foreseen perfection, reproduced in a Christ-like way*. If Egyptian art contains
within it the aspiration to become like stone, then Gothic art simply contains
the aspiration to become like the tree of life, like the vine of Christ; and both
styles of architecture as unique styles radically came to an end in this imitatio
of theirs. Historically, all styles which developed in addition to these contain
variations of these two orders: that of severity and that of profusion, but only
in Egypt and Gothic were they radically processed out and related so powerfully and divergently to their religious basis of stonemasonry. These are the
decisive characters of the architectural forms pyramid and cathedral
themselves; they both remain as the attempted construction of the depictiveness of a perfect space: on the one hand of silent death with crystal,
on the other of the organic excelsior with tree of life and community.

*Further and individual examples of guiding space in
ancient architecture*

So old is the problem of what building should ultimately adhere to. For
building not only satisfies the need for somewhere to live and so on, it
certainly does not seek to be merely pleasing in other respects either. Neither
in the zealous nor in the handicraft sense of this word, in the all too
gluttonous sense. How closely architecture is connected with the respective
social conditions, with the power that is to be displayed, with influence.
And how immanently building as such is not merely a particularly
superstructural, but a pictorial, and hence objective art. As such, however,
it adheres, like all pictorial art, to the visible world, absorbs it, reshapes
it in an experimental-substantial way. But where are the visible, i.e.
naturalistic forms which a builder could find to use as a model in the same
way as a painter or sculptor? There are a great many gaps here of course,
the architect only finds details to use as a model, scarcely however the
peculiar whole in which they are used: the house. Of course, even for
its lay-out architecture may learn something from an egg, a honeycomb,
a nest. Organic examples have been used from time immemorial for ornamentation, acanthus, lotus, shell, the pillar is a trunk, the dome may be
modelled on the cave, the interior of the cathedral on the forest. The
architrave rests on top as a slab of rock (the Lion Gate in Mycenae still

shows this origin), in general the distribution of force and weight, the basic business of statics, is of course subject to naturalistic laws. The builder has always been half an engineer, indeed into no art, apart from music, do so many mathematical and physical relationships enter from outside, even into its foundations not just into its details, and in no art have they been so greatly respected, for the sake of statics and of harmony. Certainly therefore, all this is true: and yet the house itself, this complete and unified element of his work, had to be invented or discovered by the architect in accordance with guiding images which do not lie in *what is immediately given* in the outside world, at least not in its fixed immediacy. Music, which of course likewise possesses very marked mathematical-physical foundations, but far less immediate models of the world than architecture, once imagined in this situation a harmony of the spheres. And it did so, instructively enough, not without an ancient oriental influence, that is, from the same cosmic standpoint which, as we have seen, also ordered Babylonian and Egyptian architecture from the point of view of a cosmic scale. The astronomical harmonic theory admittedly hindered rather than promoted the development of music, in contrast to the faith in a cosmic scale in architecture. This faith in a scale brought this art, as one that was objective from the start, the whole heathen half of its realm. It gave it, as an objective art but one which could not be found in the immediately given outside world and which removed the very homelessness of man, a cosmic house, a foothold and a specific image of perfection. And if Egypt is the most radical approximation to it, then astral-geometrical and inorganic-crystal elements have certainly continued to influence architecture long beyond that time. Their influence here is on both a small and a large scale, in the noble desire and search for pure forms as well as in the clarified order which is only partially described by the term classical. As far as the most beautiful individual forms are concerned, they are of course always introduced from the life from which they may be taken, but also then preferably geometrized. Thus the egg itself, although it is certainly a detail, provides a static model, which can be traced down to the modern streamline. Thus in classical times the wavy and even serpentine line was geometrized as the most perfectly beautiful:'the serpentine line, by its waving and winding at the same time different ways, leads the eye in a pleasing manner along the continuity of its variety', as the painter and aesthetician Hogarth had decreed in his famous 'Analysis of Beauty', 1753, and in which Lessing's theory of art followed him. Thus in the epigonic classicism of the nineteenth century the golden section was characterized by particularly clear geometrization, whereby even in architectural beauty, for it to be one, a whole has to be related to its larger part as the latter to the smaller one. While the school of the formal aesthetician Herbart traced this relationship throughout the structure of plants, animals, crystals and the planetary system, throughout the chemical mixture of substances and the formation of the earth's surface (Zeising, Aesthetic Investigations, The normal relationship of chemical and morphological proportions, 1856), a completely new, though formalistically emptied harmony of the spheres was applied to pictorial art in order both to regulate and to explain its beauty. The same, only very much more distinguished series ultimately also includes, from this standpoint, the 'divinae proportiones', which the Renaissance of Vitruvius and geometry in the sixteenth century sought to follow, in Vasari, Pacioli and Vignola; a crystal speculation which took its essential features with great logical consistency from the 'Timaeus', as Plato's 'most Egyptian' work. Not only is the builder of the world or demiurge to be found in it, but his fruit is perfectly geometrically ripe, beginning with the triangle of the basic components right down to the various polyhedrons in which the universe is situated. The model in all geometrized forms is ultimately, instead of details, one going right through the cosmos, believed to be going right through it, simply a kind of canonical world building. Its geometrical shape is now to be the ordering hold as such for the divinae proportiones in architecture itself, as one of visible clarity and Euclidean calm. And it is further evident that not only the clarity but even more so the latent astral myth in every crystalline hold, house, canon can and indeed must lead to the utopia of Egypt, often by way of classicism. It was not without good grounds, not without background, that Ledoux, the greatest classical architect, built in nothing but cubes, spheres, pyramids, ellipses. Roman architecture, as the most powerful example of powerfully classical architecture, itself contained, stemming from Etruria and the Roma quadrata, this geomantic-geometric, cosmometric contact. It was carried out most decisively in Egypt, then Babylon, but it went on shaping below these peaks, and the 'imitatio mundi', however secularized, also became a formative, binding article of faith for the Romans. Even Vitruvius, who is so remote from the Roma quadrata of primitive times, still ultimately founds the three things which he required of a perfect building, the firmitas, utilitas, venustas, in astronomical terms, i.e. cosmomorphically. The entire ninth book of his work De architectura, which was so widely accepted in the Renaissance, deals prominently for all its sobriety with astronomy and astrology, with the phases of the moon, with the zodiac and the seven planets, with the influence of the position of the stars on the earth. And a hundred years after Vitruvius there occurred in Roman architecture both a renewed contact with the cosmometric legacy of Etruria and an overdue importation of the Helios myth, when a builder from Damascus erected the *Pantheon* in Rome, this dome-cave and celestial dome at one and the same time. This is why, as nowhere else in a classical edifice, the *visible-canonical house of the world* believed in by the pagans is discernible in this late example. For the very curve which appeared in the Pantheon is not the comfortable or predictable one which had already given form to the Greek treasure-houses, the Roman store-rooms, and even the installations of wells and fountains; instead it is magically designed and this gives it special antiquity. Thus the sphairos of the Pantheon appeared long before in the ancient temples of the penates, in the circular altar, in the circular form and even in the domed roof of the temple of Vesta. Equally the egg-shape of the Roman circus, and even the curve of the Colosseum were not without connections with natural myths; after all, large-scale Roman architecture as a whole, far more than Greek, preserved contact with ancient guiding forms of a chthonic-Uranian kind, in short with a canonical building of the earth and cosmos. Without this considera-tion of social mediations, and hence in this case of the respective religious ideology, and particularly utopia, the basic architectural styles cannot be understood any more than they can without a thorough knowledge of their social foundations. Even the golden house of Nero, this model for so many later wondrous palaces, had according to the description of Suetonius a ceiling perforated as if with stars and an ebony circle in the middle of it 'which constantly rotated, day and night, like the universe'. Connections also run from the Colosseum to the heavy cylinder of the Castle of St Angelo, connections which were only understood and sought again under Hadrian. So the *Pantheon* had to reflect the universe all the more, with its dome and starry rosettes, with seven planetary niches and the eye of the sun looking in from above; Dio Cassius openly called the building 'a simile of heaven'. The Stoic-astrological cosmos, though no longer the highly stereometric one of the Egyptian pyramids and temples, is its architectural object. It is still full of undisturbed, paganly perfect heaven, thus without the protest which occurred soon afterwards of the myth of the Logos against the astral myth, of Christ against the cosmocrators (Eph. 6, 12). And the world-dome of the Pantheon is only apparently repeated in that of the mosque; for like the Christianity that arose, Islam, which is based on the Bible, also believed that the essence of this world passes away, it has a Day of Judgment as well, another order at bottom. The Pantheon is therefore not, as Spengler's interpretation would have it, the first mosque on European soil, but the *last pure astral structure*. The mosque of Omar in Jerusalem, the Hagia Sophia, the palace chapel of Charlemagne in Aachen give the central structure and the dome a very different meaning: they follow no world-circle, but rather a harbouring in the inward-ultramundane God. The same harbouring which the constant circular form of the apse also retained later, when the dome vanished in the Christian world, an apse which encloses with Christ against the world. *World perfection*, on the other hand, was the architectural correlate which astral-mythic architecture used as its model, a model employed in all its so powerfully varied forms. As no longer so world-like, as Christ-like in intention, the severity of Byzantium is the first ultimately to detach itself from the severity of Egypt.

Because from now on a house of the other side is intended, the building emulates it. This building is no longer pagan, it has established itself at the *exit* to this existing world. And the much acclaimed entrance to the same world, with which the Bible begins, was only apparently contrasted with this emphatic house of exit. The Bible praises its God precisely as a world-maker and above all as one who is very satisfied with his work as it is. This image of the world-builder is not originally from the Bible however, it is itself still pagan, that is to say, it grew on a different soil from the Judaeo-Christian one. It is not even found everywhere in the pagan legends of the creation; neither the Greek nor the Norse nor the Babylonian mythology of the gods portrays the Supreme Being as a world-sculptor. The latter is namely chiefly Egyptian and stems from Memphis, from the artistic centre of Egyptian religion. The sculptors' workshops, which were regarded as sacred, were there, the supreme god of Egypt: Ptah presided over them as a tutelary god there, and his priesthood ruled there as the most powerful in the Old Kingdom; the prototype of the *world-creator*, who was *very different from the God of Exodus, Yahweh*, is in fact the sculptor-god of Memphis: Ptah. Such an artist-god as world-sculptor is only found in Egypt (cf. on Ptah as demiurge: Breasted, History of Egypt), and only from the Ptah-concept in Yahweh did emulation of the world-architect and apparent emulation of his cosmic work also arise in a biblical-Christian intention. The Priestly Code of the fifth century, which constitutes the first chapter of the biblical Genesis, retained on this point the story of the creation from the Yahwists of the eighth century, just as the latter retained the cosmogony from Memphis.

Babylon, which usually exerted so much influence on biblical myth, definitely only introduced God as an organizer into the Bible, though admittedly as one who now reinforced the creator Ptah in Yahweh more than ever. The Babylonian imperial god Marduk joined the world-founder Ptah as a founder of an order, the excellent cosmic regent joined the excellent cosmic founder, already completing everything flawlessly from the very entrance and beginning of the world, with the separation of the waters of heaven and earth, with the development of the earth. Only now was the entrance of the world, precisely its alleged perfection, which did not seem to need any house on the other side, *nor any Exodus from that which exists*, also posited in the Bible. Only now in the biblical story of the Creation did the mud of the Nile modelled by Ptah become the waters of the deep, stars were posited which govern the seasons, separating and ordering determinants of a ruling-regional kind entered the work of Ptah, the sequence of the days of the Creation. In short, the familiar biblical work of Creation arose, with the world-architect from Egypt, the organizer from Babylon, a work whose legendary excellence admittedly introduced a semblance of cosmomorphy even into non-pagan architecture. But this excellence is only mentioned once in the Bible (Genesis 1, 31), and the work of art of the world itself, that completed by the supreme God, stems precisely from the *opposite land in the Bible*: from Egypt-Babylon. For even Yahweh as God of the Exodus from Egypt stands as an alien measure to the existing world, his Canaan is not the cosmos. All the more hostile, not to say rebellious is the attitude of the God of Isaiah to the finished cosmos, above all to that with which the Jews are favoured on earth, who promises a new heaven and a new earth so that the previous ones, i.e. those of Genesis, are no longer remembered (Isaiah 65, 17). And only *to this house of the other side, the Canaan which the Exodus was supposed to have in front of it, was non-pagan architecture, as anti-Egypt par excellence, assigned.* Even the ancient and hence cosmotheological architectural images in Amos, in the Book of Job, and in some of the Psalms are no match for this Exodus conception, they are already surpassed there and then by another hope, another ground-plan. Though Amos 9, 6 says: 'It is he that buildeth his stories in the heaven, and hath founded his troop in the earth'; the 104th Psalm praises heaven as a carpet, the earth as a panelled floor, and Job 38, 4–6 presents Yahweh as drawing a guide-line for the founding of the earth, plants the feet of the earth into foundations, lays a corner-stone for it. The lay-out of the Tabernacle is likewise handed down with a certain analogy to world-perfection: the Holy of Holies corresponded to heaven, the outer sanctuary to the earth, the courtyard to the ocean, the seven-armed candlestick to the seven lights of heaven. Even Solomon's temple in the continual numerical details of its proportions and parts recalls the sacred geometry which is familiar from the stepped temple and pyramid and which still recurs in the astral-mythic starry remnants of the heavenly Jerusalem. But all this means as little as the zodiac in the Gothic wheel window or the apparent similarity of the Byzantine dome to that of heaven; the alien element is still subjugated, the palace of Ptah is converted into the church of the exodus. Even the gnostic emanation of light, which streams into the later, Gothic architectural symbol, is crucially different from the reflection of the universe, and hence from the Pantheon in any form; since it comes in Christian gnosis from the 'second aeon', from the aeon of a future world. Thus on the whole this much is certain: the architectural dream of a better world has as its riverbed and mouth, as far as the history of religion is concerned, sun-worship in Egyptian terms, exodus in biblical-prophetic terms – precisely out of the Egypt of the former world. This cannot be expressed more clearly within this ideology than it was in Maimonides, in a passage on architecture full of historically immanent, and hence relevant ideology of the matter. Maimonides comments on the legend that Abraham chose the western side for his sanctuary on Mount Moria, and he concludes as follows: 'The reason for this is that the faith which prevailed in the world at that time was sun-worship, that the sun was venerated as a god and therefore all people undoubtedly turned towards the east. That is why Abraham on Mount Moria, namely at the place where his sanctuary was, turned towards the west, so that he turned his back on the sun' (Führer der Unschlüssigen III, Meiner, 1924, p. 275). This is a correction made by anti-Egypt, anti-Babylon of the east point in which, even for Columbus, the world was created and the earthly paradise was supposed to lie. But above all in which astral myth was founded, i.e. the myth which ultimately regarded the guiding space of architecture as cosmic-geometrical. Whereas within the biblical-Christian architectural ideology, chiefly in its architectural symbolism, that direction of the world had to be rejected where the external sun rises, but that direction increasingly chosen where it dies and sets together with the existing world order. From Augustine throughout the Middle Ages and above all in the Gothic period, church architecture is therefore celebrated as a depiction of that other architecture which sought to bear the inscription not of centred order but federative freedom, here conceived as 'freedom of the children of God'. The Gothic style lay radically in this direction, this attempt at a *new world-structure carved out of rock and stone like a human community*. Its architectural image of hope was the 'water of life', the 'tree of life', of which the final chapter of the Book of Revelation spoke to medieval people. This was then to be the 'new heaven', but also the 'new earth', in the anticipating ante-room as which the cathedral was conceived. With the huge moving vertical line of the tower and the pillars, with the painted light from window-panes in the interior, through which a very different world, a Christian world was to emerge for medieval believers. So much, ultimately, for the aspiration to become like stone or conversely like the tree of life in the radical fully-composed aspect of ancient architecture. The problem is simply how the guiding spaces crystal or tree can still function, have to function, after the deduction of their religious ideology, as well as after an architecture totally nullified by late capitalism. They always represent alternatives, alternatives which – now almost without religious ideology – were abstractly appeased in Greek classicism. But the point is to overcome them in concrete unity; in a clarity which does not destroy the profusion, in a crystal order which does not exclude the freedom of living ornamentation but makes it its content.

II. Building on Hollow Space

New houses and real clarity

Surgical tongs for delivering babies must be smooth, but sugar tongs certainly must not.

Ernst Bloch, *Spirit of Utopia, 1918*

These days houses in many places look as if they are ready to leave. Although they are unadorned or for this very reason, they express departure. On the inside they are bright and bare like sick-rooms, on the outside they seem like boxes on movable rods, but also like ships. They have a flat deck, portholes, a gangway, a deck rail, they have a white and southern glow, as ships they have a mind to disappear. In fact, the sensitivity of western architecture goes so far that it sensed Hitler's war quite a long time in advance, in a roundabout way, and prepared for it. But even the ship form, which was purely decorative, does not appear real enough to

the motif of escape of most people today in the capitalist world of war.
For some time houses have been projected in it without windows, artificially lit and ventilated, steel through and through, the sum total is an
armour-plated house. In general there is an increase, whereas modern
architecture when it first arose was fundamentally orientated towards the
outdoors, towards sunlight and public life, – there is an increase in the
need to live in sealed security, at least in housing space. The essential feature
with which the new architecture began was openness: it broke the dark
stone caves, it opened up fields of vision through light glass walls, but
this will towards an adjustment with the outside world was undoubtedly
premature. The de-internalization turned into hollowness, the southern
pleasure in the outside world did not, at the present sight of the capitalist
outside world, turn into happiness. For nothing good happens here in
the street, in the sun; the open door, the tremendously opened windows
are threatening in the age of growing fascism, the house prefers to become
a fortress again, if not a catacomb. The broad window full of nothing
but outside world needs an outdoors full of attractive strangers, not full
of Nazis; the glass door right down to the floor really requires sunshine
to peer and break in, not the gestapo. Also hardly unconnected with the
trenches of the First World War, but above all with the admittedly futile
Maginot lines of the Second, was the development of the plan for an
underground city – as one of security. Thus instead of the skyscraper,
projected 'earthscrapers' beckon, shining badger's setts, a rescuing cellar
city. Up in the light, though, the less real but decorative escape plan of
a flying city appeared, utopianized in Stuttgart, also in Paris: the houses
rise in spherical shape on a mast, or they hang as veritable balloons on
wire cables; in the latter case the floating buildings seem particularly
detached and keen to depart. But even these playful forms merely show
that houses as caves on the one hand, on stilts on the other, must be dreamed
again.

But what if a leap into brightness is nevertheless to be demonstrated
on such a basis? Which was in fact attempted in terms of structural
engineering, but now with the *affirmed* uncomfortable desire for nothing
but windows and equally stripped clear houses and appliances. Of course,
this kind of thing claimed to be a purging of the mustiness of the previous
century and its unspeakable decoration. But the longer it went on, the
clearer it became that it also remained at the stage of this mere omission
and – within the late bourgeois vacuum – had to remain there. The longer
it went on, the more clearly the motto emerges as an inscription over

the Bauhaus and that which is connected with it: Hurrah, we've run out of ideas. Where a life-style is as degenerate as the late-bourgeois one, a mere architectural reform can only manage to be no longer disguisedly but deliberately soulless. This is the effect as soon as no third element between plush and steel chair, between post offices in Renaissance style and egg-boxes, seizes the imagination any more. The effect is all the more chilling when it has nothing quiet-cornered about it but only the kitsch of light; however clean, namely vacuum clean it may indisputably have intended to be when it started out. Adolf Loos in Europe and Frank Lloyd Wright in America drew the first lines in negation of the epigonic tumour. Wright admittedly also with hatred of the city, one which was partly anarchistic and partly healthy, dividing up the murderous super cities into 'home towns', into a 'Broadacre City' with ten times as much space for everybody as they are used to having. Conversely though, Le Corbusier praised a high-rise urban 'housing machine', he epitomizes together with Gropius and also lesser creators of the New Objectivity* that part of the art of engineering which claims to be so progressive and which so rapidly stagnates, so rapidly ends up on the scrap-heap. That is why for over a generation this phenomenon of steel furniture, concrete cubes, and flat roofs has stood there ahistorically, ultra-modern and boring, ostensibly bold and really trivial, full of hatred towards the alleged flourish of every ornamentation and yet more schematically entrenched than any stylistic copy in the nasty nineteenth century ever was. Until it then ended even in France in the proposition of such an eminent architect in concrete as Perret: 'Ornamentation always conceals a structural defect.' A would-be classicism, which is almost Romantic, is evident here, partly due to the geometrical forms, partly due to the idea that the citizen's first duty is to keep quiet, and partly due to abstract humanity. Le Corbusier's programme 'La ville radieuse' everywhere seeks a kind of Greek Paris ('Les éléments urbanistiques constitutifs de la ville'),† he illustrates by means of the Acropolis a kind of universally human spirit ('le marbre des temples porte la voix humaine').‡ But Greece has here become an abstraction as never before, just like the 'être humain' which is not further differentiated, and to which the structural elements are supposed to refer in a purely functional way. Even the town planning

---

* 'Neue Sachlichkeit', the artistic movement around 1925 which, in contrast to Expressionism, sought to represent objective reality.
† 'The urbanistic constitutive elements of the city.'
‡ 'The marble of the temples carries the human voice.'

of these stalwart functionalists is private, abstract; because of sheer 'être humain' the real people in these houses and towns become standardized termites or, within a 'housing machine', foreign bodies, still all too organic ones; so remote is all this from real people, from home, contentment, homeland. This is and must be the result as long as an architecture does not concern itself with the ground which is not level. As long as the 'purity' consists of omissions and unimaginativeness, the serenity consists of a head-in-the-sand policy, if not of deception, and the silver sun, which seeks to sparkle everywhere here, is a chromium-plated misery. Everywhere here there is architecture as surface, as an eternally functional one; whereby even in its greatest transparency it reveals no content, no budding and no ornament-forming blossoming of a content. Though this abstractness combines excellently with glass, and could be curiously fashioned in it, a vacuum cut in air and light, neo-cosmically out of the void. Thus Bruno Taut, a disciple of Scheerbart, sketched a 'house of heaven' (cf. 'The City Crown', 1919), the ground plan consists of seven triangles, the walls, the ceiling, the floor are made of glass, the lighting makes the house into a colourful star. Precisely in emulation of the 'pancosmist' Paul Scheerbart, who had first universalized glass architecture, the whole earth was ultimately to be converted into crystal. And as an example of the new transparency Taut quoted the lines from Claudel's 'The Tidings brought to Mary': 'Into the waves of divine light the builder raises with calculated wisdom/the stone skeleton like a filter/And gives the whole edifice the water of a pearl.' Numerology along with the most modern materials also found a place in Taut's programmes, with the astral element ultimately above colourfulness; thus the adventure of an Egypt composed of the void arose here, arose in vain. Alongside it again raged a Gothic composed of the void, with rays and pencils of rays without content shooting up like unbridled rockets. Pure functional form and exuberance without any contact are thus dualistic but also complement one another, so that the mechanical style chills and relieves, but the imagination becomes all the more homeless and decays more than ever. Whereas in ancient architecture the very three principles cited by Vitruvius: the utilitas and the firmitas, which were never lacking, permeated themselves with the venustas or imagination and thus ornamented the structure throughout, in detail and as a whole. But in disintegration functional form and imagination no longer combine either, not even when the latter, as in the work of many Expressionist painters – as painters, not architects – was a monstrous and often significant one. Contact with more than the surrounding bourgeois void or semi-void was of course certainly sought, it was mostly called one with the 'laws of the universe' half in terms of engineering technology, half without any proper rhyme or reason: but however interesting the results in painting and also sculpture may have been, a Taut and Scheerbart approach in architecture remained fruitless. Precisely because the latter, far more than the other pictorial arts, is and remains a social creation, it cannot blossom at all in the hollow space of late capitalism. Only the beginnings of another society will make genuine architecture possible again, one both constructively and ornamentally permeated on the basis of its own artistic aspiration. The abstract engineering style never becomes qualitative on any account, despite the catchphrases which its literati pin on it, despite the bogus freshness of 'modernity' with which polished death is administered like the gleam of morning. The technology of today, itself still so very abstract, does not lead us out of the hollow space even as an aesthetically cultivated technology, as an artistic substitute; on the contrary, this hollow space permeates the so-called art of engineering, just as the latter necessarily increases it through its own emptiness. The only significant thing about it is the trend towards departure in these contemporary phenomena of their own accord, the house as ship in fact. Of course, further factors of sudden change are preparing themselves here too, to the same extent as the blossoming new relations to man and nature in a new society are mature and clear enough also to find expression in architectural ground plans and ornaments. Full of heritage, without historicism, especially – as now goes without saying – without the infamous stylistic copies, the gnarled romanticism of the Gründerzeit. In contrast to the Extreme Box and kitsch, what counts is simply the purification of all surviving sources, the cultivation and river-bed preparation of all rising sources into sculptural abundance. This is preceded by the radical differentiation of architecture from the machine. And even the relatively most interesting aspect of today or yesterday: the utopia of the glass structure, needs forms worthy of transparency. It needs formations which retain man as a question and crystal as an answer still to be mediated, still to be erected. The builder will then perhaps give his work 'the water of a pearl', but finally also a lost, less transparent cipher: sculptural abundance in nuce – ornamentation.

Town plans, ideal towns and real clarity again:
permeation of crystal with profusion

Combined with others, houses no longer look as if they are ready to leave.
The good builder needs groups, squares, a town, and it should no longer
need to disappear, it should be planned for the long term. This is a hope
of tomorrow, and where the morning is already breaking, of today, but
it is as old as architecture itself, remains inscribed in it and self-evident.
Town planning is therefore by no means confined to modern times, in
fact although it frequently occurs in the latter, even before the last century,
it is also oddly thwarted in them. For bourgeois society is of course a
calculating one for the sake of profit, but on account of its anarchic economy
also a disordered one, one of economic chance. That is why precisely the
industrial towns and the residential areas of the last century, which we
owe to the magnaminity of building speculation, are thoughtlessness and
planlessness per se. The only uniform thing about them is their dreariness,
the stone gorge, the bleak line of streets into the void, the kitsch of their
own miserable style or stolen flashy style; the remaining lay-out, however,
is anarchic like the profiteering which underlies it. Whereas precisely the
so-called evolved towns of the pre-capitalist period, owing to their more
regulated mode of production, by no means arose at random. Clear town
plans have come down to us from antiquity, even from the time before
Alexander, the rapid founder of towns from the Nile to the Himalayas.
Deliberate provision here characterized architects from the start, even
amazingly close to social construction. Aristotle thus mentions an architect
Hippodamos, in memorable duplication of architectural and political
planning: 'Hippodamos, the son of Euryphon, from Miletus, who invented
the division (diairesis) of towns and cut through the Piraeus... was at the
same time the first man who, without being a practical statesman, undertook to say something about the best political constitution' (Politics II,
chapter 8). So old therefore is contact between architectural and political
planning in general: the said Hippodamos had likewise planned a diairesis
on political foundations into purposes of worship, public benefit, and private
property, and had almost socially underpinned his building plan. Furthermore, the extravagance of planning was not lacking which had always
been a part of megalomania and which reckoned with its frenzy of building,
but in fact it was a mania with a plan and method. Alexander and his
master builder Dinokrates dreamed of carving out the entire foothills of

Athos into a colossus which could be colonized; in its left hand the mountain statue was to carry a town, in its right a bowl which collects all the rivers of the mountains and pours them into the sea as a classical Niagara. This is an urban fantasy which cannot be matched even in deliberation, not just in extravagance, by any constructive-Baroque fantasy of a neo-feudal kind. Town plans, although of a half geomantic, then astrological order, existed when Augustus caused Rome to be transformed from brick into marble, and when Constantine reconstructed Byzantium into a royal capital. And not least the Middle Ages, claimed by Romanticism and its rehash to be so particularly 'instinctive', is rich in town planning sui generis. With precise forethought the early medieval settlement was centred on the castle; colonial towns in southern France and eastern Germany even show a regularly repeated planning. Though it remains true, for all the individualistic contingency which then exploded in the architectural anarchy of the nineteenth century, that only capitalist calculation, this other side of the commercial society, caused efficient urban utopias to emerge in particularly large numbers. This is in pathetic-constructive contrast to the same economic anarchy to which this calculation, as an abstract law above chance, itself belongs. Above all before the French Revolution, when the mass of individual small and middle managers was not yet emancipated, when the manufacturing period posited a general bureaucracy which regulated everything, the anticipated lay-out was successful, the chessboard, the ring, in short a literal urban mathematics of planning and new foundation. However wildly the cartouche may have bulged out on the individual building, however boldly the group of buildings was orientated towards a winding veduta: like the ground plan of individual Baroque buildings, the group lay-out planned by this urban mathematics was also strictly symmetrical. The garden of Versailles and Descartes reigned here, not Galli-Bibiena; only the Rococo removed this symmetry. The chessboard lay-out of a Baroque new foundation like Mannheim, of which Goethe, who otherwise despised the Baroque, could say in 'Hermann and Dorothea' that it was a cheerful and friendly building, stands in an almost non-contemporaneous, almost classical contrast to the organically excessive style of Baroque architecture. This is the same tension as that in the refined discussions of Baroque society itself: what it found most interesting of all were human passions, and only one thing could compete with this: the interest in mathematics. Thus even siege engineers and builders of palaces and churches went together: many of the most eminent Baroque architects, Hildebrandt, Balthasar Neumann, Welsch, Eosander, came from the field of military functional building and continued to supervise this field, alongside their architectural fantasy. The Baroque tolerated in an astonishing fashion this juxtaposition of intoxication and bourgeois calculation, of counter-reformation and military geometry; the latter was victorious, reverting to a Renaissance model, above all precisely in town planning. Everywhere here the same contrast is to be found in which the mechanization of the conception of the world culminating in the seventeenth century also stands to excessively organic Baroque ornamentation. Of course, the mathematics of this period is also one of movement, the functional concept wins through, Fluxions and differential calculus, the veduta of infinity. But the conception of the world itself is in Descartes, and especially in Spinoza, an inorganic one, a fundamentally mechanical one; thus what prevails in the architect's plan of Baroque philosophy is crystal clarity wherever possible, more geometrico. Alongside the organic ornateness in sculpture, architecture and also literature there thus arose the mathematical façade: clarity, crystal; in fact we can say that alongside the 'Gothic' of Baroque architecture stood the 'Egypt' of Baroque thought (most strikingly in Spinozism). Moreover, this crystal character very easily combined with all tendencies towards order and hispanicizations in the neo-feudal Baroque. This is shown even in the difference between the utopian images of architecture which emerged in the novels of an ideal state of the Renaissance and then of the Baroque. Whereas the liberal social utopia of Thomas More embellishes its best state with detached houses, low buildings, and dispersed garden cities, a hundred years later Campanella's authoritarian utopia displays blocks of flats, multi-storey buildings, a totally centralized townscape. Mathematical compass measurement per se prevails here – with concentric walls, cosmic wall frescoes, and a circular lay-out as a whole – in consequence of the further, even astrologically determined utopia of order. Beyond this however, since the examples of town planning in the Baroque a geometrical design has generally remained the password of every bourgeois ideal town and calculated town. With the exception of those very periods which experienced no town planning at all any more, hence of the second half of the nineteenth century when town planning was not only thwarted but totally eliminated by the individual profit economy. Up till then, however, and then again in the period of monopoly capitalism, with an economy which was directed so to speak and imperialized, a cult, bordering on the Egyptian model, of regular lay-outs, parts of a building, and townscapes prevails again and again. At the same time this excluded, apart from some luxurious curved streets of villas in residential districts, all contact with the Gothic townscape, with the angularity and deep cosy profusion of old German towns. The attachment no longer provided by capitalist society was to be replaced or even newly modelled by urban geometry. The latter now became the *utopia of all modern bourgeois urban construction*; as may immediately become apparent even individually from some of its most significant examples. They contain as a whole the contrast to the economy of chance, and in such a way that they increase along with its anarchy, but they also increasingly contain the apologetic endorsement of its alienation and soullessness. They contain in the most felicitous cases, i.e. in the bare programme outside the uncovering realization, the *problem* of an urban crystal behind which concrete order (the order for what) is of course repressed or still concealed.

So what was definitely sought was to give disorderly life the framework of a clearer life. The earliest design of this kind arose in 1505, it stems from Fra Giocondo: the dream city is round, in the middle lies a circular space with domed buildings, from which the streets radiate. In 1593 Scamozzi, the builder of the procurators' offices in St Mark's Square, projected a regular urban polygon with corresponding gates, equal halves and quarters (Palma nuova near Udine was afterwards laid out in this way). With Vasari il Giovane, 1598, the città ideale becomes a combination of rectangular and radial lay-out: the main square with directional building lies in the middle, eight radial streets open out from it, with gateways as their goals, and further streets are arranged in a rectangular network. Piranesi (1720–1778), who has been valued for far too long merely as an etcher of Roman ruins, used early classicism to furnish an ideal city, not just in its lay-out but also in the features of its houses and ornamental figures, with that symmetry which was increasingly lacking in bourgeois society. Soviet Russian architecture even incorporated certain elements and municipal architectural utopias of Piranesi ('penseur dans le domaine de l'architecture'* the Soviet architect Sidorov called him), particularly arched halls and the lay-out of squares, the construction of towers and proportions of height. Probably the oddest designer of future settlements ever to occur in the history of utopian architecture is the French revolutionary architect *Ledoux*, a man who has only been fully appreciated today (cf. Kauffmann, From Ledoux to Le Corbusier, 1933); he does not make classicism as imposing as the Empire style did, but he makes it all the more varied. Ledoux (1736–1806) designed the ideal town of Chaux, and with regard from the

---

* 'Thinker in the domain of architecture.'

first to a commune organized according to occupations. Thus the formation of buildings is dispersed into smaller groups and concentrated at the same time; the modern pavilion system appears. Instead of the formation of a city centre and an endless periphery, Ledoux plans green spaces everywhere with work centres and within them an 'eloquent architecture' expressing its use. The ideal town contains various types of building corresponding to the occupation of the inhabitant (house of the woodcutter, field watchman, merchant and so on); it even contains a 'house of passions' (a kind of temple of sexual emancipation), a 'house to the glory of women', and a 'house of harmony'. But with the geometry and stereometry of these houses a limit is in fact set to the relative dispersal again; above this dispersal stands the characteristic utopia of order of all modern town plans. The geometrical allegory which Ledoux bestows on his buildings points to this kind of utopia of order, in geometrical terms leading the way, in Egyptian terms leading astray. Thus despite the pavilion system a military geometry reminiscent of Campanella's city prevails, and even astrological allusions are not lacking. The woodcutter lives beneath a pyramidal roof, the field watchman in a spherical house depicting the earth, and the 'ville naissante' as a whole is surrounded by an ellipse corresponding to the orbits of the planets. The pathos of attachment thereby also ultimately surfaces in Ledoux' ideal town; and surprisingly, anticipatorily in the midst of the French Revolution. Ledoux called the builder the 'rival of God'; this is a splendid self-confidence in human creation; but the world which he seeks to form in such a Promethean way fits snugly into the order of a cosmos which is seen as complete, moreover as geometrically complete. Just as Piranesi combined classical motifs with his ideal urban geometry, Ledoux did the same with Masonic-Egyptianizing motifs: their content is admittedly utopian collectivism, but even here it is located in the body of a crystalline, all too crystalline urban utopia. The 'chiming with the cosmos' which arched over the humane architectural purpose and its expression even in Taut, and in Le Corbusier, – this secularized astral myth, which was touched upon not only in platitudes but also in the idolatry of a superficial framework, accordingly demonstrates its effectiveness in the urban utopias of the entire modern era. Its effectiveness on mathematical grounds in *capitalist calculation*, and on sentimental grounds in the *feeling of contrast to the growing economic and cultural anarchy*. Hence the attraction to crystal as the most obvious contrasting severity, and hence, alongside estimating and calculation, the power of geometry which at least seems to be divested of the rampant human muddle. Most recently though, this has been joined by a particularly defamiliarized motif, in itself the *only original* and also significantly effective motif in utopian terms of the *art of engineering as architecture*. Or rather of the art of engineering which is responsible for the demise of architecture as a real art and from which it must arise again on the threshold of a more concrete society. What is meant here is the new connection of the old utopia of crystallization with the *desire to de-organize*. This kind of thing is precisely connected with the abstract technology itself with which the new architecture is so closely involved, and also gives to the crystalline urban utopia de-organization sui generis, one familiar from bordering technological fields. Thus, corresponding to the machine which no longer resembles human beings there are the house without an aura, the townscape of affirmed lifelessness and remoteness from man, of pencils of rays as such or other imitations of projective geometry. Functionalist architecture reflects and doubles the ice-cold automatic world of the commercial society anyway, of its alienation, of its human beings subject to the division of labour, of its abstract technology. In fact, just as technology may possibly penetrate into the non-Euclidean realm, so architectural space, in so far as it promotes abstract 'compositions', particularly in glass structures, displays the unmistakable ambition to portray an imaginary space in the empirical one. Expressionism experimented with the problem of producing spatial figures by means of rotating or oscillating bodies, which figures no longer have anything in common with perspective visual space anyhow; an abstract architecture which aspires to be super-cubic, as it were, occasionally seeks similarly remote ordered patterns, which do not appear organically or even mesocosmically any more. Of course, the space of these solids of revolution remains just as Euclidean as every other, and there is a long way to go in architecture, even in terms of symbolic suggestion, as regards so-called an-Euclidean pangeometry (cf. Panofsky, Vorträge der Bibliothek Warburg, 1927, p. 330). All that remains important is that the crystalline element predominates in all town plans since the Renaissance, including those of the otherwise so organically magnificent Baroque, seeks cosmic contacts, but also seeks some bold examples of extra-organic remoteness, although, as in technology, still without any material contact, despite all 'chiming with the cosmos'. At those points of course where Expressionism did not merely cast, as it so often did, excesses of pure subjectivity into the empty air, it also experimented with the problem of an object-based expression, which was at the same time profoundly appropriate to the human subject, in highly abstracted forms of work, in an 'ego crystal forest'.

More completely and more legitimately, i.e. linked with a still rising bourgeois society, mannerism in the Baroque and against it (Correggio, Tintoretto, El Greco, but also even Michelangelo) not only placed the highest subjectivity of 'mood' and expressive value alongside the harshest boldness of statuary modelling, but drove it into the latter. And today there arises, as has long been ripe for discussion, the vast architectural problem of *a 'Gothic' in crystal*, as if the entire crystal character in spatial art, instead of ultimately leading merely into an Egyptian clarity of death, were malgré lui a particularly sharply crystallizing Humanum. The result, or rather: the problem of the result therefore remains this: *How can human profusion in clarity be rebuilt? How can the order of an architectural crystal be permeated with the true tree of life, with humane ornamentation?* A synthesis between the architectural utopias of Egypt on the one hand and Gothic on the other is impossible, it would be a silly epigonic fantasy, yet there is an original third element, which has never appeared before, beyond rigidity and exuberance, both in the social structure and in architecture. After all, the strength of Marxism lies precisely in the fact that it posits order to the end that room should be made for human profusion; the contents alternatively arising in all earlier abstract social utopias: subjective freedom (More) or constructed order (Campanella) are in Marxism – not synthesized, but rather productively mediated and thus cancelled and raised into a third element: the constructed realm of freedom itself. Even with respect to the ordered patterns of nature, Marxism is far removed from subjectless-undialectical depictiveness, and hence from any 'chiming with the cosmos'; the concrete tendency is instead a humanization of nature. Thus the spatial art of a classless society will hardly remain abstract-crystalline, as a contrast to economic anarchy (which will have disappeared anyway). Even in the old town plans, in Piranesi, in Ledoux, a spatial premonition occasionally appears, a totally new though classically encapsulated one, which leaves the abstract or deserted crystal form far behind it. Non-formalistic glass sculpture and glass architecture likewise occasionally extends, as noted above, into unfamiliar architectural form, spatial form; this presses forward within it, strange curves and stereometries press forward within it, in an ostensibly cosmic but in reality human expression. A human form of anticipation begins here in the midst of crystal, perhaps by means of it, but right through it; it begins with extroversion to the cosmos, but bending it back *into the lineament of a homeland*. Architecture as a whole is and remains an attempt to produce a human homeland, – from the sedate residential purpose to the manifestation of a more beautiful world in proportion and ornamentation. According to Hegel's true and not merely idealistic definition, architecture sees it as its task to work inorganic nature into such a shape that it becomes allied to the mind as an artistically valid outside world. The mind, in other words: the human subject, which is itself still in search of that which can be called allied to it, this phenomenon always develops in various societies different angles, arches, domes, towers of an earth concentrated towards man. The architectural utopia is thus the beginning and the end of a – geographical utopia itself, of all this searching for precious stones in the druse of the earth, of the dreams of an earthly paradise. Great architecture sought to stand as a whole like a constructed Arcadia and more; and if it brought something lamentable, tragic mysteries with it, as in the Gothic period, then this was only in order to contribute it to the difficult harmony. The wealth was enormous, drawn from a few basic elements, the alternative was enormous between a pillared hall in Karnak and Sainte Chapelle in Paris, between our image of homeland in stone on the one hand, in strut frames and an influx of light on the other. But a protective sphere, a homeland built in advance: *this is what the outlines of a better world suggest as far as its actual construction in architecture is concerned.* The aesthetic form emerges here, as an encompassing one, so that all other pictorial forms have room and classification within it: the paintings on the wall, the sculpture in the niche. The encompassing element furnishes a homeland or touches on it: all great buildings were sui generis built into the utopia, the anticipation of a space adequate to man. And the thus erected Humanum, transposed to strictly significant spatial form, is as a task both migration from the organic and humane into crystal, and above all permeation of the crystalline with the buoyancy developed within it, Humanum and profusion. When the conditions for the order of freedom are no longer partial, the path finally becomes open again towards the unity of physical construction and organic ornamentation, towards the gift of ornamentation. It becomes open in reality for the first time, without Egypt on the one hand, Gothic on the other, i.e. that which is thus described as crystal or tree of life, having to be alternated over and over again, mixed or envied in isolation. The crystal is the framework, indeed the horizon of repose, but the ornamentation of the human tree of life is the only real content of this encompassing repose and clarity. The better world, which the grand architectural style expresses and depicts in an anticipatory fashion, thus consists very unmythically, as the real task vivis ex lapidibus, of the stones of life.

ELDORADO AND EDEN,   39
THE GEOGRAPHICAL UTOPIAS

The way the earth is now,
The earth need not remain.
To spur it again
Search, till you know.   *Brecht*

It seems so natural to man to cross the limits of space with his imagination,
to sense a something beyond the horizon where the sea meets the sky, that
even in the age when the earth was still regarded as a flat disc or one which
was only slightly concave on the surface, people could be led to believe that
beyond the cordon formed by the Homeric ocean there was another dwelling
for mankind, another oecumene, just like the Lokaloka of Indian myth a ring
of mountains which is supposed to lie beyond the seventh sea.

A. v. Humboldt

For the Lord thy God bringeth thee into a good land, a land of brooks of
water, of fountains and depths that spring out of valleys and hills; A land
of wheat, and barley, and vines, and fig trees, and pomegranates; a land of
oil olive, and honey;   *Deuteronomy 8, 7f.*

The first lights

It is easy to wish we were far away from a bad place. But the road out
of it is less obvious, it must first be laid. The level terrain which stretches
away on all sides is just as difficult for the right path as the mountainous
terrain which blocks it off externally. That is why we lose our way, one
of the bitterest situations and a strange one at that. It lies in the extension
of wanting which lacks or as yet lacks ability, of the bud which never
properly bursts into bloom. The man who has lost his way stands between
the permanent wish and the impermanent or elusive path. But the danger
in which the traveller is placed by losing his way, the danger of death,
is also the toll he pays for the New. It is paid wherever anything new
is sparked out of the darkness, the march there is decidedly away from
the comfort of our bed. Security becomes all the more negligible, the more
the familiar span of sensory perception decreases. But how significant the
first light is then, how reassuring beyond all previous measure. The desert

has not swallowed us up; things we have never seen before, which on the wrong path had frightened us, become downright enjoyable on the right path, the one made right. The instinctive desires for loot and for marvels here astonishingly often merged or went hand in hand. The earth in the distance becomes Indian, it rises fantastically beyond the habitual world. The sail releases us from the mainland, and makes the high seas navigable. Things are not only to be invented but also discovered, an extremely substantial dream now sends men out to this end.

Inventing and discovering; characteristic of geographical hope

If things are not only to be invented but also discovered, what is the leap between the two? It consists in the fact that the one changes things and intervenes in them, whereas the other merely seems to find them and to show them. The ship that arrives on a completely foreign shore definitely has not formed it. Consequently it seems as if the series of actual plans for construction, medical, social, and technological, is interrupted here. In *geographical* terms, the inventor is only found as a liar, at most in the amiable figure of Münchhausen, but not as the maker of something that has never been before. Perhaps in the long run Münchhausen came to believe he had seen the countries he sets foot in, by repeating the stories over and over again; they themselves did not see him. They are not improved by the dreams which are attached to them, they do not contain the questionable character, but also one worth questioning, of the abstract fairytale of an ideal state. Discovering, on the other hand, does not seem to contain any dream at all any more, unless it is one which is immediately corrected by the so-called facts; but the discoverer adopts a purely contemplative attitude. Invention is the act whereby something new is made (glass, porcelain, gunpowder); discovery is the act whereby something new is found (America, Uranus), which is only new for the subject arriving on the scene. Of course the inventor mostly presupposes the discoverer, but he does not remain contemplative like the latter, whom we also call an explorer. This is also why the word explorer has equally been applied to those who cross Africa or travel to the North Pole and to theorists (natural scientists, even Goethe scholars),* who are responsible or seem to be responsible for taking things as they are. So discovering also seems to be

* The German word 'Forscher' employed by Bloch in these instances can mean both 'explorer' and 'researcher'.

748   OUTLINES OF A BETTER WORLD

methodically synonymous with uncovering, with removing the cover, and
beneath this cover there then lie the findings for the mapping out of an
allegedly fixed being. A strenuous counterexample to the inventor or homo
faber has finally even been supplied by phenomenology à la Scheler and
in fact – because of the purely accepting element in this phenomenology
– in favour of the explorer or discoverer, as the epitome of the homo
contemplativus. Here the difference between inventor and discoverer is
frankly stated to be one between modern and medieval 'disposition', further
still: an attempt is made to explain it by a process as remote from inventing
or discovering as that of election. When the modern homo faber elects
a Member of Parliament or President, it is only the votes of the majority
that make them so; they are created, electing is here producing. Whereas
when the German king was elected by a majority of freemen, and then
of the Electors, he was not created – at least according to the fiction and
also the ideology –, but he is merely found out and revealed as an already
existing 'secret king'; electing is here discovering. And this is also the
way, mutatis mutandis, the phenomenologist as discoverer wants to keep
things: essential objects are viewed singly and thus presented to the mind;
the only active element here is the 'selection' which emphasizes parts, sides,
factors of overall objective reality for attention or not as the case may be.
This is a strange epistemology, an utterly reactionary one, directed against
changing the world, but one which underlines the difference between
invention and discovery, or finding, through its hatred of all acts of intervention and new formation. The discoverer therefore appears inactive all
along the line, he seems as contemplative as he does conservative, in contrast
to the inventor. And there is also undoubtedly a sharpness of contrast in
the average bourgeois consciousness as soon as it thinks about the disposition
of an Edison, say, or about the disposition of a traveller to the North
Pole. Despite the fact that, as mentioned above, the inventor mostly presupposes the discoverer, indeed that an inventing which is ignorant of
existing circumstances and laws before it overturns them will remain fruitless
or at best will only reach its goal by chance, and then not the one intended.
Despite the instructive ambivalence which is already present in linguistic
usage, when it recognizes not only a geographical discoverer, that is, a
discoverer of something that has long existed, but also a discoverer of
artificial indigo or of Salvarsan.* Also despite that existence which, as it
belongs to a world capable of change and by no means static, very often

---

* Arsenical compound for the treatment of syphilis.

prevents its discoverer from remaining a passive 'world eye'. Nevertheless, a difference between invention and discovery, indeed between the homo faber as ultimate 'world destroyer' and the homo contemplativus as ultimate 'world revealer', was transformed into an absolute rift. Thus – to return to the most typical manifestation of the discoverer – *geographical* utopia certainly seems at first sight as if it was not homogeneous with the medical, social, and technological utopias.

But this is an illusion, because discovering definitely wants and is able to change things. Even the obsession with profit, the curiosity about unknown distant lands drive us off into the realm of the unfamiliar. Even on a gentle journey, a gleam appears and lures us on, a gleam which certainly did not lie on the familiar road or is merely for inspection. All previous values in life are changed by discovery, at least for the traveller, and then for the group or the country which sends him out. The earliest changes towards a better life occurred, even for the consumers, not only through the inventions at home but through their exchange over incredibly long distances, and therefore through routes discovered for world trade. The shells of a type of snail which is only found on the Mediterranean turn up in rock-tombs of around 8000 B.C. near Nördlingen; cowrie shells from the Indian Ocean in graves of around 1000 B.C. on the Baltic coast of Germany. The Hallstatt culture, which flourished in the Salzkammergut between 1500 and 500 B.C., obtained both northern amber and African ivory in exchange for salt and combined both on pieces of jewellery. The earliest discoverer was probably the trader, and therefore not a contemplative type; Phoenician merchants ventured out the furthest. All discovery contains as its first, if not its only stimulus the elimination of intermediate trade which makes everything dearer, and therefore finding a direct route for oneself; as well as finding totally new commodities. When Columbus sailed for India, he even had a real Eden in mind. It is not surprising, from this point of view, that discoveries brought dreams with them just as strongly as changes. Though the goal appears as something which already actually exists, and its content: gold, silver, tin, amber, ivory and so on, even the fabulous things it expects, the all-surpassing marvel of distant lands, only has to be fetched. But does not *health*, the medical goal-content, also seem to be a buried existing possession which merely has to be restored? Does not the happy island stand *fixed on the horizon* even in social utopias by no means only as a fiction but (at least in older utopias) as an existing remote land of happiness which can even be discovered at home at any moment, as soon as the obstacles are cleared away? Did not even technological dreams have their chambers of the edifice of nature in whose existence they believed and which were only waiting to be entered? Did not such an intense experimental system as alchemy have an existing and merely hidden golden essence in mind, which only had to be conducted out of its prison of lead? In all these instances a kind of waiting existence is intended, and it defines the type of the older utopia, as noted above, without it thereby ceasing to be a utopia. Even the more modern utopia, for all its rejection of what is essentially already real and thus pre-ordered, does not operate in a vacuum but wholly in a space full of the real Possible. Concrete technological utopia in particular is, as noted above, not partheno-genetic but seeks to deliver nature of creations which lie as possibilities in her womb. Thus discovery, even in its geographical form, is nowhere directly opposed to invention, a familiar utopian structure runs through them both. In fact, just as an already fixed and ontological positing of perfection is hardly consistent with utopian consciousness (such a positing is mythological, not utopian), a discovering factor must just as certainly be at work in every utopia if it does not want to be a chimera in another, abstract fashion, a factor which is mediated with the objectively discoverable and not merely the producible. The element that is thus discoverable is, in concrete utopia, admittedly not a buried existence or a remote existence in the sense that even without the man who arrives on the scene it is actually already reality and fully complete. But rather the discoverable element in every concrete utopia concerns a future existence: one of the legitimate tendency, one of the latent goal-content in objective-real possibility. And the geographical utopias were eminently those of the new road, the new commodities and goods, especially of such an extreme dream-content as the finding and unlocking of an Eden. In this respect every other utopian intention is even indebted to that of the geographical discoveries; for each of them has at the centre of its positive hopes the topos: land of gold, land of happiness. It allows each of them to be called an embarkation for Cythera, an expedition to Eutopia, an experiment of the New World; wholly geographically, wholly with the will of Columbus' ship. Even if discovering does outweigh inventing and developing in the geographical utopias, or at any rate outweighs them far more than in the social and technological, and also architectural utopias, and therefore in those 'voyages of discovery' where man first leads a country out of a real-possible condi-tion into an actual one. But then: if the geographical utopias have a more modest appearance, that of discovering what already exists, it is precisely this which, instead of being modest, has a *quite specially daring reason*. It is the same one which unites medical utopias, in this respect, with geographical ones, i.e. *health* as a merely buried possession in the former with *Eldorado-Eden* as a merely hidden-remote one in the latter. It turns out in the end that the alleged existence of these two goal-contents even *indicates quite extremely utopian intentions in both fields*. Simply to want to find lost health, simply to want to reach hidden countries, these only seem a modest utopian ambition. For precisely behind this modesty, behind that of the obstacles or distances which are merely cleared away, a basic utopia is at work which is much too fantastic to manifest itself as openly as the social or technological utopias. It is namely as follows! The basis of the medical wishful dream contains the *abolition of death*, the basis of the geographical one contains nothing less, namely the finding of magical central goods like the Golden Fleece, indeed the *finding of the earthly paradise itself*. It was still supposed to exist somewhere, gold and blessings poured from it on to the countries around it, and thus the basic material purpose of the voyage of discovery was very often, immediately and quite astonishingly inflated to the highest degree. Substructure and superstructure are also so indistinguishably cross-connected here that it is impossible to know where Eldorado ends and Eden begins or vice versa. Columbus at any rate firmly believed that the islands he had discovered were those of the Hesperides and that Eden lay hidden beyond the country around the mouth of the Orinoco. And this surpassing basic goal, once it was believed to have been attained, gave such totally different values to the world that it was fundamentally wrenched out of its old status. Columbus even speaks of the New Heaven and the New Earth which had been attained by him; expedition was secession, an exodus out of the old into the new, not just an extension of the mother country or the stationary supplement of an unknown to the known. Apart from economic motives and inherent in them, of which more will be said later, there was a fantastic superstructure of paradise on earth here, which for its part activated people and was anything but contemplative. Otherwise it would have been impossible for the discoverer, and particularly Columbus, to have been virtually substituted as a witness and emblem for ars inveniendi. In alchemical works of the seventeenth century, Columbus is the master who sailed out beyond the Pillars of Hercules to the golden Gardens of the Hesperides. He stands for the alchemical journey, for the magus who seeks paradise in the curse of the earth. Even in the eighteenth century, 'golden America' appears under this aspect on alchemical title-pages, as much invention as discovery. And even wholly outside these fantastic delusions or fantasies, the Pillars of Hercules, with the plus ultra, provided Bacon with a metaphor, they even formed the frontispiece of his book 'Novum Organum' as the pillars which were sailed beyond. Likewise, discovering is itself actively utopian, it not only lifts its object out of our ignorance but where necessary also out of the twilight of its own unmediatedness and unexposure. The specifically geographical discoverer is contemplative only in so far as he gives up action at the final point, as soon as he thinks he has found it. In the accomplishment of geographical utopias, action is replaced by a phenomenon which has previously been lacking in all the others, namely – arrival. When Columbus thought he had set foot in India, on the very side where it seemed to him to lie closest to the earthly paradise, the utopian-active intention veered round accordingly, it seemed on the threshold of fulfilment. This does not prevent the most powerful image of distant lands hovering in the mind at the beginning of the journey as well as during it, an image which reached into activity more forcefully than any other. Wherever a journey to the earthly paradise provided the most expectantly stimulating illusion and idea, with Marco Polo and especially with Columbus, discovery is a centrally utopian venture. That is also why the ages of discovery, from Alexander to Columbus, made such a homogeneous contribution to the social utopias; it goes far beyond the fable of investiture. All in all then: the business of human hopes possesses its own horizon in the horizon of the great voyages of discovery; the earth has indeed become fairly familiar, but the Eldorado which Jason and Columbus had in mind is yet to be found.

Fairytales again, the Golden Fleece and the Grail

It is not surprising that here too the fiery owl is much on the wing. Lunatics talk of a land at the other end of the world and wish themselves fabulously into it. Very old images like this often circulate in the same delusion, they then always seem as if they came from foreign parts. The surroundings of the lunatic are then not only moved by superstition but carried away over a long distance. Flowing water is crazily moved by a hand which did not grow here, there is the northern storm-hopper, the dog of the south with its motionless head. But a really healthy old Bavarian folk superstition makes even the echo unfamiliar and magical: it was regarded as a special, and as it were particularly clever type of rock which catches the sound and imitates it. This rock and related things are now at work far down in the ravines, strikingly reminiscent of the marvels of the old sailors' yarns. These too show horror and temptation together, above all they show knowledge of treasures which are only to be found in distant lands. These fairytales include the bird Roc, Polyphemus and dragon-like serpents, Krakens as big as an island, countless land and sea marvels. But they also include the valley of diamonds, which are picked up by Sinbad the Sailor, there is a wonderful forest on Wak-Wak, the most easterly magic island, where supernatural girls adorned with all charms grow out of big flowers. The earth here always has its summer only in distant lands, the best fruits are cooked up there. The nautical yarn paves the fantastic way to them and is itself the most fantastic of all fairytales; an enormous fairground booth, with nothing but the South Seas inside. Nowhere has the fairytale mingled so easily with credited reports as in travel sketches and images of distant lands; geography is the region where absolutely everything was regarded as possible. Thus there is not merely a connection transcending time and space between Sinbad, Odysseus and Herzog Ernst, the man who allegedly travelled through Asia. There is also one between Odysseus and the world fairytales to be found in great geographers like Pliny and Pomponius Mela, in encyclopaedists like Isidore of Seville or Beauvais. A fake like Sir John Mandeville's fictitious journey round the world, around 1355, strengthened its claims to credibility not least by a number of well-established fabulous stories (especially about India and China), which the knight claims to have seen and experienced for himself. Since the world has few blank areas to show any more, the geographical fairytale is left with the underground realm: the treasure-cave, or the realm completely above ground: outer space. The familiar realm moves in that direction: thus Jules Verne dreamed as a boy that the island of Teydeau near Nantes, on which his parents' house stood, had been washed away by the waves and that he could sail on it far out across all the oceans of the world, with sails between the trees. In the colportages of Kurt Lasswitz, which followed those of Jules Verne, the foreign parts so sorely missed even come floating along in interplanetary guise. As in the Columbus story about the other side: 'On two planets' (Martians land at the North Pole, cancel gravitation at will); as in the astrophysical report: 'Stardew. The plant from Neptune's moon'. The discovery of the Indo-Chinese spice islands also once had a plant in mind, although a considerably more profitable one, which did not grow in one's own country, indeed all geographical dreams of distant lands circled around the treasure which is lacking in the familiar world.

As noted above, people believed they would find strange, useful things even at home. But only because their own country was still eerie itself; it had a lot of blank areas. There, ravines or mountains, and deserted houses were not only haunted by the dead and other visitors from beyond the grave, but the wishing purses and wishing dice, the breeding pennies and lucky shillings were also to be found there. One of the most charming fairytales by Musäus (The Treasure-hunter) is devoted to the mandrake which is said to open all locks; it grows in the most inaccessible spots deep in the forest. But the conjuring books were wishing purses and mandrakes in litteris, they too were hidden somewhere in forgotten vaults or, which amounts to the same thing here, brought over from oriental monasteries, from a long way off. The preface to one of the most famous of these books, the 'Liber secretus', from the thirteenth century, reads as if it brought a piece of oriental Faust into one's own home: 'This is the book by which one can see God in this life.... This is the book by which one can see hell and purgatory without death. This is the book by which every creature can be subjected except the nine orders of angels. This is the book by which all science can be learned' (cf. Thorndike, A History of Magic and Experimental Science, 1928, II, p. 285). The so-called God-given writings are of a similar order, as a fiction which set thousands of seekers in motion and legitimated several hallucinating lucky finders in the eyes of their believers. As was finally the case with the founder of the Mormon sect, the 'discoverer' of hermetically written gold plates from Canaan in a hill near New York. Late antiquity already provided the symbols for proven delusory colonial produce: a document falls from the sky or is washed up on the coast as flotsam and jetsam or is found in the coffin of a distinguished figure, that of Cleopatra or Cyrus for instance. Typical in such documents is the warning not to give them to the ignorant and uninitiated, but also typical is the belief that the heavenly powers which sent the book from a fantastic distance lead the worthiest person to find it. And the hiding-place at home thus becomes the same, in its chthonic-subterranean form, as exotic remoteness and distance are in Uranian form. But of course, despite wishing purses and falling or immured God-given writings, the two most glittering wishful possessions which now appear: *the Golden Fleece and the Grail*, were conceived solely in terms of exoticism. They occur solely as these distant treasures in fairytale and legend, as the most famous of all, and a part of their fame is precisely the long and difficult journey to find them, the call to go in search of this paragon of all marvellous things. In fact, since the voyage of the Argonauts, a very old fable, the belief becomes typical that the best thing of this kind is not only a very long way away, but its exotic wishful-dream treasure itself awaits discoverers who have come from a long way off. The Golden Fleece hangs in Colchis, a remote spot on Greek soil, the Christian Grail is even hidden in such a removed Somewhere that the only person who will find it is the one whom the Grail itself leads to its hiding-place. The Fleece and the Grail are accordingly high symbols of the sun, no longer chthonic-subterranean ones. The Fleece is admittedly guarded by a creature from the underworld, the dragon, yet it hangs visibly beneath the sky, on an oak tree. The Grail is admittedly always veiled and surrounded by the heaviest taboos, yet it floats freely in the air itself like the stars, an Eldorado as a chalice and foaming inside, a fragment of light par excellence. In contrast to wishing purses and mandrakes, underground treasure-hunting and immured marvels, the purely astral origin of the myth of the Fleece and the Grail also points to this Uranian expanse. After all, the Fleece was originally the brilliant glow which surrounds the hero and which grants him victory. The Grail especially, in its astral-mythical origin, long before its Christian interpretation, is the source and magic cauldron of daylight itself, the sun in other words. But it must be peeled and extracted from the clouds: Indra in Indian myth and Thor in Germanic myth were the heroes who conquered the cauldron of the sun with their lance of thunder. Only later did it become the Christian symbol of the bowl in which Joseph of Arimathea caught the Saviour's blood, that other hot drink from the other sun; and it is no longer conquering gods, not even, as with the Fleece, the warlike Jason, but the quiet Sunday's child Perceval who is on his way to the utopia of the chalice of the Grail. To the same one, incidentally, which also appears in Hoffmann's fairytale about the Golden Pot; and there too the realm to which the magic cauldron belongs and which it pours out lies far away – in Atlantis. Thus, ultimately, all treasures which send people off on their travels are horizontally distant ones and do not lie vertically beneath their feet in the ground at home. They were admittedly thought to exist, yet at the same time they were regarded as so remote that they were also mythologically accorded the virginity of something as yet unseized, and hence of something which does not yet exist in all its glory. This is so both in fairytale and legend as well as in the intention of the ostensibly so very different voyages of discovery. These too are treasure-hunting, as we know, but they have the characteristic of a *horizontal treasure-hunting*, and the characteristic which is already seen in the myths which preceded them: precisely that of being an extraordinary blend of Eldorado and Eden, of substructure in the superstructure as it were, of superstructure in the substructure. People dug for the treasure itself now in a westerly, now in an easterly direction, until the spherical shape of the earth was discovered and made it a matter of indifference which direction they steered in, but: whether they were lured by the golden apples of the Hesperides to the west or, as was mostly the case, by the marvels of India to the east, the strange unity of gold and Fleece, gold and Grail, gold and paradise always remained operative. Both the legendary dream-journeys and those that were actually carried out used it as a navigational guide, in the hope of loot and marvels all at once.

Island of the Phaeacians, the bad Atlantic, location of the earthly paradise

It is noticeable that fear is particularly closely related to happiness here. The Greeks placed almost all their fabled carefree regions next to equally terrible ones. Monsters lurk in front of fragrant groves, there are dangerous waters around the island of the Phaeacians and that of the Blest. Particularly around the latter: beyond the Pillars of Hercules there lies the notorious 'mare coagulatum', the curdled sea. The crafty Phoenicians made powerful use of the terror of the Atlantic, so that foreign traders were deterred from travelling to the English tin-mines. They themselves are known not to have cared about the curdled sea, nor even about claims concerning a perpetual calm, yet the legend of the unnavigable western ocean persisted for hundreds and thousands of years. It joined the other unusually gloomy sea legends of Greece, those of the Sirens, the coiling Echidna, the howling Scylla, and surpassed these sea monsters, which were localized in any case, in vagueness and invisibility. The crafty Phoenicians only exploited this horror of the west anyway, it was not a new invention; mere business lies from Tyre would not have remained plausible for so long. Instead, Punic cunning resorted to a very old astral archetype and superimposed itself on it: death dwells in the west, where the sun goes down. The underworld is there, as is the heathen Golgotha, and the sun-god meets his end there; Babylonian myth speaks of the west as the 'nocturnal sea-prison of the sun'. And according to a Syrian version of the Hercules legend, Hercules died at the very spot where he had erected his two pillars. This kind of thing in fact lived on even in the case of myths that were extinct, assumed a scientific disguise if necessary, and fortified itself with actual observations, with greatly exaggerated ones. There were fields of seaweed west of the Azores in fact, Columbus noticed them, but for Plato, Aristotle and Theophrastus the entire Atlantic became a sea of mud, governed by perpetual night. There was also the fear of a giant whirlpool, which was said to have its gullet somewhere out in the ocean and which seemed to cause the ebb and flow of the tides that the Greeks and Romans found so uncanny. The legend of the sea of mud and darkness was so tenacious that it even deterred the Arabs and their commercial capital, in an almost incomprehensible fashion, from sailing the Atlantic. The Greeks and Romans were no great seafarers, but the Arabs certainly were; the terrors of the sea did not usually deter them, they served instead, as the tale of Sinbad shows, to add spice to their courage, success, and recollections. Yet the same Arabs who get to know the Indian Ocean, and the marginal seas of the Pacific on voyages by no means confined to the coast, and who even got as far as the Philippines, did not even venture out on to the Atlantic Ocean as far as the Azores, Madeira, the Canary Islands (which were all discovered or rediscovered in the end by the Portuguese); despite possessing its Spanish and Moroccan coastline. The great Arab geographer Edrisi drew up a world map on silver around 1150; the Niger is known to him and the island of Borneo, but on the West African coast his knowledge does not extend beyond South Morocco for reasons stated above. And Edrisi does not dispel the Greek fables for instance, but he adds new ones: the waters of the Atlantic give off a noxious stench, they contain a vast number of invisible reefs and also demonic islands. It was said of one of them, Satanaxoi by name, that a giant fist reached out of the depths of the ocean every day and dragged down the ships; for Edrisi this is part of a geography of Hell, right beside the Isles of the Blest, which were likewise said to lie in the western sea, and in spite of them. Not least, the Arabs warned of the plus ultra in the west through a very curious fable of their own: through the old fable of the statue. A mysterious statue is said to stand on an island of the Atlantic, with its right arm raised in warning, and written on the base are the words: 'Beyond me there are no more countries to be explored.' Ibn Khordadbeh, geographer and general postmaster of the caliphate in Baghdad, first tells of this inscription, in the ninth century; Edrisi canonized the fable, according to him there are even six of these statues, and they all point a warning finger at the desolate expanse beyond them. The fable itself may stem from the embellished, and in this case carved Pillars of Hercules, which Pindar mentions, in the third Nemean ode, where they already bear the inscription: Non plus ultra. This strange

frontier sculpture, very much against tradition, was also even transferred
to the Indian Ocean (cf. the bronze horseman in the tale of the magnetic
mountain in the Arabian Nights), though admittedly it only marks the
eastern geographical boundary of the world, without any taboo behind
it. Thus the main station of the bronze horseman is and remains in the
Atlantic, only there was the outstretched arm interpreted as a warning,
not as a challenge or signpost for example. And although the Gardens
of the Hesperides also lie in the same sea of darkness according to Edrisi,
that did not make the darkness any more interesting or dialectical. And
the fable of the dangerous Atlantic ocean persisted up to the time of
Columbus, it was one of the strongest objections to the *western sea route*
to the wonderland of India; for it seemed unthinkable that such disfavour
was placed before those marvels. The Greeks also failed to make any
connection between the taboo of deterrence and the Isles of the Blest, as
dialectically elementary as this is, and as often – not to say, as essentially
– as it was established precisely in topics of paradise. Scheria, Homer's
island of the Phaeacians, lies untouched in the same sea where Scylla howls;
nobody reflected that the same Pillars of Hercules on which the Non plus
ultra stands were called the Pillars of Saturn in the most ancient days of
Greece, and were thus named after the god of the Golden Age. Hence
the horror of the west was not illuminated by the earthly paradises within
it, and the taboo of the statue did not tempt any Arab to break it. It was
in vain that the black death ship of the Phaeacians and the radiance of
Scheria both lay in the same place: 'Truly a light streamed out, like sunshine
or moonlight/Through the high dwelling of the illustrious ruler, Alcinous'
(Od. VII, 84f.). It was in vain that even the astral myth of the dying
sun, from which the horror of the west ultimately stemmed, contained
its own Hesperidean light apart from the darkness: Gilgamesh, Hercules
hasten with the sun beyond its setting, in order to gain immortality at
the point where the sun rises afresh. But such a connection between the
sea of mud and the island of the Hesperides only became fruitful in the
Christian world. For only the Christian-geographical legend and utopia
believed it knew *why the earthly paradise is kept unenterable*, and the fact
that it was unenterable was stressed geographically. A function now appears:
Eden lies behind a cordon of terrors, the cordon full of terrors lies around Eden.
The horror of the Atlantic was therefore interpreted differently by Church
Fathers than it was by Arabs: it was connected with the cherub's sword.
And he did in fact prevent anyone from entering Eden, but not from
approaching it. Clemens of Alexandria (Stromata V) was the first to link

darkness and masses of seaweed with the forbidden entrance to the earthly paradise (thought to be on the south side of the earth). Most of the other Church Fathers adopted this; only then was a dialectical relationship introduced into the sea of darkness, and above all an attraction which broke the barrier and the statue.

Much else combined to produce the dream of the rich lost land. Of the land beneath a happy latitude, and to which legend and hope are mutually directed. It is not just a question of fetching a Golden Fleece from it – with the remainder being left behind as immaterial, as a barbarous shore. The goal is rather a complete happy island or a land of happiness in absoluto, without any unwanted remainder. In one of these utopian accounts the usually so distant land of wine or land of milk and honey has even materialized astonishingly close at hand: in the account of Canaan. The Promised Land is here represented as thoroughly defined and present in geographical terms, it waits beyond the desert in assured, if unexplored splendour. And it seems, after the scouts had brought the grape back with them, like a second earthly paradise after the first one that was lost. In fact for the Children of Israel in those days it was the first one itself: for the detailed myth of the Garden of Eden, at the beginning of history, only reached them at all in Canaan itself, from Babylonian sources. Thus Canaan tangibly appears on the earth, not or not yet as the Garden of Eden, but as the spot where one is closer to heaven than usual. And a connection was also developed there which was added to the realm of happiness: the connection of Eden, the geographical wishful realm of happiness, with a wishful age in which it is attained. This was the Messianic connection: only at the end of history does *Canaan* appear *complete*, with Mount Zion in the middle; time itself is the possible ship to paradise regained. Of course, happiness was already there in the beginning, for the Greeks in the form of the Golden Age, in the Bible as the original sinless state in Eden. But both are lost, and therefore are only approaching again from the future, above all in the very spirit of Messianism which is not to be found among the Greeks, and is only an episode with the Romans (as in the prophecy of the divine child in Virgil), but in the Bible is endowed with total power over time. And this biblical wishful age flows out into the wishful dream of an absolute kind: at the end of time the earthly paradise is open again. It appears again and can be entered because the new Jerusalem descends to earth (Revelation 21, 2), yet only at the end of time. Meanwhile of course the *first* paradise, the actual Garden of Eden, has remained totally intact on earth, and although *entry* is forbidden, the *search for its location*, and the *sojourn in its external surroundings* are Christian and permitted. This belief that the earthly paradise still exists somewhere, that its vicinity and neighbourhood can be entered without breaking the divine commandment, was always active in the medieval expeditions. And Genesis itself was regarded as the guide, since it names rivers which do not circle in Paradise for instance but issue from it into parts of the rest of the earth which are actually named. These are the Pison, the Gihon, which flows around Ethiopia, the Hidekel, which flows outside Assyria, and then the Euphrates (Genesis 2, 11–14): for the legendary-utopian geography of the Middle Ages, all these waters still had to bring the blessings of paradise with them somewhere and spread them over fallen Creation. In other ways too, Eden was seen as the archetype of a magic garden, which inexorably spreads a fragrance and radiance across its boundaries. The Alexander of the French and German romances of Alexander the Great stood before the wall of this garden in India, smelt its fragrant scents, glimpsed its radiance through fleeting openings, and strove in vain to conquer Eden. The effect of these romances (beginning with the imaginary biography of Alexander by Pseudo-Kallisthenes around 200 A.D.) can never be over-estimated; Alexander, India, Paradise, these three huge concepts firmly shored each other up. And the medieval encyclopaedias: the 'Speculum naturale, doctrinale, historiale' of Vincent de Beauvais, the 'Imago mundi' of Pierre d'Ailly, which decisively influenced Columbus, all these books kept the conviction alive that there was still an enclave of unfallen nature on earth. The Church had left the question of determining the location of this enclave open, and had likewise given a free rein to reveries or speculations about its content. The only thing that was generally agreed was that the earthly paradise lay *in the east*, in accordance with Genesis 2, 8: 'And the Lord God planted a garden eastward in Eden.' Even the first sentence of the Bible: 'In the beginning (bereschith) God created the heaven and the earth' was used as evidence of the eastern location of Paradise; for the word 'bereschith' was taken to be able to mean not merely 'in the beginning' but also 'in the Orient'. Speculation was divided as to whether this East was to be sought in the northern or southern hemisphere; all that was certain in both cases was a connection with Canaan, with Jerusalem as the fixing point. And this point of connection given in the Bible even dislodged the classical tradition, according to which the Isles of the Blest lay in the Atlantic instead; rather, the *western tradition*, together with the dialectical fear of the Atlantic, *was blended with an eastern Jerusalem*, particularly after the discovery of the spherical shape of the earth, and thus subsumed under the eastern utopia. The famous mappa mundi in Hereford Cathedral, drawn up at the end of the thirteenth century, shows the earthly paradise on the meridian of Jerusalem; Dante, who assumed the spherical shape of the earth, even transferred it to the *antipodes of Jerusalem, to the South Seas*. This fitted in well with classical speculations about a large counter-earth in the south; Aristotle had taught it (Metereolog. II, 5), the Roman geographer Pomponius Mela spoke of an alter orbis beyond the ocean which separates north and south, and Cicero (Somnium Scipionis, cap. 6) likewise counts two habitable zones (cinguli), of which the still unknown southern one must conceal innumerable marvels. For Aristotle (as for Edrisi) the southern part of the earth was admittedly uninhabited, although it consisted of dry land, whereas Albertus Magnus, exactly like Cicero, posits a thoroughly populated large southern continent. Dante himself however, who in the 'Divine Comedy' with its captivating Arcadian description of the earthly paradise had kept alive the longing for it like no other poet before him, over and above every romance of Alexander, Dante assumed, despite the antipodes of Jerusalem, a 'terra inhabitabilis' below the equator, the 'mondo senza gente'. And because he transferred the earthly paradise to the top of the Monte Purgatorio, the exact latitude and longitude (near the antipodes of Jerusalem) had also become worthless for those expeditions which merely endeavoured to reach the environs of the 'nobilissimi loci totius terrae'. For in Dante there is no land in the southern hemisphere apart from Mount Purgatory, only water; the land has hidden at the bottom of the sea for fear of Lucifer, who fell from heaven here (Inf. 34, l. 122f.). Then the 'Divine Comedy' (the details of which, according to the intention of the poet, aspired to truth as well as to beauty) teaches that even the surroundings of the earthly paradise have become taboo. They are only accessible to the dead, not to the living, in fact, as the unique Odysseus episode shows (Inf. 26, l. 136ff.), only to those who are not destined for Hell or even for Heaven, but precisely for Purgatory; the mountain is out of bounds for the rest of the dead. And the earthly paradise itself (Purg. 28), on the top of Mount Purgatory, is for Dante, who almost invariably follows Thomas Aquinas, no place of residence even for the souls of the departed; it is merely a place for passing through. In Thomas Aquinas, the earthly paradise belongs to the 'status viatoris', not to the 'status recipientis pro meritis', and is therefore not somewhere to stay, it does not rank among the 'receptacula salutis'. Yet it is nevertheless described in Dante on the analogy of the Island of the Blest, an eternal morning in the southern forest, and situated on the earth, as the subtropicum of earthly bliss. Thus it was that the power of poetry still populated the 'terra inhabitabilis' of its theory in the most humane way: how often must Columbus, before he set out on his voyages to Eldorado-Eden, have connected the lines from Dante about this morning radiance with his own imago mundi. And Dante's theoretical restriction of the earthly paradise to the top of a mountain inaccessible to all living beings did not dispel the general belief in a continental location of the earthly paradise, nor the hope that living beings could reach its vicinity. On this point, however, the legend of Alexander had a more powerful influence, and it did not point to a postmortal island but to a populous continent in the southern sea. It pointed to India, it pointed to the overland route, and later to the sea route to the earthly paradise in Asia. That is why there was no major river in Asia which had not been connected with one of the biblical streams of Paradise; such as the Ganges, such as, in Marco Polo, the Oxus. The overland route and the sea route to the earthly paradise were thus chiefly orientated *towards India*, to the tropically mysterious land, full of marvels of another existence compared with the European-Near Eastern world. The ancient world and then the Church Fathers placed their Fortunate Isles essentially in the Atlantic, the Middle Ages essentially added these too to India or allowed India, the geographical utopian space par excellence, to extend as far as them. And in the end the voyage west itself, owing to the spherical shape of the earth, was not inconsistent with the south-easterly location: ex oriente lux, in the Christian Middle Ages the earthly paradise was explained by means of India, through all the oceans of seaweed.

Voyage of St Brendan, the kingdom of Prester John; American, Asiatic paradise

It remained there even when the ship steered a westward course. As was natural in the case of Irish and Norman seafarers; no eastern ocean lay on their doorstep. Moreover, the Isle of the Blest continued to have an effect, the wholly Atlantic and not yet Indian one. Yet for medieval legend it is still viewed in an Indian light, the Greek one alone was not mysterious enough. The contradiction between the Greek tradition, which located the land of the blessed in the west, and the biblical one which sought it in the east, admittedly did not break out yet in these early days, despite all the fluctuations, but the still so Atlantic Isle of the Blest already had an equally oriental look about it. One of the liveliest medieval legends of the sea steers exclusively towards this island: the voyage of St Brendan. The voyager himself, St Brendan, is historically documented, he was abbot of an Irish monastery and lived in the sixth century. It was the age of sea-hermits, that is, of monks who fled to lonely islands (as the Egyptian monks fled into the desert), to lead a life of contemplation there. The Faroes and Shetland Islands were discovered in this way, and some real experiences may underlie Brendan's legendary voyage too. But the utopian longing for the golden Somewhere of an enclave of happiness which escaped the Fall features far more lavishly in it and its legend. The legend of the Navigatio St Brendani dates in the existing version from the eleventh century, but it is much older, on that occasion it was revised from a sermon of the ninth century, was recorded in many more versions, was translated into almost all European languages, and kept the awareness of an island of paradise alive for centuries (cf. Babcock, Legendary Islands of the Atlantic, 1922, p. 34ff.). The content resembles an epic religious adventure; Brendan hears the voice of an angel in the night: God has given you what you are looking for, even the Promised Land. He mans a boat, sails westwards from Ireland for fifteen days, finds a palace with sumptuous food and invisible hosts, sails on for seven months in an unspecified direction, and finds an island with countless herds of sheep. When the crew attempt to roast a sheep on the fire, the island sinks; it was the back of an enormous whale, and the fire had interrupted its rest. After a host of fresh adventures, full of poisonous fish and fire-breathing sea-serpents, fiendish birds and even entrances to Hell, Brendan reaches an old island-hermit far out in the Atlantic who knows the way to the Promised Isle. Here a predecessor of Brendan's also turns up, Meruoc, who had made the voyage to the Promised Land a long time before; he concealed himself so thoroughly that he can live 'in the first home of Adam and Eve', i.e. in the earthly paradise, despite the curse. A further sign of the approaching paradise is the insula uvarum, the wine island of Bacchus, on which the sailors spend forty days, to load their ship with grapes in the end. Brendan reaches the island that was promised to him, saints live there who have been expecting him, he wakes a mysterious giant in the cave of sleep: the earthly paradise, behind the dark sea of the Atlantic, has been opened up. After seven years Brendan and his crew of monks return via the Orkades, bringing their account of the 'Promised Land of Saints', this vine-growing India in the west or right through the west. So much for the most famous sea yarn of the Christian Middle Ages and one which was completely believed, in

terms of its result, for centuries. Most of the Hanseatic towns cultivated
the worship of St Brendan, from 1476 to 1523 the legend of the fortunatae
insulae Brantani and their discovery was printed thirteen times in Germany,
and an American researcher, C. Selmer, has even connected the name
Brandenburg with the cults of St Brendan. The utopian isle is marked
on most medieval maps, it still appears on Mercator's map in 1569, indeed
in the sixteenth century the island was quite seriously handed over by the
Portuguese government to Luis Perdigon, an adventurer, who just as
seriously prepared to conquer it. And even in 1721 an expedition left the
Spanish port of Santa Cruz in Teneriffe to find the Ila de San Borondon.
What is and remains odd is the interweaving of this legend with traditions
from a non-Christian sphere of utopias, far beyond the Isle of the Blest.
Of course it is not surprising to find borrowings from contemporary Arabian
folk literature; the whale which submerges when a fire is lit on its back
appears as an octopus in the tale of Sinbad. But rather, it was part of the
whole classical learning of Irish monasteries to take over ancient sea legends,
like the unique collection in Plutarch. These are the legends about the
Isle of the Blest as the Island of Saturn (Island of Kronos) in the 'Kronian
Sea' around Britain; Plutarch recalled these legends both in his treatise
'On the Face in the Moon' and in his dialogue 'On the Decline of Oracles'.
Mention has already been made of the fact that the Pillars of Hercules
were formerly called the Pillars of Saturn, and hence Kronos; Plutarch
now describes, in connection with Saturn and his Golden Age, sacred islands
in the vicinity of Britain which are inhabited by the souls of heroes, and
particularly one 'where mild air prevails and Kronos-Saturn, imprisoned
in a deep cave, slumbers under the care of Briareus' (Briareus, a powerful
hundred-handed seagod, was like Kronos a son of Uranus). The sleeping
Saturn now appears again in the voyage of St Brendan as the giant
mentioned above, whom the saint wakes up in the cave, and the 'marvels
of the Kronian Sea' were already reflected in the island of the Golden Age.
Of course, the Britannic sea could not persist as the location of the island
of Paradise for any length of time, warmer and more easily navigable points
of the compass won the day. Thus St Brendan's isle moved further and
further south from the fourteenth century on, towards the Canary Islands.
On his famous globe drawn up in 1492, Martin Behaim shifts the island
so far to the south-west that it almost comes to lie in the latitude of Cape
Verde: 'This is the island', he says, 'on which Saint Brendan landed in
the year 565 and which he found to be full of marvellous things.' Alexander
von Humboldt remarks here with cool precision (Kritische Untersuchungen,

1852, I, p. 410) that this constant changing of the location of such an
untraceable island was connected with the progress in navigation produced
by trade in the Mediterranean. At the same time, though, there was also
the taboo surrounding the lost paradise and which only makes it possible
for the saint to enter it in St Brendan's legend itself: St Brendan's isle
thus became not merely a cartographically wandering island but one which
was inherently indeterminable, and which is only glimpsed in the distance
all the time. This belief was partly supported by an observation on the
Canary Islands: from time to time people there imagined they saw a mountainous country on the horizon towards the south-west – without its ever
having been reached. As Humboldt indicates, Viera, the historian of the
Canary Islands, imparted lengthy details about all the attempts which had
been made from 1487 to 1759 to land on the imaginary island. The mirage
was also seen at various points further to the north, even on the Azores;
Columbus knew the reports about it, almost forty years before his voyage,
as he indicates in his diary for 1492. From the moment it was first observed,
the phenomenon was interpreted as St Brendan's isle; the fact that it was
unattainable did not destroy the belief in it but rather seemed to confirm
it. And, in a more detailed way, there is a counterpart to this in China;
as proof that the vanishing Isle of the Blest, this land of happiness or land
of the Grail reserved solely for him who is worthy of it, represents if not
a roving fable then an archetype distributed over time and space. The
Chinese géographie moralisée knows of Fortunate Isles in the gulf of
Pe-chi-li; seen from a distance, they resemble clouds; when they are
approached, the ship is driven away by the wind; if they are reached
all the same, they sink into the sea; but the sailors, not called upon to
make a landing, are sickly when they come back. The supposed Island
of St Brendan was not regarded as profoundly as this by the fifteenth
century, but the distant image remained characteristic of it, as did the
fairytale of a magic land appearing over the horizon again and again. The
fairytale persisted, while people's eyes had long been wandering towards
the east, the decidedly biblical site of the earthly paradise. Towards the
actual direction of the east too, not merely – as with St Brendan – in
terms of the oriental tone and magical content, towards Asia, from which
the Three Wise Men came. And where that represented by St Brendan's
island was not supposed to be a lonely isle but – according to the equally
persistent legend – a complete world state full of well-being. St Brendan's
promised land thus saw its lustre transferred to the *Asian continent*, to the
huge kingdom now to be considered, which was unattainable in a very

different way, the Saturn- and Christ-kingdom of the so-called Prester John.

In any case it was not important for either merchants or knights to retire to a lonely island. They were in search of riches and broad profitable land, neither of which lay in Niflheim but on the way to the Holy Sepulchre and beyond. But Franconian power was dangerously threatened there a few decades after the capture of Jerusalem, a second crusade had failed, and a third was uneasily and uncertainly being prepared. This atmosphere saw the arrival of three mysterious letters around 1165, they allegedly came from Asia, from a powerful Christian ruler. He modestly called himself Presbyter John, but praised in an arrogant and bragging tone the power and marvels of his state, the greatest on the earth. According to the letters, his kingdom extended eastwards 'to the rising of the sun', westwards 'to the Tower of Babel'. A tremendous ally thus seemed to arise against the Saracens, the gift from heaven of a second front in the east. The letters were addressed to Pope Alexander III, to Emperor Frederick Barbarossa, and to the Byzantine Emperor Manuel; the two emperors seem to have mistrusted the message, the Pope rather less so, because he answered it, even if it was rather late. He sent his personal physician Philip, who had a good knowledge of the Orient, as a special envoy to Prester John, the lord of India, the lord of a kingdom which, as the message said, enclosed the earthly paradise; a legation was sent off to a phantom. The text of the papal reply has survived, dated Venice, the 27th September 1177, twelve years after receiving the Indian message; from which delay it is clear that the Pope's initially slight faith in the priest-king had grown along with the Saracen threat itself. For the people, Prester John was a certainty long before this; his letter was widely circulated in various copies, it was translated into French, German, and even Hebrew, and Europe bowed before the new hope of Asia. The papal reply was addressed: 'Carissimo in Christo filio illustri et magnifico Indorum regi, sacerdotum sanctissimo';* though Philip, the bearer, was not even able to report that the marvellous kingdom was nowhere to be found, for he never returned to Rome, the expedition was lost without trace. Hence the letter of the alleged priest-king was kept thoroughly topical, as far as its contents were concerned; it speculated not only with the military interest of a third crusade, as noted above, but also with the fables and wishful images of the East that were going round, and thus with the actual geographical utopia of the Middle Ages. If the legend of St Brendan had clung to the Isle of the Blest, in a western direction, the new message clung to the legend of Alexander

---

* 'Dearest brother in Christ, illustrious and magnificent King of the Indians, most blessed priest.'

and to the orthodox eastern orientation of the earthly paradise, which had prevailed in the High Middle Ages. The forged letter contained nothing that was not already familiar from classical, oriental, and medieval images of India, but it combined them in a complete and seductive way. India: this was a very broad concept in the Middle Ages, it extended (as it already did in Pliny) as far as the gulf of Tonking, and even embraced East Africa with Abyssinia for a time, Marco Polo also calls a Persian prince King of India. But India also proved its worth all the more as a highly mysterious concept, as the home of untold geographical marvels; the banal seemed to have been removed from nature itself there, and every escape-wheel from the clock of nature. The impossible, of a grotesque and utopian kind, seemed to be the real there, as in the medieval tapestries when they portray magic forests with the unicorn. There were thought to be mountains beyond the Indus, and they were also transferred there, their stones were emeralds, and their dust was musk; trees bore green birds as their fruit, human heads which cried and laughed grew on others. In the twelfth century a manuscript was circulating, attributed to St Jerome, about precious stones, their healing properties and other marvellous qualities, and this book characteristically begins with the description of a voyage to India, through the Red Sea (whose perilousness here replaces the terrors of the Atlantic), to the fantastic realm a whole year's journey away. To the home of the carbuncle, of the gold mountains guarded by gryphons, of the great man-eating ant which digs for gold at night, of the trees which grow in the sea, and of copper rain (cf. Thorndike, A History of Magic and Experimental Science, II, 1929, p. 238ff.). The main source of fables of India was again and again, as mentioned above, the translations and revisions which the classical romance of Alexander by Pseudo-Kallisthenes underwent in the Middle Ages; and its details by no means referred to Buddha and asceticism, as in the renaissance of interest in India in the nineteenth century, but on the contrary to the monstrosities and ecstasies of the quantum of world and gods in which Hindu legend abounds. All this had joined the legend of Alexander, an absolutely exorbitant one at that time, outside the habitual groove of the world. The letter of the priest-king himself found supposed support in the 'Nativitas et victoria Alexandri Magni' of Presbyter Leo, around 950, above all in an alleged letter from Alexander to Aristotle (cf. Kleine Texte zum Alexanderroman, edited by Pfister, 1910, p. 21ff.), where the miraculous way of life of Rama everywhere becomes the everyday life of the Macedonian. Leo recorded Alexander's journey through the air, his journey to the depths of the sea, and traditions were handed down of the prophetic trees of India, a tree of the moon that spoke Greek, another of the sun that spoke an Indian language; – such fantasies were grouped around the king's oriental campaign. Many of them are also echoed in the letter of the priest-king, are repeated, a complete dream arsenal of geographical fairytales and exceptions to everyday life. People are named in it who conjure up, saddle, and bridle aerial dragons, and ride off on them into the distance; the praises are sung of marvellous stones which heat up or cool down as required and illuminate all objects within a radius of five miles at night, stones which convert unconsecrated water into milk or wine, stones which gather fish around them, tame wild animals, kindle enormous conflagrations, extinguish enormous conflagrations. But Prester John's letter (the text of the copy addressed to Emperor Manuel is the one that survives) adds totally incomprehensible marvellous beings of its own, heightening the nonsense and the temptation: 'I, Presbyter John, the lord of lords, surpass all others walking beneath the heavens in virtue, wealth and power. Seventy-two kings pay tribute to Us...Our magnificence holds sway in the three Indias, and Our lands extend as far as the further India, where the body of the holy apostle Thomas lies...Our land is the home and dwelling-place of elephants, dromedaries, camels, of the Meta collinarum (!), Cametemnus (!), Tinserete (!), of panthers, forest asses, white and red lions, of white bears, white Merules, cicadas, silent gryphons, of tigers, Lamias, hyenas, wild horses, wild asses, wild oxen and wild men, of horned and one-eyed men, of men with eyes at the front and back of their heads, of centaurs, fauns, satyrs, pygmies, as well as giants forty cubits high, Cyclops and women of a similar nature, and of the bird called the Phoenix' (Oppert, Der Priesterkönig Johannes in Geschichte und Sage, 1864, p. 36ff.). Thus the entire stock of marvels in medieval bestiaries and books of precious stones has been located in the kingdom of Prester John in India, even the white bears of the high north, which people had only heard about in Europe in the eleventh century; the white elephant, on the other hand, which is actually found in India, is missing. Equally boastful and unreal is the description of the imperial palace: 'Its foundations and walls are made of precious stones, and the best, purest gold serves as cement. Its sky or roof consists of the clearest sapphires, mixed here and there with gems of dazzling topaz...Thirty thousand people dine at the Emperor's table every day, the table is made of emeralds, supported by four pillars of amethyst...Outside the palace there is a door of crystal framed with gold, this portal lies towards the east, is a hundred and thirty cubits high and opens and closes by itself whenever Our Excellency repairs to the palace.' In the profusion of these constant superlatives and curiosities there are also lakes of sand in which the most astonishing fish are found, rivers of precious stones, clothes of salamander skins which are cleaned with fire, the herb apsidios which drives out unclean spirits, so that the land does not contain a single person possessed with the Devil. But also above all – a serious ray of hope in the crude glare of all these fables – there is no poverty and no crime in the kingdom. Admittedly a magic mirror hangs in the vicinity of the castle square which reveals all conspiracies in the provinces and adjacent lands. Admittedly a sort of palace of the poor is mentioned, built by Prester John's father, where every hungry man who enters it immediately feels full, as if he had just finished the most lavish meal. But the priestly kingdom in the east does not cease to be a focus of almost all medical, social and technological utopias in the Middle Ages because of these admissions and palliatives. And this unity exists precisely because in it the geographical wishful image of all wishful images played on the hopes of medieval people and through all grotesquerie shone before them in a superstitiously moving, hopefully overhopeful way: the earthly paradise. A spring rises on the highest mountain of Prester John's kingdom which bestows the gift of youth for three hundred years; but Pison, the river of Paradise mentioned in Genesis, flows broadly through the capital with gold and onyx. In fact, it is such a visible piece of unfallen and permanently sacred nature that it stops flowing and rests on the Sabbath. Thus, with reports like these, the letter introduced distant marvels that were almost celestial into a Europe haunted by unrest and social decline. Into the land of catastrophic crusades, of sermons calling for repentance by Bernard of Clairvaux, of chiliastic heretical sermons by Joachim of Fiore, of the beginning war against the Albigensians. As great as the magic effect of this géographie utopisée was though, the fact to which it refers is just as dry and simple. There was indeed a Christian prince in Asia, not with a golden palace but with capable soldiers and a power that was short-lived. Yeliutashi, a Nestorian Christian, chief of the Turkish tribe of Kerait, who had already conquered West Turkistan, totally vanquished the Moslem sultan of the Persians Sandshar at Samarkand in 1141. A mere two years later the victor died, his realm collapsed, it was overrun by the Mongols who had previously been obliged to pay tribute to him; it was one of the temporary grand military-feudal structures, so many of which were harboured in the region of the Central Asian steppes one after another in the Middle Ages. But this short episode furnished the prototype for the legend of Prester John, and moreover for a legend which, as is remarkable here, had already developed in outline before the three letters. The news of the Moslem defeat filtered through to the west, the historian Otto von Freising heard of it from a Syrian bishop in 1145, and even in this first account the Nestorian Turkish prince was turned into a descendant of the Three Wise Men, into St George who defeated Islam. This was joined by hazy ideas about Mongolian theocracy, passed on by travelling merchants; thus the military-geographical utopia of Prester John finally developed at the same time that its prototype, the radiant Expected One, was already dead. This is the now transparent external cause of this legend itself; – *the purposive-factual cause*, which produced the conspicuous mystification of the letters, admittedly appears considerably more obscure. Their author is completely unknown, the social mission behind the forgery, assuming there was one at all, can hardly be guessed at with plausible reasons. A French historian, de la Roncière (The discovery of Africa in the Middle Ages, 1929), admittedly declares that the letter is 'a forgery perpetrated by Bishop Christian of Mainz between 1165 and 1177, in which the legend of Alexander the Great was used'; but all the evidence for this hypothesis is lacking. Almost as little is known about the purpose of the mystification, despite a very interesting interpretation by Olschki in terms of a *political* utopia ('Der Brief des Presbyters Johannes', Hist. Zeitschrift, Vol. 144, [1931], p. 1). According to this, the garb of geographical fable was only padding, exciting and accessible, it was only a stimulus and a recommendation. There was a political purpose behind it: the tormented Europe of Frederick Barbarossa was to be presented with an ideal portrait of the opposite kind, a picture of the secure and peaceful life of numerous nations under a theocratic government which provides and maintains both material and moral welfare. Hence the profusion of humane touches besides the swaggering ones: the abolition of private property, the realm without discord and war, the tolerance towards the numerous non-Christians within the realm under a Christian priest (with the characteristic omission of the Moslems). Hence the simple title of presbyter for the head of such a vast state (in connection with attacks against the idolization of the Byzantine emperorship). In its exotic atmosphere, Prester John's letter would therefore be a similar ruse to Montesquieu's 'Persian letters', for example (which were admittedly addressed by fictitious Persians from the West to the East); but the substance of its ideas could possibly come from the direction of Bernard of Clairvaux and the reformed order of his Cistercians. A good many things support this interpretation, it would give point and relief to an otherwise incomprehensible aplomb; though it is not clear what kind of a utopian value tolerance under the puritanical Cistercians could have provided. In Bernard of Clairvaux's will, the document 'On Contemplation', there are indeed many calls for simplicity on the part of the priesthood, but the religious zealot and inquisitor of heretics, the enemy of the dialectician Abelard (he caused the downfall of the latter precisely because of his investigatory comparisons of doctrines and authorities) was all the less inclined towards any kind of tolerance. That sort of thing is more likely to be found in the camp of heretics from the South of France, among the Cathars, perhaps also among the Knights Templar, and consequently among Christians or semi-Christians under Arabian influence. They had certainly been exposed to something of that sceptical-tolerant attitude which was usual among contemporary Arab philosophers (Ibn Tofail, Averroës) and which can be seen in the oriental parable of the three rings, which was circulating in the West for the first time around then. And only Christian heresies could contain these earliest seeds of religious tolerance, the same tolerance with which, strikingly enough, the letter is actually filled. Thus the opponents of Bernard and papism are more likely to be hidden behind the fictitious priest-king, Arnold of Brescia for instance or, since he was hanged ten years before the appearance of the letters, the disciples of his heretical preachings and prophecies who survived him. At any rate, the letter exercised no political influence as far as we know, but solely a geographical-utopian one. The social priestly kingdom is not recalled in any later political utopia, but rather it was precisely the so-called exotic padding which had a lasting effect: the message uniquely but powerfully appealed to the fantasy of Eldorado-Eden. From now on, merchants, adventurers, missionaries went in search of the kingdom for centuries on end, no less a person than Marco Polo made the supposed marvel of the east one of the goals of his journey, and thus he almost took up the legation of Philip in his own way. When the supposed priest-king could no longer possibly be alive, unless it was by means of the spring of eternal youth in his kingdom, people were spinning yarns about his descendants, as they were around 1221 about a priest-king David, the grandson of Prester John. Only in the fourteenth century did the geographers transfer the marvellous kingdom from Asia to Abyssinia, but the belief remained fresh and was so still when the Congo was discovered in 1485; for it was now suspected to be the land containing Pison, the river of Paradise. The vast extensibility of the concept of India to all possible wonderlands in medieval geography also enabled the kingdom of Prester John to be transferred to the Congo. The Portuguese even sought this kingdom on the west coast of Africa, even

Vasco da Gama set sail for it, rounded the Cape of Good Hope, and discovered on his voyage not the Presbyter of course, but the real East Indies. At the same time, though, the legend of Prester John faded, too many failures had occurred, above all the feudal-theological make-up of the thing became alien to the incipient bourgeoisie. Ridicule and disbelief increased, as in 'Don Quixote', where the land of Prester John, 'which neither Ptolemy described nor Marco Polo set eyes on', is classed and equated with the nonsense in the tales of chivalry. Also the western direction, which had never wholly been forgotten since St Brendan anyway, increasingly appealed to reason and not just fantasy since the blocking of the eastern route by the Turks. A synthesis recommended itself, facilitated by the spherical shape of the earth, between the Hesperidean direction and the eastern paradise. Columbus thus united the western dream handed down by classical tradition with the eastern dream from the time of the crusades. The Atlantic alone now leads to the 'rising of the sun' again, to the place where India really ought to begin, and which Columbus still thoroughly believed to be the remaining piece of paradise on earth.

Columbus at the Orinoco delta; dome of the earth

Many a coast has also been discovered by chance, often without any consequences. A crew which landed or rather was stranded after being driven off course rarely found its way back. Even when the Greenlander Ericson reached the American coast around 1000, without intending to, this remained episodic. This coast was discovered eleven times before Columbus, once even from Eastern Asia, but because this was all just a matter of chance, nothing came of it. There had to be a mandate and plan behind the voyage, the new land had to be a goal. Of course, the goal was not always as far away or even as extravagant as that of Columbus, the boldest traveller and dreamer in one. The Phoenicians exclusively sought markets, not marvels, and Pytheas sailed round Britain as an explorer, not as a fairytale hero. The Carthaginian Hanno, who sailed round the west coast of Africa about 525 B.C. as far as Senegal, and even as far as the Gulf of Guinea to the so-called mountain of the gods in what is today the Cameroons, wrote his extant report as an army officer, not as a mystic. Magellan only had 'el passo' in mind, the passage through America into the Pacific Ocean, the whole continent from north to south was probed at that time to find it. And despite his fierce doggedness, despite the risk

of the first circumnavigation of the world which he accomplished, Magellan
was also more of an adventurer than a dreamer; he did not need to overshoot
his goal in order to hit it. And anyway, if the Turks had not obstructed
the overland routes to India, if the Spanish feudal and luxury economy
had not needed gold in order to improve its constant balance of trade deficit,
above all with the Orient, if the impoverished hidalgos, who later so quickly
turned into the white gods of murder, had not desired to see in Eden
primarily the Eldorado which would make them rich overnight, then the
whole search for paradise would not have had a single ship at its disposal,
and Columbus would not only have been regarded by his opponents as
Jean de la lune, but he would have remained so historically. All of this
is true, and yet it did not dispel an obsession even in the case of Magellan
which stems even more strongly from the romance of chivalry than from
the much later entrepreneurial initiative first developed by the Dutch and
English. This obsession made the reaction to scepticism really fanatical,
to the shipowners first of all, and then – not just in the case of Columbus,
but in that of Magellan as well – to the captains of the escort ships and
their own crew. As surely as even a homo religiosus like Columbus would
never have been able to find a ship to set sail for his Eden without an
economic mission behind him, this mission could never have been fulfilled
without the traveller's mystical obsession with his goal. In fact, both
Eldorado in Eden and Eden in Eldorado uniquely coincided here, as neither
before nor since; and Columbus, being the utopian-religious dreamer that
he was, supplied the courage for Columbus the admiral. The wind which
drove his caravels through the terrors of the Atlantic into what he believed
was Eden did not merely blow towards utopias, they sucked it towards
them. The premonitions in antiquity of another continent would have
remained literary fantasy as they had previously done for so long *without
a new economic motive, but also without Eden as a stimulus*. Columbus praised
Seneca's allusion that one day the girdle of the ocean would break and
Thule would no longer be the outermost part of the earth, and Plutarch's
suggestion that the moon, if it was a mirror of the earth, still indicated
an undiscovered continent in its dark patches; but even these reports,
strengthened in their authority by the Renaissance, would not have enabled
the horror of the Atlantic to be overcome, nor encouraged the voyage
into the dreaded void. The belief in the earthly paradise, and this alone,
finally spurred on the man of action to risk the western voyage with
full awareness and planning, and finally fulfilled Seneca's prophecy. And
the material interest, that of feudal colonization, did not clash with the

underlying idea here; the latter, stretching from Seneca to Dante, rather provided the interest with boldness of imagination. But the fact must also be taken into account that the Renaissance in which Columbus lived was not only the age which rediscovered antiquity but also, like every turning-point in society, a new culmination of chiliasm. The latter was even a far more genuine fulfilment of the Renaissance than the rebirth of antiquity; Advent is the political-religious light surrounding the so varied excitement from Rienzo to Petrarch, from Münzer to Grünewald, even Dürer, and is the maritime aura surrounding Columbus. The horizon of the earth was immeasurably broadened by the voyages of discovery, but it was also supposed to be raised closer to heaven, with the approach to the eastern or solar point of Creation, to be discovered closer to it. As is obvious, the admiral thus exhibited very forcibly what the positivist Mach later called, post festum, 'the proliferation of imaginative life'; only he took it much further. Columbus believed more firmly than anyone in the earthly paradise, at the physically and metaphysically highest point of the earth; this was the coast of his Atlantic.

This alone supplied the strength to break the spell of the notorious western ocean. Columbus did find masses of seaweed, but not the darkness, nor was there any warning statue. Birds played a curious role, however: the admiral changed his initial westerly course towards the south-west because a flock of parrots flew in that direction in order, as he assumed, to sleep in the bushes on a nearby piece of land. Never, said Humboldt, has a flight of birds had more momentous consequences; for on the previous course, the latitude of the Canary Islands, the admiral would have reached Florida. Instead of the bewildering network of islands, he would immediately have touched the broad breast of the continent, and the north would have been colonized by Spaniards. As we know, right up to his death Columbus believed that he had reached India, he attempted to communicate with the natives in a thoroughly oriental fashion through an Arabian interpreter he had brought with him, and just three years before his death he wrote that from Cuba, a stretch of mainland where India begins, it was possible to get to Spain without touching any oceans. And yet with this mistake of his the man doubled the works of Creation, with a mistake which is precisely connected with the belief in the earthly paradise. For Columbus the new world was the oldest of all, this lay well-preserved in the interior of Eastern Asia, and on approaching it the spring of the first Creation had to dawn again, without any of the mess which the rest of the world has been in since the Fall. Hence nobody was more expectant than Columbus of finding signs and marvels, he hallucinated the song of nightingales in the forests of Haiti, as transfigured 'as our forebears must have heard it and as it will only return for the Blessed one day', he sensed the air of Paradise in the vicinity of the mouth of the Orinoco, and Paradise itself beyond the Orinoco delta. All this in the midst of the most exact observation, with masterly orientation by means of the astrolabe, establishing an equatorial current and also curious connections between the degree of longitude and the climate. But the famous letter from Haiti of October 1498 to the Spanish monarchs contains the following passage about the Orinoco (cf. C. Jane, Selected Documents, Illustrating the Four Voyages of Columbus, II, 1933, p. 7f.): 'I say that if this river does not come from Paradise then it comes from a distant, hitherto unknown land in the south. But I am much more convinced that the earthly paradise lies there, and I cite the proofs and authorities which I have stated above.' These proofs referred to the fact that Columbus believed he had reached the original point in the east where the first sunrise occurred after the Creation. But at the same time this point marked the peak of the earth, the 'apex terrae', related to a mystical concept, the 'apex mentis', at which, in the opinion of the scholastics, the unfallen part of the human soul comes into contact with God on high. Columbus did indeed write to the Spanish monarchs of the globe coming to a peak at the point he had reached in the east, and that it was consequently closer to heaven, 'for this elevation consists only in that *most excellent part of the earth*, from which the first ray of light emerged at the moment of Creation, namely from the first point in the east. The earthly paradise lies there from which the great rivers flow down, no mountains with sheer and rugged slopes, but an elevation on the globe (el colmo ò pezón de la pera),* towards which even at a great distance the surface of the oceans gradually rises'. Humboldt comments on this (Kritische Untersuchungen II, 1852, p. 44, note): 'It is possible that Columbus wanted to allude to a systematic idea of the Arabian geographers, to a passage in Abulfeda where he says that the land of Lanka (Ceylon), where the dome of the earth or Aryn is to be found, is situated at the equator midway between the western and eastern boundary of the earth.' But apart from the analogy of the mystical summit of the earth with the mystical apex mentis, the actual Olympus image of Paradise is also far older, it has its origin (for Columbus a legitimate one) in the Bible itself. The Garden of Eden had been sought by the Yahwist in the upper reaches of the two rivers Euphrates

---

* 'The top or stalk of the pear.'

and Hidekel (Tigris), that is on the mountain heights which form the
northern boundary of Mesopotamia (cf. Gunkel, Schöpfung und Chaos, 1895,
p. 112). We know from the legend of the Flood and its Mount Ararat that
these mountains were considered to be the highest in the world; recollections
of it appear in Isaiah 14, 14, and in Ezekiel 28, 13ff.: 'the garden of God' is
one with the 'mount of the congregation', with the 'holy mountain of
God'. In Dante too, Paradise appears as the mountain of God high above the
earthly realm, and it is not just the Bible which bears witness to it but the
mountain cult in all the Uranian religions of the earth, above all and highest
of all itself in Babylon, with the very ancient image of the mountain of the
gods. Arabian geography brought the image of the mountain of the gods,
this holy-phantasmagoric towering structure resembling an Alp of the gods,
back to earth again, to a 'dome of the earth', wholly in the style of Moorish
architecture, but Columbus restored its biblical radiance, the splendour of
Eden. Thus this dome of the earth became for Columbus the 'indicio del
paraýso terrenal', and hence he transferred it from the Ceylon of Arabian
geography to the Orinoco delta – supposedly in the neighbourhood of
Ceylon – , or rather beyond it, to the unenterable realm he had reached,
where the earth as Eden merges into the azure vault of the sky. The admiral's
letter to Ferdinand and Isabella thus closes quite openly with a theological
allusion to 'the countries which I have recently discovered and which I am
convinced in my heart are the earthly paradise (en que tengo assentado en el
ánima que allé es el paraýso terrenal)'. Indeed, the admiral astonishingly
goes even further, as for example in a letter to Doña Juana de la Torre,
likewise from the third voyage; the exaggeration in this letter becomes
apocalyptic. The letter is the product of a moment in which dejection and
exaltation are strangely mixed: 'I have served with a service which has never
been heard of or seen before. Of the *New Heaven and the New Earth* which
our Lord created, as St John writes in the Book of Revelation, after He had
spoken of it through the mouth of Isaiah, He made me the herald and showed
me how to proceed.' Moreover, with this outrageous trump card or triumph
Columbus overcompensated for the increasing hostility shown to him in court
circles, which was growing ever more dangerous. For the opponents of
Columbus felt their original scepticism confirmed when nothing came of the
great voyage to India and China but the discovery of a few islands and an
unknown race of savages; that sort of thing did not cover the costs of the
voyage. So this is presumably another reason for the colossal exaggeration of
the New Heaven and the New Earth, which is theologically untenable too; for
these marvels appear, precisely according to the Revelation of St John, not

at the peak of a discovery, but above the abyss of the end of the world. A primary and constant accompanying factor in Columbus is, however, the belief in an Eden that can be found, and that ultimately has been found; it now lay in a Christian realm. And from the riches which it would inevitably bring in the future, from the gold-bearing river of Pison which emerges into the surroundings of Paradise, a final crusade was to be equipped if the admiral had his way, and the earthly Jerusalem conquered. After which Eden and Canaan, the tree of life and Mount Zion would have all been situated together on the summit of Christianity. The fact that Eden then later only turned out to be the Antilles, that no white gods but criminals like Cortez and Pizarro then penetrated into the continent beyond, that the earthly paradise as a whole is not a fact but a problem of hope and a latency: this does not rob the intention pursued by Columbus of its strength and dignity.

South land and the utopia of Thule

A simpler dream of navigation appears in a more corporeal form, the southern one. Like migratory birds, coming from the colder countries, it is directed towards the sun. The east too was always simultaneously conceived in terms of the most favourable latitude, as much midday sun, much summer. And the further south it was, the more unexpectedly Italian, Arabian lustre seemed to increase. The climatic torment of the tropics was well-known of course, but it did not have a deterrent effect; because it was mitigated by distance or the brief astonished visit. It was not known, however, that the cold increases again in the southern hemisphere too. But this remained undiscovered at least until Magellan had penetrated south into the vicinity of the stormily icy Cape Horn. Nevertheless, the inclination towards increasing warmth and light, which is so deeply ingrained in human nature, persisted, that inclination towards a profane Eden so to speak, requiring no faith. And not even the driving magical additive was wholly lacking: the seat of the *source of life* in general was presumed to lie in the south, which knows the early spring earlier and from which the summer approaches. The direction in which an officer of Columbus himself, Ponce de León, sought this mythical source of life is instructive in this respect. Namely not at the eastern point of an earthly paradise, but in the tropics as such, right where he was; and a Red Indian legend was enough for him to expect the waters of eternal youth in Florida. As

closely as this spring is linked by tradition with the vicinity of Eden, and
hence, since the legend of Alexander, with India, it is just as surely the
tropical element, and not the consecrated one of that India, that led to
hopes of finding the water of life in that particular spot. The reputation
which this water enjoyed, so very different as it was from holy water,
was also therefore corporeally profane, appropriate to the longing for the
south. It flowed through the gallant conceptions of the Middle Ages and
the Renaissance, wholly in the halcyon sense of southern hope. It ran
through the 'jardins de plaisance' of medieval graphic art and literature,
it is even revealed in Titian's related allegory, very unjustly called 'Heavenly
and earthly love', where not an angel but Cupid stirs the tropical water,
'egrediens de loco voluptatis', as the Church said of this vigorous, non-
Christian baptism. So this mythical element also streamed into the *Terra
australis*, far below the equator, at the antipodes of cold. The semi-official
medieval doctrine of the terra inhabitabilis, south of the equator, admittedly
stood in the way of the Terra australis itself. But since Albertus Magnus
had already attacked the authority of Aristotle and Edrisi so forcefully on
this point, since he denied that the southern half of the earth was wholly
covered with water, at the same time he theoretically made space for the
fantasy of the southern continent. And Marco Polo finally went along
with it in practice, when he thought he would be able to locate the Terra
australis. Java, Sumatra, the lush Sunda islands were assumed to lie off
the coast of the continent, the Indian Ocean was presented as an inland
sea, with its richest coast in the south. Perhaps Malayan and Chinese legends
also contributed to this location, recollections of the prehistorical Gondwanaland – a Sodom and Gomorrha of the tropics – which, destroyed by fire,
sank in the area of the Indian Ocean. At any rate, the ancient archetype
now assumed specific shape through this location beyond the richest islands
in the world; – people saw the feet of the giant and guessed the rest. The
disappointment though, long after Marco Polo, was great, but the dream
of the Terra australis had also strongly faded in the meantime. Australia,
on which Dutchmen first set foot in 1606, and the extent of which was
fairly well established by Cook in 1770, turned out to be the most modest
of continents, a complex of deserts. The water of life and the climax of
a sun kingdom from the other side vanished, Gondwanaland sank once
again. Yet a separate geographical utopia once stood in this image of the
south, one with a radical Cimbric and Teutonic migration as it were. And
ultimately south land is the hot tertiary period, a utopian reminder of the
migratory bird and even the dinosaur in man in contrast to the winter

land. The southerly direction, and what was expected in pursuing it, is thus charged with a profusion of life which was not afraid of becoming monstrous. That is why imaginary utopian voyages to the south land never lost this innate orgiastic character: Foigny's 'The Australian land experienced', of 1676, portrays the inhabitants of the southern continent as hermaphrodites; Rétif de la Bretonne's 'Australia discovered by a flying man' has the intention of superimposing an orgiastic Rococo on to a tropical Sodom, with unknown sins located in the unknown. The utopia of the southern continent itself, luxuriant as it is, is empirically the most unfounded, but it retained the archetype of animal paradise.

On the other hand, the opposite inclination towards the north seems almost corporeally incomprehensible. Whereas the south wind tempts and promises us, the cold and darkness are menacing, our first reaction is to flee from them. The route to the north therefore seems almost paradoxical, there is no Cimbric and Teutonic migration on it. For the same reason that the icy mountains of the Alps, this piece of Greenland between the Danube and the Po, were the last to be visited, or even loved. And yet human civilization migrated more and more up from the south towards the north. Its course goes from the Nile and Euphrates to Athens and Rome, to France, Germany, England, and Russia. Civilization not only moves from east to west, but far more regularly from south to north, and the struggle with the harsh climate had the same hardening effect as that with the Ice Age in primeval days. There is no temptation to invade this region as in the Cimbric and Teutonic migration, but it happens, a creative expansion, one which has still not come to an end; its next act should be the rise of Siberia. And above all, despite the darkness and cold the north does not lack a peculiar *attraction*; economically this was based on the interest in raw materials (tin, furs, amber and more), but it also persisted for reasons of many a contrasting ideology outside the business sphere. Distinct signs of this are already evident in Tacitus, he gives the first sentimental picture of the north. For his 'Germania' not only idealizes a primitive people, it also shows a small counterpart of that freezing yearning for the sun, it shows consternation in the face of the huge chilly forests, and the 'harsh sky'. But a veritable Thule is evoked much later on in German literature, in the Sturm und Drang revolt against the 'unnaturalness' of a neo-feudally romanizing system of rules. Instead of the sculpture of the south, the 'wild Apollo' sought storm-clouds, flying moonlight, and brooding overcast expanses. This satisfied the enthusiasm for northern regions which was aroused by Ossian, and it is characteristic that a forgery which was itself sentimental could trigger it off. Not the poet Macpherson, but the mask of the old skald Ossian, another Prester John as it were, acted on northern Europe at that time, acted like a message. And not just like one out of northern literature by any means, but like one out of the *world of Fingal's Cave and the Hebrides themselves*, into which the fictitious poet led the way. It was a world of soft and at the same time enormous heroes, a nature consisting solely of reeds, rocks, moors, lakes and winds, an elegiacally remembered and waning one, yet surrounded by that sunset glow, those storms and passing clouds which can only occur on the northern heaths, close to the sea, which bring the message: Thule. Herder experienced the Ossian utopia in a way which was canonical for his age, namely from on board ship and from the perspective of the sea, from a coastal perspective: 'Floating between the abyss and the sky, daily surrounded by the same endless elements and just taking note now and then of a new distant coast, a new cloud, an ideal region of the world – now with the songs and deeds of the ancient skalds in my hand, my soul completely filled with them, in the places where they occurred. . ., now at a distance passing the coasts where Fingal's deeds occurred and Ossian's songs chanted melancholy, beneath these very currents of air, in the world of silence' (Extract from correspondence about Ossian, 1773). The essence sought after in this way reaches down into the Gothic novel, where it has been preserved in its most popular form; it reaches up (as Spengler discovered in the truest sentence he ever wrote) into the deep midnights over whose approach Faust keeps vigil at his desk, and into which the colours of Rembrandt and the strains of Beethoven fade away. But the essence itself reaches beyond these cultural spheres in a way that is still thoroughly object-based, precisely into the cloudy world of the north by whose light it is illuminated, into the utopian realm of this world as a paradise without a zephyr. Thus there was and is a real geographical utopia even here; it does not merely dwell on a globus intellectualis, it clings to real fixed points of the northern oceans, to Fingal's Cave, the Hebrides, Iceland, and from there it constructs Niflheim. 'To roam over the heath, with the stormy wind whistling in your ears bearing the ghosts of your fathers in steaming mists in the dim light of the moon' – this affinity from Werther's Sufferings, the attraction of the north thus equally ranks alongside that of the south, in fact it surpasses it by virtue of its overcast character. The more so as this very overcast element or northern magic never lacked a strange added ingredient, one from a very different direction, namely from that of the east again, from the utopia of India and the Orient. It is certainly not the opulence, but the great fairytale tone, the element of mystery lacking in the purely southern utopia, that allows a real point of utopian contact between the Orient and the territory of Ossian. The real connections: ancient trading, oriental and northern ornaments, Christianity in the Edda, these are not so important in the present case, although they obviously also have an effect on the actual *utopia* of Thule. More important is the fact that the objective atmospheric elements from which every daydream develops were able to migrate from the oriental locality with such elective affinity into the northern one. This accounts for the unmistakable correspondence between the world of veils and the world of mists, between the biblical and the highly wintry Christmas landscape, between the Apocalypse and the frontierlike-cryptic manner in which the Edda presents its twilight of the gods. *Mount Olympus cannot be imagined at all beyond the Mediterranean world, but smoking Mount Sinai accords well with the north, as does the cloud and the pillar of fire.* Hence Macpherson also takes his language in equal measure from the Psalms, Milton's biblical tone and the extant Gaelic songs. And thus from the frontier situation that is called mystery this veiled element in the Orient is added to the overcast atmosphere in the north: ultima Thule accords in a very particular way with the final frontier, with the end of the world. The overcast atmosphere of Thule thereby simultaneously discloses itself in its frontier sense itself: it is, as Herder says, 'an outlet of the world into sublimity'. The corporeally so incomprehensible inclination towards the north thus becomes clear: the attractions of the south and of the north affect different sides of human nature, its Midsummer Day in the case of the former, its Christmas in that of the latter. To the south a profusion of life utopianizes itself geographically, which certainly knows death but emphasizes neither it nor the countermove against it; to the north a magic of death utopianizes itself geographically, which contains within it a complete destruction of the world, but also seeks to overcome it, with a paradoxical homeland. Thule is the geographically dialectical utopia of a world which is ending and perishing, but with the constantly interwoven contrasting images of the stormy night and the castle. Thule in the northern ocean is the mysticism of bad weather, with the open fire in its midst. With Herder and Ossian there stirred 'the harp, the gloomy one,/Shrouded in the grey of dawn,/Where the sun rises resounding,/From waves whose heads are blue'. Thus this kind of geographical utopia also remained in the high north, it was not made groundless by what was discovered to exist.

Better abodes on other stars; hic Rhodus

There is also the lure of another sea apart from the horizontal one, namely the vertical one above us. Air space was admittedly inaccessible for long enough, but then it is transparent, it does not hide its Beyond. It particularly does not hide it at night, countless tiny sparkling coasts then emerge. And an age-old wish aims at sailing these coasts and landing on them. Up till now this wish has undoubtedly been even more extravagant than that of Columbus was, although it is less mythical. At any rate it touches on the ancient archetype according to which the stars are the seat of better characters. What draws people up to this Above does not even necessarily presuppose inhabitants of course, in the secularized form it has assumed. The lure of outer space is satisfied in one respect with the fact that man is able to imagine himself as a visitor on these distant heavenly bodies and that he will find, if not something more perfect, then at least something extremely peculiar up there. The imaginary traveller does not even need to be carried away for this, apart from taking his body and his sense organs up there with him intact into such totally changed circumstances. All the rest, in so far as it does not refer to inhabitants or even to their perfection, but simply to extreme peculiarity, is not even hypothetical, but it is true, this is where the most outlandish foreign parts really begin. The sky on the moon becomes black, the stars shine fiercely in the daytime, the sun beats down in a dazzling bombardment, unmitigated by any veil of air. A wall of blackest shadow stands immediately next to the light there, all in a silent wilderness; the vast globe of the earth rises above the rings of craters, with large cities as points of light. On the smaller asteroids our body would weigh almost nothing at all, and one jump would be enough to take us into outer space; on large dense heavenly bodies, however, our body would lie chained by gravity, it would be like granite. Then the day on pale Saturn, with the countless bodies that make up the ring above us, then the view from one of the moons of Jupiter towards the planet, which half or entirely fills the sky. There is all this and much more that is still inconceivable, virgin territory at an inaccessible, imaginary distance. And the most outrageous things of all occur on the myriads of fixed stars themselves, on these explosive blossoms and lights of cosmic development. The peculiar is thus *one part* of the astronomical lure, it continues the obsession with the 'curious' which the Baroque period had for alien zones. In this, the sky is a sheer physical wonderland or terra secreta outside the earth, precisely because it is a terra inhabitabilis. But of course the *other part* of the lure, the part in which the sky still has a lasting effect as the seat of transfigured characters, posits *habitability* instead of mere peculiarity, and in fact adds the meaning: *Mars, you have a better time of it*. This inhabited and also better element was at first sought on the moon, as it was by Kepler. Kepler regarded the craters seen through the telescope, which had just been invented, as huge cities with circular ramparts. Then, when the airless and waterless satellite was found to admit none of the forms of life at least, Mars was chosen as we know, and its canals surpassed the city ramparts, even in their assumed technological perfection. The similarity, which so quickly became popular and was indeed relative, of conditions of life on Mars with those on earth certainly encouraged the assumption that the planet was a terra habitabilis. Added to this there is the older solidification of the surface of Mars, in comparison with the earth, in keeping with the smaller size of the planet. Accordingly its possible civilization could very well have a 'start' of several million years over the earth, provided that length of time is roughly equal by and large to length of development. The majority of these Martian fantasies are correspondingly more ones of civilization than cultural and even messianic ones; thus they did not so much take the place of 'India' as that of 'America' in the planetary heavens. The neighbouring earth of Mars reflects in the images of the analogous imaginative powers which are brought to bear on it virtually the position and also the status of the utopias of 'America' prevailing on the earth at the time. That is why the numerous legendary geographies of Mars are also much more easily accompanied by an element of triviality than the older ones concerning heavenly earths. And among these older ones, after Kepler's imaginary and utopian migration, that of Kant stands out in particular; from his pre-critical period, as it goes without saying. In the speculative appendix to his 'Natural History and Theory of the Heavens', Kant also wanted to open up far more remote planets for an advanced world. According to him, the truly 'blissful regions' are not to be found, like Mars and Earth, at a medium distance from the sun, but only at the furthest remove of the outer planets. Jupiter and Saturn are singled out in this way: the decreasing density of matter in both, and the remoteness of the sun, seemed to the philosopher to be the foundations of a purer world so to speak. An idolatry of the north is unmistakable here, with Jupiter and Saturn in place of Tacitus' 'Germania' as it were. Even a variation on the utopia of Thule is discernible to some extent: not in the direction of Ossian, not at all, but in the direction of an arctically,

super-arctically transposed Stoic philosophy. A genuinely Kantian aversion
to softness and zephyrs, to sensual glow, the subtropical, and the undutiful
thus migrates to its planetary Super-Königsberg. And Kant ventures the
analogy : 'that the perfection of the spirit world, as well as the material
one, grows and advances in the planets, from Mercury all the way to Saturn
or perhaps even beyond it (if there are other planets) in a proper succession,
according to the proportion of their distances from the sun' (Werke,
Hartenstein, I, p. 338). The pre-critical Kant here imagined a totally
extravagant counterpart to Newton's formula of the decrease in gravity
as the distance is squared; that is, with the decrease in gravitational attraction
the attraction of purity is supposed to grow, in accordance with the
imagined contrast between gravity and spiritual light. These then are some
of the ways in which an orbis habitabilis populated the magic of the starry
sky technologically or also in moral wish-fulfilment. The depths of the
heavens were thereby induced to modify an element of the earthly paradise,
though admittedly one which was an illuminated earth again and again,
one which had been raised to its master level as it were. Kant himself
later expressed this reference back to man and earth very convincingly and
yet without loss of genuine height, in his 'Dreams of a Spirit-Seer': 'When
we talk of the heavens as the abode of the Blessed, then the common notion
likes to place it high overhead in the immensity of space. But we do not
consider the fact that our earth, viewed from these regions, also appears
as one of the stars in the sky, and that the inhabitants of other worlds
could point to us with just as good reason and say: Look up there, that
is the abode of eternal joys and a heavenly residence which is prepared
to receive us one day. For you see, a strange delusion always causes the
high flight taken by hope to be linked with the concept of rising, without
considering the fact that, however high we have risen, we still have to
sink again in order likewise to gain a firm foothold in another world'
(Werke, Hartenstein, II, p. 340). Behind all of this lies the belief, by no
means sinking itself, that *the earth itself* can contain within it the better
existence on other stars, if there is one or will be one. So that the sidereal,
in a utopian sense, does admittedly have its lure or a symbol up above,
but must be sought and can be pursued here below, among human beings.
In the 'secrecy of the firmament of the earth', as Paracelsus says with a
paradoxical combination or cross-combination of firmament with earth.
If there are inhabitants on other stars, then technologically at least they
possess no considerably greater perfection; for no so-called Martian giant
has landed on earth as yet. The world which the earth might gain through

contact with other hypothetically inhabited planets has been purely left up to human beings and their rocket propulsion. The distant sparkling points of light did indeed first make human beings look up at the sky, the star-studded heavens supply the prototype of peace, sublimity, and serenity, yet on the earth this image is also a task and a goal – hic Rhodus, hic salta, here is the dome, rise here.

The Copernican connection, Baader's 'central earth'

But what if the dome were only to stand very much apart? If it is so hidden away in a corner that its self-importance is all in vain? Columbus still regarded the earth as the centre of the world, a generation later it was dethroned from it by Copernicus. Whereby man too, and not just his scene of action, moved out of the centre of the world. It becomes immaterial, almost absurd by cosmic standards, how highly the grain of sand sublimates and exalts itself. The dome grows on a planet which is 'distinguished' by nothing in astronomical terms, and this revolves around a fixed star of no more than medium size. But at first this debasement did not yet have the total dimension that it acquired later on and which it has recently relinquished again. The preface to Copernicus' work, which he admittedly did not write himself, had recommended the heliocentric system only to promote an improved method of carrying out astronomical calculations. It was enough for the proposed hypotheses 'si calculum observationibus congruentem exhibeant'.* This reservation was made at the time in order to soften the clash with the Bible, it is misinterpreted today, but as a statement of conscientious physics it remains highly remarkable long before Einstein and especially Mach. For the astronomical advantage of the heliocentric theory over the geocentric one is in fact its arithmetical simplicity. It made no less than eleven motions in the Ptolemaic system superfluous, Kepler supplied the enchantingly clear rules of orbit, and Newton provided a foundation for the whole thing by formulating the laws of gravity. The system merely presupposed a stationary space in which absolute motion and absolute translational velocity really occur, and are clearly determinable and measurable. Though it is now precisely this premise which has been dropped: for in no way can the motion of a body be proved against an empty stationary space or even against a stationary ether filling

---

* 'if the calculations prove to be in agreement with the observations'.

that space. In other words, according to the elementary principle of relativity: when two observers are moving at uniform but different speeds, each of the two can claim with exactly the same justification that relative to the empty space he is at rest, and there is no method of measurement in physics to settle the matter in favour of one or the other. Applied to the solar system, the choice of the body conceived to be at rest and that conceived to be in motion is likewise open as regards the *kinetic* relation; things only change here in the respective, specific *causal* relation. This purely physical realization must thus on no account be confused with absolutely false epistemological conclusions of a very different origin, namely with physical idealism and fictionalism, but this is exactly why it cannot be rejected as fictionalist in its *purely physical detection* either. Because therefore with the discarding of an empty stationary space no motion occurs against it, but merely a relative motion of bodies against one another, and its detection is dependent on the choice of the body assumed to be at rest: providing the complexity of the calculations involved does not make this appear impractical, the earth could still be assumed to be fixed, and the sun to be in motion. There is of course all the less reason for this as precisely the causal explanation from the mass of the sun allows an explanation of gravitational motion, and consequently points to the sun as the *physical* centre; thus it stands in the right physical spot from a methodological point of view as well. The theory of Copernicus still remains most depictively valid even when the relativity of motion permits no absolute detection of motion and rest at all. But now to something else which has nothing at all to do with physics, namely concerning the problem of the situation of the earth *as the arena of human history*: is astronomy simply *all there is* and *the total matter itself*? Since the earth as a satellite and the sun as a stationary point of reference are after all determined relative to one another, is there no other 'point of reference' absolute as before? Such that man's earth would still remain in the 'middle of things' or central, in a different context to the astronomical one and in view of the role which the earth plays not just in celestial mechanics alone. Indeed it is significant that another such 'point of reference' has never ceased to exist, despite the clockwork mechanism reinterpreted by Copernicus. Nor does it by any means lie outside science, it only lies outside the old mechanics which has been made total and which is in any case untenable as this totality. Consequently, another system of reference to that of the mechanically total one, one of *human importance*, has by no means removed our planet from the 'middle of things', in this relation. In other words, since the relativity of motion stands beyond doubt, a humane and an older Christian system of reference, while it admittedly does not have the right to interfere with astronomical calculations and their heliocentric simplification, does however have its own methodological right to hold this earth fast for the *context of humane importance* and to rearrange the world around the events that occur and can occur on the earth. This and this alone remains here as the humane element from the 'Ptolemaic strain' in the Bible and also in Augustine: with the civitas Dei which fights its utopian way through and out into the open on the earth, not on the sun. The biblical order claims to be free of relativity, since it is not dealing with mechanical problems of motion, but with *problems of status*. And it needs no empty stationary space or stationary ether to determine them, but solely the invariant of a utopian Humanum. Thus the earth is here the centre in the sense of the 'central meaning' around which the world revolves. The earth is then by no means predominantly regarded as the provinces; on the contrary, for the patriots of humane civilization it becomes at the same time the capital of the universe.

It is only becoming this capital for them of course, it is only ripening into it. Nobody in recent times has given such a sanctimonious expression, but one which is not merely limited to that as we shall see, to this kind of central earth as Franz Baader. Baader's geocentric hope means the earth tinged with Christ, a tinging which begins in man and progresses from here to his arena and the rest of nature. The world is accordingly not a pantheistic statue of God, or even the absurdity of an infinite statue, but the earth is rather a modest cave in which the god was born. His work 'Foundation of Ethics through Physics', 1813, – namely through a transformed physics – formulates this as follows: 'For really man ought to be the open point in Creation in an even higher sense than the sun is, and if he therefore becomes such a point again, if the higher life freely and unrestrainedly dawns in him again, then it is easy to understand how every lower nature which steps into the sphere of illumination and influence of this re-opened sunny being will also immediately disclose its own previously sealed life, and how man, like that Orpheus in the fable, will therefore spread harmony and blessings around him even in the lower forms of nature and at least in his individual sphere will anticipate, as it were, that natural state (as natural transformation), whose general establishment is apodictically demanded by ethics in the idea of the highest good' (Werke V, p. 32f.). This is the basic tone; the problem of a humanized relation to nature, even if distorted with a tendency towards mysticism, is unmistakable. And from this point of view the disparagement of the earth only seems correct if measured numerically and according to size, but by no means if measured according to weight (in the sense of humane importance). Thus: 'The earth stands a degree further outside or deeper than the rest of the heavenly bodies, and therefore beneath these...And yet this earth holds the most exquisite things in Creation hidden and buried within it, which is why it is aptly compared with the mustard seed in the Gospel which, although it is the smallest among the seeds, will still spread its growth across the entire sky...The earth is in the material order of things what man is in the higher order of things, and just as man is unique in the universe, there is only one earth. Both, man and earth, are the secret workshop, place of learning and of reorganization of the central beings and their sensibility...The uniqueness of the earth and its destiny in the system of the world is most closely associated, and not merely from the temporal point of view, with the uniqueness of man and his destiny. Thus the modern non-conceptual idea of the heavens as a countless, uniform, and hence superfluous repetition of the same solar systems and so on also falls back into the nothingness from which it arose' (Werke IX, p. 282, XIV, p. 44, III, p. 317). The Stoics once explained their division of the philosophical sciences into three parts as follows: logic was the fence, physics the garden, and ethics the fruit. For the Christian Baader, this fruit is apocalyptic and thus the garden is not physics as such, but the earth on which Paradise already existed once, as a sign of what it can be. Thus: 'Even if this age is merely the winter of eternity, man is still able, like a judicious gardener, to produce even in the midst of this icy winter at least a few individual blossoms of eternity, even if they are only fleeting and quickly close again: hereby modelling that paradisial state of nature outside himself, if he already modelled it more permanently within himself' (Werke II, p. 121). The isle of St Brendan and the Paradise of Columbus lay wholly or predominantly in another world beyond *known space*, but not in another world beyond *time as it has developed so far*: Baader added to the old dreams the truly biblical one of a *plus ultra of time*. Baader was of course absolutely tied down to mythology himself, indeed overflowing with it, his earth of light in the centre of things is also always one that has been restored, one that used to be good; but the *Novum Eden* is not absent from the work of the expectant geosopher, as the result of a process. His earth alchemy, apart from being expert in appealing to the original state of things, was expert in 'fermentation', in 'silver gleams' of a future metal, and also in a 'vigorous feeling of freedom', precisely of the sort that was known not to exist in the mythical Paradise. The following statement corresponds to this: 'It is a basic prejudice of human beings to believe that what they call a future world is *a thing created and completed* for man, which exists without him like a ready-built house which man only needs to enter, whereas instead that world *is a building of which he is himself the architect, and which only arises through him*' (Werke VII, p. 18). The earth of the centre is therefore not only to be found at the locations of Athens, Jerusalem, and Mount Zion. Instead, the centre stands in a world which is only just becoming, although in a world laid out and obtainable on the earth. The reference point of importance, the thoroughly non-astronomical one, is thus joined by the most violently utopian one of a bliss that is home. In its secularized form it is called *heaven on earth*, apocalyptically it was called *earth* (with nothing but Jerusalem) *in heaven*. In both hopes the world actually revolves around the earth, even if it revolves around one which is still becoming, around a place of pregnancy and birth of more and different light. Likewise, in numbers and size this Bethlehem is one of the smallest among the towns of Judaea, but in weight of value it surpasses the universe. All the millions of light years are shorter than Goethe's life, and the space they traverse is empty, but the earth is the utopian essence of the universe. The period of human history on it is just as much the full golden period as the space fashioned by the earth is the golden space of the universe, i.e. the one amassed on its substance. Hic Rhodus, hic salta, here is the dome, rise here:– thus this portrays at this end not merely love and commitment to the Utopicum of an earthly paradise, but an awareness of the substance of the earthly arena, an awareness which by no means sees itself devalued by the astronomical, merely astronomical infinity on all sides. Apart from its size the universe is certainly full of meanings and ciphers, full of far more tenable ones than the figures of the zodiac were for example, which were imagined by ancient astronomy. But if these ciphers – those of inorganic nature as a whole – have a meaning, then it refers, qua meaning, just as certainly to the affairs and semantic contents of the inhabited earth. In the silent reticence of the world extra terram this meaning is not expressible at all, it remains frozen renunciation unvoiced within it. A utopian central earth, however, may contain and concentrate it – with a St Mark's Square which now looks even more essential than the entire inflation of merely astronomical infinity; with an Acropolis for which its thoroughly rebuilt space suffices to form within it a pre-appearance of the most humane space.

Geographical line of extension in sobriety;
the fund of the earth, mediated with work

It looks as if almost all distant coasts have been discovered. Few habitable
lands are still unentered, and the Blue Flower* has not been found. Thus
nothing, or almost nothing has survived of the geographical dream in its old
form. Nevertheless, the earth has not been fully learnt nor, in spatio-temporal
terms, fully experienced. It is so only in its given breadth, not in the given
task of its depth direction, its discoverable line of extension. This line runs
through the mediation, through the interaction between man and earth,
through this still absolutely unclosed transaction. It runs through economic
geography, through the political, technological, and cultural kind, yet
precisely through the earth space and earth object itself, it runs through
economics, politics, and technology not just as purely social processes. But
the earth itself also plays a part in the metabolic exchange between man and
nature, in an interaction with an equally powerful and changeable share of
nature. Climate and existing raw materials objectively determined the particular human world that arose; and this human world never lay on the moon,
never purely in the mind. It lay on the earth, which supplied the physical
possibilities for human work and was itself changed by this work for this
very reason, into an agrarian, and finally into an urban and industrial landscape. Thus apart from a few vast deserts, high mountains, primeval forests,
and for the time being also the Antarctic, almost all areas of the earth's
surface came within the radius of human action, were changed by the state
of society and according to the state of society, have a fresh say in it, in short,
they have become earth in a line of extension which is just as varied as it is
unfinished. Most splendidly, Soviet society gave its natural sciences and technology the task of rebuilding nature. Here the business of clearing which
began with the first farmers culminates in a way which was previously
inconceivable; plants, rivers, and the climate find themselves changed, even
the tundra is transformed into cornfields. The Soviet Union is hereby helping
enormously to shape the features of the cultivated land of which the earth is
capable and in which it has been expanding since it was first cultivated. In
inhabited regions, geography without and before man does not exist any more,
but this is precisely why this very geography continues to be historically
comprehensive – as both an arena and a framework. Just as the mechanical

* The unattained Romantic ideal in Novalis' novel 'Heinrich von Ofterdingen'.

world (the world of work transformers to serve human advantage) represents a kind of unnatural physics: so in almost the same way the metabolic interchange between man and earth creates a kind of supernaturalized geography. With the difference that technology far more easily passes into the realm of cunning and overpowering, can be far more contactlessly and abstractly calculated than the authentic *landscape product* of human work. This can of course also look artificial enough, in a technological context, but earth nature collaborates even in the industrial landscape more visibly, and possibly more inhibitively than electrical nature in the dynamo. The earth still remains the arena and framework even for such an extensive rebuilding, and a powerful and visible part of the material content as well. So this is precisely why there is a concrete utopia of the future condition of the earth (compared with ancient geography) in every geography of improvement, a utopia which has its frontier ideal in the dreams of the earthly paradise – an ideal not devalued by fantasy and mythology. This utopian fund lives without mythical wrapping in the Totum (itself always only a latent one) of political-cultural geography, after physical geography has been traversed and is adequately known. There are still lots of children in Gaia, and she changes with them; just as the language of geographical nature is not yet an extinct one, and the face of the earth is not yet a hippocratic one which can only be accepted as the past. With and through the changes made by human beings, the Pleistocene and Holocene epoch, and the Quaternary period of our planet can still be followed by the Quinternary period, with a better attained fund of what the earth, no geological antiquarium, still potentially contains. The earth as a whole, in its latency, is the *unfinished setting of a scene in a play which has by no means been written as yet in our previous history.*

If the changes are bad of course, then the land affected by them merely looks violated. This is particularly apparent in the hideous streets and suburbs which are a legacy of the nineteenth century. They stand out as scabs and sores on the landscape, or rather: the latter is totally destroyed. And health, clean air, light, the casual green of the trees along with it; it is almost odd to find all this still in the open countryside. The capitalist age built the endless streets, the profit-houses, all the spooks so fleetingly conjured up that it is astonishing to find they are still there in the morning. Unless it is as the façade of Hell, fading, shrivelling up, not built on the good earth and belonging to it. If the earth itself is included, as a so-called green belt or in the dispersals of the garden city, then this pastoral looks as if even the trees were fakes. The artificial desert which interrupts the landscape as the urban form of the nineteenth century is stronger than the nature added in a calculated way, which here serves only as a compensation; the emptiness and reification, the abstractness and cadaverousness are stronger. But this is not to say that the opposite: the good, the non-abstract change, can boast of appearing as if it were merely embedded in existing nature; as if it were indigenous, in the so nearly provincial, so easily reactionary sense of the word. As if rebuilding of the planet earth did not remain the utopian watchword, instead of such hesitant indigenousness. We must push off from it instead, we must definitely take to the ships, not just with the ancient energy of the voyages of discovery, but also with the intention towards the geographical line of extension, towards the ultraviolet area of the spectrum. The geographical line of extension thoroughly emerges from artificiality as much as it does from indigenousness; for its goal remains the world mediated with man and inclined towards his goals. An image secularized respectively from the pagan, then Christian notions of the earthly paradise is the *ideal landscape*; but this always appeared as a nature both changed and corrected, and delivered into a friendliness of its own. Thus it always towered into the social, technological and architectural utopias, even when the forces of production were sufficiently developed not to need any dream-fields with a thousandfold fruit. Thus the ideal landscape, not as fields but as earthly garden, surrounded the diverse pleasures and dreams of a life beyond work, from the Arcadia of antiquity to the gentle or illustrious pastoral of the Baroque. And although in many places only subjective fantasy may have had a hand in this kind of super-earth, it remains conspicuous that it was precisely the most meticulous realism, that of Homer, which furnished and was able to furnish the most radiant model of an ideal landscape: in the description of the island of Calypso. From which it follows from this angle too, in contrast to abstractness outside nature and to false indigenousness: in all improvements of a concretely possible kind there is a realism sui generis at work, and this has its source in none other than *geographically objective material, that is objectively utopian, objectively latent*. The fund of object-based possibility which is here called the earth assures that the geographical line of extension can be the road to a wholly new country, although located in the world. The intention towards such an ideal landscape, hence the real geographical utopia, is admittedly a most extreme one, as noted above, yet the consequence of a non-utopia in this area seems no less extreme and dreadful either. For if the line of extension towards the humanizable earth is taken away completely, then every human installation into the world ultimately remains futile. An abstract idealistic isolation of human works on and in the earth, a nihilistic lack of contact then follow inescapably from the absence of the geographically objective line of extension. As high as this line ultimately presumes to aspire to borderline ideals, like the earthly paradise of Columbus, its negation leads just as terribly into total isolation of human goals on earth, in the world, and beyond this it leads into the void. Above all in the second half of the nineteenth century, a boundless centrifugal sense of the universe, without the weightiness of earth in it, predominantly generated a sense of forlornness. The human devaluation called capitalism was thus ideologically strengthened by the quantitative devaluation of the human arena in general, which is simply termed the ocean of the world. This is seen most clearly in Schopenhauer, concerning the alleged paltriness of the little earth: 'In infinite space countless shining spheres, around each of which about a dozen smaller illuminated ones revolve, which, though hot inside, are covered with a cold congealed crust, on which a layer of mould has produced living and discerning beings:– this is the empirical truth, reality, the world' (Werke, Grisebach, II, p. 9). The optimism of Copernican infinity in Giordano Bruno and in Spinoza still had room for man, precisely in his 'eroico furore' in the one case, and in his 'amor dei (sive naturae) intellectualis' in the other; the nihilism of the declining bourgeoisie, however, by making life on earth into a dead end, causes the humane geographical dimension to be completely devalued in the astronomical one, without containing any point of reference of its own. And this therefore remains, through the *mistrust* of the Humanum in the world, the extreme consequence of the *chosen geographical dead end*. In contrast to the *consequence of the chosen line of extension*, which, if it allows a glimpse into distant earthly shores, *intends reception and homeland* there. That there is thus on this earth simultaneously the space for a new one and that not only time but also space contains its utopia within it: *this is what the outlines of a better world suggest as far as a geographical Eldorado-Eden is concerned*. The bodies and houses, electric power stations and St Mark's churches ultimately also belong to earthly matter and its organization; they are embraced by the whole of the earth and penetrate with their own utopia into the geographical one. Above all the architectural spatial utopia is as such also one of the earth; and the wishful landscapes which art reveals, if not through buildings then through the windows of painting or literature, even as wishful landscapes are nevertheless still simply – landscapes. *Eldorado-Eden therefore comprehensively embraces the other outlined utopias*; even the broadly transcendent element, the 'house of the other side', still had a place in the horizon of the earth. Indeed even where the belief prevailed that the earth, in conjunction with the rest of inorganic nature, occupies a place in which it does not belong, this very place remains, even after the rejection and removal of the false ways it was filled: as the spatial possibility of a new heaven and a new earth. The intention towards the earthly paradise thus focussed on a golden space which could still be expected in the outflowing world, at the delta of the world.

WISHFUL LANDSCAPE PORTRAYED   40
IN PAINTING, OPERA, LITERATURE

Painting is surfacing in another place.   *Franz Marc*

The writers whom we call eternally or absolutely good and who inspire us possess a common and highly significant hallmark: they take a certain path and also call upon you to follow them, and you feel, not with your intellect, but with your whole being, that they have a goal...The best among them are realistic and show life as it is, but since every line is permeated with the awareness of the goal, as if with sap, apart from life as it is you also feel life as it has to be, and this captivates you.   *Anton Chekhov*

Beauty is life as in all reality it ought to be, until it has to be.
                                        Chernyshevsky

Videtur poeta sane res ipsas non ut aliae artes, quasi histrio, narrare, sed velut alter deus condere.*   *Julius Caesar Scaliger*

The moved hand

It leads nowhere at all merely to feel in a beautiful way. This remains inside, has no way out of itself, is not communicated. But equally the inner voice is presupposed wherever there is artistic form. A self must be behind the paint that is applied, a hand which applies it. A feeling passes through the moved hand, adapts itself to what is painted. Just as on the other hand creative talent only proves itself to be such through the fact

* Poetry is clearly seen as a special thing not like other arts, such as history, narration, but as if another God created it.

that it is disposed towards forms from the start, and finds nothing at all within itself which does not insist on its fully shaped place. Thus the craft is not added to the creative inner voice as something different, even alien, but is the inner voice that girds and prepares itself. If, on the way between the self that is capable of something and the craft of which it is capable, something gets lost, then it was not worth much. The inner voice, as soon as it has something to say, always speaks outward expression; then they both speak of one another. A picture is therefore also heard, not merely seen, it narrates what we see in it. And first of all in a friendly way, what is colourful as such has a cheerful effect.

Flower and carpet

The hand begins delicately and neatly here, sets out. What the pencil draws must be clear, what the brush fills in, colourful. Light must be able to shine through, what is fine particularly teaches and betrays ability. Painting is therefore best learnt with flower and glass, every good picture has a glimmer of flower painting in it. And, allied to this, it has a carpet in it, this flowerbed full of balanced colours. Only beyond this pure, mastered fineness and through it do things emerge in painted form. They are now reborn and formed out of colour, flower and carpet emerge as things, first of all as still life. In this the tablecloth becomes transparent to itself, as does the plate, the fruit, the meat. Such things can never do enough, through the continuing build-up of colour, to be like linen, to be porcelain, juicy. No silk we have touched is as smooth and shining as that which is skilfully painted, no steel more masculine, more glittering than that which has passed through blue. Likewise, an otherwise often diffuse element, as in the carpet, is held close together by a continuous harmony of colour. Nothing disturbs and is disturbed, everything acts there and then, is allied and affiliated to itself, because born of colour as a whole. The latter is the original dough here, and it reduces that created by it in each case, no matter how different it is in real life, to a common denominator of colour. The nuances of aprons and cups are based on the same underlying white, the lobster and the rose on red. The still life is trained by the flower, becomes a bouquet which presents itself. It goes without saying that it itself, like everything in it, is of small dimensions.

Still life composed of human beings

It may be a feature of nearness in general that it is narrow and gives that
impression. A small surface contracts, makes a pleasantly *comprehensible*
circle. It paints an existence which can easily become musty in real life,
but is strangely warm when presented as a painting. Tame comfort plays
a part here, which is usefully content, but also pleasure in the secure circle
and within it. This is above all the case where the circle is gained by our
own efforts and life within it is not cramped but secured and enclosed,
and thus exhibits peaceful warmth. As in the Dutch interior picture,
everything becomes a parlour here, even the street, a stove is always burning,
even outside in the spring. Vermeer, Metsu, Pieter de Hooch portrayed
such cosy living, a home sweet home still without any mustiness. The
wife reads a letter or confers with the cook, the mother peels apples or
watches over her child in a courtyard. The old lady walks down the street
along a high wall, overlooked by gabled roofs on the other side, nothing
else happens, sunbeams pour through the small silent scene. And in the
actual interior the silence becomes entirely that expressed by cooing doves
in an old enclosed courtyard; it is structured by light falling in at various
angles. 'A mug of beer' (Amsterdam) shows the obliquely lit chamber
in which a woman, with infinite calm, is pouring out her beer; to the
right the view leads through the open door into the living room flooded
with light and through its window-frame out into the open air. The light
falling in at three different angles opens the narrowness and homeliness
without enlarging it; the room is primary in all pictures compared with
the figures, but it encloses them, is only there for its nearness. The objects
of bourgeois comfort calmly reveal themselves, the brass lamp shade on
the wall, the red tiles, the brown armchair. Everywhere there is an orderly
way of life per se, a tidiness of the house and a cheerfulness of mind. Even
the vanishing lines are delimiting, even the view through the windows
does not extend beyond a hundred or two hundred metres in Hooch. A
junk shop of happiness appears, and it has the effect here of a treasure
chamber. Nothing but domestic everyday life is painted in the Dutch genre
picture, but for all its nearness it is also presented in just the same way
as a sailor may see it from a distance when he thinks of home: as the small,
sharp painting which bears homesickness within it. Corresponding to this
on the other hand is the fact that there are very often maps of the world
hanging on the wall in these pictures, with the ocean looking in, which

of course first dispenses all this domestic comfort by virtue of Dutch world trade. Pieter de Hooch also painted fashionable rooms in which ladies dance, dine, and play music with cavaliers. The colour in the arches and pillared fireplaces becomes less warm in these, it is bluish and grey, the red of the costumes is hard. But even in the court pictures there is still Lilliput, an elfin manner which protects and is itself protected. Illness, wildness, loudness, disruptiveness can neither be seen in the charming format nor does it seem as if care itself could ever visit it. Rooms and windows looking out on to the street are painted as if there were no disruption in the world. The grandfather clock strikes nothing but the evening hour, nothing is more than man can cope with, nothing is in a hurry.

Embarkation for Cythera

So placid is this nearness, but it is a feature of distance to be restlessly cloaked. To bind the searching glance to itself, to attract people precisely in so far as it is *veiled*. The feeling is then erotic longing, when painted this longing is departure, romantic journey; thus every portrayal of erotic distance already expresses seduction. A fundamental picture of this kind is Watteau's 'Embarquement pour Cythère'; even its title is clearly utopian. Young men and ladies are waiting for the barque which will bring them to the island of love. The way of passing the time in those days was the reason why Watteau's picture, that of an excellent but not exactly first-rate painter, is able to give such a sensually striking delineation of wishful landscape. Even through precious-erotic diminution the Rococo period gives instead a concentrating, at least isolating impression. Watteau painted his picture three times; the first version is based on a mere stage impression, the pastoral play 'Trois Cousines' (which lingered in the memory right down to Offenbach's 'La Périchole'). The arrangement of the figures is still wooden in the first version, the feeling still conventional, the time of day still uncertain, the air not yet charged with expectation. On the face of it, the theme of the second and third version also seems conventional, in other words it stems from the era of the secrets of the deer-garden and boudoir, one treated and coined thousands of times. In this respect its basis is merely the lecherousness of the court life of those days and an interchangeable entertainment which was often more like eroticized boredom. But how extraordinarily the picture has put things right in the meantime, how clearly an archetype of the romantic journey

appears in the fashionable subject. Particularly in the second (Paris) version
there is dream and group formation in prospect: an enchanting landscape
surrounds the couples, the contours of the park have already become blurred,
the love-barque waits on the silver water, distant mountains stand in the
twilight, invisibly but directly the night of the island influences the movement and fore-pleasure of the picture. The third (Berlin) version is less
perfect, because the bijou element in it is too pre-arranged and familiar. It
not only has the foreground decorated more richly, but above all the love-
ship, with the motif of cherubs who hover about the sail. The barque is
more visibly ready, the ship's mast with the sail of amorettos brings a
clearer line into the background which is becoming blurred. The direct juxtaposition of rosy red and sky-blue around the sail is emphatic sweetness, acts
as a flag of the promise sent across by the island of love. But even here
embarkation for Cythera is merely hinted at or no more than the embarkation
itself, with merely anticipated happiness. This distinguishes Watteau's
picture from all other portrayals of sensuality, especially from those where
Cythera appears as already attained. A large picture of this kind extensively
influenced Watteau in form and colour: the 'Garden of Love' by Rubens (in
Madrid). But precisely this picture by the so much more powerful painter
shows repose, almost habit of happiness; whereas Cythera never was or has
gone. Voluptuous women are grouped in Rubens in golden brown before
massive grotto architecture, flanked by the red and black of two standing
couples; with cherubs at intervals overhead, they strongly fill the canvas. Just
as the sultry air is charged and forms the flesh of cherubs, just as even the
stone of the portal is eroticized, like the sculpture on the fountain which
spurts water from its breasts: so there is pleasure as an emblem here, coitus
as timeless mastery. The whole garden is transformed into it, in a simply
existing and hence monumental way; pillars by the portal are women's
thighs, Cupid reaps. But embarkation for Cythera is only suggested where
fore-pleasure is portrayed, with very different gardens from those of the
firmly existing land. And this is exactly why such pictures need a state of
suspense, a sail, a cloudy state, a cloaked expectation and its light. When the
curtain parts, behind it there is not so much the garden of love, with present
colours, a majestic yes, as wishful landscape ante rem, woman as expectant
landscape itself. Giorgione's 'Sleeping Venus', Goya's 'Naked Maya' preserve
the light around Cythera. In Goya it radiates undiminished from the white
cushions, the sensually cool flesh-tint, the lines of love: this nude also lies on
an island. Precisely so-called impure thoughts are purely those of these
pictures themselves, are the pleasurable utopian ground where their figures

lead, in which they lie. But Cythera makes it seem as if there were nothing in the world apart from the shining and the outline of woman.

Perspective and large horizon in van Eyck, Leonardo, Rembrandt

That distance which leaves the view open is not hiding anything, but is representationally richer. Even where the painted prospect is hazy, nothing is circumscribed but a measure is given precisely for *expanse*. As soon as the this world began to become infinite instead of the next world, the wishful landscape of open distance appeared in the picture. It gazes blue-green through windows and arches, through opened grottos; the expansive view from the mountain begins. What was previously only fit for the cathedral: to be depth of the third dimension, now becomes pictorial space: the world as nave. Depth can now also be brought into the picture plane, by the latter appearing as a section through the cone of vision; thus it is as if the observer is looking through a window, the picture plane itself is like an open window. The point where the perspective lines meet lies at infinity; the lines running in the middle part continue even beyond the horizon, something new surrounds the figures: a centrifugal space. This expanse, wishful expanse thus becomes clear even as early as the end of the Middle Ages: in the Paris Madonna of *Jan van Eyck*. The perspective serves a first veduta, framed by architecture: the landscape itself appears as a window space of the house. And for the first time the rule of the vanishing point is consciously observed in van Eyck's picture, the translation of objects seen in depth on to a flat surface begins. Between the Madonna and the figure of her donator* the prospect extends through three arches of a splendidly decorated hall, and thus a distant land crammed with treasures opens up, interrupted and enclosed by pillars. In masterly detail, with all the spatial-utopian emotions engaged of which the loosening of an as it were horizontal abyss is capable. A city becomes visible, gables and towers, a cathedral, a broad square with steps, a crowded bridge, a river furrowed by tiny boats, in the middle of which, on an island which is smaller than a child's fingernail, rises a palace surrounded by trees with numerous little bell-towers. Beyond all this a world of green hills runs towards the horizon, on which snowy mountains dimly glow, and last of all there lies the non-frontier of a sky fading away

---

* The figure of the donator is Chancellor Rolin. The Louvre picture is known as 'The Madonna of Chancellor Rolin' in English. It was painted by van Eyck around 1425.

in the clouds. It is a perfect dreamland, although in the line of extension of multi-layered reality. This is not Bruges or Maastricht or Lyon, or whatever other cityscapes of the time people have come up with; on the contrary, the perspective displays a Gothic ideal city without walls, in the apse of infinity. Soon there was also room for the veduta of *nature*, in Piero della Francesca, with the new value of the horizon in the Renaissance; but Leonardo da Vinci provided the full, open original for the dream value of perspective. Distance with mysterious colour creates in *Leonardo* a space in which sculpture ends, only light is divided, into almost unknown objects. The 'Virgin of the Rocks' displays cavernous darkness, Gothically jagged edges and ridges, but the grotto breaks up, and the eye wanders without transition into a secluded river valley. The figures in his 'St Anne, The Virgin and the Infant Christ with a Lamb' are strictly arranged into a pyramid, but the landscape behind them turns into a wildly broken mountain massif, it is half haze, half solid, an indeterminable other world of clearly laid-out objects. This distant character completely penetrates the portrait of the Mona Lisa herself; through the dream of the background, corporeality is admittedly gained for the figure in the foreground, yet at the same time also lost again. For Mona Lisa herself repeats the form of the landscape in the rippling of her gown, the dream-heaviness of the background in her eyelids, the congealed, uncanny, paradoxically opaque ether in her smile. *The landscape is here as important as the figure*, is a related, if not the same hieroglyph. In the spirit of Leonardo's philosophically expressed conception of the world: 'Every part has a tendency to be united with its whole again in order to escape imperfection. And it is necessary to know that this very wish is precisely the quintessence, companion of nature, and man is the model of the whole world'. The distant landscape is likewise called Mona Lisa and is her – a fantastically jagged mountain labyrinth in the softest light, with lakes, pale fields, and rivers between it. Mona Lisa gazes from there, and she also gazes towards this distance, towards its outspread or entire mystery, in a greenish-blue, smoky light.

But where everything is smoky from the start, how is it possible to look into the distance? This is achieved by the dark ground, out of which the picture is painted, itself defamiliarizing things. And by the light in which they stand itself coming, and being reflected, as if from sheer background. Thus *Rembrandt*, the most powerful painter of distant gleam which is mirrored in nearness, even leaves Saskia half in darkness, and the man with the golden helmet wears its metal as light only gathering, indeed leading down into the dark. The brilliant patches in Rembrandt are, purely in terms of painting technique, never applied in a shiny and as it were flat way, they are a relief to whose grainy elevations the bright colour simply adheres, while the depressions, the given substance of nearness as it were, remain filled with the darkness of the priming coat or with brown varnish. From the given element of night on the one hand, from the merely reflecting element of light on the other, stems the true rarity and preciousness of this light, its captivating brilliant gleam superimposed on night. Corresponding to this was the complicated technique of dark-grounding and over-painting which Rembrandt followed throughout his entire work; its first triumph, which already contains all this, is significantly in a picture of the Passion, in the Munich Entombment of Christ. People and even things stand in solitude in the expanse of dark space, the colours come solely from a mysterious reflection of inner light in the world and behind the world, from a paradox of final light. Thus it stems neither from the sun nor from an artificial source of light, nor is the existing world, together with any supernatural world which is believed to exist, at all capable of dispensing this not earthly, not unearthly light. The previous distance, the cosmically open perspective is obliterated by dark space, it creates a ring-shaped assembly of the figures, itself almost undifferentiated. Only in secular pictures of groups and landscapes, like the Night Watch and the River Landscape with Ruins in Cassel, is the ground criss-crossed with lances, a castle, and clouds, and scaffolding with straight lines stretches out in the Night Watch. Whereas the portraits and the pictures with a Christian subject essentially show the undifferentiated darkness outside, the acosmic loneliness inside, indeed the late Rembrandt, who no longer painted landscapes, frames his work completely with the powerfully concealing, sombrely sheltered dark tone which here means universe and infinity. Nevertheless, even the darkness of this background is streaked with golden brown, the group of figures stands in a sfumato perspective of both black and gold, the light works into the darkness, chromatizes even here, penetrates from a strangely existing Nowhere. Thus Rembrandt's paradoxical light is not to be found anywhere in the world, but nor has it emanated, despite its continuous reflection, from any ancient metaphysics of heavenly light: it is *perspective light of hope*, deeply led down into nearness and desolation, answered. The open cosmic perspective is obliterated by dark space, but the light which both contrasts with it and mysteriously breaks through from loneliness and blackness paints the truth of hope or of the brilliance which is not there at all, in the dark-groundings of the existing world. This volatile in-shining, only mediated by reflections,

constitutes the exotic nature of Rembrandt's illumination, the echo of
a fairytale distance in which the objects receptive to it or belonging to
it are pictured very near. This alone is the source of the glimmering element,
but also the love of the flashing in silk, pearls, jewels, and the golden
helmet. This alone is the source of the necessary Arabianization in the
pictures of Saskia and of Jews: the distance of light speaks most audibly
through the fairyland of the Orient; a transcendental Baghdad glows in
the night. And this alone is ultimately the source, in the depths, of light
not as an element of the world nor of the supernatural world but as a
mystical expression of Being of the figures accompanying it. This is most
quietly the case in the Munich picture of the Resurrection, with Christ
right down at the bottom edge, palely shining, and also escaped from and
superior to the mythological heavenly light which breaks down behind
the descending angel: an Ex oriente lux which itself is only beginning
to rise and is reflected from this corpse in extreme remoteness. All
Rembrandt's pictures, even the secular ones, are composed from out of
the background, and his colours – of night, incense, myrrh, gold – paint
the perspective: hollow space with sparks.

Still life, Cythera and broad perspective in literature: Heinse, Roman de la Rose, Jean Paul

A picture tells us of what we see in it as simultaneity. And a poem perceives
and can let us see what it tells in its succession. Above all if it allows
itself to be guided by a desired type of picture, by the still life, but then
by departure, by the big wide world. The *literary* species of *still life*, which
is of course now seen totally nostalgically, is the *idyll*. Even the tiniest
thing is honoured in it and becomes good, for where there is no affluence
all things must serve for the best. As in the work of Andersen: tongs,
kettle, and candle are alive, the room itself is a little fairytale, all the gadgets
live in it. The idyll runs a modest kitchen, cultivates carefree conversa-
tions, contains pleasant fortunes throughout. Of course, like the painted
still life of human beings, it can also bring with it that tame comfort which,
extremely useful for our masters, cuts its coat according to its cloth. Also
it is no accident that the idyllic comes from the old pastoral and bucolic
poem, in which a sated stratum glossed over the restricted life led by those
who had not chosen it for themselves. A life which even with the much-
vaunted sour milk and bread they did not lead that satiated, that neatly

and beribboned by any means. And yet the later, bourgeois idyll also gave room for thoroughly good things which only found themselves so desirable in this Biedermeier-like circle. A homely element in fact, as if one had returned there from far away, a domestic peace, a country garden, 'with gently breathing coolness'. The humming of the bees surrounds the withdrawn life in the day, the humming of the tea-kettle at night; this is so in Voss's 'Luise', and in moderation, despite the bad luck appropriate here, in Goldsmith's 'Vicar of Wakefield'. Distant lands occur here only as tea, the storms outside thunder in the chimney and specially contribute to the At-Home, the wicked are reduced to eccentrics and thus add the spice to comfort. But in contrast to the idyll in the space beyond its confinement the *literary* species of erotic *exodus*, of *Cythera* appears sweeping, sweeping away. The south presented itself above all for this, the sound of the lute, wine, friends and their girls, the purple night, columns lit by torchlight. In the eighteenth century the south was perceived against this background not by Winckelmann and his followers, but rather by Wieland and his successors; even Romanticism, in the work of E. T. A. Hoffmann, did not change much in this. Italy is here above all the melodious and erotic land, the longed-for land of free and liberated love, not of Apollonian marble. As in a document of the late Sturm und Drang, which is still very strangely indebted to the Rococo period, in *Heinse's* 'Ardinghello and the Fortunate Isles', 1787, an archaeologically formed and also half pornographically utopian formation. Attempted or inflamed in it is a wishful dream of the Ver sacrum, as follows: 'It went deeper and deeper into life, and the feast became more sacred, eyes glistened with tears of joy...The greatest bacchanalian storm roared through the hall, like thundering cataracts of Senegal and the Rhine, where one no longer knows anything about oneself and grandly and omnipotently returns into eternal glory...Everlasting spring, beauty and fertility of sea and land and health of water and air.' Not the first lascivious antiquity, but probably the first Dionysian one is described in this Cythera novel; so that Wieland himself, in whose work the Graces were never without a satyr but nor was the latter ever without the Graces, rejected Heinse's novel as priapism of the soul. In the end Ardinghello founds an ideal state of lust on the islands Paros and Naxos, in which nothing but this lust remains, nothing but this goddess penetrates into the various grottos and temples. Arcadia, since Theocritus the ancient bucolically longed-for essence of escape, is thus turned wholly without happiness in confinement into the erotic magic islands on which the hot nights surrounded sheer bucolic existence. That is why

Heinse's Cythera could also live off so much earlier pastoral poems, which had blossomed again anyway in Italy, in the Renaissance, and above all off Tasso's 'Aminta', the first and at the same time most perfect example, with fauns, nymphs and satyrs, with an enchanted grove and the shot from Cupid's bow, with a cool temple of Diana and the choral song of the shepherds about the Golden Age, as that of free love. In the ancient pastoral and bucolic poetry, however sentimental it was, at least in that of the Renaissance, this was also the durable, enduring wishful essence: the Golden Age with classical features, which contain oriental ones as well. In such a Renaissance the original of the fictional Cythera is located, just as the Renaissance drew its magic gardens in turn from Saracen, Saracen-Gothic recollections, as those in which the bucolic for its part borders on the tropical, on the intemperate zone. The unveiled distance of Cythera contains such intemperate nature in the most intimate form: as love, and only in the garden of love blossoms, in this wishful landscape of the Orient, that to which almost every bucolicon has tended since the crusades and from which it returns adorned. Thus it is no accident that even that *source-book of Cythera*, to whose space the Ardinghello-like element may also belong, developed in the context of Saracen love-culture and its chivalric legacy: namely the Gothic *Roman de la Rose*. For this source-book, more precious than all Rococo and full of paradoxically scholastic naturalism, only fully reveals itself as the history of the manifestation of the land of love. Moreover this was joined by allegory, in its medieval vividness: concepts become persons, and therefore in their combination a drama; that which appears frosty today was at the time full of resonant cross-references through the sensory world of multiplicity, full of life. The embarkation for Cythera was also extended now, had its dangers and problems, and thus became the ars amandi, with quodlibets from all the then existing sciences. The Roman de la Rose, begun by Guillaume de Lorris, completed by Jean de Meung, from the late thirteenth century, sings the praises of this path to pleasurable nature in over twenty thousand lines. The poet himself comes to the garden of love, Lady Idleness opens the gate for him, his heart is wounded by Amor, Bel-Accueil invites him to the roses. But now an intrigue develops, a wall is erected around the roses, Danger and his companions guard the gates, with a lament by the lover Guillaume de Lorris closes his wistful book. But now, in the sequel, Genius, the 'chaplain of nature', advises an advance with a whole army of love; this call of his mixes Jupiter and God the Father, Venus and the Holy Virgin, Jesus mysticism and the most cheerful pornographic materialism. Nature prescribes the laws of human behaviour, but this is something which does not lie founded outside our self in the other world and in church norms, but in man and this world of his. Genius preaches against virginity and sodomy, threatens with hell all those who do not heed the dictates of nature and of love, promises the faithful life without end in an efficient Mohammedan Zion, irradiated by Jesus and the loveliest women. Encouraged by the words of Genius and protected by Venus, the platoon of love invades the garden, on towards the hidden virgin, who 'is more perfect than the statue of Pygmalion'; Jealousy, Shame, Fear and other allegories of emotion put countless obstacles in the way, but Courteousness, Frankness, Kindness, and above all Bel-Accueil again (the son of Courtoisie) liberate the rose of love from its fortress, and entrust it to the lover. 'Ci est le roman de la Rose/où l'art d'amors est tote enclose';* the vaginal allegory of the rose forms the ground of utopian pleasure in the Gothic Cythera. Digressions on the duty of man to propagate himself are scattered throughout, together with rich satire, astronomy, nominalist philosophy of nature, geographical fairytales, theories about money and the circulation of money, about classical heroes, about the origin of subservience, about communist utopias. 'Chascune por chascun commune/Et chascun commun por chascune':† the social unrest of the fourteenth century casts its light ahead of it. Especially in that part of the poem which Jean de Meung already wrote for the rising bourgeoisie, with ruthless questioning, and turning to nature. A Rousseau of the Middle Ages speaks out in the midst of the feudal ars amandi, advocates the original state of things through the metaphors of free love. So far did Cythera extend in a work of literature, so frivolously and subversively, so learnedly and with such cryptic elegance – Cupid at the end of the world.

There is distance everywhere here, but a distance still tenderly veiled for us. When it appears for itself, it becomes very great foreignness, now dawning in itself. Its form is then *fictional perspective*, in the south, and all the more so in the north. The oceanic feeling is part of it, as one of boundless expanse and as a Yes within it flowing through everything. When mists fall, the expanse appears as an Ossianic landscape, as that which in its intensified form has been called the utopia of Thule. And yet which is again by no means merely northern, as noted above, but strongly fragrant, full of veils, half-open doors, oriental smoke. *Jean Paul*, outside his idyll of permanent, now subterranean now far-reaching wishful perspectives and changing panoramas, though he sees even Italy in a smoky light, even the azure sky and especially

---

* 'This is the romance of the Rose/where the art of love is all enclosed.'
† 'Every woman in common for every man/And every man in common for every woman.'

the curiosities, unfamiliarities, and sublimities of the world which are
enormously allegorized by him, displays in almost all his landscapes the
double gleam of night and east (here again mediated by the Bible). His
distance is the most unrestricted of all those that are familiar, even when it
goes into the *abyss*, whispers on in it, in endless beginnings: 'A tower
full of blind gates and blind windows stood in the middle, and the lonely
clock in it spoke to itself and sought, with its iron rod carried to and fro,
to split apart the wave of time which ran together again and again – it struck
a quarter to twelve, and deep in the forest an echo murmured as if in
sleep...'. Then the description of an object which does not murmur of
Hades but really roars it out, of the *landscape of Vesuvius*: 'The morning was
breaking, and in the midst of its dark winter we set out on the journey to
the fiery gorge and smoky gate. As if in a steaming city that has been burnt
down, I passed close to caves upon caves, close to mountains upon mountains
and on the trembling ground towards an eternally working gunpowder
factory with its magazine. Finally I found the throat of this land of fire, a
large glowing valley of steam, again with a mountain – a landscape of craters,
a workshop of the Day of Judgement – full of shattered fragments of the
world, of frozen, burst rivers of hell – an enormous mountain of the debris
of time – but inexhaustible, immortal as an evil spirit, and giving birth to
twelve months of thunder for itself beneath the cold pure sky. All of a
sudden the broad steam rises more darkly red, the thunderclaps merge more
wildly, the heavy cloud of hell smokes more fiercely – suddenly morning air
blows in and drags the blazing curtain down the mountain.' Night horrors,
ruins, Tartarus are the wishful lands of negative infinity, as Lethe of estrange-
ment; but the deeper Pluto is, the higher Phoebus Apollo is too, the sun of
the infinite Fingal's Cave of the world. In Jean Paul's 'Titan' the hero
has such a distant view into *Apollo's day*: 'The Alps stood linked together
like fraternal giants of the prehistoric world far in the past and held out
high to the sun the glittering shields of the icebergs – the giants wore
blue belts of the forests – and at their feet lay hills and vineyards – and
between the vaults of vines the morning winds played with cascades as
with watery taffeta ribbons – and on the ribbons the overcrowded surface
of the lake hung down from the mountains, and it was bordered by a
foliage of chestnut woods...Albano turned round slowly in a circle and
looked up into the air, down into the depths, into the sun, into the
blossoms; and on all the heights alarm-fires of powerful nature were
burning, and their reflection in all the depths – a creative earthquake beat
like a heart beneath the earth and drove forth mountains and oceans' (Titan,

1st Cycle). The Italy in 'Titan' was for Jean Paul not a visual idea or even a confirmed present as for Goethe, and even for Heinse; it remained in distant magic, beyond it lay continuingly significant successfulness – the intransitory is only a metaphor.* And in Germany, love, moon, and spring give the hero of 'Titan' an always exaggerated look, i.e. driven into premonition and hope, as when the gardens of a prince exalt to a *terra australis*: 'But look down, fiery man, with your fresh heart full of youth, on to the marvellous, immense magic Lilar! A dawning second world, as soft tones paint it to us, an open morning dream stretches out before you with high triumphal gates, with whispering mazes, with fortunate isles – the bright snow of the sunken moon lies solely on the groves and triumphal arches and on the silver dust of the spring-waters, and the night welling from all waters and valleys floats above the Elysian fields of the celestial realm of shadows, in which the unknown figures appear to earthly memory like local Otaheiti shores, pastoral lands, Daphnean groves and islands of poplars' (Titan, 23rd Cycle). This form of distant landscape obeys human beings and reflects them in an enthusiasm of the strangest of all Being-beside-oneself, namely one composed of identity; a utopian reception occurs, through the ciphers of great nature. The sphinx of strangeness is cleared up, becomes tolerable and sublime, in mythical but manlike images. Morning and evening red become the colour of a perspective which seeks to extend far beyond the circular line of the horizon: 'Nocturnal voices promise to guess the answer to the vast riddle of the world, and in the far distance mountain peaks are uncovered by flying mists on which man can look far into the longed-for other world.' This is a rimless cosmos, and thus it is assigned both to chaos and to an infinity filled over and over again, and which is endless precisely because of this fullness.

*The wishful landscape of perspective in aesthetics;
status of the matter of art according to its dimension
of depth and hope*

The word points differently from the start when it aims very far. It is taut, has a premonition which has nowhere yet become solid and enterable. Literary expression has been running along perspective lines for four hundred years, and it is wrong to understand this phenomenon, *which has difficulty in limiting itself*, merely as romantic. It is even more wrong to want to

* Cf. Goethe's 'Faust', Part II, 12104-5. 'Everything transitory/Is only a metaphor.'

eliminate this wishful movement, and that which is and remains tendentious, from art. In a classical and later very epigonic fashion; so that the will in art goes to bed and this art 'has everywhere reached its goal'. Whereby art would therefore contain no authentic wishful landscapes and would also not have to be classified respectively according to these, its most vehement Objects. The essential feature of the bourgeois-classical aesthetics which has arisen in this way is not hope (and will aroused by it), but contemplation (and enjoyment satisfying through it). The beautiful here demolishes the subject-matter in an illusionary way through the form, and moreover through the form which is indifferent to the subject-matter, even to a tendency of the matter. The pure aesthetics of contemplation begins in Kant with the concept of the 'disinterested pleasure in the mere mental image of the Object' (no matter whether the latter materially exists or not). It becomes metaphysical in Schopenhauer when disinterested pleasure blossoms as an incipient release of man from the will to life. Being then remains terrible of course, but seeing is blissful, especially in the 'pure world-eye of art'. In Schopenhauer, this art immediately opens up bliss in appearance, which is precisely why 'art has everywhere reached its goal' here. Thus classical aesthetics (and Schopenhauer's 'pure world-eye' definitely belongs to it, even in the – itself satisfied – reception of music) restricts relations with the beautiful to pure contemplation and the beautiful itself to its purified forms. It restricts the Object of the beautiful to a region which is wholly purged of the interests of present and of future existence. Art is always a sedative here, not an appeal, not even a comforting song; for this too presupposes the restlessness of the will. The world is always justified as an aesthetic phenomenon here, and evenly so, at the level of idealistic and therefore so beautifully rounded perfection of form. The damage of mere desire for contemplation is so extensive that even the 'garland of the beautiful' in Hegel's Aesthetics, however much it is a content-laden, historically woven and varied one contrary to formalism, hangs in the ether of contemplative appeasement. Indeed, a certain kind of formalism and therefore abstract appearance (with uninterrupted, and thus chiefly antiquarian unity of thinking) is a danger wherever even the aesthetically grasped reality, together with its riches, is definitively interpreted with a few categories which almost always remain the same, reduced to a defused schema. Such a conceptual tapestry of mere uniform contemplation, applied to everything, is a danger even for much attempted Marxist aesthetics, even where this thinks of itself as quite realistic, on the basis of an always enclosed semi-concept of reality. Even in Lukács an abstract appearance of idealistic rounding still occasionally operates, a fully-constructedness which is, however, alien precisely to dialectical materialism. As the doctrine of an unfinished world and the real, i.e. *processively open* wealth of reality precisely in view of its totality. Which is therefore why art which is material in terms of content *together with its theory* certainly cannot avoid being an art which is non-wrapped, a perspective art, one of real instead of merely alleged process. And therefore why art which is material in terms of content together with its theory certainly cannot avoid being an unclosed one, but a *portrayal of the tendency and latency of its Objects occurring* in the manner of the *pre-appearance driven to an end* (cf. Vol. 1, p. 210ff.). Because of this pre-appearance art is also definitely not a whole, but everywhere only a perspective on to it, a perspective worked out in the portrayed Objects themselves on to the immanent perfection of these Objects. Hence Lessing's statement by the painter in 'Emilia Galotti', a utopian-entelechetic statement: 'Art must paint as plastic nature – if there is one – conceived the picture: without the waste which the reluctant matter inevitably makes, without the ruin with which time fights against it.' Art is fundamentally defined as real pre-appearance, as an immanent-perfect one – in contrast to religious material. This pre-appearance becomes attainable precisely through the fact that art drives its subject-matter to an end, in plots, situations and characters, and brings it to a stated resolution in suffering, happiness and meaning. The statement thus attained is admittedly less than the subject so to speak on one point, namely from the angle of its immediate tangibility, but it is at the same time always more than this subject, namely from the angle of its immanent executability, of its concentrated-intrinsic execution. This kind of thing is precisely the opposite of an idealistic correction, though also the opposite of a mere reproduction, one approaching after a fashion the so-called fullness of perfection of the real; just as if the world, which it is a question of changing in all other cultural functions, were an unattainable masterpiece for art alone. Instead it is only the predisposition to this, the objective-real possibility for this, such that a strikingly painted forest, a strikingly dramatized historical action certainly surpass their subject in substantiality, and indeed are only striking as works of art by being able and having to surpass the subject in attainable pre-appearance. Pre-appearance itself is this attainable element by virtue of the fact that the job of driving to an end occurs in the dialectically so ramified and open space, in which every Object can be aesthetically portrayed. Aesthetically, i.e. in a more immanently successful, more materially genuine, more essential way than in the immediately natural or also immediately historical occurrence of this Object. Thus the watchword of the aesthetically attempted pre-appearance runs: how could the world be perfected without this world, as in Christian-religious pre-appearance, being exploded and apocalyptically disappearing. So art drives world-figures, world-landscapes, without them being destroyed, to their entelechetic limit: only the aesthetic illusion detaches itself from life, whereas the aesthetic pre-appearance is precisely one because it stands itself in the horizon of the real. But this means contents, meant in a utopian-real way, not those of an illusionistic abstract appearance in which perfected game-playing is consumed. This classifies, as goes without saying, the pre-appearance according to the measure and status of its utopian significant subjects, and not least it creates, instead of the artistic enjoyment which penetrates nothing, a *relation to cognition*, in the highest form to the *matter of comprehended hope*. Indeed, this relation is so conspicuous and inevitable that finally even classical aesthetics could not avoid it and began to express it anyway in objective-idealistic terms. As when Schiller, in the Kallias letters, defines 'beauty as freedom in appearance'. This kind of thing brings an Objective sense into abstract appearance, even if freedom within it could only be the same as that which had elapsed into game. And in Kant, if not the beautiful then definitely the sublime goes beyond the formalism in which the aesthetic, as a mere As If of contemplation, is usually held. Even the sublime remains this As If of course, without a desire for its existence allegedly arising, without the aesthetic in general being conceived as possible definiteness of Being. Nevertheless, the 'Critique of Judgement' says not so completely without desire and interest: 'The sublime is that which even just to be able to conceive it proves a capacity of the mind which surpasses every yardstick of the senses', and, concerning the object: 'The sublime is therefore nature in that one of its manifestations whose contemplation brings with it the idea of its infinity' (Werke, Hartenstein, V, p. 258, 262). And infinity is here none other than that which brings with it the premonition of our future freedom; whereby in fact the sublimities are assigned after all to the desiring capacity again, and thus break through the formalism of pure abstract appearance. What *the old aesthetics* called *sublimity* is in fact particularly suited to breaking through disinterested pleasure. If anything was capable of making the classical-harmonizing concept of beauty anxious and thoughtful about itself, it was the category of sublimity on which the beautiful directly borders for the Greeks as well, and especially in the great art determined by religion. For an undeniable element of the sublime is terror, which dialectically switches into elevation; and this terror assigned the will to itself on the subject side just as matter-of-factly as it did the material depth on the object side. Thus Goethe can say that shuddering is the best part of mankind; thus there is in sublimity both an objectivity which inspires this drama and in fact the same objectivity which inspires the highest confidence, namely the premonition of our future freedom, our freedom destined for no trifles nor comprised of them. All this therefore breaks through even in classical aesthetics, as soon as it touches on the category of sublimity or, against the grain, is touched upon by it, the disinterested aspect and the surface of pleasure. In fact even at the level of a much more urbane consternation than that in which shuddering is the best part of mankind the abstract appearance became untenable; there was always an interference of the subject. Thus Goethe himself pointedly distinguished among the Objects which produce a poetic effect none of closed abstract appearance, but those which are representative or symbolic, in so far as they converge on a *material depth common to them*, just as the latter, with its unity and universality, signifies itself in the poetic Objects, and lays claim to itself. Here the most alien element to interest-free harmonism is clearly postulated: the *Objective perspective in the significative direction of the object itself*. It is demanded even where sublimity does not first interrupt the formal tapestry of indifferently produced pleasure, where emotion does not first reach into the depths to feel the vastness. Where the nearer tendency-interweavings, latency-substances of an age are portrayed through and in its people, situations, and themes in a perspective-entelechetic way. Precisely because Goethe totally objectively demands: 'In art and science as well as in deeds and actions everything depends on the objects being purely conceived and treated in accordance with their nature', precisely because of this genuine insistence on reality, namely on an entelechetically full one, we find the following further remark in the author of Faust, concerning more than the already manifest fullness of the real: 'Probability is the condition of art, but within the realm of probability the highest ideal must be supplied which does not otherwise appear' (Essay on the relief of Phigalia). And the background of perspective, the *gold ground of art* is and remains – in accordance with the category of pre-appearance – a real-possible wishful landscape; this lies, however different its qualities and hierarchies, in the windows of art. It extends to that still immanent art which is lit by a world which is not yet there and stands in pre-appearance as a Faust-heaven, i.e. as an attained identity of the Object with the content of human buoyancy. But even within the broad span of this series, realism in art is no descriptive or explanatory stock-taking, but it holds up, in an activating way, a mirror of immanent anticipation, it is tendential-utopian realism.

All this prevents the beautiful from being calmly received and enjoyed.
Wanting is already presupposed in the reception, so that the latter can
be one concerning man. Entertaining people and feeding a fire, both can
and must be related. The moved will could be removed least of all from
shaping itself, from the production of the beautiful. Thus even from the
standpoint of the pathos of creation, that inscribed in the bourgeois world
from the beginning, the differently bourgeois, i.e. the formal pleasure of
contemplation was frustrated. Art appeared from this angle particularly
as active reworking, one which definitely expanded and essentially increased
the world. Thus, as we have seen, the French revolutionary architect Ledoux
even called the builder a rival of God. And long before that the humanist
Scaliger took the word poetry in the both literal and Promethean sense
of ποιεῖν: the poet is 'factor', indeed 'alter deus'. So that Scaliger himself
defined the poet as someone who does not retell what already exists like
an actor, but creates and founds like another God: 'Videtur poeta sane
res ipsas non ut aliae artes, quasi histrio, narrare, sed velut alter deus
condere.' This Prometheus metaphor of the artist ran from 1561 on, the
Faust period in which Scaliger's poetics appeared, through Bacon and
Shaftesbury, to Klopstock, to the Sturm und Drang, to Herder and the
young Goethe: a classification based on will throughout; a classification
based on genius, in which the courage for the creator spiritus appears,
but no sedative of a pure, receptive-contemplative world-eye, as in the
later classical definition. Thus 'freedom in appearance', even from the
production side, does not become illusion but object-based essentiation of
what is portrayed in the sense of deep human closeness, to which art in
its way leads and brings the world. In its way: in the stated way of aesthetic
pre-appearance, whereby essential material which has not yet emerged but
is treated without any illusion as having emerged and existing is carried
such an important step towards being born and existing. So even from
this standpoint no formalism exists for which its autarkical perfection of
form is the sole perfection. The landscape of hope, even in the terrifying
vision, is rather the aesthetic omega: Hegel called this, in objective-
idealistic fashion, infinity in the finite, here it is called, in utopian-realistic
fashion, human identity in the other, in the driving alteritas. This is the
same as the *goal-definition* by virtue of the symbol, in contrast to the allegory
which as identity relation in the other, expressed by what is other, is a
path-definition. Art in its path *is thus just as thoroughly allegorical* as, with
regard to the goal governing the path (with regard to unity and universality,
which is ultimately only one in so far as it is humane), it *remains indebted*

to the symbolic. And, as art, it both immanently reflects if necessary the distance from what is right and, with other Objects immanently driven to an end, in a pre-appearance that has become positively possible, risks a Paradiso. Only since Marx, for the attainable part, this is no longer a risk which absolutely must remain in pre-appearance. For the attainable part, this means, together with the building site whose activity belongs to the beautiful which is not merely contemplated.

Painters of the residual Sunday, Seurat, Cézanne, Gauguin; Giotto's land of legend

Back now to pictures again, and first to those which simply travel into a better world. Namely into an outdoors as escape from daily toil, in Sunday pleasure. Thus *Teniers* placed his poor dice-players and card-players beneath the linden tree, broad-mouthed, with their happiness in a beer mug. *Pieter Brueghel* painted his Land of Cockaigne exactly as the poor folk always dreamed it to be. As an eternal Sunday, which is one because there is no sign of any treadmill, and nothing beyond what can be drunk, eaten boiled or roasted is to be found. A peasant, a knight, and a scholar in the foreground, the first two full and asleep, the scholar still with open mouth and eyes, expecting a roast pigeon or the piglet which stands at the back and already carries the carving knife with it. What a long way from here, what a leap in manners, attitude and spirit from these pictures of louts to another wishful scene of epicurean happiness: to *Manet's* 'Déjeuner sur l'herbe'. And yet what is painted and relaxing as a day of enjoyment, a day of aesthetic pleasure, is related to this in the most different tone, even in the bourgeois one, even in the aristocratic one. Manet's wishful scene already had its model in Giorgione's 'Concert in the open air', as a pastoral of naked women, men enjoying music, and secluded nature. Manet repeats the scene, though without music, and certainly without Venetian gold tone; yet here too the garden of Epicurus gathers and assembles. Soft light, as only Impressionism could create it, flows through the trees, surrounds the two couples, the naked woman and the one undressing to bathe, the dark male figures. What is portrayed is an extraordinarily French, extraordinarily lingering situation, full of innocence, supreme ease, unobtrusive enjoyment of life, and carefree seriousness. On the whole, through the fair scenes to the bourgeois tranquillities – in the wood, on the promenade or even in an imagined vale of Tempe – there

runs that category which can be described as that of *Sunday pictures*; its
subject is: an immediate other world beyond hardship. Though this subject
can no longer easily be painted in the nineteenth century; Manet's 'Déjeuner
sur l'herbe' forms an exception precisely with regard to its naivety and
presence. Its unstale Sunday would already hardly be possible any more
with petit-bourgeois subjects, characteristically it cannot do without artists
and their models.

The real bourgeois Sunday, even as a painted one, thus looks less desirable
or even less varied. The *negative* foil to Manet's 'Déjeuner sur l'herbe',
in other words: the *merriness that has become powerless*, is given in *Seurat's*
promenade piece: 'Un dimanche à la Grande-Jatte'. This picture is a single
mosaic of boredom, a masterpiece of the longingly unsuccessful and distanced
element in the dolce far niente. The picture portrays a bourgeois Sunday
morning on an island of the Seine in the vicinity of Paris, and in fact:
it now portrays this solely in a scornful way. Figures rest in the foreground
with vacant faces, the group of the others forms for the most part wooden
verticals, like puppets from the toy-box, intensively preoccupied with
strolling stiffly about. Then there is the pale river, with sailing boats, a
rowing regatta, pleasure steamers, a background which despite its fun rather
seems to belong to Hades than to the sun. There is sheer hapless idleness
in the picture, in its light matt and watery space, in the expressionless
water of the Sunday Seine, as the object of an equally expressionless
brooding. There is the Land of Cockaigne here too, but such that with
the working world every world, indeed every object seems to fade into
watery tepidness. The result is bottomless boredom, a petit-bourgeois and
infernal utopia of distance from the Sabbath in the Sabbath itself; Sunday
proves to be merely a tormented demand, no longer a brief gift from the
Promised Land. Such a bourgeois Sunday afternoon is the landscape of
painted suicide which does not become one only because it even lacks
resolution towards itself. In short, this kind of dolce far niente is, in so
far as it still has any consciousness at all, the consciousness of total non-
Sunday in the residual utopia of Sunday. The bourgeois Sunday picture
of the nineteenth century could nowhere recover from the negative foil
portrayed in this way, with almost the sole exception of Manet's 'Déjeuner
sur l'herbe', this echo of the Renaissance preserved as an aristocratic
bohemia. After all, the negative foil was present for a long time in society
and in its dopo lavoro objects before it was painted belatedly and therefore
in such a radically characteristic way. The historical pictures of past
abundance and festivity, these Sunday evening operas introduced on to

canvas, merely confirmed, by the fact that they were so worthless and mendacious as paintings, the wistful Hades of the arrived feast day. And on the other hand it was confirmed by the merciless art with which a sparing, rigorous painting in the manner of Marées sought to present, or rather to conjure up the other world beyond hardship. In Greek pictures full of noble gestures, solitary grace, with posed orange groves, with supposed statuary figures plucking and offering golden fruits, with precious buildings of repose and yet, as is obvious, with theatricality here too. This disappeared only when really genuine painting did not merely cultivate, in a naive fashion, the greatest technical rigour, but above all when it simplified its objects, i.e. restricted them to those in which even in the bourgeois world a *positive* image of Sundayness was still possible. This occurs above all in *Cézanne*, with resignation and restriction to a rustic little world and to a greatness of nature seen in equally simple-monumental terms. Only in this way did a *tranquillity of Sunday which remained highly laconic* become both materially concrete and monumental. This even, if not predominantly, in the portrayal of plucked fruits, and further in the reserved landscape paintings and their Dorically maintained Elysium. The Epicurus of a 'Déjeuner sur l'herbe' is at an end, the Gardens of the Hesperides which have become academic are not observed: instead there appears in the picture the most substantial corpus of repose that is known in the nineteenth and especially in the twentieth century. Cézanne transforms even his still lifes into places in which things are rigorous and sedentary, in which happy ripeness has settled. What has been plucked in these pictures, the apples, lemons, oranges, are not fruits any more, although they are painted as such with extreme care and precision, they are witnesses to a heavy contentment, brought from Hesperian landscapes on to the tablecloth of the feast day. Here everything is still life and nothing, for Cézanne condensed whole worlds of repose into these small creations, statuary ones in which harvest has occurred, in which an Elysian Ceres puts her hands in her lap. Cézanne's heroic figures and landscapes are also just as reassured, just as ordered in the restriction to mere detail, thoroughly architectonic. Nudes lie built in stone or rise like pillars into the air, stand between the trees, in Byzantine rows, or built into a background of foliage ('Les Ondines') as into a niche. The masterpiece 'Grandes Baigneuses' bends the trunks which frame the picture right and left into Gothic arches, leaning on them rise standing nudes, they turn into reclining ones towards the middle and the ground, a Sunday space par excellence fills the arch itself: beach, meadow, water, village landscape, high clouds. Things and people thus become building stones of different form and different weight, destined to produce and to support a picture building. Each thing finds its place, is inscribed in it with firm strokes, with those of its shape. Even pure landscape paintings like 'L'Estaque' build up what is theirs in a balance which had not been achieved since Giotto. Reddish-brown tiled roofs, green treetops, a crimson-blue gulf, yellowish-purple hills, and a turquoise-blue sky together yield more than unity of surface, the colours also model out the geological structure beneath the flesh, as a sure ataraxy of the landscape. The repose of a settled nature appears, but of course precisely with restricted or sharply clipped objects and on the whole distant in every respect from the conflicts of the large city. An agrarian world uncontemporaneous with developed capitalism and its objects arises, a provincial landscape with profoundly viewed extensions into cheerfulness and order. Thus Cézanne's equilibrium, his repose reminiscent of Giotto, precisely this in fact, is also certainly a reserved Sunday of the world, a utopia which can only still be moulded in bays and the most sparing formal rigour. Thus if Sunday is intended *in breadth and for every day as it were*, with a portrayal which does not model out its objects as if it was digging for treasure, then given Europe had to be abandoned. Then all that presented itself was that world which a so much more inferior and more affectuous painter like *Gauguin* sought and found as it were, far from Europe, fleeing from it, *in a very remote and primitive other world beyond hardship*. Happiness and colour on Tahiti: this kind of thing now comes into the late Sunday picture, a long-lost piece of south land. This dream had first appeared when Tahiti with its seemingly paradisial innocence was discovered in 1606, and it had found new nourishment in the Europe of Rousseau through Cook and the fine, eloquent accounts of Georg Forster. The Sunday feeling already sought tropical accessories at that time and precisely these: 'Through Forster's charming description of Otaheiti', says Alexander von Humboldt in his 'Aspects of Nature', foreseeing Gauguin, 'particularly in northern Europe a general, I could say yearning interest had been aroused for the islands of the Pacific.' Even the differently located or novelistic feelings which have been circulating here since Rousseau: Saint-Pierre's 'Paul et Virginie', the novel of palms and innocence, or the 'The Indian Hut', even this kind of Robinsonade (with no return) is paid out by Gauguin in late illustration. As such the Tahiti still particularly uncontemporaneous with capitalism is now painted, and the subjects seem indiscriminately paradisial as it were: a pair of children among flowers, a young rider and girls who await him, a Maori house between palms, effortless fruit-picking.

Everything lies in fiery brown repose, a south, admittedly still seen in Parisian brunettes, but they have shed the native Eve, melancholy is dissolved or transformed into silence and distant vacancy. 'Nature For Us', this most fundamental background of the Land of Cockaigne, is indicated by a paradisial region and so less fundamentally put in the picture. The Sunday on Tahiti is bought with primitiveness, and this primitiveness is rewarded with carefreeness – at least in Gauguin's pictures. But: terra australis *in Europe* and without primitives, this workday as Sunday has not yet been painted anywhere; for it would be the classless society. Dostoevsky's despair caused a recollection of Claude Lorrain's picture 'Acis and Galatea' to appear at various times in his novels, which is always described by his heroes as the 'Golden Age' (cf. Lukács, Der russische Realismus in der Weltliteratur, 1952, p. 147). Modern bourgeois painting, full of senti-mental distance, could not yield much more than such Arcadian-mythical Sundays in *an attained Cythera itself*. Painted Eden in the modern age must always equip itself with the sentimental resignation of a mere Arcadia, that is, with a Sunday to flee to, which for this very reason also only has a dualistic relation, not one of assimilation and relaxation, to the workday. The Middle Ages too, even in its happiest and relatively most harmonious period, transferred the peace of what has come good, as we know, beyond every world; only there did the olive leaf and the peace of the Sabbath grow. So too in the picture when it projects this other world on to an observable Here: the happiness of the Nunc stans remained – however little it was dependent for medieval consciousness on restriction, and especially on artificial primitives – in the *land of legend*.

At that time of course the feeling of having faithful support there was all the more certain. The religious picture believes in its wishful place in existing sacred events, only erring man excludes himself from it. The picture becomes an exhortation to order, to the same order which the depicted sacred material paints for wavering life. The world of perspective is ulti-mately alien to this, not merely for technical reasons. Canonical medieval painting is not familiar with an espressivo any more than its predominant two-dimensional style is familiar with perspectives; and both for related reasons. For both are a matter of the subject and of its distance, not of the religiously possessed object and its absolute There. Distance and projection are mere tensions in what has long been decided, and come good through Christian fulfilment. No external nature makes itself available for this of course, but rather that woven by legend (sacred history); most completely in *Giotto*. Not least because Giotto, standing at the end of the

Middle Ages, summarizes the latter for this very reason, in its hierarchy
and its reference to legends, with a painted finale. So more than ever here
everything finds its believed support and place, every movement is allocated
to it and built into it. Even angels in flight, precisely these stick and rest,
there are no longer any crowds and accidents in the picture, its objects
have taken their seats. The naturalistic appears only at the edge of this
order: in contrast for example to the nature mysticism of the other order,
the Tao order, in Chinese landscape painting. The naturalistic is an
instrument or, as a mountain outline, an ornament which serves to frame
the figures (Paduan frescoes 'Joachim's dream', 'Flight into Egypt'). Even
the external architecture is simply a co-ordinate system to the internal one
of the pictorial structure: the loggias and terraces, the thrones and halls
are a spiritually erected sphere of activity (Florentine frescoes 'Annunciation
to Zachariah', 'The Assumption of St John'). Thus there appears in Giotto's
ideal space not merely *extreme repose*, but a painted existence of an absolutely
certain kind: *mystical gravity*. Especially Giotto's maturest work, the
'Apparition of St Francis to the Chapter at Arles' (Florence, S. Croce),
gives such repose: with a continuous horizontal, a dividing vertical line,
and gives such gravity: with the weight of the self-communion of the
seated monks, with the unshakeable position of the saint in the middle.
According to Thomas Aquinas, angels are not contained in space like a
body, but they themselves contain their space, and they enclose it instead
of being enclosed by it; comparable to this, in Giotto every sacred event
itself posits the place where it is located, and the division of the surface
of the picture is strictly orientated to the weightiness of the event occurring
within it. A third element after repose and gravity therefore follows from
this: the construction of the picture occurs from the standpoints of the
value-based hierarchy portrayed. The figures are distributed in the space with
precise consideration of their weightiness; corresponding to this is the fact
that even their degree of reality is graded according to their spiritual value.
That is to say: the higher an event in the spiritual hierarchy, the more
'really', which here means: more really in conceptual terms, it is painted.
This even though we know that Giotto's age also perceived him in
naturalistic terms; Ghiberti praised him for having abandoned the style
of the Greeks and for having introduced naturalness and gracefulness. The
beginnings of bourgeois emancipation were thus perceived in Giotto, and
with them picturesque detail, clearly descriptive narrative, and individual
characterization; thus even Boccaccio's 'Decameron' asserted that nature
produced nothing which Giotto was not able to imitate. But in fact these

examples of naturalism are only such when compared with the Byzantines and also with Cimabue; they are none within the Gothic diversity of being and the hierarchy of being beneath which the diverse, by being built in, is all the more triumphantly bowed. In this respect Giotto totally conforms to the Thomist world-picture, the equation of valuations with levels of being, of the degree of reality with the hierarchical status. This strangely optimistic theory fills the whole conceptual 'realism' of the High Middle Ages, it is also the sole premise of the ontological proof of the existence of God (God is therefore by far the most real being because he is the most universal and most complete). Thus even Giotto's art succumbs to the ontological-hierarchical conviction: he paints robes, rocks and the like flat, almost two-dimensional, but the reality increases towards the centre of the composition (which centre does not necessarily coincide with the middle of the picture). Giotto thus supplements the spatial hierarchy of his objects most vividly with hierarchy of being: only this conveys to repose and gravity that particular dignity of value which stems from believed Being-More. Even the superficiality to which the naturalistic, and also architecture is usually subordinated in Giotto, with regard to the unum necessarium: land of legend, can in this way, by underlining an event of value, ultimately become central. The mountain outline which serves as an ornament in the 'Flight into Egypt', as a background to the travelling figures also repeats their outlines and signs itself like them into eternity. But all this occurs solely in the land of legend for which sacred history has succeeded, and instead of perspective in the Renaissance sense it exclusively contains hierarchy of successfulness and composition steering towards it. Thus in this painting a utopia of Christianity is formed as existing, in fact as already by far the most real; corresponding to the enormous optimism of the proportionality of being and value. This optimism has shattered, the specific utopia of Giotto's world has thoroughly turned into a mere *mythology* of a utopian kind. Its builtness also immediately shattered with the end of the medieval feudal-theocracy, it even broke in internal-religious terms. Grünewald's world of Christ, the Baptist not cathedral one, presents the Bible legend solely as explosive and the centre (resurrection in the Isenheim altar) solely as that of the most glaring paradox. But even in his day Giotto's land of legend lay on that narrow ridge of equilibrium which was stretched out more in heaven than on earth and which the modern age lost as much as abandoned. The perspective of mere premonition, a precise but dawning one, which appears in the background of the Mona Lisa and even in the absorbing distant centre of the Baroque, expresses more appropriately the existing *wishful state*, and also the lasting incurableness. Though not the governing *wishful content*, which is not one of distance, most importantly, nor one of endlessly moved motion, but one of repose. That is why even in this wishful landscape, final landscape which has become truly monumental, despite its skipped distance, its mythological hypostasis, there appears a measure of all that which can be truly painted; there appears the *painted gold ground of every movement: peace*. Even the 'Flight into Egypt' exhibits it, and especially the 'Apparition of St Francis to the Chapter at Arles', with the homogeneity of a successfulness which has also fully composed the heterogeneous. This kind of presence, this reposefulness and spatiality, this gravity and monumentality, with every object in its value-place, remains an iron corrective to every later order. The repose painted thus is certainly only a corrective, it is no concrete attainedness, let alone guarantee of the being of its content. A fixed ontology is also by no means contained in this corrective as in Thomas Aquinas and so many philosophers of closedness and enclosedness. What is attested in Giotto is therefore solely the ultimate primacy of rest over motion, of space over time, of spatial utopia over endless temporal utopia, of the form of arrival over perspective. Legend and its land here wants to make the situation into situationlessness and composes each of its events, with the strictest gradation, into a hierarchy of the Ultimate, in which everything portrayed seems to be ordered in correspondences which are both promised and have occurred long ago.

Land of legend in literature: as celestial rose in
Dante's 'Paradiso', as transcendental high mountains
in the Faustian heaven

The features of the Ultimate were rigorously painted, but only hesitantly expressed. Their language faltered among nothing but psalms and songs of praise or did not venture into the vast Sunday. No definition from the objective-real world could be applied to the absolute one without caution and mere signifying. Only where the highest visionary power with regard to the invisible existed could a celestial land of legend also be provided with words, but with approximated ones. Dante and Goethe thus concluded their works solely with indirect images of heaven, the one in contemplation of a given faith, the other in the faith of a transparent contemplation. However, even the medievally secure *Dante* avoids the directness which great contemporary painting displayed towards heaven. Giotto's visible order of visible objects becomes in the final cantos of 'The Divine Comedy' a highly symbolic sketch of unnamable contents. The paradise of the saints in Giotto's 'Last Judgement' is festively clear, the thrones of the patriarchs stand austerely, an arena of angels' heads and gleaming gold rises solidly behind the thrones. Whereas Dante's geography introduces figures and solidities from the objective-real world into the 'Paradiso' only with metaphorical language, and finally symbols from a very distant utopia of space. Consequently, 'The Divine Comedy' also transforms its architecture of the seven heavens from the sphere of fixed stars downwards into the wishful mysteries of a space of both inward and ultramundane depth. Even the external figure of light does not correspond to it, at least not that which appears in the sun and in the mere starfire of the heaven of fixed stars, only striving towards the Empyrean. For the sun (in Dante equated with the cardinal virtue of wisdom) is indeed the place where the Theologians reside who have become immersed in the infinite light of God; nevertheless, the circle of the sun is by no means the Empyrean, in fact (a particular difficulty for the interpretation of Dante's hierarchy of heaven) the circles of Mars, Jupiter and Saturn are placed above it as circles of courage, justice and temperance. This means that in Dante's space there is a utopia which in its highest manifestation may correspond to the sphere of the sun, but instead of this reveals itself in a special *symbolic form which is by no means astronomical any more*. As such there appears in the Empyrean, above the 'final drive of the world ring towards pure light', the *rose of heaven*:

> Light is there above, through which is clearly rendered
> the creator visible to that creation
> whose peace, alone in seeing him, is engendered.
>
> And extending in a circular formation
> to such a girth that its circumference would seem
> too large a girdle for the sun's illumination.
>
> The whole of its appearance, fashioned by a beam,
> reflects from the peak of the primum mobile
> from where its vigour and potential stream.
>
> And as the hillside seems to put on a display
> in the water-mirror, admiring its image
> when its greenery and flowers are in full array,

so I saw, floating above the light, stage by stage,
mirroring themselves in more than a thousand tiers,
all those of us returned to that high vantage...

Thus in the form of a white unblemished rose
the sacred host was then revealed to me,
the very bride that Christ with his own blood chose.

('Paradiso', Canto 30, 31)

The souls of the crusaders form a crucifix, the angels the great flower
of light; everything is the form and yet everything the symbol of a
Venerabile that is a rose and then again is not. The utopia of space has
become spacelessness in the Empyrean: nearness and distance can here neither
give nor take more ('Presso e lontano, li, ne pon ne leva', Par. 30, l. 121);*
there thus remains even in the rose only the perfect circular form of
fulfilment. This is not the rose of love from a secular literature at all any
more, not even the Rose of Mary, although Dante, at the level of the
heaven of fixed stars, calls the mother of God this (Par. 23, l. 73f.): the
most perfect figure remains outside space. Shortly before Dante, Pietro
da Mora, cardinal of Capua, published a treatise de rosa; in this the most
perfect flower from time immemorial figured three times: for the chorus
martyrum, for the virgo virginum, and for the mediator Dei et hominum.
While Dante's symbolism of the rose also exactly concurs with this trinity
(cf. Olschki, Sacra doctrina e Theologia mystica, 1934, p. 20squ.), it
certainly does not do so with regard to the wishful landscape: spatial figure
of the rose itself; this stands in the hyperspace of the Empyrean solely
for the *circle of everywhere*. And within it, as the now no longer separating
but solely connecting wishful dream, the flower of paradise can be grasped
with a single glance (Par. 30, l. 118), indeed it is graphicness itself; in the
highest part of paradise, cognition is necessarily superseded by vision. The
courage to describe the indescribable, which is not even indescribable,
therefore even progressed to the image of a swarm of bees, as which the
angels present themselves, as which they settle in the calyx of the rose
of heaven and fly up to God (Par. 31, l. 7ff.). Then again ancient architectural images are chosen: the leaves of the rose appear as tiers (di banco
in banco) of a vast amphitheatre. The rose is able to be all this because
it is chosen as a spatial symbol of a perfection which can no longer be

---

* 'Near and far, over there, neither add nor take away'.

compared with any space at all other than that which the circling around
the central core describes, and which thus has as its simile all roundness
that is purely forming itself.

Otherwise a whiff of the things of this world penetrated its way across
here only in passing, a pleasant whiff. They themselves are essentially
abandoned, in Dante's eyes the earth lies ridiculously small below him
(Par. 22, l. 152), only its deeds reach up. This changes in *Goethe*, where
the rift between Here and Yonder comes to an end even for the land of
legend, by virtue of contemplation which has become secular. Faust enters
the infinite by striding into the finite on all sides, although again in a
mountaineering way. The *heaven in Goethe's Faust* remains totally drawn
from earthly perception and holds fast to it, though again always symbolically, indeed ('Everything transitory is only a metaphor') with particularly
pronounced symbolism, reflected almost more than in Dante. Only: the
scene of the Faustian heaven, which is so figurative, is and remains of
this world, is that of the high mountain, of the Alpine massif full of ravines
in the blue. Dante of course, on the peak of Mount Purgatory, also had an
earthly landscape as an almost celestial one. Up there lay the earthly paradise,
and there was spring breeze, birdsong, hidden in the leaves, ambrosial
forest, with Lethe and Eunoë as rivers of blessing (Purg. 28, l. 1ff.). To
the deadly forest of sin at the beginning of Hell (Inf. I, l. 2ff.) a forest
of God is opposed here, in the morning; the pine-grove near Ravenna
served, in Dante's memory, as a model. However, the thus animated and
illustrated earthly paradise is in Dante totally different from the heavenly
one, it is a mere place of transit, for souls which are ready for admission
to the heavenly paradise. Eden only belongs to heaven in so far as it is
the lowest situated space to which the veiled Beatrice can still descend
to greet Dante. Consequently, the use of images from nature here by no
means signifies the same as in Goethe; in Dante they only adorn and describe
a natural place, though a transfigured one, they do not become transparent
without a rift for the place of glory. Its region was in Dante a rose without separating space, in Goethe however even the highest region is and
remains further intensifying space, is the transcendent-transcendental high
mountains, and in fact those which were only conquered, almost revealed
in Goethe's age. Alpine nature surrounds the blessed boys who float through
the firs like little morning clouds, greets the angels 'misting around rocky
heights', contains the pure radiance above the peaks. A mountain cathedral,
rising out of ecstatic precipices into the ether, that is Goethe's vision
of heaven, and precisely as an incessant range of high mountains, with

constantly new spheres up above. Even this active-infinite system, a
Protestant striving one tensed into constantly new premonitions as well,
thus upholds, in contrast to Dante, the earthly connection, the geography
of upward striving and of ever new peaks. The framework remains that
of the high mountains, not of the circle; the final Faustian landscape remains
transcendent, not transcendental, both in the lasting ability to become of
its figures and in the continually ramifying Upward. The ages and societies
part here, the feudal one in Dante, the capitalist-Protestant one in Goethe:
Dante completed a well-conducted arriving journey, Goethe's Faust gropes
further for his goal even in heaven. In Dante the figures are finished, the
status termini has replaced the status viae, a definitive position, except
in the Purgatorio, and even this has its precise measure. Dante's figures
are definitely the past in the shape of eternity, and the landscape of this
immortality is so constituted; whereas the immortal element in Faust is
conceived in the chrysalis condition, that is: expecting sheer future in the
form of eternity. Instead of spiritual hyperspace, with every soul in the
place of its revealed-finished quality, a new space of influence opens up,
instead of a completed utopia of space the utopia of time as well, still lasting
within that space. And to the temporal utopia of the Faustian heaven there
corresponds in fact the infinity of the striving endeavour, with immortal
premonition at its core; at the highest point of Dante's Paradiso however,
at the goal to which all wishes turn, longing ends ('L'ardor del desiderio
in me finii', Par. 33, l. 48).* Visio beatifica Dei and the primacy of the
vita contemplativa over the vita activa absorb the will into themselves;
indeed the longing of the Dante-subjects is not only destroyed by divine
contemplation and through the rose of heaven, the longing, as one which
has likewise become eternal, is without a future and has reached the end,
even ends in – Hell. Even the worst situation becomes through its eternity
situationless, like the existence of the gods, and therefore blessed in the
formal sense. Hence Hegel's very bold formulation, but valid for Dante:
'Even his damned in Hell still have the salvation of eternity – io eterno
duro stands over the gates of Hell –, they are what they are, without
remorse and desire, do not speak of their torments – these do not concern
us and them as it were, for they last for ever –, but they only remember
their opinions and deeds, firmly self-consistent in the same interests, without
lamentation and longing' (Hegel, Werke X³, p. 107). But the repose which
even applies to Hell in Dante does not even apply to heaven in Goethe's

---

* 'I put an end to the ardour of my craving.'

Faust, let alone to the chrysalis condition; not even the eternity of happiness is here one of repose. Even arrival still remains process here, with rising full gain, even salvation does not cease here to contain a Tantalus sui generis, a kind of Tantalus of happiness. Even heaven yields no ready goal-content, there remains instead an infinitely striving distance from it, and there also remains of course that not scrupulous but rich premonition which passes over again and again to untested horizons. The scrupulous distance is Protestant, as noted above, as resolutely as the faith in attainability and contemplatable goal-form has remained arch-Catholic. The Protestant Faustian heaven corresponds, despite its Catholic clothing, to Lessing's proposition that truth is only for God alone, the striving for truth is for man; and related to this is Kant's doctrine of the eternally only approximative movement towards the ideal. Whereas Dante's heaven, this total exposition of arrival, corresponds with equally great fidelity to the ultimate faith in Sabbath and rest of classic medieval philosophy, represented above all by Dante's master Thomas Aquinas. In Thomas there is no endless approach to the ideal at all, but human creatures are thoroughly capable of attaining by means of grace that divinae bonitatis similitudo for which they are destined. So whereas in the Protestant Faustian heaven the goal perpetually moves and therefore distances itself so much that it almost ceases to be one, in Dante's Catholic heaven it stands so firmly and eternally in central repose as if in its own essence it was no goal at all, i.e. in correlation to a path, but an absolute self-composure and perfection of Being in and for itself. But although in Dante-Thomas repose is thus reified and ontologically hypostasized, as in Faust-Lessing-Kant the infinitely striving distance from it, a primacy of Dante's Paradiso over the Faustian heaven still emerges *on the one hand*, where this *infinite striving* is concerned. It is *the utopian primacy of rest*, as the schema of fulfilment, over motion, as the schema of unfulfilled striving for something; whereby Dante's land of legend, like that of Giotto, stands as a corrective to every intention-perspective which does not destroy itself in bad infinity of approaching any more than in infinite variability. The infinity which appears as scrupulosity if not as ultimate non-wanting of arrival and successfulness is a caricature of the historical-utopian conscience and by no means this conscience itself. This is precisely why the rose as Dante's symbol of rest has a utopian primacy over the infinitely ramifying symbols of elevation in the Faustian high mountains; for utopia is accordingly not one of itself, but one of its no longer utopian content – as one that is attained. *On the other hand*, of course, the primacy of circular rest over Faustian motion changes the moment attention is no longer paid to the scrupulous infinity of elevation to ever higher spheres but simply to the *element of premonition* within it, i.e. of utopian certainty that no previously supposed or even hypostasized final symbol buys up sorrow, fulfils hope, or adequates the subject with the substance. The thus preserved motion is then not a reified one, not one of a running amok made absolute in eternal distance, but it proves for all its faith in the finally attainable goal, indeed precisely because of this faith, the consciousness of the *still lasting unachievedness of the goal and of its substance*. So in this respect the Faustian high mountains, with ever higher and as it were more authentic peaks, contain a darker blue of utopian conscience. The Faustian heaven contains from this standpoint the conscience of an arrival-content whose day has not yet come, whose medieval mere day of legend together with a transcendental Empyrean have disappeared. And that is precisely why, in the non-transcendent transcendence of premonition, even Dante's realm of rest shines only as the *corrective* to a perfection, but at no point of the content that has remained aesthetic as the former image-fulfilment of what can be signified with the category of heaven. The element which is not indifferent in literature either, nor can be shunted off into artistic enjoyment, affirms itself in this way: even such a high wishful landscape of the All as Dante's rose of heaven, even this revelation of an All has long become insufficient with regard to its Absolute or final essence. Each revelation of great religious art had its truth, in so far and as soon as it possessed it, solely as a substitution for the still outstanding, still consistently utopian real content of what was meant in general and can continue to operate solely in this way. For the seriousness of atheism, against which no reality of the other world and God whatsoever can hold out any more, except as a hypostasis which has become shallow or even simply as a historicizing art industry, art religion industry, – this seriousness is the basic condition for every centrally comprehended utopia. It is also the basic condition for the possible inheritance of the still relevant, and in utopian terms (not mythical-ontological ones) still valid contents of former religious art and of religion itself. *For it is solely the experimenting utopian form, and nowhere now the maintained real form of the Absolute, whereby roses of heaven, described gods, the Empyrean and other intentional contents represented as perfect remain in the memory of hope.* Atheism as a whole both created the intentional contents of the final utopia from the already existing reality and sharpened the intention towards these contents, without mythology and part payment. But heavenly rest of course, interpreted as a corrective, indicates to the utopia of motion, and precisely to that which is conscientious, what it has in it itself as its most radical intention: the end of intention, the infinity of content, not of the path. The will of utopia is on the right path only when it does not allow the elevation to higher spheres to be blocked by temporary cases of fulfilment, yet believes just as rigorously in an end, time-stop, arrival. When it believes in nothing more than the objectively founded *possibility* of this arrival, but therefore also in the power to hasten it and not to renounce it for the sake of the path. Precisely the final form of the highest moment, which Faust increasingly sought and of course continues to make eventful in heaven, as something still insufficient: precisely this final form has no higher sphere above it any longer, indeed no sphere at all any more alongside others. Dante's land of legend gives the densely successful rose, Faust's land gives mountains above mountains in the outspread blue – in the former the mystery is the existing solution, in the latter the solution is the still remaining mystery.

Splendour, Elysium in opera and oratorio

Sound hovers, it is not clear where it is located. Equally it is not very plain what it expresses, completely different words have been set to the same tune. Yet a sound can also express better than any colour or words that transition where we no longer know whether it is a lament or a consolation. Music on the whole does not stick at it, certainly not in a major key, but not in a minor key either. It has a totally lonely but long-drawn-out, undying light in the pain it states, and for seriousness it has a song which covers even the hardest step of the grave* as one towards hope. The fact that music exists at all, as a path or way out pre-figured nowhere else, shines through and already surpasses the materials to which it turns. To which it turns in a searching, hovering fashion though, so that the solution is not yet binding; except for a few great musical statements. The path of music is longer than that of painting, and even that of poetry; thus it is by no means as objective as other arts, although referring far more intensively to objects which do not lie in the horizon of sensations and ideas but of emotions. But at the same time, since all emotions are pressing for a solution, this means that, of all the arts, music is most geared to this and, by virtue of the consoling character of its hovering above, most powerfully capable of giving a pre-appearance of outflow. Though also in a most carefree way, at least in the form of music

---

* This is *grave* in the musical sense.

which is not so rigorous, i.e. where cadenza and finale press towards *radiance* anyway, towards the *visibility* of radiance. in the opera. As such, like the oratorio, the opera is only a form in which the instrument of the human voice can join in and, without causing a traffic obstruction, is heard to advantage. But over and above this the opera posits visible action; its singing instruments have risen above the orchestra, and are people in a scene. And in addition, since the Baroque period in which it first blossomed on a wide scale, the opera has served the festival, imposing display, and elevated existence. It is intent, even more decidedly than the finale of a symphony, on *happiness*, on triumph, even though possibly on a silent, exhaling triumph. Even the cool experiments in the manner of classical antiquity with which the opera began in *Florence*, indeed by means of which it was invented, showed a surprising desire for the bright ending and its land, despite the elegiac material they chose. Peri's 'Eurydice', 1600, ended cheerfully, and a little later Monteverdi's 'Orfeo' admittedly restores Eurydice's sad return to the underworld, but Apollo places the couple among the stars. More than ever the splendid *Baroque opera* needs the per aspera ad astra in its music: nothing better filled the festive sets, nothing allowed more lavish ceremonies, more evident splendour of the happy end. The orchestra as yet possessed no crescendo, but precisely the jerky changes in the intensity of tone allowed the formation of terraces of sound, and above all an abrupt contrast. Together with the individual, the dramatic solo now arose and the vertical line of the chord, with the cadenza effect of victory which it alone made possible; the dominant and tonic effect was supported by harmonic innovations like the Neapolitan sixth, one of the most powerful means of expression in Baroque opera, precisely with regard to appearing triumph. A quiet Arcadia was still undoubtedly more natural to the Renaissance opera when it began in Florence, and it followed pastoral plays at least as much as it did antiquity; but the Baroque opera made an apotheosis out of it. The Baroque operas themselves are forgotten, and like the novel, the tragedy, and even the poetry of this period have not yet attained the modern esteem which arose for Baroque buildings and also Baroque sculpture. This selectivity concerning the different values of individual kinds of art in the same period is strange and unprecedented; yet constant espressivo, and constant maestoso obviously has limits in the afterripening, it enforces fractions and rations in which it can be absorbed. Even masterpieces like Scarlatti's 'Theodora', like Purcell's 'Dido and Aeneas', and even Handel's 'Julius Caesar' have not yet become really reproducible as full-scale creations, in their grand tone and background.

Josef Fux, the author of the famous 'Gradus ad Parnassum', had composed a festival opera in 1723 for the king's coronation in Prague which was performed by a hundred singers and a two-hundred-strong orchestra: not a sound of such colossi, or even of such assiduous lavishness comes across to us any more. But the structural technique of the *opera form itself* hardly ever forgot this Baroque radiance in the bad and good sense; after all, even from the cradle opera was directed towards the Elysian, and then towards the splendid. The magnificent style of the Scarlatti aria: sustained initial notes with large intervals which are followed by a lively movement, – this style was of course mocked in Mozart's 'Così fan tutte' (Fiordiligi's aria), but it has an influence down to Weber and beyond. Not in the opera buffa, but rather in the opera seria, even Mozart serves up the grand scene from the Baroque, the theatrical one that transcends all everyday life, with the radiance of terror and apotheosis; hence the storm at sea in 'Idomeneo', and the burning of the Capitol in 'Titus'. Neither are adequate Mozart operas of course, and the Elysium of this genius lies, instead of in apotheoses, in the garden music of 'Figaro', but even the 'Magic Flute' (with the final stage direction: 'The whole theatre is transformed into a sun') ends in the tone of triumph, land of triumph, to which the Baroque opera was committed. Monteverdi's 'Apollo', after all the darknesses of operatic fate, places the couple again and again among the stars: the opera is optimistic, and the significant exceptions to this are none or merely prove the rule. All the more so in the *nineteenth century* (when the bourgeoisie was striving for imposing radiance and adopted the instrument of the opera for this purpose) when Spontini and Meyerbeer, and especially Wagner started baroque festivals, high dramas with a borrowed aurora or one of their own. At the same time the banality of the grand scene came to the fore here, in so far as victoria is trumpeted within it in a too contrived way, and the dangerous mixture of risk and convention in the victorious operatic finale; a danger which can incidentally also arise in a so much higher style: precisely in the symphonic finale. Nothing is more urgent in operatic composition than to be ready before dramatic climaxes and low points with an idea which is worthy of the great moment and especially of the blissful moment, but nothing in the nineteenth century was more threatened by the routine of the theatrical effect either. Theatrical effect, said *Wagner*, the master of resounding silence, but even more so of the colossus, is effect without cause; this phenomenon or non-phenomenon therefore advanced above all into the great outbursts, great conclusions of acts and closing vedutas of the opera. Theatrical effect was still most suitable where incidental music of the left hand, music as accompaniment to the spectacle was permissible anyway: in ballet, and above all in the Being-beside-oneself of the *bacchanal* (that can be combined with ballet). The garden of love made into music here still contained a legacy of festiveness in which the set is a large part of the attractive and lecherous business itself. The embarkation for Cythera, the fine hesitant one, is far off, unless it rings, isolated backwards and forwards, in Offenbach's introductory music to the barcarole, in his luxurious Evoës and in his 'latest concerto' of Orpheus, but the gardens of love and magic islands of the Baroque certainly appear, both coarsened and magicized, in the great bacchanals throughout, especially in that of the Paris 'Tannhäuser'. Here is a masterpiece of desire and of nothing else in the world, an abyss of satyriasis, demonized down from strains of Tristan, and far off in the abyss, from the shore which it does not have, the song of the nymphs wafts across, the brothel radiance of a higher order, with a rose of hell. Yet more dubiously in fact than in the bacchanal the salute of beach and radiance could be at hand where climaxes of operatic action, where above all conclusions of acts and the landscape of the finale are also to be made present. The various consecrations of swords, prayer scenes and trumping conclusions in Meyerbeer and therefore also in Wagner here became a cliché. A cliché in statu nascendi in the case of Siegmund's lovesickness and Siegfried's sword-song, the entry of the gods into Valhalla and all the other transportable fortissimi of something allegedly right or wonderlandish which now seems to break through and yet remains merely rhetoric, effect without cause, a braggart tone. Verdi, although likewise belonging to the age of Meyerbeer, kept himself freer from the cliché of such climaxes precisely by delivering it in the minor parts and confining it to them, so to speak. Thus, to give a single example, the triumphal march in Aida sparkles, being kept as superficial as it should be, but the moment afterwards when Amneris crowns the victor with laurels does not sparkle musically, and the love-scene between Othello and Desdemona when the Pleiades touch the ocean, when space grows small and the world grows deep, differs in this low point of its own characteristically from the contrived climax of the conclusion of another act, between Siegmund and Sieglinde, when the Volsungs' blood glows in flood. The Wagner of 'Tristan' certainly does not need to be directed into the piano mood and the wholly extraordinary, he is a teacher of the piano mood and of the aurora to night beyond compare, but the convention of the climax, from 'Rienzi' to the 'Ring of the Nibelungen' and beyond, is the satanic angel who beats this wicked great genius with his fists. The satanic angel is the imposing radiance of the Baroque in the midst of the bourgeoisie, in its German alliance with stale, refurbished, romanticized feudalism; thus the stated danger of false pre-appearance of radiant outflow, outflowing radiance became in Wagner just as clear as genuine pre-appearance certainly also emerges again and again in the operatic wishful landscape, by virtue of music and by virtue of a *work of genius in music*. And it is not for example as if the spectacle as such, with fortissimo, which is so powerfully familiar from the Baroque, were incompetent from the start at the climax, and possibly even at the low point; the incompetent aspect of it remains essentially only the cliché, which is always so easily combined with emptiness in what is pompously wonderful. The fact that the pompously wonderful as well, even that which is particularly heightened, can be effect with cause, a powerfully fulfilled tonic even in opera, as soon as the contrived zest is absent: this is shown in the last act of the 'Meistersinger' by the chorus of the 'Awake', this unexpectedly mighty reddening dawn, after every intensification of day already seemed to have come. And even the fine, more mysterious reddening dawn becomes free wherever a climax, a pause without the cliché of pretending to be a climax, shows its landscape: as even in the drumbeats surrounding Senta's first encounter with the Dutchman; as in the quintet of the 'Meistersinger'; even as in the violin strains of the Good Friday meadow. This is the legitimate thing about significant opera in general: the fact that, out of the tonic radiance native to it as also out of tragedy and especially out of happiness, it can cause a solution to arise in the action which the spoken word lacks in this expansive oceanic element. With what grand-arched jubilation the bliss-making melody ends and also does not end in the final bars of the 'Götterdämmerung', the opposite land to the bombastic entry into Valhalla which is here also musically purified. There is high time in the opera, resoundingly represented wishful land which it well befits if by virtue of the still hovering sound, as in the most powerful of all operas: in 'Fidelio', it rises above a nameless ocean with nameless joy.

All this presupposes a taut sound of course, which surprisingly slackens. The raging then dies down in such a way that it flows out into the entering song of rest. But this outflow is still itself filled with the preceding unrest, and thus the song which reproduces it is characteristically hot. And the danger here always remains a sensational entry of the tonic (in a further sense than the fundamental harmonic one). But there is still an often smaller, always cool melodic region where a kind of *silvery* released element itself emerges from the action in opera. As an Arcadian melody, without previous overheating, as an anteroom to the wishful landscape where one forgets the wishing one has had. A seemingly modest and certainly striking example of this is provided by the roundelay strains in *Gluck's* 'Orpheus', above all the Elysium scene: 'What a clear sky covers this place'. Gluck gave more than the melodious sensuality of the Neapolitan school here and also more than the dramatic contrast to the agitations and unhappinesses of his infernal chorus, on the contrary: there is over-dramatic lento here, transparently simple at the same time. Elysium emerges, beyond vanquished death, in Orpheus' glance at the clear sky and its softer light, in the transfigured major key of the roundelay, and then chorus, to the strains of which Orpheus greets Eurydice. This is the model of *seraphic rest* in the opera, but especially in the *oratorio* (to which Gluck's 'Orpheus' half belongs); there is nothing majestic about it, only peace, peace, as the Koran says. The classical manifestation of what can be called arrival style in music may not of course flourish in theatrical forms and hence forms of action at all, in so far as they also extend into the oratorio. It is rather wholly applied to tranquillitas animi, and its musician: *Palestrina* is the master of such transfiguration. Its pure rainbow sound already lives in the secular madrigals of Palestrina's youth, it triumphs in the sudden simplicity of his masses, as soon as the dogmatic keyword sounds. The rhythm is reduced to a minimum of movement, chromatics are avoided, as the expression of individually broken feelings and feelings of distance. Melody and polyphony are totally cleared up, the four-part movement here has an absolutely assertive effect, and shows ruling simplicity: homophony (often revelling in pure triads) does not interrupt but crowns a masterly counterpoint obtained from the Dutch. Palestrina seeks an echo of that which Saint Cecilia hears, of whom the legend says that she had already heard the choirs of angels on earth. Such auditio beatifica corresponds to Thomas Aquinas' and Dante's ideal of a visio beatifica Dei; it corresponds even more precisely to Augustine's ideal of music as a praeludium vitae aeternae. The Palestrina style was thus the only one to indicate in practical terms what had remained theory in the musical ideal of the whole Middle Ages, a learned though devout theory of paradise. Palestrina's art is really applied to the wishful image of the singing of angels, his music was in fact heard as the echo of heavenly strains. Since Augustine, music had been theoretically celebrated as this echo, he himself had ascribed to the hymn-singing of the Church a share in his own conversion, he himself had first reinterpreted the ancient harmony of the spheres, this astral-mythic psaltery, as the singing of angels, as a paradise sound in no longer planetary but human-like form.

This singing of angels will incorporate and surround those redeemed by the Lord, and so all earthly music which takes its inspiration from this Above is for Augustine an open gate of heaven, precisely a 'praeludium vitae aeternae, ut a corporeis ad incorporea transeamus'* ('De musica' VI, 2). Augustine was thus the one source of the Elysium dream in the medieval view of music; but the other was Dionysios Areopagita, he already made music wholly into the language of angels itself, i.e. here: into a hierarchically graded message. Music was now for the first time to deal totally with the connections of the heavenly and human harmony; it descends from paradise to the musica mundana, the cosmic harmony, then to the musica humana, the harmony of body and soul, and returns to paradise. All this was still astral-mythic throughout of course, an astronomical theory of music, rebaptized in Christian terms, and its influence on real music was slight throughout the whole of the Middle Ages. Now, in Palestrina an intention towards a musica coelestis won through in practice, so that Pius IV here ventured a superlative which, wholly in the spirit of Augustine, sought and was able to find the praeludium vitae aeternae only in a musician, not in painting or literature: 'Here a John in the earthly Jerusalem gives us a sensation of that song heard by John the apostle in the heavenly Jerusalem, prophetically enraptured.' The choirs of angels of course are a hypostasized mythology, like the rose of heaven, and musica coelestis belongs solely in the great human history of hope and its postulated spaces, not in the existing heaven which had so largely been invented as deaf. Thus no music since Palestrina has dared to reproduce this musica coelestis as a possession; precisely as music, all examples of sanctus and gloria were expected to be appeals or conjurations and not pretended reflections, not even in the most timid pianissimo. Beethoven certainly has seraphic elements as the final word, but always as incomprehensible elapsion or as a promise of the Benedictus which has come to the hope. There is of course music of arrival in Beethoven throughout: its most significantly fulfilled form sounds where Leonora removes Florestan's chains, with a presentiment of the highest moment; but the arrival and its land never spread to angelic spheres. 'He must dwell above the stars': the misterioso of this chorus from the Ninth Symphony is stirred and surrounded by the empirical doubt of a mere Kantian postulate of God, it does not land in transcendental perfection which has been and can be sung to an end. Music therefore shares to a particularly strong degree the destruction of the heavenly

---

* 'prelude to the eternal life, so that we may cross from the corporeal to the incorporeal'.

certainty of Being, yet in such a way that, through non-renunciation as at the same time through the stated ambiguous hovering above which nevertheless aims with wishful emotion, wishful solution, through its tendency-object in other words, music was able to give the strongest pre-appearance of what has come good. Of a humanly possible Elysium for which there is as yet no concretion, but in which there is no mythology either. The utopian distance strikes into the immediacy of musical self-contact, the nearness of this musical landscape is in turn charged with significances of an extremely humanized distant world. Music thus has that paradoxical perspective that its objects appear ever greater, and therefore nearer, the more they move towards the horizon on which music lies and forms hope. Even the rest announced by Palestrina has become insufficient in face of the much further ranging wishful and volitional phenomenon of Beethoven. But it too remains in turn a corrective for an andante-finale, however rarely possible, whose arrival causes the music to sound both silent and great.

Contact of the interior and the boundless in the spirit of music: Kleist's ideal landscape; Sistine Madonna

Even portrayed happiness is reluctant to be known and agreed beforehand. It thus points in an unfamiliar direction, not just into the narrowness which we know or into the expanse which belongs to greatness. But in both of these a third destination also rises, one which is pointed out not least in musical terms: the unfathomable. This category unites cave and expanse, interior and perspective, containing and surpassing both. The *interior* is paradoxical, it does of course contract seductively into the narrow, near, and secret, but at the same time it contains significant horizon in this narrowness. Images of spatial contraction, of the formation of houses and interior space as a whole ultimately share in an intensive element which, when added to it, first makes the expanse incapable of losing itself and substantial. Thus no interior remains simply this, and no significant idyll resigns itself as happiness to confinement; in both there is also the opposite of, or the switch into, the universe. In other words, into an amalgamated universe, with golden space and golden time, into small infinity. And the great image of expanse on the other hand: the *perspective of infinity*, this conversely does not merely proceed to expanse. The content of longing in distance and the oceanic element in perspective do not remain simply cosmic, nor is the height of the Paradiso supra-cosmic. Instead, in the extensively sublime, even in its deserted aspect, a secret path here curves back to the fountain of most intensive nearness. What is boundless and the deepest nearness are mutually in league with one another, what is unfathomable in lonely distance teaches the cave again and the latter an expanse again as around the castle of the king of Thule. Heinrich Kleist indicated such a lesson, in the most appropriate way, in an uncanny-canny one, precisely by means of an extensive image; he calls it 'Impressions before Friedrich's sea-landscape'. Kleist describes a sea-scape by the Romantic painter, one beyond the terminus humanitatis, but a whispering merging begins: 'It is glorious to look out on to a boundless waste of water in an infinite loneliness by the seashore beneath a gloomy sky. Part of this, however, is the fact that one has gone there, that one has to go back, that one would like to go across, that one cannot, that one misses everything that makes for life and yet hears the voice of life in the roaring of the tide, in the blowing of the wind, in the drifting of the clouds, and the lonely shrieking of the birds. Part of this is a demand made by the heart and an injury, if I may put it like this, inflicted on one by nature. But this is impossible in front of the picture, and that which I ought to find in the picture itself I only found between me and the picture, namely a demand which my heart made upon the picture, and an injury which the picture inflicted on me; and thus I myself became the Capucin, and the picture became the dunes; but that on which I was supposed to look out with longing, the sea, was completely missing. Nothing can be sadder and more uncomfortable than this position in the world: the only spark of life in the wide realm of death, the lonely centre in the lonely circle. The picture lies there with its two or three mysterious objects like the apocalypse, as if it had Young's Night Thoughts; and since in its uniformity and endlessness it has nothing but the frame for a foreground, it is as if, when one contemplates it, one's eyelids had been cut away. Nevertheless, the painter has undoubtedly broken completely new ground in the field of his art; and I am convinced that with his spirit a square mile of sand from the Mark Brandenburg could be portrayed, with a berberis bush on which a lonely crow is fluffing up its feathers, and that this picture would be bound to create a truly Ossianic effect. In fact, if this landscape was painted with its own chalk and with its own water, then I think one could make foxes and wolves howl with it: the strongest evidence which can be produced without any doubt in praise of this kind of landscape painting.' The infinity in which the world has ended and the dark lonely man in whom every gaze has perished of nearness thus exchange faces. As such Caspar David Friedrich's manner of painting is not like this, on the contrary: its constant longing for expanse tears nearness and distance roughly apart, without a painted intermediate world between the two. But by this very means Kleist's creative consternation in front of the picture can describe such a tremendous arc between nearness and distance, centre and circle. Kleist's soundless apocalypse contains the spark of life anew, in an unfathomable abyss in which man and nature both are, and both no longer are. The eye disappears by looking at the picture, the viewer disappears together with his distance, the picture injures the man standing outside it, 'as if one's eyelids had been cut away', but it also injures the sea, for 'that on which I was supposed to look out with longing, the sea, was completely missing'. Something it is hard to name appears, going out from the viewer to the Capucin, going back from the sea to the dunes; both, Capucin and dunes, become one, the 'lonely centre in the lonely circle', the unfathomable abyss of the inconspicuous with 'truly Ossianic effect'. There is happiness in this, that of Thule, but again no agreed, arranged happiness at all, with a locality that can be catalogued, particularly not this. A central wishful landscape arises all the more strangely, to the howling of foxes and wolves, at the edge of an ending world, in this laconicism: a subject-house, 'with its two or three mysterious objects'. As the only ones which remain in the lonely circle with the lonely centre, and furthermore certainly as Objects, but as those about which there is nothing alien any more. So that we can equally, indeed more accurately speak of an object-house: and all the more so because of the depth-extension of its natural Objects, of a house concentrating subject and object. Of all descriptions of pictures this one has most penetrated into the painted hiatus between subject and object, has filled it with destruction and with an unusual night- or mist-piece of Jerusalem.

Only we cannot see or breathe here, in this so very nearest remote region. Kleist's description is one of the most profound, but the familiar sun no longer rises, and another one does not yet become visible. And Friedrich's sea-landscape can give only in such central impressions, such description powerfully experiencing things through, that which great painting communicates in its own horizon: the unity of man and distance, the return of perspective into the manifold Mona Lisa and of the latter into the perspective of the manifold edges of the world. Nevertheless, all humane-transcendental painted spaces become almost conventional compared with that described by Kleist, with a single exception, the – space of the Sistine Madonna.

It is different from the space which is usually painted, and thus the Sistine Madonna is the boldest picture and the landscape in it the most mysterious. There is no so-called southern space here, the firmly constructed stage, nor so-called northern space, with the varying structure determined by the events within it. There is geometrically clear unity, in the spirit of southern space, in Raphael's picture, but it determines no place at all for the figure within it, neither in nearness nor distance, neither in this world nor the other world. The Madonna hovers equally before and between and behind the peculiar curtain which frames her aura in the picture. She rises while she descends, and descends while she ascends, her space is that of abduction and of homecoming. The relation of the Madonna gloriosa in Faust to this hovering one is obvious: in the gentleness of an outspread mystery, in the receptive inner world of immensity. Franz Marc has said that pictures are our own surfacing in another place, and here, in the placelessness in which interior and perspective mutually merge and permeate themselves with a dissolved other world, *a whole existence* surfaces *in the other place*; here there is nothing more than the wishful landscape of this Everywhere, of this permeatedness with homeland. A limit of art is also reached here of course, if not ventured beyond; for religious art is none at all in so far as it is always on the point of doing away with the appearance which exists for the senses, without which appearance nothing can be portrayed aesthetically. Wishful landscape of beauty, of sublimity as a whole remains in aesthetic pre-appearance and as such the attempt to complete world without it perishing. Such virtual perfection, the object of every iconoclasm and of course itself perforated in religious art: *this rises, suo genere geographically, in the wishful landscapes, placed far ahead, from painting, opera, and literature.* They are often mythologically cloaked and disguised, but never remain settled and sealed in this; for they intend human happiness, a sense of its space having been well placed and having turned out well, from the idyllic to the still mystical space. Pre-appearance gives this aesthetic significance of happiness at a distance, concentrated into a frame. For the happiness imagined in Kleist, powerful enough to make foxes and wolves howl, deep enough to satisfy the demand made by the heart and to dispel the injury done to us by nature, in an unalienated world: – for this utopia in the utopian element itself the situationless landscape is certainly one of the most exact spatial symbols, in the pre-appearance of the picture. But everywhere the wishful landscape is such that everything which happiness needs is present; no less and equally no more than that. It will be incumbent upon socialist art to see that this auroral feature in the picture of the real is also always communicated. Corrected and correctly placed, nocturnal day, as the cheerful Greeks themselves called the reddening dawn. The wishful landscape in art has this colourful foreglow up its sleeve, indeed has it as an Object after it is planted in the world and may grow, but has not yet ripened.

WISHFUL LANDSCAPE AND WISDOM   41
SUB SPECIE AETERNITATIS AND OF PROCESS

What do I have,
If I do not have all, the young boy said,
Is there here a case of less and more?
And is your truth just like the senses' bliss
A simple sum we can possess in greater
Or smaller form and always still possess?
Or is it not alone and undivided?

Schiller, The Veiled Image at Sais

If a single truth prevails like the sun, that is day.

Hamann, Aesthetica in nuce

The concept is the fence, physics the garden, ethics the fruit.

Chrysippos the Stoic

The search for proportion

There is no thinking for its own sake and never has been. Thinking began with wanting to recognize a situation in order to know one's way around in it. Behind this thinking stood fears and above all wishing needs which are to be satisfied, and moreover by means of a short cut, deliberately. There is no path here which has not been made into one, so that people may walk on it and arrive where they wish to go in accordance with their interests. For which they have set out with light above their work in a world half mediated with them. This results in wishful lands even in cognition, above all where life is surveyed as a whole, and hence philosophically, and is to be brought to what is to be fled, what is to be sought. For the first really free thinking, which was Greek, began

precisely with what is to be fled, what is to be sought as a whole. It tried
to sketch its world clearly according to the proportions of this right wish,
of the wish for what is right. Thus if we take the so-called seven sages,
all of them already distinguished in their rules and main points the thinking
to which they could *adhere*. It was the middle course in life and in the
circumstances of things, it was not yet the 'authentic' in general; but this
very middle course was now decisive and stressed that in which things
really run in accordance with bon sens. In so far as, in the opinion of
these sages, things are ideally as they should be, in the extract offered
to them by the world. Thus Bias, Solon and other men of epigrams above
all praised contentment and no remorse, a 'nothing too much' which may
portray the Greek way of the Tao, of the rhythm of life. On the plane
of everyday life of course and in a retracted way: the sense of these epigrams
portrays as it were a still life in the form of thought and of calmness as
a protective house. And the ground of anxiety on to which and towards
which all this was drawn even subsequently is the transitoriness and frailness
of life, the uncertainty of all its conditions. Through the whole of early
Greek thinking there runs the lament of Simonides that human beings
drop like leaves in the forest; but equally the assumption runs throughout
that everything is preserved most calmly and for the longest time in the
middle. Thus the seven sages were called such because their thinking sought
in disorderly life proportion and harmony, in which there was a blessing.
Indeed, with new ability it furnished the key to something durable, to
presumably the oldest sense of what was called φύσις: to be unageing,
to hold together. Fools give themselves a lot of futile trouble over that
which has lost all proportion, in which there is no blessing, but the
aforementioned sages, usually sceptical in everything, backed what was
well-balanced. It was in fact to be human and material bon sens at one
and the same time, in the most desirable way. It was to be the equilibrium
of the pointer in the scales of circumstances, the orderly way of life where
things are all right as they are. Through this world goes that which has
been designated again and again, from the Stoics to Goethe, as 'recovery'
per se and its support. It coincides here attractively with true Being itself,
as the land of the simplicity which always composes itself between extremes.
Where the true is confined to that which constantly thinks itself into what
is right and is so as good world. Even though the latter does not lie there
as calmly as house, home, and garden make it seem.

The 'authentic' in primary matter and law

Great thinking went out to things more sharply as soon as it occurred. Enlightening, against antiquated custom, otherworldly mist, but also against mere sensory appearance. And trust was put in the fact that essence could be found and that, even as water, it could be walked on. In other words, something existed to which, as friendly matter, as sustaining physis, man was related in the 'authentic'. The antithesis that like can only be perceived and especially recognized by like runs even in purely epistemological terms trustingly through so-called pre-Socratic thinking. It tacitly underlies that of Thales and clearly underlies that of Heraclitus, though it only became conscious in Empedocles. So that we can only grasp the cold through the cold, and the hot through the hot, hatred only through hatred, love through love and so on in corresponding areas of man and world. Which then led, in Plotinus and in Goethe, to the great expansion into bilateral perfection: 'If the eye was not sunlike, it could never see the sun.' The information about this elective affinity can be as different as the restless *fire of life* in Heraclitus and the motionless *sphere of Being* of the Eleatics; a common feature, however, is the equation of this 'authentic' element or original matter with that in which an 'authentic' element in man has its motion, its true essence. Thus Heraclitus says that the more dry and fiery the soul is, the better it shares in the rational primary fire ('Die Fragmente der Vorsokratiker', Diels, fr. 118). Thus Parmenides says that Themis and Dike, i.e. the goddesses of unwavering justice, lifted the veil where the unchanging Hen kai Pan sits enthroned, 'the unshakeable heart of well-rounded truth' (fr. 1). These value-tinged sketches of the essential are contradicted least of all by the amazingly economic reflection in Heraclitus: 'All things are an exchange for fire and fire for all things, as are commodities for gold and gold for commodities' (fr. 90). For in this statement an early commodity thinking in the Ionian trading cities comes together with gold as an allegorical permanent value precisely by making itself cosmic. Like gold itself, the always precious fire now shines, 'made by no god and no man, proportionately going out again and again, and igniting again and again' (fr. 30); but conversely the static Hen kai Pan is also removed from every change. Empedocles was of course the first to formulate consciously the elective proposition that only like could perceive and recognize like. And even here it is by no means confined to hot or cold, but poses as the key to nothing less than something volitional in the turnover of things themselves. Thus Empedocles not only goes sympathetically to the elements but also to a kind of life of value between them: 'With our earth matter we perceive the earth, with our water the water, with our air the divine air, with our fire the destructive fire, with our love finally the love (of the world) and its hatred with our sad hatred' (fr. 109). Thus for the first time basic emotions like love and hate are here found in the motions, separations, and connections of four elements. Nothing less in fact than the volitional intensive element, 'interest' itself was thereby designated for the first time as an objectively motive factor in the world – a fermenting landscape full of destruction, but ultimately full of construction. For however much νεῖχος, hatred, disturbs and destroys the universe, and separates again and again that which is beautifully taking shape, unrest is likewise still the strongest seeker of rest in the Empedoclean *emotional matter*. Ultimately φιλία, love, brings the elements together again into a true wishful land, until they are all united in complete harmony. This harmony constitutes in its most perfect form the sphairos, as the last, victorious counterpart to the whirlpool of hate. With all this Empedocles approaches the basic Heraclitean idea of struggle as the father of all things. And he defuses this idea again of course, since for him struggle is not only no father but more a Moloch, so that precisely the productive dialectics of Heraclitus is lost. But it is lost simply in the premature anticipation of total harmony – with the lull, prophesied utterly in the manner of a wishful image, in the restored essence solely moved by love. 'O Iris' bow! above rushing/Waters, when the wave in silver clouds/Flies up, as you are, so is my joy' – this free rendering by Hölderlin in his Empedocles does in fact renew the rainbow light in this elevated landscape. Like is recognized by like, i.e. not just the earth by what is earthy, but also the ether by the highest element: by the airy matter of the soul.

This is a powerful wish, together with the outside world that is supposed to correspond to it. On solid, consciously materialist soil, however, stands the most sober and most important so-called pre-Socratic philosopher: Democritus. The physis is disenchanted of all mythical features, but it is also thereby illuminated in the ad valorem sense, namely in a wholly uniform friendly way. The darkest element of the demonic: Moira, the old goddess of fate, is intentionally recollected, but victoriously recollected. Fate becomes totally understandable causal necessity. This gives the sole explanatory reason for everything that happens in the world, and the Ananke, the *necessity illuminated* as such, is now without spectres and clouds, a new wholly cooled ether as it were and one in all motions, manifestations

of matter, even now. This recognition causes according to Democritus
what is most worth striving for and happiest in man, the γαλήνη, the
calm at sea (Diog. IX), but equally the wishful image of calm is that of
the lawfully ruled landscape itself. The fine and gentle motion of the 'fire
atoms' which form the human soul not only gives calm happiness but
also opens up – again recognizing like with like – the world; so this world
itself is one of the even course, the inevitable yet transparent constraint
of causes. Epicurus and Lucretius later stressed the fearless element in this
landscape, and the Stoics – with an even stronger praise of necessity –
trust in the world. The eternal essence in Democritus is the totality of
the atoms moving through their heaviness and forming the world. But
there is no doubt that there lies in this natural necessity an interpretation
of it at the same time which satisfies the wish for happiness; it lies in
the prospect: cheerful fate.

Kant and the intelligible kingdom;
Plato, Eros and the pyramid of value

It was only fairly late that thinking focused on man, indeed began with
him. The Sophists brought this inner glance so to speak, though one which
originally was not at all inward in the later and above all German sense,
but a sceptical one. It belongs to the Athenian enlightenment which is
different from the preceding one in the colonies in that it brings the sought-
after 'authentic' element into the subjective factor. And crushes that element
within it either more or less individualistically, as in the case of the Sophists,
or instead seeks to investigate it within it afresh by means of philosophical
craft (σοφός, the wise man, originally means craftsman), as in the case
of Socrates. But he too remains subjective or anthropological: 'I can learn
nothing from the trees, but I can learn from people in the city.' The physis
therefore ceases to be the first consideration, in its place the soul, the mind,
and the spirit are now to be primary. Idealistic consciousness begins and
now covers – in however many forms, in a more or less reactionary way
also letting in mythical consciousness again – the world. Of course the
idealism thus exposed, despite its irredeemable biases and exaggerations
in the spirit, has become one of the most important antithetical enzymes
of philosophical development, precisely for materialism itself. It became
important both because of the subjective approach, and hence the epistemological spur, which since sophistical scepticism can no longer be stopped,

and because of the abundance of definitions which the constant consideration precisely of what is logical in the world was able to reveal. However much this logical element was stood on its head, i.e. was turned from a material predicate into an all-sustaining subject. And it naturally follows that a new perspective of wishful contents, i.e. here: of *ideals*, also belongs to the authentically experimenting abundance of idealisms – pouring from the subject, but possibly also from the tendencies of the object. And it must be further emphasized here that the struggle between materialism and idealism in the history of philosophy cannot be divided as simply as a struggle between two sports teams. Here Dessau against Schwerin, here Dynamo against Turbine, here materialists against idealists, the latter with a capital I, and the others with a capital M on their shirts. But the struggle frequently takes place within significant philosophies themselves: not in the case of Socrates, not in the case of the so sharply distinct grand idealist Plato (who characteristically does not even mention Democritus), but rather in the Stoics, in Aristotle, Leibniz, and Hegel. As also in the case of the greatest man in the series of the subjective factor running on from Socrates, in *Kant*. For his 'Theory of the Heavens' of 1755 was almost purely mechanical and materialistic, his 'Critique of Pure Reason' is totally idealistic in its approach, a transcendental one, yet its Object is exclusively Newton's mechanics, and the idealistic ideas: God, freedom, and immortality are expelled from science. Instead, as 'ideas of the unconditional' which simply do not occur in the existing world of unbroken conditional connections, they are to preserve an unreal place in faith, together with all – still unreal – images of perfection in the ideal (and ultimately in the highest good). So Kant does admittedly want to 'do away with knowledge in order to make way for faith', but what is to be done away with is by no means *all* knowledge, least of all the highly recognized one of mechanics, but above all the false, dogmatic knowledge which deals with the 'ideas of the unconditional' as if they were more than mere 'transcendental appearance', as if they were existing, empirical reality. And through this reduction of the 'authentic' to an 'Absolute', which can ultimately only be aspired to, in the world, a particularly accentuated wishful landscape, which here means a landscape of perfection, in fact appeared in philosophy – with retained materialism in Being, and abstract-postulative idealism in obligation. There thus arises of course – *in the midst of the materialistic-idealistic coalition* – a new realm of two worlds, an all too mechanistic and a really all too detached, intelligible one. Significantly, however, the tenor of his 'faith' is stated precisely by the pre-critical and thus not yet so dualistic Kant as one which is by no means merely unworldly. 'I do not find that any attachment or any other inclination which has crept in before inspection robs my mind of tractability towards all kinds of reasons for or against, with one single exception. The scales of reason are not completely impartial after all, and one arm of those scales which bears the inscription: *hope for the future*, has a mechanical advantage which means that even light reasons which fall into the pan belonging to it raise speculations on the other side which are inherently heavier. This is the only error which I probably cannot correct and which in fact I also never want to correct' (Träume eines Geistersehers, Werke, Hartenstein, II, p. 357). This kind of thing refers of course there and then apparently only to – departed souls and the future world of this sort, yet in reality an intelligible realm is implied in this significant statement, to which the access is not death but history in cosmopolitan intention. Just as precisely the later Kant expressed the 'hope for the future' to the effect that 'the human race has always been progressing towards something better and will continue to progress in this way' (Streit der Fakultäten, Werke VII, p. 402). In the sense of the beautiful ideal of a realization of the moral law, 'which we do not *foresee* as an empirical completion, but on to which we *look out* only in the continuous progression and approach towards the highest good possible on earth, i.e. we are able to make preparations for it' (Religion innerhalb der Grenzen, Werke VI, p. 234f.). Ultimately this perspective of hope in Kant aims at a moral kingdom of God on earth, elucidated by the citoyen. German misery admittedly tore this wishful image again and again off the historically varying reality, and thus it remained in Kant particularly strongly within inwardness and eternally distant abstractness. However, this abstractness and distance outlined no 'other world' in Kant himself, but exclusively a heaven in the humaneness which was working its way up and was to be promoted. This humaneness is served by the postulates which apply the ideas of the unconditional (God, freedom, immortality) purely to morality. It is served by ideals as the 'regulative concepts of what is wholly complete and perfect in the field of human reason'. Postulates, ideas of the unconditional and ideals thus represent a wholly unique starry landscape, a star-studded sky of pure practical reason. And the analogy of the image even extends to the fact that all these stern lights, like the stars, radiate their sublimity only in a purely normative way, without empirically illuminating the gaps in the night sky. 'This is the situation with the *ideal of reason*, which must always be based on definite concepts and serve as a rule and a prototype, whether of compliance or assessment' (Werke III, p. 392). Kant definitely protests against belonging to those who kindled their light from Plato, but his own idealism means of course that he transferred Platonic prototypes or ideas partly from metaphysical Being into moral obligation. They now shine ahead within it in pure, all too pure future, in the unmediated sky of good will and ultimate moral purpose.

The purity which is not to be found here was sought forwards, but was first sought upwards. The latter is the mythical way, it had been abandoned in the Ionian and Sicilian trading cities. The Athenian enlightenment in particular, when it declared in the case of the Sophists even the earthly authorities to be bogus, had certainly announced that there was no celestial Above, and there were no gods. *Plato*, however, is the aristocratic and mythical setback to this, but as goes without saying precisely regarding the height, indeed particular luminosity of the most dangerous and greatest idealist, he is not this alone. It was easier for Plato, as a wishful thinker like none before him, to believe in the invisible than in the visible, and the Upwards became for him a longing, an Eros, a competitive striving, and finally of course a so-called vision of the invisible. As if the world lay in twilight and only the conceptual prototypes within it were the true, the solely real, that which fulfils in non-sensory purity. A wishful land through and through, with much reactionary relation to Spartan order, much sentimental relation to Egyptian repose, and a wishful land which as the realm of figures and types covered the world, conceptually doubled it, hierarchically divided it, and idealistically concealed it. Precisely because of the strong wishful character here, however, a great deal of very emotional material is also involved, until the apparently so purely spiritual vision is reached. Hence the longing which does not believe at all that it will meet the like thing that it seeks to grasp in something available to the senses. Hence the Eros which is by no means merely to consist of like things but also of the spur of unlike things, of the existing deficiency, and thus, driven dialectically again and again, neither has nor does not have the treasure of the right thing, but seeks it. Not least the image of the Agon is also of such an emotional nature, the image of the contest in which the nevertheless still amiable, indeed playful Eros, as Plato portrays it in the 'Symposium', becomes in the 'Phaedrus' the all-beginner, all-creator. If the Eros of the 'Symposium' (203 C-E) stands in the transition from not-having to having and vice versa, as 'the son of wealth and poverty, with the characteristics of both', in the 'Phaedrus' (247 B, C) it is a wing and a team of horses, as the agent driving on to perfection, 'very steeply

up the path to the vaults of the heavens, and the vaults themselves now
circle with the gods themselves around the great Being, colourless and without form and intangible'. The *love* of wisdom looks up there, a dialectical
vision in so far as it embraces, above all in the 'Parmenides', certain opposites
like the Many and the One, the unlike and the like and is not also, as in
Heraclitus, an objective dialectics through the totality of the world. Instead
the whole world remains in a dualism of two spheres, of which the upper one
merely shines into the dark space of the lower one. Though also associates
with all its geometrical figures and quantitative-qualitative types within it,
offering that beauty which still goes into the neo-Platonism of Faust's mono-
logue: 'How heavenly powers rise and then descend,/To each their golden
pails extend!/With fragrant blessings winging/From heaven through the
earth all swinging,/Through universe harmonious ringing.'* This kind of
thing remains monistic in Goethe despite all transparency, with an embracing
or rather vanquishing of every echo of an image of two worlds by Spinoza's
spacious natura sive deus. In Plato, however, the Jacob's ladder landscape
and later church-window landscape of the world is clearly one from light
to night, from night to light. In Plato the world is totally inexplicable
in terms of itself, indeed does not exist at all in itself, as empty space:
only μέθεξις, accepting participation in the ideas, and παρουσία, com-
municating currency of the ideas, give things their characteristics, their types,
their palm-like, leonine quality, beauty, and goodness high up. And in a
cloudy form, in mere imitation, compared with the pure Jacob's ladder, of
the pyramid of ideas rising with ever truer Being to ever higher perfection.
After all, its apex is supposed to be the *idea of goodness*, as the sole and
final definition projecting into the mystically indefinite element of the
highest Being. At the same time this idea is supposed to be the purposive
cause of the whole methexis and parusia, herewith reverting to the strong
wishful character which, as we have seen, accompanied Plato's apparently
so contemplative vision from the start, with longing, Eros, and Agon. From
this standpoint, from the standpoint of the supreme idea of goodness (Plato
calls it, not without purposive cause itself, τὸ μέγιστον μάθημα, his most
important piece of instruction) Plato's reforming activity seeks to justify
itself, together with the hierarchical utopia, as does his momentous equation
of ever higher perfection with ever more existing Being and vice versa.
The latter equation is even supposed to make the wishful landscape of
Platonism into an ever – more real one, the higher it rises into the ether of

* 'Faust', Part I, 449–53.

the Ideas; an idealistic hypostasis (the more perfect, the more real) which ultimately has a continuing influence right down to Anselm's proof of the
existence of God (ens perfectissimum – ens realissimum), and in fact into the
Being-for-itself, ever more impervious to reality, of the 'absolute spirit' in
Hegel. And this provides at the same time the most decisive foil (e contrario)
for the ideal but not real definition of the Kantian 'final moral purpose'; which
of course, like all Kant's 'normative prototypes', presupposes Platonism,
together with its theory of two worlds, yet leaves out precisely the being
real, especially that rising with the ideals. The ideal land in view of the last
idea, that of goodness, is the same, but such that in Kant it stands in hope
and in unfortunately only an endless approach towards its realization, whereas
in Plato it stands in the strongest reality, removed from all Becoming. Above
all in the work of his old age, the 'Philebos', Plato developed the idea of
goodness as such a teleologically real central sun, with the double entrances:
pleasure and insight together, simply as 'what is desirable for all and (really)
perfect per se' (61 A). And the centripetal pull towards it ultimately itself
provided the heliotrope for the *Eros and Agon Platonism* which continued to
have an effect in otherwise so little dualistic but really teleological philosophies
like those of Aristotle, Leibniz, and Hegel. Eros in Aristotle is the impulse
(ὁϱμή) of matter to form, at its highest point to pure form = God; thus
the world shines here as self-embodying form. Eros in Leibniz is the inquiétude
poussante or tendency of the monads towards ever more alert, more copious
reflection (repraesentatio) of the universe; thus the world shines here as a self-
brightening phenomenon of light. Eros in Hegel is the penetrating power
of the dialectical shaping, reshaping, out of the Hades of the abstract In-itself
through the jungle of the physical Beside-itself to the Being-for-itself of
culture; thus the world shines here as process of its self-emptying, self-
amalgamating spiritual substance. All these are idealisms in the ethereal direction of their wish and their aim, yet idealisms which would not only not have
become objective ones without the hierarchical Platonic realm but which have
enriched the knowledge precisely of the world from within itself far beyond
Democritus and Democritism. Namely through transforming incorporation
of the originally so static pyramid of ideas into an emerging succession;
whereby in fact a new, by no means exhausted perspective appeared: that
of immanent teleology.

Bruno and the infinite work of art; Spinoza and the world as crystal

And now thinking turns outward again, so that it looks at matter once

more. This occurred in the newer, bourgeois attitudes in so far as they
were given over to this world and nothing else any more. In so far as
they wanted to go into the garden of this world and not just to work
in it but also take pleasure in it. Thus Thales had caused the fertilizing
water, and Anaximenes the invigorating air to flow around everything,
and both already did this with religious devotion to the world. Matter
was enhanced and animated, there was even room in it for the ethereal
and for this in particular. But this never occurred more beautifully, and
above all more broadly than in the vision of *Giordano Bruno*, which finally
again seeks to be a materially immanent one like that of the first Ionian
thinkers (Bruno deliberately praises them), but is a distant vision here.
The appearance of the habitual becomes too narrow in the age of discoveries
and the Copernican revolution: 'It is obviously foolish', says Bruno, 'to
think there are no other creatures, no other senses and no other intellect
than those familiar to us.' A wish, itself vast, into the boundless now
begins, il eroico furore, an oceanic feeling, a cosmic consciousness, as if
on a great mountain-top with the clouds beneath one and only the sun
and the stars above one, around one. Thus Bruno steps forward, a
philosophical minnesinger of infinity, in the spirit of Copernicus, but far
beyond and above him, for even the ceiling of the heavens cracks, to which
the latter had left the fixed stars attached. The perspective into this-worldly
infinity began earlier in pictures, in the large horizon in Jan van Eyck,
than in thought; despite large preparations in Alain de Lille, and especially
in Nicholas of Cusa. This new space, a centrifugal space, is now completely broken all around the earth, not just on the horizon but also into
the zenith: the earth disappears, but also the sun as the centre, and there
remains only the infinite sphere whose centre is everywhere. In addition,
'minimum' and 'maximum' are now to harmonize in comprehensive
infinity: the minimum as a point, atom, monad, the maximum as the
universe in which this individual profusion is framed. Not numerically
framed as in a dead space, but so that the inexhaustible activity of the
principle inherent in the world posits an equally rich and varied profusion
of formations. At the same time, however, the *entirety* of the universe
is again celebrated as the balancing out of all these differences, so that
intoxication with the world, which has climbed so high, really does see
and would like to see all the clouds of existence beneath it. Hence also
the differences between light and shadow and above all the shadows
themselves; this is now to balance itself out in harmony, sub specie toti,
in just the same way as like and unlike, motion and rest, and ultimately

possibility and reality. The latter above all: the denial of a separate, still existing possibility in the *entirety* of the world, maintaining as it were the finished emptiedness of the universe as one which is closed, – denotes a strange interruption in the perspective of infinity in Bruno himself; and this precisely in accordance with the wishful image of a *cosmically existing perfection*. For only finite things are, according to Bruno, not everything they can be, indeed for him the formative power inherent in things never wearies of creating new forms, but in the entirety of the universe the possible and the real are supposed to coincide perfectly, because it is itself perfection. For if it still contained an unrealized possibility, if all the possibilities had not been realized in it, then – so Bruno argues – it would lack something, and thus would not be perfect. But Bruno thereby applied not only the classical concept of harmony and that of the Renaissance to the universe, with art which has supposedly everywhere achieved its goal, but also the ens perfectissimum of scholastic theology. And in addition, against all prospects of open unrealized elements in the world, the divine 'Possest', 'Can be' of God in Nicholas Cusanus, as the absolute reality in which ipso facto all possibilities are realized. Thus Bruno once again introduced a finiteness into his infinity, namely that of being statically enclosed in the extent and entirety of the universe itself; at this point therefore, towards the future, the ceiling of the heavens is not yet broken. The temptation to this is of course – as goes without saying in the great anti-theist – not theology, but ultimately the great wishful landscape of the world as a *completed work of art*. And the work of art points to the artist, to something divine as artist – in world-immanent and workmasterly terms precisely in the heart of nature itself. But Bruno has thereby again employed possibility, if not in the Totum of the world, then at least for every individually shaping element within this Totum, and above all for the workmasterly element within it: the 'natura naturans'. This is the fire of life which formatively runs through things, the πῦϱ τεχνικόν of Heraclitus, but *inseparably linked with matter*. Matter is the birth-giving womb, it contains all its forms and designs potentially, and brings them to light at the same time with its *own potentiality*: 'Thus we attain a more worthy view of the Godhead and this Mother Nature who produces, preserves and incorporates us again in her womb, and we will henceforth no longer believe that any body is without a soul, or even, as many lie, that matter is nothing other than a cesspit of chemical substances' (Werke, 1909, VI, p. 120f.). Matter has other 'dimensions' in the form of man, others in that of the horse, others in the form of the myrtle, others in that of the eye: but

it has the potential for all this equally and at the same time the potentiality
to shape it thoroughly and to mould it. It is the same material principle
which is formative in metals, plants, and animals, and which thinks and
organizes in human beings, except that it manifests itself in an infinitely
various way. Logically, Bruno calls the distinction: formless matter,
immaterial form a pure abstraction and abolishes it. Instead, he celebrates
matter itself as the 'dator formarum', as Mother Nature (natura naturans)
and Nature of Forms (natura naturata) in one; he thus completes the
'naturalization' of Aristotle, which had been driven towards more and
more emphatic materialism by his follower Strato, by his commentator
Alexander of Aphrodisias, by Avicenna and Averroës, by Avicebron and
the Amalrikans. Towards a qualitative materialism though, one in which
matter largely appeared in man's image, in the life-image and creator-image
of Renaissance man, with a Renaissance dimension. The world-matter
in Paracelsus was also so full of forging 'Vulcanus', so full of 'water spirits'
in Jakob Böhme. 'Among the properties innate in matter, motion is the
first and most excellent, not just as mechanical and mathematical motion,
but even more as the drive, vital spirit, vigour, as the agony – to use
Jakob Böhme's term – of matter': this sentence from Marx's 'Holy Family'
is equally true of Bruno, together with the statement: 'Matter smiles on
the whole man in poetically sensuous lustre.' In fact this statement is
particularly true of Bruno, of the world as a work of art. Of the wishful
image of man as a child in Mother Nature, of the enthusiasm which wants
to know it is in agreement with the this-world of infinity. Where the
universe stands for the All and nature already seems to belong completely
in the place it occupies.

Even the thinking which does not guard against being edifying purifies
itself as bright thinking beforehand. The mirror of cognition is checked
for stains or uneven patches before it is worked with. First came the check
for sensory delusion, later and more importantly there followed that for
impure logical components, and in addition for those of an emotional kind.
Bruno believed there was no reason to clarify thinking other than by
smashing windows and expanding in all directions. But *Spinoza*, when
he likewise took the mysterious path outwards, wrote his moral essay 'On
the improvement of the intellect'. This essay is moral and not merely –
as goes without saying in the most unequivocal of all rationalists –
epistemological; but he seeks all the more eagerly to purge the intellect
itself of the turmoil of the emotions which cloud and weaken it. And
to them belongs everything which lures towards transitory possessions

(sensual pleasure, riches, external honour), unlike the lasting possession and Object of a true life. To them belongs everything which is clear only as such a lure, unlike the genuine clarity that is gained in certainty through unerring intellect and that solely provides constant joy. So no wishes whatsoever seem to have any place in it either, since wishing, above all as hoping, involves that uncertain element which is detrimental to joy and to the pride of cognition. Spinoza tried to remove all such 'inadequate emotions' as vehicles of 'inadequate ideas' even more clearly in his 'Ethics'; and consequently not just remorse and the like, as something depressing, but also hope and the like, as something uncertain (Eth. III, Table of Emotions 12). In fact, inadequate ideas without any real reference are also supposed to lie in all qualitative and value judgements, like: 'good, evil, order, confusion, hot, cold, beauty and ugliness' (Eth. I, Appendix). And yet the same philosopher outlined in his system one of the most cheerful landscapes of order in the world – precisely on the basis of what he calls rational clarity. Not without inconsistency (it is often particularly noticeable in Spinoza, since he develops different chains of thought so consistently that they cannot be harmonized any more) there is now after all a knowledge of good and evil, indeed one linked with emotions: 'The knowledge of good and evil is nothing other than the emotion of joy or sorrow in so far as we are aware of it' (Eth. IV, Prop. 8). And even more than this: the judgements about perfection and imperfection are admittedly supposed to be purely subjective, 'modes of thinking' with false, purely anthropomorphic measurement (Eth. IV, Intro.), but perfection itself is characterized as so objective that Spinoza can say: 'By reality and perfection I understand the same thing' (Eth. II, Def. 6). That is, there are supposed to be no value judgements about perfection because there is no measurable More or Less of perfection at all in the sense of opinions, but only a More or Less in the sense of reality (Eth. V, Prop. 40) and no objective-real imperfection at all. So one looks here, against the grain, into the most perfect desideratum – a non desiderando, into a so *perfect wishful landscape of philosophy that it leaves nothing to be desired any more*. All this results for Spinoza from the sole kind of knowledge which he allows: from that sub specie aeternitatis and its perspective. As an absolute greatness of contemplation, cursing nothing, ridiculing nothing, but knowing everything in the form of eternity, which is also the form of the comprehended necessity of everything: 'Things could be produced in no other way and in no other order by God than that in which they have been produced' (Eth. I, Prop. 33). It is therefore not a part, as in Bruno, of the infinite creative power of the natura naturans to form precisely the imperfect as well alongside the perfect, but: 'From what has gone before it clearly follows that things are produced in their highest perfection by God; since they have necessarily followed from the given most perfect nature' (Eth. I, Prop. 33, Note). Necessarily followed, which means here: just as mathematics is regarded as an exemplary kind of knowledge of necessity, so things have followed more geometrico, with the same apodictic consistency, from the God-nature. Accordingly even human actions and drives (however much they may be denounced for the most part as 'inadequate emotions' or neo-Stoically as 'perturbationes animae') are also regarded 'as if investigation had to do with lines, areas and bodies' (Eth. III, Intro.). Spinozism is from here in fact the Novum: *mathematical* pantheism; which distinguishes it particularly clearly from the enthusiastic pantheism of Bruno. But it does not distinguish it from the powerful immanence of Bruno (with Avicenna and Averroës behind him), which in Spinoza rather becomes only world-figure, likewise concerning and containing natura naturans, natura naturata: 'Namely that by natura naturans we have to understand that which is in itself and is comprehended through itself, or such attributes of substance which express eternal and infinite essentiality. But by natura naturata I understand everything which follows from the necessity of the nature of God or of each of God's attributes, i.e. all the modes of the attributes of God in so far as they are regarded as things' (Eth. I, Theorem 29, Note). Deus sive natura is, as naturing, therefore just as much the ground or the implied perfect world as it is, as natured, the same sequence in terms of content or the explicated perfect world. 'I work at the buzzing loom of time/And weave vivid clothes for the Godhead sublime':* this statement by Goethe's Earth-spirit does of course separate his terrestrial essence from the universal Godhead, but it definitely contains as a whole the jubilant identity of natura naturans and natura naturata. And in the depths of Spinoza's world, to which the unity of amor fati and amor dei intellectualis turns, that silence reigns in which the tide of life and the storm of action die down, into harmony. The vast wish-fulfilment reigns of 'Above all summits there is peace',† and Goethe's other seraphic statement is conceived: 'For all urging, all struggle is eternal rest in the Lord God.'‡ So the thinker who sought to purify the intellect totally of everything which does not belong to the intellect finally noted down the most solemnly beautiful landscape of wishful feeling in his universe. The world stands here as *crystal, with the sun in the zenith, so that nothing casts a shadow.* No God thrusts here from outside, Spinoza in his

---

* 'Faust', Part I, 508–9.
† From Goethe's 'Wanderers Nachtlied'.
‡ 'Zahme Xenien VI'.

'Theological-political Treatise' protests brilliantly against the view that knowledge can be learned from religion, that deus sive natura should be confused with the image of gods in any religion: thus he is not only a mathematical pantheist, but a pantheistic materialist. With nothing but 'world which has made itself' (Eth. I, Appendix), with worldliness of the highest consciousness, and consciousness of the highest worldliness. Time is missing, history is missing, development is missing and especially every concrete multiplicity in the one ocean of substance. But Spinozism gives – and this constitutes its unique altitude – a picture of the world which seems to have no subjectivity because it is wholly filled with perfect object-substance, and no purpose because the perfect does not need one. Spinozism stands there as if there was eternal noon in the necessity of the world, in the determinism of its geometry and of its both carefree and situationless crystal – sub specie aeternitatis.

Augustine and goal-history; Leibniz and the world as process of illumination

The thinking that looks outwards skirts along the edge of things. If this movement is essentially a *temporal*, forward-directed one, it entrusts itself to a flux, not to rest. The prospect is then one of progress, and rest itself is not in the rounded whole but only in an outflowing, late on, probably even right at the end. It is characteristic that Heraclitus, the philosopher of flux, called time the 'first body', and in fact he was preceded in this line even earlier by orphic-mythical thinking. Pherekydes, one such orphic, had thus placed Chronos at the beginning of things and caused fire, the breath of air and water to spring from him, in other words nothing but things that have been moved; Zeus, the heavens, and Chthonia, the depths of the earth, here stand only in the second rank. He was followed by Heraclitus with his strange yet trend-setting propositions; the gods disappeared, the in every sense original Kronos-Chronos remained. But at the same time a second feature of the perspective beginning with time and running within it was laid down here: namely the vision of Becoming as a value-stressed *becoming light*. As we have seen, Empedocles had in any case declared something as thoroughly interested and therefore value-stressed as 'hate and love' to be the agent of motion, of the separation and combination of substances. And from this standpoint a view was now possible which emphasized actual *historical time* in the world, with rest only in the initial and final state of the world. In between lies the intervention

of separating hate, and furthermore in three periods: that of the emerging
separation of substances, that of their total severance by a complete
preponderance of love; after which the whirlpool of process, evenly freed
of hate and love, of the motion of separation and combination, again flows
into the 'sphairos of harmony'. But flows into it again as a temporal sphere;
for even the sphairos is transitory, because severing hate invades it again and
again and sets the life of nature in motion, together with re-combining love.
The peculiar contribution of Empedocles is therefore that he not only introduced concepts of value into the contemplation of nature, but that he tried
above all to divide up the motion of nature into periods through the
alternating proportional shares of hate and love – with the ultimate extinction
of both in a kind of worldlessness in general. Mythical definitions also
undoubtedly lay behind this as well, as in Heraclitus' theory of time as the
'first body' and especially in the Chronos who began everything for
Pherekydes. In fact, the mythical definitions of the Heraclitean body of time
even have the same mythical origin as the powers of hate and love in
Empedocles, namely a Persian one. 'Boundless time' is at the head of the
genesis of the world in the Zendavesta too; and in Persian myth the counter-
movements of hate and love act more than ever as those of the destructive
Ahriman, of the bright Ormuzd. And this Persian dualism, renewed many
centuries later by Mani and his sect, in turn stirred so many centuries after
Empedocles a late classical thinker who was a – Manichaean, before he became
a Church Father: *Augustine*. It is therefore no leap over historical abysses at
all if now at this point, almost over the heads of all the Greek philosophers
who lie between them, Empedocles and Augustine move closer together –
linked by Persian myths, as thinkers of a *struggle of process*, of a perspective
of the triumph of love, the triumph of light. And Augustine's clear mission:
to make room in society for Christ as against Caesar, naturally particularly
sharpened the duality of hate and love, darkness and light. And furthermore,
the total insertion of Ahriman or the devilish element into the pole of hate,
and Ormuzd or the divine element into the pole of love vastly dramatized
the world-process; from an alternating process relationship of hate and love
it is turned into a *battlefield between Satan and Christ*. This new perspective
appears, world-historically harnessed between the Fall and the Last Judgment,
in the twenty-two books of Augustine's 'De civitate Dei', a single preparatory
activation of feudal-clerical society and much more besides. So that this book
displays yet another context and content than that of social utopia which has
already been dealt with, – a content which fires, excites and aims at the whole
of history. The repose posited as given of a Hen kai Pan, as a sphere or later as

a mathematical crystal nature, is now over. But the eternal recurrence of a cycle is also over, with no other result at all in its dynamics than a sphairos which shatters over and over again through the power of hate. On the contrary: world history is unique, together with its climax Christ; it becomes the sphairos (here the 'Sabbath rest of the world'), and is portrayed as a no longer disturbable triumph of the lux aeterna. The path of history is now to proceed to this end, according to Augustine, in six epochs (articuli temporis) through night to light, through a journey of war and pilgrimage by the chosen few and their kingdom of God right through the civitas terrena of sinful creation (and fallen nature). The goal itself of course is ready given here, and already existent high above, indeed for an omniscient God history conversely does not exist as process: 'All happenings have already happened in praedestinatione Dei... ideo nihil recens sub sole'* (De civ. Dei XII, 14). And with a further, purely spatial colouring, if not elimination of the category of time: 'The civitas Dei is as far removed from the civitas terrena as the sky is from the earth' (l.c., V, 17). So that therefore the historical process of light may finally stand as a merely pedagogical one, as one of mere progressive *light-finding* instead of progressive *light-kindling itself* occurring in the matter. But it is precisely this which, for all the rejection of human hubris, is intended in Augustine's perspective and has influenced – not ecclesiastical history of course, certainly not, but rather heretical history. Most of all with the *directedness of time*, as time which is irreversible in terms of salvation history, but also which cannot be arrested in any previous civitas Dei mode. After which this directedness came back to life precisely in the work of the man who took Augustine's kingdom of God most seriously of all, in Joachim of Fiore, the Isaiah of the thirteenth century. For whom the status of light even from the point of view of its existence is one which is only coming up, so that it is not now found by means of the formation of historical stages, but is *itself coming to birth*. And at work in this directedness is Augustine's proposition of the restoration of the human like-ness at the end of history, which decisively fired heretical history. Namely because of the sharply eschatological emphasis it possesses despite the 'restoration' (the mere restitutio in integrum) and despite the rejection cited above of all historical production (regarding the kingdom of God). This vast proposition, *clearly containing something new*, of a wishful land was effective above all: *'We human beings ourselves will be the seventh day'*, 'Dies septimus etiam nos ipsi erimus, quando eius fuerimus benedictione et sanctificatione pleni...'†

---

* 'in God's predestination...and so there is nothing new under the sun'.

† 'We ourselves will be the seventh day, when we will be filled with his blessing and sanctification...'.

(l.c., XXII, 30). But on the path towards this Augustine remains the greatest discoverer right up until Leibniz of the objective function of time: furthermore as a function of the world itself, despite the mythologically fixed connections. For Augustine ultimately stressed, in a distant vision of process which was unavoidable again and again, nothing less than the *mutability of the world* which makes this process possible. And this in the literal, both negative and ultimately complex positive sense of the concept of changeability – as a fall into the transitory (corruptio, defectus), but above all also as a progression (augmentatio, profectus) of deliverance. Though here Augustine's concept of time (and this first philosopher of history was accordingly also the first to think deeply about time) is strangely shackled both to mere reality based on experience and to the image of the hour-glass simply trickling down. Time trickles as it were out of the retort of the future through the narrow crack of the present incessantly, inexorably into the retort of the past; whereby an image of gravity, an image of anti-flight simultaneously gets under way. In this respect the depraving element, indeed the character of death in the lapse of time now also predominates, seen from this standpoint, the transport out of vague future through the so narrow actuality of the moment down into an increasingly accumulating No-Longer-Being of the past. Changeability, conceived along these lines predominantly as corruptio and defectus, therefore signifies in its time merely an imperfection in Being, a defect, indeed a downright evil; Augustine thinks he is able to devour this kind of changeability with the nothingness out of which the world was created and into which 'all things can also pass away, quae ex nihilo facta sunt'* (l.c., XII, 8). But Augustine advances from the falling of this hour-glass time thoroughly dialectically to time as a pilgrimage, to movement out of the defectus into nothingness towards the profectus into expectant fullness. If the temporal being of creatures and the world sinks into the past again and again because of their share of nothingness, *temporal being as unfolding* proceeds into the future again and again, from which its existence and ultimately an ever truer one accrues. According to Augustine's mythology, of course, only the creator mundi himself, i.e. God, keeps us above the abyss and ultimately saves us from the abyss; otherwise there would not be any process upwards. But this is also the way in which events, instead of merely flowing away into the specific nothingness of the past, move into the unfolding of the future, into the realization of its possibilities, especially of the possibilities of salvation pre-arranged for it. Though their content lies for Augustine once again totally

* 'which are made from nothingness'.

outside temporality, it is Being without any time: 'Observe the changes of things, and you will find Erit et Fuit; think of God and you will find Est, in which Fuit et Erit cannot be' (In Joh. ev. tractatus 38, 10). The crystal of repose thereby even rises out of all dissonances of time, but as a crystal of the *end of history*. Thus it is the one most alien to pantheism, it is not one of a cosmic curve, but of the thoroughly transcendental depths, not one of space but of eternity. 'Nunc stans aeternitas': this is for Augustine the original light which only breaks through after a totally ended historical-cosmic illumination.

A thinking which is charged with time mostly also proves to be humanly charged. For passing away and arising are not only looked at but at first experienced in a particularly close and involved way in one's own body and being. Even if time is by no means the form of the inner mind, but a material mode of existence through and through, its consciousness still unlocks more than that of space a striving and Where To in Being. In all thinkers who look outward and are nevertheless full of subjective movement we therefore find the motion of things as an equally aroused motion. A tangle of emotional and world events takes place which had first been indicated in Empedocles by 'hate and love'. But which also arose in the great progressive thinker of development Aristotle as ὁϱμή, i.e. as the stated 'urge of matter towards form', and then as a 'self-realization of form in matter'. And which finally in antiquity fulfilled Augustine's world-perspective of a struggling pilgrimage, with farewell to the old society and with the formation of signals for the new society. All this now intensifies with the incipient bourgeois-self-confident and so subject-rich, ultimately dynamic consciousness of the modern age. In so far as it appears precisely as *tendency to light*, as *light in tendency* and not already as spatial completion of light. An essential feature from Eckhart to Hegel in this predominant temporal landscape of philosophy (in other words Non- or Not-Yet-Spinozism) is the co-operation of self-illumination and world-illumination, such that the Fiat lux assists itself and echoes on in both. There is *Eckhart*: the ground of everything that is declares itself, man is its highest word, and in him it returns as a recognized ground back into itself. If non-thinking creatures are the footprints of the ground which has turned out well, then the thinking soul is its likeness, its likeness released from all unclear darkness. *Paracelsus* follows, or the doctrine of the ground as the creative force of nature itself, inside and outside, in the fever and in the storm, in man and in the world. But man is the highest undertaking of this natura naturans, and it is up to him to reinforce and to purify ever further the Becoming of things. God wants everything he has laid out and left imperfect to be brought to completion: the doctor as philosopher, the philosopher as doctor thus stands wholly in this process of purification. The purification occurs in a very broad sense alchemically: both as a removal of impure elements and as a heightening of virtus, efficiency, fullness of life. All this is to occur through truth to nature, that is, the 'imagination' true to the natura naturans, which knows all about 'quintessence'. This means in turn: about the extraction of the vital essence from everything, about the continuation of the 'maize of the great world'; even the Last Judgement is thus understood in moral-chemical, chemical-moral terms. *Jakob Böhme* follows – precisely related in such processing out – or the doctrine of the manifestation of the dark original ground through quaking, kraken, quality on towards the kingdom of light. 'If one wants to talk of God, what God is, one must diligently consider the forces in nature.' But these (and this kind of thing had no longer been heard since Heraclitus) are themselves a struggle between opposites. Thus to begin with: 'Nature has two qualities in it, a lovely, heavenly and holy one, and a fierce, hellish and thirsty one' (Aurora, Preface 9); this is still reminiscent of the old Manichaean duality. But then comes the continuation: 'All creatures are made from these two sources, and everything which grows out of the earth, which lives and wells out of the force of these qualities... For through its double source everything has its great mobility, running, racing, welling, sprouting and growing' (l.c., Chap. 2, 1); this consequently passes from the Manichaean to objective dialectics. With seven 'welling spirits' or 'natural forms', from the dry and bitter through the fire of lightning to warm light, to the peal of joy right up to the whole corpus naturae and to Christ in man, 'a thousand times greater than the Father', i.e. than the undeveloped beginning or original ground. Thus the self-explication of the ground here is not only its *self-knowledge*, as in Eckart, but apart from this its *self-correction*. As a theme which, minus the chemical nights and days with which it was coloured in Paracelsus and Böhme, became everlasting from here on in the philosophy of process.

But now of course, although all this definitely intended thinking of light-becoming, it had not escaped from the fermentation of the latter. Its powerful internal and external weather therefore still formed no separate strict counterpart to the Spinozism of the crystal. This counterpart is first given in that landscape, illuminating itself so vigorously and extensively, which is described by *Leibniz*. Consequently by the thinker of genetic enlightenment, by the perception and explication of the world-content developing in ever clearer, ever more distinct reflection. Nevertheless,

Leibniz definitely stands in the landscape of process entered by Paracelsus and Böhme; among so many riches he has this specifically German Renaissance dimension even to a considerable degree. Leibniz's enlightenment, in keeping with its rationalistic spirit, abandoned the fermenting system of retorts, and a foaming gold-cooking is replaced by a continuous intensity-sequence of light-increasing, but in fact: this light-increasing forms precisely in Leibniz the *world as process of illumination*, the landscape of its perfectibilité. Five main points particularly stand out in the present connection here, they all show man, time, and world once again as intertwined and related to the process of growing light. Firstly all Being is supposed to consist here of mental power-points, each of them a totally internal life which has no windows, but finding in itself, namely reflecting, everything outside. Secondly these monads are characterized in this reflection by an appetitus, a tendency, for they are conceived as cosmopolitans of the Enlightenment, they are all of the race which strives out of darkness into light, and for Leibniz there is nothing but this appetitus of light. Thirdly the tendency, as 'inquiétude poussante', runs *explosively*, particularly when constricted, and Leibniz here uses the arch-processive, long unheard equation of open space and – future: 'Just as, in the elastic body which is constricted, its greater dimension lies as striving, so in the monad does its own future state', and further, in a reply to Bayle in 1702: 'One can say that in the soul, as everywhere else, the present is big with the future.' In such definitions, objective dialectics above all attained more clearly than ever before the closest connection with process, indeed as a process essentially mediated with the future, not only with the past (cf. Ernst Bloch, Subjekt-Objekt, 1951, p. 123f.); despite the block against the genuine future, against what is in reality new, which even Leibniz displays. Fourthly the tendency, precisely as an immanent one peculiar to the monads themselves, possesses its Where To as What For; it cannot even be conceived without such a *purposive relation*. Leibniz differs above all even in this point from Spinoza and no less from Bacon and Hobbes, who all rejected the category of purpose; Spinoza called it the refuge of ignorance. However, this rejection was directed chiefly against the equation of teleology and theology, i.e. against transcendental purpose-setting by a divine will, by divine Providence and the like. But Spinoza himself by no means avoided the category of purpose when he saw it at work in naturalistic terms, i.e. in the work of man, not in a so-called work of God: as for instance in the definition of the state as a machine built by men for the purpose of their welfare. And however much Leibniz ultimately seeks to found his concept of purpose, i.e. with a metaphysical limiting concept, in a divine purpose-setting of the best of all things possible, just as little does he cancel out the causal determinism in it which has no exception; instead this prevails in order to fulfil the purpose, as in a machine. And the concept of purpose is in fact applied to immanent tendency, as a Where To connection between the natural and the moral world. It guarantees the perfectibilité of the world, and therefore not just the harmony of all the activities of the monads but the ever brighter representation of the universe in the monads, right down to the transformation of the world into the highest brightness of its content. Fifthly, for the first time since Aristotle, Leibniz opened up with genuine ideas of process the concept of *possibility* again, conceived both as 'disposition', 'dispositio' to unfolding in every monad, and as a 'realm of infinite possibilities', of which the existing world is a partial realization. The 'disposition' is the virtual containment of the predicates within the subject, again with sharp reference to the tendency: 'Omne possibile exigit existere'.* The 'realm of infinite possibilities' on the other hand, from among which the existing world constitutes a partial realization, signifies despite the purely theological location given to this realm by Leibniz an enormous horizon of possibility, which also in fact extends into the existing world itself (by virtue of the 'dispositions' within it). So much in this connection, that of the landscape of process, for the five main points of a *theory of world development sub specie perfectionis instead of a theory of world perfection sub specie aeternitatis*. Since Leibniz portrays an inorganically-organically-humane graduated structure of the universe as the climax of illumination, he also posits the process of this climax, the pluralistically dynamic process, as just as much a formation of tiers towards perfection. 'Every substance is like a world by itself and like a mirror of God or rather of the whole universe which it, each in its own way, expresses' (Philos. Schriften, Gerhardt, IV, p. 434), – namely in an ever clearer and more distinct way. Thus the independence of forces and the self-development of things continuously rise and intensify, with the ultimate purpose of a clarity which represents both the 'machine of God' and the 'state of God', that is, of the highest perfection. 'By virtue of this harmony the paths of nature lead to grace of their own accord' (Monadologie, § 88): this is Leibniz's utopia of world-process in place of Spinoza's unity of nature and grace and as against Augustine's transcendental influence of grace. The 'dark ground' of course, the 'gloomy non-ground' of Jakob Böhme has likewise been omitted in this rationalism, as one ab ovo usque finem. Only the later *Schelling* referred to it

---

* 'Everything possible demands existence.'

again, not without a very differently obscure, namely reactionary brief, but apart from this not without the strength of the memory that precisely in the striving, volitional, dynamic element of Leibniz's tendency there lies something other than the mere logos of the Ratio. Hence Schelling's distinction between the positing, volitional That-element and the rational What-element in process (indicated in Aristotelian terms as the difference between the ὅτι and the διότι, expressed in scholastic terms as the difference between the quodditas and the quidditas). 'The first Be-ing, this primum existens, is therefore at the same time the first contingent element (original contingency). This whole construction therefore begins with the genesis of the first contingent element – what is unlike itself – , it begins with a *dissonance* and probably must begin in this way' (Schelling, Werke X, p. 101). If we leave aside the 'falling away' mythology, added to this by Schelling, of this first Being, an incalculable process element is certainly considered along with the intensity factor of process conceived as Böhme's 'non-ground'. For if the growth of cosmic brightness as such only had *rational* elements, then there would be nothing at all which hastened growth with an *intensive* agency. Furthermore, if the process did not have to produce and to manifest something which is by no means already ab ovo quidditas, there would be no process at all either, in fact there would not even be Leibniz's category of relation in it. Instead of this, and especially instead of the differences in brightness within a purely logical quidditas, there would be no differences and connections at all, but the collapse of all relations into processless identity. As is also wholly consistently the case in Spinoza's total rationalism in accordance with its radical elimination of process. But how significantly even the concept of process in Böhme ultimately stems from a darkly intensive upward struggle and its aurora; how conspicuously both a *healing process* and a *judicial process* are encompassed in the whole category of process, how both are referred to something negative which is to be healed and corrected by means of process. And the process in each of these forms must – be gained; for it refers back to something unfinished, something which ought not to be, which forms the foundation of this process without this process being founded on it. Which is why *Hegel* in particular – as remote as he was from Scheiling's Irratio, and however much the latter criticized him in particular – certainly adopted and recognized the old Böhmean 'resistance' from the standpoint of a non-ground. And which is moreover why Leibniz's intentions towards dialectics were so dynamically sharpened by Hegel, namely by transferring the process-driving agent into negation. Because the latter, as 'a nocturnal and turning point of existence', both tautens and breaks each time, an element of the non-ground is constantly sent into Leibniz's continuum, though also logicized by it again. But a sourdough, an element of blackness is thereby added to Leibniz's perfectionism, indeed to the idea of process as a simply self-interpreting self-love, self-knowledge of God out of perfection: 'This idea descends into edification and even into insipidity if the seriousness, the pain, the patience and work of the negative element is lacking in it' (Hegel, Werke II, p. 15). The negative element, this enormous driving power, is in Hegel's perspective of process for this very reason the 'inequality of substance with itself', because the positive element is only the 'essence' completing itself through its development. The essence as That-Which-Is in reality, this authentic element or in Hegelian language: Absolute therefore moves entirely to the peak of genetic world-preservation, that is, to its end. Temporality thus triumphs as a true production centre, at least in the world of historical Becoming-for-itself; thus essence lives in its Being-for-itself only as a goal. The world of process as a dominant to this tonic now becomes a total *blossom-fruit-archetype* in contrast to that of crystal: 'It must be said of the Absolute that it is essentially result, that it is what it is in reality only at the end' (l.c., p. 16). Here, of course, the renewed utmost logicization causes Hegel's philosophy of process to adjust its world purely to the idea, so much so that even every intensive-material element together with difference and negation is supposed to consist of spirit and nothing but spirit. Likewise, as in Leibniz, indeed more than in him, all predicates of the 'result' are far from being actually arising Nova, on the contrary they are already fixedly contained in every stage and simply not yet clear and distinct. This is the old barrier of contemplation and anamnesis even in philosophies of process, which has been preserved right up to the gates of Marxism. Anamnesis always remains conservative and thus prevents the real depiction of real processes, i.e. those working into the New. Nevertheless the line from Eckhart to Hegel, even the previously so transcendentally harnessed philosophy of history of Augustine, opens up a single dispersal from juxtaposition and even superimposition to succession, from space to time and calmly back to final form as result; – it is the line of Gothic instead of Egypt in philosophy.

The watchful concept or the 'authentic' as a task

If there is no thinking for its own sake, it must be clean for this very reason. Precisely because it has a need and volition behind it, this volition and its being-thought is only possible as a progressive one in each case, not as a cheerless one. The thinkers cited above thus stood on the heights of their age, though with a different status of themselves and their age and above all with a differently unerring glance into the core of the apparent world spirit. But all sought, idealistically and especially materialistically, in concrete aiming, the That-Which-Really-Is, to which man can cling. So that he did not stumble five steps from his house into darkness and thickets, but paths were made, the path was recognized as a real connection, and the sought-after essence became a tangible concept. It is characteristic of the great feature in philosophizing here that the essence which was thus displayed as presence, namely as house and hold, was to be an All in which each human concern and all external manifestations are comprised. The information about this Totum (we only have to think of Heraclitus' fire and then of the fixed sphere of being of the Eleatics) is so different that foolish confusers of substantial research with withered catechism thought they could call the history of philosophy the strongest refutation of philosophy. In reality the various great concepts, as those which portray non-transitory ideology of transitory conditions or even hired championings of social retrogression and decline, by no means depress to the point of relativism. Instead these great world concepts, often in transitory guise, with so much idealistic but also with mechanistic wetness behind the ears, represent sectors in succession or in juxtaposition and, expressed less statically, respective frontal areas of reality, complementing one another. Thus the sweeping Leibniz says he has never found a totally false idea anywhere, and if something like this is also far too sweeping, Hegel is still free of such objectivistic secondary stress of the universal, when he firstly only permits significant step-forming ideas as such and secondly treats these as progressive revelations of the world-content. His mistake is to portray these revelations as concrete reproductions of his abstract-logical categories, his merit is to have finally liberated the history of philosophy from a kind of intellectual collection of anecdotes, whereupon it becomes recognizable as a progressive unfolding of scientific world-consciousness. In addition, there is a further peculiarity of great philosophies, which has hardly been sufficiently taken into account up till now: the driving-to-an-end of their basic ideas, with the volitional, social-biased basic impetus in and behind it. This driving-to-an-end in fact constitutes the specific wishful landscape in philosophies, i.e. the perfection to which a promising motif of knowledge, a suggestive side of the world devoted to it, has been boosted. This was partly alleviated and partly concealed in its utopian character by the formal driving-to-an-end of logical consistency and the architectonic-total kind in the system. Alleviated because the logical consistency incorporates the volitional-emotional kind, like the steam of the locomotive which carries off the hot gases and thus promotes the draught in the boiler. The perspective of a utopian-completed kind is concealed by the rounding off – interrupted almost only in Kant – of a closed system in the fabric of doctrines of philosophy elaborated along pre-Marxist lines; which is why that which is distinguished as the 'authentic' appeared both as ready existing and as factually closed, and therefore without Front and Novum. The old spell of Platonic anamnesis is again at work throughout here, the theory that all learning is only a re-remembering of what was seen long ago and That-Which-Timelessly-Is; this antiquarian spell also conceals in the shape of the closed system the by no means antiquarian element in each perspective on to the 'authentic' or essence. Yet this perspective as such exists everywhere, and in fact: it is, sub specie toto, sub specie aeternitatis, one in which one of the great archetypes of the world as a whole (motion, rest, ocean of matter, light, crystal) is boosted into an image of the end, an image of perfection. Thus Heraclitus, Parmenides, Democritus came close, as did Bruno and Spinoza, and Leibniz in a different way – nothing but putting the world, in various sectors or even fronts, to the test of essence. And above all in the already *always* sorrowless and daybright materialism, in Bruno's world-tree, in Spinoza's midday crystal there rises the self-perfecting consciousness, there rises the critical optative: *If only it were so! If only the world were as full of enthusiasm as in Bruno, as full of shadowless crystallization as in Spinoza!* If only this intensification, indeed over-intensification of something which exists only in fragmentary form signified a solution of the world mystery! Such an optative holds good despite the total lack of history in Spinoza, which alone would cause the fragmentary Almost-Not in the projected midday crystal to be comprehended and pursued in a Not-Yet. The optative holds good despite the rationalistic dogmatism of the system, despite the pantheism which posits the denied God of heaven as the affirmed one of nature and which, as Feuerbach rightly says, represents the negation of theology from the standpoint of theology. But Spinoza's substance in its radiant repose – cum grano salis similar to Giotto's and Dante's repose in art – will appear as a *corrective* of Leibniz's goal of unrest and process. How remote, therefore, the thus conceived notation and distinction of philosophical images of perfection is from relativism and especially from the subjectivist abjurations of truth which are called pragmatism or fictionalism. But how remote, too, the notation cited above is from the non-dialectics which already regards the 'authentic' element and essence of things or even simply the Totum as a static completion – with the perspective only as an intending glance at or towards it and not also as an *object tendency itself*. The decision here runs: the optative, which strikes with more or less consternation according to the philosophical approximations to this essential element, has to become a *task* in order increasingly to recognize and increasingly to manifest the 'authentic' in the same feature. To put it another way: the essential element needs people for its ever more identical presentation; and this most thorough theory-practice is the moral of the corrected wishful landscape in philosophy.

From this point of view nothing is more false than the unexamined proposition that something is too beautiful to be true. It must be examined, which is a duty and without which certainly nothing can be affirmed about this beautiful thing from the start, but cannot be denied about it in this way either. Which means that more than anywhere else the watchful concept belongs here with a value-substance, even the highest, with which That-Which-Truly-Is has been provided. This concept is by no means the destructive one in terms of value, in the manner of a miserable and ultimately all the more subjectivist positivism, but it is more sharply than anywhere else (for corruptio optimi pessima) the correcting one. That is why Aristotle described the scientific statement as a proposition which precisely in contrast to the wishful proposition appears as true or false. Which only means of course that wishful propositions of a negative or positive kind, even if they refer to something objectively possible, refer to something which has not or not totally occurred and does not or not totally exist, so that they are not or not fully affirmable or deniable with regard to this. But rather all wishful propositions in so far as they can be treated scientifically move in the sphere of more or less great probability towards falsehood or truth; and furthermore, this probability is determined according to the degree of more or less great objective possibility in the content of the wishful proposition. Possibility therefore, that is, partial existence of conditions which is still by no means already sufficient for their realization, this constitutes the sphere in which nothing whatsoever can be too beautiful not to be true in the future at least, according to the conditions. Indeed in which truth, precisely as one of essence, with the full and very old golden sound of Being-In-Truth, possibly does not even have to beware of being edifying. Possibly of course, and this means in fact: after *correction* by detailed knowledge of the really occurring process, of the objective-real possibility in which the whole process-reality is substantiated as one of process-capacity itself. This correction came through Marx, and here least of all it extinguished the task of the world being changed into wished-for and humane recognition and of essence becoming that of an embracing At-Home. Without haste, not skipping pages in order to get to the end more quickly; without inflation of individual factors and sectors in order to impoverish the world in an idealistic but also vulgar-materialist way. Without idealistic reification of abstractions as a whole, which turn the world on its head, make the predicate into the subject and seek the primacy in the mind instead of in the interests and material conditions. But finally also without any above-mentioned after-effect of anamnesis in cosmic style, just as if the 'authentic' had already been produced and was stationed not just as ens perfectissimum but already as ens realissimum. Precisely because this is not the case, is fundamentally not yet the case, the watchful concept and its practice operates during the correction and after it just as tirelessly as mindfulness of the Verum Bonum, with truly highly-organized matter in view. Thus the world then stands of course with a crystal light of Spinozism in *philosophical pre-appearance*, which sees the world without anything unessential, more than this: without truly real unessential mischief. In the horizon of the task which proceeds from the amor fati to the control of comprehended destiny and from the amor dei intellectualis to world-devotion, but to the right kind and to that of a right world.

Two wishful propositions:
teachable virtue, the categorical imperative

Sober thinking is particularly splendid if it is not narrow as well. Bold thinking is particularly precious if it also knows the frontiers it is extending. And yet there are cases where it is necessary to shoot not just beyond the barriers but even beyond the goal in order to hit it. Just as conversely it can be a formula of total baseness to take things as they are, with a view to leaving them like that. There are therefore not only great conceptions of the world but also individual philosophical propositions which are false purely with regard to the facts and which yet, because even more about them leaves something to be desired, are not totally finished with regard to the truth. Whether it is that even concerning them, in them the wish arises: if only it were so! Or even whether it is that these propositions, at least partly, are false with regard to the facts because they have asserted something that is not yet due, in a hasty way, because they came too early. Here too the wish is then father to the thought, but not, as so often in other cases, to a foolish, extravagant, probably even lying thought, but to a thought rushing on ahead, even though in an exaggerated way. Such a thought can later also seem much more sober than many poor imitations and pieces of advice from what happens to exist at the time, which in their day thought they were ever so effective. Of course, the dry assessment of how things are and stand at present is indispensable and cannot be dry enough. But it is one thing to note the state of things is bad, and another to affirm it or even simply to consider it to be irremediable. Thus even one of the Seven Sages says: 'Most people are bad', which is not far from Hobbes' opinion, which until recently was almost overwhelmingly correct, that man is a wolf to man. But it is all a question of not agreeing with such opinions; of recognizing the causes from which they will not spring nor need to spring for ever; knowing how bad so many things still are, but knowing more deeply how good they could be. The latter is in fact to be found, in a hasty way, also often in an abstract wholesale fashion, in some otherwise not at all very comprehensible philosophical propositions; as for example in Socrates' proposition that nobody voluntarily does wrong. Such propositions share their, shall we say: cheerful haste with many wishful propositions of a much lesser kind; and they still have the defect that they do not seem to be conscious of their wish at all. But these propositions are so designed that they simply ironically conceal the wish, together with the well-known distance from the assertion and the land in which they are indigenous. This makes their seriousness related to the so particularly invisible and unobtrusive one of humour, which again is not at all hasty but rather stretches a point, because it takes misfortune even less, much less seriously than itself. Though the propositions of the kind intended and cited above by no means have a smile in common with humour but rather an empirically often so incomprehensible yet never precipitate, thoroughly well-housed elapsion. So that in them not just thoughts but also things sit easily side by side, in well accentuated pre-appearance. Which therefore does not hover in the air or would not have to if things were already on the right track everywhere.

Let us take the proposition that no man voluntarily does wrong. By saying this, *Socrates* is asserting much more than just this, virtue is teachable and learnable. He is also asserting more than the uniformity of virtue and insight, in the sense that true virtue consists in knowledge or, somewhat restrictively, that ultimately all virtues are only one: knowledge. And this knowledge for Socrates is only allowed to be one of goodness anyway, since nothing can be learnt from the trees, but rather from people in the town, and a knowledge of trees and things even more remote from the right style of living, which is all that matters, is of no use at all. For all its narrowness, this leads Socrates in his apologia even to the sublime remark that he does not know whether death is an evil but he does know that wrongdoing is one. And since this is totally knowable, teachable, and learnable, Socrates now goes on to the very much more extreme assertion, which sounds almost absurd at that time and place, that a man is totally incapable of doing what is wrong if he knows what is right. The knowledge of goodness as such is always the stronger, and cannot be overcome by any desire any more; so in order to arouse moral efficiency and εὐπραξία, happily general usefulness of behaviour, it is not the will but solely the understanding which has to be improved. Socrates of course, as a genuine enlightener, thereby acquitted man of a mere dull and often brute origin. The Kantian cry is his own: 'Enlightenment is the emergence of man from his self-inflicted minority.' But like the desire, the *defiance* not to want and not to do precisely what is good is not seen or admitted either. 'I am determined to prove a villain', says Richard III, so, wholly contrary to the high doctrine of Socrates, he still certainly has the psychological freedom of choice to do evil even though he has recognized it (and evil is in fact only a changing concept of good). The *circumstances* in particular are wholly omitted in which people live and by which their will is far more strongly determined than by the ABC, however illuminating, of moral knowledge. No more needs to be said here about what sounds nonsensical and is in fact actual nonsense in Socrates' proposition on virtue and knowledge, and it was only said in order to set off its relevant sense here, despite everything. Undoubtedly the wish is father to the thought in this proposition, yet in fact a wish which is not nonsensical itself, one which is not erroneous for ever, but merely one which was pronounced too early. If the circumstances are put in order which keep human beings from doing what is good, indeed from unfalsified ideology-free under-standing of it, then the determining influence of understanding on action is certainly no longer difficult. It is not even necessary to wait until the circumstances (they are fundamentally those of property) have all changed, for their changing itself, if it is concrete, is dominantly determined by the understanding of what is right. Sheer misery only becomes a revolu-tionary force through the notion which it gains of its situation and of true eupraxia, and the moral duty to change here springs of course inevitably from a knowledge which precisely in this decisive case is not least a knowledge of 'virtue'. So the proposition of Socrates cited above is of course not yet true at that time and place, but it has the advantage as it were of becoming and being able to become ever more true. Socrates did not say without further ado that man is good, but he said virtue was the only *true* human Being. And in order to do what is true voluntarily, firstly nobody must be compelled any more to suffer or carry out evil involuntarily, namely on pain of destruction, and secondly the good must certainly have been both recognized and admitted. In a finally friendly relation, one possible as friendly, of human beings to human beings, in this 'eupraxia' so prematurely accepted by Socrates what is known to be good can first and foremost make itself inevitable. Thus no man will in fact voluntarily do wrong if in accordance with the wishful image of this proposition the circumstances are changed which made it nonsensical because they prevented it.

Now let us take the much more desirable proposition that man is never merely a means but is an end. *Kant* teaches this, and the fact that for the time being this is only the statement of a demand is unfortunately obvious. Given an individual turn this Should-be runs: 'Man is unholy enough, but humanity in his person must be holy to him.' Given a social extension this Should-be runs: 'Act in such a way that the maxim of your will can simultaneously count as the principle of a general legislation, i.e. that in the attempt to conceive the maxim of this action as a generally obeyed law no contradiction emerges.' This kind of thing then becomes a downright command, the categorical imperative, as is well-known, the allegedly inherent-autonomous law of pure practical reason a priori. And once again – mutatis mutandis as in Socrates' proposition about knowledge and virtue – embarrassment, indeed rejection and consternation all arise together. Depending on whether the landscape of this moral proposition is considered directly, at that time and place, or in utopian terms, in its intended and legitimately intendable future-substance. In Kant's moral proposition what first leap to the eye as both strange and untenable are its all too inward quality, its coldly formal quality, its Prussian citoyen-like amalgam. But with so much distance from the old Adam and residue of earth that Jean Paul, precisely with regard to this moral proposition, could say that Kant was a complete radiant system of fixed stars all of a sudden. Undoubtedly the categorical imperative is strongly *inward*, crucial to it is the frame of mind in which people act, as good will in itself. In addition this frame of mind is portrayed in a very Prussian fashion as one in which not even any warmth, any inclination to do right is allowed to occur, on pain of not being pure. The only feeling it is allowed is the very bitter one called respect, for the moral law which simply commands. Something pure has rarely been frankly masked out of sheer purity in such an unfriendly and indeed sour way, such a gloomy reaction to something so good. Undoubtedly the categorical imperative is also strongly *formal*, i.e. its dutiful frame of mind is supposed to prove itself in the form, not in the content of wanting. Nor is its criterion, any more than its impetus and its motive, supposed to be an ingratiating one, one which does not characterize the moral command for its own sake and thus distinguishes it from all mere 'advice of cleverness', all squinting at secondary purposes and also consequences. The latter gave only impure imperatives, which changed depending on the situation and were therefore hypothetical, whereas the true moral commandment, commanding unconditionally, is and must be simply a categorical one. And for this very reason a criterion according to Kant must be a purely formal one, i.e. one absolutely free from situational fluctuations and historical changes of its empirical content, indeed such a very formal one at that time and place that Kant cannot name any ethical criterion at all any more, but solely one from – formal logic. It is simply that of non-contradiction; whereby the capacity of a maxim to be conceived as a generally obeyed law has its morality measured and decided solely by the permanent unity of what is thus conceived. Accordingly, man can only not want people to lie in general because it contradicts the concept of the statement for it to be a lie. Or man can only not want a deposit to be embezzled because it contradicts the concept of the deposit, as a sum destined to be given back, for it to be embezzled. In fact hardly any ethics has ever started out more formally, not even the most laborious ethics of reflection; again out of sheer purity the virtue of the pure frame of mind always needs a collegium logicum, as the testing laboratory of its metal. And finally the categorical imperative is undoubtedly also strongly *ideological*, namely a Prussian walking-stick plus the idealized realm of the bourgeoisie. The Prussian walking-stick, incorporated into his own frame of mind, was even often felt to be the more powerful element in Kant's moral proposition and thus either rejected, by the victims of bounden duty, or praised, by the provost marshals and indeed those driving people to the slaughter. As if in fact the absolute moral law, simply commanding towards the natural impulses of the human creature, did not look wholly unlike the will of the absolute monarch, simply commanding towards the underling human creature. Be that as it may, far more clearly than the walking-stick at any rate, Kant's moral proposition, ideologically conceived, contains the idealized realm of the bourgeoisie developing out of the middle citizen. It contains no monarch, but the formal equality of all before the law, against class privileges, and all the more against privileged masters' morality; all this reflected with German, non-revolutionary abstraction. The citoyen who had raised himself in the ideology of the French Revolution in an unmediated-ideal way above the real businessman of the bourgeois class was now spiritualized or cerebralized more than ever into a humanity in the sublimely general sense. And here again, amazingly brief cross-connections consist of such great normative height with precisely this real businessman; as in the above-mentioned example of criteria for the general conceivability of a maxim, in the example of the deposit. In this respect, of course, Kant's moral proposition is then not at all merely formal either, not at all merely pure practical reason without any regard to empirical motives, to a heteronomous sanction, i.e. one lying outside its self-legislation. Instead this sanction decides the question as to which maxims are suitable for the principle of a general legislation, ultimately by no means unempirically nor in an unconditionally autonomous way. In other words, it decides according to the consequences which would result from the general validity within bourgeois society. This is then so much the bourgeois dimension of Kant's moral criteria that, precisely as far as the deposit and its contradiction to being embezzled is concerned, the question does not occur to Kant at all which Hegel, who certainly was not unbourgeois, saw very early on in terms of radical content: 'But what contradictions would lie in the fact that no deposit existed at all?' (Werke I, p. 352). So much therefore for a transitoriness in a so deeply relevant moral proposition, in one which admittedly shows the character to call to a gathering, to an inwardly general, formally con-curring gathering, like a new peal of bells despite all ephemerality, as laconically as bells and yet without any formless singing in the ears, but celebrates a duty which predominantly seems to effect rather Königsberg in Prussia than the Marseillaise, or contains it at that time and place.

But what if even Kant's so rigid-seeming proposition was precisely ahead of its time? If in its direction it contained a boldness and a happiness which are only waiting to be able finally to appear? If its questionable element was again at the same time a background from which something extremely worth questioning and more than that with near future stood out? After all, Kant's above-mentioned demand, which *underlies everything else*, never to regard man merely as a means but always as an end at the same time is not exactly bourgeois; it cannot be fulfilled at all in any class society.

For each of these societies was based, though in different forms of
association, on the master-servant relationship, on the use of people and
their work for ends which are by no means their own. Man as the only
end: however general this humane element and especially the abstract notion
'humanity in man' may be in Kant, and incidentally continued to be up
to and including Feuerbach, exploitation is absolutely denied by it. Only
morally denied, of course, Kant's practical reason lacks all real practice
because of the German misery, but it rings the judgment bell for exploitation
from the standpoint of principle. And it does so both for the overexploitation of man and the predatory war which is inseparably connected
with it: all this with projection from the standpoint of the moral principle,
but also from the standpoint of a future which is approaching it. The
categorical imperative does not remain rigid either, any more than it remains
or may ultimately remain confined to the idealistic realm of the bourgeoisie.
Illuminating in this respect is a real thunder and lightning proposition
from the 'Dispute of the Faculties', 1798, a very late work in other words,
without mercy for bourgeoisie and feudalism together: 'Since, for the
omnipotence of nature or rather its supreme cause unattainable to us, man
is only a trifle. But the fact that the rulers of his own kind also take him
for one and treat him as one, partly by burdening him like an animal,
as the mere instrument of their purposes, and partly by lining him up
in their quarrels with one another in order to *have him slaughtered - that
is not a trifle but a reversal of the final purpose of creation itself*' (Werke,
Hartenstein, VII, p. 402f.). The final purpose of creation: with this concept
Kant does not mean any empirical reality, but no theological sham reality
either; he means the Should-be of the moral law and its realization by
the historical and above all future development of the human race. But
here - and this founds precisely the thundering ethics of the proposition
cited above -, but here a stratum is touched on which is most particularly
charged with utopian pathos in Kant. Whereby the mere idealization of
an ideological kind (that of the realm of the bourgeoisie), as certainly as
it exists at that time and place, is pervaded with a very different signature.
It is, logically speaking, the signature of value-concepts, in this case of
a Should-be that by no means unconditionally surrenders to what is only
once given. And does not do so precisely because the value-concepts in
question (and only those of a real value, hence progressive-humane ones,
are concerned here) bear the wishful, volitional and tendency contents of
a rising class which has not yet attained full power and thereby at the
same time imply, given sufficient thoroughness, the radical content of the

whole human struggle for liberation. Such a value-concept is then not merely abstracted from finished facts, but from tendencies; consequently it cannot readily be corrected, refuted or confirmed by an existing *latitude* of experience either, but so to speak only by its *tendential longitudinal extension*, i.e. by the reality, *situated in events*, of what is coming up and capable of victory. But not only the already mature socialist value-concepts are of this kind, in an eminent fashion, but the radically bourgeois-revolutionary ones were also of this kind, with obvious distance, beyond their addition of ideologically transitory or even merely illusionary components. Thus the contents of bourgeois-revolutionary Natural Right, for instance, in so far as they refer to inalienable human dignity, were refuted by no given fact of right and state at the time; on the contrary, Rousseau refuted this given fact. That something can be all the worse for the facts if a theory does not agree with them: this proposition, so untenable in all non-normative concepts, is thoroughly tenable and not even grotesque in the area of a progressive-concrete Should-be. In fact, it constituted the glory of Rousseau's Natural Right, in contrast to the merely draped one of a Christian Wolff or even a Pufendorf, that it by no means sought a touchstone of its rightness in the existing 'empiricism', as one of feudalism; for the bourgeois revolutionary, this touchstone would rather have been an attestation of its mistakenness, indeed betrayal. And now let us consider the proposition of the categorical imperative, since it definitely belongs to those of the Should-be, of the humane 'final purpose of creation', in a correspondingly right way sub specie aeternitatis vel substantiae humanae, in Kant's own approximative sense. Then it follows precisely for the Kantian moral proposition: it sketches a Should-be *which, against the grain at that time and place, is not even approachable in any class society*. Kant cited the freedom from contradiction as a criterion in order to be able to conceive a maxim of behaviour as a generally followed law; of course, this is terribly formal. But if the contradiction is not covered in the *concept* and especially in concepts of mere business ethics (as in the example of the deposit that cannot be embezzled), if it appears instead in the *volitional maxim itself*, then it actually does become a criterion which can decide the moral enforceability or non-enforceability of an action as a generally valid one. And this decision then makes it impossible to obey the *categorical imperative as a whole*, and hence not just its individual trial problems, in the class society. For no proletarian can want the maxim of his behaviour to be able to be conceived as the principle of a general legislation, which also includes the capitalists; that would not be morality but betrayal of his brothers.

The craziest contradiction in the moral way of thinking would be caused by this very means, indeed the radical prevention of the categorical imperative by itself. But it prevents itself according to Kant's so unambiguously judging testimony solely in a society whose rulers treat man 'partly by burdening him like an animal, as the mere instrument of their purposes, and partly by lining him up in their quarrels with one another in order to have him slaughtered'. It prevents itself no less in the purely capitalist world that arose after Kant, in the world of deception which Hegel called the 'spiritual animal kingdom'. Thus the categorical imperative contains within it a Humanum which is so little merely abstractly general and so clearly also anticipatorily general that it is not accommodated with its human landscape in any class society. On the contrary, this axiom, with the unmistakable optative behind it, seems almost like an *anticipatory formula directed towards a non-antagonistic society, that is, to a classless one, in which real generality of moral legislation is possible for the very first time*. Only here, with the individual maxim as an equally general principle, is that transformation of 'forces propres into social ones' to be found, as prophesied by Marx; in accordance with a *solidarity that has become possible* in a total way. The categorical imperative thus becomes, beneath stars which it calculated so to speak but could not yet see, the element of a formula for classless solidarity; its apparently grey field is in fact full of distant enthusiasm.

The proposition of Anaximander or world which turns into likeness

No thinking without deprivation, but constant surprise at something takes it further. Surprise and astonishment not just at particularly abruptly emerging things, but also at familiar things. It can thus become precisely conspicuous, apart from the How of a Being, that anything is at all. So the world is encountered as alien, and this alien element itself gives the impetus to think further and further about it. That is why the so richly variable assertion by Empedocles cited above: that only like can understand like, has not remained uncontradicted. At least not for the thinking of the *question*, of the transformation of the familiar into something conspicuous and by no means self-evident; in fact this kind of thing is then already supposed to begin with grasping as perceiving. That is why Anaxagoras claimed the contrary to Empedocles: the properties of objects were only graspable by means of the opposite element in us; like could therefore only be experienced and comprehended through unlike. This is followed by the uncommonly fine remark with a good knowledge of disturbance: because of the opposite element in it every perception proceeds μετὰ λύπης, i.e. connected 'with reluctance'; also of course (from the same contrast) only the visible reveals the invisible (Diels, fr. 26a,). Certainly only the cold perceives the hot, the bitter the sweet and vice versa, just as only the sick man notices, e contrario, what the health imperceptible to the healthy man is. In fact, astonishment itself presupposes an inconsistent relationship to the world, though not one which has and seeks to remain inconsistent. To the world in which the Un-at-home, the unhomely element admittedly no longer predominates, as in the primitive, but has remained as a spur to questions, as a perceptibility of something not wholly evident, not wholly crystalline in the world which now exists or has existed up to now. Thus Anaxagoras significantly supplemented the Empedoclean dictum of likeness with the dictum of relative unlikeness between cognizing subject and object. And moreover with a momentous regard to what the world leaves to be desired, so to speak, in the way of logical but also metaphysical evidence. After all, the logical crux has always been the individual and particular in relation to the general, the Many in relation to the embracing One. Precisely the individual and particular, the factual Many of phenomena has always been a stumbling block for the epistemological equation of thinking-Being and, as must be added, in a way which fruitfully disturbs idealism. This disturbance became totally apparent in late medieval nominalism, when the factually individual and Many exploded the 'universals', in other words the generic concepts which appeared so homogeneous to logical thinking. The rift, wholly irrevocable for idealism, between logical-general evidence and fact-based individual datum was then stated more precisely in Leibniz's distinction of 'vérités éternelles' of a mathematical-moral-metaphysical kind and the 'vérités de fait' underivable from them, i.e. the not logically obvious but empirically obtrusive truths of experience. Only Hegel noted the dialectical unity in the contrasts of the individual and general which had become abstract, and Marx grasped them in material terms; whereby everything effectively particular is that of something general and everything concretely general is that of something particular. But the other spur of the question of unlikeness, that of the non-evidence of the many individual, above all that of world-being itself as a by no means panlogical, by no means crystalline-completed one, this spur did not disappear even in materialistic terms and least of all in revolutionary-materialistic terms. There is after all, as was to be seen, precisely in revolutionary ideals a Should-be with evidence (and by no means just a logical evidence, but a humane one in mediated terms and in terms of content), which does not lower the flag or surrender the sword to the mere Factum if it is inadequate to the ideal. Instead the revolutionary reason is admittedly an anticipation corrected by damage but never destroyed by it or even merely refuted au fond. The real unity of thinking (in this case of a revolutionary-total kind) and world-being must rather first be found; it is least of all dialectically already a given fact, but in the most eminent sense a dialectical task. Up to the frontier landscape of the fulfilment of this task the historical process holds good, whose continuance would not exist if something did not exist which ought not to exist. The true thought, still uncompleted for this very reason, is the art of the right way home in this On-the-way.

But the astonishment remains effective, interferes for so long in the trend. It sells itself only dearly, namely at the price of a Being prematurely passed off as 'authentic'. Which now has to appear all the more precious, although in view of the bad way in which so much of the world still finds itself this Being can only be deeply tentative pre-appearance. Unlike-like, like-like – it is significant now that precisely the first surviving proposition of one of the earliest European thinkers contains painful astonishment of the unlike and afterwards harmony. Namely the proposition of *Anaximander*, it is as capable and in need of the indication of its darkness and its sought At-home as not many later ones are. The proposition, for all the darkness in it, is that of a materialist who sought to explain the world in its own terms, an earthy but by no means simple materialist. His thesis runs in the translation given by Diels (Die Fragmente der Vorsokratiker, 1912, p. 15) as follows (fr. 9): 'The beginning of things is the infinite (ἄπειρον, the misshapen, inexhaustible primal matter). But that which gave them birth (γένεσις) is also the direction of their death in accordance with necessity (χρεών). For they pay one another (ἀλλήλοις) a penalty and forfeit (δίκην καὶ τίσιν) for their wickedness (ἀδικία) according to the order (τάξιν) of time.' The problem of this proposition is obviously first the multiplicity of individual things (τῶν ὄντων, of That-Which-Is in the plural), and then, in accordance with necessity (χρεών, perhaps also: custom), their passing, hence the very un-illuminating aspect of transitoriness, particularly including man. The 'solution' to the problem is first characterized by penalty and forfeit, hence by a kind of reparation for the emergence of things in their multiplicity; and then in the passing of things their return into the Apeiron is probably also implied. Even though the important word ἀλλήλοις (i.e., paying a penalty and forfeit 'mutually to one another' and not to the Apeiron itself) is certainly not interpolated, although it is missing in the doxograph Simplikios, the Apeiron as final place of return (as later Heraclitus' primal fire which again becomes 'undivided') is nevertheless the background of this going under, going to the bottom of things. The separate things emerging from their measure but also having emerged from the Apeiron must therefore pay δίκη(forfeit, probably in a more general sense: justice) for their ἀδικία (wickedness, in a more literal and more general sense: injustice) according to the τάξις (order, probably rather: respective penalty norm) of time (cf. in the sense which appears amazingly related: 'World history is the Last Judgement'). Dikē itself, which thus prevails according to the order of time, was regarded in myth, according to the record of Herodotus, as one of the three Horae, together with Eunomia, well-orderedness, and Eirēnē, peace; but more instructive is the fact that the Horae, one of which Dikē became, were originally goddesses of the air and wind, and then changed into those of the seasons, after which Dikē, who was also cited by name as the daughter of Chronos and no longer of Zeus, could then easily take over even in allegorical terms the justice of chronological order, the Last Judgement as world history. The counterpart to Dikē, the Adikia who is persecuted by her, is particularly very closely associated with Anaximander's world of unlikeness, and world of evidence which is only just establishing itself. Adikia, injustice, is, as stated above, firstly the multiplicity of individual things and secondly, precisely connected with this separation and its inflation which follows from it, their transitoriness. This therefore leads in Anaximander to the amazing fact of a very early objective dialectics, but before we go into this an assurance is in order, concerning the landscape of perspective. Nothing may be detected in a philosopher, especially in an early one, which is not inherent in his own work, in a verifiable way; there is no hermeneutics, apart from a cheeky and decadent kind, hence apart from its opposite, without the sound art of reading, which is called philology in the narrow sense. But in a philosopher, in so far as he is significant, i.e. capable of cultural heritage, there is this element inherent precisely within himself: not just to have thought at that time and place, and hence to have formulated in philosophy not just his own time but also a permanent concern of the times, and to have put it in philosophical perspective. On the other hand, great thinkers and indeed everything great that has been created would merely be sleep of the past, a quite superfluously woken sleep or rather: a sleep resorted to by those asleep themselves to increase their own drunkenness, defeatist drunken drowsiness; instead of past philosophers being quoted as those who are not past, namely from the point of view of their undischarged element, which extends its influence into the future space of such thoughts which continue to operate. Thus the same also goes for the early, already identified dialectics of Anaximander, the witness of light, a dialectics which is thoroughly verifiable and collected precisely in the astonishment over the *Adikia*.

Decisive here is his doctrine as to how the various things materialized in such a transitory way. Just as hot and cold, density and thinness emerged from the Apeiron which is itself featureless, but these opposites combine further into the elements, into water, earth, air, and fire. But this also gives rise to the state of a lasting imbalance of these elements in relation to one another, in fact an encroachment, a preponderance ($\grave{\alpha}\delta\iota\varkappa\acute{\iota}\alpha$) of one over the other, so that the hot seeks to displace the cold and vice versa, so that water or earth threatens to suppress the air or fire threatens to suppress everything else, and to take its place. Or, as the Physics of Aristotle says wholly in the spirit of Anaximander against the association of air and infinity in Anaximenes: 'If a single element were infinite, the others would have ceased to exist'. But in fact the world consists of nothing but a changing preponderance of elements and also the separate things formed from them: so that it operates in nothing but such intensified differences, and always newly heightened contrasts. So an objective dialectics is quite unmistakably evident here, obviously also one which interpreted the relationship of the cosmic elements out of the ever-changing preponderance of Demos and urban nobility in the Ionian trading cities. The dialectic thus appeared as an Adikia repeatedly corrected and directed in the destructibility of separate things, in the frailty of living things, and in the cycle of matter; but it is also evident in the extinction of the Adikia, namely in the ultimate relationship of separate things to the Apeiron. These justly destroy one another, because the *over-intensified difference* of their separate being wears itself down until it annihilates itself; but things are also destroyed because their *separate being as a whole turns into likeness at one end of the world*, and cancels itself out in the contrastlessness of the Apeiron. That is then where the unison is, attained by the Dikē which with time brings everything to light and more than this: which brings it into light, into the harmony of the infinite. And at the same time a very unusual oriental note is sounded here; unusual because for the Greeks the infinite (as something misshapen, unplastic) was otherwise always something negative. Only in late Hellenism, and hence precisely in the unrestrained invasion of the Orient, did the revaluation of the infinite reach the very highest, at least very highest theological category. Only in fact Anaximander's perspective into an Apeiron did not first need the false, late Hellenistic patriarchal air; the character of the θεῖον, of the divine, which he gave precisely to his primal matter as the in-finite, was still based very directly on the mysticism of the Orient. Though in Anaximander, the materialist, the infinite is never the infinite of a God or even of a Nirvana but always that of a primal matter, of one that is undefined. And that is why Aristotle's observation about this Apeiron is both well-informed and particularly important here: in the undefined primal matter of Anaximander – as in the Aristotelian definition of matter – everything consists 'of That-which-is potentially (δυνάμε), but not That-which-is actually' (Metaph. XII, 2). But beyond this the earliest surviving dictum of European philosophy gives later, indeed final perspectives in a very varied way – and this, vastly premature, even as far as harvest and peace. The dictum is charged with loneliness and far-reaching thoughts, in a first concept of matter as *potentiality* it simultaneously displays the first philosophical wishful and intentional image *of identity* – against the differentness of human beings from the world and of the world from itself.

Lightness in the depths, joyfulness of the phenomenon of light

No thinking without deprivation, yet occasionally everything around it becomes cheerful all at once. This already occurs as soon as people are capable of taking even an inconvenient thing lightly. And this taking-lightly possibly points to a by no means self-evident capacity for being light in things themselves. Its place is not wit, which is often merely subjective, the unexpected lightning comparison of seemingly incompatible facts and Objects. Its place is rather humour, the readiness of facts and Objects themselves no longer to hold their gravity as so important, or at least not as so exclusive and final, in human beings who are themselves ready for and above all capable of this. Both of course, wit and humour, have the fact in common that they widely thrive precisely in cheap and cheapest versions. Or rather: they grow rife and grimace in accordance with the stock of laughter which is undoubtedly greater in the foolishness of the subject than in the objective world. Berlioz even observed that there is more laughter in the madhouse than anywhere else; he could have added the shrieks and bursts of laughter of Dionysian bourgeois female and male conformists. Not just brutal seriousness has all livestock on its side, but also the petit-bourgeois urge for amusement and that which satisfies it.

W. Benjamin remarked aptly and conclusively on this strange case that
humour was a plant which could be found in very large and very worthless
numbers in the lowlands, but which became all the rarer and especially
all the more precious the higher the site on which it occurred. Humour,
in such noble and in less noble form, is in turn noted in several regions,
alongside its higher or lower situation, but alongside those regions of stylistic
attitude usually only or almost only in works of *art*, not of *philosophy*.
This is all the more striking as the phenomenon of the wise man, but
also wisdom as such contain a re-emphasis, and precisely a smiling one,
of what is important, a re-emphasis which has always appeared as the wishful
landscape of a deep taking-lightly, and hence is associated with humour,
of a particularly precious kind. Lao Tzu, the wise man, admittedly warns
against taking things lightly under certain circumstances: 'The weighty is
the root of lightness/By taking things lightly we lose the root' (Tao-té-ching,
Saying 26), but he warns only against lightness in the sense of levity, indeed
of giddy frivolity, which causes a ruler 'to take the world lightly'. Whereas
in the Tao-té-ching itself the advice of the tender, effortless, and unassuming
man shines out concerning all that the element of being truly light in the
course of things means, in the true playful rotation around the true centre.
And this advice shines out full of unassuming modesty against everything
dressed up, against heavily armed and thus not merely brutal seriousness.
Likewise, even on this side of Lao Tzu's quietest Tao: 'The fact that humour
is possible does not mean smiling amidst tears in the sense that, always
locked in dreams anew, we could lead a happy and refined existence, while
the basis of the world is unchanged, really sad. But its making-light and
accentuation means precisely – and here a fine mysterious ray of light,
a knowledge nourished only from within, inexplicable, supported by
nothing, and mystical, flashes into life – that something is not right in
it, that the tears are not to be taken wholly seriously compared with our
immortal soul, however horribly real they may appear together with the
world-basis from which they stem; that Goethe's statement: 'Verse that's
good, like rainbow's arc, is drawn against a ground that's dark', is probably
true of deep utterances but not of the most essential ones; that therefore
dreaming, the apparently so illusory ability to hope, the significant lightness
of being, which is admittedly answered but by no means guaranteed, and
incomprehensible delight as such, – is closer to the truth and reality which
does not need to be the world-basis than all the oppressive, verifiable, and
indubitable features of factual circumstances with their entire, sensorily
most real brutality' (Ernst Bloch, Geist der Utopie, 1918, p. 75f.). The

important connection of humour with joyful, indeed most joyful contents, which do not exist only as if they do not yet exist, is beyond doubt at any rate, even if these contents are so distant that they can be hoped for almost solely against hope itself. Biting humour even behaves as if the contents of its strangely significant joyfulness were secret and not yet there, but like the final state ringing through. This is so even when the daughter from Elysium did not come striding up the steps for a very long time, and all the more so when humour does not need any message at all from Elysium. For above all in fact, humour (it is not for nothing that one of its most droll and thoughtful borderline cases is so-called gallows humour) has no guaranteed confidence-being or even a fixed otherworldly-being whatever in the space of its Just-so. The total Just-so does not of course go so far that it could say for example: I would not know that the existing world existed if it did not exist, that is, if it did not force itself upon me empirically. But I know that what was formerly meant and designated by the divine exists, although nothing of the kind actually exists, indeed because nothing of the kind actually exists. For such a statement would not only be pure idealism, but a reified utopianism kept permanent as well, with alienation not only towards an inadequately existing world but towards every realization and its reality in general. Just as if the Just-so had to remain a King John Lackland on principle so to speak, on its honour. Or as if every realization of perfect evidence, of evidence of the perfect caused a blemish; even far beyond the well-known melancholy of fulfilment, even beyond the Romantic reification of dreams. But humour, which is in fact the *most unassuming of all utopias*, and at least has them in it, does not reify itself, and its cheerful Just-so does not aim at something outside reality, but stresses precisely within it its possible final state ringing through – full of lightness, full of liquor of the ability to be different, being different in essence, without becoming fixed, without escape, and also without any supra-world of a noisy or solemn jubilation. In a word: humour is characterized exclusively by transparency of that lightness and peacefulness of Being which gives the lie to gravity. And this without lightness already having empirical confirmation on a sufficient scale or even needing a supra-empirical guarantee (trust in God).

All brightening up follows from the light, but at the same time precedes it. It accompanies the rising even in a *double* fashion, first as particularly carefree dissolving of the outmoded, and then as a greeting of what is coming up. The *dissolving element* is busy in the old and with it only merrily, as with a land which occasionally itself begins to disappear easily, indeed comically. 'So that mankind cheerfully departs from its past', *Marx* says of this; this is true, since even bloody despots, in whom a declining society abounds, cast a comic shadow. And the cheerful farewell is all the more true where really great material of what is past and outmoded dissolves unceremonially in the face of the New, as material for laughter. 'History is thorough and goes through many phases when it buries an old form. The last phase of a world-historical form is its comedy. The gods of Greece, who were already once fatally wounded in tragic terms in the bound Prometheus of Aeschylus, had to die once more in comic terms in the Dialogues of Lucian' (Marx, 'Introduction to the Critique of Hegel's Philosophy of Right'). This means therefore that the cheerfulness of the farewell occasionally needs some assistance, and this is then called satire. *Hegel* himself, in idealistic dialectics, had given the cue for the disappearance of each antiquated landscape of pre-appearance, and for the emergence of each new aesthetic one, in triple form: as dissolving of 'symbolic art' in the epigram, of 'classical art' in satire, of 'romantic art' in a totally erupted farewell through humour. 'The spirit only works around in objects as long as there is still something secret and unrevealed in them . . . But once art has revealed on all sides the essential world views which lie within its conception as well as the sphere of the content which belongs to these world views, it has shaken off this substance destined on each occasion for a particular nation and a particular time, and the true need to incorporate it again only wakes with the need to turn *against* the substance which has been solely valid up to now; just as in Greece, for example, Aristophanes rebelled against his own times and Lucian rebelled against the whole Greek past, and in Italy and Spain, in the departing Middle Ages, Ariosto and Cervantes began to turn against chivalry' (Werke X², p. 231f.). This sort of thing therefore characterizes humour of the *first, critical kind* (and both the epigram and satire are then only its pointed or sharply ribbed manifestations); it actually creates farewell space, and it also posits the ridiculousness which effortlessly finishes off and kills. But humour remains and becomes much more important, namely, in the *second, positive kind*, belonging to the *rising* of light, as a *land in what is coming up, and therein still secret and unrevealed itself.* It is the thoroughly surprising fact here that Hegel himself, who erected a wholly closed system after all and left open nothing at all within it that was still secret and unrevealed, nevertheless grants to humour, apart from a critical character, one which frankly points beyond everything. At least in art and beyond it, apparently beyond and over to religion, more specifically: to the retreat of man into himself; but for him humour as

humanism is unavowedly always something unclosed. It is the dissolving
of circumstances sung to an end precisely as that which is itself not sung
to an end, as the circulation of an absolutely future lightness in the effort
and gravity of process. This although the thinker of memory and circles-
in-circles seeks to keep future things absolutely unconceptual and without
light: 'The past is the preservation of the present, as reality, but the future
is the opposite of this, or rather the formless... so no form whatsoever
can be viewed in the future' (Werke XIV, p. 105); – but humour displays
in its fluidity, even in Hegel, transparency of form which has not become
manifest. This precisely explains Hegel's aversion to merely arbitrary
humour, to 'saucy and brilliant wryness, the cometary world of smells
and sounds, without a core, the game in unrealistic tones of the hollow
spirit'; this explains the classification of true humour with depths which
lie very far out. Hegel notes this trend towards the latter, a trend which
has never been wholly indicated by any existing path, and never been wholly
authenticated by any existing significant Object, as 'an unaffected, light,
inconspicuous strolling on, which in its insignificance gives precisely (!)
the highest concept of depth, and since it is in fact details which swirl
up in disorder, the inner connection must lie all the deeper and drive out
the light-spot of the spirit in what is isolated as such' (Werke X^2,
p. 228). Hegel posits here, with the function of strolling on, merely a
certain and not the highest humorous literature for the utopian phenomenon
of lightness that is humour per se, yet not only the classification with a
highest concept of depth is described but also – which explodes the mere
aesthetics of humour – with light-spots everywhere. In fact it is the joyfulness
of *light* which is everywhere contrasted with gravity here too and which
in this whole system so alien to the future, malgré lui, again and again
with further-pointing, further-signifying transparency allows a glimpse
of formations of lightness, far beyond aesthetics. Brightness breaks forth
everywhere where 'the inward-turning nocturnal point of negative unity'
veers round in a positive direction. As in the philosophy of nature: when
light is the first 'to cheer the gravity of being beside oneself' and consciousness finally bursts the crust. As in the philosophy of history when, after the
wild splendour of the oriental rising of the light, Greece 'emerges in its more
beautiful naturalness, freedom, depth and cheerfulness, like the bride from
the chamber'. As in the philosophy of religion where Hegel apparently seeks
to make the phenomenon of light culminate in an elapsed way: 'All sorrow,
all care, this sandbank of temporality, hovers in this ether, whether in
the present feeling of devotion or of hope. In this region of the spirit stream

the waters of Lethe, from which Psyche drinks, in which she sinks all
pain, forms all hardnesses and darknesses of time into a dream-image and
transfigures them into the brilliant light of the eternal' (Werke XI, p. 4).
The narrower relation to the spirit of humour, namely to an unassuming
cheerfulness, is here abandoned of course; the fine flashing and shining
of humour, although it cannot be world-shattering by any means, also
comes from a very different peace from that made by Hegel's philosophy
with an imperfect world. But precisely the element which has not been
sung to an end itself, and hence the still objectively utopian element is
at work around all these successive 'light-spots' (contra gravity), together
with a positive element of the final state, without the misuse of which
Hegel's philosophy could not have been so poorly apologetic, and without
the use of which it could not have been so finely optimistic. So much
here for the *second, positive kind* of philosophically shining transparency,
thoroughly belonging to the greeting of something that is coming up,
although the past-bound thinker buried it in a closed system. But even
in the light-spot of optimism, it is only since *Marx* that the past has not
only been brought into the present and the latter again into the contemplated
past, but both have been brought on to the horizon of the future. And
what is conceived in the optative: lightness-cheerfulness-peacefulness is not
only set on its feet by Marxism but referred to its hands. For more than
a promise that all that is claimed to be full of light could be so is not
to be found, alongside the wish that it may be so, in the closed systems
of light even from the point of view of cheerfulness. We must here recall
Spinozism once more, the world claimed to be crystal, and the vast
philosophical utopia must be considered which would like to form and
does form the final conclusion of such wisdom: 'There is nothing in
nature which is contrary to intellectual love or can eliminate it' (Eth. V,
Prop. 37). Such a proposition of light is in its very extremeness without
empirical meaning, but in fact a promise is implied in it, and with it the
extremeness no longer alien to meaning, though remaining vast, of the
task of keeping the promise thus implied approximative. So that the At-
home in this world, the this-world of every At-home, which is lit in the
utopian dimension of such propositions, does not remain unproven even
empirically by changing the nature of history and the world. There is
certainly no lack, in the empirical process, of inward-turning or even less
inward-turning nocturnal points of negative unity, but even less of light-
spots, despite and by means of these Negativa, and of light in latency.
The landscape of the truly essential, with positive resoluteness of its content,

is a wholly dawning borderline content; but this lies in the material process, and the process goes with brightening up of its content. And this is precisely why the philosophical overall views in the *wish for penetrating knowledge* also involve the *will for the truly essential*; – it is not the evening to end all these days yet, nor the day to end all these mornings. Philosophies are their age, expressed in ideas, but their *great themes*, because they can never be exhausted and cannot even be wholly formulated in a single epoch, lie far beyond each respective age and even society. They lie in the concern of the age, the concern of the process in general – and the most central of these themes of process is Verum Bonum. Man as a question about it, a world as an answer to it: *this is, again suo genere geographically, the wishful landscape in philosophies.* Only the truth of essence in *breakthrough* is its path and goal, as the pleasant truth without illusion.

EIGHT-HOUR DAY, WORLD IN PEACE,   42
FREE TIME AND LEISURE

Look up: the chimney is smoking.   *Brecht*

I have convinced myself by experience of the truth of the quotation in the Bible and made it into my lodestar: But seek ye first the kingdom of God, and his righteousness; and all these things shall be added unto you.*
       Hegel, Letter to Major Knebel, 30th August 1807

Even in northern regions, if we at least consider the example of the oldest and greatest nations, it seems man should not allow himself to be degraded into a beast of burden by deprivation but be content with the little that nature can give him there or emigrate; and if anywhere work is required from one church bell to the other if one wants to live, then only faulty state constitutions and state administrations are to blame for this, a consequent disproportionate distribution of what nature amply gave for all, and feigned needs which nature is not obliged to satisfy; and the strange fancy can only be influential in the sermons and catechisms of the precious Christian north that even in eternal

---

* The English of the Authorized Version seems to be the exact inversion of the biblical quotation Hegel cites, which could be translated 'Seek first for food and clothing and the kingdom of God will come to you of its own accord', which is perhaps more in keeping with the spirit of Bloch's epigraph. We have given the Authorized Version here. Matthew 6, 33.

life there is no rest, but rather our energies are still to be exercised on higher
objects in further spheres of activity. The paradises of the orientals have nothing
of this, and someone who must know better than we do what things are
like there does not place the blessed at a loom again for example, but rather
at the table with Abraham, Isaac and Jacob.

Johann Peter Hebel, The Jews

The realm of freedom begins in fact only where working which is determined
by deprivation and external expediency ceases; it therefore lies in accordance
with the nature of the matter beyond the sphere of actual material production.

Marx, Das Kapital, III[2]

The whip of hunger

Let us return to a simpler spot again. To the ground at our feet, which
is mostly hard. In previous social life lives the suffering which longs most
powerfully for a remedy and dreams it most exactly. Hunger forces us
to work, but this work wears us out in its own way exactly like hunger.
The entrepreneur who is eager for his profit does not know what this
sort of work is, that of the servant; artists and scientists do not know
any more about it either, though for different reasons. For it is *drudgery*,
imposed, imposed for alien purposes; only the proletarian and the employee
know the whole dreary extent of this drudgery. Work has furthermore
become more monotonous than before, where at least a whole piece was
still to be made with love. A piece which gave the craftsman the pleasure
of being created and skilfully completed. Whereas the worker who, through
the division of labour, increasingly lost sight of the whole piece, makes
only a part, day in, day out the same part of the same screw, without
love, with hatred, mitigated only by desolation, and with the same flick
of the wrist. The wish has always existed to shake off imposed work,
or at least to reduce the time which is spent on it. But dependent people
never succeed in this or not for long.

From the casemates of the bourgeoisie

The poor man always has to earn every mouthful the hard way first. The
master is one by squeezing the servant dry, by living off his work. With
the goods which the worker produces beyond his own requirements (kept

extremely low) the master finances his leisure. From the beginning of the ownership of a plough and a field this exploitation divided people into two kinds, two classes, and it has become broader and stricter than ever. If progress in goodness and happiness is often dubious in historical terms, that of *squeezing people dry* is not; it occurred by and large more and more aridly and blatantly. The Greek slave was looked after better than the serf, and the latter better than the modern labourer. For the slave was at least the livestock of his master, and so he was fed and had his stable. Whereas the serf had to look after himself, in so far as he was left with any time to do so and the owner of the village left him a bowl. In 1525 the German serf who had taken for himself the freedom of a Christian man hung on the rope. Or he stumbled with his eyes gouged out and his tongue torn out through the Holy Roman Empire until he perished in a ditch. Even the situation of the journeymen approached that of the peasants towards the end of the Middle Ages, to the same extent that the master turned from a patriarchal foreman into an early capitalist exploiter. In Danzig in around 1550, striking journeymen had their ears cut off, and in Florence they were branded by the hangman and flogged out of the city. Individuality was under way only in the higher strata, coming from the capital of merchants and princes, but at the bottom the wholesome bonds prevailed. The conqueror certainly did not admit to all children of the earth that the highest happiness was personality; the dream of it was punishable by torture and death. Until at last even freedom of movement began, man as the free owner of his labour. As a partner with equal rights of the contract of employment which he concludes with the capitalist; eye to eye, tooth for tooth. The blessings, described by Engels, of the early industrial age arrived; after the slave, the serf, and the gradually swallowed-up journeyman, the proletarian appeared. If the situation of the working class was miserable up till then, it now became hellish; the proletariat around 1800 began on the level of the galley slave. Often even four-year-old children were forced to work, in dark mine tunnels or in the muggy stinking cotton factories, the usual age for beginning work was eight or nine years old. Working hours for children lasted six to ten hours, from the age of thirteen to eighteen they increased to twelve hours, women and men over eighteen stood at their machines for their profiteers from five o'clock in the morning until eight o'clock in the evening, and often longer. The women suckled their children while they operated the machine, there were no breaks for eating, the pitiful wage mostly disappeared on rent anyway. Capital opposed any change of this hell, more conservatively than any feudal lord ever did;

profit remains relentless. When people wanted to take children under nine years of age out of cotton mills because the iron foundries which could not use any children became philanthropic, the pious English textile manufacturers proved that cotton spinning would have to perish if it could not use the little workers 'who crawl around with ease beneath the machines and on the one hand can do the cleaning and on the other can tie on the threads'. It was irrelevant for churchgoers that many of the little workers died in accidents; uninteresting for the classical land of democracy that only a fraction of the consumptive or scurvy-mouthed workforce reached the age of forty and none of them the age of fifty. Jonathan Swift, who knew his England, was already making the differently bitter proposal a hundred years before this, when no industry was as yet devouring everything around it, that in order to control the misery of children one might fatten the fruits of the womb of poverty for the tables of the rich: 'It would encrease the Care and Tenderness of Mothers towards their children, when they were sure of a Settlement for life, to the poor Babes, provided in some Sort by the Publick, to their annual Profit instead of Expence; we should soon see an honest Emulation among the married Women, which of them could bring the fattest Child to the Market.'* This proposal, stylized as a petition to Parliament and adorned with many quotes from the Bible, was prophetic; industry even devoured children under six years old, and by no means well-fed ones.

The parents of these children were still not provided for, of course. Although, something which Swift could not foresee, they also shared in the blessings of British trade. The worker namely had to spend his six hours of free time in having to earn all over again the wages that had been paid out to him, in other words: in the initial stages of this capitalism, he very often received his wages not in cash but in goods in kind, in products of his own factory, in umbrellas and the like, which he first laboriously had to turn into money on the market. What a sublime form of making out of the wage-slave an unpaid salesman as well; even the wages still served profit in the so-called truck-system. The only means of forgetting this unprecedented misery was spirits; occasionally wild despair broke out, machines were wrecked, factories set on fire, – with little other effect than the death penalty, which was imposed for such convulsions from 1811. In his work: 'The Condition of the Working Class in England', Engels allowed this condition to speak for itself, with the result: 'Rising

* Bloch's text does not appear to be a direct quotation from Swift here, unless he is using a very free translation. We have included the closest example from 'A Modest Proposal'.

capitalism did not achieve, as it had promised, the greatest possible happiness, but the greatest possible misery of the greatest possible number.' A demonic world arose, that anti-Cockaigne, exact down to the last detail, which capitalists need in order to prepare for themselves their own relative Cockaigne. Or as Marx sums it up: 'In capitalist society free time is produced for one class by transforming all the lifetime of the masses into working time.' Misery and big business are inextricably connected, slums and hunger with the capitalist unleashing of the forces of production. The profit drive has made itself absolute in capitalist society; formerly a scourge, it now became a cannibal, formerly a means in the service of feudal consumer needs, it now became an absolutely unlimited end in itself. And if the greatest possible misery of the greatest possible number changed here and there in the epoch of high capitalism and then imperialism, it did so only during a respective boom. The crises which went ever deeper and especially the rising mass murder in the business of wars showed that the cold heart of the capitalist economy did not change its temperature, nor can change it objectively. Thus through war everything is made up for again which was previously lost in terms of misery for example, and more – according to the law of maximum profit. Even around the middle of the eighteenth century, hence shortly before the Industrial Revolution, the ten-hour working day was regarded as normal in England. Whereas, after the victory of the bourgeoisie, it needed enormous struggles before even this older standard finally returned in 1847, a hundred years later, fought for step by step. And the ten-hour bill of 1847 (with a working day that had become considerably more intensive) certainly was not accepted on humanitarian grounds. But even where these appeared, in the sentimental sheen which so becomes a rich biblical nation, it was for the most part only the clever product of a particular interest and an observation which obtruded itself precisely on the manufacturing class. For it turned out that the quality of the products steadily sank as a result of the degeneration of the factory population and therefore became uncompetitive in comparison with countries which had begun their overexploitation only recently. This was joined by the deterioration of the sailor material for the merchant navy and the navy; even the whip which ruled for so long on English ships could not cure consumption and scurvy. The English family magazine novel had blushingly called the slums 'the dwellings of vice and poverty'; but now they had also become dangers to profit. Thus philanthropy became almost inevitable, after all its Christian-industrial oblivion, interest made philanthropy inevitable. The ten-hour day became normal again, it also formed the limit to concessions of course, one which was repeatedly susceptible and only reluctantly recognized. Especially something as subversive as the eight-hour day stood outside human civilization; it flowed from laziness and lechery, it testified only to 'the awful growth of selfishness among the mass of the people'. Even in 1887, at the end of the so-called Haymarket revolt in Chicago, four workers were hanged whose sin had been to proclaim the eight-hour day. The American general public regarded them as common criminals. Until the labour movement which was gaining strength finally gave a new impetus to love of mankind, an even more unpleasant one than sinking competitiveness and deteriorated soldier material. Germany was regarded as the centre of the labour movement at that time, its social democracy at least successfully gave this impression, the law against the activities of the Social Democratic Party* had not been any use, instead the ancient Roman remedy of throwing panem et circenses to the plebs now recommended itself to the upper classes, so that they hoped to prevent revolutionary acts by part payments. There thus arose the widespread social welfare legislation under Wilhelm II (England, undaunted by its Labour Party, and especially America followed very slowly), and finally 1918 was to be swaddled and duped before it was suffocated. The eight-hour day was the minimum demand of the class-conscious proletariat; there was nothing for it but to consider this demand with a wink. But then the crisis came and brought a lot more capitalist free time, namely unemployment. Then came ultimately the legacy of crisis and no revolution: fascism, and it again brought the twelve-hour day to light. Such is the circle, this is how it finally had to turn out: slave-driving to war production, with mass graves for relaxation; unemployment in peace, with famine for wages.

All kinds of alleviation through benefaction

At least the poor man has the advantage of looking dirty. He is not a pretty sight, he seems reproachful even when he is silent. The poor man may tug at the heartstrings but not of course at the pursestrings; the master does the latter in order to alleviate the misery off which he lives. Especially when, as noted above, sentimental feeling accompanies and embellishes economic interests. Also the ruling class, with this feeling, often describes very exactly the ugly existence of poverty, it denounces from time to time

---

* Bismarck's law of 21 October, 1878.

the brutality of its own representatives, namely as a stupid one. The clever man gives charitable gifts and certainly charitable opinions which are open to the idea of an eight or even two-hour day, and of happiness for all, as a beautiful dream. The liberal bourgeoisie emotionally takes note of neediness, partly for the sake of something to talk about, partly in order to reform it. The latter with *household remedies* which by no means undermine the fund, the fund of wealth from which the beneficent gift comes after all. Big business was never short of kind-hearted writers with an aesthetically troubled glance at misery, least of all in England. Galsworthy, himself a capitalist frigate, thus describes, in a novel which as lucus a non lucendo is called 'Beyond', a piece of contemporary London almost as Engels had described it, at least a London which has remained as it was in Engels' time: 'The usual route from the station to Bury Street was "up", and the cab went by narrow by-streets, town lanes where the misery of the world is on show, where ill-looking men, draggled and overdriven women, and the jaunty ghosts of little children in gutters and on doorsteps proclaim, by every feature of their clay-coloured faces and every movement of their underfed bodies, the post-datement of the millennium; where the lean and smutted houses have a look of dissolution indefinitely put off, and there is no more trace of beauty than in a sewer'. But this awareness of missing beauty causes the heroine of the novel, the moved heroine, incidentally also a huntress and a friend of Polyhymnia, to do nothing more than – found a kindergarten. This is simply reformism or the liberation of the proletariat by the riders who are sitting on it. Enough of this, enough about a philanthropy which moans and indeed accuses while at the same time producing the stuff of the accusation. How nimbly, with how much rhetorical cant the patriotic English historian Macaulay speaks about the horrors of the East India Company, about beastly exploiters like Warren Hastings and his successors, about the wretchedness of the Indian masses: 'They had been accustomed to live under tyranny, but never under tyranny like this. They found the little finger of the Company thicker than the loins of Surajah Dowlah....It [the English government] resembled the government of evil Genii, rather than the government of human tyrants ....and the palanquin of the English traveller was often carried through silent villages and towns, which the report of his approach had made desolate.' But the intellect which drives forth such truthful descriptions is always as sharp as a chisel of soap, and it gets to the bottom of the matter as imperturbably as the patroness of a charity soirée; but it developed that awe-inspiring cunning which proposes to relieve the crimes against colonial slaves by the export of spirits, and those against the proletariat at home by means of chloroform. This is that level-headed technology of the millennium which a stirred bourgeoisie bequeathed to the social democracy of all countries. Without the millennium having come noticeably closer which Galsworthy rightly misses in the London slums. The wolf assumes grandmother's voice, the crocodile sheds tears, the Gestapo practises Winter Aid, * Wall Street fights for the free nations. And an untold number of petit bourgeois, who have not learned anything from experience, and also living intellectually from hand to mouth, still believe, almost more than ever, in the lies, clichés and distortions which were not only invented by the old fascism but which a new fascism, with the same goal, is increasing by its so-called Atlantic freedom. And what is liberally stale has now become totally perverted and poisonous, so that here the difference between west and east is falsely changed from that between capital and work into one between alleged freedom and alleged constraint. This kind of thing sees itself supported by a social democracy of soft Henrys who are not at all so soft when it comes to shooting at those for whom freedom is no cliché and revolution is no snail. All these alleviations of misery stifle the awareness of misery and of that which will change it, especially in its urban morass. A proven contribution to this is also the inner life, the wholly unpolitical one, which the sons and daughters of the educated classes, above all in Germany, have cultivated for so long and have so abruptly paid for. The leisure which they had to some extent in advance of the workers, and the bit of light which the habit of education could have bestowed, thus itself turned into a fund to increase their own ignorance and to support the general ignorance. These average educated people were very often and very gladly familiar with a Galsworthy or his other European relatives, but they had hardly heard the name of an Engels, and in the case of Marx they could only think of the line: a political song is a nasty song,† or the maxim that nobody is perfect. This kind of thing did not even belong to the momentary shooting stars let alone to the fateful starry hours of humanity in which educated people, who like fools are always with us, took delight. Thus all the social workers and other organizations had a clear conscience about begging from door to door and in the street, they developed it themselves and had it developed for them. Until the greatest alleviation of misery was called Hitler and spoke more than ever of spiritual values.

---

* A relief organization for the needy in winter during the Nazi period.
† A bourgeois cliché after Brander in Goethe's Faust, Part I, 2092.

It goes to show that a den of robbers cannot be reformed, it can only be cleaned out and radically destroyed. Together with cheap sympathy and philanthropy towards Christian robbery with murder. Action alone makes what is feigned in sentimental books come true, revolutionary power alone makes room for educated, fully educated kindness.

Bourgeois pacifism and peace

Even the noblest dream nursed by the bourgeois has to pay for its half-heartedness. It is the ancient dream of *eternal peace*, a genuine maternal utopian goal. But the means of attaining it have always been of the most unsuitable kind, and the soil in which the matter was to prosper was an unchanged field of blood. A society which is in itself geared for battle and intrinsically antagonistic cannot found any eternal peace. Despite all inclinations to it in the populace and occasionally even at the top, at least as long as the bourgeois is earning smoothly. But the wish for peace, an unconditional one, is only natural to the peasant, worker, and petit bourgeois, as the born and not unavailable candidates for the grave of the unknown soldier. The wish becomes all the more natural the more exactly it is associated with the insight into the obligation to die for alien interests. Which only scantily masquerade as the cause of the fatherland, which meant here: the imperialist aims of a minority. The fight for free time is then automatically associated with the fight against the most dangerous and most inhuman slave-driving, against that of organized murder. The ruling bourgeoisie, however, only irregularly had epochs when it seemed to become alienated from war. Or rather, when it applied war solely to colonial soil, against Filippinos, Indian mountain tribes, negroes from the Congo and the like. Whereas above all the Anglo-Saxon lands of capital, as the most well-worn capitalisms used to the technique of tough deceitful negotiations or treaty-instruments, sought reconciliation with great powers for a long time, politics of the open door. Thus it is no accident that England, the home of compromise, had apparently defeated the feudal pathos of arms by a civilian spirit or eliminated it from the constitution. There thus arose that deceitful and temporary variety which can be called stock market pacifism: war in or with Europe appeared too risky, and even in the case of a victory too full of heavy losses in business terms to be able to be seriously ventured upon. Thus, typically enough, Anglo-Saxon sociology, far beyond the Victorian Age, almost equated war and feudality, war and the Junker, war and the Samurai. Spencer's* sociology calls on the full armour of its so-called theory of evolution to prove that war solely belongs to the primitive and feudal state of society, to constraint, tutelage, and strangely also to otherwise scarcely feudal centralization. Whereas it is in keeping with the most special interests of the industrial period to eliminate superannuated militarism like a foreign body – war is the ultima ratio of kings, not of the bourgeois. Therefore the deportment of Spencer's sociology released the white dove from debit and credit, or at least from credit; peaceful competition, as they used to say, unites the business offices. It was thus on this basis, under the direction of England and an earlier North America, that bourgeois pacifism spread. Well-meaning and vague, short-winded and composed of misunderstandings of itself, and also having been useful as a quasi 'peace in our time', for the purpose of tolerating and indeed promoting Hitler. For capitalism is certainly not the sort of lamb it was made out to be by the Spencer-sociologists, and risks do not frighten the entrepreneur when the destruction of competition is the goal. Even alleged militarism as such, which had survived in Germany and Japan from a pre-capitalist feudal past, would have declined long ago to a showpiece if it had not had the freshest imperialist mandate behind it precisely in these two countries. So war and peace are no opposites any more in the age of monopoly capitalism; they both stem from the same business, precisely from this, modern war itself comes from capitalist peace and bears its ghastly features. The fight for marketing areas, and competition fighting by every possible means, are written into capital, hence it cannot keep any eternal peace, hence imperialisms necessarily form the explosive atmosphere of a permanent pre-war period, and the declaration of war itself (recently it can be lacking too) becomes mere release. Only a sentimental, then a slovenly, then a roguish idealism can therefore water the plant of peace on bourgeois master-heights; it conceals here only the preparations for attack, si vis bellum, para pacem, if you want fascism, speak about freedom. Indeed the very civilian spirit has become so identical with big bombers in late capitalism that only imperialism, as the last capitalist phase, has brought war to the perfection that is called total. The diverse Wall Street wars are total not merely because they by no means occur only between armies any more but because they choose, with particular heroism, what is defenceless as a sacrifice. The full churches and women and children had not been terrified of the armies of knights, but they find no mercy from the fury of the

---

* Herbert Spencer (1820–1903), English sociologist who anticipated much of Darwin's theory of evolution.

imperialist bourgeoisie, particularly from the latter. Likewise, what remains of pacifism in the womb of the upper bourgeoisie and condemns aggression, aggression itself fabricated in the White House and in the Vatican by nothing but stock brokers, Tartuffes, and Franco priests, has become not just roguish idealism but pure swindling. Thus peace prospers in capitalist soil like a lamb in the slaughterhouse; the dream of peace can no more be fulfilled in capitalist terms than that of love of man in general. Of course, wars are not inevitable if a unified and sufficiently powerful action on the part of their prospective victims intervenes, but even then they remain a constant threat, at best a mere *non-war*, by the skin of its teeth, the preservation of which requires constant vigilance. Only socialism radically removes war and the seeds of new wars contained in every capitalist peace agreement. Peace is no party matter, in the age where it is constantly under threat it is a matter for mankind par excellence, but a mankind without Nimrods. The will for free time from war, and hence for pacifist leisure, will only wholly get a chance together with that taming of imperialist maximum profit which ultimately means its abolition. Otherwise the absence, even *impossibility* of wars of aggression will never turn from a highly desirable state of affairs into a normal one.

So this is what emerges here as soon as a fox is set to watch the geese. At the same time the foxes themselves had to admit that peace is an ancient dream, though not a beautiful one for them. The cry of Berta von Suttner: 'Lay down your arms'* moved in such an ancient and above all often pictured longing that pacifism almost possesses the tradition of a *separate utopia*. A utopia which, though it is also occasionally contained in the social ones, still by no means coincides with them. For the dream of peace is found to be particularly elaborated in those very writers who have left behind no elaborated sketches for the best state at all; as in the ancient Israelite prophets, as in Kant. Equally it belongs to revolutionary Natural Right: Grotius, the founder of international law, pictures peace simply as the normal state of things. And before it amounted to stock market pacifism and its illusion, the dream of peace was close to the young bourgeois enlightenment and its alliance against princes, against masters' wars and wars of religion. The whole irony of capitalist destiny was involved in making precisely the French Revolution, with the popular army which it had to form for its defence, into the origin of universal conscription. Pacifist utopia appeared most forcibly of all in Kant, and not in fact in

---

* Title of the life-story of Baroness Berta von Suttner (1889).

a social-utopian connection, but its light was kindled from morality. The sketch 'On perpetual peace', 1795, does not allow politics to take a single step without first having paid homage to ethics, in its absolutely commanding form. 'Politics says: Be as wily as serpents; ethics adds (as a qualifying condition): and as guileless as doves' (Werke, Hartenstein, VI, p. 437); the combination of both is difficult, but a requirement about which, according to Kant, no dispute is possible. Ethical politics, political ethics would then secure eternal peace, as soon as the state is formed in all great nations as if it had come about through a voluntary agreement of its subjects. The constitution which thus arises is the republican one, it alone has 'apart from the integrity of its origin, having sprung from the pure source of the concept of justice, the prospect of the desired result as well, namely eternal peace' (l.c., p. 417). But Kant, even when he now aims at a single world republic, despite all rigour of morality has hard-bitten bon sens enough to content himself with a substitute among the existing piratical states: the league of nations. 'For states, in relation with one another, there can be no other way, in accordance with reason, of getting out of the lawless condition that contains sheer war than by giving up their wild (lawless) freedom, just like individual human beings, complying with public compulsory laws and thus forming an (admittedly always growing) international state, which would finally comprise all the nations of the earth. But since they certainly do not want this, in accordance with their idea of international law, . . . in place of the positive idea of a world-republic (if everything is not to be lost) only the negative surrogate of a league averting war, persisting and always spreading, can check the flood of the law-shunning, hostile inclination, but with the constant danger that it will erupt' (l.c., p. 423f.). This pessimism differs at least from the trustfulness of those pacifists who saw peace and not the armaments industry promoted in an American 'world-republic'. Kant's pessimism, in view of his dream of peace, stems of course not only from the true assessment of the law-shunning states but just as much from the Decalogue and the prophets. Both addressed themselves without illusion to the man who has become a wolf to man; the Decalogue with the sharp commandment: 'Thou shalt not kill',* the prophet Isaiah with the extremely distant promise: 'and they shall beat their swords into plowshares, and their spears into pruning-hooks.'† This is messianic, and it did not entrust or confuse the king of the Assyrians, and certainly not the modern priests of Baal either, with the realm

---

* Exodus 20, 13.
† Isaiah 2, 4.

of peace. This kind of thing in fact can only befall the 'defence community' of wolves, the pacifism of deception, the same deception which lyingly changes the victim of aggression into the aggressor and manufactures atom bombs for the salvation of civilization. To sum up: the ancient dream of peace presupposes almost even more cogently than any other element of social utopia clear supports and correction. Even in the First World War, simply from looking at the Prussian Junkers, it became clear that pacifism does not consist in ending existing wars at any price but in radically preventing future ones. In the Second World War, which has not finished and has merely shifted the aggressor from Berlin to Washington, it becomes obvious that militarism, however much it was able to count on the preserved brutality of Junkers, as in Prussia or Japan, does not come from feudal barbarism but from the most modern property relations, and the radical prevention of future wars will not succeed in the long run without a permanent removal of monopolistic interests. The swords will only certainly become ploughshares when the soil over which the plough passes belongs to all; not an hour earlier, nor an hour later. Capitalist peace is a paradox which spreads fear more than ever and which enjoins the nations to defend the cause of peace to the utmost, most strenuously; whereas socialist peace is a tautology.

Technological maturity, state capitalism and state socialism; October Revolution

How hesitantly word gets around among those in the centre that things could be better managed. The small trader, after all, under the illusion of being independent, still largely exists with this illusion. And the happiness of free competition, although neither the former nor the latter exists any more, has still by no means ceased to mean something here. The man with his own little business, the vast amount of senseless middlemen, the employee who cannot help being industrious although it does not get him anywhere any more, they all still believe in the cause which has become partly watery and partly bloody: private industry. In their precarious situation, of course, they believe in it more stubbornly than firmly, at least they are inwardly still private, drag this remnant around with them. They are therefore just as much a hindrance to themselves as to the consciousness of the other overdue and no longer private mode of production and exchange. Now, however, even the Babbitt begins to feel something rather new as soon as he admires the *technological* enterprise which seems as bright as day, instead of the economic machinery that he cannot see through. He sees the factories kept running collectively, namely by masses of workers, about which there is nothing private at all apart from the firm. He sees the effortlessly operating machines, spewing forth goods upon goods, and the sales life which is all the more arduous for that reason and often stagnant as soon as goods become commodities. He sees how the machine saves or could save human work, if only things were not so desolate in the profit economy itself. He sees how there are factories even now, particularly chemical ones and those of the food industry, which look as deserted as on a Sunday because machines with a particularly high capacity perform the work there. This is the peculiar propaganda which technology was able to make even within such a dull-witted stratum as the normal petit bourgeoisie, and also sometimes strangely carries through. The machinery already stands, for all its artificiality, as the fragment of another society in this one, a fragment whose production capacity is no longer accommodated and is in fact distorted in the private industrial form of appropriation. Not least technologists themselves became and are becoming aware of this parti- cular role, however clumsily. Indicative of this was therefore the appearance of so-called technocrats, a short-lived but amazing one, originating in the land of overproduction. The American engineer Howard Scott developed one of the most extensive programmes of free time out of a professional technological interest, in other words out of a one-sided insight into existing production capacity. According to Scott the power of machines is even already large enough to make a two-hour day possible, one picked up from the machine not the proletariat (whose demands rarely went so far). Of course, wherever 'technocracy' goes beyond such statements it is social-dilettante gossip, but these utopians untouched by any Marxism still expressed what every practician encounters every day. What the inventor, the hygienist, and not least the modern architect encounters when he thinks in terms of breakthroughs and collective settlements: the technological possibilities, indeed realities of today are being artificially curbed by means of a super- annuated economic system. The social balance of power releases technology only for purposes of war, for the production of means of death; but the power of this production alone already indicates how lavishly the manufacture of food as a means of life could prosper. Previously incredible things would be ready for this, above all in organic chemistry, in a technology which no longer merely aims at the processing of raw materials but at the synthetic formation of these raw materials themselves. This began on a large scale with aniline instead of vegetable dyes; artificial saltpetre, artificial oil, artificial rubber followed; plastic may inevitably replace steel in cars, railway carriages, and perhaps in machines themselves. Artificial fertilizers and artificial irradiation are on the way, or could be, which stimulate the soil into thousandfold fruit, in a hubris and 'anti-Demeter movement' beyond compare, with the synthetic borderline concept of a cornfield growing on the flat of the hand. In short, technology as such would be ready, almost already able, to make us independent of the slow and regionally limited work of nature on raw materials, independent even of wide transportation (cf. A. Lowe, The Trend in World Economics, The American Journal of Economics and Sociology, 1944). A new super-naturation of given nature would be due, even though with the familiar dangers of technological artificiality handed down by the bourgeoisie and abstractly intensified. But – and this remains sociologically decisive for all reddening dawns of synthetic chemistry – : the thus facilitated omnipotence of production is the most impossible one in the capitalist system of appropriation and distribution. It would bring the overproduction which exists anyway to a level for which neither existing monopoly capitalism nor its *state capitalist* form latent within it, with nothing but robots under centralized exploitation, would be a match. This kind of thing is at the same time a final sign that technological maturity on its own still has no socialist significance at all. However much it has overhauled its mother, private capitalist society, and however visibly the private form of exploitation proves to be superannuated compared with the long since collectivized forces of production even in purely technological terms, in the *means of production*. But the means of production alone do not make people happy, the proletariat must rather have them first, must have seized possession of them. Without this socialization precisely the most highly developed means of production bring crisis after crisis, or they arm imperialist war, or they promote total, state capitalist enslavement. Progress – a category which has been reduced in existing society exclusively to technology – is never linear as one which occurs in a uniform and hence real way; it proceeds instead in a leap which posits a change of direction. This leap is merely suggested by the ever more highly developed means of production that is the machine. The proletariat draws the collectivist conclusion, and against this the bourgeoisie cultivates even more latent plans apart from terrorism and war: monopolistic state capitalism.

It would not be the first time that the falsifying enemy seeks to cure itself by what is growing against it. But even in 'purely human' terms it is different in a number of ways whether a mine is nationalized from below or from above so to speak. Everywhere a 'controlled economy' becomes inevitable, but the difference is the most enormous precisely here:

whether monopoly capitalists or producers will be the subject doing the organizing. In the first case state capitalism arises or the mere functional change of private ownership of the means of production, in the second case socialism arrives or the transfer of this private property to the real, namely producing collective. Both structures have the common element so to speak that they rise on the ruins of free competition, of the liberal market mechanism. But both structures display beyond this all too formal similarity the vast difference, hushed up by social democracy, that socialism presupposes that revolution whose very absence alone makes state capitalism possible. The latter received its form through the two world wars, in which output was regulated from above for the first time since the manufacturing period. It receives its content through the growing state-development of monopoly capital, through the transition of the previously subjective firm into the state as the now quite officially and totally executive committee of the ruling class. State capitalism here combines full, indeed sharpened exploitation with the most drastic changes in previous private industry; all this with an illusion of collectivism. This illusion can even mean that the capitalist economy controlled from above claims to be socialist; it did this in the various fascist coups d'état, but it also does so, often well-meaning but always wrong, in reformist terms. As in the old short-sighted delusion of the 'peaceful growing of capitalism into socialism', this Bernsteinism which has already been dreadfully refuted twice, in 1914 and 1933. In a period of prosperity and a laboriously maintained peace, capitalism (which constantly has within it the opposite of prosperity and peace) may pose as liberal again, after it has nevertheless shown its grotesque fascist face; but an intensification of the state is always immanent in the controlled profit economy of monopolism. And in the socialist economy this intensification, contrary to all popular opinion, does not appear because this economy is controlled in socialist terms but because it touches on state capitalism or – with a view to a supposed short cut – makes instrumental use of it and incorporates it. It is of detective-utopian importance to sketch on the horizon the changes of which state capitalism could be capable if it is allowed time and space. And in fact everything stays as it was in the main point, in exploitation, and the crises immanent in capitalism are simply wrapped up in gun-cotton. The first change would concern the *market*, which would cease to be a free, open one. Human beings no longer face one another as agents of barter, but the total state contains exclusively those who give the orders and those who are dominated. Into its hands passes the control over price fixing and the quality of goods which had been exercised up to then by the free market to some extent. The second change would concern *production itself*, after the freedom of the market is at an end together with its competition. There is a prospect of full employment, though with a necessarily lower standard of living for the masses. There is a prospect of relative economic security, as a result of the adjustment of production to consumption, as a result of a regulated profit economy; however, security is bought by the army of workers and employees being totally transformed into slaves instead of into co-owning comrades. Even the residual capitalists are restricted in their freedom, 'public need before private greed', which only means however that the monopolists restrict Manchesterist private greed so that their own public need itself remains all the more formidably preserved. A *capitalist collective* arises, composed of the greatest robbers in industry and distribution, from the high civil and above all military bureaucracy; all other people, in the whole world, in the vast complex of state capitalism, whose centre would be America, would become objects of a control which the world has never seen before on such a large scale and with such thoroughly rationalized strategy. The total prison, with undernourished robots insured for life, the prospect therefore which Manchester capital always lyingly portrayed as that which threatened in socialism, is precisely its own. And there is the additional piquancy that the attempt is made to introduce the economic system to which fascism corresponds, and the fascism which corresponds to this economic system, from America, where even the word capitalism is still an honorary title and the state is not, under the trade-mark of – freedom. These therefore are among other things the horizons of state capitalism, ultimately of the same state capitalism which is in the habit of calling socialism 'red fascism' because it is on its guard against the murderous intentions of imperialism. So that therefore the liberals of the expired epoch of free competition romanticize out a 'third path' which would liberate them from the mildly unloved fascist alternative and the genuinely hated socialist alternative. The alternative seems to them to be an equal one between 'totalitarian regimes'; which is not even formally true in view of the dictatorship of the proletariat, let alone in respect of the goal of freedom of this dictatorship, the solely and really total goal. The difference between the two 'controlled economies' is therefore obvious despite the malice or also the great foolishness which mix it up; it marks the utmost contrast of social content: of *abolished exploitation* on the one hand, and of *totally rammed-in* exploitation on the other. And state capitalism threatens as a possibility, indeed as an already begun reality only as long as people put up with it and stand for it. The profoundly low level of wages which seems inseparable from state capitalism, and the lasting incapacitation would be unbearable in the long run, – even if fascism does not enter the land of no return in a final world war which it provokes and, in accordance with the law with which it fell in, must continue to provoke. In all respects, however, something results from the evil latency of state capitalism which helps fascism and makes it almost concrete, the tendency towards the capitalist collective in the vacuum of disappeared free competition: thus state capitalism is *the long-sought element of reality in otherwise so insubstantial fascism*. The latter uses anachronism and the dull rage of its protest in the seduced masses, but it is eminently up to date in its leadership. It is not merely spookish here, it is also the real ape of a real tendency, that towards socialization of the forces of production; fascism made state capitalism formidable as a real alternative. And this is joined by the *most central danger* of the delusion of order, and indeed socialism, with which the capitalist collective has draped itself and may drape itself again – *state capitalism beneath the mask of state socialism*. Hence above all the forgery of security, indeed liberation from the struggle for life which has become horrifying; what is lost in the way of free time and freedom seems to come in again through a guarantee, through guaranteed employment, through subsidized leisure. If there is anything in which the average American citizen in particular, the former risk-taker par excellence, is even more interested than he is in profit-making, it is life insurance; even the former capitalist pioneer will unhesitatingly take security in exchange for vanished advancement, and fascism seemed and seems to guarantee this security at least for the Babbitts of all zones as if it were – the future state. It was a grave flaw that the existing possibilities of state capitalism have been so little worked out in socialist literature itself; an even graver one that the mountainous contrasts to socialism have not found any sufficient analysis. Through the *first flaw* fascism came as a complete surprise, through the second social democracy was reassured about its inactivity and about the allegedly dialectical optimism it showed for the big companies. Capitalism seemed, as is well-known, to change into socialism of its own accord as soon as it was further synthesized; indeed even the Prussian militarizations of economic life, which began in 1914, the so-called ideas of 1914, appeared as socialism here. Through the *second flaw*: the insufficient distinction between state capitalism and – temporary – state socialism, it was made particularly easy anyway for social democracy and the rest of the bourgeoisie to overlook its own state capitalism, by

simply imputing it, qua 'controlled economy' one way or another, to the
– Soviet Union. If this is malicious deception, it certainly would not even
have found a spurious reason for its formalistic distortions if the difference
between state capitalism and the intermediate stage: state socialism had
not been left in intentional but also in unintentional vagueness. Indeed,
the non-distinction is so old that it could even appeal to the one-sided
pathos of order in centralist social utopians and, in the case of anarchists,
even actually did appeal to it. As will be remembered, even in Saint-Simon
a state-capitalist line ran parallel to the socialist one; the 'capacité administrative', exercised by industry, here appeared as the germ of the socialist
future state. For the Saint-Simonist Louis Blanc, state monopoly and governmental socialism even amounted to completely the same thing; Blanc
planned national workshops with state credit so that each could produce
according to his abilities, and could consume according to his needs. The
older utopians, if they did not yet distinguish state capitalism and socialism
as prison and revolution, admittedly had the excuse of a not yet surveyable
capitalist development; and even later utopian novelists, like Bellamy, when
they found their organized bourgeois state to be socialist, had the freedom
of dilettantism. But even in 1939 an alleged 'Economics of Socialism' is
found in America, in H.D. Dickinson and others; in this the possibilities
and forms of state capitalism are thoroughly thought out, not as abstract
utopia, but fairly close to the monopolistic tendency: and the investigation
nevertheless runs as one via – socialism. It is as if socialism corresponded
to the caricatures which the anarchists paint on to it; as if it were fundamental centralization and nothing else; as if it were state per se and not
Soviet. And it does not need to be repeated here: socialism in its scientific
form bears the clear distinguishing features on its brow: as act it is revolution
of the proletariat, and therefore destruction of the capitalist class per se;
as goal it is classless society, and therefore organized freedom. The Soviet
Union is still in the process of an act of construction, and consequently
still a state, even a harsh one, but simply one without an economy based
on capital. Thus, for the purpose of the abolition of all private ownership
of the means of production, there can at worst so to speak be state socialism
there, but never in the long run genuine, regular state capitalism. And
even state socialism, in so far as it appears, is in the process of an act,
and consequently temporary and for demolition; for the goal at work in
the act is the dying away of the state. The October Revolution of 1917
posited for this goal the proletarian dictatorship, the epoch after Lenin's
death established the strongest state- and military power as a safeguard:

nevertheless the end of force in this kind of force is inescapably immanent. Whereas in bourgeois liberalism, which once so highly conspired and so deeply revealed itself, it was always only the capitalist apparatus of force that was hidden and present. From the first, the worker in the capitalist class-state only had the freedom to starve if he did not bow to the dictatorship of profit, and he would not have achieved either the right to strike or even the eight-hour day, the same rights which state capitalism will take from him again, if he had not bloodily wrested them from the so-called Statue of Liberty through organization. Whereas the land of socialist construction employed all its vast power to this end and must unerringly use it so that power over people comes to an end. So that instead of freedom of trade, with which liberalism has lured and deceived, freedom from acquisition may arise. So that instead of the so-called state under the rule of law, which because of its rotten class content has become wholly a state under the rule of illegality, no state at all is necessary any more. The order which is still possible in late capitalism, that of state capitalism or fascism, consists solely of atrocities of order, and the freedom, with self-alienation that has become total, persists solely as a suppressed, if not missing freedom. Again it is evident, more sharply than in the case of beneficence and pacifism, more terribly perverted: in the late bourgeoisie peace becomes war, order barbarism, leisure emasculation and desolation. The high drama of fascism thus still hardly proves to be exhausted in its state-capitalist possibilities, although restricted in them. The Soviet Union was the very troublesome contemporary of fascism at Stalingrad; a Soviet Union in inviting maturity will put an end to this state capitalism everywhere.

Delusions of free time: toughening up for business

In the evening the oppressed man finally relaxes, becomes free as it were. He is allowed to recuperate, and he is allowed to do so because even a worker gets tired. He receives free time after the trials and tribulations of the day, to feed and oil himself as a machine. The hours after work and Sunday mean: recuperation of working power; man is never an end in the acquisitive society, always a means. Whatever is done with the hours after work, privately or in accordance with ancient custom, merely embellishes the bourgeois end: reproduction of working power. All the more varied of course are the dreams which now settle in the *hours after work* of the oppressed man. They would like to be fulfilled there, as in a place where at least a hollow space arises. Fresh air is taken in, alcohol washes down the dust, card-playing kills time, and is moreover the desire not just to succumb to chance but to be able to play with it and even to win something off somebody else. This has the double effect here that the working day, the business day is abandoned and at the same time its forms continue in a 'lightened' way. *Sociability* as a whole largely repeats the relations between people and things which predominate in society and constitute it in each case. These relations prevail even in the downtrodden class that has come off badly, although it has or could have particular interest in distinguishing the hours after work from the working day in terms of form and especially of content. But this kind of thing is not simple, not even where a contrasting will exists; sociability as the form of play in a society confirms this society even in escaping it. And sociability keeps people up to scratch all the more, the less those who have come off badly lament existing social conditions themselves but only the singular place they occupy in them. Indeed as we have seen: pleasure then serves as a substitute for what has not been attained in the capitalist struggle for life and its approved forms. The drive to win in card-playing and the poker face imperative for it, together with its straight and crooked paths, is in sport the assiduity, transferred there, of competition that appeared free. To the same extent that this competition is made economically impossible, the *contest in sport* beckons. It beckons not only its practising enthusiasts but much more, by means of empathy with the sides, the thousands upon thousands of Sunday spectators at the professional match. It is true that even Greek wrestling matches and medieval tournaments had displayed 'competition': but it was not a busy one as yet. This contest reflected, in the upper class of the time, no economic struggle, its participants rather resembled that 'high-minded' man whom Aristotle praises for 'going hesitantly and idly through life except where an honour or a work require him'. The emotion was the desire of distinction not of friction, it was Eros for the goal, with the loser as the 'second winner', not as a rival who goes bankrupt from the stock exchange. Mutatis mutandis this kind of contest is also possible in a post-capitalist society; the Soviet Union is already using it today. Whereas the pleasure taken in sport by capitalist employees necessarily displays all the features of competing in its contest, in other words: of the substitute in the form of play for the socially disappeared free competition. It is not admitted by capital that this competition (make way for efficiency, the marshal's baton in every knapsack)*

---

* Bloch adapts a German phrase here to mean that everyone is a potential leader of men.

is economically outmoded; it was, after all, the strongest seductive charm of capitalism, above all in the 'land of unlimited possibilities'. Thus, in so far as it still works with the illusion of free competition, capital promotes sport, which mobilizes this illusion in free time. As if in this way at least the body was accorded its rights, as if in this way at least man were still worth something in this field, even as if a bit of Greece appeared, called the Olympic Games, a festival of free people not of slaves. And the promoted sociability of sport dopo lavoro does not remain confined to forged freedom; it has other merits as well in capitalist terms. Even where capital is no longer capable of feigning free competition to its employees, even in the confessed state of new serfdom sport is made useful for delusion. In this case not for the individualist kind but for the collective kind, though it must be noted: for the collective kind in the service of the firm, and ultimately of monopoly and state capitalism. This is the spirit of pre-fascist and fascist 'organization of free time', concerning gymnastics. Big businesses have long used the love of sport in their employees to form a particularly faithful 'following' for themselves. This now no longer returns in free time to the individual illusion of competition, on the contrary: the following has to lead the colours of its capitalist business to victory itself; thus sportsmen are transformed into 'industrial relays'. Here too only the Soviet Union and the people's democracies have produced the genuine spirit of a collective contest: namely because the businesses themselves have become collective property. The fascist state finally even annexed to itself the return to nature; it is now called 'military sports'. This saw the end of the evening walk of the longing for fresh air, of the art of moving paralysed limbs. But the initial reasons for this end already lie in the fact that free time has always been regarded by the bourgeoisie only as hidden service and permitted as such. Strength through joy, taken to its logical conclusion this simply means: repair of the worn-out commodity of working power by means of cunning dopo lavoro. And everything is done to see that the commodity does not have any harmful ideas in the joyfully filled free time. To see that the wistful consideration of possibilities is canalized and remains as subordinate as the little position of the person doing the considering himself. Free time therefore ultimately serves stupefaction here, whether with an apparent laissez faire, laissez aller (on capitalist strings) or with forms which fascism imposes, with garlands for oxen to be slaughtered. It must be noted that it is not the fact that a form is also sought for free time which is lamentable and detestable but that, with such content, it comes from the enemies of the people. Sunday and even the contact with nature thereby remain closer than ever within the capitalist workday and its interested parties. So that the commodity of working power does not shake off its commodity character even during recuperation; the long arm of capital embraces the man at the machine and at the supper table, in the sports stadium and in the holiday-hospital of nature. Nevertheless the rebellious desire, desire for something different, does not fail to appear in the long run, nor even in the hours after work; for human beings are not a commodity. Nor is their laziness, this sole residual fragment of paradise, as Schlegel said, truly a backward-looking prophet in this respect. But above all their vigour, and not just their laziness, seeks without exception a state where even the clock, as the hand of duty, lives for the moment.

Residual older forms of free time, spoiled, but not hopeless: hobby, public festival, amphitheatre

There is still a part of man which is not or not wholly sold. 'I enjoy myself', idleness is at least nicely put into words in English. Dolce far niente, a Being, not just a word, already gives life without work as such an inner charm. Provided that we also have the external means for it or even without them know how to have as many holidays as possible. Further provided that we can bear nothing more easily than a series of beautiful days, and are therefore not spoiled for pleasure. Because work has burnt us out and we have time and example neither for the grace nor the peace of happiness. You are like a flower, this is admittedly difficult in a society which even in its leisure-class, precisely in it, displays few flowers, except carnivorous ones. But it is evident that even in the holiday ruined by capitalism there are still half sheltered spots. There still lives a not wholly saleable patch or patchwork of man which is not wholly suitable for the business of reproduction. And in him certain traces of more fulfilled leisure have survived from *older times*, from pre-capitalist ones, worthy of being considered and indeed possibly re-functioned under changed circumstances. Because of its pre-capitalist features this kind of thing is also far less incorporated into capitalism, although obviously usable and falsifiable. What are meant here are such various entertainments after work as the *private hobby*, the *public festival* (mostly grouped around former church festivals), and then the whole complex of culture which is becoming communal: the *amphitheatre for all*. Man is therefore not wholly betrayed wherever

a part of him is still not wholly sold and enjoys itself. The *hobby* brings
the quietest of these idle pleasures, there is a rather lonely but always easy
ride on this hobby-horse. Do-it-yourself enthusiasts, allotment holders,
along with so many other varieties of play, act out in their favourite pursuit
the profession which they have missed or which does not exist at all in
the seriousness of life. This kind of thing often merely turns out stunted,
but from a distance work without constraint opens up with it, a private
appearance of what activity with pleasure and love could mean. Where
the almost chance profession, the job, satisfies the fewest people, as in
America, there are therefore the most hobbies. And the favourite pursuit
will only disappear when it constitutes the correct profession itself one
day. Until then we can learn from the hobby how fulfilled leisure is privately
dreamed, as work which appears like leisure. But when the most private
of idle pleasures turns into the most public and throws the whole activity
away which does not belong to the hobby, there then appears from ancient
times the most effortless favourite pursuit: the *public festival in boisterous
folklore*. It still thrives more or less in rustic regions, and also in cities,
where traditional customs, encapsulated or immigrated, have continued
to be preserved. Parades, carnivals, and church festivals then fill up no
empty space of Sundays and holidays but make these really into such.
Countries with a Roman-pagan base are richer in such festivals than
northern ones, and Catholic ones are more talented at them than the
Protestant ones of the work ethic. America, with three million Italians
in New York, displays through them the difference between living and
dead joy even in one and the same spot. Living joy is that which in the
case of numerous church festivals has migrated over from Palermo or Rome,
from Bari or Naples; dead joy is the fun of the Yankee world, from the
juke-box to the cocktail-party. Italy, France, Austria, Bavaria and the
Rhineland have still preserved enclaves in the general capitalist mechanical
response by virtue of the classical subsoil and the Catholic tradition, i.e.
intervals of a feeling for life for which time is not yet money and merriment
as yet no whitewashed grave. Public festivals have perhaps wholly survived
only in Russia, so that the Soviet Union was not only able to take them
over but first allowed the popular life and the popular joy in them to arrive
and return home in the new society. Yet even in France the bourgeois
mechanics has deformed, it brought about a harsh contrast between the
conventional and the naive gaieté parisienne. The domestic Sunday of the
petit bourgeois is almost never more than furnished despair; and the publicly
manifested Sunday, even in the land of the devout Epicurus? 'One only

needs', writes Jean-Richard Bloch about a kind of civilization which has even spread its veneer over Paris, 'one only needs to stroll through our parks and gardens and over the boulevards of our cities on holidays to encounter these pitiful bourgeois families in thousands of examples, who, dusty and bored, drive a few idle, sullen, hypocritical children before them.' The memory of the Sunday misery which Seurat painted in his promenade piece 'La Grande Jatte' (cf. Vol. II, p. 814) also belongs here, and the comparison of these incurable groups of strollers, indeed of the whole watery-desperate promenading with God in France.* How juicily even the old kermis pictures of the Dutch emerge in this contrast, and all the wishful dreams attached to church festivals and carnivals as well, in which Sunday afternoon, instead of being the best time for suicide, could give room for collective enjoyment of life, after all the workday misery. The workday was even more arduous than today, but an unoppressed capacity for joy gained shape on feast-days, that which can be won and filled only communally. We only have to read the description of the Saint Roch festival in Bingen, in Goethe's journey 'On the Rhine, Main and Neckar in 1814 and 1815', this splendid health and contentment, to see masterly joy in the most faithful mirror. The public festival here certainly released wishful dreams of festivity, but they lacked the play-acting and also melancholy-sentimental element which characterized the festive utopias of the leisure-class, despite the greatest radiance and pre-appearance. This means that public festivals stand in contrast to deprivation, but feasts of our lords to boredom. And the latter cannot be combatted with relaxation but again only with effort; hence Heine's paradox of the *'brave comrade in arms* of a dolce far niente'. Conversely, public festivals display no artificiality, not even when, as is often and particularly the case in Italy, they have modified the forms of the governing Baroque. While pastorality and the posed Arcadian element are clearly lacking here, and an element of naivety and antiquity, a bit of the final procession of Dionysus is added instead. Dionysus is a releasing god, thus his public festival has now proved to be fit for a re-functioning, for one which is by no means clerical any more. This holiday world celebrates joys for which in fact there becomes real occasion only later, i.e. liberation of the people is anticipated. Hence the easy transition from the dance around the linden tree to that around the liberty tree of the French Revolution, hence the always latent element from the end

---

* Bloch has in mind the idiom 'To live like God in France' which is equivalent to the English 'To live like a king'.

of 'Fidelio': Hallowed be the day, hallowed be the hour. It is not inconsequential that the Saturnalia of all peoples are based on the memory of a Golden Age, and hence of the freedom, equality and fraternity of the early communist gentes. The re-functioning of the public festival into a real dopo lavoro therefore revives in its programmatic newness very old tendencies: on the soil of the carnival, of the St Roch's day, the St John's day, united in the re-presenting of a thoroughly transparent occasion, of something free from pain. Is not the festival of the storming of the Bastille at home on the old soil? And hence the festival of the October Revolution and the political spring festival of the first of May? The holiday has certainly refreshed itself here with relics of the parade, the procession, indeed re-functioned church-banners. There thus remains in the public festival a certain hope for the dopo lavoro that has become fundamental and is becoming ever more fundamental. All the more so as the ground on to which the festivity was and is applied, alongside the traditional-cheerful content in whose memory the festival is 'observed', was and is still unobserved hope.

That which presses for more cultivated joy does not seem quite so inviting. And which is fed or *fobbed off* there, with cultural presentation for everyone. With the so-called cultural treat which the bourgeois world provides on Sundays and holidays. The treat seeks to occur beyond sporting contests and the cinema; thus it ranges from concerts, in which there is pale ale, to plays and books which are free of all alcohol. Needs, life and forms from older times are also present in the cultural Sunday, of course. But incomparably more than in the case of the surviving public festival they are crossed by orders from above, by interested diversion. If the sports business still feigns free competition and if the whole of free time regulated by capitalism is so arranged that the commodity of working power does not become conscious of itself even during its recuperation, then this endeavour naturally continues in bourgeois presentation, but also in an *administering of cultural assets* which still occurs in a bourgeois and especially petit-bourgeois way. Though there is no doubt here about a continuing pre-capitalist existence of these ways of filling free time as well. This traditional element is far sounder than in sport, where the Greek-democratic pleasure can be redirected to very different toughening up, and ultimately stupefaction. Beethoven, even if he is packaged into the so-called cultural treat, with reduced price and content, refuses to be mocked. The fire of Prometheus and the milk of the bourgeois-pious way of thinking remain, even when administered in social-democratic popular education, incompatible with one another. The old places where the people had no cultural treat but was involved in the work, stirred by the subject itself, indeed revolutionized and wholly absorbed in it, were called *amphitheatres* in antiquity, and *mystery stages* in the Middle Ages. But the very form of modern higher holiday activity reveals the character, or rather: the non-character which lies even in the phrase popular education evening itself. This is clearance sale, this is dross and staple commodity, this is an endeavour to turn Mozart into a stick of rock, Goethe into a philistine, and the Ninth Symphony into a non-denominational Sunday sermon. Valuable information was and is served up to a so-called general public from all areas, without problems, without centres, at best with the effect of staunchly orthodox boredom. Such cultural transmission resembles a promenade concert in small spas, and the Sunday supplement in the great bourgeois conformist press. The initiator into this educational philistinism was David Friedrich Strauss in those days, and thousands of even more cheerful people of his type have been at work in Sunday culture since then. The wild and the sublime sun of the originals has set, or is at least veiled, even in those presentations which connect the popular with the cheaply saleable instead of with popular energy and ancient popular imagination to be invoked, and long active in dance, fairytale, and brooding reflection. The still current danger of the bourgeois social-democratic cultural park is indicated when its David Friedrich Strauss speaks like a chorus of a hundred thousand senior primary school teachers: 'Alongside our profession we seek to keep as open as possible our appreciation of all higher interests of mankind...We aid our understanding of these things through historical studies which are now made easy even for the non-scholar by means of a series of attractively and popularly written historical works; in addition, we seek to extend our knowledge of nature, for which generally comprehensible aids are not lacking either; finally we find in the works of our great writers, in the performances of the works of our great musicians a stimulus for mind and soul, for imagination and sense of humour, which leaves nothing to be desired.' The plush age of the nineteenth century which regarded itself as a purple age is past, but – with undeniable offshoots into the contradictio in adjecto of a petit-bourgeois communism – educational philistinism is not out of circulation. The background remains the museum world of the previous century, with art as illusion, illusion as ideal. And it is ultimately the same background which in its fully elaborated development, as purely epigonic, purely contemplative space of consciousness, is still called *historicism*. Precisely the latter is the principle of the parasitic cultural treat or the servability of dead education; with history as repeatedly considered past, with culture as something to fill an evening. Historicism elegantly delivers what capital demands in its interest and disseminates in 'culturally pedagogical' terms: it delivers into the educated leisure-time of the petit-bourgeois masses the paralysed muse, the no longer far-striking Apollo. Historicism thought it had a Hegel as a forerunner, but Hegel in particular opposed a limine this museum of alienation, with those who are alienated themselves as guides: 'The living spirit. . . demands, in order to reveal itself, to be borne by a related spirit. It brushes past the historical behaviour that sets out from any interest in knowledge of opinions as an alien phenomenon and does not reveal its inner self. It can be a matter of indifference to it that it has to serve to enlarge the remaining collection of mummies and the general pile of contingencies' (Werke I, p. 168). Thus only the epigonism of the nineteenth century turned history into a warehouse and a museum, a place for all tastes or, not much better, a canon designed to stifle. Apart from hideous copies, the subjectless diligence of this age certainly also produced monumental works of historical erudition, so that a material collection of fidelity on a small scale and dubiousness on a large scale could hardly be accomplished any more like that built up by the historicism of the nineteenth century. But instead of the living legacy there arose a lull in knowledge and contemplation, which paralysed or dangerously diverted even existing productivity – historicism is in all fields the wisdom of those who are unfruitful. Really experienced history, namely that experienced in terms of forming history oneself, provides no legacy for its own family vault or for the contemplative Sunday room. It is rather, to use Ludwig Börne's splendid metaphor, a house which has more staircases than rooms, it resembles rather an unfinished suburb than a numbered field of debris, it only approaches at all from a communal future, not from the past made into a grave, namely concluded. Thus in fact the *example of the future in the past* is the only one that pleases, inspires and teaches. Like this of course and only like this, but absolutely like this, there can and must be a linking up, beyond corruption, with the evening cultural consciousness, without lies, without illusions, beneath other stars. A society which as such will itself stand beyond work will of course, for this very reason, no longer have any separate Sundays and holidays, but just as it will have the hobby as a profession and the public festival as the finest manifestation of its community, so it will also be able, in a happy marriage with the mind, to experience with it its *festive weekday*. So that no classless educational philistine emerges; so that precisely education remains on the Front, instead of in epigonism. The care of existence remains enough, even if the shabbiest, that of acquisition, is abolished; neediness remains enough which presses for information and for the five thousand years of the history of civilization, as a single, unfinished, continuing day. But the more society is economically in accord, and the slighter its antagonisms stemming from this source are, the more exactly the genuine discordances of existence then emerge, those worthy of human beings, for the illumination of which culture in fact has its plan of campaign, and will have it more than ever. It was often rounded but never closed, never a sum of finished products; precisely the great educational works prove their continuing surplus over the submerged ideology within which they arose. The art of hearing singing in the air then no longer appears as an escape or even as an interested deification of something poorly available; it no longer appears as a hasty solution of social contradictions in a shining game, but the pre-appearance of what is right emerges with a continuing effect, alone with a continuing effect. This is the afterripening of every great work after it has been plucked from the tree of its age and this tree itself has long disappeared; kingdoms pass away, a good verse remains and says what – lies ahead. This pre-appearance so little suited to be a staple commodity will therefore operate all the more when the inauthentic other reflection, that of mere class ideology, is taken from it. As far as this very pre-appearance is concerned, as joy and doctrine of a true dopo lavoro, it was said above, on the problem of the encounter of the utopian function with ideology, with itself pre-appearing significance: 'Thus it is always only the shaping dream-force towards a better world which is culture-creative, or the utopian function as one which ventures beyond. This function posits in ideology for the first time what can be named without cliché and hypocrisy, and without property, illusion and superstition, and it alone forms the substratum for the cultural legacy'.* And: 'The parasitic enjoyment of culture reaches an end through insight into the more and more adequate trend towards our becoming identical and through commitment to this; cultural works open up strategically...They are now, from the point of view of the philosophical concept of utopia, not an ideological prank of a higher kind, but the attempted path and content of known hope' (cf. Vol. I, p. 153ff.). And if there is still a part of man which is not or not wholly sold, this is also the same one which has not yet become free for itself. It therefore

---

* Though this quotation is similar to the content of the section in Volume I 'Encounter of the utopian function with ideology', it is not directly quoted verbatim. It may be a quotation from an earlier draft of the book which was not emended during Bloch's revisions.

seeks its absolution not least in *leisure*; culture thus forms, in the *leisure that is its work*, instead of illusions of *the hours after work* substances of real *free time*. For nothing is more threatened and more hopeful than this, nothing needs more cultivation than this human, still all too little human field.

The surroundings of free time:
utopian Buen Retiro and pastoral

Heinrich:	We forget.
Paul:	But something is missing.
Jacob, Heinrich, Joe:	Wonderful is the approach
	of evening
	And fine are the discussions
	of men by themselves.
Paul:	But something is missing.
Jacob, Heinrich, Joe:	Fine is the calm and the peace
	And pleasant is the harmony.
Paul:	But something is missing.
Jacob, Heinrich, Joe:	Marvellous is the simple life
	And matchless is the grandeur
	of nature.
Paul:	But something is missing.

Brecht, Rise and Fall of the City of Mahagonny

We sense still or again how we wish to spend our free life. But apart from the How of free time it is a question of its Where, of the more beautiful *free space*. Even in the case of the festival and the educational evening the usual surroundings are changed and embellished. Especially a longer period of leisure requires a decided change of space, what is called striking tents. The distance from business which is called holidays must literally be one, a change of air, of paths, of things themselves. And the space around this free time, without work, is longed for and regarded as the protective space of the simple-unrestrained life: free-time space is then nature devoid of human beings but not hostile to human beings, in short that utopianized into an idyll. This is particularly true of those evening hours after work called the evening of life, and hence of dopo lavoro as consummate holidays, of Buen Retiro. And the nature around it which is itself contented so to speak appears as the Arcadian content which positively fills, automatically as it were, the absence of business and perhaps even of pleasures. It does not need to be stressed that nature in this sense of simplicity and at the same time fulfilment is a social utopian category; that it belongs to society precisely because it contrasts with the latter and its artificiality, even emptiness. As this category it had been varyingly – in the older wishes for free space – played off by Diogenes against the polis, by Rousseau against the fortress of feudalism, by Ruskin against mechanical capitalism. With ever-varying content, simply according to the character of each society and its civilization from which the Robinsonade pushed off. And yet it must be emphasized, simply to understand the peculiar unquestionableness of all dreams of *free space*, in contrast to the so often embarrassed elaborations of dreams of *free time*: there is a common matter-of-fact element in the Arcadian contrasting wishes which almost has as much staying power as the nature sought by them. And despite the vast preponderance of the merely social utopian element, of the social assurances and the contrast in the pastoral picture: the landscape before the gates, this objective factor, nevertheless constantly presented itself for such a picture. Arcadia was located from the first beneath trees, beside springs and other elements of paradise, not in the city, however shimmering. A trace of this very old utopia of free space still shines in every harmony with nature and that which the city-dweller expects and receives from it. Like the public festival in Romance and Slavonic countries, the joy in nature may well have been most ardently developed and preserved in Germany. But dopo lavoro demands everywhere, in its dreams of space, a portion of the great Pan; and he certainly provides a hall for leisure.

Live hidden away, this piece of advice is just as dangerously isolating as it is harmlessly quiet. It refers first to the settler's smallholding for which the lonely countryside gives room, but then also to rural repose. Freud's theory of sleep makes a certain contribution to the particular dopo lavoro of this quietness, as that of the country. For according to this, the wish for sleep aims at turning away from the outside world, the libido-occupation of objects, the object-occupation of the libido decreases, libido and ego-interest are again united, in full narcissism. This produces the strongest possible recuperation, namely that of the psychological return to the womb, to objectless isolation. And in fact this sheds light on the peculiar security which the person who has escaped from the city may find in nature. He does not feel disturbed by existing objects; there thus arises in the quietness founded by this a particular protective space, in fact a *maternal space* of leisure. Similarly, writing at night and writing in the country also have this seclusion in their favour: quietness and darkness, the two grave sisters, or rather: narcissism coats even natural objects themselves, so that they not only fail to disturb but seem like a part of the ego; then, in the illusion of total fusion, the tensions between ego and non-ego completely fall away. Then the object ceases to be one to be overcome by work, as is particularly the case in capitalist enterprise and in its relation to materials. Then there is even a hint, in the face of nature, of that prelogically happy animism which Byron expresses as follows: 'I live not in myself, but I become/ Portion of that around me; and to me/High mountains are a feeling.' The holiday feeling in nature is thus not necessarily the lonely soul and its mother, despite the narcissism, and possibly solipsism underlying it. The Being-alone-with-oneself, indeed, Being-alone-without-oneself in nature can rather have total object-occupation, only not one in fact so very much alienated from the self. The free space beyond work then itself becomes one beyond hardship; in its repose, above all the inorganic kind, and the blue overhead it gives material for this. And precisely this feeling of non-alienation in quietness, in the landscape which absorbs, has also always bestowed on nature its very particular character of refuge, the *character of peace*. It joins – again at first only as a social category – the protest against artificiality, which the nature-lover believes he leaves behind him. Often with self-deception, as when the ruling class administers the enjoyment of nature wholly as sleep. Often with defeatism, as when the bustle on the human plane is declared to be incurably bleak and the great Pan is to resolve social contradictions. But often the repose of nature arrives on the scene as a real call for what is right, as a corrective to everything tormented in which there is no health, and to everything artificial in which there is no blessing. Leisure, on its heights, would like to look as set apart as this quiet working, as devoid of all trivialities. Together with the Muses who possibly inhabit these heights: the murmuring of the mountain-spring on Parnassus and Helicon is in Greek mythology, with more than mythological significance, the natural basis of the Muses. And the quietness of nature, that which belongs to Olympus, was still stressed as a basis of the immense, the elevated, and the sublime itself even when no animism whatsoever was preserved any more. The neo-Platonist Iamblichos remarks that we can recognize the gods by their silence and human beings by their talk, and so the noise (the futile unrest) grows ever louder the further we withdraw from the light of heaven. This is an experience of nature which has remained as it were naively alive even beyond mythology: precisely with regard to the heights, the isolation of the heights. Up there, since the aesthetic discovery of the Alps, the great mountains hold their elapsion upright, surrounded by sun and silence. Above all the upward-looking stars stand up there, above an earth that has become invisible, indeed reduced to one single lowland; sublimity and silence per se are associated through them with the peaceful character of a thus crowned nature. Omnia sub luna caduca: this means in this connection, despite a star-worship that can hardly be re-experienced any more, that the vast depths above the moon impress us as total situationlessness, as total other world beyond hardship. 'The broad heaven which spreads above the ignominious baseness of the earth': what Tolstoy's seriously wounded Andrei Bolkonsky thus sees and experiences on the battlefield of Austerlitz concentrates a symbolic experience of millions – in the evening hours after work that have become a night of celebration for them.* Even if later, with the eyes of the city, only that firmament remains which conceals a void. The starry sky ultimately gives the male component to the maternal feeling in nature, it gives the *component of sublimity* to that peaceful character with which precisely astonishment at nature on a grand scale communicates. And the experience of the starry sky gives even more to the pastoral: it indicates that the demonic in nature, only apparently alien to the pastoral or only in its idyllically choice manifestations (precisely Beethoven's Pastoral Symphony contains the thunderstorm), – that this great warning against narrowness and abstractness of civilization may also belong to an unfathomable abyss of the heights, not just to darkness in nature. Felt natural sublimity as a whole gives a significant contact with such elements which are still sealed or unincorporated, and not a contact which only lies in the mind of man instead of also in the mountain-, ocean- or sky-object of this specific astonishment. The pastoral maintains as a whole, above its individualism of escape, its ideology of contrast, its utopia of longing, this contact with objective material, with that which in fact only presents itself in rural nature, never in the city. This kind of contact is certainly not yet the same as a depiction valid even if only in iridescent reflection, but circulating within it, even where it is still densely furnished with mythology, are elements of an objective-latent free space, indeed of one in – nature itself. Precisely also Judaeo-Christian hope, this death of the great Pan, was not able and did not wish to renounce the pastoral completely. Easter stands wholly in the spring, Christmas takes the rising sun, if no longer as its content, then certainly as its accompaniment. The growing world-hatred in the Bible from Deutero-Isaiah on does not stand in the way of this, a world-hatred

---

* Bloch coins the word 'Feiernacht' here as an intensification of 'Feierabend' (evening hours after work), and as a contrasting echo to 'Feiertag' (holiday).

which extended from the will of political upheaval to that for a radical upheaval in nature. For although natura naturata is here only a blocking crust, although earth and heaven here occupy a place which does not befit them but only the new heaven and the new earth, although in the new heaven no moon and no sun shine any more and the Heavenly Jerusalem is no Arcadia or even Elysium any more, but an eternal city: nature still remains even in this both non-pagan and select pastoral, in that of Christian myth, full of significances, full of ciphers which – as high mountain, as living water, as tree of life, as precious stones – are delivered to the apocalyptic city. A different world now stands in the place which the existing one occupied and for whose new spatial premises pure water, high mountain, and crystal light are transparent. The Baroque period constantly sang the praises of this wholly non-pagan pastoral in the existing one of delight in nature; as in Angelus Silesius: 'So blossom, frozen Christian, May is at the door,/You'll stay forever dead, if now you don't bloom here' (Cherubinical Wanderer III, rhyme 90); as in Jakob Böhme: 'The powers of heaven always work in images, plants, colours, to reveal holy God, so that he may be recognized in all things' (Theosophical Missives I, § 5). Thus even the Christian intended explosion of nature cannot avoid transposing categories like May, images, plants, colours into its Sabbath, so that it is not only an outwardness like sheer inwardness, but equally an inwardness like sheer outwardness. How much more than this a relation to nature which has become less or differently transparent may prove leisure in the indelible pastoral. In fact, if it wants to encounter its pastoral above all in depictability and not just in iridescent reflection, this probation ultimately still has a particular problem in its way. Namely that of the double consciousness of our age with regard to nature: the mechanical on the one hand, the qualitative-aesthetic on the other. It is the problem of dualism which has opened up between the modern, purely calculatory, and therefore totally quality-free content of physics on the one hand and the nature in landscape-experience, as a totally qualitative one. Images, plants, colours, and especially beauty, sublimity, repose, and peace are just as unreal in the mechanical aspect which appears as urban physics so to speak, as they characterize in landscape painting, and also the older qualitative philosophy of nature, a content of the relation to nature of leisure. Only once in the history of reflected Arcadia has a bridge emerged between the two positions: we can say: between the *mechanical standpoint* and the *qualitative vantage point*. This occurred in Schiller's essay on naive and sentimental poetry, where nature can be celebrated in Galileo's sense, but also in Shaftesbury's sense as 'the calm working from within itself, the existence according to its own laws, the inner necessity, the eternal unity with itself'. The miracle approaches that even contrasts like that between Newton's and Goethe's nature appear reconciled here, but of course: the equation does not combine mechanical calculation and qualitative feeling for nature, but it occurs on the basis of a 'conformity with laws' in both cases. But this conformity with laws only forms an apparent bridge, in factual terms it has itself a double, mutually divided sense. In calculation it is that of merely external necessity, which proceeds on the chain of causality. In Schiller's image of nature it is that of the formative-inner necessity, which proceeds in the organism of naivety, in the qualifications of substantiality. Thus there is of course no synthesis between mechanical and landscape nature; a nature without qualities is far more alien to that of forests, mountains, and luminous stars than the Christian negated one was. And precisely Schiller's non-synthesis between the mechanical and the qualitative particularly indicates the problem, the truth, not worked up as it were, of the pastoral view on bourgeois soil. It concerns a different sector of nature than that appertaining to mathematical natural science, but it relates to it in a pre-capitalist, in a not yet post-capitalist way. The pastoral view, the view into forests, mountains, and oceans, has – like the public festivals – kept alive a great, wonderful element of non-mechanical response which one day can and will enter into concrete leisure; however, the access to it is, as a pre-capitalist one in a capitalist age, still largely archaic-romantic. There is in it just as much conjuration of a submerged objectivity as astonishment and meeting of one coming up undischarged, i.e. of a *truth of the pastoral* on which precisely leisure has to prove itself and can prove itself. But only a no longer abstract economic system will bring, even in matters of nature-experience, that elimination of the differences between city and country which among its other consequences also *contains the elimination of the dualism between urban and landscape physics.* The pastoral itself, with the whole inheritance of a not exploited but loved nature, here keeps in view, in its archaic-romantic cloak, a utopian kind of restful land – without the battlefield of Austerlitz. A restful land in which something is missing of course, because man is not yet at rest in it himself and the humanization of nature still in fact lies mostly in mere – pastoral. Only active leisure in all areas will bring us closer to a receptive nature, one not just depicted sub specie of business; human freedom and nature as its concrete surroundings (homeland) are mutually dependent.

Leisure as imperative, only half explored goal

The path there is an economic one, masters and servants have to go. Social order eliminates both, in the same accomplishment, and much more as well. Previous economic contradictions disappear, discordance that remains produces no external and filthy misery any more. The differences between manual and brain work, between country and city disappear, but above all, as far as possible, those between work and leisure. They only acquired this harshness through capitalism anyway; pre-capitalist production knew work with more share in works made by hand and joy with less dreariness. Socialism, by removing from work the drudgery for others, has already largely taken the alienation from it. But only a classless society contains the basis to liberate work, that reduced to a minimum, from the curse of alienation completely and leisure from the devil's blessings of the 'Grande Jatte'. It eliminates the expropriation of work from man, that in which the worker feels himself to be expropriated, alienated, a reified commodity, and is therefore unhappy in his work. The classless society removes from leisure, by means of the same re-expropriation, the unlived emptiness, the Sunday thoroughly corresponding (and not contrasting) to the dreariness of work. It removes from leisure above all the *false* kind, nurtured by that type of ideology which belongs to illusion and consequently ends in cliché and total fraud. This ideology began only with the appearance of master and slave, is solely posited with the class society based on the division of labour and disappears with it, as separation of social being and consciousness. The origin of this ideology, as Marx presents it, explains precisely its end without resurrection: 'The division of labour only really becomes division from the moment when a division of material and intellectual labour occurs. From this moment on, consciousness can really imagine it is something other than the consciousness of prevailing practice, that it really represents something without representing something real – from this moment on, consciousness is capable of emancipating itself from the world and giving itself over to the formation of "pure theory", theology, philosophy, and morality. But even if this theory, theology, philosophy, morality etc. enter into contradiction with prevailing conditions, this can only occur through the prevailing social conditions having entered into contradiction with the prevailing force of production' (Deutsche Ideologie, Dietz, 1953, p. 28). With these sentences Marx unequivocally cites class division as the origin, and class society as the support of ideology, though of course, – and this motif now becomes crucially important: 'theology, philosophy, morality et cetera', hence ideology, could also 'enter into contradiction with prevailing conditions'; there thus remains ideology which is *not mere illusion, mere lies*. It is the latter as false, particularly as exploited false consciousness of prevailing practice, but not as the contradiction, finally cited by Marx, of theory with prevailing conditions. That is, as the expression of a contradiction into which the prevailing social conditions have entered with the prevailing force of production, and above all vice versa. So possibly this is the place for that ideology in a very *different sense*: not for an obscuring-justifying one, but for a revolutionary-contrasting one. It surfaces precisely in the *change* between class societies and all the more so in the *elimination* of class society as a whole. This kind of ideology, with regard to its militant intention and for the most part its contents, is solely related as a contrasting one to the social basis on which, i.e. against which it has arisen. It does not reflect and justify this basis, it conversely brings to consciousness the not yet fully developed elements of the new society which have not yet achieved political breakthrough, and which have ripened in the womb of the old one. It accomplished this in the past, because of the then still unrecognized driving forces of history, with various illusions, but never with any *purposeful intention* of obscuring. On the contrary, this kind of ideology was produced on the basis of a thoroughly honest, revolutionary-progressive mandate, and even its illusion bears heroic-utopian features. And its positive function is to activate the still by no means properly existing basis of the new society, freed from the ice, with the power of theory; otherwise the appearance of this basis would be much more difficult, much more untidy. And therefore: *this kind of ideology*, that of the formerly revolutionary 'contradiction with prevailing conditions', continues to remain alive with the fire and the goal-images of its contradiction, namely an anticipatory-humane one. Thus the ideology of the French Revolution, minus illusions, minus the realm of the bourgeoisie idealized in them, carries on working in the space of progressive consciousness; thus especially the ideology of the German Peasant War, minus its mythological components, has a goal-fire in it which non-obsoletely strikes into the revolutionary conscience, and particularly also into the imagination of this conscience. And going on to *leisure*, the thus characterized, not easily satisfied ideology is not only the startling pike in a possible fish-pond of leisure, but it prevents the latter from being a fish-pond at all, in other words: a happiness as bed of ease instead of as expedition and fullness of life. The contradictions in socialist society, and especially in the future classless one, are no longer antagonistic ones, but just as they do not cease as non-antagonistic ones nor does the function of ideology to take care of discordances within the leisure generally made possible and to make anticipatory provisions for their solution. Even if these discordances have finally become purely human ones, ones worthy of human beings, and hence concern the only true existential cares. No activation of a new basis is then necessary any more, this task was solved by the socialization of the means of production, but rather the ideology that has become communist has the function of activating the ever richer and deeper fashioning of human relations. For there is precisely in leisure still a powerful career of solidarity, indeed it is only starting to begin. Thus the ideology of illusion completely passes away, but not however, in any way, that of the social-moral shaping of political consciousness. In all its main features, even in the areas of art and the more distant superstructure not predominantly related to nature, this kind of ideology will be an *ethics*. The new neediness of leisure itself thus produces a new superstructure above a new planned non-economy. It produces an ever more essential ideology of interhuman illumination – and this precisely in the purified service of leisure, for the promotion of its humane contents.

But all that is discordant and is to be considered goes far beyond the social range. Even where the relation to the economic substructure and its upheavals is either not a direct one, or where no superstructure at all exists. As in language, in logic, general dialectics, as well as – because of the outside world here visibly independent of human beings – in natural science (minus its philosophical theories). Now there are of course precisely in the physically organic character of human beings extremely powerful elements by virtue of which nature is admittedly independent of man but not man of nature. The most powerful of these elements is to be found in death, and likewise it forms the distinct field of a contradiction, even of a particularly harsh one, which is by no means merely a social one. In fact, death illustrates nothing short of a double contradiction, which is admittedly indicated by such intensity and quality in social pressure and the reaction to it, but does not occur at all in such a *pronounced* form. That *contradiction* is meant here in which the negation lies both as a protesting one in the subject which denies what opposes it, and in the opposing objectivity, a hindering and even destroying one. And both in fact operate most harshly in death as the *natural phenomenon* of discordance per se (in view of the normal will to life, work, and light); and the double contradiction operates, even if less sharply, by no means in death alone. For socially inexhaustible conflicts are also gathered around the position of man in the universe as a whole. That is, around the lasting disparateness of the universe (of its size in space, of its emergence and passing in time) to so many human ranks of purpose, particularly to those on this earth which are radically and totally (regnum hominis) aimed. But the thus characterized discrepancies definitely do not belong to any superstructure either, because they are not socially produced; – but does their consciousness therefore not belong to an ideology either? Undoubtedly these discrepancies do not belong to one in the usual sense, do not belong to it with regard to their objective natural component. However, these kinds of discrepancies have produced in fact a *very special structure* of ideology-formation in the consciousness that is startled by them. A structure which does not react to social contradictions, nor to the incorporated and domesticated relation, as it were, of human beings to nature, but precisely to nature from the side of its negation or even disparateness to human beings, to their creatural and culturally developed, indeed particularly culturally sharpened purposive concerns. In any case, the philosophical inquiries which have been issued about the position of man in the cosmos belong to ideology (in keeping with the philosophical theories within natural science). But beyond this the notations of contradictions with by no means interhuman conditions and the various formations of thought or wishful thinking for their reso-lution again form an *ideology of a separate kind*, one which is socially only partly co-determined (as in mythology). This different quality holds good despite the obvious tangle which permits no isolation whatever of the connection with nature in the relation of human beings to human beings and to nature. Nevertheless, a nature not only independent of man but also far less mediated with human beings than in the social metabolism necessarily works towards the stated distinction. A significant unity with the social ideology of illumination exists though: namely *anticipation*. So that both kinds of ideology also predominantly contain utopia, both as anticipatory formulation of a new society in conformity with the forces of production and above all also as consideration of the radical-total human ranks of purpose and their position in a mediated universe. 'Only thus can the as such useless, anarchic and all too literary element of intellectual creations be brought into a framework and into relief at all, by means of a historical-teleological background which assigns to everything that human beings create above themselves in the way of works a flux, current, direction, salvational value and a metaphysical place, the place of genuine socialist ideology, the place of the great plan of campaign of civilization and culture' (Geist der Utopie, 1918, p. 433). What is meant here, that which could therefore be called the *ideology of the Absolute*, now leads immediately towards leisure again, in accordance with *its final contents, which are nevertheless incessantly distributed in it*. The spur of the overpowering and probably even painful astonishment at a world which contains so much death and such vast disparateness, the motor of the knowledgeable hope of the character in process of the equal world, as one of the heliotropic matter which human beings are and by which they are surrounded: both, astonishment and hope, occupy and substantiate leisure all the more purely and exactly, the freer from acquisition and ultimately from work it has become such a leisure in order. Cultural production, despite all its lands of significance, has so far addressed itself only sporadically to the problem of the outlines of a better world. But this problem and its content will immediately become systematic as soon as the beautiful and great work not only finds social living ground again but as soon as, in a living ground finally undivided in social terms, the contribution of the ideology of deception and diversion, together with the flat enjoyment of free time corresponding to it, indeed culture as mere beautiful illusion, is finished. Once the state and all government over human beings have disappeared, the government and guidance by teachers will also find enough freedom and leisure to make people eager for the total contents of freedom. To give a human answer to the extremely naked question of leisure, to the *problem and essence*, thus appearing clear at last, of its ever more concrete contents. Striking out in the right direction leads into the terra incognita of leisure as into a terra utopica. But this striking out becomes the same as a striking impact, namely on the outstanding consideration of what human beings want in general and how the world as answer is related to this. Towards this, after the expiry of its previous prehistory, runs the interest of active leisure and of its incipient main history, as humanized history itself. Real leisure lives solely off the content of Being-oneself or of freedom, presently expected at any time and made present in good time, in a likewise unalienated world; only then comes land.

GLOSSARY OF FOREIGN TERMS

Greek (transliterated)

aporia: doubt, perplexity
aristoi: aristocratic quality (*lit*: best)
diairesis: division
dynamei on: What-Is-in-possibility
dynaton: capable
elphis: hope
eschaton: the last things
eudaemonia: happiness
hen kai pan: one and all
kairos: occasion, opportunity, the right time
logos spermatikos: engendering word
melos: melody
oecumene: the whole world, the merging of all nations
peripeteia: sudden change
polis: city state
proskunesis: worship
zoon politikon: political animal

Latin

ab origine: from its origin
ab ovo: from the beginning
absconditum: the thing that has vanished
actus purus: the pure act
ad calendas apocalypticas: until the time of the apocalypse
ad libitum: as far as desirable
ad oculos: to the eye
ad pessimum: in a pessimistic direction
ad valorem: according to its strength
alter deus: the other god

alteritas: multiplicity
alterius juris: according to another law
amor Dei: love of God
amor dei intellectualis: intellectual love of God
amor fati: love of fate
analogiae entis: the correspondences between things
a nihilo contracta: assimilated from nothing
anima candidissima: most candid soul
anima mea: my soul
ante rem: before the event
apex mentis: the apex of the mind
apex terrae: the apex of the earth
a posse ad esse: from potential to being
appetitus socialis: social appetite
arpeggio ante lucem: the arpeggio before the light
ars amandi: the art of love
ars combinatoria: the art of combination
ars demonstrandi: the art of demonstration
ars inveniendi: the art of invention
ars magna: the great art
artes liberales: liberal arts (in the Middle Ages)
a se esse: being to itself
auditio beatifica: blessed hearing
augmentatio: augmentation
aut Caesar aut Christus: either Caesar or Christ

bona valetudo: good health

caccatum: stained, soiled
cantus firmus: sure song
caput mortuum: dead head
caritas: charity, love
carpe aeternitatem in momento: seize eternity in the moment
carpe diem: seize the day (live for the day)
carpe diem nostrum in mundo nostro: seize our day in our world
causa aequat effectum: cause equals effect
causa finalis: final cause
causa sui: for its own sake
chorus martyrum: chorus of martyrs

circenses: circuses
civitas Christi: the city of Christ
civitas Dei: the city of God
civitas terrena: the earthly, sinful city
cogitatio: thinking
cogito ergo sum: I think therefore I am
collegia fabrorum: college of masons
comes: comrade
communes notiones: common ideas
communis opinio: common opinion
compunctio cordis: the contrition of the heart
conditio sine qua non: an indispensable condition
contemplatio: contemplation
contradictio in adjecto: opposite to what is next to it
Corpus Christi: the body of Christ
corpus permixtum: adulterated body
corpus verum: true body
corrumpere: to corrupt, corruption
corruptio, defectus: corruption, disintegration
corruptio optimi pessima: the worst things are a corruption of the best
credo quia absurdum: I believe because it is absurd (the leap of faith)
crucifixus sub Pontio Pilato: crucified under Pontius Pilate
cum grano salis: with a grain of salt
cum ira et studio: with passion and partiality
cur deus homo: why does god become man

dator formarum: the giver of forms
definitio: definition
de jure: according to the law
de nobis res agitur: the matter in question is ourselves
de profundis: of the depths
descendendo ad opera: by getting down to business
destillatio, solutio, purefactio, nigredo, albedo, fermentatio, projectio
   medicinae: the distillation, solution, purefaction, blackening, whitening,
   fermentation and projection of medicine
destinatio: destination
deus absconditus: vanished god
deus optimus maximus: greatest and best god
deus spes: god is our hope

dies irae: day of wrath
disjecta membra: scattered limbs
divinae bonitatis similitudo: the likeness to divine goodness
divina proportio: divine proportion
docta spes: educated hope
doctor angelicus: the angelic doctor
doctor ecstaticus: the ecstatic doctor
doctor subtilis: the subtle doctor
donum inventionis: the gift of invention
dux: commander, leader

ecce homo: behold the man
ecclesia perennis: eternal church
ecclesia philadelphia: church of brotherhood
ecclesia triumphans: the church triumphant
eductio formarum ex materia: extraction of form from matter
egrediens de loco voluptatis: emerging from the place of pleasure
ens perfectissimum: perfect being
epitheton ornans: decorative epithet
eritis sicut deus: you will be like God
et in Arcadia ego: and I too am/have been/will be in Arcadia
ex cathedra: edict from the authority (bishop)
ex contrario: from the opposite
exempla docent: examples teach
ex encyclica: edict from an encyclical (pope)
exercitia spiritualia: spiritual exercises
ex ingenio: from character, personality
existere: to exist, existence
exitus letalis: departure through death
ex machina: by divine intervention
ex oriente lux: light from the East
expressivo: expressively
exprimatio: expression
ex una voce plures faciens: making many things from one voice
ex uno judicio plures faciens: making many things from one judgement

facies hippocratica: shrunken and deathly appearance
factum brutum: bare fact
facultas agendi: individual justification (*lit.* the ability to do something)

fiat lux: let there be light
fides: faith
fieri: to be done
figura animae: form of the soul
figura Dei: form of God
figura virtutum: form of the virtues
finis ad quem omnia: end to which all things move
florealia: flower festivals
fortuna vertit: fortune changes
fruitio: fruition

generatio aequivoca: of dubious generation

hic et nunc: here and now
hic Rhodus, hic salta: here is Rhodes, here rise
homo absconditus: vanished man
homo contemplativus: contemplative man
homo faber: man as maker
homo homini homo: man being man to man
homo homini lupus: man being a wolf to man
homo religiosus: religious man
horror pulchri: fear of the beautiful
horror vacui: fear of the void

idola theatri: idols of the theatre
imitatio deorum: the imitation of the gods
imitatio mundi: the imitation of the world
impietas: impiety, disrespect
impossibilium nulla obligatio: under no obligation because impossible
in aeternum damnatus: damned for eternity
incipit vita nova: the new life begins
in concreto: in concrete terms
in corpore: in substance, as a whole
incredibile dictu: incredible to relate
in fluxu nascendi: in the process of birth
in gloria et jubilo: in glory and jubilation
in litteris: literally
in nuce: in a nutshell
in realitate: in reality

in spe: to be hoped for
in statu nascendi: in the state of birth
intellectus: intellect
intermissio legis: legal loophole
intimum, summum, apex mentis: inmost, uppermost, peak of the mind
in toto: as a whole
in tyrannos: against tyranny
ipso facto: in the fact itself

justificatio: justification
justitia: justice

laboratorium Dei: laboratory of God
laudabiliter se subjecit: he subjects himself in a laudable manner
lex continui: law of continuity
lex divina: divine law
libertas amicorum: the freedom of friendship
libertatem perfectam: perfect freedom
liquidas sorores: liquid sisters
locus minoris resistentiae: place of least resistance
lucus a non lucendo: light that does not light
lux aeterna: eternal light
lux nova: new light
lux pura: pure light
lyra Apollinis vel Solis: the lyre of Apollo or the Sun (god)

magia naturalis: natural magic
magisterium magnum: the great teaching
magnum opus et strenuum: the great and strenuous work
mappa mundi: map of the world
materia prima: prime matter
mathesis: (from Greek) science, mathematics, astrology
mediator Dei et hominum: the mediator between God and man
medicina mentis: medicine for the mind
meditatio: meditation
memento mori: a remembrance of death
mens bona: good mind
mens sana in corpore sano: a healthy mind in a healthy body
misera contribuens plebs: the people pooling their miseries

moralitas musicae: morality of music
more geometrico: in geometric fashion
mors aeterna: eternal death
mundus situalis: world fixed as it is now
musica coelestis: heavenly music
musicae personae: musical characters
musica humana: human music
musica instrumentalis: instrumental music
musica mathematica: mathematical music
musica mundana: wordly music
mutatio specierum: the mutation of the species
mutatis mutandis: with suitable or necessary alteration
mysterium tremendum: tremendous mystery

natura facit saltus: nature makes leaps
natura naturans: nature naturing
natura naturata: nature natured
natura sive deus: whether nature or god
nervus rerum: the nerve, pulse of things
neque in plano via sita est: nor is the path on the flat
nobilissimi loci totius terrae: the most noble place on the whole earth
nolens volens: willing or unwilling
non liquet: it will not dissolve
non omnis confundar: let me not be utterly confounded/destroyed
non plus ultra: that which cannot be bettered
non possumus non peccare: it is impossible for us not to sin
norma agendi: legal prescription
nova instauratio scientiarum: new instauration of the sciences
numen: heavenly power, divinity
numerus clausus: limitation of numbers
numinosum: numinous
nunc aeternum: the eternal now
nunc stans: the stationary moment, the captured now

omnia sint communia: let everything be in common
omnia sub luna caduca: everything under the moon is mortal, fallible
orbis: globe
ordines angelorum: the orders of the angels
ordo cognitionis: order of cognition

ordo sempiternus rerum: the eternal order of things
origo: root, origin

paradisi voluptatis: paradises of pleasure
pars mentis aeterna est intellectus: the eternal part of the mind is the
    intellect
pars pro toto: part for the whole
pater familias: father of the family
pater noster: our father
pavor nocturnus: night-fear
pax Americana: American peace
pax Britannica: British peace
pax capitalistica: capitalist peace
pax Romana: Roman peace
per aspera ad astra: through difficulties to the stars
per definitionem: by definition
per definitionem calculi: by the definition of calculations
per se exitus: exit through oneself, suicide
perfectio motus: perfect motion, the completion of motion
perturbatio animi: disturbance of the mind
phantasma bene fundatum: well-established fantasy
phantasma utopicissime fundatum: a fantasy established in a most utopian
    manner
pharos: lighthouse (at Alexandria)
pictum: painted
plus ultra: that which is capable of being bettered
poesis a se: creation through itself
poetica tempestas: poetic storm
post festum: after the celebration
potentia-possibilitas: potentiality-possibility
praeludium vitae aeternae: prelude to the eternal life
pretium justum: just price
primae noctis: feudal right of the first night (droit de seigneur)
primae possibilitates: first possibilities
primum agens materiale: first agent of matter
primus inter pares: first among equals
profectus: progression

qua: as

quale: essence
quendam vultum et gestum: a certain mien and gesture
quidditas: whatness, What-Essence (Bloch)
qui es in coelis: that art in heaven
quietas in fuga: quietness in the fugue (*lit*: quietness in flight)
quodditas: thatness, That-ground (Bloch)
quos ego: those whom I affect

ratio: reason
rebus sic stantibus: as things now stand
rebus sic imperfectibus: things thus being imperfected
rebus sic imperfectis et fluentibus: in the imperfect and fluid state of things
receptacula salutis: refuges of salvation
recta ratio: the right reasoning
regnum Christi: the reign of Christ
regnum homini: the reign for man
regressio: regressive material
res finita: finite thing
restituto in integrum: putting back together again, making whole again
Roma quadrato: the Roman square

sacerdos: priest
sacramentum plenum: full sacrament
sal philosophicum: philosophers' salt
saltare fabulam: to perform a play
sancta: the sacred
satis est: that is enough
seculis: ages
sed: but
sensus: physical sense
signatura rerum: the signature of things
signifer sanctus Michael: Michael the holy standard-bearer
si vis bellum para pacem: if you want war prepare for peace
socialis vita sanctorum: the social existence of the saints
societas amicorum: society of friends
sol invinctus: sun unchained
solus ipse: the individual himself
spes: hope
spes quae speratur: hope which is hoped

status quo ante: the status quo before
status recipientis pro meritis: state of receiving on merit
status termini: end state
status viae: transitional state
status viatoris: transitional state
studio: study
sub Iove frigido: under an icy Jove
sub specie: under the eye of
sub specie aeternitatis: in the long eye of history (*lit.* in the sight of eternity)
sub specie aeternitatis vel substantiae humanae: in the long eye of history
    or human substance
sub specie toti: under the eye of all
sui generis: of its own or peculiar kind
sui juris: according to its own law
summum bonum: the highest good
suo modo: after its fashion
suprema spes: supreme hope
sursum corda: lift up your hearts
suum cuique: to each his own
suum esse conservare: to preserve one's being

terminus a quo: starting-point
terminus ad quem: finishing-point
terra australis: southern country, Australia
terra inhabilitabilis: uninhabitable country
terra utopica: utopian country
tertium non datur: there is no third possibility
theatrum mechanicum: mechanical theatre
totaliter: in a total way
toto coelo: everywhere, across the whole sky
tranquillitas animi: tranquillity of the soul
transcendere: to transcend, transcendence
tua res agitur: it is your concern
tuba mirum spargens somnum: the trumpet scattering its amazing sound

ubi bene, ibi patria: where good, there the fatherland
ubi lux, ibi patria: where light, there the fatherland
ultima legislatio: ultimate legislation
unio mystica: mystical union

unitas: oneness
universitas litterarium: university of studies
unum necessarium: the one thing necessary
unum verum bonus: the one true good
unus Christianus nullus Christianus: the solitary Christian is no Christian
urbs: city
usque ad finem: right to the end
ut aliquid fieri videatur: so that something may be seen to be done

vade-mecum: a book that can be carried for reference along the way
ver sacrum: sacred spring (season)
verum bonum: true good
via regia: royal road
virgo optime perfecta: the virgin of sheer perfection
virgo virginum: virgin of virgins
virtus: virtue
virtus-ingenium: virtuous talent
vis dormitiva: dormant strength
visio: perception, vision
visio beatifica Dei: beatific vision of God
vita activa: the active life
vita brevis, ars longa: life is short, art is long
vita contemplativa: the contemplative life

French

acte accessoire: act of accessory
après nous le déluge: after us the flood
au dessus de la melée: above the rabble
au fond: basically
cloches du monastère: monastery bells
concert à la vapeur: steam concert
corriger la fortune: to correct fortune
donneurs d'avis: givers of advice
durée: duration
échappé de vue: vanished from sight
égalisation des classes: the equalization of classes
épater le bourgeois: to shock the bourgeoisie

état d'âme: state of mind
être humain: human being
femme introuvable: the woman who cannot be found
férocité et verve: ferocity and spirit
forces propres: one's own powers
grâce à l'homme: thanks to man
inconscient supérieur: superior unconscious
inquiétude poussante: pressing anxiety
jardin de plaisance: garden of pleasure
juste milieu: proper medium
laissez faire, laissez aller: let things be done, let things go
la nuit et le moment: the night and the moment
l'art pour l'art: art for art's sake
l'art pour l'espoir: art for hope's sake
la ville radieuse: the radiant city
le néant: nothingness
l'homme machine: machine man
liberté: freedom
malgré lui: in spite of this
mystères de l'infini: mysteries of the infinite
naturel dictionnaire de la nature: the natural dictionary of nature
papillons: butterflies
paradis artificiel: artificial paradise
pensées fugitives: fleeting thoughts
petites perceptions insensibles: perceptions too small to be discernible
petit propriétaire rural ou industriel: the little rural or industrial proprietor
portière: door-curtain
possibilités éternelles: eternal possibilities
prévoir: to foresee, a foreseeing
propriété: property
résistance à l'oppression: resistance to oppression
sans la barbe limoneuse: without the muddy beard
souvenirs de Varsovie: souvenirs of Warsaw
sûreté: security
vérités de fait: factual truths
vérités éternelles: eternal truths
violence créatrice: creative violence

Italian

adagio: quietly, softly
amoretti: little Cupids
atto puro: pure act
dolce far niente: sweet idleness
dopo lavoro: after work
espressivo: expressively
grave: with gravity, solemn
lento: slowly
maestoso: stately
martellato: hammered
misterioso: mysteriously
mondo senza gente: uninhabited world
oprare: to work
pastoso: soft, sticky (from 'pasta' dough)
piano: softly
presto: fast
prevenire: anticipate, an anticipation of what is coming
sostenuto: sustained
sostenuto assai: sustained effort
trepassar del segno: venture beyond the limits
vedere: to see
veduta: a view (with a full perspective)
virtù ordinata: regulated virtue
vivace allegro: at a lively pace

Spanish

buen retiro: happy retreat
hidalgo: Spanish knight, junker
passacaglia: an early dance tune (of Spanish origin)

NAME AND TITLE INDEX

Clair, René
 Chapeau de paille (Straw-hat)
  408
 Gaslight 408
Claudel, Paul 405
 L'annonce faite à Marie (The Tidings
  brought to Mary) 736
 L'homme et son désir (Man and his
  Longing) 405
Clemens of Alexandria
 Stromata 758
Cleopatra 328, 704, 754
Cocteau
 Orpheus and Eurydice 426
Collini 390
Columbus 732, 749, 750-2, 758, 760,
 762, 772, 773, 774-7, 782, 785,
 788, 793, 1026
Comenius 528, 636, 717
 The Labyrinth of the World and the
  Paradise of the Heart 639
Comte, Auguste 474, 567-8
Confucius 1191, 1196, 1221-8, 1261
 Lun-yu 1221
Conrad, Joseph
 Typhoon 661
Constantine 739
Cook 778
Cooper, James Fenimore 353
Copernicus 785-6, 848
Correggio 744
Cortez 777
Coué, Emile 453, 1158
Creuzer, Friedrich 160, 1363
 Symbolik und Mythologie der alten
  Völker (The Symbolism and
  Mythology of the Ancient
  Peoples) 160-1
Cromwell, Oliver 1276
Cusanus (see Nicholas of Cusa)
Cyrus 754, 1232, 1240, 1263
Czepo, Daniel 1299

Däubler, Theodor 101
Dahn, Felix
 Ein Kampf um Rom (A Struggle for
  Rome) 379
Dalcroze 394
d'Alembert 655

Dali, Salvador 365, 366
D'Annunzio
 Il Fuoco (The Fire) 1002
Dante Alighieri 89, 218, 761-2, 774,
 820-7, 832, 864, 1317
 The Divine Comedy 98, 158, 333,
  821-7, 992, 1119, 1121, 1130-1;
  Inferno 761, 1023-7, 1130, 1297n;
  Purgatorio 761, 954, 1121;
  Paradiso 94, 122, 126, 214, 776,
  813, 821-7, 835
Danton 1010
Danziger 588
Da Ponte 1008
Darius 1240
Darwin 469, 646, 894n
Daumier 473, 476, 1023
David of Dinant 207, 236
Davy 686
de Bonald 566
Debussy 105, 107
Decian 506
Déclaration des droits de l'homme
 (Declaration of the rights of
 man) 541
Defoe, Daniel
 Robinson Crusoe 816
Dehio 301, 957
Delacroix 377
de la Roncière
 La découverte de l'Afrique au moyen
  âge (The discovery of Africa in the
  Middle Ages) 770
de Maistre 566
 Étude sur la Souveraineté (A Study of
  Sovereignty) 566
della Porta
 Magia naturalis 651
Democritus 256-7, 285, 841-2, 843, 847,
 864, 1364
Descartes 72, 123-4, 147, 212, 257, 667,
 739, 740
 Meditations 72
Desmoulins 933
Deutsche Zeitschrift für Philosophie xxv
Dickens, Charles
 The Old Curiosity Shop 692
Dickinson, H. D.
 Economics of Socialism 903

Racine 546
Iphigénie 211
Rameses II 1124
Raphael 1347
School of Athens 709
Sistine Madonna 836-7, 1310
Rasputin 630
Rawley, William 654n
Reich, Wilhelm 633
Reichenbach
Physikalisch-physiologische
Untersuchungen
(Physical-physiological
investigations) 633
Reinach, Salomon 1128
Reinhardt, Max 621
Reitzenstein
Das iranische Erlösungsmysterium (The
Iranian Mystery of the
Redemption) 1240
Das mandäische Buch des Herrn der
Größe (The Mandaean Book of the
Lord of Greatness) 1245
Rembrandt 800-2, 999
Entombment of Christ 801
Man with the Golden Helmet 800
Night Watch 801
Resurrection 802
River Landscape with Ruins 801
Saskia 800
Renard, Maurice
Docteur Lerne 439
Rétif de la Bretonne
La découverte australe par un homme
volant (Australia discovered by a
flying man) 779
Reübeni, David 600
Reuchlin 1349
Reuleaux 662
Reventlov, Franziska 66, 467
Ricardo 545, 557, 580, 621, 1329
Richard of St Victor 1299, 1302
Richardson, Samuel 151
Richelieu 524
Richter
Literary Works of Leonardo da
Vinci 649
Rienzo 774
Rilke, Rainer Maria 959, 1202, 1290

Duineser Elegien (Duino Elegies) 990n
Robespierre 933, 1010
Rodbertus 555, 620
Roland, Madame 933
Rolin, Chancellor 799
Rosenberg
Mythos des zwanzigsten Jahrhunderts
(Myth of the Twentieth
Century) 584
Rosenkranz
Psychologie 125
Rousseau 68, 389, 535, 537-40, 541, 546,
549, 597, 816, 873, 915, 951, 976
Confessions 92
Contrat social (Social contract) 527,
537-40
Emile 538, 539
Ruben
Geschichte der indischen Philosophie
(History of Indian Philosophy) 676
Rubens 1099
Garden of Love 798
Rückert 928
Ruge xxviii, 155, 195, 251, 1363
Ruskin 551, 613-14, 615, 617, 915
Russell, Bertrand 668, 697
Rutherford 663
Ruysbroek 1300

Sabbatai Zewi 328, 600, 1185, 1269
Sacco, Nicola 1173
Sachs, Hans 1083, 1085
St Boniface 1274-5
St Brendan 763-4, 765, 766, 772, 788
St Germain, Count 455, 460
St Jerome 767
Saint-Pierre, Bernadin de
Chaumière indienne (The Indian
Hut) 816
Paul et Virginie 816
Saint-Saëns 398
Saint-Simon 474, 476-7, 479, 480, 528,
545, 551, 560, 563-8, 576, 577, 578,
616, 970
Nouveau Christianisme (New
Christianity) 567
Réorganisation de la société européenne
(Reorganization of European
society) 564

"FIGHT AGAINST RATS" 466